Proverb
Wit &
Wisdom

PROVERB WIT & WISDOM

A Treasury of Proverbs, Parodies, Quips, Quotes, Clichés, Catchwords, Epigrams and Aphorisms

LOUIS A. BERMAN

with assistance by
Daniel K. Berman

A PERIGEE BOOK

A Perigee Book
Published by The Berkley Publishing Group
200 Madison Avenue
New York, NY 10016

First edition: March 1997

Published simultaneously in Canada.

The Putnam Berkley World Wide Web site address is http://www.berkley.com/berkley

Library of Congress Cataloging-in-Publication Data
Proverb wit & wisdom : a treasury of proverbs, parodies, quips,
    quotes, clichés, catchwords, epigrams and aphorisms / [compiled by]
    Louis A. Berman ; with assistance by Daniel K. Berman. — 1st ed.
        p.   cm.
      "A Perigee book."
      Includes bibliographical references and index.
      ISBN 0-399-52273-5
      1. Proverbs.   I. Berman, Louis A.   II. Berman, Daniel K.
    PN6405.P74   1997
    082—dc20   96-27373
                                                                CIP

Printed in the United States of America

10 9 8 7 6 5 4 3 2 1

This book is dedicated to the memory of Sydney J. Harris. Reading his columns, in the Chicago *Daily News* and the *Chicago Sun-Times*, made commuting more enjoyable, and also whetted my appetite and shaped my interest in proverbs, proverb commentaries, and proverb humor. His columns reminded newspaper readers that there are timeless issues worth pondering, as well as topics of the day to keep abreast of.

Contents

Acknowledgments

I HAVE BEEN generously encouraged and assisted in completing this book. Thanks are due to my computer helpers Jim Niels and Sally Comfort. My thanks also go to my daughter Jennifer, who helped me find the literary agent, Ed Knappman, who saw the potential of my first draft, and helped me shape it into a viable book. Thanks to my son Daniel for lending his editorial skills, for contributing some apt quotes, and for lending his expertise in Chinese culture. Thanks to my publisher, John Duff, for his judgment and patience. Thanks to my good friend Professor Louis Marder for double-checking all the Shakespeare quotes for accuracy, and for his moral support. Thanks to Professor Wolfgang Mieder for his encouragement and help. Proofreader, adviser, sounding board, chauffeur, and helpmate: my wife, Helga Kauf-Berman, has helped directly and indirectly in more ways than I can list, to make this book the offspring of our partnership.

I welcome hearing from users of this book who want to reach the author. Is your favorite proverb, proverb twist, or quotation missing?

Do you have a suggestion for the next edition? Have you spotted an error or omission in these pages? Whatever your contributions, comments or criticisms, I would be happy to receive them and hope to acknowledge your letter. Please address: Louis Berman, Box 6014, Wilmette, Illinois 60091-6014.

Quotations from the writings of Sydney J. Harris are reprinted with permission of the estate of Sydney J. Harris. Verses by Robert Dennis are reprinted with permission of Crown Publishers, Inc. Verse by Felicia Lamport reprinted by permission of the author. Verse by Richard Armour copyright by the author and reprinted by permission of John Hawkins & Associates, Inc. I share with my fellow quotations-collector Otto L. Bettmann the confession he appended to his book *A Word from the Wise* (Harmony Books, 1977): "The quotes in this book have been collected over many years. At times, in the excitement of the chase, I may not have taken the time required for complete authentication. If any holders of rights have been inadvertently overlooked, I offer my apologies and the promise of adjustment."

Introduction

WHY COMBINE A dictionary of proverbs with a collection of quotations and proverb humor? Because proverbs and quotations go together like singing and dancing, like food and wine, like coffee and cream. The distinction between proverbs and quotations may be clear to scholars and to specialists, but not to the rest of us. "Love thy neighbor as thyself"; is it a proverb or a quotation from the Bible? "All men are created equal"; proverb, or quotation from the Declaration of Independence?

The best quotations of all times may be viewed as amplifications or commentaries, either pro or con, on familiar proverbs. What better way to organize quotations than by the proverb they touch on? What better way to draw out the full meaning of a proverb than to relate it to the thoughts of notable authors, philosophers of all ages, and anonymous wits?

A special contribution of this book is its focus on *proverb humor*: the jokes, twists, parodies, and humorous verses that celebrate or lampoon the proverbs of our culture. It's easy to understand the impulse to question proverbs, to quarrel with proverbs, or to make fun of proverbs. Proverbs, like parents and teachers, purport to tell us what to do—what we must always do, what we may sometimes do, what we cannot ever do, how to cope with a harsh reality, how to get along with all kinds

of people. We both value this advice and resent it, and the fruit of this ambivalence is the gentle humor, piercing wit, and savage satire that have always been directed against proverbs. This book documents that perennial revolt, in which the weapons are humor, wit, and satire.

Think of this book as five books in one: a book of (1) proverbs familiar in contemporary America and their origins, (2) parallel proverbs of other cultures, (3) quotations so familiar, they function like proverbs, (4) familiar sayings, which do not appear in most dictionaries of proverbs, and (5) humorous "twists," verses, and witty or serious commentaries on all the above.

It is the inclusion of these twists, parodies, and commentaries that makes this collection unique.

Since ancient times, each generation has challenged the wisdom of its elders. In the New Testament, "Love thine enemy" is very likely a deliberate reversal of the Biblical commandment to love thy neighbor (Leviticus 19:18). Shakespeare also twisted and lampooned the proverbs of his time. For example, in *The Merchant of Venice*, Gobbo accidentally meets his blind old father and shamelessly teases the old man for not recognizing his own son. Gobbo twists a familiar proverb, saying to his father, "It's a wise father who knows his own son." In *Much Ado About*

Nothing, Dogberry gravely allows that "comparisons are odorous."

Shakespeare was not the only Elizabethan to engage in proverb-bashing. In 1616, Nicholas Breton published a two-part booklet titled *Crossing of Proverbs,* in which he poohpoohed a hundred proverbs of that time. Here are a few examples of Breton's proverbs (his commentaries are parenthesized and in italics; spelling has been modernized):

Fortune favors fools. (*Not so; there are fools enough, but there is no fortune.*)
A good housewife is a jewel. (*Not if she be a scold.*)
Nothing so necessary for travelers as languages. (*Yes; money.*)

More often, Shakespeare's characters cited proverbs as nuggets of wisdom, for he lived during England's heyday of proverbs, when every schoolboy was required to memorize a collection of Latin maxims called *Sentertia Pueriles.*

Proverbs are born, grow, and change. The wording of proverbs changes to keep up with changes in our language. Today, many proverbs of English origin are phrased somewhat differently in Britain than in the United States. The British say "Appearances are deceptive"; Americans say "Appearances are deceiving."

With time, proverbs sometimes change in meaning, too. For example, the proverb "The exception proves the rule" originally meant that the exception *tests* the rule. To many, this proverb now reminds us that in this world every rule has an exception, and when we do find an exception to some rule, we know that the rule really belongs to this world.

One of the most dramatic changes a proverb has undergone from ancient to modern times involves the ancient Roman proverb "To err is human." Around the sixteenth century, the elaboration emerged, "To err is human, to repent is divine, to persevere is diabolical" (*Dictionary of Proverbs in England in the Sixteenth and Seventeenth Centuries,* by Morris Palmer Tilley). In 1711, Alexander Pope wrote "An Essay on Criticism," in which he once again reworded the ancient Roman proverb, as "To err is human, to forgive is divine." After almost three hundred years, Pope's variation is the one most frequently cited.

This book not only lists Alexander Pope's version of this ancient proverb but also records how Mark Twain, Josh Billings, and about two dozen other wits, known and unknown, have altered Pope's sentiment.

Virtually every humorist and comic has hurled a barb or aimed a teasing word against a proverb. In the pages of this book, you rub elbows with famous, lesser-known, and unknown authors of all times. Some writers made the proverb a prime target; the list would include Charles Lamb, Ambrose Bierce, G. B. Shaw, George Jean Nathan, Arthur Guiterman, and Ogden Nash. Other wits and popular philosophers have also enjoyed rephrasing familiar proverbs—improving upon them or giving them new meaning. Ben Franklin, publisher of *Poor Richard's Almanac,* was not only a proverb collector but also tinkered with them. A hands-on printer, Franklin shortened proverbs, perhaps to save typesetting time. Thus, "He that goes a-borrowing goes a-sorrowing" became "Borrowing brings sorrowing."

This is a book of *proverb humor* as well as a dictionary of proverbs. In these pages, carefully crafted witticisms appear side by side with unintended bloopers (such as Ronald Reagan's remark, "Reality is a stupid thing"), and all are classified by the proverb to which they are related.

Unlike traditional dictionaries of proverbs, this book does not document the history of proverbs in meticulous detail. Happily for everyone interested in proverbs, Oxford University Press has published *A Dictionary of American Proverbs* (1992), under the editorship of Wolfgang Mieder, dean of proverb scholars. There readers can find the archaic, obscure, and quaint as well as a most thorough documentation of the American proverb.

An important difference between this dictionary and Mieder's is organization. For example, in this book the wisecrack "A press agent is a man who hitches his braggin' to a star" is listed under "Hitch your wagon to a star." In Mieder's dictionary the wisecrack appears under "agent."

Another recent proverb dictionary is deserving of a special mention: I have found Stuart and Doris Flexners' *Wise Words and Wives' Tales* especially useful for the authors' close attention to the question of what a proverb *means*.

Without limits, this book would have become not a collection, but an accumulation of bits and pieces. Thus, I have limited my selection to sayings that I judged to have a ring of familiarity in our times to the American ear. Twists, jokes, verses, and commentaries have been included only if they are really funny, or at least mildly amusing (often a subjective opinion), or provocative without being maliciously offensive.

Sprinkled through the pages of this book are "proverb twists" taken from picture postcards, relics of a bygone era before the telephone was within reach of most people, and a medium by which ordinary people kept in touch with kith and kin. Proverb humor was a favorite topic of postcard creators.

Proverb Wit & Wisdom is a book to enjoy—for browsing, for reference, or for locating the perfect witticism to brighten up a letter, an announcement, or a speech. An audience deserves to be repaid for its patience, with an occasional flash of humor (original or not). As one wit put it, "Many speakers confuse the seating capacity of an auditorium with the sitting capacity of their audience."

About This Book

THE CORNERSTONE OF this book is a comprehensive collection of proverbs and quotations familiar to most Americans today. Familiar sayings such as "Always is a long time," "It's great to be alive," "Anything can happen," and "Never assume" have been included. Excluded are figures of speech (e.g., "Cool as a cucumber"), though they are sometimes called proverbial expressions. For the defining purposes of this book, a proverb offers a universal truth (e.g., "Beauty is in the eye of the beholder") or piece of wisdom, not a description of a particular situation (e.g., "Pretty as a picture"). Also excluded are proverbs that deal with health, farming, superstitions, and weather prediction, which may be better suited to a volume dedicated to folk wisdom.

ARRANGEMENT BY KEYWORD

Quotation hunters will discover that classification by saying makes it easy to find exactly the thought they're looking for. For example, here you will find quotations about money under twenty-four different sayings, so that quotations are arranged by *theme*, (e.g., "Money has no smell") rather than by general topic (e.g., money, love, work, etc.).

In this collection of about fifteen hundred main entries, each entry is listed alphabetically by a keyword, which is capitalized, and which is not necessarily (and not usually) the first word of the saying. Here are ten examples from the beginning of the book:

1. ABSENCE makes the heart grow fonder.
2. Should auld ACQUAINTANCE be forgot . . . ?
3. It pays to ADVERTISE.
4. Don't sell AMERICA short.
5. APPAREL oft proclaims the man.
6. There's no harm in ASKING.
7. You must take the BAD with the good.
8. No matter how you slice it, it's still BALONEY.
9. A thing of BEAUTY is a joy forever.
10. BLACK is beautiful.

Keywords are a useful way to classify proverbs because the wording of proverbs has no fixed form. For example: "You must take the bad with the good," "One must take the bad with the good," "Take the bad with the good," or "Always take the bad with the good." No matter how the proverb is said, however, it includes the word *bad*, which makes *bad* a good keyword.

When a proverb explicitly states its subject (as in examples 1, 3, 4, 8, and 10 above), there is no question about what is the keyword. But sometimes the choice of keyword is not so obvious. Example 5 is about both *ap-*

parel and *man*, 7 is about both *bad* and *good*, 9 is about both *beauty* and *joy*. In such cases the first of the pair is usually chosen as the keyword.

Many proverbs are metaphorical, and do not include the actual subject. "When the cat's away, the mice will play." What should be the keyword: cat? mice? play? As the proverb goes, there are no easy answers (in this case, it's *mice*).

Since the reader might not know the meaning of foreign-language words—and hence the keywords—main-entry sayings in another language are alphabetized according to the first word of the saying.

ABBREVIATED NOTE ON PROVERB ORIGINS

Because one's natural curiosity often raises the question "Where did this come from?", the origin of most sayings is documented. Absence of documentation means that the origin is recent (nineteenth or twentieth century), unknown, or in doubt.

Where possible, the approximate date and origin are indicated, without duplicating all the scholarly material contained in existing sourcebooks, which are listed in the Bibliography. Instead, many proverbs are followed by a brief note on the year and place of first citation. For example:

ENOUGH is enough. *1546, Heywood*

The earliest occurrence of this proverb (with a possible variation in wording) is the 1546 book by J. Heywood, as listed in part I of the Bibliography.

Fair EXCHANGE is no robbery. *1546, 0-71*

The earliest occurrence of this proverb (with a possible variation in wording) appears in a 1546 source as indicated in the *Concise Oxford Dictionary of Proverbs*, page 71. All abbreviated citations are listed below.

B   Stevenson, Burton. *The Home Book of Proverbs, Maxims, and Familiar Phrases*. New York: Macmillan, 1948.

BJW Whiting, Bartlett Jere. *Modern Proverbs and Proverbial Sayings*. Cambridge: Harvard University Press, 1989.

EAP Whiting, Bartlett Jere. *Early American Proverbs and Proverbial Phrases*. Cambridge: Belknap Press of Harvard University Press, 1977.

F   Flexner, Stuart, and Doris Flexner. *Wise Words and Wives' Tales*. New York: Avon Books, 1993.

Heard in . . . Noted by a field researcher in a study (approx. 1945–78) conducted by the American Dialect Society under the direction of Margaret M. Bryant, as noted in *A Dictionary of American Proverbs*, edited by Wolfgang Mieder and others (Oxford University Press, 1992). For example, "Heard in Mississippi" means the saying was recorded by an American Dialect Society field worker in Mississippi and appeared in *A Dictionary of American Proverbs*.

K   Keyes, Ralph. *Nice Guys Finish Seventh: False Phrases, Spurious Sayings, and Familiar Misquotations*. New York: HarperCollins, 1992.

M   Magill, Frank N., and Tench F. Tilghman. *Magill's Quotations in Context.* 2 vols. New York: Salem Press, 1965.

M69 *Magill's Quotations in Context.* Harper & Row, 1969 ed.

MD   Morris, William, and Mary Morris. *Morris Dictionary of Word and Phrase Origins.* New York: Harper & Row, 1977.

O   Simpson, John A., ed. *Concise Oxford Dictionary of Proverbs.* New York: Oxford University Press, 1982.

OE   Smith, William G., ed. *Oxford Dictionary of English Proverbs.*

O2   Smith, William G. *Oxford Dictionary of English Proverbs.* 2nd ed. New York: Oxford University Press, 1952.

T   Tilley, Morris Palmer. *A Dictionary of Proverbs in England in the Sixteenth and Seventeenth Centuries.* Ann Arbor: University of Michigan Press, 1950.

TW   Taylor, Archer, and Bartlett Jere Whiting. *A Dictionary of American Proverbs and Proverbial Phrases, 1820–1880.* Cambridge: Belknap Press of Harvard University Press, 1967.

W   Mieder, Wolfgang. *American Proverbs: A Study of Texts and Contexts.* Berne: Peter Lang, 1989.

WM   Mieder, Wolfgang, ed. *A Dictionary of American Proverbs.* New York: Oxford University Press, 1992.

The reader may note a certain unevenness in citations given (or absent) throughout this book. Many citations are the words of unknown wits. Rather than pepper the pages with *Anon.*, I simply give no indication of authorship where none is known. In some cases I cite the author and name the poem, essay, play, or book in which the line appears. In many cases, only the author's name is given, and the source is not. In these instances it probably means that the citation was found in a secondary source.

The Nature of Proverbs

AN EASY WAY to belittle proverbs is to observe that for practically every known proverb, you can find one that says exactly the opposite. Hence, goes the argument, proverbs cancel each other out and their net value is close to zero.

If it is true that "Absence makes the heart grow fonder," can it also be true that "Out of sight [is] out of mind"? If it is good advice to "Know thyself," is it also good advice that "Ignorance is bliss"? If "Money isn't everything," can it also be true that "Money makes the world go 'round"?

As one skeptic has commented, "Proverbs should be sold in pairs, a single one being but a half-truth." In her preface to the 1983 *Penguin Dictionary of Proverbs*, Rosalind Fergusson acknowledges that "folk wisdom is often contradictory" and admits that two contradictory proverbs "cannot both be true." She concludes:

> Perhaps it is a mistake to regard proverbs as a source of accumulated wisdom. Perhaps they are better seen as a collection of tags that enable thoughts to be communicated and exchanged, without effort of formulation. . . . [Proverbs are] preformulated ideas, ready for instant use in an appropriate situation.

Leo Rosten, who has written extensively on proverbs, seems in substantial agreement with Fergusson's position that proverbs are mainly of rhetorical value. In his *Treasury of Jewish Quotations*, Rosten describes proverbs as ready-made witticisms, traditional bon mots that infuse color and life into the speech of ordinary people. The truth is this: people quote proverbs "the better to express themselves." Adages are the wit of the inarticulate: What we get from proverbs, he writes, "much more than instruction . . . is . . . delight, pleasure in the precision of phrasing, the music of alliteration, the felicity of verbal counterpoint and balanced construction. . . ."

It should be pointed out that this is *not* the traditional attitude toward proverbs. There is a long tradition that regards proverbs as the carrier of the wisdom of the folk, the "discoveries of the wise." In Elizabethan England, schoolboys memorized hundreds of proverbs and maxims, in English and in Latin. In part, it is a reflection of this cultural attitude that the plays of Shakespeare are so rich in proverbs, proverb allusions, and proverb jokes.

In contrast to the position of Fergusson and Rosten, the contemporary proverb scholar Wolfgang Mieder expresses a more traditional attitude toward proverbs when he writes, ". . . proverbs are small pieces of human wisdom that have been handed down from generation to generation and that continue to be applicable and valid even in our modern technological age" (*Prentice-Hall Encyclopedia of World Proverbs*).

Of course, many proverbs do have a rhetorical charm: many have rhyme and rhythm and evoke colorful images. But is that their *major* contribution to our culture? Does the fact that proverbs contradict each other cancel out their net value as "small pieces of wisdom"? Or does this very fact, that proverbs contradict each other, convey an important message about the nature of reality? If so, what is the message?

Simply put, the message conveyed by contradictory proverbs is that *life is contradictory* and that what is true or good or wise is true or good or wise only in a certain context, only under certain circumstances. Thus "Circumstances alter cases" becomes a key proverb.

"Circumstances alter cases" means that for a proverb to be a *complete* statement, it must be preceded with the qualification "Sometimes." Think of every proverb as an elliptical statement; the full statement would be something like "*Sometimes* absence makes the heart grow fonder" or "*Sometimes* out of sight means out of mind." *Sometimes* money makes the world go 'round, or *sometimes* money isn't everything. Circumstances alter cases (sometimes).

The idea that circumstances alter cases is *contained* in many proverbs: Beauty is in the eye of the beholder, Everyone knows where his own shoe pinches, It all depends on whose ox is gored, Where you stand depends on where you sit, You judge your neighbor by yourself, or You measure other folks' corn by your own bushel. Circumstances alter cases is a basic concept in folk wisdom and tells us why proverbs do, in fact, contradict each other.

Interestingly, the proverb "Circumstances alter cases" was adopted by Rev. Joseph Fletcher to explain the basic idea of "situation ethics," as set forth in his *Situation Ethics, the New Morality*.

In his book, Fletcher raises the classic moral problem: Must ethical principles begin with the assumption that there are "eternal and absolute" principles of right and wrong? Does the attitude that "everything is relative" undermine a fundamental belief in the concept of right and wrong?

Ethicists have always struggled over the question of whether ethical principles must have an absolute validity. Some have proposed an alternative, Fletcher notes, which has been variously labeled antinomianism, situationism, contextualism, occasionalism, circumstantialism, and actualism.

Fletcher explains: "These labels indicate . . . that the core of the ethic they describe is a healthy and primary awareness that '*circumstances alter cases*,'—i.e., that in actual problems of conscience the situational variables are to be weighed as heavily as the normative or 'general' constants." This does not mean that because every case is different, anything goes. Fletcher's long discussion of this problem may reasonably be summarized by the maxim "Temper justice with mercy."

In the world of practical affairs, we are accustomed to living with contradictions of all sorts. We blow on our hands to warm them up and blow on hot food to cool it off. A physician recommends that one patient eat less and that another eat more. A child psychologist suggests that one parent be more lenient with his or her child and that another be a little stricter. In many ways, much of life may be described as a search for striking a balance between opposing forces: finding activity that balances work and play, finding a love that balances lust and tenderness, exercising money habits that balance generosity and thrift, cultivating a mind that is open to new ideas but not closed to old ideas.

The balancing of opposing forces seems to be built into nature's design of things—opposing forces of gravity and inertia keep the planets in orbit, the antagonistic action of flexors and extensors results in exquisite muscular coordination.

The special contribution of Gestalt psychology to the psychology of visual perception has been an emphasis on the fact that *the perception of an object depends on the total perceptual field*; one must understand the total *pattern* (gestalt) in which an event is embedded before the psychological meaning of the event can be understood. This may be seen as a special case of circumstances altering cases: the surroundings alter the object.

Gestalt psychologists are fond of presenting ambiguous figures to demonstrate how ambiguous isolated events can be. For example, is Figure 1 a vase or a pair of profiles?

Figure 1

Add a pair of parentheses and two dots (Figures 2 and 3) and you can remove the ambiguity, but *where* you place these details makes all the difference in the meaning that the figure takes on!

Figure 2   Figure 3

Social psychologists have studied the influence upon perception of *internal* factors, rather than external, surrounding factors. In a landmark psychological experiment of 1947, Bruner and Goodman demonstrated that to a child from a poor home, a quarter actually looks bigger than it does to a child from a well-to-do home.

Circumstances alter cases. Perhaps this is the message of Ralph Waldo Emerson's words, "A foolish consistency is the hobgoblin of little minds." F. Scott Fitzgerald put it this way: "The test of a first-rate intelligence is the ability to hold two opposed ideas in mind at the same time, and still retain the ability to function."

From each according to his ABILITIES, to each according to his needs. *Karl Marx (1818–83), Criticism of the Gotha Programme*

Communism might be likened to a race in which all competitors come in first with no prizes. *James Lyle Mackay*

From each according to his inability, to each according to his greed. *Peter's Almanac*

The inherent vice of capitalism is the unequal sharing of blessings; the inherent virtue of socialism is the equal sharing of miseries. *Winston Churchill*

ABSENCE makes the heart grow fonder. *

. . . of the other fellow.

. . . for Somebody New. *Popular song of the 1930s*

. . . and presents work well too.

. . . A pretty and poetic thought, but quite misleading. If the person is not around to annoy you, the heart might feel fonder for a short time, but any prolonged absence weakens the bond of love. *Marlene Dietrich*

Absence does not live up to its reputation.

Absence makes the heart go yonder.

Absence makes the heart grow heart trouble. *Title of a poem by Ogden Nash*

Absence makes the mind go wander.

Absence sharpens love, presence strengthens it. *English proverb*

Absinthe makes the heart grow fonder. *Line in a Marx Brothers film, written by S. J. Perelman*

Absinthe makes the tart grow fonder! *Hugh Drummond, in The Vintage Years, by S. Hicks*

Abstinence makes the heart grow fonder.

Anything you lose automatically doubles in value. *Mignon McLaughlin*

Friction makes the heart beat faster. *Erica Jong, reviewing a book on sex technique, in New York Times, June 23, 1992*

God gave us our memories so that we might have roses in December. *James M. Barrie*

It's amazing how nice people are to you when they know you're going away. *Michael Arlen*

Love knows not its depth till the hour of separation. *Kahlil Gibran*

Sometimes people are easier to love after they die.

The same wind snuffs candles yet kindles flames; so, where absence kills a little love, it fans a great one. *François de la Rochefoucauld*

*The first line of an anonymous poem published in 1602, says Burton Stevenson (B-4). Flexner (F-4) gives the earliest form of this saying as the words of the Roman poet Sextus Propertius (ca. 26 B.C.): "Always toward absent lovers love's tide stronger flows."

ACCIDENTS will happen in the best-regulated families. *Charles Dickens (1812–70), David Copperfield*

. . . that's how lots of families get started.

Actresses will happen in the best regulated families. *Oliver Herford*

Most accidents happen at home—maybe we oughta move.

If accidents happen and you are to blame,
Take steps to avoid repetition of same.
Dorothy Sayers, The Teeth of the Evidence

Should auld ACQUAINTANCE be forgot . . . ? *Robert Burns (1759–96)*

ACTIONS speak louder than words. *Poor Richard's Almanac, 1766*

. . . but not as often.

All talk and no do.

It's always the ones who talk loudest who do the least.

Them as talks most does least.

A superior man is ashamed if his words are better than his deed.

Actions lie louder than words. *Carolyn Wells*

As I grow older, I pay less attention to what men say. I just watch what they do. *Andrew Carnegie*

At the day of judgment we shall not be asked what we have read but what we have done. *Thomas à Kempis, Imitation of Christ*

Do not offer advice which has not been seasoned by your own performance. *Henry S. Haskins, Meditations on Wall Street*

Fair words butter no parsnips. *1639, Clarke*

Few things are harder to put up with than the annoyance of a good example. *Mark Twain*

Help with deeds, not with words. *Desiderius Erasmus, Adagia*

I am not yet so lost in lexicography, as to forget that words are the daughters of earth, and that things are the sons of heaven. *Samuel Johnson, A Dictionary of the English Language*

I have no words; My voice is in my sword. *Shakespeare, Macbeth 5.8.7*

I'd rather see a sermon than hear one any day. *Edgar A. Guest*

If you are of the opinion that contemplation of suicide is sufficient evidence of a poetic nature, do not forget that actions speak louder than words. *Fran Lebowitz, Metropolitan Life*

If you don't live it, you don't believe it.

I'm not much of a talker, but I'm not much of a doer either. © *Ashleigh Brilliant*

It is more important to watch how a man lives than to listen to what he says.

It is not enough to have a good mind. The main thing is to use it well. *René Descartes, Discourse on Method*

It is well to think well; it is divine to act well. *Horace Mann*

It isn't the whistle that pulls the train. *Vermont proverb*

Judge men not by their opinions, but by what their opinions have made of them. *Georg Lichtenberg*

Most men had rather say a smart thing than do a good one. *Josh Billings*

My life is my message. *Mahatma Gandhi*

People may doubt what you say, but they will believe what you do.

Plans get you into things, but you got to work your way out. *Will Rogers*

Religion is a way of walking, not a way of talking. *W. R. Inge*

Say nothing and saw wood. *Vermont proverb*

Saying is one thing and doing another. *1603, T-586*

Sayings remain meaningless until they are embodied in actions. *Kahlil Gibran*

The great end of life is not knowledge but action. *T. H. Huxley, Technical Education*

The man who has a right to boast doesn't have to.

The shortest answer is doing. *1640, Herbert*

The smallest deed is better than the grandest intention.

What you say can mean anything, but what you do means everything. © *Ashleigh Brilliant*

Well done is better than well said. *New England proverb*

Wisdom is knowing what to do next, skill is knowing how to do it, and virtue is doing it. *David Starr Jordan*

Wit without employment is a disease. *Robert Burton, Anatomy of Melancholy*

Words can never express what words can never express. © *Ashleigh Brilliant*

You can preach a better sermon with your life than with your lip. *Oliver Goldsmith*

You'll never plough a field by turning it over in your mind. *Irish proverb*

See also DEEDS not creeds; TALK is cheap.

Sweet are the uses of ADVERSITY. *Shakespeare, As You Like It 2.1.12*

A stumble may prevent a fall. *1732, Fuller*

Adversity introduces a man to himself.

All misfortune is but a stepping stone to fortune. *Henry David Thoreau, Winter, Jan. 20, 1841*

By trying we can easily learn to endure adversity. Another man's, I mean. *Mark Twain, Pudd'nhead Wilson's New Calendar*

Do not be afraid of defeat. You are never so near to victory as when defeated in a good cause. *Henry Ward Beecher*

Every successful person has had failures, but repeated failure is no guarantee of eventual success. © *Ashleigh Brilliant*

Failure teaches success. *1902, WM-195*

Fractures well cured make us more strong. *Ralph Waldo Emerson*

I thank God for my handicaps, for, through them, I have found myself, my work, and my God. *Helen Keller*

I'll say this for adversity: people seem to be able to stand it, and that's more than I can say for prosperity. *Kin Hubbard*

If you have not known poverty, heart-hunger and misunderstanding, God has overlooked you, and you are to be pitied. *Elbert Hubbard*

It has been said that misfortune sharpens our wits, but . . . it often simply dulls them. *Friedrich Nietzsche*

It is not true that suffering ennobles the character . . . it makes men petty and vindictive. *W. Somerset Maugham*

Joys are our wings; sorrows our spurs. *Jean Paul Richter*

No man should praise poverty but he who is poor. *Saint Bernard*

One way to keep happy is to learn to enjoy trouble.

Pain nourishes courage. You can't be brave if you've only had wonderful things happen to you. *Mary Tyler Moore*

Pleasure makes us acquainted with each other, but it takes trials and grief to make us know each other. *Vermont proverb*

Some defeats are only installments to victory. *Jacob A. Riis*

Suffering isn't ennobling, recovery is. *Christiaan N. Barnard, New York Times, Aug. 28, 1985*

Sweet are the uses of advertising.

Sweet are the uses of the other fellow's adversity.

The common idea that success spoils people by making them vain, egotistic and self-complacent is erroneous—on the contrary it makes them, for the most part, humble, tolerant, and kind. It is failure that makes people bitter and cruel. *W. Somerset Maugham, The Summing Up*

The Lord sometimes takes us into troubled waters not to drown us, but to cleanse us.

There is no useful generalization about adversity: It drives some men to God, some to the devil, and others to the dogs. *Sydney J. Harris*

There's nothing like failure to give you success. *John Trent*

'Tis held that sorrow makes us wise. *Alfred, Lord Tennyson, In Memoriam*

We could never learn to be brave and patient, if there were only joy in the world. *Helen Keller*

What makes our opponents useful is that they allow us to believe that without them we wouldn't be able to realize our ideals. *Jean Rostand, Journal d'un Caractère*

A woman is like a teabag—you can't tell how strong she is until you put her in hot water. *Nancy Reagan*

You've got to learn to survive a defeat. That's when you develop character. *Richard Nixon, Dallas Times-Herald, Dec. 10, 1978*

Know how sublime a thing it is
To suffer and be strong.
Henry Wadsworth Longfellow, The Light of Stars

It pays to ADVERTISE.

. . . A store that advertised for a watchman was burglarized that night.

A codfish lays ten thousand eggs a day, but it is done silently. A hen lays one egg and cackles. Nobody eats codfish eggs and nearly everybody eats chicken eggs.

Advertising begins when the first crying child advertises his wants to his mother, and ends only with the epitaph on the headstone in the village cemetery. *Edward S. Jordan*

Advertising is legalized lying. *H. G. Wells*

Advertising may be described as the science of arresting human intelligence long enough to get money from it. *Stephen Leacock*

Advertising is . . . the cheapest way of selling goods, particularly if the goods are worthless. *Sinclair Lewis*

Advertising is the rattling of a stick inside a swill bucket. *George Orwell*

Doing business without advertising is like winking at a girl in the dark: you know what you are doing, but nobody else does. *Ed Howe*

If you would have your business rise
Don't forget to advertise.
For the man who has some goods to sell
And gently whispers it down a well
Will not entrap the elusive dollar
As he would if he'd climb a tree and holler.

In good times, people want to advertise; in bad times, they have to. *Bruce Barton*

It's a great art to know how to sell wind. *Confucius*

Many a small thing has been made large by the right kind of advertising. *Mark Twain, A Connecticut Yankee in King Arthur's Court*

ADVICE is cheap.

. . . because supply always exceeds demand.

. . . unless you take it.

. . . and the best advice is, "Don't give it."

. . . Too bad it interferes with our plans.

. . . except when you consult a doctor or lawyer or tax accountant.

A good scare is worth more to a man than good advice. *Ed Howe*

A word of advice: don't give it. *A. J. Volicos, as quoted in Reader's Digest, Apr. 1947*

Advice is what we ask for when we already know the answer but wish we didn't. *Erica Jong*

Advice is worth what you pay for it.

Advice of old men is as the sun in Winter; it enlightens without warming. *Luc de Clapiers de Vauvenargues*

Advising a fool is like striking cold iron. *Greek proverb*

Don't give me advice, give me money. *Spanish proverb*

Don't think people judge your generosity by the amount of advice you give away.

Even those who do not display any acuteness and acumen in other respects are experts in the algebra of other people's affairs. *Arthur Schopenhauer, Counsels and Maxims*

For the first half of your life, people tell you what you should do; for the second half, they tell you what you should have done. *Richard Needham*

Give neither advice nor salt, until you are asked for it. *English proverb*

Good advice costs nothing and is worth the price. *Walter A. Benz*

He who gives advice is a bigger fool than he who takes it. *H. W. Thompson, Body, Boots and Britches*

I always pass on good advice. It is the only thing to do with it. I have found the best way to give advice to your children is to find out what they want and then advise them to do it. *Harry S. Truman, May 27, 1955*

I have lived some thirty years on this planet, and I have yet to hear the first syllable of valuable or even earnest advice from my seniors. *Henry David Thoreau, Walden*

I let the American people down, and I have to carry that burden for the rest of my life. My political life is over. I will never again have an opportunity to serve in any official position. Maybe I can give a little advice from time to time. *Richard Nixon*

I sometimes give myself admirable advice, but I am incapable of taking it. *Mary Wortley Montagu*

If you can tell the difference between good advice and bad advice, you don't need advice.

Medicine is like advice—easy to give, hard to take. *A. I. Silverman, The Wit of Medicine*

Never invest your money in anything that eats or needs repainting. *Billy Rose, New York Post, Oct. 26, 1957*

No man will take counsel, but every man will take money; therefore money is better than counsel. *Jonathan Swift*

No one really listens to anyone else, and if you try it for a while you'll see why. *Mignon McLaughlin*

No one wants advice—only corroboration. *John Steinbeck*

One gives nothing so freely as advice. *François de la Rochefoucauld*

The land is never void of counselors. *African proverb*

The surest way to lose a friend is to tell him something for his own good. *Sid Ascher*

The people sensible enough to give good advice are usually sensible enough to give none. *Eden Phillpotts, as quoted in Reader's Digest, Dec. 1951*

The worst waste o' breath, next to playing the saxophone, is advisin' a son. *Kin Hubbard*

To be good is noble, but to teach others to be good is nobler—and less trouble. *Mark Twain*

Too bad that all the people who know how to run the country are busy driving taxicabs and cutting hair. *George Burns*

Unasked-for advice smells bad. *Heard in Maryland*

What a pity it is that nobody knows how to manage a wife, but a bachelor. *George Colman, Sr., The Jealous Wife*

What is easy? To give advice to another. *Thales*

When a man comes to me for advice, I find out the kind of advice he wants, and I give it to him. *Josh Billings*

Pressed for rules and verities,
All I recollect are these:
Feed a cold to starve a fever.
Argue with no true believer.
Think-too-long is never-act.
Scratch a myth and find a fact.
Stitch in time saves twenty stitches.
Give the rich, to please them, riches.
Give to love your hearth and hall.
But do not give advice at all.
Phyllis McGinley

ADVICE that ain't paid for ain't no good. 1546, Heywood

Bought wit is best. *1585, T-735*

Free advice is worth what you paid for it.

Good advice is one of those insults that ought to be forgiven.

If you want to get rid of somebody, just tell 'em something for their own good. *Kin Hubbard*

AGE before beauty. 1843, WM-12

There's no cure for old AGE.

A man is young if a lady can make him happy or unhappy. He enters middle age when a lady can make him happy, but can no longer make him unhappy. He is old and gone if a lady can make him neither happy nor unhappy. *Moriz Rosenthal, seventy-five-year-old pianist, as quoted in Reader's Digest, Jan. 1937*

Advanced old age is when you sit in a rocking chair but can't get it going.

After a certain age, if you don't wake up aching in every joint, you are probably dead. *Tommy Mein, quoted by Herb Caen in San Francisco Chronicle, Jan. 6, 1986*

Age comes in on little crow's feet.

Age is a very high price to pay for maturity. *Tom Stoppard, Rosencrantz and Guildenstern Are Dead*

Age mellows some people; others it makes rotten. *Heard in Arkansas*

All passions are extinguished with old age; self-love never dies. *Heard in Indiana*

By staying alive too long, you could seriously damage your health. © *Ashleigh Brilliant*

For what crime is old age the punishment? © *Ashleigh Brilliant*

I have everything now I had 20 years ago—except now, it's all lower. *Gypsy Rose Lee, Newsweek, Sept. 16, 1968*

I've looked that old scoundrel death in the eye many times but this time I think he has me on the ropes. *Douglas MacArthur, before undergoing surgery from which he never recovered*

Intellectual blemishes, like facial ones, grow more prominent with age. *François de la Rochefoucauld*

Men grow old, pearls grow yellow, there is no cure for it. *Chinese proverb*

Nature abhors the old. *Ralph Waldo Emerson, Essays*

Old age ain't for sissies. *Bette Davis*

Old age comes at a bad time. *Sue Banducci*

Old age is a shipwreck. *Charles de Gaulle*

Old age is the only disease you don't look forward to being cured of. *Citizen Kane*

Old age is when work is a lot less fun, and fun is a lot more work.

Old age is when you feel bad in the morning without having had any fun the night before.

Old age is when you know all the answers and nobody asks you the questions.

Old age is when you look at the menu before you look at the waitress.

Old age is when you read the obituaries before the sports page.

Old vessels must leak. *1613, OE-473*

Should we slow down because we're getting older, or hurry up because we'll never get any younger?

The ego is willing but the machine cannot go. It's the last thing a man will admit, that his mind ages. *Will Durant at age ninety, New York Times, Nov. 6, 1975*

The only good thing about it is you're not dead. *Lillian Hellman (attributed)*

There is no cure for birth or death save to enjoy the interval. *George Santayana*

There's no use wishing to be younger; just concentrate on getting older.

They tell you that you'll lose your mind when you grow older. What they don't tell you is that you won't miss it very much. *Malcolm Cowley*

Time is a dressmaker specializing in alterations. *Faith Baldwin, Face Toward the Spring*

We neither get better or worse as we get older, but more like ourselves. *Robert Anthony, Think Again*

When you begin to notice how well you feel—that is a sure sign of age. *Sydney J. Harris*

Wrinkles are beds that the gods have dug for our tears. *Émile Augier*

Years steal fire from the mind. *Lord Byron, Childe Harold's Pilgrimage*

Youth is beauty, even in cattle. *Egyptian proverb*

We are but older children, dear,
Who fret to find our bedtime near.
Lewis Carroll

Whatever poet, orator, or sage
May say of it, old age is still old age.
Henry Wadsworth Longfellow, Morituri Salutamus

Senescence begins
And middle age ends
The day your descendants
Outnumber your friends. *Ogden Nash, as quoted in Reader's Digest, Sept. 1971*

See also ALL MEN are mortal; There's a remedy for everything except DEATH; Grow OLD gracefully; We get too soon OLD and too late smart.

It's great to be ALIVE.

Everything that lives is holy, life delights in life. *William Blake*

Bite your tongue. Get a cinder in your eye. When you feel good, you feel nothing. *R. Buckminster Fuller*

ALL for one, and one for all. *Alexandre Dumas père (1802–70), The Three Musketeers*

Be ALL that you can be. *U.S. Army recruitment advertisement*

Being it all is hard work,
Having it all makes up for it.
Caption of a poster, signed Betsy von Furstenberg, showing a fashionable lady loaded with shopping bags; seen in Manhattan, 1988

Make the most of yourself, for that is all there is to you. *Ralph Waldo Emerson*

The hand, the heart and the head form a triangle that can bring untold happiness, if used together. One alone is not much service, any more than one blade of a scissors. *William C. Hunter*

See also Hitch your wagon to a STAR.

It is not good for man to be ALONE.

. . . but sometimes it is a great relief. *John Barrymore*

. . . [but] when God created two sexes he may have been overdoing it. *Charles Merrill Smith*

A bachelor washes his own dishes, makes his own bed, puts out his own garbage, and then, a month or so later, has to do it all over again.

A bachelor's life is no life for a single man. *Samuel Goldwyn*

And yet when all, all, all is said about the horrors of marriage, we still must admit that single people don't seem any happier. *Richard Needham*

Every man should take unto himself a wife, but he should be careful whose wife he takes. *Old postcard*

If you can't stand solitude, maybe you bore others too. *Bob Gordon*

It's a lonesome washing when there's not a man's shirt in it. *Vermont proverb*

Our language has wisely sensed the two sides of being alone. It has created the word "loneliness" to express the pain of being alone. And it has created the word "solitude" to express the glory of being alone. *Paul Tillich, The Eternal Now*

Man without woman would be like playing checkers alone. *Josh Billings*

Solitude is more enjoyable when you have someone to talk about it with.

Hell is oneself;
Hell is alone, the other figures in it
Merely projections. There is nothing to escape from
And nothing to escape to. One is always alone.
T. S. Eliot, The Cocktail Party

See also A good WIFE and health are a man's best wealth; MAN is a social animal.

ALWAYS is a long time. *Heard in Illinois*

Don't sell AMERICA short.* *J. Pierpont Morgan (1837–1913)*

*After the money panic of 1907, by these words America's financial genius, J. P. Morgan, expressed his faith in America's ability to weather the worst financial storms, and tried to reassure Wall Street colleagues less stout-hearted than he.

When you're ANGRY, count to ten.*

A man that does not know how to be angry does not know how to be good. Now and then a man should be shaken to the core with indignation over things evil. *Henry Ward Beecher*

When you are right, you can afford to keep your temper, and when you are in the wrong, you cannot afford to lose it. *Sign on the wall of Mahatma Gandhi's room at Sevagram, India, according to Ambassador Chester Bowles*

Anger has no eyes. *Hindu proverb*

Anger punishes itself. *John Lyle, Euphues, 1579*

Do not plunge thyself too far in anger. *Shakespeare, All's Well That Ends Well 2.3.222*

If you kick a stone in anger, you'll hurt your own foot. *Korean proverb*

Man is a rational animal who always loses his temper when he is called upon to act in accordance with the dictates of reason. *Oscar Wilde, The Critic as Artist*

No revenge is more honorable than one not taken. *Spanish proverb*

Temper is one thing you can't get rid of by losing it.

The best remedy for a short temper is a long walk. *Jacqueline Schiff*

The best way to know a man is to watch him when he is angry. *Hebrew proverb*

The only good thing about anger is that it proves you have feelings. © *Ashleigh Brilliant*

When a wise man is angry, he is no longer wise. *Talmud*

When angry, count four; when very angry, swear. *Mark Twain, Pudd'nhead Wilson's Calendar*

When a man is wrong and won't admit it, he always gets angry. *Thomas Haliburton*

When angry, write a nasty letter . . . but wait a day before you mail it.

When I am angry with myself, I criticize others. *Ed Howe*

When you complain about your neighbor's faults, count ten . . . of your own.

*When angry, count ten before you speak, if very angry, count a hundred. *Thomas Jefferson (1743–1826), Ten Commandments*

Be kind to ANIMALS.*

Be kind to dumb people. *Don Herold*

Find some other way of proving your manhood than by shooting defenseless animals and birds. *H. Jackson Brown, Jr., Life's Little Instruction Book*

The angels smile when we are kind to a bird. *Opie Read*

To hell with whales—save the dollar. *Bumper sticker seen in Seattle, 1991*

Be kind to all dumb animals
    And give small birds a crumb;
Be kind to human beings too.
    They're sometimes pretty dumb.
Rebecca McCann

*The compassionate treatment of animals is an important theme of the Hebrew Bible. The Fourth Commandment designates the sabbath as a day of rest for humans and work animals alike. Among the many laws of compassion to animals is the commandment "Thou shalt not muzzle the ox when he treadeth out the corn" (Deuteronomy 25:4). The rabbis commented, humans "may be forbidden to consume that which they harvest, but animals must be allowed to feed if they so desire, for while men can understand deprivation, animals cannot" (Erich Isaac, *Forbidden Foods*, p. 38). Psalms 36:6 praises God for preserving "man and beast."

A soft ANSWER turneth away wrath. *Proverbs 15:1*

. . . but hath little effect on a telephone salesman.

. . . but just as often it provokes even more wrath from the person who resents your refusal to argue. *Sydney J. Harris*

Keep your words soft and sweet—you never know when you might have to eat them.

Soft drinks turn away company.

Short ANSWERS save trouble.

See BREVITY is the soul of wit.

There are no easy ANSWERS.

. . . No easy answers to what? To unclear questions? To questions not properly asked? To stupid questions? *Garry Wills*

All simple statements are wrong. *Frank Knight*

Life is an unanswered question, but let's believe in the dignity and importance of the question. *Tennessee Williams*

What is important is to keep learning, to enjoy challenge, and to tolerate ambiguity. In the end there are no certain answers. *Marina Horner*

Go to the ANT, thou sluggard; consider her ways, and be wise. *Proverbs 6:6*

See Mind your own BUSINESS; Tend to BUSINESS.

ANYTHING can happen.

. . . Even a rich man can knock at a poor man's door. *Russian proverb*

Don't lay any certain plans for the future; it is like planting toads and expecting to raise toadstools. *Josh Billings*

Genuine bons mots surprise those from whose lips they fall, no less than they do those who listen to them. *Joseph Joubert, Pensées*

Life is what happens to you while you're making other plans.

Nothing is certain but uncertainty. *Latin proverb*

The most precious thing in life is its uncertainty. *Yoshida Kenko, Essays on Idleness*

There is only one thing certain and that is that nothing is certain. *G. K. Chesterton, as quoted in Reader's Digest, June 1922*

What's going to happen will happen, and what isn't is liable to happen anyway. *Heard in Illinois*

You understand human nature when you are never surprised by anything it does. *Vernon Howard*

What we look for does not come to pass.
God finds a way for what none foresaw. *Euripedes*

See also Never the ROSE without the thorn.

ANYTHING worth doing is worth doing well. *Lord Chesterfield (1694–1773), Letters to His Son*

. . . so first ask yourself, Is it really worth doing?

A work ill done must be done twice. *1659, Howell*

Anything worth doing has probably already been done by someone else.

Anything worth doing is worth hiring someone who knows how to do it right.

Doing a thing well is often a waste of time. *Robert Byrne*

Doing little things well, enables one to do big things better. *Old postcard*

Good enough isn't good enough.

If a thing is worth doing it is worth doing badly. *G. K. Chesterton, What's Wrong with the World*

If a thing's worth doing, it's worth doing late. *Frederick Oliver*

If a thing is worth doing, it's worth doing slowly . . . very slowly. *Gypsy Rose Lee*

If it's worth doing, it's worth overdoing.

It takes less time to do a thing right than to explain why you did it wrong. *Henry Wadsworth Longfellow*

One of the rarest things that man ever does is to do the best he can. *Josh Billings*

The sad truth is that many of the backbreaking achievements reported in the *Guinness Book of World Records* weren't worth doing in the first place.

There are only a few ways of doing a thing right, but the ways of doing a thing wrong are infinite. *Peter's Almanac*

There is nothing so fatal to character than half-finished tasks. *David Lloyd George*

There is nothing so useless as doing efficiently that which should not be done at all. *Peter F. Drucker*

What is the difference between effectiveness and efficiency? Efficiency is getting the job done right; effectiveness is getting the right job done.

What is worth doing at all is worth doing well, and what is worth doing well is worth doing at once, so that you may have an early start to do something else better. *Old postcard*

What is worth doing is worth the trouble of asking somebody to it. *Ambrose Bierce*

What's worth doing is worth doing for money. *Joseph Donohue*

Whatever is worth having is worth cheating for. *W. C. Fields*

Whatsoever thy hand findeth to do, do it with thy might; for there is no work, nor device, nor knowledge, nor wisdom, in the grave, whither thou goest. *Ecclesiastes 9:10*

When a thing is not worth overdoing, leave it alone! *Henry H. Haskins, Meditations on Wall Street*

Do nothing by halves
Which can be done by quarters
F. R. Scott

If a task is once begun
Never leave it till it's done.

Be the labor great or small,
Do it well or not at all.

Good, better, best;
Never let it rest
Until your good is better
And your better best.

ANYTHING worth having is worth working for.

Anything worth having is a thing worth cheating for. *W. C. Fields*

If a thing is worth having, it's worth fighting for; on that principle the institution of marriage was founded. *Captain Billy's Whiz Bang, Apr. 1922*

APOLOGIES never made anything better.

Sorry doesn't mend it.

Never APOLOGIZE.

. . . The right sort of people do not want apologies, and the wrong sort take a mean advantage of them. *P. G. Wodehouse*

APPAREL oft proclaims the man. Shakespeare, *Hamlet* 1.3.72.

. . . to be what he is not. *Henny Youngman*

A woman's apparel oft proclaims her man.

Apparel off proclaims the woman.

See also CLOTHES make the man.

APPEARANCES are deceiving.* 1526, T-16

. . . but disappearances are even more so. *Peter's Almanac*

A red-nosed man may be no drunkard, but he will always be called one. *Chinese proverb*

A straight stick is crooked in the water. *1589, WM-563*

All that looks good ain't. *Heard in New York*

An honest look covereth many faults. *1642, Torriano*

Bees are not as busy as we think they are. They jest can't buzz any slower. *Kin Hubbard*

Every one's faults are not written in their foreheads. *1678, Ray*

Experience teaches you that the man who looks you straight in the eye, particularly if he adds a firm handshake, is hiding something. *Clifton Fadiman, Enter, Conversing*

Fair without, false within. *1200, OE-187*

Judge a man not by his clothes, but by his wife's clothes. *Thomas Dewar*

Judge not according to appearances. *John 7:24*

In order to become the master, the politician poses as the servant. *Charles de Gaulle*

Nepotism is only kin deep. *Peter Hillmore, London Observer, Oct. 20, 1985*

Never judge from appearances. *16th century*

Rosary in hand, the devil at heart. *Portuguese proverb*

She who appears to be a dumb blond may be a bright brunette.

Snow on the roof doesn't mean there's no fire in the furnace.

Strip away the phony tinsel of Hollywood and you find the real tinsel underneath. *Oscar Levant*

Th' feller that agrees with ever'thing you say is either a fool er he is gettin' ready to skin you. *Kin Hubbard*

The bait hides the hook. *1579, Lyle*

The best proof that appearances are deceiving is that the dollar bill looks exactly as it did fifteen years ago. *Wall Street Journal, ca. 1925*

There hain't nothin' as disappointin' these days as catchin' up with a girl an' findin' out she's an old woman. *Kin Hubbard*

Misleading are appearances.
　One's true self is within—
A corpulent outside may hide
　A soul that's starved and thin.
Rebecca McCann

*Appearances are deceptive. *British equivalent*

See also You can't tell a BOOK by its cover; NOTHING is simple.

APPETITE comes with eating.

. . . but thirst goes away with drinking. *François Rabelais*

Scratching and eating wants but a beginning. *1598, T-588*

APPETITE makes the best sauce. *ca. 1375, WM-23*

Appetite grows by what it feeds on.

An APPLE a day keeps the doctor away. *1866, 0-5*

. . . if you aim it right.

. . . and use tomatoes on bill collectors.

A worry a day drains vitality away.

An apple a day makes 365 a year.

An onion a day gives your diet away. *Knickerbocker Press, ca. 1925*

I gave up eating an apple a day when it occurred to me that the doctor doesn't make house calls anymore.

Motto of a Bible-reading family: A chapter a day keeps the devil away.

When the oranges are golden, doctors' faces grow pale. *Japanese proverb*

If an apple a day
Keeps the doctor away,
They'll soon be condemned
By the AMA.
Joan Liftin

*Flexner (F-9) notes that one of the tales of the Arabian Nights tells of a magical apple of Samarkand, which supposedly could cure all ailments. In 1612, Thomas Cogan, in *The Haven of Health*, advised eating an apple to quench "the flames of Venus": "He that will not a wife wed, Must eat a cold apple when he goeth to bed." Mieder (1993, pages 162-168) discusses the history of this proverb, and offers humorous variations of it.

One bad APPLE can spoil the barrel. *1340, 0-194*

There is no pack of cards without a knave. *16th century*

The APPLE doesn't fall far from its tree. *Ralph Waldo Emerson**

. . . and when it does, too often it rolls down-hill.

Joke all you please about the old family album, but it gave a prospective bridegroom a purty fair idea o' the gang he wuz marryin' into. *Kin Hubbard*

Pedigree may be of some use to racehorses, but what use it can be to man is a mystery to me. *Josh Billings*

The nut doesn't fall far from its tree.

You can't choose your ancestors, but that's fair enough—they probably wouldn't have chosen you.

The pedigree of honey
Does not concern the bee;
A clover any time, to him
Is aristocracy.
Emily Dickinson

With him for a sire, and her for a dam
What should I be, but just what I am?
Edna St. Vincent Millay

*Emerson was referring not to the parental influence, writes Flexner (F-9), but to "the tug that often brings us back to our child-hood home."

See also BLOOD will tell; Like FATHER, like son; The TREE is known by its fruit.

There are a few rotten APPLES in every barrel.

There is little choice in a barrel of rotten AP-PLES. *Shakespeare, The Taming of the Shrew 1.1.137*

Don't upset the APPLECART.

Why not upset the apple cart? If you don't, the apples will rot anyway. *Frank L. Clark*

APRIL showers bring May flowers. *1555, T-603*

. . . but when it's coming down in buckets, it's hard to think of the goddamn May flowers.

. . . and May showers bring flooded base-ments.

A cold April and a wet May fill the barn with grain and hay. *1659, Howell*

An ARMY marches on its stomach. *Napoleon (1769–1821)*

An army, like a serpent, travels on its belly. *Frederick the Great (attributed)*

Give them great meals of beef and iron and steel,
They will eat like wolves and fight like devils. *Shakespeare, Henry V 3.7.162*

The best troops would be as follows: an Irish-man half drunk, a Scotchman half starved, and an Englishman with his belly full. *19th-century general*

Join the ARMY and see the world.

. . . meet interesting people—and kill them. *Pacifist badge, 1978*

What goes AROUND comes around. *African American proverb*

See also CURSES, like chickens, come home to roost.

ART for art's sake. *Latin proverb*

. . . makes no more sense than gin for gin's sake. *W. Somerset Maugham*

All art is quite useless. *Oscar Wilde, The Picture of Dorian Gray*

There is no such thing as a moral or immoral book. Books are well-written, or badly written. That is all. *Oscar Wilde, The Picture of Dorian Gray*

ART imitates nature. Seneca (1st century A.D.)

A pro is someone who makes it look easy. *Paul Henderson*

All I know is that within every man and woman a secret is hidden, and as a photographer it is my task to reveal it if I can. *Yousuf Karsh*

Art apes nature. *1533, T-19*

Art lies in concealing art. *Ovid, The Art of Love*

Art not only imitates nature, but also completes its deficiencies. *Aristotle*

Copy nature and you infringe on the work of our Lord. Interpret nature and you are an artist. *Jacques Lipchitz, New York Times, April 28, 1964*

Each time you go on the stage you have to do it as if it's the first time. *Lou Jacobi*

It usually takes me more than three weeks to prepare a good impromptu speech. *Mark Twain*

No great artist sees things as they really are. If he did, he would cease to be an artist. *Oscar Wilde*

No television performance takes as much preparation as an off-the-cuff talk. *Richard Nixon*

The mind conceives with pain, but brings forth with joy. *Joseph Joubert, Pensées*

The perfect hostess is like a duck: calm and serene on the surface but paddling like hell underneath.

To be natural is such a very difficult pose to keep up. *Oscar Wilde*

When something can be read without effort, great effort has gone into its writing. *Enrique Jardiel Poncela*

When plastic surgeons make real people look like Hollywood film images, nature imitates art.

Without art, the crudeness of reality would make the world unbearable. *G. B. Shaw*

Secure the shadow 'ere the substance fade, Let Nature imitate what Nature made! *Advertisement ca. 1850 for the daguerreotype, the first practical method of taking photographs*

See also What is ART?

ART is long, and time is fleeting. Henry Wadsworth Longfellow (1807–82), A Psalm of Life

. . . except when you're at a PTA meeting. *L. L. Levinson*

Ars longa, vita brevis. ("Art is long, life is short.") *Hippocrates*

Ars longa, vita herring. *Graffiti*

I love a statue old and still
    Ancient moods pervade it.
It's strange how much more real it is
    Than is the hand that made it.
Rebecca McCann

See also LIFE is short; TIME flies.

I don't know what ART is, but I know what I like.

Everyone wants to understand painting. Why don't they try to understand the singing of birds? People love the night, a flower, everything that surrounds them without trying to understand them. But painting—that they must understand. *Pablo Picasso*

Modern medicine makes me believe in progress, but modern art revives my doubts. © *Ashleigh Brilliant*

What is ART?

A guilty conscience needs to confess. A work of art is a confession. *Albert Camus, Notebooks*

An artist cannot speak about his art any more than a plant can discuss horticulture. *Jean Cocteau, Newsweek, May 16, 1955*

Art is a lie that makes us realize the truth. *Pablo Picasso*

Art is an action against death. It is a denial of death. *Jacques Lipchitz, Chicago Tribune, June 4, 1957*

Art is the illusion of spontaneity. *Japanese proverb*

Art is the triumph over chaos. *John Cheever, The Stories of John Cheever*

I dream for a living. *Steven Spielberg, Time, July 15, 1985*

I make pictures and someone comes in and calls it art. *Willem de Kooning*

I would have it written of me on my stone: I had a lover's quarrel with the world. *Robert Frost*

Perfection itself is imperfection. *Vladimir Horowitz, Newsweek, May 17, 1965*

Poetry is man's rebellion against being what he is. *James Branch Cabell*

The essence of all art is to have pleasure in giving pleasure. *Mikhail Baryshnikov, Time, May 19, 1975*

The object of art is to give life a shape. *Jean Anouilh*

The true function of art is to . . . edit nature and so make it coherent and lovely. The artist is a sort of impassioned proofreader, blue-pencilling the bad spelling of God. *H. L. Mencken*

What garlic is to salad, insanity is to art. *Augustus Saint-Gaudens*

What is art? A semblance of the truth more beautiful than the truth. *Opie Read*

When I was a little boy, they called me a liar, but now that I am grown up, they call me a writer. *Isaac Bashevis Singer, Time, July 18, 1983*

When power leads man toward arrogance, poetry reminds him of his limitations. When power narrows the area of man's concern, poetry reminds him of the richness and diversity of existence. When power corrupts, poetry cleanses. *John F. Kennedy, last major public address, dedication of Robert Frost Library, Amherst College, Oct. 26, 1963*

See also ART for art's sake; ART imitates nature; I don't know what ART is, but I know what I like.

ASHES to ashes, dust to dust. *The Book of Common Prayer*

Ashes to ashes, and clay to clay, if the enemy doesn't get you, your own folks may. *James Thurber*

Ashes to ashes, dust to dust, if heaven doesn't get you the other place must. *Heard in U.S. and Canada*

Eulogy by an absentminded minister: Only the shell is here; the nut has gone.

See also ALL FLESH is grass.

What you don't ASK for, you don't get.

Freedom is never voluntarily given up by the oppressor; it must be demanded by the oppressed. *Martin Luther King, Jr., Why We Can't Wait*

Who waits on fortune's knock will rarely win; Who calls on fortune, some day finds her in. *Arthur Guiterman*

See also GOD helps those who help themselves; HELP yourself.

There's no harm in ASKING.

Lose nothing for want of asking. *16th century*

Never ASSUME.

Always verify your references. *1918, OE-9*

Assumption is the mother of screw-up. *Angelo Donghia, New York Times, Jan. 20, 1983*

Most of our assumptions have outlived their uselessness. *Marshall McLuhan*

Never assume the obvious is true. *William Safire, Sleeper Spy*

Remember to distrust. *1664, T-568*

Supposing is good, but finding out is better. *Mark Twain.* "Quoted as a favorite maxim of his," says Burton Stevenson (B-309).

See also I'm from MISSOURI . . .

There are no ATHEISTS in a foxhole. *William T. Cummings, 1944*

. . . not because people are hypocrites . . . [but] because times like those bring us face to face with our limitations. We who are usually so self-confident, so secure in our ability to control things, suddenly learn that the things that matter most in our lives are beyond our control. *Harold S. Kushner, Who Needs God*

. . . and there are, apparently, no atheists in the Ku Klux Klan. God sometimes moves in mysterious ways, His lip service to exact. *Mignon McLaughlin*

A man cannot become an atheist by merely wishing it. *Napoleon, Maxims*

By night an atheist half-believes in God. *Edward Young, Night Thoughts*

In case of atomic attack, the federal ruling against prayer in schools will be temporarily suspended. *Cold War graffiti*

Misfortune teaches us to pray. *Slovakian proverb*

Once on shore we pray no more.

People in trouble remember Allah. *Hausa (West African) proverb*

Pray for one hour before going to war, for two before going to sea, for three before going to be married. *Indian proverb*

Some pray to the gods only when in trouble. *Japanese proverb*

The chamber of sickness is the chapel of devotion. *1616, Draxe*

There are no atheists in an audit.

There is no such thing as an atheist. Everyone believes he is God. *Alan Ashley-Pitts*

Vows made in storms are forgotten in calms. *1732, Fuller*

When it thunders the thief becomes honest. *1640, Herbert*

Who saileth not, knoweth not what the fear of God is. *1591, Florio*

See also The DEVIL was sick, the devil a saint would be . . .

Out of the mouth of BABES.*

. . . comes cereal.

. . . come words we should never have taught them.

*Out of the mouth of babes and sucklings hast thou ordained strength. *Psalms 8:2.* Out of the mouth of babes and sucklings thou hast perfected praise. *Matthew 21:16*

See also CHILDREN and fools speak the truth.

Don't throw out the BABY with the bath-water.*

Don't empty the baby with the bath.

No bathwater is ever thrown out without some species of baby goes down the plug-hole with it. *1955, BJW-24*

*A 16th cent. German proverb, says Meider, who devotes an entire chapter (1993, pages 193–224) to this proverb.

Stay in your own BACKYARD.

Don't forget your raisin. *Southern U.S. proverb*

Oh, let us love our occupations,
Bless the squire and his relations,
Live upon our daily rations,
And always know our proper stations.
Charles Dickens, The Chimes

See also Let the COBBLER stick to his last; It is a wise CHILD that knows its own father; Mind your own BUSINESS.

You must take the BAD with the good.

See Never the ROSE without the thorn.

No matter how you slice it, it's still BALONEY.* *Alfred E. Smith, campaign speech, 1936; F-692*

Baloney is the unvarnished lie laid on so thick, you hate it. Blarney is flattery laid on so thin you love it. *Fulton J. Sheen*

*Since the 1920s, *baloney* has had the connotation of nonsense, possibly an Italian American distortion of the word *blarney*, conjectures Tad Tuleja.

A BARGAIN is a bargain.* *1553, T-29*

*Like "An honest man's word is his bond" or "A promise is a debt," this proverb expresses the English legal principle that an oral agreement is binding.

See A PROMISE is a promise.

It takes two to make a BARGAIN. *1598, 0-234*

. . . but just one may make a profit.

. . . and a lawyer to write the contract.

Make the best of a bad BARGAIN. *1589, T-46*

About the time one learns how to make the most of life, the most of it is gone. *Akron Beacon Journal, ca. 1925*

Gnaw the bone that has fallen thy lot. *1678, T-58*

BEAR and forbear. *Epictetus (1st to 2nd century A.D.)*

Be willing to have it so. Acceptance of what has happened is the first step to overcoming the consequences of any misfortune. *William James*

He who doesn't accept the conditions of life sells his soul. *Charles Baudelaire*

In 1932, at the height of the Great Depression, Pope Pius XI implored believers to endure hard times in a Christian spirit of penance and resignation, and quietly await the hour of mercy and peace: "Let the poor and all those who at this time are facing the hard trial of want of work and scarcity of food, let them in a like spirit of penance suffer with greater resignation the privations imposed upon them by these hard times and the state of society, which Divine Providence in an ever-loving but inscrutable plan has assigned them. Let them accept with a humble and trustful heart from the hand of God the effects of poverty, rendered harder by the distress in which mankind is now struggling. . . . Let them take comfort in the certainty that their sacrifices and troubles borne in a Christian spirit will concur efficaciously to hasten the hour of mercy and peace." *Pius XI, Encyclical of 1932*

Self-restraint is feeling your oats without sowing them. *Shannon Fife, as quoted in Reader's Digest, July 1950*

The ideal man bears the accidents of life with dignity and grace, making the best of the circumstances. *Aristotle*

If you can't BEAT 'em, join 'em. *1941, WM-371*

. . . If you can't join 'em, start your own league.

If you can't beat 'em, call 'em names. *Old postcard*

If you can't convince them, confuse them. *Harry S. Truman, undoubtedly describing the tactics of his political opponents*

It gets embarrassing when you can't lick 'em and they won't let you join 'em.

It's probably better to have him inside the tent pissing out, than outside the tent pissing in. *Lyndon B. Johnson, on J. Edgar Hoover, New York Times, Oct. 31, 1971*

A thing of BEAUTY is a joy forever.*

A garden is a thing of beauty and a job forever.

A thing of beauty can be a great expense.

A thing of beauty keeps you broke forever.

A thing of duty annoys forever.

Face it: a thing of beauty is a joy till sunrise. *Harvey Fierstein, Torch Song Trilogy*

The nakedness of woman is the work of God. *William Blake, The Marriage of Heaven and Hell*

You don't have to be a thing of beauty to be a joy forever. *Flip Wilson*

What is lovely never dies.
But passes into other loveliness.
Thomas B. Aldrich, A Shadow of the Night

We shirk our duties,
And our home ties sever;
A string of beauties
Is a joy forever.
A Fisherman's Rhyme

*A thing of beauty is a joy forever:
Its loveliness increases; it will never
Pass into nothingness.
John Keats (1795–1821), Endymion

BEAUTY is in the eye of the beholder. 1878, F-15

. . . and so is dullness.

A book is a mirror: if an ass peers into it, you can't expect an apostle to look out. . . . He who understands the wise is himself wise. *Georg Lichtenberg*

A fool sees not the same tree that a wise man sees. *William Blake, Proverbs of Hell*

A generous man is merely a fool in the eyes of a thief. *Henry Fielding*

A man has generally the good or ill qualities which he attributes to mankind. *William Shenstone, Essays on Men and Manners*

All looks yellow to the jaundiced eye. *Alexander Pope, An Essay on Criticism*

An evil eye can see no good. *Danish proverb*

Ask a toad what is beauty? . . . a female with two great round eyes coming out of her little head, a large flat mouth, a yellow belly and a brown back. *Voltaire*

Asses would rather have hay than gold. *Heracleitus*

Bad eyes never see any good. *Heard in Florida*

Beauty is in the heart of the beholder. *Al Bernstein*

Beauty, like supreme dominion
Is but supported by opinion.
Poor Richard's Almanac, 1741

Error held in truth has much the effect of truth. *George Iles*

Guilty men see guilt written on the faces of saints. *Heard in Illinois*

Humor is in the funnybone of the beholder. *Fred Metcalf*

Illusion is the first of the pleasures. *Voltaire*

It is only in appearance that time is a river. It is rather a vast landscape and it is the eye of the beholder that moves. *Thornton Wilder, The Eighth Day*

It's innocence when it charms us, ignorance when it doesn't. *Mignon McLaughlin*

Jail is jail for thieves. . . . For me, it [is] a palace. *Mahatma Gandhi*

Junk is anything that has outlived its usefulness. *Oliver Herford*

Logic is in the eye of the logician. *Gloria Steinem*

Look at everything as though you were seeing it either for the first or last time. Then your time on earth will be filled with glory. *Betty Smith, A Tree Grows in Brooklyn*

Love is a great beautifier. *Louisa May Alcott*

Love is an attempt to change a piece of a dream world into reality. *Theodor Reik*

Love is the delusion that one woman differs from another. *H. L. Mencken*

No two people read the same book. *Edmund Wilson*

Nothing is beautiful from every point of view.

Obscenity is whatever happens to shock some elderly and ignorant magistrate. *Bertrand Russell, Look, Feb. 23, 1954*

One thing about baldness: It's neat. *Don Herold*

Pornography is in the groin of the beholder. *Charles Rembar, End of Obscenity*

Some women are not beautiful—they only look as though they are. *Karl Kraus, Aphorisms and More Aphorisms*

The idiot looks at the mirror and sees a scholar. *Heard in Illinois*

The lesson intended by an author is hardly ever the lesson the world chooses to learn from his book. *G. B. Shaw, Man and Superman*

[The lover says] "How beautiful you are, now that you love me." *Marlene Dietrich*

The optimist makes his own heaven, and enjoys it as he goes through life. The pessimist makes his own hell and suffers it as he goes through life. *William C. Hunter*

The woman one loves always smells good. *Rémy de Gourmont*

The world is a looking glass, and gives back to every man the reflection of his own face. *William Makepeace Thackeray*

There is only one beautiful child in the world, and every mother has it. *Stephen Leacock*

'Tis the good reader that makes the good book. *Ralph Waldo Emerson, Society and Solitude (Success)*

To the drunkard, no liquor is bad; to a merchant, no money is tainted; to a lecher, no woman is ugly. *Talmud*

Ugliness is a point of view: an ulcer is wonderful to a pathologist. *Austin O'Malley*

We don't see things as they are, we see things as we are. *Anaïs Nin*

We find what we look for in this world. *Ella Wheeler Wilcox*

We must respect the other fellow's religion, but only in the sense and to the extent that we respect his theory that his wife is beautiful and his children smart. *H. L. Mencken, Minority Report*

What is grass to the lion is flesh to the horse. *Turkish proverb*

What is pornography to one man is the laughter of genius to another. *D. H. Lawrence, Pornography and Obscenity*

What we see depends mainly on what we look for. *John Lubbock*

Whatever interests, is interesting. *William Hazlitt*

A jest's prosperity lies in the ear
    Of him that hears it, never in the tongue
    Of him that makes it.
Shakespeare, Love's Labour's Lost, 1.1.871

Two men look out through the same bars:
One sees the mud, and one the stars.
Frederick Langbridge, Cluster of Quiet Thoughts

See also It also DEPENDS on whose ox is gored; One man's MEAT is another man's poison; Where you STAND depends on where you sit.

BEAUTY is its own excuse for being. *Ralph Waldo Emerson* (1803–82), *The Rhodora*

God don't like ugly. *African American proverb*

See also ART for art's sake.

BEAUTY is only skin-deep. *1613, T-35*

. . . as any alligator would be happy to tell you.

. . . but it's only the skin you see. *A. Price, 1978*

. . . but ugly goes to the bone. *19th century, F-16*

. . . but it's a valuable asset if you're poor or haven't any sense. *Kin Hubbard*

. . . in the eye of the beholder. *A maxim mixture by Diane Crosby, in Jeff Davis County (Ga.) Ledger*

. . . which is okay for this superficial world we live in.

. . . What do you want—an adorable pancreas? *Jean Kerr*

Always remember that true beauty comes from within—from within bottles, jars, compacts, and tubes. *Peter's Almanac*

Beauty is a short success, but while it lasts it is quite pretty. *Josh Billings*

Beauty without grace is a hook without bait. *Ninon de Lenclos*

Better a girl has beauty than brains, because boys see better than they think. *Josh Billings*

It's a good thing that beauty is only skin deep or I'd be rotten to the core. *Phyllis Diller*

More women are wooed for their complexions than for their characters. *Arnold Haultain, Hints for Lovers*

Most beauty is like the strawberry—soon out of season, but exquisite while it does last, and like the strawberry, ain't perfect without a good deal of sugar. *Josh Billings*

The peacock is a beautiful bird, but it takes the stork to deliver the goods. *Old postcard*

The saying that beauty is but skin-deep is but a skin-deep saying. *Herbert Spencer, Essays (Personal Beauty)*

The skin of a hippopotamus is two inches thick. With a face like that he needs it. *Herbert V. Prochnow*

Virtue is but skin-deep. *New England proverb*

One man's BEAUTY is another man's ugliness.

See BEAUTY is in the eye of the beholder; One man's MEAT is another man's poison.

As you make your BED, so you must lie in it. 1590, O-143

. . . Simply a lie. If I have made my bed uncomfortable, please God, I will make it again. *G. K. Chesterton*

As you have made your bed, why lie about it?

Early to BED and early to rise makes a man healthy, wealthy, and wise. 1496, F-48

Be the first to the field and the last to the couch. *Chinese proverb*

Early to bed and early to rise ain't never no good if you don't advertise.

Early to bed and early to rise and you wear what belongs to the other guys.

Early to bed and early to rise take most of the zing out of living. *Leo Rosten*

Early to bed and early to rise and your girl goes out with other guys.

Early to bed and early to rise is a sure sign that you're fed up with television. *Henny Youngman*

Early to bed and early to rise is the curse of the working class. *Pappy Maverick, TV show*

Early to bed and early to rise makes a man healthy, wealthy, and despised.

Early to bed and early to rise makes a man healthy, wealthy and apt to get his own breakfast. *Franklin P. Jones*

Early to bed and early to rise makes a man mighty tired by afternoon.

Early to bed and early to rise makes Jack a dull boy. *Judge, ca. 1925*

"Early to bed and early to rise" is either a thing of the past or a thing that ain't come—it certainly don't exist in these parts now. *Josh Billings*

Early to bed and early to rise, and you'll miss seeing a great deal that doesn't go on during the daytime. *Roanoke Times, ca. 1925*

Early to bed and early to rise or the boss will promote the other guys.

Early to bed and early to rise—till you get enough money to do otherwise. *Peter's Almanac*

Early to bed and early to rise; that's okay for other guys.

Early to rise and to bed makes a male healthy and wealthy and dead. *James Thurber, Fables for Our Times*

Early up and out won't pay off nearly as well as working far into the night. *Leo Rosten*

Late to bed and late to rise keeps a twinkle in the eyes.

Most men who go to bed early and get up at the crack of dawn are found in the world's inferior jobs, have little money, and are of an elementary mentality. *George Jean Nathan*

Rise with the sun, instead of sitting up until midnight with the daughter. *Old postcard*

Well enough for the old folks to rise early, because they have done so many mean things all their lives they can't sleep anyway. *Mark Twain, Notebook*

Late to rise and late to rest
Unfits a man to do his best.
Arthur Guiterman

The BEE that gets the honey doesn't hang around the hive.

. . . Only a hen can lay around and make money.

A tethered sheep winna get fat. *English dialect*

The dog that trots about finds a bone.

Here's a maxim to remember
    If you's have your business thrive.
"The bee that gets the honey
    Doesn't hang around the hive."
Old postcard

BEGGARS can't be choosers. 1546, Heywood

Tiggers should not be tarrowers. *English dialect, EMW-173*

BEGINNER'S luck.

Fools are lucky.

A good BEGINNING makes a good ending. 1300, O-97

Be pleasant every morning till ten o'clock; the rest of the day will take care of itself. *William C. Hunter*

The BEGINNING is the hardest. *ca.* 1500, WM-45

A good beginning is half the battle. *1415, WM-45*

A good lather is half the shave.

All things are difficult before they are easy. *Fuller, 1732*

Beginning is easy—continuing is hard. *Japanese proverb*

Getting things done is largely a matter of getting things started. *Heard in Ontario*

Kissing a girl for the first time is like getting the first olive from a jar: after the first one, they come rolling out. *Heard in Oklahoma*

The first sip of broth is always the hottest. *Irish proverb*

The first step is the hardest. *1596, O-82*

The worst is first. *1672, T-41*

Well BEGUN is half done. *Latin proverb*

There is an old saying "well begun is half done"—'tis a bad one. I would use instead—Not begun at all until half done. *John Keats, letter, 1817*

See also The BEGINNING is the hardest.

BELIEVE only half of what you see, and nothing of what you hear. *ca.* 1205, WM-46

. . . but which half?

I can believe anything provided it is incredible. *Oscar Wilde, The Picture of Dorian Gray*

If you keep your mind sufficiently open, people will throw a lot of rubbish into it. *William A. Orton*

Merely having an open mind is nothing. The object of opening the mind, as of opening the mouth, is to shut it again on something solid. *G. K. Chesterton*

You can't BELIEVE everything you hear.

. . . but you can repeat it anyway.

See also BELIEVE only half of what you see, and nothing of what you hear.

Ask not for whom the BELL tolls.*

. . . You might get an answer you don't especially like. *Ernst Angst*

. . . and you will pay only the station-to-station rate. *Howard Kandel*

An insult to one man is an insult to all, for it may be our turn next. *Josh Billings*

There is no they, only us. *Bumper sticker*

*. . . never send to know for whom the bell tolls; it tolls for thee. *John Donne (1572–1631), Devotions*

Better BEND than break.* **1666, *Torriano***

I'd like to believe it, but I guess I won't. Broken legs heal, but bowlegs don't. *John Heywood*

Blessed are the flexible, for they shall not be bent out of shape. *From a tour leader's Ten Commandments for Travelers*

*This phrase is an allusion to the fable of the Willow and the Oak.

All is for the BEST in the best of all possible worlds. *Voltaire (1694–1778), Candide**

Because everything is for the best it does not follow that it is for our best. *L. de V. Matthewman*

But all shall be well and all shall be well and all manner of thing shall be well. *Julian of Norwich, 14th-century nun; source of a passage in Little Gidding, by T. S. Eliot*

For all our folly, we are a splendid, promising form of life and I am on our side. *Lewis Thomas, The Fragile Species.* Dr. Thomas continues: "I do not agree with this century's fashion of running down the human species as a failed try, a doomed sport. At our worst, we may be going through the early stages of a species' adolescence, and everyone remembers what that was like."

Just in proportion to the outward poverty is the inward wealth. *Henry David Thoreau, Autumn*

Man is lazy by nature, so God gave us children to get us up early. *Henny Youngman*

Material wealth is God's way of blessing people who put Him first. *Jerry Falwell*

Optimism cuts a sorry figure in this theatre of sin, suffering and death. *Arthur Schopenhauer*

Optimism. The doctrine or belief that everything is beautiful, including what is ugly. *Ambrose Bierce*

That some good can be derived from every event is a better proposition than that everything happens for the best, which it assuredly does not. *James K. Feibleman, as quoted in Reader's Digest, May 1971*

The optimist proclaims that we live in the best of all possible worlds; and the pessimist fears this is so. *James Branch Cabell, The Silver Stallion*

The sun shines after every storm; there is a solution for every problem, and the soul's highest duty is to be of good cheer. *Ralph Waldo Emerson*

Life is a glorious cycle of song,
A medley of extemporania;
And love is a thing that can never go wrong;
And I am Marie of Romania.
Dorothy Parker, Comment

An optimist is a guy
that has never had
much experience
Don Marquis

*Voltaire wrote this with satirical intent, but the Roman philosopher Marcus Aurelius was apparently serious when he wrote: "Whatever happens at all happens as it should."

The BEST is the cheapest in the long run.

Cheap is cheap.

Cheapest is dearest. *Yiddish proverb*

Ill ware is never cheap. *1611, Cotgrave*

The best is best cheap. *1546, Heywood*

The longest is the shortest.

You've probably seen the words [by John Ruskin] displayed on a little plaque by the cash register of some store you've been in: "There is hardly anything in the world that some man cannot make a little worse and sell a little cheaper, and the people who consider price only, are this man's lawful prey." The stores with that legend displayed usually charge too much. *Andy Rooney*

The BEST is yet to be.*

Although living to a ripe old age may not guarantee health, wealth, and happiness, it certainly beats the only alternative.

If the worst is yet to come, don't wait for it. *Old postcard*

Modern marriage slogan: Cheer up! Divorce is yet to come. *Life, ca. 1925*

No man or woman really knows what perfect love is until they have been married a quarter of a century. *Mark Twain*

Old friends, and old wine and old gold are best. *1576, OE-470*

Old wood is best to burn, old horse to ride, old books to read, and old wine to drink. *1580, OE-473*

The point of living, and of being an optimist, is to be foolish enough to believe the best is yet to come. *Peter Ustinov*

The older the tree, the sweeter the sap.

There is more felicity on the far side of baldness than young men can possibly imagine. *Logan Pearsall Smith, Last Words*

There's many a good tune played on an old fiddle. *English proverb*

Whatever aging people say to the contrary, we all regret our youth once we have lost it. The famous wisdom that is supposed to be ours in old age doesn't help us a bit. *Marlene Dietrich*

Winter is on my head, but spring is in my heart. *Victor Hugo*

You ain't heard nothin' yet. *Al Jolson, a saying that became his signature line, from The Jazz Singer*

*Grow old along with me!
The best is yet to be,
The last of life, for which the first was made.
Our times are in his hand.
Who saith, "A whole I planned,
Youth shows but half; trust God: see all, nor
be afraid!"
Robert Browning (1812–89), Rabbi Ben Ezra

Behaviorist B. F. Skinner does his deadpan best to correct Browning's promise: "Browning's Rabbi Ben Ezra was unfortunately wrong; old age, 'the last of life,' is not the part 'for which the first was made.' We do not live in order to be old, and for young people to expect that 'the best is yet to be' would be a great mistake." (B. F. Skinner and M. E. Vaughan, Enjoy Old Age)

The BIGGER they come, the harder they fall. *Robert Fitzsimmons, before a boxing match of 1902, when he faced a much heavier opponent.* Flexner (F-23) notes that despite his cheery prediction, Fitzsimmons went on to lose the match, "but that did nothing to discourage use of the saying."

The bigger the summer vacation, the harder the fall.

The bigger they are, the harder they hit.

The whale is endangered, but the ant is doing very well, thank you.

See also The higher they CLIMB, the harder they fall.

A BIRD in the hand is worth two in the bush. *Aesop (6th century B.C.)*

. . . but this is not the opinion of the bird.

. . . Yes, but a bird in a good restaurant is worth ten of either of them. *Stephen Leacock*

A Bible in the hand is worth two on the shelf.

A bird in the hand can be messy.

A bird in the hand could bite your wrist.

A bird in the hand is a certainty. But a bird in the bush may sing. *Bret Harte*

A bird in the hand is bad table manners. *Wall Street Journal, ca. 1925*

A bird in the oven is worth two in the butcher shop. *Russell T. Blackwood, Jr.*

A book in the hand is worth two in the library.

A burden in the bush is worth two in your hands. *James Thurber*

A cuff on the wrist is worth two on the ear.

A feather in the hand is better than a bird in the air. *1640, Herbert*

A foot on the brake is worth two in the grave.

A girl in the cab is worth a dozen in the choir.

A girl on the knee is worth two on the phone. *Old postcard*

A hair on the head is worth two on the brush. *Oliver Herford*

A handkerchief dropped is worth two in the hand. *Heard in Mississippi*

A job in hand is worth a dozen in prospect. *Malcolm Forbes*

A man in the house is worth two in the street. *Mae West*

A ring on the finger is worth two on the phone. *H. W. Thompson*

A trout in the pot is better than a salmon in the sea. *Irish proverb*

An ace in the hand is worth two in the deck.

Better for birders, but for birds not so good. *John Heywood, Epigrams upon Proverbs*

Colonel Sanders' bird in the hand is finger-lickin' good.

It is a proverb of this world only, and is not true on the broad field of eternal things. There our bird in the bush is worth all the birds that ever were in mortal hands. *Charles H. Spurgeon, Salt Cellars*

One today is worth two tomorrows. *Poor Richard's Almanac*

Sign in a florist's window: A rose in the hand is worth two on the bush.

Two in the bush is the root of all evil. *Elbert Hubbard*

Water afar off quenches not fire. *1586, T-708*

Wine in the bottle does not quench thirst. *1640, Herbert*

The bird that feeds from off my palm
Is sleek, affectionate, and calm,
But double, to me, is worth the thrush
A-flickering in the elder-brush.
Dorothy Parker, Ornithology for Beginners

See also Better an EGG today than a hen to-morrow; Don't count your CHICKENS before they are hatched.

It's an ill BIRD that fouls its own nest.* Latin proverb

Do not cut down the tree that gives you shade. *Persian proverb*

Do not spit in the well—you may be thirsty by and by. *Russian proverb*

Don't quarrel with your bread and butter.

For the first time in the history of the world, every human being is now subjected to contact with dangerous chemicals, from the moment of conception until death. *Rachel Carson*

Mud not the fountain that gave drink to thee. *Shakespeare, The Rape of Lucrece*

Pollution is nothing but resources we're not harvesting. *R. Buckminster Fuller*

*The word *ill* is popularly used to mean sick, which would suggest that the bird in a be-fouled nest must have bowel trouble. No! Here ill means evil, wrongheaded.

See also Don't KILL the goose that lays the golden eggs.

The early BIRD catches the worm. *1636, Camden*

. . . and the wise worm knows the value of laziness.

. . . the early fish gets worm, hook, and all.

. . . and he is more than welcome to it.

. . . and the Early Christian is got by the lion. *W. R. Inge*

. . . and the fisherman with a flashlight gets the night crawlers.

. . . but the guy who comes along later may be having Lobster Newburg and crepe suzettes. *Charles Merrill Smith*

. . . Don't be fooled by this absurd saw; I once knew a man who tried it. He got up at sunrise and a horse bit him. *Mark Twain, Notebook*

Art Linkletter: What do you think of the saying "The early bird gets the worm"?

Kid: He's welcome to it. I tried it once and it tasted like cold spaghetti. *TV show*

By always rising early in the morning you won't make the dawn come any earlier. *Spanish proverb*

For latecomers, the bones. *Latin proverb*

If you must rise early, be sure you're a bird and not a worm.

If you're a bird, be an early bird
And catch the worm for your breakfast plate.

If you're a bird, be an early bird
But if you're a worm, sleep late.
Shel Silverstein

Sleep late; worms are for birds.

The early fish catches the worm, hook and all. *Puck*

The early bird gets the late one's breakfast. *Mrs. Chamberlain, 1882*

The early bird suffers from insomnia.

The early bird wishes he could have gotten someone else to get up first.

The early tire gets the roofin' tack. *Kin Hubbard*

The early worm is for the birds. *Peter's Almanac*

Well enough for old folks to rise early, because they have done so many mean things all their lives they can't sleep anyhow. *Mark Twain*

Why doesn't the early worm get the bird? It's a poor rule that won't work both ways.

I like the lad, who when his father thought
To clip his morning nap by hackneyed phrase
Of vagrant worm by early songster caught,
Cried, "Served him right! It's not at all surprising:
The worm was punished, sir, for early rising."
John Godfrey Saxe

She was one of the early birds,
And I was one of the worms.
T. W. Conner

BIRDS of a feather flock together. *Aristotle (384–322 B.C.), Rhetoric*

. . . How can birds flock any other way? *Henny Youngman*

It is the wretchedness of being rich that you have to live with rich people. *Logan Pearsall Smith, All Trivia*

There are people who, if they ever reach heaven, will commence at once looking for their own set. *Josh Billings*

When cockroaches give a party, they don't invite chickens. *Jamaican proverb*

You can tell a man who boozes by the company he chooses. *Heard in Indiana*

Don't sell your BIRTHRIGHT for a mess of pottage.*

*Allusion to Esau's bargain with Jacob. *Genesis 25:30–38*

Don't BITE off more than you can chew. *1200, F-180*

The soundest advice that a man can heed: Don't plant more garden than your wife can weed.

Don't BITE the hand that feeds you. *1711, WM-54*

. . . or lick the boot that kicks you.

Don't bite the hand that lays the golden eggs. *Samuel Goldwyn (attributed)*

Don't bite the hand that has your allowance in it. *A child's ending of the proverb*

If you pick up a starving dog and make him prosperous, he will not bite you. This is the principal difference between a dog and a man. *Mark Twain, Pudd'nhead Wilson's Calendar*

There are times when parenthood seems nothing but feeding the mouth that bites you. *Peter De Vries*

Take the BITTER with the sweet.*

All sunshine makes a desert. *Arabic proverb*

He who drives an ass must of necessity smell its fart. *African proverb*

Life is made up of marble and mud. *Nathaniel Hawthorne, The House of the Seven Gables*

The . . . family seems to have two predominant functions: to provide warmth and love in time of need and to drive each other insane. *Donald G. Smith*

You can't have two hills without a valley. *1583, WM-201*

You don't have to die; heaven and hell are in this world too. *Japanese proverb*

Life to have its sweets must have its sours. Love isn't always two souls picking flowers. *John Masefield*

*An ancient idea, with many variants: Take the rough with the smooth, Take the lean with the fat, Take the bad with the good.

See also Every CLOUD has a silver lining; Never the ROSE without the thorn.

BLACK is beautiful. *Stokely Carmichael, 1966*

. . . The redefining of ourselves as "black" places us closer to those people called white, because we, too, now claim race as identity. Black Power sounds like the roar of independence but it is the whimper of submission. To make our primary definition the color of our skin is to imitate white people, not be free of them. *Julius Lester, Lovesong*

Black Is Dutiful. *Sign on the wall of the West African Hair Groomers, New York City, expressing their commitment to service*

Spice is black, but it has a sweet smack. *1721, Kelly*

The blacker the berry, the sweeter the juice. *Heard in California, Colorado, Illinois, and Oregon*

Count your BLESSINGS.

. . . and let your neighbor count his. *James Thurber*

. . . but first be sure they're yours.

. . . Some of them may be missing.

Good cheer is something more than faith in the future; it is gratitude for the past and joy in the present.

If you can't be content with what you have received, be thankful for what you have escaped.

Inflation lets you live in a more expensive neighborhood without ever moving.

Reflect on your present blessings—of which every man has many—not on your past misfortunes, of which all men have some. *Charles Dickens*

Small favors thankfully received.

Summer is better than winter because you don't have to shovel sunshine.

Think of the ills whereof you are free. *Joseph Joubert*

What I'm looking for is a blessing that's not in disguise. *Kitty O'Neill Collins*

You will not know how many things you can be glad for until you begin counting your neighbors' troubles. *Old postcard*

In the kingdom of the BLIND, the one-eyed man is king. *Desiderius Erasmus (1466–1536); O-43*

. . . and the two-eyed man is lynched. *Ernst Angst*

Like the BLIND men and the elephant.

See Where you STAND depends on where you sit.

None so BLIND as those who will not see. 1546, Heywood

. . . any one except his wife.

You see, but you do not observe. *Arthur Conan Doyle*

When the BLIND lead the blind, they all go head over heels into the ditch.*

When the blind lead the blind, they both fall into matrimony. *George Farquhar*

*And if the blind lead the blind, both shall fall into the ditch. *Matthew 15:14*

Follow your BLISS. *Joseph Campbell*

When making your choice in life, do not neglect to live. *Samuel Johnson*

BLOOD is thicker than water. ca. 1412, WM-57

. . . and blue blood is thicker than glue. *BJW-56*

. . . and dirtier. *Richard Shattuck, The Snark Was a Boojum*

. . . and so is toothpaste.

. . . but money is thicker than blood. *BJW-56*

. . . but water's wider, thank the Lord, than blood. *Aldous Huxley, Ninth Philosopher's Song*

Home is the place where, when you have to go there, they have to take you in. *Robert Frost, The Death of the Hired Man*

I hope that when the time comes, I'll be a good mother-in-law. I have only one qualification for it: I always love the girls who love my sons. *Mignon McLaughlin*

BLOOD will tell. 1850, O-22

. . . but often it tells too much. *Don Marquis, A Roach of the Taverns*

Snobs talk as if they had begotten their ancestors. *Herbert Agar*

You can't get BLOOD out of a stone.* 1435, O-21

It's hard to get a stocking off a bare leg.

Sue a beggar and get a louse. *1639, Clarke*

You can't get wool off a frog. *Vermont proverb*

*A legal maxim, on the collection of debts.

You can't get BLOOD from a turnip. *1666, Torriano*

. . . or water from a bone.

. . . or wine from a cork.

Don't try to get blood from a locust. God didn't put it there. *African proverb*

Don't rock the BOAT.

Bureaucracy defends the status quo long past the time when the quo has lost its status. *Laurence Peter*

Conformity, humility, acceptance—with these coins we are to pay our fares to paradise. *Robert Lindner*

Conservatism is adherence to the old and tried against the new and untried. *Abraham Lincoln, Cooper Union address, 1860*

Good things flow from status quo. *Don Cameron*

Hell hath no fury like a bureaucracy scorned. *Milton Friedman*

If you are going to sin, sin against God, not the bureaucracy. God will forgive you but the bureaucracy won't. *Hyman G. Rickover*

Innovations are dangerous. *Heard in Illinois*

One of the greatest pains to human nature is the pain of a new idea. *Walter Bagehot*

Progress is a nice word. But change is its motivator and change has its enemies. *Robert F. Kennedy*

See also Don't make WAVES; Don't go out on a LIMB.

If a BODY kiss a body, need a body cry?*

If a body trust a body—and fail to get prompt pay;
May a body ask a body, Please remit today?
Old postcard

If a body meet a body
And quite circumspect
Kissed a body, would that body
Do you think object?
Old postcard

*Gin a body kiss a body,
  Need a body cry?
  Robert Burns (1759–96) Coming Through the Rye

What's bred in the BONE will come out in the flesh. *1470, O-25*

See BLOOD will tell.

You can't tell a BOOK by its cover.

. . . and you can't always go by its jacket blurb.

. . . but if it's in a plain wrapper, you're entitled to your suspicion.

. . . but make sure your own cover makes a good impression.

. . . especially if it's a paperback.

A rough shell may have a good kernel. *New England proverb*

An ill-dressed person may or may not be a bum, but a person who is always well-dressed is a crook.

As soon as I hear a name, I feel convinced I can guess what the owner looks like, but it never happens, when I actually meet the man, that his face is as I had supposed. *Yoshida Kenko, Essays in Idleness*

Beware of false prophets, which come to you in sheep's clothing, but inwardly they are ravening wolves. *Matthew 7:15*

Empty vessels sound most. *1547, T-697*

Fair face, foul heart. *1548, T-198*

Half the work that is done in the world is to make things appear what they are not. *E. R. Beadle*

I have known a vast quantity of nonsense talked about bad men not looking you in the face. Don't trust that conventional idea. Dishonesty will stare honesty out of countenance any day of the week, if there is anything to be got by it. *Charles Dickens*

Judge not according to the appearance. *John 7:24*

Just exactly in proportion that a man undertakes to make a reputation by his personal appearance, just in that proportion is he a dead beat. *Josh Billings*

Look not on the flask but on what it contains, for there may be a new flask filled with old wine, and an old flask which contains not even new wine. *Judah ha-Nasi*

Many a man who seems to be on Easy Street is only on Easy Payment Plan. *Virginian Pilot, ca. 1925*

Most important ideas aren't exciting, and most exciting ideas aren't important.

Straight trees have crooked roots. *1580, T-682*

The fish does not go after the hook, but after the bait. *Czech proverb*

You can never tell the depth of the well by the length of the pump handle. *H. W. Thompson*

You can't tell a book by its author. *Howard Kandel*

You can't tell a book by its lover.

You can't tell a book by its movie.

You can't know a wine by its barrel. *1651, Herbert*

O judge not a book by its cover
Or else you'll for sure come to grief,
For the lengthiest things you'll discover
Are contained in what's known as a Brief.

See also APPEARANCES are deceiving; Beware of false PROPHETS; THINGS are not always what they seem.

Of making many BOOKS there is no end.

I am not yet so lost in lexography, as to forget that words are the daughters of earth, and that things are the sons of heaven. *Samuel Johnson, A Dictionary of the English Language*

Ye must be BORN again. *John 3:7*

How can we tell when a sin we have committed has been pardoned? By the fact that we no longer commit that sin. *Rabbi Bunam, in Tales of the Hasidim, by Martin Buber*

If your religion does not change you, then you had better change your religion. *Kin Hubbard*

Man's main task in life is to give birth to himself. *Erich Fromm*

Neither a BORROWER nor a lender be. *Shakespeare, Hamlet 1.3.75.*

. . . unless the interest rates are in your favor.

. . . but if you must do one, lend. *Josh Billings*

Lend money to a bad debtor and he'll hate you. *Chinese proverb*

BORROWING brings sorrowing. *Desiderius Erasmus (1466–1536)*

A ready way to lose your friend is to lend him money. Another equally ready way to lose him is to refuse to lend him money. It is six of one and a half dozen of the other. *George Jean Nathan*

Before borrowing money from a friend, decide which you need more.

Borrowing, like scratching, is only good for a while. *Yiddish proverb*

Debt is slavery.

Give money, never lend any. The giving makes ingrates only, the lending makes enemies. *Alexandre Dumas*

He that doth lend doth lose a friend. *William Hazlitt*

He that goes a-borrowing goes a-sorrowing. *1470, O-96*

In borrowing an angel, in repaying a devil.

It costs more to borrow than to buy. *Josh Billings*

It's better to give than to lend, and it costs about the same. *Philip Gibbs*

Lend only those books you never care to see again. *H. Jackson Brown, Jr., Life's Little Instruction Book*

Make friends with your creditors, but never make creditors of your friends.

Money borrowed is money spent. *Heard in California and Colorado*

Money lent to a friend must be recovered from an enemy. *German proverb*

Pay your debts; God made man out of dust, and dust settles.

The borrower is servant to the lender. *Proverbs 22:7*

The holy passion of friendship is of so sweet and steady and loyal and enduring a nature that it will last through a whole lifetime, if not asked to lend money. *Mark Twain, Puddin'nhead Wilson's Calendar*

The surest way to get rid of a bore is to lend money to him. *Paul Louis Courier*

Them ez borrows, sorrows. *E. R. Sill*

There is no practice more dangerous than borrowing money. *George Washington*

Who wants to borrow can come tomorrow. *Yiddish proverb*

I once had money and a friend;
    My friend was short of cash.
I lent my money to my friend.
    (Did I do something rash?)
I sought my money from my friend,
    Which I had wanted long.
I lost my money and my friend.
    (Did I do something wrong?)

The BOSS gets all the credit and the help gets all the blame.

An executive is a man who believes in sharing the credit with the man who did the work.

See also One does all the WORK and the other takes all the credit.

Don't send a BOY to do a man's work.
1932, WM-65

It's a good rule never to send a mouse to catch a skunk or a pollywog to tackle a whale. *Abraham Lincoln*

One boy's a BOY, two boys' half a boy, three boys is no boy at all. *1930, WM-66*

One boy is more trouble than a dozen girls. *1848, O2-475*

You can take a BOY out of the country, but you can't take the country out of the boy. *Heard in Illinois, Indiana, and New York*

You can take a boy out of Brooklyn, but you can't take Brooklyn out of the boy.

You can take a Jew out of the *galut* [i.e., exile], but you can't take the *galut* out of the Jew.

The shepherd smells of sheep even when he becomes a nobleman. *Greek proverb*

Boys will be boys. *1601, O-24*

. . . and so will a lot of middle-aged men. *Kin Hubbard*

. . . but the girls are giving 'em a hot contest for the privilege. *Arkansas Gazette, ca. 1925*

. . . but why do men have to remain boys so much longer than women remain girls? *Sydney J. Harris*

Boys will be boisterous.

The fact that boys are allowed to exist at all is evidence of a remarkable Christian forbearance among men. *Ambrose Bierce*

The old notion that "Boys will be boys" has given way to the new demand that boys must grow up. *TV newscaster, Oct. 14, 1992, on a* college's efforts to eliminate racial slurs from fraternity songs

Until the age of sixteen, a lad is a boy scout—after that he is a girl scout.

See also You're only YOUNG once.

BRAGGING saves advertising.

You have to do a little bragging on yourself even to your relatives—man doesn't get anywhere without advertising. *John Nance Garner*

See also Don't HIDE your light under a bushel.

None but the BRAVE deserve the fair. *John Dryden (1631–1700), Alexander's Feast*

None but the brave desert the fair. *Addison Mizner.* In *Rome Wasn't Burnt in a Day,* Leo Rosten calls this "one of the finest puns I know."

None but the brave deserve affairs.

Only the brave dare ask the fare. *J. Hobday*

Cast your BREAD upon the waters.*

. . . if you like soggy bread.

. . . but don't expect it to come back toasted and buttered.

*Cast thy bread upon the waters: for thou shalt find it after many days. *Ecclesiastes 11:1*

Know which side your BREAD is buttered on. *1546, Heywood*

You can't help liking this boss; if you don't, he fires you.

Whose bread I eat, his song I sing. *German proverb*

The BREAD always falls buttered side down.* *1876, O-25*

. . . and if it's a sandwich, it falls open.

The windshield wiper on the driver's side always streaks and wears out first.

When numbered pieces of toast and marmalade were dropped on various samples of carpet arranged in quality, from coir matting to the finest Kirman rugs, the marmalade-downwards-incidence . . . varied indirectly with the quality of the carpet . . . the Principle of the Graduated Hostility of Things. *Paul Jennings, Even Oddlier*

*This proverb surfaced a hundred years before Murphy's Law: "If anything can go wrong, it will."

You've buttered your BREAD, now eat it. ca. 161 B.C., B-1968

You've buttered your bread, now lie in it. *Heard in Indiana*

BREVITY is the soul of wit. *Shakespeare, Hamlet 2.2.90*

. . . and laughter is the goal of wit.

A little word is a bonny word. English dialect variant.

Brevity is the soul of lingerie. *Dorothy Parker*

Don't waste your breath. *Vermont proverb*

Good things, when short, are twice as good. *Baltasar Gracian, The Art of Worldly Wisdom.*

I don't care how much a man talks—if he will only say it in a few words. *Josh Billings*

If I am to speak for ten minutes, I need a week for preparation. If fifteen minutes, three days. If half an hour, two days. If an hour, I am ready now. *Woodrow Wilson, answering the question of how long it takes him to prepare a speech*

Impropriety is the soul of wit. *W. Somerset Maugham, The Moon and Sixpence*

Let thy speech be short, comprehending much in few words. *Ecclesiastes 32:8*

Men of few words are the best men. *Shakespeare, Henry V 3.2.40*

No speech can be entirely bad if it is short.

Office sign: Be brief, we have our living to make.

One o' the finest accomplishments is makin' a long story short. *Kin Hubbard*

Short answers save trouble.

Some speakers confuse the seating capacity of the meeting place with the sitting capacity of the audience. *Noel Wical*

Speeches that are measured by the hour will die with the hour. *Thomas Jefferson*

Talk less and say more. *Vermont proverb*

The first rule of public speaking is to speak up, the second is to sit down. *Evan Esar*

The great art of writing well is to know when to stop. *Josh Billings*

The minute a thing is long and complicated it confuses. Whoever wrote the Ten Commandments made 'em short. They may not always be kept but they are understood. They are the same for all men. *Will Rogers*

To make a long story short, there's nothing better than having the boss walk in. *Wall Street Journal*

To make a speech immortal, you don't have to make it everlasting. *Leslie Hore-Belisha,* as quoted in *Reader's Digest, Oct. 1955*

When a fellow says, "Well, to make a long story short," it's too late. *Don Herold,* as quoted in *Reader's Digest, Feb. 1958*

How eloquent the orator
Who says enough—and nothing more.
Arthur Guiterman

All BRIDES are beautiful.

She got her good looks from her father; he's a plastic surgeon. *Groucho Marx*

Don't cross the BRIDGE before you get there. *1850, O-45*

. . . but there's nothing wrong with a little foresight.

Don't cross a bridge before it's built.

The hardest thing to learn in life is which bridge to cross and which bridge to burn. *David Russell*

We cross our bridges when we come to them and burn our bridges behind us, with nothing to show for our progress except a memory of the smell of smoke. *Tom Stoppard, Rosencrantz and Guildenstern Are Dead*

Don't cross a river till you reach its brim;
Yet come prepared to row or wade or swim.
Arthur Guiterman

Don't burn your BRIDGES behind you. *1923, WM-71*

. . . unless you're sure you can swim.

If it ain't BROKE, don't fix it. *Bert Lance*

If it Ain't Broke, Break It. *Title of a book on unconventional business wisdom, by Robert J. Kriegel and Louis Palter, 1991*

Never tamper with a hit. *Show business maxim*

Babbling BROOKS are noisy. *1574, WM-512*

Shallow streams make most din. *1721, Kelly*

A new BROOM sweeps clean.* *1546, Heywood*

. . . when properly handled.

. . . but wouldn't you rather have a broom that sweeps dirt?

. . . but the old brush knows the corners. *Irish proverb*

. . . but the old broom knows where all the dirt is.

. . . but never trust an old saw. *James Thurber*

New grooms sleep keen. *L. L. Levinson*

*Notes Tilley (T-68), "Spoken of new servants, who are commonly very diligent; and new officers, who are commonly very severe."

Am I my BROTHER'S keeper? *Genesis 4:9**

A person who borrows books becomes his brother's bookkeeper.

A rancher who built a thriving business out of breeding cattle and pickling corned beef was horrified to learn that his only barrel maker intended to retire. Aware that barrel making is a dying art, and a replacement might be impossible to find, he pleaded with his valued worker to stay. Back came the rhetorical question: "Am I my breeder's cooper?"

As long as there are human beings, there will be the idea of brotherhood—and an almost total inability to practice it. *Sydney J. Harris*

Don't be too nosy. You are your brother's keeper, not his bookkeeper.

Everyone believes in "brotherhood"—if he can pick the brothers; but the whole point of the concept is that we have no choice in the matter. *Sydney J. Harris*

First they came for the Jews. I was silent. I was not a Jew. Then they came for the Communists. I was silent. I was not a Communist. Then they came for the trade unionists. I was silent. I was not a trade unionist. Then they came for me. There was no one left to speak for me. *Martin Niemöller*

I have never been indisposed to do whatever might be in my power in favor of those whose misfortunes have been unavoidably brought upon them without any fault of their own. *George Washington*

If we are not our brother's keeper, let us at least not be his executioner. *Marlon Brando*

The quizzical expression of the ape in the zoo comes from wondering whether he's his brother's keeper or his keeper's brother.

Those who set out nobly to be their brother's keeper sometimes end up by becoming his jailer. Every emancipation has in it the seeds of a new slavery, and every truth easily becomes a lie. *I. F. Stone*

My brother is not my keeper.
But when he can, he keeps me down.
Neil Rathgelo, 1975

*Jealous because God had favored Abel's sacrifice over Cain's, Cain slew Abel. "Where is thy brother?" God called to Cain, who answered a rhetorical question with a rhetorical question: "Am I my brother's keeper?" (This was, no doubt, the very first time that a question had been answered with another question.)

The BUCK stops here.* *Motto displayed on the desk of Harry S. Truman (1884–1972)*

The buck stops with the guy who signs the checks. *Rupert Murdoch*

*In the game of poker, the buck is a token object which is passed to the person who wins a jackpot, to remind him that when it is his turn to deal the next hand, he must start another jackpot.

It is easier to pull down than to BUILD up. 1577, O-185

Any fine morning, a power saw can fell a tree that took a thousand years to grow. *Edwin Teale*

Any jackass can kick down a barn, but it takes a good carpenter to build one.

It's easier to dump the cart than to load it. *Heard in Wisconsin*

It's easier to tear a hole than to mend one. *Russian proverb*

It's easy to describe why
That guy is such a pain,
But to see the fellow's good points
Is harder on the brain.

BUSINESS before pleasure. 1640, O-28

Pleasure before business. *Frank Gruber*

The trouble with mixing business and pleasure is that pleasure usually comes out on top.

See also You can't mix BUSINESS and friendship.

BUSINESS is business. *18th century*

. . . Eat and drink with your relatives; do business with strangers. *Greek proverb*

A childlike faith may do in religion, but it won't do in business. *Frederick H. Seymour*

A friendship founded on business is better than a business founded on friendship. *John D. Rockefeller, Jr.*

Bargain like a gypsy and pay like a gentleman. *Serbo-Croatian proverb*

Bankruptcy is a legal proceeding in which you put your money in your pants pocket and give your coat to your creditors. *Joey Adams*

Business is a combination of war and sport. *André Maurois*

Business? It's quite simple. It's other people's money. *Alexandre Dumas the younger*

Business: the art of extracting money from another's pocket without resorting to violence. *Max Amsterdam*

In business be exact; 'tis better thus;
In friendship you may then be generous.
Arthur Guiterman

It is well known what a middleman is: he is a man who bamboozles one party and plunders the other. *Benjamin Disraeli*

Let us prey.

Live together like brothers, but do business like strangers. *Arab proverb*

Sentiment has no place in business—except for the man who sells greeting cards.

The bazaar recognizes neither father nor mother. *Turkish proverb*

The merchant has no country. *Thomas Jefferson*

The notion that business is clothed with a public interest and has been devoted to the public use is little more than a fiction intended to beautify what is disagreeable to the sufferers. *Oliver Wendell Holmes, Tyson v. Banton, 1927*

The usual trade and commerce is cheating all round by consent. *1732, Fuller*

There are very honest people who do not think that they have had a bargain unless they have cheated the merchant. *Anatole France*

A Christian is a man who feels
　　Repentance on a Sunday
For what he did on Saturday
　　And is going to do on Monday.
Thomas Russell Ybarra

Everybody's BUSINESS is nobody's business. *17th century*

A pig that has two owners is sure to die of hunger.

Everybody's work is nobody's work. *1611, Cotgrave*

He that serves everybody is paid by nobody. *1611, Cotgrave*

What's everybody's business is nobody's business except the journalist's. *Joseph Pulitzer*

In BUSINESS, there are no friends and no enemies.

See BUSINESS is business.

Mind your own BUSINESS. *1532, T-73*

. . . and give other folks an opportunity to mind theirs. *Elbert Hubbard*

A man is likely to mind his own business when it is worth minding. When it is not, he takes his mind off his own meaningless affairs by minding other people's business. *Eric Hoffer, The True Believer*

Busy souls have no time to be busybodies. *Austin O'Malley*

Don't be dipping your lip in another's porridge. *Vermont proverb*

Don't worry over what other people are thinking of you. They're too busy worrying about what you are thinking of them.

If we devoted as much attention to our own affairs as we freely give to those of others, we and others would be gainers. *L. de V. Matthewman*

It seems like one of the hardest lessons to be learned in this life is where your business ends and somebody else's begins. *Kin Hubbard*

People who mind their own business succeed because they have so little competition.

He that tilleth his land shall have plenty of bread: but he that followeth after vain persons shall have poverty enough. *Proverbs 28:19*

Seest thou a man diligent in his business? he shall stand before kings. *Proverbs 22:29*

Some folks mind other people's business because their own business isn't worth minding.

Speak not of my debts unless you mean to pay them. *1651, Herbert*

The fellow who courts trouble often marries her. *Old postcard*

The hardest thing about business is minding your own. *Old postcard*

There are two reasons why people don't mind their own business: either they haven't any mind, or they haven't any business.

To keep your teeth in good condition, see your dentist twice a year and mind your own business. *Ann Landers*

What ain't your duty ain't your business. *Heard in Oregon*

What is privacy if not for invading? *Quentin Crisp*

Take care of your BUSINESS, and your business will take care of you.

See Keep your SHOP, and your shop will keep you.

Tend to BUSINESS.

Business is like an automobile. It won't run itself, except downhill.

It has been my observation that most people get ahead during the time that others waste. *Henry Ford*

See also Mind your own BUSINESS.

There's no BUSINESS like show business.

No business is so riddled with lawsuits, claims and counterclaims, broken contracts, dishonored obligations, threats, curses, feuds, and interminable petty bickerings.

No other business is so cruel to the people it no longer needs.

No other business engages in so much public boasting about its "big heart" and indulges in so much private malice with its little head.

No other business so ruthlessly exploits the young, the ignorant and the emotionally underprivileged and has such bland disregard for the canons of taste and decency.

There's no business like show business—and it's a good thing there isn't. *Sydney J. Harris*

You can't mix BUSINESS and friendship.

[This] prudent maxim . . . is not so much a testament to the power of money as it is a confession of the fragility of most friendships. *Sydney J. Harris*

See also BUSINESS before pleasure; BUSINESS is business.

If you want to get a job done, give it to a BUSY man.

. . . The other kind has no time. *Elbert Hubbard*

. . . He'll have his secretary do it. *Calvin Coolidge*

Who is more busy than he that hath least to do? *1616, Draxe*

BUY cheap, and sell dear. *Thomas Lodge, 1595*

. . . collect early, and pay late.

Cut your losses and let your profit run.

Everyone loves a bargain.

In business . . . while loss spells failure, large profits do not connote success. Success must be sought in business also in excellence of performance . . . in the improvement of products . . . in bettering the conditions of workingmen . . . and in the establishment of right relations with customers and with the community. *Louis D. Brandeis*

We all like to see everybody make a little profit . . . a very little. *Cullen Hightower*

See also No one was ever ruined by taking a PROFIT.

Let the BUYER beware.

The buyer has need of a hundred eyes, the seller of but one. *Italian proverb; O-29*

See also CAVEAT emptor.

Don't monkey with the BUZZSAW. WM-78

A man does not rub buttocks with a porcupine. *African proverb*

Don't tempt fate.

Never scratch a tiger with a short stick. *Peter's Almanac*

Never tread on a sore toe. *H. G. Bohn*

See also Don't ask for TROUBLE.

Let BYGONES be bygones. *1546, Heywood*

. . . but any person capable of doing you one dirty trick is capable of doing you another, and usually does. *George Jean Nathan*

Forgiving our enemies has the same refreshing effect upon our souls as it does to confess our sins. *Josh Billings*

No use harping on the past! Play the music of today. *Old postcard*

Those who cannot forget are worse off than those who can't remember.

See also FORGIVE and forget; It is no use CRYING over spilt milk.

Give unto CAESAR the things which are Caesar's, and unto God the things that are God's.*

*Render therefore unto Caesar . . . *Matthew 22:21*

See also Praise the LORD and pass the ammunition.

CAESAR'S wife must be above suspicion.*
Latin proverb

*Caesar actually did divorce his wife because she was (innocently, perhaps) involved in a scandal. (Flexner, F-29, describes the nature of the scandal.) Not to worry; she was not his only wife.

Let them eat CAKE.*

Poverty is an anomaly to rich people; it is very difficult to make out why people who want dinner do not ring the bell. *Walter Bagehot*

*Did Marie-Antoinette respond to the news that "the country people have no bread" by replying, "Then let them eat cake"? The answer is complicated by two facts: (1) the Queen suggested, according to the story, that the country people eat *"de la brioche,"* which is not exactly cake, but more like a scone; (2) according to Burton Stevenson (B-275), the story was recorded about two years before Marie-Antoinette arrived in France!

You can't have your CAKE and eat it too.*
1546, Heywood

. . . unless you bake two cakes.

. . . but you can't eat cake unless you have it.

An independent is someone who wants to take the politics out of politics. *Adlai Stevenson*

Free love is sometimes love but never freedom. *Elizabeth Bibesco, Haven*

He longs for war but dislikes the battle. *Arabic proverb*

What men desire is a virgin who is a whore. *Edward Dahlberg*

What we want is brand-new ideas that don't upset our old ideas. *Peter's Almanac*

What I want is to feel brave and adventurous, without actually having to risk anything. © *Ashleigh Brilliant*

You can't sell the cow and have the milk, too. *Vermont proverb*

You cannot eat your cake and have it.
So the cautious wise ones wail.
But I shall eat mine willy-nilly
Otherwise it might get stale.
Rebecca McCann

*The exact meaning of this proverb is "You can't have your cake if you've eaten it." Heywood's 1546 rendering was "Wolde you bothe eate your cake, and haue your cake?" In the 19th century, two versions appeared: "One cannot eat one's cake and have it, too," and "You can't have your cake if you eat it."

It is easier for a CAMEL to go through the eye of a needle, than for a rich man to enter into the kingdom of God. *Matthew 19:24*

. . . The impossibility is not alleged but the rarity is emphasized. *Thomas Aquinas*

'Tis as hard for a rich man to enter the kingdom of Heaven as it is for a poor man to get out of Purgatory. *Finley Peter Dunne, Mr. Dooley's Opinions*

Better to light a CANDLE than to curse the darkness.*

. . . but if you're in a munitions plant, just curse the darkness.

I have lost more than a friend. I have lost an inspiration. She would rather light candles than curse the darkness, and her glow has warmed the world. *Adlai Stevenson, tribute to Eleanor Roosevelt, 1962*

*Motto of the Christopher Society, and believed to have been authored by its founder, Rev. James Keller. When asked if that was true, Christopher director Father Richard Armstrong declared, "Our motto is an ancient Chinese proverb." (MD-56-57)

You can't burn the CANDLE at both ends.* *1611, Cotgrave*

It all depends on the person. Winston Churchill, even at sixty-eight, works eighteen hours a day, including Sundays, drinks a pint of wine at lunch, several whiskeys and sodas at dinner, and a spot or two of brandy at night, smokes strong cigars all day long, gets hardly any sleep, jumps hither and yon across the seas, and yet seems to get things done pretty well. *George Jean Nathan*

It is better to burn the candle at both ends, and in the middle too, than to put it away in the closet and let the mice eat it. *Henry Van Dycke*

My candle burns at both ends;
    It will not last the night;
But, ah, my foes, and, oh, my friends
    It gives a lovely light!
Edna St. Vincent Millay, First Fig

I burned my candle at both ends,
And now have neither foes nor friends;
For all the lovely light begotten,
I'm paying now in feeling rotten.
Samuel Hoffenstein, parody on Millay's parody

My candle burns at both its ends;
Where can I set it down, my friends?
Richard Armour

With cards and dice and dress and friends,
My savings are complete;
I light the candle at both ends,
And thus make both ends meet.

*According to Burton Stevenson (B-78), this proverb warned against dissipating one's fortune.

When the CANDLES are out, all women are fair.

See At night all CATS are gray.

CANDY is dandy, but liquor is quicker.*

Candy is dandy, but depravities won't give you any cavities. *L. L. Levinson*

*The original meaning of this phrase is suggested by the title of the Ogden Nash verse from which it is taken: "Reflections on Ice-Breaking."

You can't be too CAREFUL.

A conservative is a man who does not believe that anything should be done for the first time. *Frank A. Vanderlip*

Be afraid and you'll be safe. *Irish proverb*

Much heed does no harm. *1639, Clarke*

Measure twice, because you can only cut once.

Don't believe in superstition; it brings bad luck.

There is always a danger for those who are afraid of it. *G. B. Shaw*

To avoid risks, stay in bed. And even then you can't be sure.

Transcendental meditation is evil because when you are meditating, it opens space within you for the devil to enter. *Billy Graham, Ms. magazine, 1977*

Warning: Your local police are armed and dangerous. *Graffiti*

If wisdom's ways you wisely seek,
    Five things observe with care:
Of whom you speak, to whom you speak,
    And how and when, and where.
Old Farmer's Almanac, 1851

See also Take a CHANCE.

CARPE diem.* *Horace (65–8 B.C.)*

He who lives in the present lives in eternity. *Ludwig Wittgenstein*

People say that life is the thing, but I prefer reading. *Logan Pearsall Smith*

*"Seize the day." The Latin poet goes on to advise that one "trust little in tomorrow." Thus Horace anticipated "Enjoy yourself,

it's later than you think," "Make hay while the sun shines," "Never put off till tomorrow what you can do today," etc. At best, these sayings remind us that each moment is too precious to waste; at worst, these words have been used to push reluctant maidens into foolish acquiescence.

"Carpe diem" was the motto of the passionate literature teacher in the 1989 Academy Award–winning film *Dead Poets Society.*

Carpe diem is also a category of poetry that advises (implores? seduces?) the reader to enjoy the pleasures of youth before youth passes away. For example, these lines from Shakespeare's *Twelfth Night* (2.3.48–53):

What is love? 'Tis not hereafter;
Present mirth hath present laughter
    What's to come is still unsure.
In delay there lies no plenty;
Then come kiss me, sweet and twenty,
Youth's a stuff will not endure.

See also DO it now; STRIKE while the iron is hot.

Don't put the CART before the horse. *Latin proverb*

She put the heart before the course. *George Kaufman, of a college girl who eloped*

The real question . . . is: which was the cart and which the horse? Leonard Woolf, *Downhill All the Way*

Take the CASH and let the credit go. *Omar Khayyam, The Rubiyat*

Take the Money and Run. *Title of a movie by Woody Allen*

A CAT may look at a king. *1546, Heywood*

. . . and a dog can bite him in the leg.

Even a Honda can scratch the fender of a Rolls-Royce. *Spoken by a Japanese businessman to Justin Wintle*

The cat may look at a king, they say
But rather would look at a mouse at play.
Arthur Guiterman

Care killed the CAT.

Let care kill a cat,
We'll laugh and be fat.
1600, T-82

They say it was care killed the cat,
That starved and caused her to die;
But I'll be much wiser than that,
For the devil a care will care I!
Maria Edgeworth

Don't let the CAT out of the bag. *18th century*

. . . after the barn door is locked. *Honey Flexner*

There are more ways than one to kill a CAT.

. . . than choking her with cream. *Charles Kingsley, Westward Ho!*

There are more ways than one to skin a CAT* 1678, *Ray*

. . . without tearing its hide.

. . . but never mind telling me about it.

There's more than one way to kill a chicken than to kiss him to death. *Heard in Mississippi*

*Mieder (WM-346) lists eleven variants of this proverb.

Who will bell the CAT? *Aesop (6th century B.C.)*

Who should tell the lion it has bad breath? *Tunisian proverb*

At night all CATS are gray. *1546, Heywood*

All women are the same when the lights are out. *Plutarch*

Joan is as good as my lady in the dark. *T-1525*

The lady of my heart is one
Who has no peer beneath the sun;
But mortal truths have mortal sequels
Beneath the moon I know her equals.
Samuel Hoffenstein

CATCH-22.* *Title of a novel by Joseph Heller, 1961*

Any club that would accept me as a member, I wouldn't want to join. *Groucho Marx*

Office memo: Firings will continue until morale improves.

The average tourist wants to go to places where there are no tourists. *Sam Ewing*

*Heller's hero tries to convince an army psychiatrist that he should be discharged as mentally unfit for service. The "catch-22" is that if he is intelligent enough to know that he is crazy, he is fit for continued service.

See also You can't WIN.

CAVEAT emptor. ("Buyer beware.") *Latin proverb*

. . . which can be loosely translated as "Honesty is the best policy but it hasn't caught on yet."

Caveat venditor. *Eugene Ehrlich, on the consumer rights movement*

A market is a place set apart for men to deceive and get the better of one another. *Anacharsis*

Beware of too great a bargain. *New England proverb*

Don't give too much for the whistle. *Poor Richard's Almanac*

Everything is worth what its purchaser will pay for it. *Publilius Syrus*

He praises who wishes to sell. *Shakespeare, Love's Labour's Lost 4.3.236*

If you would not be cheated, ask the price at three shops. *Heard in New York*

In a horse trade, you got to know either the horse or the man. *Vermont proverb*

No man cries stinking fish. *1660, T-423*

Nobody really loves to be cheated, but it does seem as though everyone is anxious to see how near he could come to it. *Josh Billings*

Nothing is as irritating as the fellow who chats pleasantly while he's overcharging you. *Kin Hubbard*

The purchaser . . . is a child who must be protected against his own mistakes, while the seller . . . is the big, bad wolf lying in wait for Little Red Riding Hood. *Eugene Ehrlich*

The melon seller declares his melon sweet. *Philippine proverb*

Watch the butcher when he weighs the roast; otherwise you'll buy his hand. *Heard in New York*

When you sell to your neighbor or buy from your neighbor, you shall not wrong each other. *Leviticus 25:14*

Who buys has need of a hundred eyes, who sells has enough of one. *1640, T-493*

Without some dissimulation, no business can be carried on at all. *Lord Chesterfield*

See also BUSINESS is business; BUY cheap, and sell dear.

A CHAIN is as strong as its weakest link. *1868, O-34*

. . . and the longer the chain, the more weak links. *Laurence Peter, commenting on the Curse of Bigness, the theme of The Peter Pyramid*

A chain is no weaker than its missing link. *e. e. cummings*

No brain is stronger than its weakest think. *Tom Masson*

One rotten beam can make a whole house collapse. *Russian proverb*

The thread breaks where it is weakest. *1640, Herbert*

Take a CHANCE.

. . . when the odds are in your favor.

. . . but don't bet anything that you can't afford to lose.

. . . but remember that gambling casinos are run not by gamblers, but by businessmen.

. . . but remember that the highest branch is not the safest roost.

A great deal of talent is lost in this world for the want of a little courage. *Sydney Smith*

A ship in port is safe, but that is not what ships are built for. *Grace Hooper*

Any life truly lived is a risky business, and if one puts up too many fences against the risks one ends by shutting out life itself. *Kenneth S. Davis, as quoted in Reader's Digest, Apr. 1952*

Courage is doing what you're afraid to do. There can be no courage unless you're scared. *Eddie Rickenbacker*

Do not be too timid and squeamish about your actions. All life is an experiment. *Ralph Waldo Emerson*

During the first period of a man's life the greatest danger is: not to take the risk. *Soren Kierkegaard, Journal*

Everyone has talent. What is rare is the courage to follow the talent to the dark place where it leads. *Erica Jong*

Everyone who loves is vulnerable to the pain of grief, for love means attachment and all human attachments are subject to loss. *Joyce Brothers, Good Housekeeping, Jan. 1971*

First weigh the considerations, then take the risks. *Helmuth von Moltke*

I believe in getting into hot water. I think it keeps you clean. *G. K. Chesterton*

If the creator had a purpose in equipping us with a neck, he surely meant us to stick it out. *Arthur Koestler*

If we don't grow, we are not really living. Growth demands a temporary surrender of security. *Gail Sheehy*

If you risk nothing, then you risk everything. *Geena Davis*

If you'll always say no, you'll never be married. *1721, OE-9*

If you're careful enough, nothing bad or good will ever happen to you. © *Ashleigh Brilliant*

If you're never scared or embarrassed or hurt, it means you never take any chances. *Julia Sorel, See How She Runs*

It is not enough for a man to know how to ride, he must also know how to fall. *American Indian proverb*

It's better to risk trusting the wrong people than never to trust anybody at all. © *Ashleigh Brilliant*

Many a man who takes a chance would be mighty happy to put it back. *Heard in North Dakota*

One man plus courage is a majority.

Only those who dare to fail greatly can ever achieve greatly. *Robert F. Kennedy*

Only those who risk going too far can possibly find out how far one can go. *T. S. Eliot*

Security is mostly a superstition. It does not exist in nature. . . . Life is either a daring adventure or nothing. *Helen Keller*

Success has a simple formula: do your best, and people may like it. *Sam Ewing*

Success is that old ABC—ability, breaks and courage. *Charles Luckman*

Take time to deliberate; but when the time for action arrives, stop thinking and go in. *Andrew Jackson*

The biggest mistake of all is to avoid situations in which you might make a mistake.

The one thing worse than a quitter is the person who is afraid to begin.

The power of choice must involve the possibility of error that is the essence of choosing. *Herbert L. Samuel, Belief and Action*

There is always a multitude of reasons both in favour of doing a thing and against doing it. The art of debate lies in presenting them; the art of life lies in neglecting ninety-nine hundredths of them. *Mark Rutherford, More Pages from a Journal*

We must dare, and again dare, and forever dare. *Georges-Jacques Danton*

Whenever you see a successful business, someone has made a courageous decision. *Peter F. Drucker*

Why not go out on a limb? Isn't that where the fruit is? *Frank Scully*

You cannot pluck roses without fear of thorns, nor enjoy a fair wife without danger of horns. *Poor Richard's Almanac*

You can't get honey unless you take a chance on getting stung. *Old postcard*

You may be disappointed if you fail, but you are doomed if you don't try. *Beverly Sills*

You must do the thing you think you cannot do. *Eleanor Roosevelt*

The more things CHANGE, the more they stay the same. *Alphonse Karr, Les Guêpes, 1849*

Every revolution evaporates and leaves behind only the slime of a new bureaucracy. *Franz Kafka (attributed)*

Just because everything is different doesn't mean anything has changed. *Irene Peter*

Nothing is clearer in history than the adoption by successful rebels of the methods they were accustomed to condemn in the forces they deposed. *Will and Ariel Durant*

Politics, as hopeful men practice it in the world, consists mainly of the delusion that a change in form is a change in substance. *H. L. Mencken, Prejudices, 4th ser.*

Revolutions have never lightened the burden of tyranny, they have only shifted it to another shoulder. *G. B. Shaw, Man and Superman*

Take off the dateline and one day's paper is the same as the next. *Marshall McLuhan, Understanding Media*

The less things change, the more they remain the same.

What the first philosopher taught, the last will have to repeat. *Henry David Thoreau, Journal*

What we call "progress" is the exchange of one nuisance for another nuisance. *Havelock Ellis*

When smashing monuments, save the pedestals—they always come in handy. *Stanislaw J. Lec, Unkempt Thoughts*

There is nothing permanent except CHANGE. *Heracleitus (5th century B.C.), Fragments; F-969*

See All is FLUX.

CHARITY begins at home. *1383, O-34*

... but should not end there. *1732, Fuller*

... and justice begins next door. *Charles Dickens, Martin Chuzzlewit*

... but sympathy travels abroad extensively.

... often with a third-class envelope in the morning mail. *Changing Times*

A bone to the dog is not charity. Charity is the bone shared with the dog, when you are just as hungry as the dog. *Jack London*

Charity and beating begins at home. *Francis Beaumont and John Fletcher, 1616*

Don't collect straw for your neighbor's roof while your own is leaking. *Russian proverb*

If charity costs nothing, the world would be full of philanthropists. *Yiddish proverb*

If you are in debt, pay your debts before you contribute to charity. *Yehuda ha-Hasid*

Let the heathens go to hell: help your neighbor. *Ed Howe*

Think globally, but act locally. *Recalled by a Letter to the Editor writer (New York Times, May 1, 1989) as the theme of Abbie Hoffman's last public speech*

When it comes to giving, some people stop at nothing.

Help the needy—all that's lent
Brings from six to ten per cent;
Place your trust in Heaven, but keep
Your money working while you sleep.
Samuel Hoffenstein, For Little Boys Destined for Big Business

CHARITY covers a multitude of sins.*

... which are committed in her name. *L. de V. Matthewman*

Charity creates a multitude of sins. *Oscar Wilde, The Soul Under Socialism*

Charity is the sterilized milk of human kindness. *Oliver Herford*

Alas! for the rarity
Of Christian charity
Thomas Hood, the Bridge of Sighs

*Charity shall cover the multitude of sins. *1 Peter 4:8.* Peter was urging Christians to repay persecution with goodness. In popular use, Flexner (F-31) notes that the saying lost this sense of forgiveness and cynically claimed that an act of charity may cover up the giver's wrongdoing.

Now abideth faith, hope, charity, these three; but the greatest of these is CHARITY. *1 Corinthians 13:13*

A part of kindness consists in loving people more than they deserve. *Joseph Joubert*

And now abideth faith, hope, money; but the greatest of these is money. *George Orwell*

At income tax time, the greatest of these is Charity.

Christianity taught men that love is worth more than intelligence. *Jacques Maritain, I Believe*

CHASTE is she whom no one has asked. Ovid (43 B.C.–A.D. 17)

A man is not honest just because he never had a chance to steal. *Yiddish proverb*

It is easier for the unattractive girl to live a life of modesty. *Marlene Dietrich*

It is easy holding down the latch when nobody pulls the string. *English proverb, probably referring to the virtue of unattractive women (EMW-171)*

Most plain girls are virtuous because of the scarcity of opportunity to be otherwise. *Maya Angelou*

What's the difference between a guy in the big house and the average guy you pass in the street? The guy in the big house is the Loser who tried. *Charles Bukowski, Notes of a Dirty Old Man*

See also OPPORTUNITY makes the thief; There but for the grace of GOD go I.

CHE Sera Sera.* *Italian proverb*

Destiny . . . a tyrant's excuse for crime and a fool's excuse for failure. *Ambrose Bierce, The Devil's Dictionary*

He that is born to be hanged shall never be drowned. *1503, T-33*

I don't believe in fatalism, only so far as fools and rascals are concerned. *Josh Billings*

If physiognomy becomes what Lavater expects it to become, then criminals will be hanged before they have committed the deeds which deserve the gallows. *Georg Lichtenberg*

Life is like a game of cards. The hand that is dealt you represents determinism. The way you play it is free will. *Jawaharlal Nehru*

Lots of folks confuse bad management with destiny. *Kin Hubbard*

Nothing underneath the sun
Merely happens; things are done.
Arthur Guiterman

When Mark Twain visited Springfield, a congressman once said to him, "Mr. Clemens, I have often thought what a pity it was that fate did not intend that Lincoln should marry Ann Rutledge. It seems that fate governs our lives and plans history in advance."

Responded Mark Twain, "Yes, had Lincoln married the dear one of his heart's love he might have led a happy but obscure life and the world would never have heard of him. Happiness seeks obscurity to enjoy itself . . ."

"Well, doesn't that prove," asked the congressman, "that what is to be will be?"

"The only thing it proves to me," replied Mark Twain, "is that what has been was." *Opie Read, Mark Twain and I*

*"What must be, must be" (O-157).

See also I am the master of my FATE; It's up to YOU.

You can't CHEAT an honest man.* *Title of a 1939 W. C. Fields movie, but not originated by Fields, says Keyes. (K-136)*

. . . but don't worry about that; you're not likely to run into one anyway.

*"A common credo among con men," says Keyes (K-136). Compare with Ralph Waldo Emerson's words, "It is impossible for a man to be cheated by anyone but himself" (*Compensation*).

CHEATERS never win.

It is a common saying in England that "Cheating never thrives": but, in America, with honest trading you cannot succeed. *R. Parkinson, Tour in America*

A shady business never yields a sunny life. *Heard in North Carolina*

See also CRIME does not pay.

CHERCHEZ la femme.* *1639, B-2587*

*"Look for the woman," a phrase that appears in the writings of Alexandre Dumas *père*.

G. B. Shaw has a character say, "Let us hunt for the woman; may I rot forever if I utter that banal phrase in my bad French." (B-2587)

See Never underestimate the power of a WOMAN.

Don't count your chickens before they are hatched.* *Aesop (6th century B.C.), The Milkmaid and Her Pail*

. . . and it's still more hateful to count them with gloating when they're hatched. *D. H. Lawrence*

Baptize only what is born. *Ukrainian proverb*

Don't count your winnings until the bookie has put the money in your hand.

First catch the rabbit, then make your stew. *Heard in Ontario*

There is a very wide difference between getting tenants and getting rent. *George Washington*

The man that once did sell the lion's skin
While the beast liv'd, was kill'd with hunting him.
Shakespeare, Henry V 4.3.93

*There are probably more equivalents to this proverb than to any other. Here are a few variants listed by Burton Stevenson (B-333):

Don't sell the bearskin before you've caught the bear. *A proverb found in many countries of the world*

Do not rejoice over what has not yet happened. *Ancient Egyptian proverb*

Don't bargain for fish which are still in the water. *Hindu proverb*

Don't build the sty till the litter comes.

Don't cry herrings until they are in the net. *Dutch proverb*

Don't give away the deer until it is caught. *Persian proverb*

Don't reckon your eggs before they are laid. *Italian proverb*

Don't spread the cloth till the pot begins to boil. [Don't set the table until meal preparation is under way.]

Gut no fish till you get them. *Scottish proverb*

The kid is not yet born. *Ancient Greek proverb*

See also PLAN ahead.

A burnt CHILD dreads fire. *ca. 1250, O-27*

. . . no more . . . than a child who has acquired a stomachache from gumdrops dreads gumdrops. *George Jean Nathan*

. . . until the next day. *Mark Twain*

A scalded cat fears cold water. *1561, T-87*

Birds once snared fear all bushes. *1579, T-50*

Cold feet are often the result of burnt fingers.

Once bitten, twice shy. *1894, B-725*

One year bitten by a snake, three years afraid of grass ropes. *Chinese proverb*

Things that hurt teach. *Latin proverb*

Unaware of proverbs,
The burnt child craves the flame.
Christopher Morley, Of a Child That Had Fever

The burnt child, urged by rankling ire,

Can hardly wait to get back at the fire.
Ogden Nash, 1940

The CHILD is father of the man. *William Wordsworth, 1807*

. . . unless the offspring happens to be a girl.

The childhood shews the man,
As morning shews the day.
John Milton, Paradise Regained

It is a wise CHILD that knows its own father.* *1584, O-247*

. . . Not at all. Alter this and make it read: It is a very silly boy who isn't on to his old man. *Stephen Leacock*

. . . and an unusual one that unreservedly approves of him. *Mark Twain, More Maxims of Mark*

Don't forget your raisin'. *Appalachian proverb*

If you ever forget you're a Jew, a Gentile will remind you. *Bernard Malamud*

If your son asks for something he shouldn't have, don't be afraid to refuse him: It's a wise father that no's his own son.

It's a wise crack that knows its own originator.

The butterfly often forgets it was a caterpillar. *Swedish proverb*

Today, it's a wise father who knows as much as his own child. *Judge, ca. 1925*

Breakfast foods grow odder and odder;
It's a wise child that knows its fodder.
Ogden Nash, as quoted in *Reader's Digest, July 1952*

*In *The Merchant of Venice* (2.2.83), Shylock's servant, Gobbo, takes a devilish pleasure in finding that his blind old father fails to recognize him. Shakespeare twists a proverb of his day, by having Gobbo tease his father with the words "It is a wise father that knows his own child."

Train up a CHILD in the way he should go: and when he is old, he will not depart from it. *Proverbs 22:6*

Give me a child for the first seven years, and you may do what you like with him afterwards. *Jesuit saying*

It takes a village to raise a child. *African proverb*

Teach your kids the value of money: borrow from them.

To bring up a child in the way he should go, travel that way yourself once in a while. *Josh Billings*

When I was a CHILD, I spake as a child . . . but when I became a man, I put away childish things. *1 Corinthians 13:11*

Credulity is the man's weakness, but the child's strength. *Charles Lamb, Essays of Elia*

Genius is childhood recaptured. *Charles Baudelaire*

If a man does not put away childish things, someone may drive over them coming into his garage.

Perhaps at fourteen, every boy should be in love with some ideal woman to put on a pedestal and worship. As he grows up, of course, he will put her on a pedestal the better to view her legs. *Barry Norman, 1978*

Some of you may remember that in my early days, I was sort of a bleeding heart liberal.

Then I became a man and put away childish ways. *Ronald Reagan*

CHILDREN and fools speak the truth. *1546, Heywood*

Honesty is just as much an art as politeness is, and never was born with a man any more than the capacity to spell the word Nebuchadnezzar right the first time was. *Josh Billings*

. . . children are generally awful liars, a tribute to their beautiful imaginations and irrepressible flights of fancy. . . . If a fool were master of the truth, in however slight a degree, he would be no fool. *George Jean Nathan*

In 1921, the *Evening Standard* reported a trial in which a witness was asked, "Are you telling the truth?" The witness replied, "Only children and fools tell the truth." *F-32*

In vino veritas.

CHILDREN should be seen but not heard.*

A child is a curly, dimpled lunatic. *Ralph Waldo Emerson*

At one time, parents taught their children to speak; nowadays children teach their parents to keep silent. *Yiddish proverb*

Children should be seen and not hurt. *Bumper sticker*

Children should be seen and not had.

Children should neither be seen or heard from—ever. *W. C. Fields (attributed)*

First you teach a child to talk; then you have to teach it to keep quiet.

Go back to reform school, you little nose-picker. *W. C. Fields*

He that has no children knows not what is love. *17th century*

My children weary me. I can only see them as defective adults: feckless, destructive, frivolous, sensual, humorless. *Evelyn Waugh*

The trouble with children is that they are not returnable. *Quentin Crisp*

The value of marriage is not that adults produce children but that children produce adults. *Peter De Vries*

Women should be obscene and not heard. *John Lennon*

*Variant of the 15th-century English proverb "A maid should be seen but not heard" (O-36).

Little CHILDREN, little troubles; big children, big troubles. *1640, Herbert*

Children are a great comfort in your old age—and they help you reach it faster, too. *L. M. Kauffman*

Children suck the mother when they are young, and the father when they are old. *1670, Ray*

Children are certain cares, but uncertain comforts. *1639, OE-92*

Premature graying is hereditary; you get it from your children.

Teenagers were invented to keep parents from wasting time on the telephone.

When they're little, they step on your toes. When they're grown, they step on your heart.

There are no illegitimate CHILDREN,

only illegitimate parents.* *Judge Leon Yankwich, in ruling on a 1928 child custody case in Superior Court of Los Angeles*

There are no dull subjects. There are only dull writers. *H. L. Mencken*

The age of CHIVALRY is not dead.*

*A remark sometimes elicited by an unexpected act of gallantry. The statement "The age of chivalry is gone" appears in Edmund Burke's *Reflections on the Revolution in France,* first published in 1790.

CHRISTMAS comes but once a year.*

Christmas comes, but once a year is enough.

Christmas is a holiday that persecutes the lonely, the frayed and the rejected. *Jimmy Cannon*

Christmas is over and Business is Business. *Franklin P. Adams*

Don't send any funny greeting cards on birthdays or at Christmas. Save them for funerals, when their cheery effect is needed. *P. J. O'Rourke*

I am sorry to have to introduce the subject of Christmas. It is an indecent subject; a cruel, gluttonous subject; a drunken, disorderly subject; a wasteful, disastrous subject; a wicked, cadging, lying, filthy, blasphemous and demoralizing subject. Christmas is forced on a reluctant and disgusted nation by the shopkeepers and the press; on its own merits it would wither and shrivel in the fiery breath of universal hatred; and anyone who looked back to it would be turned into a pillar of greasy sausages. *G. B. Shaw*

I wish my enemies would go to hell,
Noel! Noel! Noel! Noel!
Hilaire Belloc

In the United States, Christmas has become the rape of an idea. *Richard Bach, Time, Nov. 13, 1972*

Merry Christmas, Nearly Everybody! *Ogden Nash*

Next to a circus there ain't nothing that packs up and tears out any quicker than the Christmas spirit. *Kin Hubbard*

Santa Claus has the right idea. Visit people once a year. *Victor Borge*

Roses are reddish,
Violets are bluish,
If it weren't for Xmas
We'd all be Jewish.
Graffiti

Winter comes but once a year,
And when it comes it brings the doctor good
    cheer.
Ogden Nash, Summergreen for President

*Take your choice of two 16th-century "sources":

Christmas comes but once a year.
But when it comes it brings good cheer.
    or
At Christmas play and make good cheer
For Christmas comes but once a year.

CHURCH ain't over till the fat lady sings.*

The opera isn't over till the fat lady sings. *1978, WM-200*

The rodeo ain't over till the bull riders ride.

It ain't over till it's over. *Yogi Berra, on 1973 National League pennant race*

*Listed as a southern saying by Smith and Smith.

See also Don't count your CHICKENS before they are hatched; Don't jump to CONCLUSIONS.

What this country really needs is a good five-cent CIGAR.* *Vice President Thomas R. Marshall, during a 1917 Senate debate on the needs of the country.*

. . . shoved down its throat. *Harold Jones*

There are plenty of good five-cent cigars in this country. The trouble is, they cost a quarter. What the country really needs is a good five-cent nickel. *F. P. Adams*

*First said by Kin Hubbard (1868–1930), according to Laurence Peter.

CIRCUMSTANCES alter cases. 1678, O-37

. . . especially reduced circumstances. *Henny Youngman*

Almost every wise saying has an opposite one, no less wise, to balance it. *George Santayana, Life of Reason*

Circumstances alter faces. *Carolyn Wells*

The circumstances of an act make it good. *1619, T-102*

If moral behavior were simply following rules, we could program a computer to be moral. *Samuel P. Ginder*

Speech is better than silence; silence is better than speech. *Ralph Waldo Emerson*

See also BEAUTY is in the eye of the beholder; DISTANCE lends enchantment; It all DEPENDS on whose ox is gored; Where you STAND depends on where you sit.

You can't fight CITY HALL.

. . . but you can attack them. *Alan King*

He that spits against the wind spits in his own face. *New England proverb*

In the fight between you and the world, back the world. *Frank Zappa*

The world is always agin' you if you are agin' the world. *Old postcard*

See also You can't WIN.

CLEANLINESS is next to godliness. *Talmudic proverb; K-184*

. . . if not before it. *G. B. Shaw, Man and Superman*

Clean your rooms well; for good spirits will not live where there is dirt. There is no dirt in heaven. *Shaker motto*

Cleanliness is almost as bad as godliness. *Samuel Butler*

Cleanliness is next to impossible. *Phyllis Diller*

If you go long enough without a bath even the fleas will let you alone. *Ernie Pyle*

Washing should be only for the purpose of keeping the body clean, and this can be effected without scrubbing the whole surface daily. Water is not the natural habitat of humanity. *Mary Baker Eddy, Science and Health*

It is not necessary to be a pig in order to raise one. *Heard in New York and South Carolina*

Only dirty people need baths.

So far as cleanliness is concerned, in Holland it is evidently not next to, but far ahead of godliness. *P. T. Barnum, 1873*

Soap is a four-letter word.

The classes that wash most are those that work least. *G. K. Chesterton*

On Judgement Day
If God should say
Did you clean your house today?
I will say, I did not.
I played with the children
And I forgot.
Sue Wall

He that would have the fruit must CLIMB the tree.

He that will eat the kernel must crack the nut. *ca. 1500, WM-345*

The higher they CLIMB, the harder they fall. 1460, T-103

Hall binks are slithery. [The stairways of mansions are slippery.] *Scottish proverb*

He that lies on the floor doesn't fall down. *Norwegian proverb*

In the big river big fish, but sometimes you'll get drowned. *Spanish proverb*

The bigger the summer vacation, the harder the fall.

The eagle may soar, but the weasel never gets sucked into a jet engine. *Simon & Simon, TV show*

The harder you fall, the higher you bounce. *Heard in Illinois and Washington*

The higher skirts climb, the better the view.

The higher the ape goes up, the more he shows his tail. *1640, Herbert*

There is more danger of ruin in success than in adversity but the world is full of people who would take the risk. *Frederick H. Seymour*

Now that I'm almost up the ladder,
I should, no doubt, be feeling gladder.
It is quite fine, the view and such,
If it just didn't shake so much.
Richard Armour

CLOTHES don't make the man. *ca. 1500, WM-103*

. . . but clothes can break the man.

Beware of all enterprises that require new clothes. *Henry David Thoreau, Walden*

By adornment, one acknowledges his ugliness. *Kahlil Gibran*

Dress up a monkey like a bishop, it's still a monkey. *Japanese proverb*

Fine clothes make not a gentleman. *1521, T-606*

How anybody dresses is indicative of his self-concept. If students are dirty and ragged, it indicates they are not interested in tidying up their intellects either. *S. I. Hayakawa, as president of San Francisco State College, 1973*

In silk and scarlet walks many a harlot. *English proverb*

When you meet a man, you judge him by his clothes; when you leave, you judge him by his heart. *Russian proverb*

You can't always tell a gentleman by his clothes, but you can by his fingernails. *Josh Billings, 1865*

The tulip and the butterfly
Appear in gayer coats than I:
Let me be dressed fine as I will,
Flies, worms, and flowers exceed me still.
Isaac Watts, Against Pride in Clothes

CLOTHES make the man. *Babylonian Talmud, ca. 450*

. . . uncomfortable.

. . . if the right girl is wearing them. *Henny Youngman*

. . . Naked people have little or no influence in society. *Mark Twain, More Maxims of Mark*

A man should dress as though he cares how he looks, but not as though he cares how other people think he looks. *Sydney J. Harris*

Classy clothes say to the world, "I've got the bread, man, so treat me with a little respect."

Clothes and manners do not make the man; but, when he is made, they greatly improve his appearance. *Henry Ward Beecher, Proverbs from a Plymouth Pulpit*

Clothes fake the man.

Clothes make people, and rags make lice. *German proverb*

Clothes make the woman and break the man.

Even a dressed-up broomstick is handsome. *Yiddish proverb*

Fools invent fashions, and wise men are fain to follow them. *Samuel Butler, Prose Observations, 1660–1680*

Good clothes make the impression, but they don't make the man. *Josh Billings*

He who scorns to be influenced by fashion is a wise fool. *Josh Billings, 1865*

I have heard with admiring submission the experience of a lady who declared that the sense of being well dressed gives a feeling of inward tranquility which religion is powerless to bestow. *Ralph Waldo Emerson*

If you think clothes make no difference, try walking down the street without any. *Old postcard*

In my own city my name, in a strange city my clothes procure me respect. *1670, Ray*

The clothes hide the blemish. *Yiddish proverb*

There is one other reason for dressing well, namely that dogs respect it, and will not attack you in good clothes. *Ralph Waldo Emerson, 1870*

We are all Adam's children; but Silk makes the Difference. *1732, Fuller*

When you's broke, dat's de time to ack stylish, so folks won't know you're broke. *Heard in Mississippi and New York*

Every CLOUD has a silver lining. *John Milton, Comus, 1634*

. . . But not the kind of silver you can take to the bank.

. . . Even an old suit of clothes has its shiny side.

After the clouds, the sun. *Latin proverb*

Every crowd has a silver lining. *P. T. Barnum*

Every silver lining has a cloud. *Line in a Noel Coward song of the 1930s*

For every thing you have missed, you have gained something else; and for everything you gain, you lose something. *Ralph Waldo Emerson, Compensation*

I enjoy convalescence. It is the part that makes the illness worth while. *G. B. Shaw*

I reckon being ill is one of the greatest pleasures of life, provided one is not too ill and is not obliged to work till one is better. *Samuel Butler*

I've sprained my neck looking for the silver lining behind every cloud.

Ill luck is good for something. *1636, T-401*

Mumps keeps a boy out of school.

No experiment is ever a complete failure. It can always be used as a bad example. *Paul Dickson, The Official Rules*

No sunshine but hath some shadow. *1670, Ray*

Pollution is nothing but resources we're not harvesting. *R. Buckminster Fuller*

Problems are only opportunities in work clothes. *Henry J. Kaiser*

The blue of heaven is larger than the cloud. *Elizabeth Barrett Browning*

The death of wolves is the safety of the sheep. *16th century*

The father of the bride doesn't lose a daughter, he gains a bathroom; the mother of the bride doesn't lose a daughter, she acquires more closet space.

The stones that mar the hill will grind the corn. *B-395*

There are gains for all our losses, there are balms for all our pain. *Richard Henry Stoddard*

There's another advantage to being poor—a doctor will cure you faster. *Kin Hubbard*

There's no great loss without some gain. *1641, O-139*

To the pickpocket, every crowd has a silver lining.

To the undertaker, every shroud has a silver lining.

When it rains, look for the rainbow.

A heart full of joy and gladness
Will always banish sadness and strife
So always look for the silver lining
And try to find the sunny side of life.
Jerome Kern and Buddy DeSylva, Look for the Silver Lining

See also It's an ill WIND that blows nobody any good.

Don't carry COALS to Newcastle. *1601, T-106*

. . . or carry crocodiles into Egypt. *1670, T-106*

. . . or pour water on a drowned rat.

Don't bring leaves to the wood. *1659, T-257*

Don't carry glasses to Venice. *1659, T-257*

Don't bring owls to Athens. *1548, T-517*

Don't cast water into the Thames. *1611, T-707*

Let the COBBLER stick to his last.*

Before you clean up the world, think about your garage.

Every man a little beyond himself is a fool. *1677, OE-177*

Let every man abide in the same calling wherein he was called. *1 Corinthians 7:20*

*Attributed to the Greek painter Apelles (4th century B.C.), who would not allow a cobbler to criticize his paintings, except for the slippers.

A COBBLER'S children always go barefoot. *1546, Heywood*

He is like a needle that clothes people and is itself naked. *Arabic proverb*

It's a COCKEYED world.

An editor is one who separates the wheat from the chaff and prints the chaff. *Adlai Stevenson*

Are you so unobservant as not to have found out that sanity and happiness are an impossible combination? *Mark Twain*

Doctor to patient lying in a hospital bed: "Medical ethics do not allow me to assist in your death. I am, however, permitted to keep you miserable as long as possible." *P. Steiner, cartoon*

Life would be infinitely happier if we could only be born at the age of 80 and gradually approach 18. *Mark Twain*

People try to live within their income so that they can afford to pay taxes to a government that can't live within its income. *Robert Half*

The first half of life consists of the capacity to enjoy without the chance; the last half consists of the chance without the capacity. *Mark Twain*

What a half-arsed world! *BJW-703*

Why do so many children's books have large print, when youngsters see so well, and adult books have small print for adults who don't? *Sydney J. Harris*

You can't make up anything anymore. The world itself is satire. All you're doing is recording it. *Art Buchwald*

This world is very odd we see,
We do not comprehend it;
But in one fact we all agree,
God won't, and we can't mend it.
Arthur Hugh Clough, Dipsychus

When we are born, we cry that we are come
To this great stage of fools. *Shakespeare, King Lear 4.6.187*

See also LIFE is funny; TRUTH is stranger than fiction.

A man is known by the COMPANY he keeps.* *1541, O-40*

. . . away from. *Joe Creason*

. . . and a politician is known by the promises he keeps.

. . . and a woman is known by the man who keeps her.

. . . and by the enemies he makes.

A company is known by the men it keeps.

A man is known by the companies he merges. *L. L. Levinson*

A man is known by the company he thinks nobody knows he's keeping. *Irv Kupcinet*

A man is known by the company his mind keeps. *Thomas Bailey Aldrich*

A man is known by the silence he keeps. *Oliver Herford*

A woman is known by the company she keeps waiting. *Louisville Times, ca. 1925*

Be not among winebibbers; among riotous eaters of flesh. *Proverbs 23:20*

To be a big man among big men, is what proves a man's character—to be a bullfrog among tadpoles don't amount to much. *Josh Billings*

One night in late October,
When I was far from sober,
Returning with my load with manly pride,
My feet began to stutter,
So I lay down in the gutter,
And a pig came near and lay down by my
 side.

A lady passing by was heard to say:
"You can tell a man who boozes
By the company he chooses,"
And the pig got up and slowly walked away.

The flannel suit,
The Dacron smile,
The drip-dry zest that sweeps him.
You can always tell
A man these days
By the Company that keeps him.
E. Y. Harburg

*In a 1901 issue of the *Philistine*, Elbert Hubbard denounced this proverb as "the motto of a prig. . . . Little men with foot rules six inches long, applied their measuring sticks in this way."

See also BIRDS of a feather flock together; If you lie down with DOGS, you get up with fleas.

Two is COMPANY, three is a crowd.* 1706, F-188

. . . especially in a motel room.

. . . and four is a bridge game.

. . . four on a sidewalk is not allowed. *Heard in U.S. and Canada*

. . . Two, save in a love affair, is often a bore. Three is often a good party, or at least the makings of one. *George Jean Nathan*

I have three chairs in my house: one for solitude, two for friendship, three for society. *Henry David Thoreau, Walden*

In married life three is company and two is none. *Oscar Wilde, The Importance of Being Earnest*

One's company, two's a crowd and three's a party. *Andy Warhol, Exposures*

The third person makes good company. *Dutch proverb*

Two were company, and three was the result.

*The traditional form of this proverb seems to be "Two is company, but three is none." Both Oxford (O-233) and Stevenson (B-386) give four citations of this form.

COMPARISONS are odious. 1573, T-114

. . . and generalizations are dangerous.

. . . but no woman yet has become wroth over being compared to an angel. *George Jean Nathan*

Comparisons are odorous. *Shakespeare, Much Ado About Nothing 3.5.18*

COMPETITION is the life of trade. 1903, WM-109

Thou shalt not covet: but tradition
Approves all forms of competition.
Arthur Hugh Clough, 1849

When you are not practicing, remember, someone somewhere is practicing, and when you meet him he will win. *Ed Macauley*

Don't COMPLAIN.

. . . but anyone who is always feeling sorry for himself should be.

It is a good horse that never stumbles, and a good wife that never grumbles. *1530, Palsgrave*

Taint no use to grumble and complain.
    It's just as cheap and easy to rejoice.
When God sorts out the weather and sends
    rain,
    Why, rain's my choice.
Old postcard

Don't tell friends about your indigestion.
"How are you" is a greeting, not a question.
Arthur Guiterman

See also Never EXPLAIN . . .

Everyone COMPLAINS of his memory, but no one complains of his judgment.

Don't jump to CONCLUSIONS.

. . . They might jump back at you.

. . . It doesn't make for happy landings.

Draw your own CONCLUSIONS.

He who enters the tavern, enters not to say his prayers. *Rumanian proverb*

Life is the art of drawing sufficient conclusions from insufficient premises.

CONFESSION is good for the soul.* 1598, T-116

... only in the sense that a tweed coat is good for dandruff—it is a palliative rather than a remedy. *Peter De Vries*

"Confession may be good for the soul, but ... it is also a very dirty trick to play on the woman with whom you were involved. If you feel you must clear your conscience, please talk to a clergyman, a trusted lawyer, or your doctor. *Ann Landers, advice to a man who felt driven to tell his wife about an affair he had with a woman they both knew.*

Confess your sins to the Lord and you will be forgiven; confess them to a man and you will be laughed at. *Josh Billings*

Confessions may be good for the soul, but they are bad for the reputation. *Thomas Dewar*

Every time a friend succeeds, I die a little. *Gore Vidal*

Who brags about his faults, no doubt
Has little else to brag about.
Arthur Guiterman

*Spoken ironically, says Tilley (T-116), to those who boast of their ill deeds.

A good CONSCIENCE needs no excuse. 1580, B-407

A good conscience is a continual feast. *English proverb*

A good conscience sometimes needs a poor memory.

A peace above all earthly dignities,
A still and quiet conscience.
Shakespeare, Henry VIII 3.1.379

A guilty CONSCIENCE needs no accuser. 1390, O-99

A guilty conscience is the mother of invention. *Carolyn Wells*

An evil conscience breaks many a man's neck. *1678, Ray*

See also CONSCIENCE makes cowards of us all.

CONSCIENCE is that still small voice within you.*

... that makes you feel still smaller. *John Sanaker*

... that says you might get caught.

I get very poor reception. *Edgar Bergen's Charlie McCarthy, when asked why he never listened to his conscience*

Conscience has a small, still voice when it's a small, still conscience.

Conscience is a mother-in-law whose visit never ends. *H. L. Mencken*

Conscience is as much a part of man as his leg or arm. *Thomas Jefferson, 1787*

Conscience is God's presence in man. *Emanuel Swedenborg, Arcana Coelestia*

Conscience is that still, small voice that is sometimes too loud for comfort. *Bert Murray*

Conscience is the inner voice that warns us that someone might be looking. *H. L. Mencken, A Mencken Chrestomathy*

Conscience is the voice of values long and deeply infused into one's sinews and blood.

Elliot L. Richardson, 1973, on resigning as U.S. Attorney General rather than approve presidential firing of a Richardson appointee

Conscience is what your mother told you before you were six years old. *Brock Chisholm, 1949*

Going through life with a conscience is like driving your car with the brakes on. *Bud Schulberg, 1941*

If you want to be good, begin by assuming that you are bad. *Epictetus, Fragments*

If your conscience won't stop you, pray for cold feet. *Elmer G. Leterman*

Listen to your conscience, for you may be listening to God. *J. H. Rhoades, 1942*

O conscience, silent torture of the soul. *Publilius Syrus*

The difference between a moral man and a man of honor is that the latter regrets a discreditable act, even when it has worked and he has not been caught. *H. L. Mencken*

The more things a man is ashamed of, the more respectable he is. *G. B. Shaw, Man and Superman*

The New England conscience . . . does not stop you from doing what you shouldn't—it stops you from enjoying it. *Cleveland Amory, New York Times, May 5, 1980*

There's no substitute for conscience. Unless, of course, it's witnesses.

What the world needs is a good loudspeaker for the still, small voice. *Herbert V. Prochnow, as quoted in Reader's Digest, Aug. 1954*

You have to live with yourself. *Heard in North Carolina*

He who is ridden by a conscience
Is worried by a lot of nonscience.
Ogden Nash, 1940

This world would be a different sort of place
If men feared conscience as they fear disgrace.
Arthur Guiterman

There is only one way to achieve happiness
     on this terrestrial ball,
And that is to have either a clear conscience,
     or none at all.
Ogden Nash, I'm a Stranger Here Myself

*Magill (M-1011) notes that the phrase "a still small voice" appears in 1 Kings 19:12.

CONSCIENCE makes cowards of us all. 1594, O-41

A guilty conscience is the mother of invention. *Carolyn Wells*

An uneasy conscience is a hair in the mouth. *Mark Twain*

Conscience gets a lot of credit that belongs to cold feet.

Conscience is a thousand witnesses. *1550, Erasmus*

Conscience makes egoists of us all. *Oscar Wilde, The Picture of Dorian Gray*

He who is without shame, all the world is his. *Italian proverb*

The English have a proverb, "Conscience makes cowboys of us all." *Saki, Chronicles of Clovis*

The fear of being laughed at makes cowards of us all. *Mignon McLaughlin*

Let your CONSCIENCE be your guide.

. . . a silly thing to say to a good man, or a bad one. *Mignon McLaughlin*

Proselytizer: Let my conscience be your guide.

When conscience has dictated one course and passion another, did you ever regret following the injunctions of the former? *Old Farmer's Almanac, 1848*

A foolish CONSISTENCY is the hobgoblin of little minds.*

A man should never be ashamed to own that he has been in the wrong, which is but saying, in other words, that he is wiser today than he was yesterday. *Jonathan Swift, Thoughts on Various Subjects*

A wise man sometimes changes his mind, but a fool never. *Old postcard*

Any plan is bad that cannot be changed. *Italian proverb*

Art is a lie to make us realize the truth. *Pablo Picasso*

Both egoism and altruism are necessary to welfare. Both are moral motives. Right living is the right balance between them. *Herbert L. Samuel, Belief and Action*

Civilized man's brain is a museum of contradictory truths. *Remy de Gourmont*

Consistency is the last refuge of the unimaginative. *Oscar Wilde (attributed)*

Consistency requires you to be as ignorant today as you were a year ago. *Bernard Berenson*

Everyone must have two pockets, so that he can reach into the one or the other, according to his needs. In his right pocket are to be the words: "For my sake was the world created," and in his left: "I am but dust and ashes." *Rabbi Bunam*

Holding it a sound maxim that it is better to be only sometimes right than at all times wrong, so soon as I discover my opinions to be erroneous I shall be ready to renounce them. *Abraham Lincoln, 1832*

I do not believe today everything I believed yesterday; I wonder will I believe tomorrow everything I believe today. *Isaac Goldberg*

One has two duties—to be worried, and not to be worried. *E. M. Forster, London Observer, Dec. 20, 1959*

Only a fool never changes his mind. *Heard in Kansas and Ontario*

Seek simplicity and distrust it. *Alfred North Whitehead*

The best people usually owe their excellence to a combination of qualities which might have been supposed incompatible. *Bertrand Russell, Sceptical Essays*

The foolish and the dead alone never change their opinion. *James Russell Lowell, My Study Windows*

The man who never alters his opinion is like standing water, and breeds reptiles in the mind. *William Blake, The Marriage of Heaven and Hell*

The only man who can change his mind is the man who's got one. *Edward Noyes Westcott*

The test of a first-rate intelligence is the ability to hold two opposed ideas in the mind at the same time, and still retain the ability to function. *F. Scott Fitzgerald, The Crack-Up*

The truth in this observation is that consistent reasoning or action on the basis of incorrect premises may lead to disaster, and that common sense and the direct appeal to experience should be continually invoked to check the conclusions of deduction. *Corliss Lamont, Humanism as a Philosophy*

There is no happiness that is not idleness, and only what is useless is pleasurable. *Anton Chekhov*

Things that I felt absolutely sure of but a few years ago, I do not believe now; and this thought makes me see more clearly how foolish it would be to expect all men to agree with me. *F. D. Van Amburgh*

Think like a man of action, act like a man of thought. *Henri Bergson*

Those who never retract their opinions love themselves more than they love truth. *Joseph Joubert, Pensées*

*A foolish consistency is the hobgoblin of little minds. . . . With consistency a great soul has simply nothing to do. . . . Speak what you think now in hard words and to-morrow speak what to-morrow thinks in hard words again, though it contradict every thing you said to-day. *Ralph Waldo Emerson, Self-Reliance, 1841.* The Morrises (MD-226) note that the Emerson quotation does not disapprove of consistency itself, but in a foolish consistency. But as several commentaries argue, in some cases consistency itself is foolish.

You have not CONVERTED a man because you have silenced him. *Viscount Morley (1838–1923), Essay on Compromise*

*This quotation was popularized by a Ben Shahn poster memorializing the Sacco-Vanzetti case.

See Merely to SILENCE a man is not to persuade him.

That's the way the COOKIE crumbles.

See Such is LIFE; LIFE'S like that.

Too many COOKS spoil the broth. 1575, O-228

Far too many cooks spoil the broth. *Wayne G. Haisley*

I'm going to stop asking my cooks to prepare broth for me. Over the years, I've found that too many broths spoil the cook. . . . My cooks . . . also spoil the dinner. *Groucho Marx, on New Year's resolutions*

Having too many cooks on the payroll can spoil a restaurant's balance sheet.

The madam turned away oddballs and weirdos; too many kooks spoil the brothel.

Too many cooks leaves nobody to wash the dishes.

Too many fingers spoil the pie. *Heard in California, Colorado, Illinois, and New York*

Two midwives give the child a crooked head. *Persian proverb*

You measure everyone's CORN by your own bushel. 1670, Ray

Everyone is a prisoner of his own experiences. No one can eliminate prejudices—just recognize them. *Edward R. Murrow*

My idea of an agreeable person is one who agrees with me. *Samuel Johnson*

See also Great SPIRIT . . . ; It all DEPENDS on whose ox is gored; Where you STAND depends on where you sit.

A fool's COUNSEL is sometimes worth the weighing.

Listen to a fool. *Yiddish proverb*

Ask not what your COUNTRY can do for you, ask what you can do for your country.* John F. Kennedy

Ask not what you can do for your country, for they are liable to tell you. *Mark Steinbeck*

*The Morrises (MD-28) note that the challenging statement for which John F. Kennedy is remembered actually echoes two other famous Americans. Many years ago, Oliver Wendell Holmes, Jr., wrote, "It is now the moment when we pause to recall what our country has done for each of us and to ask ourselves what we can do our country in return." And Warren G. Harding said before the 1916 Republican National Convention: "We must have a citizenship less concerned about what the government can do for it and more anxious about what it can do for the nation."

My COUNTRY right or wrong.*

. . . Like saying, "My mother, drunk or sober." *G. K. Chesterton*

Each man must for himself alone decide what is right and what is wrong, which course is patriotic and which isn't. You cannot shirk this and be a man. *Mark Twain*

If you want a symbolic gesture, don't burn the flag, wash it. *Norman Thomas*

In statesmanship, get the formalities right, never mind about the moralities. *Mark Twain*

Intellectually, I know that America is no better than any other country; emotionally, I know she is better than every other country. *Sinclair Lewis*

Nationalism is a silly cock crowing on its own dunghill. *Richard Aldington, 1931*

Nationalism is power hunger tempered by self-deception. *George Orwell, 1945*

Our country, right or wrong! When right, to be kept right; when wrong, to be put right! *Carl Schurz, 1872*

Patriotism is, fundamentally, a conviction that a particular country is the best in the world because you were born in it. *G. B. Shaw, Music in London, Nov. 15, 1893*

To make us love our country, our country ought to be lovely. *Edmund Burke*

True patriotism doesn't exclude an understanding of the patriotism of others. *Elizabeth II*

True patriotism hates injustice in its own land more than anywhere else. *Clarence Darrow*

Be England what she will,
With all her faults, she is my country still.
Charles Churchill, The Farewell

*Although Mieder (WM-119) identifies this as an 18th-century Spanish proverb, these words are popularly identified with this 1816 statement of Stephen Decatur: "Our Country! In her intercourse with foreign nations, may she always be in the right; but our Country, right or wrong."

See also PATRIOTISM is the last refuge of a scoundrel; All POLITICIANS are crooked.

COURTESY costs nothing. *Ralph Waldo Emerson, 1837*

. . . Try not tipping and see. *Cynic, 1917*

Etiquette means behaving yourself a little better than is absolutely necessary. *Will Cuppy*

It never hurts to be polite.

Manners are happy ways of doing things. *Ralph Waldo Emerson*

The greatest mistake is trying to be more agreeable than you can. *Walter Bagehot*

Pleasant words are as an honeycomb, sweet to the soul, and health to the bones. *Proverbs 16:24*

You can get through life with bad manners, but it's easier with good manners. *Lillian Gish*

Full of COURTESY, full of craft. 1576, T-123

A honey tongue, a heart of gall. *1300, OE-301*

Fair words make me look to my purse. *1640, Herbert*

He who can lick, can bite.

[He who] speaketh fair, believe him not; for there are seven abominations in his heart. *Proverbs 26:25*

Many do kiss hands which they would wish to see cut off. *1666, Torriano*

Nothing is so irritating as the fellow that chats pleasantly while he is overcharging you. *Kin Hubbard*

True politeness consists in being anxious about the welfare of others; false politeness consists in being very anxious about nothing. *Josh Billings*

See also HYPOCRISY is the homage . . .

If I own a COW, the cow owns me. *Ralph Waldo Emerson*

Few rich men own their own property. The property owns them. *Robert G. Ingersoll, address to the McKinley League, 1896*

He that hath lands, hath quarrels. *1640, Herbert*

I wish I were either rich enough or poor enough to do a lot of things that are impossible in my present comfortable circumstances. *Don Herold*

If he works for you, you work for him. *Japanese proverb*

The man who owns his own house is always just coming out of a hardware store. *Kin Hubbard*

The woman you keep keeps you. *Heard in Illinois*

Many a good COW has a bad calf. 1546, Heywood

A black hen lays a white egg. *French proverb*

Deacons' daughters and ministers' sons are the biggest devils that ever run. *1855, WM-135*

Good wombs have borne bad sons. *Shakespeare, The Tempest 1.2.120*

See also The APPLE doesn't fall far from its tree; Like FATHER, like son; Like MOTHER, like daughter.

Why buy a COW when you can get milk free?* *1659, Howell*

No man chases a streetcar he's already caught.

Try it before you buy it. *Heard in Wisconsin*

What's the sense of eating prunes when peaches are ripe?

*Said to have been Elvis Presley's favorite answer to the question "Why aren't you married?"

See also There are plenty more FISH in the sea.

The COWARD dies a thousand deaths, the brave just one.*

*Cowards die many times before their deaths; The valiant never taste of death but once. *Shakespeare, Julius Caesar 2.2.32*

See It is sweet and fitting to DIE for one's country.

Give CREDIT where credit is due.

Give credit to whom credit is due. *1777, WM-125*

CREDITORS have better memories than debtors. *1659, Howell*

A creditor is worse than a master, for a master owns only your person—a creditor owns your dignity and can belabor that. *Victor Hugo, Les Misérables*

A habit of debt is very injurious to the memory. *Austin O'Malley*

Gratitude is a lotus flower whose leaves soon wither. *African proverb*

See also BORROWING brings sorrowing.

We have to CREEP before we can walk.* *1670, O-240*

*Oxford (O-240) lists several variants, including "We must learn to walk before we can run," "You must learn to creep before you go."

CRIME does not pay. *Slogan of the FBI and Dick Tracy; WM- 126*

. . . unless you really know what you're doing.

. . . You're lucky if it covers your overhead.

. . . if you can find something that is lucrative, dishonest, and legal.

Crime in the U.S. is perhaps one of the biggest businesses in the world today. *Paul Kirk, Wall Street Journal, Feb. 26, 1960*

It is no secret that organized crime in America takes in over forty billion dollars a year. This is quite a profitable sum, especially when one considers that the Mafia spends very little for office supplies. *Woody Allen*

It is wit to pick a lock and steal a horse, but wisdom to let it alone. *1659, Howell*

Make crime pay—become a lawyer.

Most criminals . . . are apprehended because they are stupid and not because of some giant balance wheel that punishes crime. Crime itself is a stupid thing and every repetition of a criminal act brings apprehension that much closer. The entire pattern of criminality is a path to a jail cell. *Donald G. Smith*

A classic bully who lived by the credo that crime pays and absolute crime pays absolutely. *Thomas L. Friedman, on Saddam Hussein, New York Times, Aug. 5, 1990*

One of the biggest lies in the world is that crime does not pay. Of course crime pays. *Watergate conspirator G. Gordon Liddy*

The only crimes that don't pay are those which were botched up. We don't know beans about the whacking number of crimes that do pay. How can we? They remain undiscovered.

   Crime pays off like crazy to bookkeepers who boodle accounts; dognappers who steal a pet, then claim the reward; buzzard Lotharios who gull lonely widows; till-tappers who ring up "No Sale"; glue-fingered glommers who helpfully reduce the inventory of department stores; talented "icemen" who peddle stolen diamonds; gandy dancers who swindle the credulous; brazen cops uncaught in their weekly collection of payoffs; and all the miscellaneous lamsters, fence-jumpers, credit-card finks and hotel hustlers who lighten the assets of the innocent and naive.

   . . . crime doesn't pay unless you're very good at it. Neither does playing the fiddle, or using a trampoline. *Leo Rosten, The Power of Positive Nonsense*

Thieves respect property; they merely wish the property to become their property that they may more perfectly respect it. *G. K. Chesterton, The Man Who Was Thursday*

To make certain that crime does not pay, the government should take it over and try to run it. *G. Norman Collie*

*The fruitlessness of crime is an ancient idea, notes Flexner (F-35). For example, around 550 B.C. Cleobulus advised: "A man may thrive on crime, but not for long."

No CROSS, no crown. *1621, T-130*

See No gains without PAINS; Never the ROSE without the thorn.

Every CROW thinks its own young ones the whitest. *1513, T-131*

Every peddler thinks well of his pack. *1611, T-529*

There's only one pretty child in the world, and every mother has it. *English proverb*

See also BEAUTY is in the eye of the beholder.

Uneasy lies the head that wears a CROWN. *Shakespeare 2 Henry IV 3.1.31, ca. 1598*

Uneasy lies the tooth that wears a crown.

Crowns have cares. *1576, T-131*

It is no use CRYING over spilt milk. *1659, Howell*

. . . It only makes it salty for the cat.

. . . Go milk another cow.

. . . There's enough water in it already.

. . . but if you must cry over spilled milk, condense it.

. . . because all the forces of the universe were bent on spilling it. *W. Somerset Maugham*

. . . When that saying was written, milk was ten cents a quart.

. . . I am not so sure. . . . A good cry sometimes serves as an anodyne and slightly alleviates disappointment and pain. Anyway, it can't do you any harm and it may help a little. *George Jean Nathan*

Any person who's always feeling sorry for himself should be.

Better to cry over it than try to put it back in the bottle.

If you should find your house on fire, go up and warm yourself by it. *Spanish proverb*

It is unwise to meditate unthriftily over spilt milk.

There's no use crying after the jug's busted. *Ozark variation*

What can't be CURED must be endured. 1377, O-46

What cannot be eschew'd must be embrac'd. *Shakespeare, The Merry Wives of Windsor 5.5.251*

What can't be cured must be insured. *Oliver Herford*

CURIOSITY killed the cat. 1909, WM-170

. . . Satisfaction brought it back.

A person should want to live, if only out of curiosity. *Yiddish proverb*

An interviewer asked Studs Terkel, "What's kept you going all these years?" "Curiosity," he replied. "I always say, if I have an epitaph: 'Curiosity did not kill this cat.' " *Chicago Tribune, Aug. 13, 1995*

Curiosity has its own reason for existing. One cannot help but be in awe when he contemplates the mysteries . . . of life. . . . It is enough if one tries merely to comprehend a little of this mystery every day. Never lose a holy curiosity. *Albert Einstein*

Curiosity has killed more mice than cats.

Curiosity is looking over other people's affairs and overlooking our own. *Old Farmer's Almanac, 1851*

Curiosity is the first step to hell. *Polish proverb*

Curiosity will conquer fear even more than bravery will. *James Stephens*

I like to listen. I have learned a great deal from listening carefully. Most people never listen. *Ernest Hemingway*

Dorothy Parker was told by a friend that her cat was sick and had to be put away. Miss Parker's not-very-sympathetic reply was, "Try curiosity."

I think, at a child's birth, if a mother could ask a fairy godmother to endow it with the most useful gift, that gift would be curiosity. *Eleanor Roosevelt, The Common Wisdom of Three First Ladies*

Mother: Stop asking so many questions. Don't you know that curiosity killed the cat? Small daughter: What did the cat want to know?

Saint Augustine, in his *Confessions*, tells of a curious soul who wondered what God did in the eons before creating heaven and earth. Came the stern reply: "He fashioned hell for the inquisitive." *F-35*

The whole art of teaching is only the art of awakening the natural curiosity of young minds for the purpose of satisfying it afterwards. *Anatole France*

The whole secret of life is to be interested in one thing profoundly and in a thousand things well. *Hugh Walpole,* as quoted in *Reader's Digest, Nov. 1947*

The CURSE of bigness.*

A business is too big when it takes a week for gossip to travel from one end of the office to the other.

A government that is big enough to give you all you want is big enough to take it all away. *Barry Goldwater, 1964*

Gigantic organizations make gigantic mistakes. *Robert Lekachman, 1987*

. . . public education will always be mediocre, for the same reason that in large kitchens the cooking is usually bad. *Friedrich Nietzsche*

The bigger the information media, the less freedom they allow. Bigness means weakness. *Eric Severeid*

The more complex the system becomes, the more open it is to total breakdown. *Lewis Mumford*

*Justice Louis D. Brandeis (1856–1941) saw "the curse of bigness" in the growth of corporate America. He warned, "When . . . you increase your business to a very great extent, and the multitude of problems increase with its growth . . . the man at the head has a diminishing knowledge of the facts and . . . a diminishing opportunity of exercising a careful judgment upon them. . . . Demoralization sets in; a condition of lessened efficiency presents itself. . . . These are disadvantages that attend bigness."

See also A CHAIN is as strong as its weakest link; LESS is more; SMALL is beautiful.

CURSES, like chickens, come home to roost. *ca. 1275, WM-131*

Injure others, injure yourself. *Chinese proverb*

Kennedy cooked the soup that Johnson had to eat. *Konrad Adenauer, on Vietnam War, 1973*

Throw rocks at the world and the world will throw back rocks at you. *William C. Hunter*

Whoso stoppeth his ears at the cry of the poor, he also shall cry himself, but shall not be heard. *Proverbs 21:13*

CUSTOM is a second nature. *1547, T-136*

Bad customs, like good cakes, should be broken. *1611, Cotgrave*

Custom in infancy becomes nature in old age. *H. G. Bohn, 1855*

Custom is the plague of wise men and the idol of fools.

Custom makes sin no sin. *1576, T-136*

Good ideas are not adopted automatically. They must be driven into practice with courageous impatience. *Hyman G. Rickover*

That monster, custom, who all sense doth eat
Of habits evil.
Shakespeare, Hamlet 3.4.37

The laws of conscience, which we pretend to be derived from nature, proceed from custom. *Michel de Montaigne, Of Custom*

When custom and reason are at odds, custom always wins out. *Napoleon*

Where is it written that shoes, socks, gloves, etc. must match? © *Ashleigh Brilliant*

The CUSTOMER is always right. *John Wanamaker (attributed)*

. . . Misinformed, inexact, bullheaded, fickle, stupid, forgetful, maybe even dishonest, but never wrong.

. . . Then why did she decide to return the merchandise for a refund the next day?

The art of showmanship is to give the public what it wants just before it knows what it wants. *David Belasco, as quoted in Reader's Digest, July 1970*

The customer is always ripe. *Peter's Almanac*

When white-collar people get jobs, they sell not only their time and energy but their personalities as well. They sell by week or month their smiles and their kindly gestures, and they must practice prompt repression of resentment and aggression. *C. Wright Mills*

A CYNIC is a person who knows the price of everything and the value of nothing. *Oscar Wilde, Lady Windermere's Fan, 1892*

A cynic is a man who, when he smells flowers, looks around for a coffin. *H. L. Mencken*

A cynic may know much but he does not know how to believe. *Paul Weiss*

An idealist is one who, upon observing that a rose smells better than a cabbage, concludes that it will also make better soup. *H. L. Mencken*

Cynic: a blackguard whose faulty vision sees things as they are, not as they ought to be. *Ambrose Bierce*

The power of accurate observation is commonly called cynicism by those who have not got it. *G. B. Shaw*

You're DAMNED if you do and damned if you don't.* 1836, M-185

Do what you feel in your heart to be right—for you'll be criticized anyway. You'll be damned if you do, and damned if you don't. *Eleanor Roosevelt*

One was never married, and that's his hell; another is, and that's his plague. *Robert Burton*

*You can and you can't,
You will and you won't;
You'll be damn'd if you do,
You'll be damn'd if you don't.
Lorenzo Dow (1777–1834), Reflections on the Love of God (the author's definition of Calvinism)

See also You can't WIN; What's the USE?

He who DANCES must pay the piper.

. . . and he who pipes must pay the plumber.

He that dances should always pay the fiddler. *1638, O-48*

In my case it so happened that a whole symphony orchestra often had to be subsidized. *John Barrymore*

It's always DARKEST just before the dawn. 1732, Fuller

. . . for the man who has been out all night drinking.

It's always darkest just before it goes totally black.

It's always dullest just before the yawn. *Life, ca. 1925*

75

The darkest hour is just before you're over-drawn. *Peter's Almanac*

Better to be an old man's DARLING than a young man's slave. *1546, Heywood*

. . . and even better to be a young man's darling than an old man's slave.

For it ne fit not unto fresshe May
For to be coupled to colde Januari.
John Lydgate, Temple of Glass

Perhaps the majority of girls would rather be a young man's slave than an old man's darling. *E. J. Hardy, How to Be Happy Though Married*

Have a nice DAY.*

. . . elsewhere.

. . . Thank you, but I have other plans. *Paul Fussell*

May you have warmth in your igloo, oil in your lamp, and peace in your heart. *Eskimo proverb*

*This old (ca. 1925) cliché was popularized in the 1950s when it became a greeting exchanged by truck drivers over citizen-band radios.

Take one DAY at a time.

I have a new philosophy. I'm only going to dread one day at a time. *Charles Schulz, Peanuts*

I try to be as philosophical as the old lady from Vermont who said that the best thing about the future is that it only comes one day at a time. *Dean Acheson, as quoted in Reader's Digest, Sept. 1950*

I try to take one day at a time, but sometimes several days attack me at once. © *Ashleigh Brilliant*

Life by the yard is hard, but by the inch, it's a cinch.

Live each day as if it were your last—and one of these days, you'll be right.

One day at a time. *Slogan of Alcoholics Anonymous*

Take it easy. That's why they made tomorrow—so we don't have to do everything today. *Barnaby Jones, TV show*

Other DAYS, other ways. *Greek proverb*

. . . like watching the old movie about the *Pearl Harbor* attack on your Sony TV.

Don't limit a child to your own learning, for he was born in another time. *Rabbinic saying*

In heaven, an angel is nobody in particular. *G. B. Shaw, Man and Superman*

Oh, would that my mind could let fall its dead ideas, as the tree does its withered leaves! *André Gide*

One of the first things one notices in a "backward" country is that children are still obeying their parents.

You can never plan the future by the past. *Edmund Burke, Letter to a Member of the National Assembly*

Rules, like men, to time must bow;
Then was then, but now is now.
Arthur Guiterman

See also HISTORY is bunk; O tempora! o mores!; Those days are GONE forever; Things are going to the DOGS.

Always speak well of the DEAD. *Latin proverb*

. . . and always speak well of your enemies; you probably made them.

Epitaph: a belated advertisement for a line of goods that has been permanently discontinued. *Irwin Cobb*

He that has too much feeling to speak ill of the dead . . . will not hesitate . . . to destroy . . . the reputation . . . of the living. *Samuel Johnson, Lives of the Poets*

It proves what they say, give the public what they want to see and they'll come out for it. *Comment whispered by Red Skelton at the funeral of Hollywood executive Harry Cohn.* "Red Skelton's comment about Harry Cohn's well-attended funeral could be his best-remembered line," writes Keyes (K-131).

It wasn't just with Mark Twain: the reports of all deaths are greatly exaggerated. *Mignon McLaughlin*

Since we have to speak well of the dead, let's knock them while they're alive. *John Sloan*

The best way to get praise is to die. *Italian proverb*

They say such nice things about people at their funerals that it makes me sad to realize that I'm going to miss mine by a just a few days. *Garrison Keillor*

Dead men tell no tales. *1560, O-49*

. . . and many who are alive aren't very informative either.

. . . which makes it easier for widows to re-marry.

A dead person has no mouth. *Japanese proverb*

Dead men don't bite. *Latin proverb*

Let the DEAD bury their dead.* *Matthew 8:22*

*Jesus implied with these words that his disciples had more important things to do than go back to their families and participate in their traditional rituals.

None so DEAF as those who will not hear. *1546, Heywood*

There are none so deaf as those who stop up their ears with impatience. *1938, BJW-157*

There is none so deaf as do not choose to hear. *1766, EAP-98*

A DEAL is a deal.

See A PROMISE is a promise.

DEATH, be not proud.*

*Death, be not proud, though some have called thee
Mighty and dreadful, for thou are not so:
For those whom thou think'st thou dost overthrow
Die not. . . .
John Donne (1572–1631)

See O DEATH, where is thy sting?

DEATH before dishonor.* *Latin maxim*

Live free or die. *Motto of New Hampshire*

*Urdang (pp. 151–53, 183) lists eighty-three aristocratic families that have adopted a motto that conveys this sentiment.

See also Better RED than dead; DO or die; He that FIGHTS and runs away may live to fight another day; It is sweet and fitting to DIE for one's country.

Nothing is certain but DEATH and taxes. 1726, WM-433

. . . but not in that order.

Collecting more taxes than is absolutely necessary is legalized robbery. *Calvin Coolidge*

Death and taxes and childbirth! There's never a convenient time for any of them. *Margaret Mitchell, Gone with the Wind*

Man is a thinking animal, a talking animal, a toolmaking animal, a building animal, a political animal, a fantasizing animal. But in the twilight of civilization he is chiefly a tax-paying animal. *Hugh MacLennan*

Now there are differences of opinion as to when death occurs, and nothing is certain but taxes.

Taxes, after all, are the dues we pay for the privileges of membership in an organized society. *Franklin D. Roosevelt*

Taxes are what we pay for a civilized society. *Oliver Wendell Holmes*

The difference between death and taxes is that death never gets any worse.

The difference between a taxidermist and a tax collector? The taxidermist takes only your skin. *Mark Twain*

The income tax has made more liars out of the American people than golf has. *Will Rogers (attributed)*

The income tax people are very nice. They're letting me keep my own mother. *Henny Youngman*

O DEATH, where is thy sting?*

Come lovely and soothing death. *Walt Whitman, When Lilacs Last in the Dooryard Bloom'd; M-161*

Death: A fate worse than life. *J. J. Furnas*

Death is nature's way of telling you to slow down. *Graffiti, London, 1978*

Death is not the greatest loss in life. The greatest loss is what dies inside us while we live. *Norman Cousins*

Death is not to be feared because it is evil; it is evil because it is feared. *Quoted as "an old proverb" by Corliss Lamont, in Humanism as a Philosophy*

Death, so called, is a thing which makes men
    weep,
And yet a third of life is passed in sleep.
Lord Byron, Don Juan

Death, the only immortal who treats us all alike, whose pity and whose peace and whose refuge are for all—the soiled and the pure, the rich and the poor, the loved and the unloved. *Mark Twain, on his deathbed, 1910*

Dying is a very dull, dreary affair. My advice to you is to have nothing whatever to do with it. *W. Somerset Maugham, last words, 1965*

. . . every individual existence goes out in a lonely spasm of helpless agony. *William James, The Varieties of Religious Experience*

Feared of dying? Were you feared of being born? *Old Farmer's Almanac, 1943*

For dust thou art, and unto dust shalt thou return. *Genesis 3:19*

I adore life but I don't fear death. I just prefer to die as late as possible. *Georges Simenon, International Herald Tribune, Nov. 26, 1981*

I am bored with it all. *Winston Churchill, last words, Jan. 24, 1965*

I look back on my life like a good day's work, it was done and I am satisfied with it. *Anna Mary Robertson Moses, Grandma Moses: My Life's History*

I think of death only with tranquility, as an end. I refuse to let death hamper life. Death must enter life only to define it. *Jean-Paul Sartre, No Exit*

I'm not afraid of death. I just don't want to be there when it happens. *Woody Allen*

Life always comes to a bad end. *Marcel Ayme, Les Oiseaux de Lune*

On the plus side, death is one of the few things that can be done as easily as lying down. *Woody Allen, Without Feathers*

Sleep is lovely, death is better still, not to have been born is of course the miracle. *Heinrich Heine*

The light of stars that were extinguished ages ago still reaches us. So is it with great men who died centuries ago, but still reach us with the radiations of their personality. *Kahlil Gibran*

The only religious way to think of death is as a part and parcel of life; to regard it, with the understanding and the emotions, as the inviolable condition of life. *Thomas Mann, The Magic Mountain*

Those who welcome death have only tried it from the ears up. *Wilson Mizner*

To desire immortality is to desire the eternal perpetuation of a great mistake. *Arthur Schopenhauer, The World as Will and Idea*

To die will be an awfully big adventure. *James M. Barrie, Peter Pan*

To live in the hearts that are left behind is not to die.

To me death is not a fearful thing. It's living that's cursed. *Jim Jones, last words, tape-recorded before his death and mass suicide of his followers at Jonestown, Guyana, Nov. 18, 1978*

Try to think of death as a learning experience. © *Ashleigh Brilliant*

We need to be reminded that there is nothing morbid about honestly confronting the fact of life's end, and preparing for it so that we may go gracefully and peacefully. The fact is, we cannot truly face life until we have learned to face the fact that it will be taken away from us. *Billy Graham*

If there's another world, he lives in bliss;
If there is none, he made the best of this.
Robert Burns, Epitaph on William Muir

Do not go gentle into that good night,
Old age should burn and rave at close of day;
Rage, rage against the dying of the light.
Dylan Thomas, 1951

The weariest and most loathed worldly life
That age, ache, penury and imprisonment
Can lay on nature is a paradise
To what we fear of death.
Shakespeare, Macbeth 3.1.27

O Death! The poor man's dearest friend
The kindest and the best.
Robert Burns, Man Was Made to Mourn

When life is woe,
And hope is dumb,
The World says, "Go!"
The Grave says, "Come!"
Arthur Guiterman, Betel-Nuts

*. . . O grave, where is thy victory? *1
  Corinthians 15:55*

See also All MEN are mortal; LIFE is short.

There's a remedy for everything except DEATH. *Miguel de Cervantes, Don Quixote*

The only real cure for snoring is deafness.
© *Ashleigh Brilliant*

See also There's no cure for old AGE.

Oh what a tangled web we weave, when first we practice to DECEIVE. *Walter Scott, Marmion, 1808; M-808*

. . . But when we've practiced for a while
How vastly we improve our style!
R. J. Pope, A Word of Encouragement

Oh, what a tangled web they weave when bras they put on to deceive.

Oh, what a tangled web we weave when first we practice to conceive. *Don Herold*

No good DEED goes unpunished.*

Anyone who proposes to do good must not expect people to roll stones out of his way, but must accept his lot calmly if they even roll a few more upon it. *Albert Schweitzer*

Beware of the man to whom you have done a good turn. *Lebanese proverb*

I taught him to swim and he drowned me. *Moorish proverb*

If you give people nuts, you'll get shells thrown at you. *Yemenite proverb*

Let your charitable gifts be anonymous gifts. These have the double advantage of suppressing at once ingratitude and abuse. *Alexandre Dumas père*

Those who do a kindness because they expect to be repaid are always disappointed. *Chinese proverb*

*Attributed to Clare Boothe Luce, Brooks Thomas, and Walter Annenberg.

See also Be good and you will be HAPPY.

A man of words and not of DEEDS is like a garden full of weeds.* *1659, Howell*

*A man of words and not of deeds,
  Is like a garden full of weeds;
  And when the weeds begin to grow,
  It's like a garden full of snow;
  And when the snow begins to fall,
  It's like a bird upon the wall;
  And when the bird away does fly,
  It's like an eagle in the sky;
  And when the sky begins to roar,
  It's like a lion at the door;
  And when the door begins to crack,
  It's like a stick across your back;
  And when your back begins to smart,
  It's like a penknife in your heart;
  And when your heart begins to bleed,
  You're dead, and dead, and dead indeed.

See also A PROMISE is a promise; PROMISES and pie crust are made to be broken.

DEEDS, not creeds.*

Deeds are fruits, words are but leaves. *1616, Draxe*

If our creeds divide us, let our deeds unite us.

If your work speaks for itself, don't interrupt it. *Henry J. Kaiser*

The truths which are not translated into lives are dead truths, and not living truths. *Woodrow Wilson, Oct. 1904*

*Motto of the Ethical Culture Society. Words of the founder, Felix Adler, were "Not by the Creed but by the Deed," 1876.

See also ACTIONS speak louder than words.

DEEP calleth unto deep. *Psalms 42:7*

. . . But also shallow unto shallow
And gets more prompt reply.
Christopher Morley

*In a disquieted mood, the Psalmist's soul is cast down, as he searches for God, and for relief from the oppression of his enemies. An infinitesimal being calls out to a hidden God: deep calleth unto deep.

The DEER that goes too often to the lick meets the hunter at last.

A pitcher that goes too often to the well is broken at last.

The best of swimmers eventually drown. *Yiddish proverb*

The best DEFENSE is a good offense. *1775, F-139*

. . . and the more offensive the better.

When you have the facts on your side, argue the facts. When you have the law on your side, argue the law. When you have neither, holler. *Lawyer's maxim*

Tender-handed stroke a nettle,
    And it stings you for your pains;
Grasp it like a man of mettle,
    And it soft as silk remains.

'Tis the same with common natures:
    Use 'em kindly, they rebel;
But be rough as nutmeg-graters,
    And the rogues obey you well.
Aaron Hill

The only defence
that is more than pretence
    is to act on the fact
that there is no defence.
Piet Hein

Delays are dangerous. *1300, O-51*

See He who HESITATES is lost.

It all DEPENDS on how you look at it.

. . . After you buy a new car, you probably see that make of car everywhere. That's because people find what they are looking for. If you're looking for conspiracies, you'll find them. If you're looking for examples of man's good works, you'll find that too. It's all a matter of setting your mental channel. *Roger von Oech, A Kick in the Seat of the Pants*

An adventure is only an inconvenience, rightly considered. *G. K. Chesterton*

Delusions help make life worth living. *William C. Hunter*

Don't lose faith in humanity: think of all the people in the United States who have never played you a single nasty trick. *Elbert Hubbard*

If things look hopeless, look and see if you aren't facing the wrong direction. *Heard in Kansas*

Immature poets imitate; mature poets steal. *T. S. Eliot, 1920*

Junk is anything that has outlived its usefulness. *Oliver Herford*

Look at everything as if it were the first and last time you'll ever see it. *Whitt N. Schultz*

Look for the ridiculous in everything and you will find it. *Jules Renard, Journal*

Look on the bright side. *19th century*

Some people are always grumbling because roses have thorns; I am thankful that thorns have roses. *Alphonse Karr*

The optimist sees the doughnut, the pessimist, the hole. *McLandburgh Wilson*

The optimist's cup is half full; the pessimist's cup is half empty. *Heard in Oregon*

The world is a looking glass, and gives back to every man the reflection of his own face. Frown at it, and it in turn will look sourly upon you; laugh at it and with it, and it is a jolly, kind companion. *William Makepeace Thackeray*

Two men look out through the same bars; one sees the mud, and one the stars. *Frederick Langbridge*

Why is it that we rejoice at a birth and grieve at a funeral? It is because we are not the person involved. *Mark Twain, Pudd'nhead Wilson's Calendar*

Work and play are words used to describe the same thing under differing conditions. *Mark Twain, More Maxims of Mark*

Work is work if you're paid to do it, and it's pleasure if you pay to be allowed to do it. *Finley Peter Dunne*

You can parody or make fun of almost anything, but that does not turn the universe into a caricature. *Bernard Berenson, Notebook*

Both read the Bible day and night,
But thou read'st black where I read white.
William Blake, The Everlasting Gospel

And, after all, what is a lie? 'Tis but
The truth in masquerade.
Lord Byron, Don Juan

You're right from your side,
I'm right from mine.
Bob Dylan, One Too Many Mornings

Infinity's taken
   by everyone
as a figure-of-eight
   written sideways on.

But all of a sudden
   I now apprehend
that eight is infinity
   standing on end.
Piet Hein

If all the world looks dreary, perhaps the
   meaning
Is that your windows need a little cleaning.
Arthur Guiterman

See also BEAUTY is in the eye of the beholder; Where you STAND depends on where you sit.

It all DEPENDS on how you take it.

Everything's got a moral, if only you can find it. *Lewis Carroll, Alice in Wonderland*

Poverty consists in feeling poor. *Ralph Waldo Emerson, Domestic Life*

Experience is not what happens to you. It is what you do with what happens to you. *Aldous Huxley, 1956*

When an optimist gets the worst of it, he makes the best of it.

Trouble's a ton or trouble's an ounce;
   Or trouble is what you make it;
And it's not the fact that you're hurt that
   counts;
   It's only—how did you take it?

You're battered on earth, well, what of that?
   Come up with a smiling face.
It's nothing against you to fall down flat;
   But to lie there—that's the disgrace.

This world is not so bad a world
   As some would like to make it.
And whether good or whether bad
   Depends on how we take it.

It all DEPENDS on whose ox is gored.*

A boil is fine as long as it's under someone else's arm. *Yiddish proverb*

A "clique" in any organization is a group I am not a member of.

A fair wage is what you pay, an unfair wage is what you get; a fair price is what you charge, an unfair price is what the other fellow charges. *Richard Needham*

A gossip talks about others, a bore talks about himself, and a brilliant conversationalist talks about you.

A lobster has very little praise for lobster salad. *Old postcard*

A minor operation is one performed on someone else.

A practical joke is like a fall on the ice; there may be fun in it, but the one that falls can't always see it. *Josh Billings*

A turkey never voted for an early Christmas. *Irish proverb*

Advice is like castor oil, easy enough to give, but dreadfully uneasy to take. *Josh Billings*

Among those who dislike oppression are many who like to oppress. *Napoleon, Maxims*

Everything is funny as long as it is happening to somebody else. *Will Rogers, The Illiterate Digest*

Fair competition is when you undercut the other guy; unfair competition is when he undercuts you. *Richard Needham*

Humility is the first of virtues—for other people. *Oliver Wendell Holmes*

I am interested in medical research because I believe in it. I am interested in arthritis because I have it. *Bernard M. Baruch, New York Post, May 1, 1959*

If men could get pregnant, abortion would be a sacrament. *Florynce Kennedy*

If the fool weren't mine, I'd also laugh. *Yiddish proverb*

If we had to tolerate in others all that we permit in ourselves, life would become completely unbearable. *Georges Courteline*

If we should find the same excuses for the faults of others that we do for our own, it would be a different world—a better one. *Old postcard*

Impiety: your irreverence toward my deity. *Ambrose Bierce*

It is easy when we are well to give good advice to the sick. *Terence*

It's amazing how radical an unemployed conservative can become. *Peter's Almanac*

It's innocence when it charms us, ignorance when it doesn't. *Mignon McLaughlin*

It's just a matter of whose ox is being goosed. *From the collection of mixed metaphors of W. Willard Wirtz*

It's worth the taxi fare to feel you don't care what happens to the fenders. *Judge, ca. 1925*

Men judge the affairs of other men better than their own. *Terence*

Morality is simply the attitude we adopt towards people we personally dislike. *Oscar Wilde, An Ideal Husband*

Never ask a barber whether you need a haircut. *Daniel Greenberg*

Never ask a salesman whether his is a good price.

No man with four aces asks for a new deal.

Now they're calling taking drugs an epidemic—that's 'cos white folks are doing it. *Richard Pryor, 1984*

Old age is always 15 years older than I am. *Bernard M. Baruch*

One has always strength enough to bear the misfortunes of one's friends. *Oliver Goldsmith, She Stoops to Conquer*

One man's wage rise is another man's price increase. *Harold Wilson, 1970*

Other people's troubles are bearable. *Yiddish proverb*

Our children seem to have wonderful taste, or none—depending, of course, on whether or not they agree with us. *Mignon McLaughlin*

Ours is not the only story, just the most interesting one. *Mignon McLaughlin*

"Peace" is when nobody's shooting. A "just peace" is when our side gets what it wants. *Bill Mauldin*

Satire is a glass, wherein beholders do generally discover everybody's face but their own. *Jonathan Swift*

Sentimentality is only sentiment that rubs you up the wrong way. *W. Somerset Maugham, A Writer's Notebook*

Tax reform means, "Don't tax me. Tax that fellow behind the tree." *Russell Long*

That which we call sin in others is experiment for us. *Ralph Waldo Emerson, Essays (Experience)*

The comforter's head never aches. *1590, T-112*

The coward calls himself cautious. *Publilius Syrus*

The difference between constructive and destructive criticism is simple: the former is what you give while the latter is what you get. *Frank Walsh*

The major flaw in democracy is that only the party out of power knows how to run the government. *Peter's Almanac*

The poor are always liberal. *Yiddish proverb*

The troubles we laugh at are seldom our own.

There is always a comforting thought in time of trouble when it is not our trouble. *Don Marquis*

Vanity is other people's pride. *Sacha Guitry, Jusqu'a Nouvel Ordre*

Vulgarity is simply the conduct of others. *Oscar Wilde*

We all have enough strength to bear other people's troubles. *François de la Rochefoucauld, Maximes*

We are all practical in our own interest and idealists when it concerns others. *Kahlil Gibran*

We are quite able, while hating sin, to pity and be charitable to the sinner—when we happen to be the sinner concerned. *L. de V. Matthewman*

We can endure agonizing pain for three years when someone else is suffering. *Japanese proverb*

What is play to the cat is death to the mouse. *Danish proverb*

What we think an unreasonable price when we are to buy, we think just and equitable when we are to sell. *Characters and Observations, 18th century*

When a man wants to murder a tiger he calls it sport: when a tiger wants to murder him he calls it ferocity. *G. B. Shaw, Maxims for Revolutionists*

When a man you like switches from what he said a year ago, or four years ago, he is a broad-minded person who has courage enough to change his mind with changing conditions. When a man you don't like does it, he is a liar who has broken his promises. *Franklin P. Adams, Nods & Becks*

When you prevent me from doing anything I want to do, that is persecution; when I prevent you from doing anything you want to do, that is law, order and morals. *G. B. Shaw*

When you want it, it's a handout; when I want it, it's seed money. When you're that way, you're naive; when I'm that way, I'm open. When you have it, it's a hang-up; when I have it, it's a priority. When you're that way, you're uptight; when I'm that way, I'm liberated. When you're that way, you're not hearing me; when I'm that way, I'm telling it like it is. When you're that way, you're being irrelevant; when I'm that way, I'm being prophetic. *Carroll Simox, at Episcopal Convention, Sept. 28, 1969*

When you tell someone something for their own good, that's advice; when someone tells you something for your own good, that's interference.

Where your treasure is there will your heart be also. *Luke 12:34*

With me, the fall of the Roman Empire is a great deal easier to bear than a fall on the ice when it is wet. *Josh Billings*

You can see a mote in another man's eye but cannot see a beam in your own. *Matthew 7:3 (rephrased)*

Mine, Yours, and Theirs

These variants of "It all depends on whose ox is gored" deserve to be arrayed by themselves:

The admirable firmness in ourselves is detestable stubbornness in others. *Peter's Almanac*

An alcoholic is someone you don't like who drinks as much as you do. *Dylan Thomas*

Cowards call themselves cautious, and misers thrifty. *Heard in Illinois*

A fanatic is one who would be an idealist if he happened to be on your side. *Peter's Almanac*

Fresh air is when you open a window; a draft is when someone else does.

Good is when I steal other people's wives and cattle; bad is when they steal mine. *Hottentot proverb*

I am an epicure; you are a gourmand; he has both feet in the trough. *Sydney J. Harris*

I am concerned. You're curious. He's nosy. *Lori A. Abrams*

I am economical; you are stingy; he is a miser. *Sydney J. Harris*

I am fastidious; you are fussy; he is an old woman. *Sydney J. Harris*

I am firm; you are obstinate; he is a pigheaded fool. *Bertrand Russell*

I am quiet. You're unassertive. He's a wimp. *Alexandra Frank*

I am righteously indignant; you are annoyed; he is making a fuss about nothing. *Sydney J. Harris*

I am sensitive. You're fussy. He's neurotic. *Michele Simos*

I am slender; you are emaciated; she is a walking skeleton. *Sydney J. Harris*

I am supporting a neighborhood venture that will accrue to my benefit because I am "community-minded"; you are supporting a venture that may harm my interests because you are a "busybody." *Sydney J. Harris*

I am thrifty. You're a bit tight. He's cheap. *Rosemary Proehl*

I am trusting. You're naive. He's a fool. *Lori A. Abrams*

I am wearing an interesting fragrance; you are overdoing it; she stinks. *Sydney J. Harris*

I have my pride; you're stuck with your vanity. *Sydney J. Harris*

I have put on a few pounds; you are filling out; he is getting as big as a house. *Sydney J. Harris*

I invest in pharmaceuticals, you speculate in drugs, he exploits the misery of the suffering.

I persuade; you educate; they manipulate. *Alan Crawford, 1970*

I take advantage of "credit facilities"; you live beyond your means; he is wildly in debt. *Sydney J. Harris*

In me it's caution; in someone else, it's cowardice. *Henny Youngman*

It's a recession when your neighbor loses his job; it's a depression when you lose yours. *Harry S. Truman, 1958.* An old saw, comments Keyes; not original (K-5).

My competitor was awarded the contract because "he put in the fix"; we won the contract because we "spoke to the right people." *Sydney J. Harris*

My dog "barks" as a protector; your dog "yaps" as a nuisance. *Sydney J. Harris*

My personal remark was intended as a "good-natured jest," but your personal remark was "in extremely bad taste." *Sydney J. Harris*

My religious convictions are based on faith, yours are controlled by fear, and his are dominated by superstition. *Sydney J. Harris*

My word is the truth; the other man's word is an opinion; the boss's word is law. *Sydney J. Harris*

Neurotic means he is not as sensible as I am, and psychotic means he's even worse than my brother-in-law. *Karl Menninger*

Orthodoxy is my doxy; heterodoxy is another man's doxy. *William Warburton*

Our own weaknesses we regard as misfortunes for which we cannot escape; the weaknesses of others we consider crimes. *L. de V. Matthewman*

The secret agent on our side is an intelligent officer; the one who's working for the enemy is a spy. *Sydney J. Harris*

When I fail to do something, I give an "explanation"; you make an "excuse"; he comes up with an "alibi." *Sydney J. Harris*

When I sell liquor, it's called bootlegging; when my patrons serve it on silver trays on Lake Shore Drive, it's called hospitality. *Al Capone*

Antics with Semantics

Sydney J. Harris (1917–86), who is well represented in the quips just listed, delighted in the wordplay he labeled "Antics with Seman-

tics." Here are a few more items that appeared in his newspaper columns at one time or another:

"Believers" tend to believe in God's vengeance for their enemies, but in God's mercy for themselves.

Every parent's son in a gang was "led wrong" by the other boys.

A highly active woman I happen to like is quivering with "animal vitality," but a highly active woman I dislike is jumping with "nervous energy."

It's a "hideous insect" to the restaurant patron who finds it in his soup, but "just a little bug" to the restaurant manager.

"Mere rhetoric" is what we would call "powerful oratory" if we agreed with what the speaker is saying.

Only strangers are "criminals"; friends are "in trouble."

A "perceived difference" is the illusion an ad agency tries to create about a product that has no real difference.

Shooting has a fascination only for those who have never faced the wrong end of the gun; if animals were armed, instead of us, all humans would proclaim the sacred creed of vegetarianism.

"Terrorism" is what we call the violence of the weak, and we condemn it; "war" is what we call the violence of the strong, and we glorify it.

*A tenant of the great Elizabethan jurist Edmund Plowden (1518–85) came to him and with a bow and a cringe, confessed: "Sir, an't please your worship, my bull has gored and killed one of your worship's oxen; I beg to know what I must do in this case." "Why, surely, pay the value of the ox," answered Plowden. "That is both law and equity." "But I have made a little mistake in the matter. It was your worship's bull that killed my ox." "Oh, it is so, then the case is altered," quoth Plowden.

See also BEAUTY is in the eye of the beholder; Great SPIRIT . . . ; Where you STAND depends on where you sit; You measure everyone's CORN by your own bushel.

The mass of men lead lives of quiet DESPERATION.* *Henry David Thoreau, Walden, 1854*

A month of days, a year of months, 20 years of months in the treadmill, is the life that slays everything worthy of the name of life. *Roy Bedichek, Adventures with a Texas Naturalist*

Few men ever drop dead from overwork, but many quietly curl up and die because of undersatisfaction. *Sydney J. Harris*

For most men life is a search for the proper manila envelope in which to get themselves filed. *Clifton Fadiman, 1960*

Men for the sake of getting a living forget to live. *Margaret Fuller*

People would rather sleep their way through life than stay awake for it. *Edward Albee*

The danger of the past was that men became slaves. The danger of the future is that men may become robots. *Erich Fromm, The Sane Society*

The difference between a rut and a grave is the depth. *Gerald Burrill, Advance, July 1979*

The parents of teenagers who play rock music live lives of noisy desperation.

The peculiar malaise of our day is air-conditioned unhappiness, the staleness and stuffiness of machine-made routine. *Eugene B. Borowitz*

The tragedy of life is what dies inside a man while he lives. *Attributed to both Albert Einstein and Albert Schweitzer in [James B.] Simpson's Contemporary Quotations (1988).*

There is only one success—to be able to spend your life in your own way. *Christopher Morley*

Commuter—one who spends his life
In riding to and from his wife;
A man who shaves and takes a train,
And then rides back to shave again.
E. B. White, The Commuter

Nothing to do but work,
    Nothing to eat but food,
Nothing to wear but clothes
    To keep one from going nude.
Ben F. King, The Pessimist

*H. Ross Perot, Texas billionaire and onetime presidential aspirant, decided to leave IBM and launch his own business after he picked up a copy of *Reader's Digest* and read this line. Whatever Thoreau may have meant, it is unlikely he intended to goad a star salesman on to become a billionaire entrepreneur.

Better the DEVIL you know than the devil you don't know. *1539, O-16**

And always keep a hold of Nurse
For fear of finding something worse.

Hilaire Belloc, Jim, Bad Child's Book of Beasts

*Flexner (F-20–21) discusses the antiquity of this thought.

Every man for himself, and the DEVIL take the hindmost. *Geoffrey Chaucer, Knight's Tale, 1386*

Every man for himself and God for us all. *1572, O2-178*

Every man for himself and to hell with everyone else. *E. F. Russell, The Great Explosion*

Give the DEVIL his due. *1589, T-153*

. . . but be very careful that there ain't much due him. *Josh Billings, 1865*

. . . said the printer's apprentice to his boss on payday.

I am a man of God and a man of the devil. To each his due. *Henry Miller, Black Spring*

We rashly demand that the devil shall have his due, forgetting that if that gentleman gets all that is coming to him it will go badly with some of us. *L. de V. Matthewman*

See also The DEVIL is not so black as he is painted.

He must have a long spoon who sups with the DEVIL.* *Geoffrey Chaucer, Squire's Tale, 1390*

*A warning, says Flexner (F-84), "against becoming involved in shady dealings of any sort."

Talk about the DEVIL and he's sure to appear. *17th century*

Speak of the devil and he comes in person. *1938, BJW-165*

The DEVIL can cite Scripture for his purpose.* *1673, WM-146*

. . . if a fairly free translation be allowed. *Ellery Queen, 1948; BJW-161*

. . . He must have gone to Sunday school.

The devil can quote Shakespeare for his purpose. *G. B. Shaw*

The devil sometimes speaks the truth. *1635, T-153*

*According to Oxford, this proverb refers to Matthew 4.

The DEVIL finds work for idle hands. *1368, O-51*

A loafer is an abomination, but a man who is busy doing foolish things is worse than a loafer. *William C. Hunter*

If the Devil finds work for idle hands, as our mothers used to warn us, how much more mischief do you suppose he finds for idle minds? *Sydney J. Harris*

The devil enters the idle man's house without knocking. *Josh Billings*

The devil finds work for idle glands. *Peter's Almanac*

The devil tempts all men; but the idle man tempts the devil. *Old Farmer's Almanac, 1865*

. . . what young people should do to avoid temptation: get a job and work at it so hard that temptation would not exist. *Thomas Edison*

See also If you've got time to kill, WORK it to death.

The DEVIL is an ass. *1631, O2-139*

The devil is a gentleman.

The DEVIL is not so black as he is painted. *1535, O-52*

. . . In fact, he is more like us than we care to admit. *L. de V. Matthewman*

. . . He does a nice business for such a lousy location. *Dan Bennett*

God created the world, but it is the Devil who keeps it going. *Tristan Bernard, Contes, Répliques et Bons Mots*

The prince of darkness is a gentleman. *Shakespeare, King Lear 3.4.148*

When it comes to making proselytes, the devil understands his business better than anyone I know of. *Josh Billings*

The DEVIL was sick, the devil a saint would be; the devil was well, the devil a saint was he. *Latin proverb*

See There are no ATHEISTS in a foxhole.

DIAMOND cuts diamond.* *1539, O-53*

*"Used of persons well matched in wit or cunning" (OE-144).

DIAMONDS are a girl's best friend. *Theme of a popular song*

Kissing your hand may make you feel very, very good but a diamond and sapphire bracelet lasts forever. *Anita Loos, Gentlemen Prefer Blondes*

It is sweet and fitting to DIE for one's country.* *Horace, Odes 3.2.13, 23 B.C.; M-550*

As my eye ranges over the field whose sods were so lately moistened by the blood of gal-lant and loyal men, I feel, as never before, how truly it was said of old, that it is sweet and becoming to die for one's country. *Edward Everett, Dedication Address at Gettysburg Cemetery, 1863*

I only regret that I have but one life to lose for my country. *Nathan Hale, last words before being hanged as a spy by the British, Sept. 22, 1776*

Call him not alone who dies side by side with gallant men. *Heard in New York*

I would never die for my beliefs because I might be wrong. *Bertrand Russell*

If it is for fame that men do brave actions, they are only silly fellows after all. *Robert Louis Stevenson, The English Admirals*

Tov lamut be'ad artsenu. ("It is good to die for our country.") *Monument inscription at Tel Hai, Israel, memorializing the last words of legendary Zionist soldier Joseph Trumpel-door*

No hero to me is the man who wins fame by the easy shedding of his blood; give me the man who can win praise without dying. *Martial, Epigrams*

Sweet honor, for one's native land to die! *John Osborne Sargent, 1893*

The object of war is not to die for your coun-try. It's to make the other poor bastard die for his. *George S. Patton*

They never fail who die in a great cause. *Lord Byron, 1820*

Who does not rather envy than regret a death that gives birth to honor and glorious mem-ory? *George Washington*

If you could hear, at every jolt, the blood
Come gargling from the froth-corrupted
lungs, obscene as cancer, bitter as the cud
Of vile, incurable sores on innocent tongues,
My friend, you would not tell with such high
    zest
To children ardent for some desperate glory
The old Lie: Dulce et decorum est
Pro patria mori.
Wilfred Owen, World War I British soldier, observing a comrade die of gas poisoning

*This sentiment has been widely adopted as a serious eulogy of "the ultimate sacrifice," but its effect clearly depends on the fact that it is torn out of its original context. It is not a complete statement, but only the beginning of a long sentence which ends, "[because] death follows even after the man who runs away and does not spare the knees and timid back of a spineless youth." Freely translated, Horace's advice to the young soldier goes: "When you are in battle, you might as well fight as if death for your country would be just wonderful, because if you turn your back and run away, then you're sure to be killed, and you'll die the death of a coward."

Comments Horace scholar Gordon Williams: "There is a curiously unpoetical realism about the qualification . . . [and] it is never quoted on memorials on which [the] line . . . appears" (*The Third Book of Horace's Odes* [Oxford, 1969], p. 35).

The famous phrase is torn from its context both in *Bartlett's Familiar Quotations* and in *Stevenson's Home Book of Proverbs* (B-1760). It is therefore not too surprising to see the phrase quoted out of context at the

Gettysburg dedication ceremony, by Edward Everett, former president of Harvard and a leading scholar and orator of his day.

Horace's "soldierly ideal" has also been adopted as the motto of the Smith family in England and of the Van Rensselaer family in the United States.

See also WAR is hell.

Never say DIE. *1814, WM-149*

. . . Say dammit!

A man may be down, but he's never out. *Slogan of the Salvation Army*

Being defeated is often a temporary condition. Giving up is what makes it permanent. *Marilyn von Savant*

It is part of the American character to consider nothing as desperate. *Thomas Jefferson*

It's never too late to say die.

Never give up.

To never despair may be godlike but it ain't human. *Josh Billings*

See also BEAR and forbear; Keep on TRUCKIN'; GRIN and bear it.

The DIE is cast. *1616, T-156*

What is to be will be, and no prayers of ours can reverse the decree. *Abraham Lincoln, ca. 1864*

See also CHE sera sera.

It won't make any DIFFERENCE a hundred years from now.

. . . A cheap philosophic half-truth. . . . It makes a great deal of difference if you plant a walnut tree . . . or a bed of poison ivy. *Sydney J. Harris*

In a hundred years, we'll all be bald.

The DIFFICULT we do promptly; the impossible takes a little longer.*

. . . Miracles by appointment only.

By asking for the impossible we obtain the possible. *Italian proverb*

Difficulty is the excuse history never accepts. *Edward R. Murrow, 1960*

Doing what can't be done, is the glory of living. *Samuel C. Armstrong*

No task will be evaded merely because it is impossible. *New York City schools chancellor, 1988*

The Difficult is that which can be done immediately; the Impossible that which takes a little longer. *George Santayana, as quoted in Reader's Digest, Nov. 1939*

The illegal we do immediately. The unconstitutional takes a little longer. *Henry Kissinger, on Watergate, New York Times, Oct. 28, 1973*

The legal we do immediately; the illegal takes a little longer. *Sign on a lawyer's door, New Yorker cartoon*

The obscure we see eventually; the completely apparent takes longer.

To do easily what is difficult for others is the mark of talent. To do what is impossible for a person of talent is the mark of genius. *Henri Amiel, Journal Intime*

Trivial matters are handled promptly; important matters are never solved.

We can lick gravity, but sometimes the paperwork is overwhelming. *Wernher von Braun*

Problems worthy of attack
Prove their worth by hitting back.
Piet Hein

*This saying has been variously attributed to the Royal Navy, the U.S. Army Air Force, and Chaim Weitzmann. Oxford (O-53) traces the saying to an 1873 quotation from Anthony Trollope's *Phineas Redux*: "What was it the French Minister said? If it is simply difficult, it is done. If it is impossible, it shall be done."

If you don't DIG it, don't knock it.

Whoso DIGGETH a pit shall fall therein.*

*. . . and he that rolleth a stone, it will return upon him. *Proverbs 26:27*

See Who lives by the SWORD dies by the sword; What goes AROUND comes around.

**DIPLOMACY is to do and say
The nastiest thing in the nicest way.
*Isaac Goldberg (1887–1938), The Reflex***

A diplomat is a man who always remembers a woman's birthday but never remembers her age. *Robert Frost*

A diplomat is a person who can tell you to go to hell in such a way that you actually look forward to the trip. *Caskie Stinnett, Out of the Red*

A diplomat is one who thinks twice before saying nothing. *Peter's Almanac*

An ambassador is an honest man sent abroad to lie for his country. *Henry Wotton*

Diplomacy: the art of jumping into trouble without making a splash. *Art Linkletter*

Diplomacy is the art of letting someone else have your way. *Heard in California and New York*

I have discovered the art of fooling diplomats; I speak the truth and they never believe me. *Camillo Benso di Cavour*

In archaeology you uncover the unknown. In diplomacy you cover the known. *Thomas Pickering*

Sincere diplomacy is no more possible than dry water or wooden iron. *Joseph Stalin*

The real diplomat is one who can cut his neighbor's throat without having his neighbor notice it. *Trygve Lie*

Every man must eat a peck of DIRT before he dies. *1603, T-411*

. . . replied the wife to answer her husband's complaint about sand in his spinach. "That's true," answered the husband, "but why so much at one time?" *1732, Fuller (adapted)*

Throw enough DIRT, and some will stick. *Latin proverb*

. . . and if dirt doesn't stick, throw sewage. *TV commentator, on "negative campaigning" in 1992 presidential race*

If it sounds DIRTY, you have a dirty mind.*

Murder is a crime. Writing about it isn't. Sex is not a crime, but writing about it is. Why? *Larry Flynt*

Nature knows no indecencies; man invents them. *Mark Twain, Notebook*

Pornography is in the groin of the beholder. *Charles Rembar, End of Obscenity*

Shame on him that shame thinks. *1546, Heywood*

To the filthy all things taste filthy. *1618, T-211*

*A rough equivalent of the Latin proverb *Pravis omnia prava*. The French proverb *Honi soit qui mal y pense* is sometimes translated as "Evil to him who evil thinks" or "Shame on him who thinks it is a shame."

DISCRETION is the better part of valor. *1477, T-158*

A daring pilot is dangerous to a ship. *Euripides, The Suppliant Women*

A man was hanged for saying what was true. *Italian proverb*

Anybody who argues with the barber should have his head examined. *Wall Street Journal*

Before you fool with a fool, be sure you have a fool to fool with. *Old postcard*

Desertion is the better part of valor. *Heard in Ohio*

Don't take the bull by the horns, take him by the tail; then you can let go when you want to. *Josh Billings*

Intelligence is when you spot a flaw in your boss's reasoning. Wisdom is when you refrain from pointing it out. *James Dent*

It's all right to look on the bright side, but it's wiser to look on both sides. *Old postcard*

Many would be cowards, if they had courage enough. *English proverb*

Men are born with two eyes but with one tongue, in order that they may see twice as much as they say. *Old postcard*

Never call a man a liar if he is bigger than you are. If you're positive that he is a liar, hire some cheap man to break the news to him. *Old postcard*

Next to knowing when to seize an opportunity, the most important thing in life is to know when to forgo an advantage. *Benjamin Disraeli*

Pick battles that are big enough to matter, small enough to win. *Jonathan Kozol*

Sometimes the better part of valor is to cut and run.

The best armor is to keep out of gunshot. *Heard in Mississippi*

Tact consists in knowing how far we may go too far. *Jean Cocteau, A Call to Order*

The better part of valor is indiscretion. *Samuel Butler*

There are several good protections against temptation, but the surest is cowardice. *Mark Twain*

When a man has not a good reason for doing a thing, he has one good reason for letting it alone. *Walter Scott*

See also He that FIGHTS and runs away may live to fight another day.

Desperate DISEASES must have desperate remedies. *Latin proverb*

Don't DISH it out if you can't take it. *1936, WM-152*

See If you can't stand the HEAT, get out of the kitchen.

DISTANCE lends enchantment.* *Thomas Campbell, The Pleasures of Hope*

A poet in history is divine, but a poet in the next room is a joke. *Max Eastman*

Bygone troubles are a pleasure to talk about. *Yiddish proverb*

All these woes shall serve
For sweet discourses in our time to come.
Shakespeare, Romeo and Juliet 3.5.52

Distances can be deceptive; sometimes when I'm close to you, I find you're very far from me. © *Ashleigh Brilliant*

Distant drum, sweet music. *Turkish proverb*

Distance, night, under an umbrella. *Japanese proverb.* Like a treatment that cures the disease but kills the patient, translation can render a foreign proverb into English, but how much of the life of the original survives? The literal translation of this proverb is too vague. The meaning of the original is enriched by a punning allusion: the word for distance, *yome,* is a homonym for daughter-in-law. In a few words, the Japanese proverb says, "Your daughter-in-law is a beauty from afar, at night, under an umbrella."

Everything unknown is taken to be magnificent. *Tacitus, Agricolae*

Faraway birds have fine feathers. *1794, WM-52*

I'm an idealist: I don't know where I'm going but I'm on my way. *Carl Sandburg.* Except for the first three words, this is an old saying.

Idealism increases in direct proportion to one's distance from the problem. *John Galsworthy*

Idealism is fine, but as it approaches reality, the cost becomes prohibitive. *William F. Buckley, Jr.*

If you would understand your own age, read the works of fiction produced in it. People in disguise speak freely. *Arthur Helps*

In heaven, an angel is nobody in particular. *G. B. Shaw, Man and Superman*

Mountains when far away appear misty and smooth, but when near at hand are rugged. *Diogenes Laertius*

Nostalgia is a seductive liar. *George Ball, Newsweek, Mar. 22, 1971*

Pain past is pleasure. *English proverb*

Perhaps, someday, even these hardships will be a joy to recall. *Virgil, Georgics*

The price one pays for pursuing any profession or calling is an intimate knowledge of its ugly side. *James Baldwin, Nobody Knows My Name*

The remembrance of past sorrow is joyful. *1576, OE-538*

Wars are sweet to them who know them not. *1550, Erasmus*

Weekends are a bit like rainbows; they look good from a distance but disappear when you get close to them. *John Shirley*

What is hard to bear is sweet to remember. *Geoffrey Chaucer, Romance of Rose*

When we get what we want, we are always disappointed to find that it is not what we wanted. *L. de V. Matthewman*

Twinkle, twinkle, little star
But stay, my darling, where you are;

Into my life if you should fall,
I'd never see you shine at all.
Samual Hoffenstein

**'Tis distance lends enchantment to the view,
And robes the mountain in its azure hue.

See also Be careful of what you WISH for . . . ; No man is a HERO to his valet; No man is a PROPHET in his own country.

The shortest DISTANCE between two points is a straight line. *1942, WM-378*

A good line is the shortest distance between two dates.

A curved line is the loveliest distance between two points. *Mae West*

The shortest distance between two points is usually under repair.

DIVIDE and conquer. *Latin proverb, adopted by Niccolo Machiavelli*

When two fight, a third one profits. *Polish proverb*

There's a DIVINITY that shapes our ends, Rough-hew them how we will.
Shakespeare, Hamlet 5.2.10, ca. 1600

There's a divinity that shapes our ends. *Erich Fromm, after a discussion with a group of Jewish college students on the psychological meaning of circumcision*

Is middle-age spread hereditary? Is there a destiny that ends our shapes?

There's a divinity that shapes our ends rough, hew them how we will. *L. L. Levinson*

DO as I say, not as I do. *1350 B.C., B-2036*

Example is the main thing in influencing others. *Albert Schweitzer*

Good sense is easier to have than use. *James Grady, Runner in the Street*

He that speaks me fair and loves me not,
I'll speak him fair and trust him not.
English proverb, 1678

I have, all my life long, been lying till noon; yet I tell all young men, and tell them with great sincerity, that nobody who does not rise early will ever do any good. *Samuel Johnson, Tour of the Hebrides*

The hardest job kids face today is learning good manners without seeing any. *Fred Astaire*

DO as you would be done by.* *1596, O-56*

My creed is this:
Happiness is the only good.
The place to be happy is here.
The time to be happy is now.
The way to be happy is to help make others
　　so.
Robert G. Ingersoll

*Lord Chesterfield, in a letter to his son, interprets this proverb not for its moral significance, but to mean that a person can use his own response to others, to be socially successful: "Take the tone of the company that you are in . . . be serious, gay, or even trifling, as you find the present humor of the company."

See also DO unto others as you would have them do unto you.

DO it now.

. . . tomorrow there may be a law against it.

Action doesn't always bring happiness, but there is no happiness without it. *Benjamin Disraeli*

After you have made up your mind just what you are going to do, then is a good time to do it. *Josh Billings*

Doing beats stewing.

Even if you're on the right track, you'll get run over if you just sit there. *Will Rogers*

If you think you can do it, begin it! Begin and the mind grows heated. Begin, and the task is completed. *Johann Wolfgang von Goethe*

If you can imagine it, you can achieve it; if you can dream it, you can become it. *William Arthur Ward*

If you wait, all that happens is that you get older. *Larry McMurtry, Some Can Whistle*

I'm torn between all the things I don't want to do. © *Ashleigh Brilliant*

Lose an hour in the morning and you will be all day hunting for it. *Old postcard*

Many a false step is taken by standing still. *Arnold Glasow*

The best way to get rid of work is to do it. *Heard in California, Colorado, New Jersey, and New York.*

The Nike athletic shoe company adopted the advertising slogan "Just do it" (. . . take up running? jogging? basketball?). Reported a company spokesperson, in a 1989 *New York*

Times article, "We've gotten letters from people around the country thanking us for helping them to stop smoking. . . . One woman said it inspired her to finally leave her husband."

The reason I never do anything is that there's always something else I have to do first. © *Ashleigh Brilliant*

The truth of the matter is that you always know the right thing to do. The hard part is doing it. *Norman Schwarzkopf*

There will be sleeping enough in the grave. *English proverb*

Thought is action in rehearsal. *Sigmund Freud, as quoted in Reader's Digest, Apr. 1973*

To liberate his staff from the evil of procrastination, an office manager put up a sign, "Do it now." By the end of the week, the office boy had pulled the plug from the copy machine, a stenographer had eloped with the boss's son, the bookkeeper had disappeared with the contents of the safe, and the office staff struck for a six-hour day. The office manager is now looking for a new motto.

Unless a capacity for thinking be accompanied by a capacity for action, a superior mind exists in torture. *Benedetto Croce*

When you come to a fork in the road, take it. *Yogi Berra*

Wisdom is knowing what to do next, skill is knowing how to do it, and virtue is doing it. *David Starr Jordan, as quoted in Reader's Digest, Aug. 1960*

You must do things you think you cannot do. *Eleanor Roosevelt*

If you've got a job to do,
   Do it now!
If it's one you wish were through,
   Do it now!
If you're sure the job's your own,
Do not hem and haw and groan
   Do it now! . . .
If you want to fill a place
And be useful to the race,
Just get up and take a brace
   Do it now!
Don't linger by the way,
   Do it now!
You'll lose if you delay,
   Do it now!
If the other fellows wait,
Or postpone until it's late,
Just hit up a faster gait
   Do it now!

When I get time
   I know what I shall do:
I'll cut the leaves of all my books
   And read them through and through.

When I get time
   I'll write some letters then
That I have owed for weeks and weeks
   To many many men. . . .
When I get time
   I'll regulate my life
In such a way that I may get
Acquainted with my wife.

When I get time
Oh glorious dream of bliss!
A month, a year, ten years from now
But I can't finish this
I've no more time.
Thomas L. Masson

See CARPE diem; He who HESITATES is lost.

DO or die. *Scottish family motto (Douglas clan)*

. . . and it is much easier than to reason why.

See also Yours is not to REASON why . . .

DO unto others as you would have them do unto you.*

. . . but better not expect others to do unto you what you do unto them.

. . . but the Golden Rule is of no use whatever until you realize it's your move. *Leo Aikman*

As I would not be a slave, so I would not be a master. This expresses my idea of democracy. *Abraham Lincoln*

Do not do unto others as you would they should do unto you. Their tastes may not be the same. *G. B. Shaw, Maxims for Revolutionists.* Eighty-three years after Shaw made this observation, Sydney J. Harris (1917–86) ruminated for eight paragraphs over the thought "that the so-called Golden Rule is only gold-plated." He advised, "A far more sensible version would be: 'Do unto others as they would have you do unto them.' This attitude requires, not the sentimental arrogance of assuming that you know what is best for them, but respect for and understanding of your cultural differences." (Sydney J. Harris, *Clearing the Ground*, 1986)

Do unto mothers. *Mother's Day advertisement*

Do unto others and do it fast.

Do unto others as though you were the others. *Elbert Hubbard*

Do unto others as you would be dung by. *P. Dickinson, 1970; BJW-171*

Do unto the other feller the way he'd like to do unto you an' do it fust. *Edward Noyes Wescott, David Harum*

Do unto yourself as your neighbors do unto themselves and look pleasant. *George Ade, Hand Made Fables*

Due unto others. *Label on a minister's box of unpaid bills*

Give unto others the advice you can't use yourself.

Here's the rule for bargains: "Do other men, for they would do you." That's the true business precept. *Charles Dickens, Martin Chuzzlewit*

On the basis of my years with the Stone Age Eskimos, I feel that the chief factor in their happiness was that they were living according to the Golden Rule. *Vilhjalmur Stefansson*

The golden rule is that there are no golden rules. *G. B. Shaw, Maxims for Revolutionists*

We have committed the Golden Rule to memory; let us commit it to life.

What is hateful to you, do not to another: that is the whole Torah; the rest is commentary. Now go and study it. *Hillel, Shabbat, 31a.* Hillel, who lived during the time of Jesus, is described by *Encyclopaedia Judaica* as "the greatest of the sages of the Second Temple period." The story is told that a heathen came to Hillel and said he would convert to Judaism if Hillel could teach him the entire

Torah "while standing on one foot." This was Hillel's reply.

Whenever I hear anyone arguing for slavery, I feel a strong impulse to see it tried on him personally. *Abraham Lincoln*

You can't hold a man down without staying down with him. *Booker T. Washington*

Sleep my baby, little elf;
Grow up honest—with yourself!
Always unto others do
What they'd like to do to you.
Samuel Hoffenstein, For Little Boys Destined for Big Business

*And as ye would that men should do to you, do ye also to them. *Luke 6:31.* Flexner (F-39) quotes parallel sayings in Babylonian, Chinese, Greek, and Hindu sources.

See also DO as you would be done by.

DO your best and bury the rest.

Efficiency is concerned with doing things right. Effectiveness is doing the right thing. *Peter F. Drucker, Management: Tasks, Responsibilities, Practices*

DO your own thing. *Credo of the 1960s**

A man's gotta do what a man's gotta do.

Don't aim for success if you want it; just do what you love and it will come naturally. *David Frost*

The man who goes alone can start today; but he who travels with another must wait till that other is ready. *Henry David Thoreau*

*Keyes (K-39) does a masterful job of tracing this hippie watchword back to this portion of Ralph Waldo Emerson's essay "Self-Reliance": "But do your own thing, and I shall know you." Keyes digs deeper and quotes from Geoffrey Chaucer (the Clerke's Tale, in *The Canterbury Tales*): "Ye been oure lord; dooth with your owene thyng."

See also Follow your BLISS; Be YOURSELF; PADDLE your own canoe; You can't PLEASE everybody.

Don't just stand there; DO something.

Don't just do something, stand there. *Daniel Berrigan, advice to war protesters of the 1960s*

It is more pain to do nothing than something. *1640, Herbert*

Passivity can be a provoking modus operandi;
Consider the Empire and Gandhi.
Ogden Nash

When you soar like an eagle, you attract the hunters. *Milton S. Gould, on why the government investigates top corporate executives, Time, Dec. 8, 1967*

It ain't what you DO, it's the way that you do it.

Copy from one, it's plagiarism; copy from two, it's research. *Wilson Mizner*

Cynicism is an unpleasant way of saying the truth. *Lillian Hellman*

If Galileo had said in verse that the world moved, the Inquisition might have let him alone. *Thomas Hardy, in The Later Years of T.H., by F. E. Hardy*

If we are polite in manner and friendly in tone, we can without immediate risk be really rude to many a man. *Arthur Schopenhauer, Parega und Paralipomena*

If you have good manners, you can get away with almost any kind of morals. *Richard Needham*

Immature poets imitate; mature poets steal. *T. S. Eliot, 1920*

In the battle for existence, talent is the punch, and tact is the fancy footwork. *Wilson Mizner*

Is it progress if a cannibal uses a fork? *Stanislaw J. Lec*

It doesn't matter what you do in the bedroom as long as you don't do it on the street and frighten the horses. *Mrs. Patrick Campbell*

Of the two, I prefer those who render vice lovable to those who degrade virtue. *Joseph Joubert, Pensées*

Sarcasm is an insult in dress suit.

Sometimes we think we dislike flattery, but it is only the way it is done that we dislike. *François de la Rochefoucauld*

When you don't know what you're doing, do it neatly.

Theirs not to reason why, theirs is but to DO or die.* Alfred, Lord Tennyson, The Charge of the Light Brigade, 1854

It is much easier to do and die than to reason why. *G. A. Studdert-Kennedy*

Nobody but a bureaucrat likes to be ruled by rules, and nobody but a bureaucrat likes to say, "I don't make the rules, I'm just here to see they are carried out." *Laurence Peter, The Peter Pyramid*

*"Do or die" is a Scottish slogan.

What you DO speaks so loudly, I can't hear what you say.

Many people live alone and like it, but more of them live alone and look it. *Gelett Burgess*

See also ACTIONS speak louder than words; DEEDS, not creeds.

A man who is his own DOCTOR has a fool for a patient.

. . . and a fool for a doctor.

A physician who treats himself has a fool for a patient. *William Osler.* Inspired by the 17th-century proverb "He that teaches himself has a fool for his master."

Who shall decide when DOCTORS disagree? *Alexander Pope (1688–1744), Moral Essays*

. . . The undertaker, very probably. *Richard Armour*

A living DOG is better than a dead lion. *Ecclesiastes 9:4*

A man's best friend is his DOG. 1709, WM-157

. . . after his mother. *T. E. Dickty, 1958; BJW-174*

. . . yet nobody wants to be compared with him. *E. Gurdy, 1975; BJW-175*

. . . but a good cow is more help at the table. *Vermont proverb*

A dog has friends because he wags his tail instead of his tongue. *Heard in North Carolina*

A dog is the only thing on this earth that loves you more than he loves himself. *Josh Billings*

A dog teaches a boy fidelity, perseverance and to turn round three times before lying down. *Robert Benchley, as quoted in Reader's Digest, Apr. 1963*

A man is the dog's best friend. *H. Whiting; BJW-175*

Animals are such agreeable friends—they ask no questions, they pass no criticisms. *George Eliot*

Beware of false friends—your dog won't desert you when your money's gone. *Josh Billings*

Don't accept your dog's admiration as conclusive evidence that you are wonderful. *Ann Landers*

If dogs could talk, perhaps we'd find it just as hard to get along with them as we do with people. *Karel Capek*

If you pick up a starving dog and make him prosperous, he will not bite you; that is the principal difference between a dog and a man. *Mark Twain*

Man is a dog's ideal of what God should be. *Holbrook Jackson*

The great pleasure of a dog is that you may make a fool of yourself with him, and not only will he not scold you, but he will make a fool of himself too. *Samuel Butler*

The one absolutely unselfish friend that man can have in this selfish world, the one that never deserts him, the one that never proves ungrateful or treacherous, is his dog. *George G. Vest, 1876, spoken at the trial of a farmer who had shot a neighbor's dog for killing farm animals*

To be sure, the dog is loyal. But why, on that account, should we take him as an example? He is loyal to men, not to other dogs. *Karl Kraus*

To his dog, every man is Napoleon; hence the popularity of dogs. *Aldous Huxley, as quoted in Reader's Digest, Dec. 1934*

The wastepaper basket is a writer's best friend. *Isaac Bashevis Singer*

Better to be the head of a DOG than the tail of a lion. *1760, Ray*

Better a live dog than a dead lion. *ca. 1390, WM-159*

Better to be a fox among geese than a goose among foxes. *Russian proverb*

Better to be a king among dogs than a dog among kings. *Heard in Kentucky*

Better to reign in hell than serve in heav'n. *John Milton, Paradise Lost*

DOG eat dog.

A criminal is a person with predatory instincts who has not sufficient capital to form a corporation. *Howard Scott*

Dog does not eat dog. *Juvenal*

Every man must be either a hammer or an anvil.

If we could create a world in which no one harmed his fellow creatures, we would achieve a breakthrough of staggering importance. People could be rude, selfish, apathetic, and completely uncaring but if no one raised a hand against his own kind, we would be a step beyond Utopia. *Donald G. Smith*

It's a nasty world out there, so it's good to come home to a loving family.

Look, we trade every day out there with hustlers, deal makers, shysters, con men . . . that's the way businesses get started. That's the way this country was built. *Hubert Allen*

Man is a wolf to man. *English proverb*

Skin or get skinned. *Old postcard*

The world is made up of two classes, the hunter and the hunted. *Heard in New York*

Drinking together in the evening we are
    human.
When dawn comes, animals
We rise up against each other.
Antimedon, The Greek Anthology, trans. Peter Jay

See also PEOPLE are no damned good.

Don't be a DOG in the manger. 1546, T-167

Don't let the tail wag the DOG.

Lo! Men have become the tools of their tools. *Henry David Thoreau*

Every DOG has his day. 1539, *Taverner*

My turn today, yours tomorrow. *Latin proverb*

. . . The kind of day depends on the sort of dog. *Old postcard*

. . . but the night belongs to us pussycats.

At high tide fish eat ants; at low tide ants eat fish. *Thai proverb*

Every dogma must have its day. *Carolyn Wells*

Today mine, tomorrow thine. *German proverb*

Give a DOG a bad name and hang him. 1706, WM-159

Call a man a thief and you license him to steal. *Josh Billings*

He that hath the name might as well enjoy the game. *O2-442*

If you have been put in your place long enough, you begin to act like the place. *Randall Jarrell, A Sad Heart at the Supermarket*

Never send a DOG to deliver a steak.

Don't set a wolf to watch the sheep. *1513, WM-164*

Never trust the cat with the cream.

See also Who will watch the WATCHMAN?

The DOG that trots about finds the bone. 1843, WM-161

See The BEE that gets the honey doesn't hang around the hive.

You can't teach an old DOG new tricks.* 1614, Camden

. . . so long as his old tricks keep working. *Seth Haven*

. . . but old fleas don't mind a new dog.

An old tree cannot be transplanted. *Vermont proverb*

Best to bend while it is a twig. *1530, T-690*

The habit of saving money is hard to acquire, and even harder to break. *Mignon McLaughlin*

The only time a woman really succeeds in changing a man is when he's a baby. *Natalie Wood*

The trick is to grow up without growing old. *Frank Lloyd Wright*

When we are young, we change our opinions too often, when we are old, too seldom. *Josh Billings*

When you're through changing, you're through. *Heard in Utah and Wisconsin*

*Some folks, with nothing better to do, enjoy expressing simple proverbs in unnecessarily wordy language, like this: "It is impossible to indoctrinate a superannuated canine in the intricacies of innovative feats of legerdemain."

Barking DOGS seldom bite. 1275, WM-157*

. . . You know it, and I know it—but does the dog know it? *Joe Weber and Lew Fields*

. . . [and] cowardly dogs bark loudest. *John Webster, The White Devil*

A bargain dog never bites. *Ogden Nash, Funebrial Reflection*

A sleeping dog never bites.

Dread silent dogs. *Russian proverb*

*Flexner (F-14) tells of a Latin proverb, "Beware of a silent dog and still water."

If you lie down with DOGS, you get up with fleas. *Latin proverb*

He who goes with crabs learns to walk backwards. *Heard in Ohio*

Live with a hog and you'll grunt like one. *Heard in Kentucky and Tennessee*

You can't root with hogs and have a clean nose. *Heard in Arkansas and Kansas*

See also A MAN is known by the company he keeps.

Let sleeping DOGS lie. *German proverb*

Let dead dogs sleep.

Let lying dogs sleep.

Let sleeping dogmas lie.

Things are going to the DOGS.

A nickel goes a long way now. You can carry it around for days without finding a thing it will buy.

Every old man complains of the growing depravity of the world, of the petulance and insolence of the rising generation. *Samuel Johnson, The Rambler*

I almost think it is the ultimate destiny of science to exterminate the human race. *Thomas Love Peacock, 1860*

I think the world is run by C students. *Al McGuire*

It isn't progress that's hurting us so much today—it's the side-effects. *Don Fraser*

It seems you can't buy anything anymore that lasts as long as the old one. *Kin Hubbard*

Men have become the tools of their tools. *Henry David Thoreau*

Nostalgia isn't what it used to be. *Graffiti*

Nothing's more responsible for the good old days than a bad memory. *Franklin P. Jones, as quoted in Reader's Digest, Jan. 1953*

Ours is the age of substitutes: instead of language, we have jargon; instead of principles, slogans; and, instead of genuine ideas, bright ideas. *Eric Bentley*

Pessimism is as American as apple pie— frozen apple pie with a slice of processed cheese. *George Will, Statecraft as Soulcraft*

Pessimist: one who, when he has the choice of two evils, chooses both. *Oscar Wilde*

Science is always wrong; it never solves a problem without creating ten more. *G. B. Shaw*

The odds are six to five that the light at the end of the tunnel is the headlight of an on- coming train. *Paul Dickson, 1978*

The probability of anything happening is in inverse ratio to its desirability. *John W. Haz- ard, Changing Times, 1957*

The world is disgracefully managed, one hardly knows to whom to complain. *Ronald Firbank, Vainglory*

The world just doesn't work. It's an idea whose time is gone. *Joseph Heller, Something Happened*

There can hardly be a stranger commodity in the world than books. Printed by people who don't understand them; sold by people who don't understand them; bound, criticized and read by people who don't understand them; and now even written by people who don't understand them. *Georg Lichtenberg*

"Times ain't as they used to be"—this has been the solemn and wise remark of mankind ever since Adam was a boy. *Josh Billings*

We are in a decaying age. Young people no longer respect their parents. They are rude and impatient. They inhabit taverns and have no self-control. *Inscription on 6,000-year-old Egyptian tomb*

We used to say that things will get worse be- fore they get better; now we say they will be worse before they're still worse. *Robert Triffin, 1974*

My granddad, viewing earth's worn cogs,
Said things were going to the dogs;
His granddad in his house of logs
Said things were going to the dogs;
His granddad in the Flemish bogs
Said things were going to the dogs;
His granddad in his old skin togs
Said things were going to the dogs;
There's one thing that I have to state
The dogs have had a good long wait.
Perennial Journeys

See also NOTHING works; O tempora! o mores!

The shortest answer is DOING. 1640, T-14

See Actions speak louder than words.

If you want a thing DONE well, do it your- self. *1541, O-240*

. . . [but] next to doing a good job yourself, the greatest joy is in having someone else do a first-rate job under your direction. *William Feather*

A committee of one gets things done. *Joe Ryan*

Command your man and do it yourself. *Ray, 1670*

Don't itch for something you're not willing to scratch for.

If you let other people do it *for* you, they will do it *to* you. *Robert Anthony, Think Again*

If you want a steak well done, order it rare.

If you want a thing well done, let it cook.

If you want something done—go. If you don't—send.

If you would be well served, serve yourself. *1659, O-200*

Who goes himself, wishes it; who sends someone else, does not care. *English proverb*

See Burton Stevenson (B-2064) for equivalents in five languages.

What's DONE is done.

It is too late to call again yesterday. *1611, T-766*

If life had a second edition, how I would correct the proofs. *John Clare*

If you had your life to live over again, you'd need more money.

No man is rich enough to buy back his past. *Oscar Wilde*

Nothing we can do can change the past, but everything we do changes the future. © *Ashleigh Brilliant*

There are three things that cannot be recalled—a spent arrow, a spoken word and a lost opportunity.

Things done cannot be undone. *1539, Taverner*

What is done can't be undone.

What is once well done is done forever.

What is done is done, and can't be mended by words.

Yesterday's gone on down the river, and you can't get it back. *Larry McMurtry, Lonesome Dove*

You can't change the past, but you can ruin the present by worrying about the future. *Peter's Almanac*

The Moving Finger writes; and, having writ,
Moves on: nor all thy Piety and Wit
Shall lure it back to cancel half a Line,
Nor all thy Tears wash out a Word of it.
Omar Khayyam, The Rubiyat

See also It is no use CRYING over spilt milk; You can't unscramble EGGS.

When one DOOR shuts, another opens. 1586, O-169

. . . which means that you live in a drafty house.

. . . but we often look so long and so regretfully upon the closed door that we do not see the one which has opened for us. *Alexander Graham Bell*

When one door of happiness closes, another opens; but often we look so long at the closed door that we do not see the one which has been opened for us. *Helen Keller*

When in DOUBT, abstain. 1884, O-59

If you are ever in doubt as to whether or not you should kiss a pretty girl, always give her the benefit of the doubt. *Thomas Carlyle*

In case of doubt, decide in favor of what is correct. *Karl Kraus*

When a man has not a good reason for doing a thing, he has one good reason for letting it alone. *Walter Scott*

Know nothing, do nothing.

When in doubt, leave it out.

When in doubt, do nowt. *1917, O-59*

When in doubt, do the courageous thing. *Jan Smuts*

When in doubt, do without. *Vermont proverb*

When in doubt, duck. *Malcolm Forbes*

When in doubt, mumble. When in trouble, delegate. When in charge, ponder. *James H. Boren*

When in doubt, say no. A *parent's advice*

When in doubt, tell the truth. *Mark Twain, Notebook.* Biographer A. B. Paine writes that when Clemens was introduced as the man who said this, he replied that he had invented that maxim for others, but that when in doubt himself, he used more sagacity (*Mark Twain: A Biography*, vol. 3, 1912, p. 1280).

When in doubt, the vague generality and a fixed smile is your best ploy. *Laurence Peter*

When in doubt, worry.

See also SILENCE is golden.

DRINK is the curse of the working class.

A man takes a drink and then the drink takes the man. *Heard in Illinois and Iowa*

Drink is the curse of the land. It makes you fight with your neighbor. It makes you shoot at your landlord—and it makes you miss him. *Irish proverb*

It's all right to drink like a fish if you drink what fish drink. *Heard in Florida*

One drink is good, two is too much, and three is not enough. *Heard in New York*

Water, taken in moderation, cannot hurt anybody. *Mark Twain*

When your drinking interferes with your work, you're in trouble. When your work interferes with your drinking, you're an alcoholic.

Work is the curse of the drinking class. *Attributed to Oscar Wilde and to American restaurateur Mike Romanoff*

See also WINE is a mocker.

If you DRINK, don't drive.

. . . You might hit a bump and spill your drink.

. . . Don't even putt. *Dean Martin*

The hand that lifts the cup that cheers
Should not be used to shift the gears.

Epitaph for a drunken driver: He put the quart before the hearse.

Constant DRIPPING wears away a stone. *Greek proverb*

Constant dropping wears the stone. *British version; O2-107*

Time's office is to . . . waste huge stones with little water-drops. *Shakespeare, Richard II 3.3:164*

DRIVE carefully; the life you save may be your own.

Don't smoke in bed. The heap of ashes on the floor may be your own.

It takes a lot of bolts to hold a car together, but only one nut to scatter it all over the highway. *Heard in Kansas*

Your first accident may be your last. *Heard in Mississippi*

A DROWNING man will grasp at a straw. 1534, O-60

Thirsty men catch at straws oftener than drowning ones do. *New York Commercial Advertiser*

What DUST do I raise!*

*According to a fable of Aesop, exclaimed by a fly who sat upon the axle of a chariot wheel.

See One does all the WORK and the other takes all the credit.

DUTY before pleasure.

. . . as the man said when he kissed his wife before calling on his sweetheart. *1938, BJW-82*

Duty is duty.

Please first and business afterwards. *1908, BJW-82*

See also BUSINESS before pleasure.

To EACH his own.

Everyone has his own pleasures. *Latin proverb*

See also BEAUTY is in the eye of the beholder; Every CROW thinks its own young ones the whitest; One man's MEAT is another man's poison.

Keep your EARS open.

. . . Even a rattlesnake will warn before he bites. *Heard in Arkansas, Georgia, and Ohio*

The EARTH is the Lord's, and the fullness thereof. *Psalms 23:6*

We don't own this land; we're just borrowing it from our children.

EASIER said than done. *200 B.C., B-2037*

The lilacs are flowering, sweet and sublime,
    with perfume that goes to the head;

and lovers meander in prose and rhyme,
trying to say
    for the thousandth time
    what's easier done than said.
Piet Hein

EAST is East and West is West and never the twain shall meet. *Rudyard Kipling (1865–1936), Ballad of East and West*

Birds sing the same in every land. *Japanese proverb*

See also The colonel's lady and Mrs. O'Grady are SISTERS under the skin.

EASY come, easy go. *Latin and Chinese proverb*

Light come light go. *1390, O-133*

Quickly come, quickly go. *1583, O-187*

Soon gotten soon spent. *1546, Heywood*

Soon hot, soon cold. *15th century*

Soon learnt, soon forgotten. *14th century*

[The rogues of this world] do not always find manors, got by rape or chicanery, insensibly to melt away, as the poets will have it; or that all gold glides, like thawing snow, from the thief's hand that grasps it.... [Here is another fallacy] which the thieves can very well afford to leave... to the losers. *Charles Lamb, Popular Fallacies*

EASY does it. *Slogan of Alcoholics Anonymous; 1863, O-63*

... sometimes.

The art of progress is to preserve order amid change and to preserve change amid order. *Alfred North Whitehead*

Take-it-easy and live-long are brothers. *Heard in Mississippi*

See also Don't burn the barn to destroy the RATS; HASTE makes waste.

Nothing worthwhile is ever EASY.

Nothing difficult is ever easy.

The most expensive things in this world are those we get for nothing. *Old postcard*

The sweetest grapes hang the highest. *German proverb*

What is written without pain is read without pleasure. (Say the Morrises [MD-596–97]: "We don't know the author of that sentence, but the thought has been stated by many writers." They give a few examples.)

See also If I own a COW, the cow owns me; There's no such thing as a free LUNCH; No GAINS without pains.

Take is EASY.

I have never liked working. To me a job is an invasion of privacy. *Danny McGoorty, 1936*

I like the word "indolence." It makes my laziness seem classy. *Bern Williams*

If you are losing your leisure, look out! You may be losing your soul. *Logan Pearsall Smith, Afterthoughts*

It is sad indeed if the people have time only to earn their daily bread; they must also be able to eat it with joy, otherwise their earning days will be short-lived. God, who is just and benevolent, wills that Man shall work, but also that he shall enjoy relaxation; Nature commands him to have exercise and rest, pleasure and pain, in equal measure. The drudgery of work is a greater affliction to the poor than the work itself. *Jean-Jacques Rousseau, letter to Jean d'Alembert, 1758*

It's impossible to enjoy doing nothing thoroughly unless you have a great deal of work to do. *Abe Martin*

Laziness is nothing more than the habit of resting before you get tired. *Jules Renard*

Loafing is something you can do without exerting yourself.

Milk the cow that stands still. Why follow you the flying? *1594, T-125*

Most men pursue pleasure with such breathless haste that they hurry past it. *Soren Kierkegaard, Either/Or*

Motto posted in the *New York Times* composing room: All the news that fits, we print.

Slow down and enjoy life. It's not only the scenery you miss by going too fast—you also miss the sense of where you're going and why. *Eddie Cantor*

Sometimes the most urgent and vital thing you can possibly do is take a complete rest. © *Ashleigh Brilliant*

Take a rest; a field that has rested gives a bountiful crop. *Ovid*

Take things as they come. *17th century*

Take-it-easy and live-long are brothers. *Heard in Mississippi*

The more careless, the more modish. *1738, OE-79*

Time is but the stream I go a-fishing in. *Henry David Thoreau, Walden*

Work is a curse—which is why I've never made it a habit. *Blaise Cendrars*

Workers of the world, relax.

You're busy? Chipmunks darting in and out
The hole are busy, too—but what about?
Arthur Guiterman

See also Take time to stop and smell the FLOWERS; Who invented WORK?

Eat, drink and be merry for tomorrow we die.*

Eat, drink and be merry for tomorrow they may recall your credit cards.

Eat, drink and be merry for you died yesterday. *BJW-195*

Eat, drink, and be quiet. *Coffee cup motto*

Eat, drink, but do not marry, for tomorrow you may die. *Captain Billy's Whiz Bang, June 1922*

Everyone should believe in something—I believe I'll have another drink.

If life is a trip on the *Titanic*, there's no point in traveling steerage.

It is better to be on pleasure bent, than to be broke. *Old postcard*

It is better to have a few mornings after than never to have a night before. *Jack Wasserman*

Let us swear while we may, for in heaven it will not be allowed. *Mark Twain, Notebook*

Live it up.

Man is the only animal that eats when he is not hungry, drinks when he is not thirsty, and makes love at all seasons.

My theory is to enjoy life, but the practice is against it. *Charles Lamb*

Part of the secret of success in life is to eat what you like and let the food fight it out inside. *Mark Twain*

Prohibition motto: Eat, drink and be merry, for tomorrow your bootlegger may get caught. *Captain Billy's Whiz Bang, Jan. 1922*

There is no fun in the graveyard; give me my flowers now. *Old postcard*

Who loves not women, wine and song remains a fool his whole life long. *Martin Luther*

Live while you live, and when you're dead
We'll plant a tombstone at your head.
Old postcard

Let us have Wine, Women, Mirth and
  Laughter
Sermons and soda-water the day after.
Lord Byron

We may live without books
What is knowledge but grieving.
We may live without hope,—what is hope but
  deceiving.
We may live without love,—what is passion
  but pining;
But where is the man who can live without
  dining?
George Meredith

If all be true and I do think,
There are five reasons we should drink;
Good wine—a friend—or being dry
Or lest we should be by and by
Or any other reason why.
Henry Aldrich

Let us drink and be merry, dance, joke, and
  rejoice,
With claret and sherry, theorbo and voice,
The changeable world to our joy is unjust,
All treasure uncertain, then down with your
  dust.
    In frolicks dispose your pounds, shillings,
      and pence,
    For we shall be nothing a hundred years
      hence.
Thomas Jordan, The Epicure

*Keyes (K-183) notes that this proverb is ac-
tually a composite of two biblical lines: "Let
us eat and drink; for tomorrow we shall die"
(Isaiah 22:13) and "A man hath no better
thing under the sun, than to eat, and to
drink, and to be merry" (Ecclesiastes 8:15).

See also CARPE diem; CHRISTMAS comes
but once a year; ENJOY yourself . . . ; All the
things I like are either ILLEGAL, immoral,
or fattening; WINE maketh glad the heart of
man.

**EAT to live, and not live to eat. 1410,
O2-167**

A minute in the mouth, two hours in the
stomach, and forever on your hips.

Brown bread and Gospel is good fare. *Puritan
proverb*

Eat a third [of the stomach's capacity], drink
a third, leave a third empty. *Babylonian Talmud*

Eat at pleasure, drink by measure. *1611,
T-545*

Eat not to dullness, drink not to elevation.
Poor Richard's Almanac

Gluttons dig their graves with their teeth.
1630, T-181

Gluttony kills more than the sword. *1535,
T-258*

Let your head be more than a funnel to your
stomach. *German proverb*

Many doctors pay their grocery bills with the
money of folks who have eaten too much.

More die by food than famine. *1584, T-227*

Some eat to live, others live to eat.

The alimentary canal is thirty-two feet long.
You control only the first three inches of it.
Control it well. *Kin Hubbard*

The lesse one eates, the more he eates, I
meane he liveth longer to eat more. *Stefano
Guazzo, 1574*

See also You are what you EAT.

You are what you EAT.

. . . maybe, and you are how you eat, for sure.

. . . [and a] good reducing exercise consists of placing both hands against the table edge and pushing back. *Robert Quillen*

A man is what he eats. *Ludwig Feuerbach, Blätter für Literarische Unterhaltung, Nov. 12, 1850*

Diet cures more than doctors. *19th century*

I refuse to spend my life worrying about what I eat. There is no pleasure worth forgoing just for an extra three years in the geriatric ward. *John Mortimer*

If you eat too many doughnuts, you'll turn into one. *A parent's warning*

Man is what he reads. *Joseph Brodsky*

My exit is the result of too many entrees. *Confession of Richard Monckton Milnes, an overindulgent 19th-century British society figure*

Take those scales out of the bathroom, madam; the right place for them is in front of your refrigerator. *Richard Needham*

Taste makes waist.

Tell me what you eat, and I will tell you what you are. *Anthelme Brillat-Savarin, Physiologie du Goût*

They who drink beer will think beer. *Washington Irving*

Vegetarians eat vegetables; what do humanitarians eat?

You are where you eat. *Pamela Fiori*

Your body is the baggage you must carry through life. The more excess baggage, the shorter the trip. *Arnold H. Glasow*

What goes past the lips
comes out on the hips.

"You are what you eat," said a wise old man;
If that's true, I'm a garbage can.

My soul is dark with stormy riot,
Directly traceable to diet.
Samuel Hoffenstein

Better an EGG today than a hen tomorrow. *Italian proverb*

Better small fish than an empty dish. *1670, Ray*

Bread today is better than cake tomorrow. *Heard in Indiana and Oregon*

Modern variant: Better a hen today than an egg tomorrow. *L. L. Levinson*

See also A BIRD in the hand is worth two in the bush.

You don't have to be able to lay an EGG to tell a bad one.

. . . and you don't have to eat the whole pie to know if it is bad.

Don't put all your EGGS in one basket. *1662, O-64*

A combined charity drive represents an effort where everyone puts all their begs into one ask-it. *Clifton Fadiman*

A group of Basques, fleeing before the enemy, were penned into a narrow mountain pass and wiped out. Which is what comes of putting all your Basques in one exit. *Franklin P. Adams*

A wise Marchant neuer aduentureth all his goodes in one ship. *Thomas More, 1513*

Behold, the fool saith, "Put not all thine eggs in one basket"—which is but a manner of saying, "Scatter your money and your attention," but the wise man saith, "Put all your eggs in the one basket and—WATCH THAT BASKET." *Mark Twain, Pudd'nhead Wilson's Calendar*

Science without religion is lame, religion without science is blind. *Albert Einstein*

The cunning hare has three holes. *Chinese proverb*

You can't unscramble EGGS. *J. Pierpont Morgan (attributed), ca. 1905; WM-178*

Broken eggs can never be mended. *New England proverb*

Once the toothpaste is out of the tube, it's hard to get it back in. *H. R. Haldeman, on Watergate*

Spilled water is hard to retrieve. *Chinese proverb*

Things done cannot be undone. *1539, T-660*

Respect your ELDERS.

A man's age commands veneration; a woman's demands tact.

The hoary head is a crown of glory. *Proverbs 16:31*

Many a man that couldn't direct you to the drug store on the corner when he was thirty will get a respectful hearing when age has fur-ther impaired his mind. *Finley Peter Dunne, Mr. Dooley on Making a Will*

Old folks know more about being young than young folks know about being old. *Peter's Almanac*

An ELEPHANT never forgets.* 1937, WM-178

Women and elephants never forget.

*Burton Stevenson (B-675) regards this proverb as a modern variation of an ancient Greek proverb, "The camel never forgets an injury."

The EMPEROR has no clothes.

Freedom comes only from seeing the ignorance of your critics and discovering the emptiness of their virtue. *David Seabury*

If all the world went naked, how could we tell the kings?

Kings are not born: they are made by universal hallucination. *G. B. Shaw, Maxims for Revolutionists*

The Clothes Have No Emperor. *Title of an anti-Reagan book by Paul Slansky, 1989*

Should an employee risk criticizing company policy, or question the quality of its products? Warns career counselor Marilyn Moats Kennedy: "The kid who said the emperor had no clothes didn't get a scholarship to Mandarin U." *Chicago Tribune, May 12, 1996*

To knock a thing down, especially if it is cocked at an arrogant angle, is a deep delight to the blood. *George Santayana, Life of Reason*

All good things must come to an END. 1440, O-3

. . . but bad things seem to go on forever.

The END doesn't justify the means.

If the end doesn't justify the means, what can? *John Maynard Keynes*

Never do evil that good may come of it. *Romans 3:8 (paraphrased)*

The end cannot justify the means for the simple and obvious reason that the means employed determine the nature of the ends produced. *Aldous Huxley, Ends and Means*

The kind of person who can foment a revolution is usually a poor civil administrator. *Donald G. Smith*

There is no right way to do the wrong thing.

Wisdom denotes the pursuing of the best ends by the best means. *Francis Hutcheson*

You are not at liberty to execute a good plan with bad instruments. *Henry Ward Beecher, Proverbs from Plymouth Pulpit*

The END justifies the means. *Latin proverb*

Does the end ever justify the means? Is the object worth the price? "It is impossible to give a meaningful answer to this very general question, unless we know the precise object that is under consideration and the exact price that is being demanded." *Corliss Lamont, Humanism as a Philosophy*

Exitus acta probat. ("The result justifies the deed.") *Motto of George Washington*

Him you cannot control by fair means, you must restrain by foul. *Publilius Syrus*

Most of the great results of history are brought about by discreditable means. *Ralph Waldo Emerson, The Conduct of Life*

The end excuses any evil. *Sophocles*

To deceive a deceiver is no deceit. *Ulpian Fulwell, Ars Adulandi*

When the end is lawful, the means are also lawful. *Hermann Busenbaum, on the Jesuit doctrine that the end justifies the means, 1650*

Win any way you can as long as you can get away with it. *Leo Durocher*

The end must justify the means:
He only sins who ill intends:
Since therefore 'tis to combat evil,
'Tis lawful to employ the devil.
Matthew Prior, Hans Carvel

See also MIGHT makes right; Nothing succeeds like SUCCESS.

All's well that ENDS well. 1250, O-244

. . . said the monkey, contemplating his tail.

. . . and all that begins badly sometimes ends worse.

All's well that ends.

A man is his own worst ENEMY.

Debt is a trap which a man sets and baits himself, then deliberately gets into. *Josh Billings*

Defend me, God, from myself. *Spanish proverb*

If you just try long enough and hard enough, you can always manage to boot yourself in the posterior. *A. J. Liebling, The Press*

Ten enemies cannot do a man the harm that he does to himself. *Yiddish proverb*

The earth is infected and we are the virus. *T-shirt saying*

When the gods wish to punish us they answer our prayers. *Oscar Wilde, An Ideal Husband*

The gods are just, and of our pleasant vices
Make instruments to plague us.
Shakespeare, King Lear 5.3.172

We see men fall from high estate on account of the very faults through which they attained it. *Jean de La Bruyère, Of the Court*

But human bodies are sic fools
For a' their colleges and schools,
That when nae real ills perplex them,
They make enow themselves to vex them.
Robert Burns, The Two Dogs

See also Be careful of what you WISH for . . . ; I am my own EXECUTIONER; We have met the ENEMY, and he is us.

Better an open ENEMY than a false friend. ca. 1200, WM-180

Better a square-shooting atheist than a false Christian. *Heard in Illinois*

We have met the ENEMY, and he is us.* Walt Kelly (1917–73), Pogo

The increasing control that science has won over external Nature makes it clear that the most serious danger at present to man is man himself and not non-human Nature. *Corliss Lamont, Humanism as a Philosophy, about*

forty years before there was widespread concern for "saving the planet"

God has given us a world that nothing but our own folly keeps from being a paradise. *G. B. Shaw, Candide*

Man has lost the capacity to foresee and to forestall. He will end by destroying the earth. *Albert Schweitzer*

No witchcraft, no enemy action has silenced the rebirth of new life. . . . The people have done it themselves. *Rachel Carson*

The differences between man's soot and nature's grime is that nature knows how to clean up after herself. *Stanford Research Institute*

The face of the enemy frightens me only when I see how much it resembles mine.

The young home-grown gangster and drug dealer . . . has taken more young black lives in recent years than the Ku Klux Klan lynched in a century. *Clarence Page, Chicago Tribune, May 8, 1996*

*This saying is a parody of the words of Commodore Oliver Perry (1785–1819), "We have met the enemy, and they are ours," to announce his victory over the British in the naval battle of Lake Erie, Sept. 10, 1813.

According to Keyes (K-14), in the 1953 introduction to *The Pogo Papers*, Walt Kelly wrote, "We shall meet the enemy, and not only may he be ours, he may be us."

See also Be careful of what you WISH for . . . ; I am my own EXECUTIONER.

Love your ENEMIES* Matthew 5:44

. . . for they will tell you your faults.

. . . It will drive them nuts.

Instead of loving your enemies, treat your friends a little better. *Ed Howe*

It's too much to ask one to love his enemy. Let's compromise on forgetting him. *William C. Hunter*

Love your enemies in case your friends turn out to be a bunch of bastards. *R. A. Dickson*

*A Hebrew precursor of this Christian commandment is expressed in Proverbs 25:21: "If thine enemy be hungry, give him bread to eat; and if he be thirsty, give him water to drink."

ENJOY yourself; it's later than you think.*
Chinese proverb

. . . None of us came with a guarantee but we all have an expiration date. *Peter's Almanac*

A man can scarcely be said to have made a fortune if he does not know how to enjoy it. *Luc de Clapiers de Vauvenargues*

All of the animals except man know that the principal business of life is to enjoy it. *Samuel Butler*

Better to do a good job of enjoying leisure than a poor job at work. *Spanish proverb*

Death is more common than life; everyone dies but not everyone really lives.

Eat coconuts while you have teeth. *Singhalese proverb*

Enjoy life: this is not a rehearsal. *Bumper sticker*

Enjoy yourself. If you can't enjoy yourself, enjoy somebody else. *Jack Schaefer*

Gather the roses, maiden, while the blooms are fresh and youth is fresh, and be mindful that in like fashion your lifetime hastes away. *Ausonius*

I had rather be a beggar and spend my last dollar like a king, than to be a king and spend my money like a beggar. *Robert G. Ingersoll, 1877*

If life is a banquet, why are so many people eating sandwiches?

If you have two loaves of bread, sell one and buy a hyacinth. *Persian proverb*

Live and scratch—when you're dead the itching will stop. *Russian proverb*

Life is a fatal adventure. It can only have one end. So why not make it as far-ranging and free as possible? *Alexander Eliot, New York Post, Nov. 28, 1962*

Sign under an office clock: It's earlier than you think.

The day that goes by without you having had some fun—the day you don't enjoy life—is not only unnecessary but unchristian! *Dwight D. Eisenhower, as quoted in Reader's Digest, Jan. 1972*

The world is his who enjoys it. *18th century*

There are two things to aim at in life: first, to get what you want, and after that to enjoy it. *Logan Pearsall Smith*

There is no cure for birth and death save to enjoy the interval. *George Santayana*

Time you enjoy wasting is not wasted time.

To enjoy is to live. *Favorite phrase of psychologist Jack D. Krasner, noted in an obituary of his death, Oct. 6, 1978*

To have slept is not to have lived. *Yiddish proverb*

Wealth is not his that has it, but his that enjoys it.

When one has had to work so hard to get money, why should he impose on himself the further handicap of trying to save it? *Don Herold*

Yesterday is gone, tomorrow may never come, today is here. *Carl Sandburg*

*This proverb rose to popularity in America with the publication in *Reader's Digest*, Nov. 1946, of "In a Chinese Garden," a reminiscence by retired medical doctor Fredric Loomis.

Sometime in the 1930s, a patient of his was on a vacation in China and wrote him a thank-you note for helping her through a personal crisis. In her letter, she noted that on the garden wall where she sat was a piece of Chinese calligraphy that was translated for her as "Enjoy yourself, it's later than you think."

Dr. Loomis took the hint. He left his busy practice for a few months' vacation and begged a dear old friend of his to come with him. When the doctor returned, he found that not only was his medical practice still flourishing but that some of his patients did not even know that he had been away. Shortly afterward, his dear old friend died, and Dr. Loomis felt even more touched about the advice his patient had seen on a Chinese garden wall.

The retired doctor's reminiscence was read by millions. He was invited to tell his story in person before clubs and societies across America. Tin Pan Alley made it the theme of a hit tune, which was played to the point of boredom. Such was the journey of "Enjoy yourself; it's later than you think," from Chinese proverb to American cliché.

The writings of Lin Yutang suggest that this saying does express an authentically Chinese attitude. In *My Country and My People*, 1935, Lin Yutang writes that in the Chinese way of life what is most important is not life after death, or Nirvana, or individual achievement, or social progress, but "the enjoyment of a simple life, especially the family life, and in harmonious social relationships. . . . There is no doubt that the Chinese are in love with life, in love with this earth, and will not forsake it for an invisible heaven. They are in love with life, which is so sad and yet so beautiful, and in which moments of happiness are so precious because they are so transient."

A student of Chinese culture advises the editor that in China this proverb may also be spoken ironically; that is to say, to chastise a person for wasting precious time.

ENOUGH is as good as a feast. *Euripides, The Suppliant Women*

The fool that eats till he is sick must fast till he is well. *Heard in Ontario*

ENOUGH is enough. *1546, Heywood*

. . . and more than enough is too much.

A man with one watch knows what time it is; a man with two watches is never quite sure. *Lee Segall*

An ass endures his burden but not more than his burden. *1599, Minsheu*

Enough is usually just a little more.

One weakness of our age is our apparent inability to distinguish our needs from our greeds. *Don Robinson*

Talk good, talk on; talk bad, stop. *Heard in Alabama and Georgia*

There never was a child so lovely but his mother was glad to get him asleep. *Ralph Waldo Emerson*

Too much spoils, too little does not satisfy. *1659, Howell*

You never know how much is enough until you've had too much.

See also the MORE you have, the more you want; TOO MUCH of anything is not good.

EPPUR si muove.*

I do not feel obliged to believe that the same God who has endowed us with sense, reason, and intelligence has intended us to forgo their use. *Galileo Galelei*

*"Nevertheless, it [the world] does move." Galileo is said to have muttered this under his breath when he was brought before the Inquisition in 1633 and forced to recant his belief in the heliocentric theory. Keyes (K-174) doubts that Galileo actually said this, and notes that the statement does not appear in writing until a century after Galileo's death.

To ERR is human, to forgive is divine.* *Alexander Pope, An Essay on Criticism, 1711*

. . . to persist in error, beastly. *George Pettie, 1576*

. . . to refrain from laughing is humane. *Lane Olinghouse*

To err is human:

. . . but when the eraser wears out ahead of the pencil, you're overdoing it. *J. Jenkins*

. . . to blame it on the other party is politics. *Wall Street Journal*

. . . to admit it, superhuman. *Doug Larson*

. . . to cheat is common. *Chicago Tribune headline, Dec. 16, 1993, of survey that 8 out of 10 MIT undergraduates have cheated at least once*

. . . but this does not make it desirable to make as many errors as possible. *Roger Williams*

. . . but to remain in error is stupid.

. . . but to admit it isn't.

. . . but to really foul things up requires a computer. *Paul Ehrlich*

. . . but it feels divine. *Mae West*

Does it bother you to hear a speaker fill his pauses with "errr"? Remember that "To errr is human."

How natural it is for a man when he makes a mistake to correct it by cussing somebody else for it. *Josh Billings*

If thou hast never been a fool, be sure thou wilt never be a wise man. *William Makepeace Thackeray*

It is human to err, but devilish to brag on it. *Josh Billings*

Lord, when we are wrong, make us willing to change; and when we are right, make us easy to live with. *Peter Marshall*

The man who boasts he never made a mistake usually has a wife who made a big one.

The only one who never makes mistakes is the one who never does anything. *Theodore Roosevelt*

To eat is human, to digest is divine. *Mark Twain*

They wouldn't make erasers if we all didn't make mistakes. *Heard in Kentucky, Mississippi, and Tennessee*

To err is dysfunctional, to forgive co-dependent. *Berton Averre*

To itch is human, to scratch divine.

To pity distress is but human: to relieve it is Godlike. *Horace Mann, Lectures on Education*

To speed is but human; to get caught a fine. *Pennsylvania Punch Bowl, ca. 1925*

We do not err because truth is difficult to see. It is visible at a glance. We err because this is more comfortable. *Alexander Solzhenitsyn, as quoted in Reader's Digest, Apr. 1974*

To err is human,
To forgive takes restraint;
To forget you forgave
Is the mark of a saint.
Suzanne Douglass, 1966

The road to wisdom? Well, it's plain
And simple to express:
Err
And err
And err again
But less
And less
And less.
Piet Hein

Some errors I forgive, though, quickly.
. . . Mine.
Richard Armour

* Pope's inspired transformation of an older proverb: "To err is human, to repent is divine, to persevere is diabolical" (T-190).

One ERROR always leads to another.

Coming EVENTS cast their shadows. *1803, WM-184*

What I am to be I am now becoming. *1936 office calendar*

EVERYBODY is wise after the event.

Hindsight is 20-20.

EVERYBODY loves a fat man.

. . . until he sits next to him in a bus.

Nobody loves a fat man. *Edmund Day, Round-Up*

Some fat men are good-natured, I suspect, because they can neither fight nor run.

Thin people are beautiful but fat people are adorable. *Jackie Gleason*

A friend to EVERYBODY is a friend to nobody. *1623, O2-227*

EVERYBODY'S doing it.

Custom makes sin no sin. *1576, T-136*

Never keep up with the Joneses. Drag them down to your level. It's cheaper. *Quentin Crisp*

EVERYONE has his cross to bear.

Each of us suffers his own hell. *Virgil, Aeneid*

Every back hath its pack.

It's a poor family that has neither a whore nor a thief in it. *1566, WM-479*

EVERYONE knows where his shoe pinches. *Geoffrey Chaucer, Merchant's Tale, 1386*

Everyone thinks his sack heaviest. *1611, T-579*

None knows the weight of another's burden. *1640, Herbert*

There is something the poor know that the rich do not know, something the sick know that people in good health do not know, something the stupid know that the intelligent do not know. *Gerald Brenan, Thoughts in a Dry Season*

See also Great SPIRIT . . . ; Where you STAND depends on where you sit; You measure everyone's CORN by your own bushel.

EVERYONE should row his own boat.

See PADDLE your own canoe.

EVERYONE to his taste.

. . . as the old woman said when she kissed her cow. *1546, Heywood*

Art is what you can get away with. *Marshall McLuhan*

EVERYTHING comes to him who waits. *1548, B-2440*

. . . especially old age. *Old postcard*

. . . except a borrowed book.

. . . except what he happens to be waiting for.

. . . except taxicabs on a rainy day.

. . . Like death, for instance.

. . . They come, but often come too late. *Violet Fane (Lady Mary M. Currie), ca. 1890*

. . . but no man wants everything. He usually wants one thing in particular—just that one which he never gets no matter how long he waits. *L. de V. Matthewman*

. . . but by the time they come, they're out of date.

. . . but you get it quicker if you go and fetch it.

All things come to the other fellow, while you sit and wait.

All things come too late for those who wait. *Elbert Hubbard*

Everything comes to him who hustles while he waits. *Thomas Edison, as quoted in the Golden Book Magazine, Apr. 1931*

He goes long barefoot that waits for dead men's shoes.

Know how to bide your time and sit tight. *Otto H. Kahn*

The secret of patience is doing something else in the meantime.

The things that come to those who wait are generally the things that no one else wants. *Old postcard*

All things come to him who waits
    If he waits in a place that's meet.
You can never catch an uptown bus
    On the downtown side of the street.

"All things come to him who waits."
    But here's a rule that's slicker
The man who goes for what he wants
    Will get it all the quicker.
Old postcard

Success may come
    To him who waits;
But, goodness, how
    It hesitates.
Robert Dennis

EVERYTHING happens to me.

Why me?

See also LIFE is so unfair.

EVERYTHING has an end. *1385, O-70*

. . . and a sausage has two. *1592, T-186*

Everything has an end and a piece of string has two.

EVERYTHING is relative.

Every mile is two in winter. *English proverb*

Some people can stay longer in an hour than others can in a week. *William Dean Howells*

Some words are not so absolute as they sound. Take the word "nothing." A woman who has nothing to wear also never has room in her closet. *John P. Grier*

The sound of a dinner bell travels half a mile a second, while an invitation to get up in the morning I have known to be three quarters of an hour going up two pairs of stairs, and then not have strength enough to be heard. *Josh Billings*

Time is relative—it depends on which side of the bathroom door you're on. *Peter's Almanac*

We all know how the size of sums of money appear to vary in a remarkable way according as they are being paid in or paid out. *Julian Huxley*

You never realize how short a month is until you pay alimony. *John Barrymore*

See also It all DEPENDS on whose ox is gored; Where you STAND depends on where you sit.

EVERYTHING that goes up must come down.

. . . except the cost of living. *Henny Youngman*

EVERYTHING takes longer than you think it will.

EVERYTHING will come out in the wash.

There is a time and place for EVERYTHING. *1509, O-225*

A fool is drunk all year, and sober on Purim [the one Jewish holiday when drunkenness is permitted]. *Yiddish proverb*

It's a sin to go to a wedding and come home sober. *Russian proverb*

When young, sow wild oats; when old, grow sage.

A windy day is not the day for thatching. *Irish proverb*

To every thing there is a season, and a time to every purpose under the heaven. *Ecclesiastes 3:1*

You can't have EVERYTHING.

. . . Where would you put it all?

He that will have all dies of madness. *1573, Sanford*

I may not yet have everything, but I already have too much. © *Ashleigh Brilliant*

You can have anything you want, but you can't have everything you want.

You can't have it both ways. *1911, F-208*

See also You can't have your CAKE and eat it too.

EVERYTHING'S got a moral, if only you can find it. *Lewis Carroll, Alice's Adventures in Wonderland, 1865*

Better a known EVIL than an unknown one. *1721, T-291*

The dread of something after death . . .
Makes us rather bear those ills we have
Than fly to others that we know not of.
Shakespeare, Hamlet 3.1.78

EVIL to him who evil thinks.

See If it sounds DIRTY, you have a dirty mind.

See no EVIL, hear no evil, speak no evil. *O-199*

. . . and eat no evil. *Nutritionist's advice*

I hear no evil, and see no evil—two out of three ain't bad.

It is better to say a good word about a bad fellow than a bad word about a good fellow. *Heard in Ontario*

It may be a sin to think evil of people, but it is seldom a mistake. *H. L. Mencken*

Nobody will tell you gossip if you don't listen. *Marlene Dietrich*

Sufficient unto the day is the EVIL thereof.* *Matthew 6:34*

*The word in the King James translation given as "evil" actually denotes trouble, adversity, misfortune. Matthew advises not to worry about having the proper food or clothing, but to have faith that God will provide for them even as he provides for "the lilies of the field." His concluding words mean, in effect, "There are troubles enough in this world."

The EVIL that men do lives after them; the good is often interred with their bones. *Shakespeare, Julius Caesar 3.2.1*

The evil that men do lives on the front page of greedy newspapers, but the good is often interred apathetically inside. *Brooks Atkinson*

The only thing necessary for the triumph of EVIL is for good men to do nothing.*

*Attributed to Edmund Burke (1729–97), in speeches by John Kennedy (1917–63), but the actual source is unclear, says Keyes (K-89–90).

Of two EVILS, choose the lesser. *Plato (ca. 428–348 B.C.), Protagoras*

Democracy is good. I say this because other systems are worse. *Jawaharlal Nehru, New York Times, Jan. 25, 1961*

. . . Brandy or gin, for instance; which will you have?

Fat sorrow is better than lean sorrow. *1678, Ray*

Marriage has many pains, but celibacy has no pleasures. *Samuel Johnson*

Of two evils, choose neither. *C. H. Spurgeon, John Ploughman*

Of two evils, choose the more enjoyable.

Of two evils, choose the one least likely to be gossiped about.

Of two evils, choose the prettier. *Carolyn Wells*

Of two evils, choose to be the least. *Ambrose Bierce*

Of two evils, when we tell ourselves we are choosing the lesser, we usually mean we are choosing the more comfortable. *Sydney J. Harris*

Politics . . . consists of choosing between the disastrous and the unpalatable. *John Kenneth Galbraith, 1969*

The poignancy of the human condition is not so much that our choices are usually between evils, rather than between good and evil, as that when we choose the lesser evil, it often turns out to be as bad as the other. *Sydney J. Harris*

When choosing between two evils, I always like to take the one I've never tried before. *Mae West*

When one has been threatened with a great injustice, one accepts a smaller as a favor. *Jane Welsh Carlyle, Journal*

EXAMPLE is better than precept. *Aesop (6th century B.C.), The Two Crabs*

A good example is the best sermon. *1732, Fuller*

Children are natural mimics—they imitate their parents in spite of every effort to teach them to behave properly. *Peter's Almanac*

He was advised to find a good example and follow it, so he became a counterfeiter.

Setting a good example for your children takes all the fun out of middle age. *William Feather*

There is just as much difference between precept and example, as there is between a horn that blows a noise and one that blows a tune. *Josh Billings*

See also ACTIONS speak louder than words; DEEDS, not creeds; PRACTICE what you preach.

A good EXAMPLE is the best sermon. *1732, Fuller*

To bring up a child in the way he should go—travel that way yourself. *Josh Billings, 1865*

See also ACTIONS speak louder than words.

The EXCEPTION proves the rule.* *1664, B-2014*

It's a bad rule that won't work both ways. *1837, WM-518*

*The original meaning of this proverb was that the exception *tests* the rule—that is, shows whether it needs more precise definition. With time, however, this proverb has taken on the additional meaning, "No rule is so general that it does not admit some exception."

Fair EXCHANGE is no robbery.* *1546, O-71*

A fair exchange is not much fun.

*Donald Bond explains that this proverb originally referred to the "forcible exchange of clothing made by a fugitive in order to disguise himself."

A poor EXCUSE is better than none. *1551, O-8*

. . . and a good excuse is one you can use over and over again.

False modesty is better than no modesty at all. *Vilhjalmur Stefansson*

It is better to offer no excuse than a bad one. *George Washington*

I am my own EXECUTIONER. *John Donne (1571–1631), Devotions*

A born loser is a guy who loses even in his fantasies.

A man's own self is his friend, a man's own self is his foe. *Bhagavad-Gita*

A man's worst enemies can't wish on him what he can think up himself. *Yiddish proverb*

A tyrant is most tyrant to himself. *1640, Herbert*

Beware of no man more than thy self. *1732, Fuller*

Every man is crucified upon the cross of himself. *Whittaker Chambers, Witness*

Fate has in store for men exactly what they are preparing for themselves. *Frederick H. Seymour*

He is most cheated who cheats himself. *Danish proverb*

If one views his problem closely enough, he will recognize himself as part of the problem.

If we were brought to trial for the crimes we have committed against ourselves, few would escape the gallows. *Paul Eldridge, Maxims for a Modern Man*

If you are in trouble and wish to find the party who is to blame for it, consult the looking-glass. *Old postcard*

Man is the only kind of varmint sets his own trap, baits it, then steps on it. *John Steinbeck, Sweet Thursday*

Most of the shadows of this life are caused by standing in our own sunshine.

None but myself ever did me any harm. *Napoleon, 1817*

The end of the human race will be that it will eventually die of civilization. *Ralph Waldo Emerson*

We are never deceived; we deceive ourselves. *Johann Wolfgang von Goethe*

See also Be careful of what you WISH for . . . ; A man is his own worst ENEMY; We have met the ENEMY, and he is us.

EXPERIENCE is the best teacher. *Latin proverb*

. . . but you learn things you don't want to know.

. . . but life is too short for a fool to complete the course.

. . . and the school of experience keeps raising its tuition fees.

. . . It gives you individual instruction. *Henny Youngman*

. . . but she sends terrific bills. *Minna Antrim, Naked Truth and Veiled Allusions*

. . . This is an argument advanced by people who have nothing going for them but experience. They also like to say, "You can't learn that in a book." (As an aside, I have often wondered how people who never read books can possibly know what can or cannot be learned in a book.) Actually, experience is a terrible teacher. Why in the world would anyone take six months to learn a thing that can be taught in twenty minutes? *Donald G. Smith*

A good scare is worth more to a man than good advice. *Ed Howe*

A handful of good life is better than a bushel of learning. *1623, T-287*

A man could retire nicely in his old age if he could dispose of his experience for what it cost him.

A man never knows how to be a son until he becomes a father.

A professor in a business course, lecturing his students, explained the difference between "education" and "experience" thus: "In reading a contract, education is what you get from reading the small print; experience is what you get from not reading it." *Sydney J. Harris*

About the best thing that experience can do for us is to teach us how to enjoy misery. *Josh Billings*

An old horse knows its way home. *Vermont proverb*

An ounce of experience is worth a pound of theory. *New England proverb*

An ounce of practice is generally worth more than a ton of theory. *E. F. Schumacher*

Analysis is not the only way to resolve inner conflicts. Life itself still remains a very effective therapist. *Karen Horney*

Before I got married I had six theories about bringing up children; now I have six children, and no theories. *Lord Rochester*

Creative activity could be described as a type of learning process where teacher and pupil are located in the same individual. *Arthur Koestler*

Evils must first be felt. *George Washington*

Experience enables you to recognize a mistake when you make it again. *Franklin P. Jones*

Experience gives wisdom to some and sadness to many.

Experience has the same effect on most folks that age has on a goose; it makes them tougher. *Josh Billings*

Experience is a revelation in the light of which we renounce our errors of youth for those of age. *Ambrose Bierce*

Experience is a school where a man learns what a big fool he has been. *Josh Billings*

Experience is an author's most valuable asset; experience is the thing that puts the muscle and breath and the warm blood into the book he writes. *Mark Twain, Is Shakespeare Dead? What Is Man? and Other Essays*

Experience is not what happens to a man. It is what a man does with what happens to him. *Aldous Huxley*

Experience is the worst teacher—it gives the test before presenting the lesson. *Vernon Law*

Few men are lucky enough to profit from their mistakes. I . . . have had fifty years of experience and I am still merrily making all the same old mistakes. *George Jean Nathan*

Good judgment comes from experience, and experience comes from bad judgment. *Larry LePatner*

I don't think much of a man who is not wiser today than he was yesterday. *Abraham Lincoln*

I learned more about economics from one South Dakota dust storm than I did in all my years in college. *Hubert Humphrey*

If we could sell our experiences for what they cost us, we'd all be millionaires. *Abigail Van Buren*

If you don't learn from your mistakes, there isn't much sense in making them. *Peter's Almanac*

Information's pretty thin stuff unless mixed with experience. *Clarence Day, The Crow's Nest*

Learn from the mistakes of others; you cannot possibly live long enough to make them all yourself.

Let the boys have a few rods of land that they may grow a few strawberries for market and thus earn a little pocket money. *Old Farmer's Almanac, 1891*

Man really knows nothing save what he has learned by his own experience. *Christopher M. Wieland*

Mistakes are the usual bridge between inexperience and wisdom. *Phyllis Theroux, Night Light*

Nothing ever becomes real till it is experienced—even a proverb is no proverb to you till your life has illustrated it. *John Keats, Letters*

Of course children should battle their parents; how else will they learn to battle the world? *Richard Needham*

One should not have to fall off of the roof to find out that it hurts. *Donald G. Smith*

One thorn of experience is worth a whole wilderness of warning. *James Russell Lowell*

The best of prophets of the future is the past. *Lord Byron, Journal*

The man who views the world at 50 the same as he did at 20 has wasted 30 years of his life. *Muhammad Ali, Playboy magazine, Nov. 1975*

The most permanent lessons in morals are those which come not of booky teaching, but of experience. *Mark Twain, A Tramp Abroad*

The person who has had a bull by the tail once has learned 60 or 70 times as much as a person who hasn't. *Mark Twain*

The thing experience teaches us is that experience teaches us nothing. *André Maurois*

The value of marriage is not that adults produce children but that children produce adults. *Peter De Vries*

The wise make of their mistakes a ladder; the foolish a grave. *Old postcard*

Today is yesterday's pupil. *1732, T-673*

Today teaches tomorrow.

We don't receive wisdom; we must discover it for ourselves after a journey that no one can take for us or spare us. *Marcel Proust*

What is all wisdom save a collection of platitudes? Take fifty of our current proverbial sayings—they are so trite, so threadbare, that we can hardly bring our lips to utter them. Nonetheless, they embody the concentrated experience of the race, and the man who orders his life according to their teaching cannot go far wrong. How easy it seems! But has anyone ever done so? Never. Has any man ever attained inner harmony by pondering the experience of others? Not since the world began. He must pass through the fire. *Norman Douglas*

Wise men learn by others' harms, fools by their own. *1670, O-72*

Wise men learn more from fools than fools from wise men. *Cato*

Years know more than books. *1651, Herbert*

You can't judge widows or horses without handling them. *Japanese proverb*

A man who is so dull
that he can learn only by personal experience
is too dull to learn
anything important by experience.
Don Marquis, "Archy on This and That

EXPERIENCE is the name everyone gives to their mistakes. *Oscar Wilde, Lady Windermere's Fan, 1893* *

Experience keeps a dear school, yet Fools will learn from no other. *Poor Richard's Almanac, 1743*

Experience teaches you to recognize a mistake when you've made it again.

The way to avoid mistakes is to gain experience. The way to gain experience is to make mistakes. *Peter's Almanac*

*Leo Rosten comments that this saying has also been attributed to Voltaire, G. K. Chesterton, Sydney Smith, and Samuel Butler, and that it is also a Jewish proverb.

See also To ERR is human, to forgive is divine.

The EXPERT is one who knows more and more about less and less. *Nicholas Murray Butler (1862–1947)*

. . . and the less he knows about more and more. *Charles Osgood, The Osgood Files (adapted)*

. . . until he knows everything about nothing at all.

An expert is someone called in at the last minute to share the blame. *Sam Ewing, Mature Living*

Never EXPLAIN: your friends don't need it and your enemies won't believe it. *Victor Grayson (1881–1920)*

Never complain, never explain. *Advice to politicians, attributed to Benjamin Disraeli, according to John Morley's Life of Gladstone*

You can't truthfully explain your smallest action without fully revealing your character. *Mignon McLaughlin*

EXTREMES meet. *Blaise Pascal, Pensées, 1662*

. . . said the zoo-goer as he saw the monkey put its tail in its mouth.

. . . and there is no better example than the naughtiness of humility. *Ralph Waldo Emerson*

An overflow of good converts to bad. *Shakespeare, Richard II 5.3.64*

Enemies, as well as lovers, come to resemble each other over a period of time. *Sydney J. Harris*

Virtue is more to be feared than vice, because its excesses are not subject to the regulation of conscience. *Albert J. Nock*

An EYE for an eye.*

*Life shall go for life, eye for eye, tooth for tooth, hand for hand, foot for foot. *Deuteronomy 19:21.* This principle, also known in Roman law as *lex talionis,* has been disparaged by many Christian writers as "primitive" and "severe," but deserves a closer look.

In the ancient world, there was no such thing as criminal law as we know it. The state itself punished only crimes against the state. Offenses against an individual were settled by private revenge or family feud, and it was for the injured party or clan to decide what price to exact in retaliation for the injury.

The Deuteronomic law replaced ruthless revenge with a rule of measure for measure. "An eye for an eye" meant that you could demand an eye from someone who has actually taken an eye, but not for the crime of peeping; "a hand for a hand" meant you could cut off the hand of someone who has cut off the hand of another, but not for stealing.

In Matthew 5:37–42, the apostle preaches that the Jewish law of "an eye for an eye" be replaced by the rule "Resist not evil: but whosoever shall smite thee on thy right cheek, turn to him the other also."

The EYE of the master does more work than both his hands. *Poor Richard's Almanac, 1744*

If you give orders and leave, the work won't get done. *Portuguese proverb*

One eye of the master sees more than ten of the servants'. *1640, Herbert*

Not to oversee workmen is to leave one's purse open. *New England proverb*

There's more to it than meets the EYE.

See APPEARANCES are deceiving; NOTHING is simple; You can't tell a BOOK by its cover.

FACTS are facts. *Robert Browning, The Ring and the Book, 1868*

A man should look for what is, and not for what he thinks should be. *Albert Einstein*

Aristotle could have avoided the mistake of thinking that women have fewer teeth than men by . . . asking Mrs. Aristotle to open her mouth. *Bertrand Russell*

Facts do not cease to exist because they are ignored. *Aldous Huxley, A Note on Dogma*

How empty is theory in presence of fact! *Mark Twain, A Connecticut Yankee in King Arthur's Court*

It is just as is and ain't no is-er. *Heard in Kentucky, Michigan, and Tennessee*

Let's look at the record. *Popularized in the speeches of New York Governor Alfred E. Smith*

No problem is too big to run away from. *Charles Schulz*

Truth is truth. *1576, T-686*

Words may varnish facts, but they cannot alter them. *H. J. Smith, 1911*

But facts are chiels that winna ding
An' downa be disputed.
Robert Burns, A Dream

FACTS are more eloquent than words.

But facts are chiels that winna ding,
And downa be disputed.
[But facts are quiet lads,
Who cannot be disputed.]
Robert Burns, A Dream

Facts speak louder than opinions.

Facts talk loud.

Facts are facts.

Facts don't lie.

FACTS are stubborn things. *Alain-René Lesage, 1715*

. . . and have upset many a perfectly good theory.

. . . but statistics are more pliable. *Fort Wayne News-Sentinel, ca. 1925*

A beautiful theory killed by a nasty, ugly little fact. *T. H. Huxley*

Don't confuse me with the facts; I've already made up my mind.

Facing it—always facing it—that's the way to get through. Face it! *Joseph Conrad*

Facts are stupid things. *Ronald Reagan, impromptu comment at the 1988 Republican National Convention, Time, Aug. 29, 1988*

If the facts do not conform to your theory, they must be disposed of. *N. R. F. Maier*

Never turn your back on reality. It surrounds you. *Stanislaw J. Lec*

Reality is for people who can't face drugs. *Peter's Almanac*

Truth is tough. It will not break, like a bubble, at a touch; you may kick it about all day like a football, and it will be round and full at evening. *Oliver Wendell Holmes, as quoted in Reader's Digest, June 1962*

See also EPPUR si muove.

FAITH is the substance of things hoped for, the evidence of things not seen. *Hebrews 11:1*

An atheist is a man with no invisible means of support. *Fulton J. Sheen, Look, Dec. 14, 1955*

A casual stroll through the lunatic asylum shows that faith does not prove anything. *Friedrich Nietzsche*

Convictions are more dangerous enemies of truth than lies. *Friedrich Nietzsche*

Faith: belief without evidence in what is told by one who speaks without knowledge, of things without parallel. *Ambrose Bierce*

Faith in a holy cause is to a considerable extent a substitute for the lost faith in ourselves. *Eric Hoffer, The True Believer*

Faith is a knowledge within the heart, beyond the reach of proof. *Kahlil Gibran*

Faith is a necessity to man. Woe to him who believes nothing. *Victor Hugo*

Faith is believing what you know ain't so. *Mark Twain, Pudd'nhead Wilson's New Calendar*

Faith is knowing there is an ocean because you have seen a brook. *William Arthur Ward*

Faith may be defined briefly as an illogical belief in the occurrence of the improbable. *H. L. Mencken*

Hope is the feeling that the feeling you have isn't permanent. *Jean Kerr*

If it weren't for faith, there would be no living in this world. We couldn't even eat hash with any safety, if it weren't for faith. *Josh Billings*

If you gain, you gain all; if you lose, you lose nothing. Wager then, without hesitation, that He exists. *Blaise Pascal*

One goldfish told the other, "Of course there is a God. Who do you think changes the water?" *Richard Needham*

Nothing that is worth doing can be achieved in a lifetime; therefore we must be saved by hope.

Nothing which is true or beautiful or good makes complete sense in any immediate context of history; therefore we must be saved by faith.

Nothing we do, however virtuous, can be accomplished alone; therefore we are saved by love.

Reinhold Niebuhr, on the three Christian virtues (faith, hope, and charity), The Irony of American History

Religion is caught, not taught. *Henrik Ibsen*

The miserable have no other medicine but only hope. *Shakespeare, Measure for Measure 3.1.2.*

The mythologist Joseph Campbell tells of a priest who once asked him, "Would you believe in God if I could prove to you that God exists?" Replied Campbell, "If you could prove that God exists, what would be the need of faith?"

The nonbeliever says: "Show me God and I will believe in Him." The believer answers: "Believe in God and He will show himself to you." *Michel Paul Richard*

The people who teach us that it is wrong to be skeptical are themselves the reasons that we should be skeptical. *Donald G. Smith*

The reason why birds can fly and we can't is simply that they have perfect faith, for to have faith is to have wings. *James M. Barrie, The Little White Bird*

What is faith unless it is to believe what you do not see? *Saint Augustine*

You can do very little with faith, but you can do nothing without it. *Samuel Butler*

There lives more faith in honest doubt,
. . . than in half the creeds.
Alfred, Lord Tennyson

FAITH will move mountains.

. . . but not furniture.

If ye have FAITH as a grain of mustard seed . . . nothing is impossible unto you. *Matthew 17:20*

I'm just moving clouds today—tomorrow I'll try mountains. © *Ashleigh Brilliant*

FAITH without works is dead. *James 2:26*

Hope is all right and so is Faith, but what I would like to see is a little Charity. *Don Marquis*

In order to be a realist you must believe in miracles. *David Ben-Gurion*

See also ACTIONS speak louder than words; DEEDS, not creeds.

Keep the FAITH, baby.*

. . . Better yet—spread it around. *Church sign*

*I have fought a good fight . . . I have kept the faith. *2 Timothy 4:7*

FAME is the spur.* *John Milton* (1608–74)

If fame is to come only after death, I am in no hurry for it. *Martial*

Honour and renown,
A spur to valiant and magnanimous deed.
Shakespeare, Troilus and Cressida 2.2.199

*Fame is the spur that the clear spirit doth raise
(That last infirmity of noble mind).
Lycidas

FAMILIARITY breeds contempt. *Aesop (6th century B.C.), The Fox and the Lion*

. . . and children. *Mark Twain, Notebook*

. . . and self-contempt breeds contempt for others.

. . . only applies to men, not to hot buckwheat cakes well buttered and maple-sugared. *Josh Billings*

. . . but you can't breed without familiarity. *Nicolas Slonimsky, Perfect Pitch*

. . . This is so—just as soon as we get familiarized with castor oil, for instance, we contempt it. *Josh Billings, 1865*

A maker of images never worships the gods. *Chinese proverb*

A platitude is simply a truth repeated till people get tired of hearing it. *Stanley Baldwin, 1924*

A president likes to keep on good terms with the press corps because unfamiliarity breeds contempt.

"As long as you remain a stranger, we will be your friend forever." This expresses the attitude of the true misanthrope, who holds that "Familiarity doesn't breed contempt, it *is* contempt." *Florence King, With Charity Toward None: A Fond Look at Misanthropy*

Familiarity breeds consent.

Familiarity breeds. *Howard Kandel*

Familiarity just as frequently leads to affectionate friendship and, even more often, to deep love and trust. *George Jean Nathan*

Getting anything changes it from being desirable to just being taken for granted.

He will never worship well the image on the altar who knew it when it was a trunk of wood in the garden. *Spanish proverb*

In politics, familiarity doesn't breed contempt. It breeds voters. *Paul Lazarsfeld*

Marriage must incessantly contend with a monster that devours everything: familiarity. *Honoré de Balzac, The Physiology of Marriage*

Most human beings have an almost infinite capacity for taking things for granted. *Aldous Huxley, Themes and Variations*

My wife said I don't listen to her—at least I think that's what she said. *Peter's Almanac*

Nothing is so good as it seems beforehand. *George Eliot, Silas Marner*

Nothing is wonderful when you get used to it. *Ed Howe*

Of course it's possible to love a human being if you don't know them too well. *Charles Bukowski, Notes of a Dirty Old Man*

Sweets grown common lose their dear delight. *Shakespeare, Sonnet 102*

The nearer the church the farther from God. *ca. 1536, T-101*

The penalty for success is to be bored by the people who used to snub you. *Nancy Astor*

There's an element of truth in every idea that lasts long enough to be called corny. *Irving Berlin*

Those near the temple insult the god. *Chinese proverb*

Though familiarity may not breed contempt, it takes the edge off admiration. *William Hazlitt, 1821*

When you have something in your hand, its charm flees. *Iraqi proverb*

Yesterday's avant-garde experience is today's chic and tomorrow's cliché. *Richard Hofstadter, Anti-Intellectualism in American Life*

Like old accustomed spots upon the wall,
Familiar faults seem hardly faults at all.
Arthur Guiterman

See also DISTANCE lends enchantment.

The FAMILY that prays together stays together.*

Comes autumn, the family that rakes together aches together.

Don't pray for lighter burdens, but for stronger backs.

If it seems a childish thing to do, do it in remembrance that you are a child. *Frederick Buechner, Wishful Thinking: A Theological ABC*

Mafia—the family that preys together.

Prayer is less about changing the world than it is about changing ourselves. *David J. Wolpe, Teaching Your Children About God*

The family that pulls taffy together sticks together.

There's plenty o' peace in any home where the family keeps scattered an' don't make the mistake o' tryin' to git together. *Kin Hubbard*

*According to Oxford (O-76), this saying was invented by Al Scalpone, British writer of radio commercials, and was used as the slogan of Father Patrick Peyton's Family Rosary Crusade. The slogan was first broadcast on Peyton's radio show Mar. 6, 1947.

Inside every FAT person is a thin person trying to get out.*

A heavy body weighs down the spirit. *Marlene Dietrich*

Every dentist would like to be a doctor and inside every photographer is a painter trying to get out. *Pablo Picasso*

Fat people are today's lepers. *Sondra Gotlieb*

In every fat book there is a thin book trying to get out.

Inside every 70-year-old is a 35-year-old asking, "What happened?" *Ann Landers*

Inside every copywriter is a novelist trying to get out. *New York Times, May 14, 1990, on an advertising man who became a novelist-publisher*

Inside every large problem is a small problem struggling to get out. Inside every small problem is a larger problem struggling to get out. *Arthur Bloch*

Outside every thin woman is a fat man trying to get in. *Katherine Whitehorn*

*Imprisoned in every fat man, a thin one is wildly signalling to be let out. *Cyril Connolly*. The inspiration for this statement and those that followed was possibly a line written by Nietzsche: "In every real man, a child is hidden that wants to play."

Like FATHER, like son. *Latin proverb*

. . . Marry son.

Heredity is something every man believes in until his own son begins acting like a darn fool. *Old postcard*

No branch is better than its trunk. *Japanese proverb*

The pumpkin vine never bears watermelons. *Belizean proverb*

There is inherited wealth in this country and also inherited poverty. *John F. Kennedy, address at Amherst College, Oct. 26, 1963*

See also The APPLE doesn't fall far from its tree; Many a good COW has a bad calf.

FAULTS are thick where love is thin. *1659, Howell*

The only thing we have to FEAR is fear itself.*

. . . but of fear itself I'm scared to death. © *Ashleigh Brilliant*

All fear is bondage. *1573, OE-195*

If I knew what I was so anxious about, I wouldn't be so anxious. *Mignon McLaughlin*

Never let the fear of striking out get in your way. *Babe Ruth*

Recalling Hitler's success in spreading the Big Lie, columnist Roger Simon bemoans man's vulnerability to propaganda and concludes, "We have nothing to fear but ourselves."

*So first of all let me assert my firm belief that the only thing we have to fear is fear itself. *F. D. Roosevelt, first inaugural address, 1933.* Keyes (K-103) lists variants of the phrase FDR popularized, from the writings of Montaigne (1580), Francis Bacon (1623), Duke of Wellington (1832), and Thoreau (1851).

Fine FEATHERS do not make a peacock.

Fine feathers make a fine bird, at night, when all cats are gray. *1931, BJW-217*

The fair feathers make fair fowls,
But some have fair feathers and look like owls. *1611, O2-202*

God makes and apparel shapes. *1670, Ray*

Dress a monkey as you will, it remains a monkey still. *1550, Erasmus*

Puttin' feathers on a buzzard don't make it no eagle. *Heard in Nebraska*

Fine FEATHERS make fine birds. *1583 (F-61)*

. . . extinct.

. . . until it comes time to fly. *Mignon McLaughlin*

. . . No! Fine birds make fine feathers.

See also CLOTHES make the man.

Every FELLOW ought to cut his own fodder.

See PADDLE your own canoe.

Good FENCES make good neighbors.* *1640, O-98*

. . . more comfortable while they gossip.

A hedge between keeps friendship green. *1707, WM-295.* Contemporary parody: A fence between makes love more keen.

Love your neighbor, yet pull not down your hedge. *1651, Herbert*

I like long walks, specially when they are taken by people who annoy me. *Fred Allen*

The fence that makes good neighbors needs a gate to make good friends. *Jacob M. Braude*

Visit your neighbor lest an unused path becomes weedy. *Heard in Ontario*

Withdraw thy foot from thy neighbour's house; lest he be weary of thee, and so hate thee. *Proverbs 25:17*

*Theme of Robert Frost's 1914 poem "The Mending Wall." Frost's message seems to be that "good fences" are apt to keep people from really knowing each other, an irony sometimes overlooked when the poet's use of this proverb is cited.

FIGHT the good fight.*

Be ashamed to die until you have won some victory for humanity. *Horace Mann, commencement address, Antioch College, 1859*

*I have fought the good fight, I have finished my course, I have kept the faith. *2 Timothy 4:7*

Let you and him FIGHT.

I have already given two cousins to the war and I stand ready to sacrifice my wife's brother. *Artemus Ward*

Older men declare war. But it is youth that must fight and die. *Herbert Hoover, Republican National Convention speech, June 27, 1944*

He that FIGHTS and runs away may live to fight another day.*

Although always prepared for martyrdom, I preferred that it should be postponed. *Winston Churchill*

Beat it while the going is good. *Old postcard*

Better to be called a coward than a corpse. *Heard in Oregon*

Courage is the fear of being thought a coward. *Horace Smith*

He who courts and runs away lives to court another day. *Henny Youngman*

He who fights and runs away lives.

He who fights and runs away may live to take flight another day. *Peter's Almanac*

He who stops to look each way lives to cross the street another day.

If God wanted us to be so brave, why did he give us legs? *Marvin Kitman*

Many would be cowards if they had courage enough. *1732, Fuller*

Of the thirty-six ways to fight, the best is to flee. *Japanese proverb*

The human race is a race of cowards, and I am not only marching in that procession but carrying a banner. *Mark Twain*

The only lions that get to be big lions are lions who know when to be a little chicken. *Malcolm Forbes*

. . . but he that is in battle slain
Will never rise to fight again.
J. Ray, History of the Rebellion

*Oliver Goldsmith's rendering of a Greek proverb on the futility of fighting a losing battle.

See also DISCRETION is the better part of valor.

No FIGS from thistles.*

*Do men gather grapes of thorns, or figs of thistles? Matthew 7:16

FIGURES don't lie.

. . . but liars figure. *C. H. Grosvenor*

. . . but a girdle condenses the truth. *Louis Safian*

Figures often beguile me, particularly when I have the arranging of them myself. *Mark Twain, Autobiography*

See also There are three kinds of LIES: lies, damned lies, and statistics.

FIGURES fool when fools figure.

I abhor averages. . . . A man may have six meals one day and none the next, making an average of three meals per day, but that is not a good way to live. *Louis D. Brandeis, Frankel, Curse of Bigness, An Interview (p. 46, McNamara)*

Mathematics has given economics rigor, but alas, also mortis. *Robert Heilbroner*

See also There are three kinds of LIES: lies, damned lies, and statistics.

FINDERS keepers, losers weepers. *Children's chant, 1824; WM-208*

See POSSESSION is nine points of the law.

Give a FINGER and they'll want a hand. 1640, *Herbert*

Allow a camel's nose beneath your tent, and his whole body will follow soon.

Give a man some cloth and he'll ask for some lining. *Turkish proverb*

Give a man a free hand and he'll run it all over you. *Mae West*

See also You're never SATISFIED.

FINGERS were made before forks.* 1567, O-80

"Once invoked to excuse eating with the fingers before others," says Flexner (F-62).

A little spark kindles a great FIRE. 1412, WM-555

A little fire is quickly trodden out;
Which, being suffer'd, rivers cannot quench.
Shakespeare, 3 Henry VI 4.8.7

See also Mighty OAKS from little acorns grow.

Fight FIRE with fire. *Michel de Montaigne, Essays*

Fire does not produce fire, it produces ashes. *African proverb*

Never wrap yourself in the false dignity of refusing to sink to someone else's level. If it is necessary to go to the gutter to make your point, then do so, but leave no volley unanswered. *Donald G. Smith*

The trouble with "fighting fire with fire" is that you can so easily end in universal holocaust. In the very act of "defeating" your enemy, you become more like him, and the values you are presumably fighting for become subverted to the aims of victory. It is not an easy question to resolve. It is one on which, as Lincoln said, good men will disagree. *Sydney J. Harris*

FIRE is a good servant but a bad master.
1580, WM-209

Is not whiskey a wonderful thing? But like fire, a good servant but a bad master. *1973, BJW-225*

If you play with FIRE, you'll get burnt.
1655, O-179

He that touches pitch, shall be defiled therewith. *Ecclesiasticus 13:1*

He who plays with cats must bear the scratches. *Algerian proverb*

Nobody has the right to shout "FIRE" in a crowded theater. *

Your liberty to swing your arms ends where my nose begins. *Quoted by Stuart Chase in Vital Speeches of the Day*

*This saying is probably a shortened, sharpened paraphrase of this 1919 legal commentary: "The most stringent protection of free speech would not protect a man in falsely shouting fire in a theatre and causing a panic" (Oliver Wendell Holmes, Jr. Schenck v. United States).

Three moves is as bad as a FIRE. *Poor Richard's Almanac*

FIRST come, first served. *1400, B-1348*

He who comes late must eat what is left.

Thirst come—thirst served. *Coca-Cola Slogan, 1932*

Who cometh late, lodgeth ill. *1573, OE-104*

FIRST things first. *Slogan of Alcoholics Anonymous; 1894, O-82*

. . . second things never. *Shirley Conran*

But should I call a caucus of my different selves, who would serve as chairman? *Christopher Morley*

How important is it? *Slogan of Alcoholics Anonymous*

If people concentrated on the really important things in life, there'd be a shortage of fishing poles. *Doug Larson*

Last gets the hash. *Heard in Kentucky and New York*

The FIRST hundred years are the hardest. *

*Life's a tough proposition—and the first hundred years are the hardest. *Wilson Mizner (1876–1933).*

A FISH stinks from the head. *1581, F-64*

The corruption of state is first discernible in the higher classes. *Winston Churchill, 1915*

Big FISH eat little fish. *1200, O-18*

The Vermin only teaze and pinch
Their Foes superior by an Inch.
So Nat'ralists observe, a Flea
Hath smaller Fleas that on him prey;
And these have smaller still to bite 'em,
And so proceed ad infinitum.
Jonathan Swift, On Poetry: A Rhapsody

Great fleas have little fleas upon their backs
    to bite 'em,
And little fleas have lesser fleas, and so *ad infinitum.*
And the great fleas themselves, in turn, have
    greater fleas to go on;
While these again have greater still, and
    greater still, and so on.
Augustus De Morgan, A Budget of Paradoxes

In Shakespeare's *Pericles, Prince of Tyre, 12.1.29*, two fishermen "marvel [at] how fish live in the sea" and how "the great ones eat up the little ones," a commentary on the human struggle that the play portrays.

FISH and visitors stink after three days.* 1580, WM-212

A guest is like rain: when he lingers on, he becomes a nuisance. *Yiddish proverb*

An unbidden guest is welcome when gone. *1546, Heywood*

Even a welcome guest is a nuisance after three days. *Japanese proverb*

Santa Claus has the right idea: Visit people once a year. *Victor Borge*

Visits always give pleasure—if not the arrival, the departure. *Portuguese proverb*

When guests stay too long, try treating them like members of the family. If they don't leave then, they never will. *Martin Ragaway*

*Since the time of ancient Rome, three days seems to be the agreed-upon limit of a visit. Around 200 B.C. the comic playwright Plautus warned, "No guest is so welcome that he will not become a nuisance after three days in a friend's house."

FISH or cut bait. 1876, WM-213

Fish or I'll cut you into bait. *1968, BJW-229*

If you wish to drown, do not torture yourself with shallow water. *Bulgarian proverb*

Shit or get off the pot.

Give me a FISH and I will eat today; teach me to fish and I will eat all my life.

You have a shilling. I have a shilling. We swap. You have my shilling and I have yours. We are no better off. But suppose you have an idea and I have an idea. We swap. Now you have two ideas and I have two ideas. We have increased our stock of ideas 100 percent. *A. S. Gregg*

There are plenty more FISH in the sea. 1573, O-83

. . . and it helps if you have the right bait.

Never run after a woman or a streetcar: there'll be another along in a few minutes. *Heard in Michigan and New York*

See also Why buy a COW when you can get milk free?

FLATTERY will get you nowhere. 1954, WM-215

A gossip is one who talks to you about others; a bore is one who talks to you about himself; a brilliant conversationalist is one who talks to you about yourself. *Lisa Kirk, New York Journal-American, Mar. 9, 1954*

A flattering mouth worketh ruin. *Proverbs 26:28*

A man that flattereth his neighbor spreadeth a net for his feet. *Proverbs 29:5*

Flattery is all right—if you don't inhale. *Adlai Stevenson, 1961*

Flattery is the floating cockroach in the milk of human kindness. *Hot Metal, TV show*

Flattery, like perfume, should be smelled, not swallowed. *Josh Billings, 1858*

Flattery will get you anywhere.

Flattery's hard to handle, but most of us would like more practice. *Malcolm Forbes*

He who cannot love must learn to flatter. *Johann Wolfgang von Goethe*

I hate careless flattery, the kind that exhausts you in your effort to believe it. *Wilson Mizner*

If a man flatters you, you can calculate he is a rogue, or you are a fool. *Josh Billings*

If a man is vain, flatter. If timid, flatter. If boastful, flatter. In all history, too much flattery never lost a gentleman. *Kathryn Cravens, Pursuit of Gentlemen*

Mountains of gold would not seduce some men, yet flattery would break them down. *Henry Ward Beecher*

Only two groups of people fall for flattery—men and women.

Remember that a man's name is to him the sweetest and most important sound in any language. *Dale Carnegie, How to Win Friends and Influence People*

Sometimes we think we dislike flattery, but it is only the way it is done that we dislike. *François de la Rochefoucauld*

The truest test of independent judgment is being able to dislike someone who admires us, and to admire someone who dislikes us. *Sydney J. Harris, as quoted in Reader's Digest, Jan. 1974*

To seduce most anyone, ask for and listen to his opinion. *Malcolm Forbes*

We recognize that flattery is poison, but its perfume intoxicates us. *Marquis de la Grange, Pensées*

What really flatters a man is that you think him worth flattering. *G. B. Shaw, John Bull's Other Island*

You can flatter anyone by telling him that he is the kind of a person who can't be flattered. *Peter's Almanac*

'Tis an old maxim in the schools,
That flattery's the food of fools;
Yet now and then your men of wit
Will condescend to take a bit.
Jonathan Swift, Cadenus and Vanessa

See also All is VANITY; PRAISE is always pleasant.

When you've got it—FLAUNT it. George Lois

Let it all hang out. *Catchphrase of Laugh-In, 1960s TV show*

Never advertise what you don't have for sale. *A parent's advice*

She laughs at everything you say. Why? Because she has fine teeth. *Poor Richard's Almanac*

With the great part of rich people, the chief employment of riches consists in the parade of riches. *Adam Smith, The Wealth of Nations, 1776.* A hundred years later, Thorstein Veblen, in his *Theory of the Leisure Class* (1899), "originated" the concept of conspicuous consumption, observing that "conspicuous consumption of valuable goods is a means of reputability to the gentleman of leisure."

See also THEM that has it shows it.

All FLESH is grass.*

We shall die all. *Sundial inscription in a London courtyard*

The steed bit his master;
　　How came this to pass?
He heard the good pastor
　　Cry, "All flesh is grass."

*All flesh is grass, and all the goodliness thereof is as the flower of the field. *Isaiah 40:6.* Compare with 1 Peter 1:24.
　　Latin scholars reminded themselves of man's mortality by displaying a human skull, called *memento mori* ("remember thou must die"). A favorite Latin proverb on this grim theme is a translation of the line from Genesis, "dust thou art, and unto dust thou shalt return": *terra es, terram ibis.*

See also ASHES to ashes, dust to dust; All MEN are mortal; LIFE is short.

You can catch more FLIES with honey than with vinegar. *1666, Torriano*

. . . Keep that in mind next time you want a swarm of flies.

. . . but nothing beats blackmail at securing the absolute allegiance. *M. A. Sharp, Sunflower*

More people are flattered into virtue than bullied out of vice. *Robert S. Surtees, The Analysis of the Hunting Field, 1846; M-714*

Tart words make no friends; a spoonful of honey will catch more flies than a gallon of vinegar. *Poor Richard's Almanac*

Vinegar never catches flies,
So don't be sour in your replies.•
Old postcard

Take time to stop and smell the FLOWERS. *Walter C. Hagen (1892–1969)*

Establishing goals is all right if you don't let them deprive you of interesting detours. *Doug Larson*

Every once in a while, take the scenic route. *H. Jackson Brown, Jr., Life's Little Instruction Book*

I think it pisses God off if you walk by the color purple in a field somewhere and don't notice it. *Alice Walker, The Color Purple*

I'd rather have roses on my table than diamonds 'round my neck. *Emma Goldman*

Lie on your back and look at the stars. *H. Jackson Brown, Jr., Life's Little Instruction Book*

Nanny goat's advice to her kids: Take time to stop and eat some flowers.

The philosophical shoplifter takes time to stop and steal some flowers.

The world is a rose; smell it and pass it to your friends. *Persian proverb*

All is FLUX. *Heracleitus (6th century B.C.)*

Wasting time is an important part of living. © *Ashleigh Brilliant*

A newspaper is lumber made malleable. It is ink made into words and pictures. It is conceived, born, grows up and dies of old age in a day. *Jim Bishop, Quill, Oct. 1963*

All things change, and we change with them. *Latin proverb*

All things change, but the nature of things doesn't change.

In the future everybody will be world famous for fifteen minutes. *Andy Warhol, 1968*

It is change, not love, that makes the world go round—love only keeps it populated. *Charles H. Brower, as quoted in Reader's Digest, Oct. 1960*

Keep changing. When you're through changing, you're through. *Bruce Barton*

My book changes so often that they say it goes to press every 20 minutes. *Amy Vanderbilt, author of The New Complete Book of Etiquette*

Remember that there is nothing stable in human affairs; therefore avoid undue elation in prosperity, or undue depression in adversity. *Isocrates*

The art of progress is to preserve order amid change and to preserve change amid order. *Alfred North Whitehead*

The only man who behaves sensibly is my tailor; he takes my measure anew every time he sees me, whilst all the rest go on with their old measurements, and expect them to fit me. *G. B. Shaw, as quoted in Reader's Digest, Sept. 1938*

The only thing sure about luck is that it will change. *Bret Harte, as quoted in Reader's Digest, May 1933*

Today's newspaper is tomorrow's fish-wrapper. *Ben Hecht*

When we got there, there wasn't any there there. *Gertrude Stein, on arriving in San Francisco*

The world's a bubble; and the life of man,
Is less than a span.
Francis Bacon, The World

See also O tempora! o mores!; Other DAYS, other ways.

A FOOL and his money are soon parted. 1573, O-84

. . . but memories of the orgy will last a lifetime. *Old postcard*

. . . and it's a wonder they ever got together in the first place.

. . . Who got yours? *Henny Youngman*

A fool and his money are soon accepted in the highest social circles.

A fool and his money are soon elected.

A fool and his money are soon partied. *Old postcard*

A fool and his money are soon spotted.

A fool and his money throw some party.

A rich man and his daughter are soon parted. *Kin Hubbard*

A widow and her money are soon courted.

He who buys what he needs not, sells what he needs. *Japanese proverb*

If a fool and his money are soon parted, why are there so many rich fools?

If a fool and his money were not easily parted, some people would never know the meaning of a real good time.

It don't make no difference what it is, a woman'll buy anything she thinks a store is losin' money on. *Kin Hubbard*

Johnny's uncle had just come for a visit and upon his departure, he gave the youngster a bright half-dollar.

"Be careful with that coin," he advised. "Remember that a fool and his money are soon parted."

"Yes, Uncle," said Johnny, "but just the same I want to thank you for parting with it." *Evan Esar's Comic Dictionary*

The feller that ventures out after dark an' his money are soon parted. *Kin Hubbard*

The man who has money to burn never has to wait long to meet his match. *Old postcard*

The racetrack is a place where windows clean people. *Cross-stitched motto that hung on the wall in the home of Virginia Kelley, President Clinton's mother, who made no secret of her fondness for horseracing*

There are two times in a man's life when he should not speculate: when he can't afford it, and when he can. *Mark Twain*

When one has to work so hard to get money, why should he impose on himself the further hardship of trying to save it? *Don Herold*

You can get poor a lot faster than you can get rich. *Bud Miller*

A FOOL can ask more questions in an hour than a wise man can answer in seven years. 1666, *Torriano*

. . . No wonder so many of us flunk our exams!

. . . [Therefore] intelligence does not consist in providing the right answers so much as it does in framing the right questions. *Sydney J. Harris*

It must have been some unmarried fool that said "A child can ask questions that a wise man cannot answer"; because, in any decent house, a brat that starts asking questions is promptly packed off to bed. *Arthur Binstead, Pitcher's Proverbs*

There are no dumb questions—only dumb answers. *Marshall Loeb*

A FOOL for luck, a poor man for children.

See The RICH get richer, and the poor get children.

Even a FOOL, when he holds his peace, is counted wise.

See SILENCE is golden.

FOOL me once, shame on you; fool me twice, shame on me.

. . . and the biggest fool is the man who fools himself.

He that stumbles twice at the same stone deserves to have his shins broke. *1552, Taverner*

If a bee stings you once, it's the bee's fault; if a bee stings you twice, it's your own damn fault. *Heard in Kansas*

If a man deceives me once, shame on him; if he deceives me twice, he's got nothing to be ashamed of. *L. L. Levinson*

If a man steals from you once, he's a fool; if a man steals from you twice, you're a fool; if he steals from you three times, chances are the thief and the agency you're paying for theft protection are one and the same.

I'll trust by leisure him that mocks me once. *Shakespeare, Titus Andronicus 1.1.301*

It is more shameful to distrust one's friends than to be deceived by them. *François de la Rochefoucauld*

Nobody but a fool gets bit twice by the same dog. *Josh Billings*

You can fool a fool the same way three or four times. *Ed Howe*

There's no FOOL like an educated fool.

A highbrow is a person educated beyond his intelligence. *Brander Matthews, Epigrams*

A learned fool is one who has read everything, and simply remembers what he has read. *Josh Billings*

Education does not make us smarter, it merely propels us further and faster in the direction of our native abilities; and if one's ability is to make a fool of himself, education can help him do a magnificent job of that. *Sydney J. Harris*

I hate books, for they only teach people to talk about what they don't understand. *Jean-Jacques Rousseau, Émile*

There is nothing so stupid as an educated man, if you get him off the thing he was educated in. *Will Rogers*

See also EXPERIENCE is the best teacher; An ounce of HORSE SENSE is worth a pound of book learning.

There's no FOOL like an old fool. *1546, Heywood*

. . . You just can't beat experience.

. . . but young fools combine foolishness and ignorance in a way that can't be beat!

As men grow older, their opinions, like their diseases, grow chronic. *Josh Billings, 1865*

Love is like the measles, all the worse when it comes late in life. *Douglas Jerrold*

Old fools are babes again. *Shakespeare, King Lear 1.3.19*

Old men are fond of giving good advice to console themselves for their inability to give bad examples. *François de la Rochefoucauld*

Some folks as they grow older grow wise, but most folks simply grow stubborner. *Josh Billings*

There's no fool like an oiled fool. *Judge, ca. 1925*

When the teeth fall out, the tongue wags loose. *Chinese proverb*

Young men think old men fools, and old men know young men to be so. *1577, O2-739*

Mexican speech is traditionally accompanied by hand gestures, and when a speaker touches his eyetooth, he signals the Spanish proverb "An old dog has very long eyeteeth"; which is to say, "Don't try to fool me; I'm too old to fall for that sort of thing."

See also There's no cure for old AGE; We get too soon OLD and too late smart.

You can FOOL some of the people all of the time, and all of the people some of the time, but you cannot fool all of the people all of the time. *Abraham Lincoln (attributed), 1858**

. . . However, you can make a fool of yourself anytime.

. . . Don't be greedy; fooling some of the people all of the time is good enough.

It is wise to remember that you are one of those who can be fooled some of the time. *Laurence Peter*

The average politician is contented with a sizeable majority. *Detroit News, ca. 1925*

The trouble with this country is that there are too many politicians who believe, with a conviction based on experience, that you can fool all of the people all of the time. *Franklin P. Adams, Nods and Becks*

We can be more clever than one, but not more clever than all. *François de la Rochefoucauld*

You can fool all of the people all of the time if the advertising is right and the budget is big enough. *Joseph Levine (attributed)*

You can fool all of the people some of the time, but the rest of the time they will have to make fools of themselves.

You can fool too many of the people too much of the time. *James Thurber, Thurber Carnival*

You can't fool all of the people all of the time, but you can fool enough of them all of the time to hold your head up in society. *Kin Hubbard*

You don't have to fool all the people all the time—just the right people part of the time.

*The saying does not appear in Lincoln's published writings, but may have been made in an unpublished speech. According to Keyes, (K-96), "Lincoln scholars don't give much credence" to claims that Lincoln said it. The saying has also been ascribed to P. T. Barnum (B-534).

FOOLS make feasts and wise men eat them. *1573, T-233*

Fools build houses and wise men buy them. *1670, T-232*

Set a fool to roast eggs, and a wise man to eat them. *1678, Ray*

FOOLS rush in where angels fear to tread. Alexander Pope, An Essay on Criticism, 1711

Before you mess with a fool, make sure it's a fool you're messing with.

[Broadway] angels rush in . . . where even fools fear to tread. *S. Dean, 1959; BJW-237*

The biggest cause of trouble in the world today is that the stupid people are so sure about things and the intelligent folks are so full of doubts. *Bertrand Russell*

Courage is often just ignorance of the facts. *Henny Youngman*

Fools rush in and take the best seats.

Fools rush in where angels fear to wed. *Poor Richard Jr.'s Almanack, 1906*

I have found a great many things in this world that were free—free to get into, but like a rat trap, not exactly free to get out of. *Josh Billings, 1865*

In the stock market, fools rush in where wise men fear to trade. *Peter's Almanac*

It is the dull man who is always sure, and the sure man who is always dull. *H. L. Mencken*

Love is an exploding cigar we willingly smoke. *Lynda Barry*

The wise man said, "It can't be done"; the fool came and did it. *Heard in Kentucky and Tennessee*

To a fool the ocean is knee-deep. *Ukrainian proverb*

FOOLS should not see half-done work. *1721, O-85*

Fools and bairns should not see half-done work. *1721, Kelly; O2-217*

What FOOLS these mortals be! *Shakespeare, a Midsummer Night's Dream 3.2.115*

All men are fools, but all fools are not men. *Heard in California*

April 1. This is the day upon which we are reminded of what we are on the other three hundred and sixty-four. *Mark Twain, Pudd'nhead Wilson's New Calendar*

Before a man speaks it is always safe to assume that he is a fool. After he speaks, it is seldom necessary to assume it. *Oscar Wilde*

Fame is proof that the people are gullible. *Ralph Waldo Emerson*

Fop: A fool, glad to be what he is. *Charles Narrey*

If you wish to avoid seeing a fool you must first break your mirror. *François Rabelais*

It is dreadfully easy to be a fool—a man can be one and not know it. *Josh Billings, 1865*

It is human nature to think wisely and act foolishly. *Anatole France*

Let us be thankful for the fools. But for them the rest of us could not succeed. *Mark Twain, Pudd'nhead Wilson's New Calendar*

Man is a clever animal who behaves like an imbecile. *Albert Schweitzer*

Man is a complex being: he makes deserts bloom and lakes die. *Gil Stern*

Man is the only animal that feels insulted when called an animal.

Man is the only animal that goes to sleep when he is not sleepy, and wakes up when he is.

Nobody ever went broke underestimating the intelligence of the American people. *H. L. Mencken (attributed).* Keyes (K-177) notes that Mencken associates say they often heard Mencken say these words. In Mencken's writings, the item that comes closest to this saying laments the stupidity of "the great masses of the plain people," not of Americans in particular.

The fools in this world make about as much trouble as the wicked do. *Josh Billings, 1865*

The idiot bakes snow in the oven and expects ice-cream pie. *Heard in Illinois*

The masses are asses. *Yiddish proverb*

The world is a paradise for fools, a purgatory or worse for others. *L. de V. Matthewman*

There are more fools in the world than there are people. *Heinrich Heine*

There is in human nature generally more of the fool than of the wise. *Francis Bacon, Essays*

What fools these morals be. *Howard Kandel*

What fools these mortals think other mortals be. *Cornell Widow, ca. 1925*

Why are there more horses' asses than there are horses? *Heard in New York and Wisconsin*

Put your best FOOT forward. *ca. 1495, WM-226*

. . . without stepping on other people's toes.

A good front is half the battle in love or war. *Kin Hubbard*

A lawyer's trick of the trade: If the facts are against you, argue the law. If the law is against you, pound the table and yell like hell.

Assume a virtue, if you have it not. *Shakespeare, Hamlet 3.4.160*

Everyone is a moon, and has a dark side which he never shows to anybody. *Mark Twain*

He who begs timidly, courts refusal. *Heard in Ontario*

Nonchalance is the ability to look like an owl when you have behaved like an ass.

Putting your best foot forward at least keeps it out of your mouth. *Morris Mandel*

Try to be the best of whatever you are, even if what you are is no good. © *Ashleigh Brilliant*

It's all right to be modest
If you have a good business,
   And money laid by on a shelf;
But if you are climbing
Your way up the ladder,
Put on a front
   That will speak for itself.
Old postcard

If you're not FOR us, you're against us.*
Let him either drink or depart. *Latin proverb*

*He that is not with me is against me. *Matthew 12:30; Luke 11:23*

See also If you're not part of the SOLUTION, you're part of the problem.

FORESIGHT is better than hindsight.

Intelligence recognizes what has happened. Genius recognizes what will happen. *John Ciardi*

The wise man must be wise before, not after, the event. *Epicharmus*

You can't see the FOREST for the trees. *1546, Heywood*

See also HINDSIGHT is better than foresight.

Nothing lasts FOREVER.

. . . [and] nothing ever goes away. *Barry Commoner*

. . . not even your troubles. *Arnold H. Glasgow*

A "good" family, it seems, is one that used to be better. *Cleveland Amory, Who Killed Society*

All human things are subject to decay. *John Dryden, Mac Flecknoe*

All that lives must die. *Shakespeare, Hamlet 1.2.172*

Cookie today, crumbs tomorrow. *Heard in Washington*

Do not try to live forever. You will not succeed. *G. B. Shaw, The Doctor's Dilemma*

Don't worry about your health. It'll go away. *Robert Orben*

Eternity is a terrible thought. I mean, where's it going to end? *Tom Stoppard, Rosencrantz and Guildenstern Are Dead*

Every civilization that has ever existed has ultimately collapsed. *Henry Kissinger*

Everything passes, everything breaks, everything wearies. *French proverb*

Fame is a vapour, popularity an accident; the only earthly certainty is oblivion. *Mark Twain*

For mortals, mortal things. And all things leave us. Or if they do not, then we leave them. *Lucian*

For riches are not forever. *Proverbs 27:24*

Glory may be fleeting, but obscurity is forever.

If things did not break, or wear out, how would tradesmen live? *1738, OE-62*

Nothing lasts as long as the suit you don't like. *Henny Youngman*

One good thing about life is it's only temporary. *Peter's Almanac*

Sic transit gloria mundi. ("Thus passes away the glory of this world.") *Latin saying*

That the end of life should be death may sound sad; yet what other end can anything have? *George Santayana, Some Turns of Thought in Modern Philosophy*

The civilization of one epoch becomes the manure of the next. *Cyril Connolly*

The Lord gave, and the Lord hath taken away; blessed be the name of the Lord. *Job 1:21*

The peacock of today is the feather duster of tomorrow. *Ezra Aranoff*

The waters wear the stones. *Job 14:19*

Things may serve long, but not serve ever. *Shakespeare, All's Well That Ends Well 2.2.60*

Time, thou devourer of all things. *Ovid, Metamorphoses*

Today's fire is tomorrow's ashes.

Treaties are like roses and young girls—they last while they last. *Charles de Gaulle, 1963*

When our first parents were driven out of Paradise, Adam is believed to have remarked to Eve: "My dear, we live in an age of transition." *W. R. Inge*

When fortune smiles
I smile to think
How quickly she will frown.
Robert Southwell

See also EVERYTHING has an end; All is FLUX.

FOREWARNED is forearmed. *Latin proverb*

'Tis half the battle to be forewarned. *1910, BJW-239*

FORGIVE and forget. *1546, Heywood*

A good memory is a valuable thing, but it is also well if you have a good forgetory. *William C. Hunter*

A retentive memory may be a good thing, but the ability to forget is the true token of greatness. *Elbert Hubbard, Note Book*

Always be kind to your enemies—nothing annoys them more.

Every man should have a fair-sized cemetery in which to bury the faults of his friends. *Henry Ward Beecher*

File it and forget it.

Forgive your enemies—but never forget their names. *John F. Kennedy*

Forgive your enemies—especially those you can't beat.

Forgiveness is a gift of high value. Yet it costs nothing. *Betty Smith, A Tree Grows in Brooklyn*

Happiness is good health and a bad memory. *Ingrid Bergman*

He who cannot forgive others destroys the bridge over which he himself must pass. *George Herbert*

It's easier to forgive than forget. *Heard in Indiana*

Never go to bed mad. Stay up and fight. *Phyllis Diller*

Nobody ever forgets where he buried the hatchet. *Kin Hubbard*

One should forgive one's enemies, but not before they are hanged. *Heinrich Heine*

People never forgive and they never forget. Sometimes they pretend to, but we doubt their sincerity. *Ed Howe*

Sign at a bar: If you drink to forget, please pay in advance.

To revenge is no valour, but to bear. *Shakespeare, Timon of Athens 3.5.39*

We believe in the spirit of forgiveness—if we owe a man and we won't pay him, let him forgive the debt. *Josh Billings, 1865*

Write injuries in sand, kindness in marble. *French proverb*

See also Let BYGONES be bygones.

To understand all is to FORGIVE all. *Madame de Staël (1766–1817)*

If doctors discover that crime is a disease, what will become of the preacher? *Frederick H. Seymour*

To know all is not to forgive all. It is to despise everybody. *Quentin Crisp, The Naked Civil Servant*

FORM follows function.

Form ever follows function. *Louis H. Sullivan, 1906*

FORTUNE favors fools. *Latin proverb*

It is to fools that the Mother of God appears.* *Spanish proverb*

*An intriguing ambiguity: does this proverb say that, like Dame Fortune, Our Lady also favors fools or that only half-wits see visions?

FORTUNE favors the bold. *Terence (ca. 195–159 B.C.)*

If someone cheats you, get your money back. If someone slanders you, call him to account. If someone makes a promise, see that it is kept, even if it means going to court or applying thumb screws. . . . If you have to be a pest, then be one, and be proud of it. *Donald G. Smith*

Whatever you can do or dream you can begin it. Boldness has genius, power and magic in it. *Johann Wolfgang von Goethe*

See also Faint HEART ne'er won fair lady.

Don't put the FOX to guard the henhouse. 1589, WM-231

When the foxes pack the jury box, the chicken's always guilty.

It's a FREE country.

. . . where a man can do what his wife pleases. *Joey Adams*

. . . but the upkeep is killing us.

**The best things in life are FREE.*

. . . Everything else makes up for it.

. . . but the second best can run into real money.

. . . and the most important things in life aren't things.

. . . until you get caught taking things without paying for them.

Anybody who thinks the best things in life are free just hasn't been caught yet.

If the best things in life are free, why is the family budget so hard to balance?

Life is the greatest bargain—we get it for nothing. *Yiddish proverb*

Sleep is the best meditation. *Dalai Lama, People, Sept. 10, 1979*

Sleep is the poor man's treasure. *Latvian proverb*

The best things in life are edible. *Jim Davis, Garfield: Words to Live By*

The best things in life are for a fee. *Peter's Almanac*

The best things in life are freaky. *Campus latrine graffiti*

The best things in life are free; and if you can afford the stuff you get with money, you've got a great combination.

The best things in life are not free but priceless. *Benjamin Lichtenberg*

The best things in life are sometimes free and usually unexpected.

*The moon belongs to ev'ryone,
  The best things in life are free,

The stars belong to ev'ryone,
They gleam there for you and me.
Popular song, by Buddy DeSylva et al., 1927

See also MONEY isn't everything.

Let FREEDOM ring. Samuel Francis Smith, America, 1831

Freedom of the press is limited to those who own one. *A. J. Liebling*

If the 1st Amendment means anything, it means that a state has no business telling a man, sitting alone in his own house, what books he may read or what films he may watch. *Thurgood Marshall, 1969*

It may be true that the law cannot make a man love me, but it can keep him from lynching me, and I think that's pretty important. *Martin Luther King, Jr., 1962*

The right to be let alone is indeed the beginning to all freedom. *William O. Douglas, 1952*

Fifty million FRENCHMEN can't be wrong. Texas Guinan (attributed), New York World-Telegram, Mar. 21, 1931

One hundred thousand lemmings can't be wrong.

A FRIEND in need is a friend indeed. Latin proverb

. . . and a friend not in need is a great relief.

. . . but who needs a friend in need? *Old postcard*

. . . but friends are for enjoying, not needing.

. . . [but] friends, if often used, wear out. *Heard in Utah*

. . . but you cannot use your friends and have them too. Never trust a friend who deserts you at a pinch. *Aesop*

A friend in need is:

> . . . a pest indeed.
>
> . . . a needy friend.
>
> . . . a friend to dodge.
>
> . . . a friend you don't need.
>
> . . . a damned nuisance.

A friend in need walks in when the rest of the world walks out.

A friend in need will keep you broke.

A friend in power is a friend lost. *Henry Adams*

A bank is a place where they will lend you an umbrella in fair weather and ask for it back when it begins to rain. *Robert Frost*

A friend loveth at all times, and a brother is born for adversity. *Proverbs 17:17*

A friend should bear his friend's infirmities. *Shakespeare, Julius Caesar 4.3.86*

A friend that ain't in need is a friend indeed. *Kin Hubbard*

A friend with weed is a friend indeed.

A real friend is one who walks in when the rest of the world walks out. *Walter Winchell*

After the verb to love, to help is the most beautiful verb in the world. *Bertha van Suttner*

Don't bore your friends with your troubles; tell them to your enemies—they'll enjoy hearing about them. *Peter's Almanac*

Fall sick and you will know who is your friend and who is not. *Heard in New York*

Friends are like fiddlestrings: they must not be screwed too tight. *English proverb*

Great opportunities to help others seldom come, but small ones surround us every day. *Sally Koch*

If a friend is in trouble, don't annoy him by asking if there is anything you can do. Think up something appropriate and do it. *Ed Howe*

If you help a friend in need, he is sure to remember you the next time he's in need.

Let me know if there's any way I can relieve your pain without increasing my own. © *Ashleigh Brilliant*

May you have more and more friends, but need them less and less. *Old postcard*

Never befriend the oppressed unless you are prepared to take on the oppressor. *Ogden Nash*

Never catch at a falling knife or a falling friend. *Scottish proverb*

Please don't put a strain on our friendship by asking me to do something for you. © *Ashleigh Brilliant*

The best time to make friends is before you need them. *Henny Youngman*

The most rewarding friendships begin when two people don't owe each other one damned thing. *Donald G. Smith*

The proper office of a friend is to side with you when you are in the wrong. Nearly anybody will side with you when you are in the right. *Mark Twain, Notebook*

There are always a few people you do a lot for, and a few who do a lot for you, but they're not the same people. *Mignon McLaughlin*

There is a chill air surrounding those who are down in the world and people are glad to get away from them as from a cold room. *George Eliot*

Think twice before you speak to a friend in need. *Ambrose Bierce*

When there is room in the heart, there is room in the house. *Danish proverb*

When trouble come, frien' run. *Heard in South Carolina*

When you lose your money, you find out who your friends are and they're not the ones you wanted. *Mignon McLaughlin*

You can fall down by yourself but you need a friend's hand to get up. *Yiddish proverb*

Say not, "God help you!" when your brother
    needs,
But let God help him through your kindly
    deeds.
Arthur Guiterman

A friend in need's a friend indeed,
    And this I've found most true;
But mine is such a needy friend,
    He sticks to me like glue.
Harper's Weekly, 1863

To give, to lend, to spend,
You may call today, my friend;
But to beg or else to borrow,
You had better call tomorrow.
Old postcard

Life is mostly froth and bubble;
    Two things stand like stone:
Kindness in another's trouble,
    Courage in your own.
Adam Lindsay Gordon

An ounce of aid is worth a ton of sorrow;
So help him now, don't pity him tomorrow.
Arthur Guiterman

He that is thy friend indeed,
He will help thee in thy need.
Shakespeare, Passionate Pilgrim

The only way to have a FRIEND is to be one. *Ralph Waldo Emerson (1803–82), Friendship*

The way to be happy is to make others so. *Robert G. Ingersoll*

Your best FRIEND is yourself.

See Every MAN is his own best friend; HELP yourself; SELF-LOVE is better than self-hate.

Your best FRIEND won't tell you. *Advertising slogan of a mouthwash*

Old FRIENDS and old wine are the best. *1616, Draxe*

As old wood is best to burn, old horse to ride, old books to read, and old wine to drink, so are old friends always most trusty to use. *Leonard Wright, Display of Dutie*

Forsake not an old friend; for . . . a new friend is as new wine; when it is old, thou shalt drink it with pleasure. *Ecclesiasticus 9:10*

The older the fiddle, the better the tune.

Those friends thou hast, and their adoption
    tried,
Grapple them to thy soul with hoops of steel.
Shakespeare, Hamlet 1.3.61

Make new friends, but keep the old;
Those are silver, these are gold. . . .
For 'mid old friends, tried and true,
Once more we our youth renew.

You can choose your FRIENDS, but you can't choose your relatives.

A father is a treasure; a brother, a comfort; a friend is both.

Fate makes our relatives, choice makes our friends. *Jacques Delille, 1803*

Happiness is having a large, loving, caring, close-knit family in another city. *George Burns*

Pick your friends, but not to pieces.

Friends are like melons, shall I tell you why?
To find one good, you must a hundred try.
Claude Mermet, ca. 1600

Love is only chatter,
Friends are all that matter.
Gelett Burgess, Willy and the Lady

See also GOD sends our relatives, but we can choose our friends.

You can't buy FRIENDSHIP.

. . . You not only can, you must. . . . Everything worthwhile has a price. *Robert J. Ringer*

Forbidden FRUIT is sweetest. *Geoffrey Chaucer, Parson's Tale, 1386*

. . . See you at the orchard.

Adam was but human—this explains it all. He did not want the apple for the apple's sake, he wanted it only because it was forbidden. *Mark Twain, Notebook*

Anyone can do any amount of work provided it isn't the work he is supposed to do at the moment. *Robert Benchley*

Forbidden fruit has no attraction until we know that it is forbidden. *L. de V. Matthewman*

Some women love only what they can hold in their arms; others, only what they can't. *Mignon McLaughlin*

There are three ways to get something done: do it yourself, hire someone, or forbid your kids to do it. *Monta Crane*

What you hear never sounds half so important as what you overhear. *Heard in New York and Ontario*

Stolen FRUIT is sweetest. A.D. 100, B-1893

A thing of booty is a joy forever. *Wayne G. Haisley*

It was not that Adam ate the apple for the apple's sake, but because it was forbidden. It would have been better for us . . . if the serpent had been forbidden. *Mark Twain, Notebook*

Kissing a girl because she is willing is like scratching a place that doesn't itch. *Vermont proverb*

Stolen waters are sweet, and bread eaten in secret is pleasant. *Proverbs 9:17*

Why do some men love wenches better than their wives? Because stolen pleasures seem sweetest. *1659, Howell*

Stolen sweets are always sweeter;
Stolen kisses much completer;
Stolen looks are nice in chapels;
Stolen, stolen be your apples.
Leigh Hunt

Beware the FURY of a patient man. *John Dryden, Absalom and Achitophel, 1681*

See Still WATER runs deep.

Don't be too FUSSY.

... It is better to have old secondhand diamonds than none at all. *Mark Twain*

See also Half a LOAF is better than none.

Ill-gotten GAINS never prosper. *1519, T-267*

... the trite consolation administered to the easy dupe, when he has been tricked out of his money or estate, [is] that the acquisition of it will do the owner no good. But the rogues of the world ... know better; and if the observation had been as true as it is old, [they] would not have failed by this time to have discovered it. *Charles Lamb, Popular Fallacies*

The first hundred dollars I ever won at poker I spent on the complete works of Homer, Dante, Shakespeare and Goethe. The first fifteen dollars I earned with a week's hard work I spent on a female tramp. *George Jean Nathan*

No GAINS without pains. *1577, WM-245*

A kick in the ass is a step forward.

Elbow grease gives the best polish.

Every dram of delight has a pound of pain. *1576, T-172*

Every gain must have a loss. *Francis Bacon, Of Seditions and Troubles*

Every sorrow has its twin joy; the fun of scratching almost pays for having the itch. *Josh Billings, 1865*

For one pleasure a thousand woes. *1573, T-545*

He deserves not the sweet that will not taste of the sour. *1535, T-645*

Industry is a better horse to ride than genius. *Walter Lippmann*

It is not enough for a gardener to love flowers. He must also hate weeds.

Learning is not child's play; we cannot learn without pain. *Aristotle*

Luck is not chance, it's toil. Fortune's expensive smile is earned. *Emily Dickinson*

Never pleasure without repentance. *1611, T-546*

No brain, no pain.

No fight, no win. *Heard in Ontario*

No guts, no glory.

No pain, no gain.

Revolutions are not made with rosewater. *Lord Byron, Letters*

Sweat and be saved. *Said to have been the favorite proverb of Theodore Roosevelt*

Sweat makes good mortar.

Take the sweet with the sour. *1546, T-645*

The gods sell us all good things at the price of labor. *Greek proverb*

The law of labor: No pains, no gains, no sweat, no sweet. *R. C. Trench, On Lessons in Proverbs*

The man who never makes a mistake is the man who never does anything. *Old postcard*

The price of progress is trouble. *Sign in a General Motors lab*

There is no hill without its valley. *1583, T-311*

There is no pleasure without pain. *1526, T-546*

You cannot learn to ice skate without being ridiculous. . . . The ice of life is slippery. *G. B. Shaw, 1911*

Tilley (T-546) lists the following 16th- and 17th-century variants:

No pleasure without pain.

No honey without gall.

No joy without annoy.

No joy without sorrow.

No mirth without mourning.

No sunshine but has some shadow.

No weal without woe.

See also Never the ROSE without the thorn; No SWEET without sweat; The best things in life are FREE.

Don't GALLOP when you're going downhill.

Don't kill a fly with a hatchet.

Don't go to a waterfall to wet a stamp.

See also Don't OVERDO it.

GARBAGE in, garbage out.* *Glossary of Typesetting & Computer Terms, 1964*

If you put tomfoolery into a computer, nothing comes out but tomfoolery. But this tomfoolery, having passed through a very expensive machine, is somehow ennobled and no one dares criticize it. *Pierre Gallois*

Purgamentum init, exit purgamentum. *Latin translation*

There comes nothing out of a sack but what was in it. *1581, WM-521*

*Oxford (O-90) explains: "Garbage is a colloquial term in data processing for 'incorrect input' which will, according to the proverb, inevitably produce faulty output." The acronym GIGO is pronounced *guy-go.*

Every man thinks his own GEESE swans. *1517, T-271*

Everyone thinks his own fart smells sweet. *1583, T-202*

The eye that sees all things sees not itself. *16th century*

The parvenu is always someone else. *Anka Muhlstein, The Rise of the French Rothschilds*

See also BEAUTY is in the eye of the beholder; CHARITY begins at home; Every CROW thinks its own young the whitest; It all DEPENDS on whose ox is gored.

When the fox turns preacher, beware of the GEESE. *1546, Heywood*

One bad GENERAL is better than two good ones. *1904, B-938*

. . . An two men ride of a horse, one must ride behind. *Shakespeare, Much Ado About Nothing 3.5.39*

All GENERALIZATIONS are dangerous.

. . . even this one. *Alexandre Dumas fils*

Every GENIUS has a touch of madness. *Aristotle (ca. 384–322 B.C.); S-940*

Every genius is a step from insanity, but insanity is not a step from genius. *Heard in New York and Oregon*

GENIUS is an infinite capacity for taking pains.*

Circumstances: The man of genius creates them, the man of talent uses them, the fool looks at them without seeing them. *Charles Narrey*

Dentistry is an infinite capacity for giving pains.

Genius has been defined as a supreme capacity for taking trouble. . . . It might be more fitly described as a supreme capacity for getting . . . into trouble of all kinds. *Eric Partridge, Dictionary of Clichés*

Genius is an infinite capacity for giving pains.

Genius is an infinite capacity for picking brains.

Genius is intensity. *Honoré de Balzac*

Malingering is an infinite capacity for faking pains.

Talent is the infinite capacity for imitating genius.

Talent made a poor appearance
Until he married perseverance.
Arthur Guiterman

Genius, cried the commuter,
As he ran for the 8:13,
Consists of an infinite capacity
For catching trains.
Christopher Morely, The Commuter

*Genius is nothing but a great aptitude for patience. *George-Louis de Buffon (1707–88)*

GENIUS is born, not made.

A genius is someone who can aim at something nobody else sees, and hit it. *Peter's Almanac*

Doing easily what others find difficult is talent, doing what is impossible for talent is genius. *Henri Amiel, Journal Intime*

Genius has the power of lighting its own fire. *John Foster*

There is no great genius without some touch of madness. *Seneca, On Tranquility of the Mind*

Vision is the art of seeing things invisible. *Jonathan Swift*

GENIUS is one percent inspiration and ninety-nine percent perspiration. *Thomas Edison, 1931*

. . . but don't confuse excessive sweating with creativity.

Everyone who really makes it does it by busting his ass. *Alan Arkin*

Genius is perseverance in disguise. *Mike Newlin*

God gives talent; work transforms talent into genius. *Anna Pavlova*

If the power to do hard work is not talent, it is the best possible substitute for it. *James A. Garfield*

If you've got the talent, you've got the energy. *Mignon McLaughlin*

Nothing comes easily. My work smells of sweat. *Eric Hoffer*

Sweat is the cologne of accomplishment. *Heywood Hale Broun, on rodeos, 1973*

There are so many things that we wish we had done yesterday, so few that we feel like doing today. *Mignon McLaughlin*

We are all such a waste of our potential, like three-way lamps using one-way bulbs. *Mignon McLaughlin*

When I was a young man I observed that nine out of ten things I did were failures. I didn't want to be a failure, so I did ten times more work. *G. B. Shaw*

It takes three generations to make a GENTLEMAN. *1598, O-90*

The English have a proverb . . . The first generation makes the money; the second goes into politics; the third is a dilettante. *TW-151*

GENTLEMEN prefer blondes. *Title of a book by Anita Loos, 1925*

. . . because they're easier to find in the dark.

. . . because blondes know what gentlemen prefer. *Henny Youngman*

. . . but take what they get. *Don Herold*

. . . and blondes prefer gentlemen.

. . . but just because a fellow prefers blondes, that doesn't make him a gentleman. *Judge, ca. 1925*

Gentlemen prefer bonds. *Andrew Mellon*

Is it possible that blondes also prefer gentlemen? *Mamie Van Doren*

That gentlemen prefer blondes is due to the fact that, apparently, pale hair, delicate skin and an infantile expression represent the very apex of frailty which every man longs to violate. *Alexander King, Rich Man, Poor Man, Freud and Fruit*

Let GEORGE do it. *

The best bet is to bet on yourself. *Arnold Glasow*

The world is full of willing people—some willing to work and the rest willing to let them. *Heard in Oklahoma*

*Archer Taylor (p.9) suggests that this expression may have originated as a vaudeville phrase. He notes that Pullman porters were frequently addressed as George.

See also HELP yourself; If you want a thing DONE well, do it yourself; Mind your own BUSINESS.

If you're going to GET ALONG, you've got to go along. *Sam Rayburn (1882–1961), advice to a young congressman, Lyndon B. Johnson*

Conformity, humility, acceptance—with these coins we are to pay our fares to paradise. *Robert Lindner*

If you are going to sin, sin against God, not the bureaucracy. God will forgive you but the bureaucracy won't. *Hyman G. Rickover*

One must make himself liked, for men are just only with those that they like. *Joseph Joubert*

We descend to meet. *Ralph Waldo Emerson*

See also Don't make WAVES; Don't rock the BOAT.

O wad some pow'r the GIFTIE gie us to see oursels as ithers see us! *Robert Burns, To a Louse, ca. 1785; F-731*

. . . we wouldn't believe it.

. . . we'd never speak to them again.

A camel never sees its own hump. *African proverb*

A neurotic is someone who's afraid to see himself as he's afraid others see him. *Mignon McLaughlin*

Every madman thinks everybody else is mad. *Publilius Syrus, Maxims*

If we could see ourselves as others see us, it would probably confirm our opinion of them. *Robert B. Fleming*

It is difficult to see the picture when you are inside the frame. *R. S. Trapp, as quoted in Reader's Digest, Nov. 1968*

Oh wad some power the giftie gie us to see some people before they see us. *Ethel Watts Mumford*

Self-portraits usually are colored. *Harold Coffin, as quoted in Reader's Digest, July 1961*

The average man thinks he isn't. *Judge, ca. 1925*

The eye that sees all things sees not itself. *16th century*

The very purpose of existence is to reconcile the glowing opinion we hold of ourselves with the appalling things that other people think about us. *Quentin Crisp*

What a blessed thing it is that we can't "see ourselves as others see us,"—the sight would take the starch out of us. *Josh Billings*

What a sad world this would be if everyone knew what their neighbors really thought of them. *Frederick H. Seymour*

You can see another's arse, but not your own. *Japanese proverb*

GIRLS who are chaste are never chased, and girls who are chased are never chaste.

A girl may be allowed to sin, otherwise she would have nothing to repent. *Russian proverb*

Girls who show their knees know all about the birds and bees. *Heard in Ohio*

If the girls won't run after the men, the men will run after the girls.

It is more blessed to GIVE than to receive. *Acts 20:35*

. . . advice.

. . . and it costs about the same. *Phillip Gibbs*

. . . and it's deductible. *Stephanie Martins*

. . . but it can be more expensive.

. . . wedding presents, for example. *H. L. Mencken, Devil's Dictionary (adapted)*

. . . [but] giving away a fortune is taking Christianity too far. *Charlotte Bingham*

. . . But the givers who cannot take in return miss one of the finest graces in life, the grace of receiving. . . . It changes one of the ugliest things in the world, patronage, into one of the richest things in the world, friendship. *Halford E. Luccock, as quoted in Reader's Digest, May 1973*

From what we get, we can make a living; what we give, however, makes a life. *Arthur Ashe, Days of Grace*

He that gives should never remember, he that receives should never forget. *Talmud*

If it is more blessed to give than to receive, then most of us are content to let the other fellow have the greater blessing. *Shailer Mathews*

It is more blessed to give and then receive.

It's loving and giving that makes life worth living. *Heard in Ontario*

Whoever is capable of giving is himself rich. *Erich Fromm*

You may give gifts without caring—but you can't care without giving. *Frank A. Clark*

I love the Christmas-tide and yet,
I notice this, each year I live;
I always like the gifts I get,
But how I love the gifts I give!
Carolyn Wells, A Thought

Better to give than take? Not so!
Far better to give than take a blow.
John Davies, 1611 (adapted)

GIVE and take is fair play. *1778, O-92*

The art of living lies in a fine mingling of letting go and holding on. *Havelock Ellis*

To be happy, give;
to be successful, take;
to be happy and successful, give and take.
L. de V. Matthewman

See also Fair PLAY.

Don't GIVE UP.

See If at first you don't SUCCEED, try again.

There is no grace GIVING that which sticks to the fingers.

Strain at a GNAT and swallow a camel.*

See PENNY wise and pound foolish. *1605, F-148*

*Ye blind guides, which strain at a gnat, and swallow a camel. *Matthew 23:24*

In both the Greek and the Latin, the passage refers to straining *out* a gnat, the process of straining wine for possible insects. Should a person who has already "swallowed a camel" worry about removing a gnat from his wine? The King James translators probably did not originate this mistranslation, but merely followed a rendering that had already become popular. See B-966.

GO with the flow.

He that follows Nature is never out of the way. *1576, OE-213*

I did not direct my life. I didn't design it. I never made decisions. Things always came up and made them for me. That's what life is. *B. F. Skinner, Particulars of My Life*

Who spits against the wind spits in his own face. *1557, WM-657*

See also Don't make WAVES; Don't rock the BOAT.

An honest man's the noblest work of GOD. Alexander Pope, An Essay on Man, 1733

An honest God's the noblest work of man. *Samuel Butler, Notebooks.* These words were also written by his contemporary, *Robert G. Ingersoll in Gods.*

God created man in his own image, says the Bible, and the philosophers do just the opposite, they create God in theirs. *Georg Lichtenberg*

God made man on purpose to fall that he might get up and be somebody on his own hook. *Josh Billings*

Man is certainly stark mad. He cannot make a worm, and yet he will be making gods by the dozens. *Michel de Montaigne*

Man is Creation's masterpiece. But who says so? Man! *Old postcard*

Man was created a little lower than the angels, and has been getting a little lower ever since. *Josh Billings*

Our Heavenly Father invented man because he was disappointed in the monkey. *Mark Twain*

Which is it—is man one of God's blunders or is God one of man's blunders? *Friedrich Nietzsche*

Man is the noblest work of God,
    And woman, with a smirk,
Or sigh, or tear or two, proceeds
    To work God's noblest work.
Old postcard

Every man for himself, and GOD for all of us. *1546, Heywood*

. . . is the cry of those who are well up in front. *L. de V. Matthewman*

Every man loves himself best. *1616, Draxe*

I must serve my own self first. *Terence*

My teeth are nearer than my relatives. *Spanish proverb*

See also The DOOR to success is always marked Push; Faint HEART ne'er won fair lady; Don't HIDE your light under a bushel; HELP yourself; Put your best FOOT forward; SELF-PRESERVATION is the first law of nature.

GOD bless America.*

. . . and it's territories.

*Irving Berlin wrote "God Bless America" in 1917, as a finale of *Yip, Yip, Yaphank.* But the composer set it aside, according to Irving Berlin expert Sol Kellerman, because Berlin was afraid critics would accuse him of flag-waving. In 1939 Kate Smith sang "God Bless America" on the radio, and

Proverb Wit & Wisdom 161

America discovered what Berlin had written twenty-two years before. During World War II, it almost became a national anthem.

GOD bless our home.

. . . as much as possible.

God bless our mortgaged home.

GOD defend me from my friends; from my enemies I can defend myself. *1477, T-246*

A man who will defraud another who confides in him is surely a greater villain than one who robs boldly at the risk of his life. *George Washington*

A tough lesson in life that one has to learn is that not everybody wishes you well. *Dan Rather*

An enemy can never sell you out because he has nothing to offer. Only a friend has this option. *Donald G. Smith*

Fortunately, not everyone who could kill you does. *Mignon McLaughlin*

God defend me from the still water and I'll keep myself from the rough. *1599, T-260*

I don't want my friends to die for me. If they will be polite, and let me alone, I will be satisfied. *Ed Howe*

Nothing is so dangerous as an ignorant friend; a wise enemy is much better. *Jean de La Fontaine*

When people won't let you alone, it's because you haven't learned how to make them do it. *David Seabury*

An open foe may prove a curse,
But a pretended friend is worse.
John Gay, The Shepherd's Dog and the Wolf

See also PEOPLE are no damned good.

GOD grant me the serenity to accept the things I cannot change, courage to change the things I can, and wisdom to know the difference. [*]

Accept half of everything that life hands you, and raise holy hell over the other half. *Donald G. Smith*

If you can neither accept it nor change it, try to laugh at it. © *Ashleigh Brilliant*

Lord, when we are wrong, make us willing to change. And when we are right, make us easy to live with. *Peter Marshall*

There is only one way to happiness and that is to cease worrying about things which are beyond the power of our will. *Epictetus*

Two things a man should never get angry at: what he can help and what he cannot help. *1732, Fuller*

For every evil under the sun,
    There is a remedy or there is none.
If there is one, try and find it,
    If there be none, never mind it.
Old English rhyme

[*]Prayer adopted by Alcoholics Anonymous, who have entitled it "The Serenity Prayer"; popularly (but wrongly) believed to have been originated by that organization. In his autobiography, *Out of Step*, Sidney Hook identifies the author of the Serenity Prayer as the German philosopher Friedrich Christoph Oetinger (1702–82). Hook documents both the original German and an English translation. An Anglican church publisher asserts

that "variations of the serenity prayer have been in common use for centuries." (K-185)

GOD help the poor; the rich can help themselves. *1721, Kelly*

God help the rich, the poor can beg. *1659, Howell*

GOD helps those who help themselves.[*] *Aeschylus, 472 B.C.*

. . . murmured the thief as he broke a window and helped himself to a TV set. *Sydney J. Harris*

. . . and the government helps those who don't. *Dan Bennett*

. . . This is dragging in God somewhat profanely. . . . Those who help themselves often succeed against what should be God's harsh judgment of them. *George Jean Nathan*

Call on God, but row away from the rocks.

Despite what Horatio Alger and his latter day prophet, C. Clement Stone, have to say about self-made success, most of us find out that pulling yourself up by the bootstraps is merely a sure way to fall on your ass. *Ed Dussault, Chicago Sun-Times, 1974*

God help those who do not help themselves. *Wilson Mizner*

God is a good worker but loves to be helped. *Basque proverb*

God may help those who help themselves, but the courts are rough as hell on shoplifters. *Leo Rosten*

God still seems to be helping those who take a big helping for themselves.

I never ask God to give me anything; I only ask him to put me where things are. *Mexican proverb*

If God helped those who help themselves, those who help themselves wouldn't have to hire expensive lawyers. *Leo Rosten*

If God helps alone those who help themselves, it is a bitter criticism of Him that He cruelly neglects those who for one reason or another cannot help themselves. *George Jean Nathan*

Obesity is a condition which proves that the Lord does not help those who help themselves and help themselves and help themselves. *Julian Brown*

Pray to God, but continue to row toward shore. *Russian proverb*

Probably as many thieves as eminences have been motivated by the old motto that "God helps those who help themselves." *Sydney J. Harris*

The Lord hears the prayer of the hustler who prays for work, but the man who prays for a job to be sent to him gets no results. *William C. Hunter*

The Lord helps those who help others.

The gods sell all things to hard labor. *Greek proverb*

The means that heaven yields must be embrac'd,
And not neglected.
Shakespeare, Richard II 3.2.29

What good is pull if you don't pull with it? *John Podhoretz, Hell of a Ride*

Without God, I can't; without me, God won't. *Saint Augustine*

*Keyes notes that in a 1991 survey, 56 percent of American polled thought the proverb comes from the Bible. It doesn't. Keyes (K-184) traces the antiquity of this proverb.

See also CHARITY begins at home; HELP yourself; Don't HIDE your light under a bushel; Put your best FOOT forward; The door to SUCCESS is always marked Push; Faint HEART ne'er won fair lady.

GOD is dead. *Friedrich Nietzsche* **(1844–1900)**

. . . but fifty thousand social workers have risen to take his place. *J. D. McCoughey, 1974*

God is not dead, but alive and well and working on a much less ambitious project. *London graffiti, 1975*

God isn't dead, he's just screening his calls. *Contemporary postcard*

God is dead, maybe; Nietzsche is dead, that's for sure.

God isn't dead, he's merely unemployed. *Walt Kelly*

I can tell you that God is alive because I talked to him this morning. *Billy Graham, 1966*

If God is dead, who will save the Queen?

If it represents progress to believe in one God rather than many, why not take the next step? *Michel Paul Richard*

In the 19th century the problem was that God is dead; in the 20th century the problem is that man is dead. *Erich Fromm, The Sane Society*

My atheism, like that of Spinoza, is true piety towards the universe and denies only gods fashioned by men in their own image, to be servants of their human interests. *George Santayana, Soliloquies in England*

Our faith has gone from God to experts. *Robert Penn Warren*

Perhaps God is not dead; perhaps God is himself mad. *R. D. Laing*

The only excuse for God is that he doesn't exist. *Stendhal*

Those who set out to serve God and Mammon soon discover that there is no God. *Logan Pearsall Smith, 1931*

What God lacks is convictions—stability of character. He ought to be a Presbyterian or a Catholic or something—not try to be everything. *Mark Twain*

When a man is freed of religion, he has a better chance to live a normal and wholesome life. *Sigmund Freud*

No matter how much I prove and prod,
I cannot quite believe in God;
But oh, I hope to God that He
Unswervingly believes in me.
E. Y. Harburg

I turned to speak to God
About the world's despair;
But to make matters worse
I found God wasn't there.
Robert Frost, Not All There

Nietzsche is pietsche
But Sartre is smartre.
Graffiti

*The boldly secular point of view made explicit in "God is dead" is hinted at, says Corliss Lamont, in such popular sayings as "God helps those who help themselves" and "Praise the Lord and pass the ammunition."

GOD is love. *

God will forgive me; it is his trade. *Heinrich Heine, on his deathbed, 1856*

God is the best part of everybody's head. *Alcoholics Anonymous*

The Jews are a frightened people. Nineteen centuries of Christian love have broken down their nerves. *Israel Zangwill*

*God is love; and he that dwelleth in love dwelleth in God, and God in him. 1 John 4:16. He that loveth not knoweth not God; for God is love. 1 John 4:8. Mahatma Gandhi turned the phrase around and said, "Love is God."

GOD is our refuge and strength, a very present help in time of trouble. *Psalms 46:1*

A lie is an abomination unto the Lord and a very present help in trouble *Adlai Stevenson*

It is the final proof of God's omnipotence that he need not exist in order to save us. *Peter De Vries*

The policeman is a never-present help in time of trouble.

GOD loveth a cheerful giver. *2 Corinthians 9:7*

I wonder what the Lord does about the cheerful giver who charges his donation to overhead an' passes it along? *Kin Hubbard*

We hear a great deal about the Lord loving cheerful givers; we wonder where he finds them. *Ed Howe*

GOD made the country, and man made the town. *Latin proverb popularized by William Cowper in The Task, ca. 1783*

I have no relish for the country; it is a kind of healthy grave. *Sydney Smith*

If God made the country, and man made the town, then it was the devil who made the country-town. *Alfred, Lord Tennyson (attributed)*

Suburbia is where the developer bulldozes out the trees, then names the streets after them. *Bill Vaughn*

The city for wealth, the country for health. *Heard in Michigan*

GOD moves in a mysterious way his wonders to perform. *William Cowper, Light Shining out of Darkness, 1779*

A God we can understand is no God.

God moves in a mysterious way his blunders to perform. *Loudwick, 1943*

He seems to have an inordinate fondness for beetles. *John B. S. Haldane*

GOD must love the common people, he made so many of them. *

. . . Lincoln might have said it, but I bet it was not until he was elected. *Will Rogers*

God must hate the common people, because he made them so common. *Philip Wylie (attributed)*

God must love the rich or he wouldn't divide so much among so few of them. *H. L. Mencken*

Poverty must have its satisfactions, else there would not be so many poor people. *Don Herold*

*Attributed to Abraham Lincoln, as a reply to a congressman from a western district who apologized for presenting the President with such a crude petition from his constituents, as "they are very common people." This story first appeared in a 1903 *New York Tribune* Sunday supplement story. The closest variation of this saying documented during Lincoln's lifetime is an 1863 entry from the published diary of Lincoln's private secretary, John Hay: "The President to-night has a dream:—He was in a party of plain people, and as it became known who he was, they began to comment on his appearance. One of them said:—'He is a very common-looking man.' The President replied:—'The Lord prefers common-looking people. That is the reason he makes so many of them.' "

GOD never sends mouths but he sends meat. *ca. 1377, WM-255*

Whenever cannibals are on the brink of starvation, Heaven in its infinite mercy sends them a nice plump missionary. *Oscar Wilde*

GOD sends our relatives, but we can choose our friends. Wilson Mizner, The Cynic's Calendar

A brother may not be a friend, but a friend will always be a brother. *Poor Richard's Almanac, 1752*

Be kind to your mother-in-law, and, if necessary, pay for her board at some good hotel. *Josh Billings*

Love your relations, but live not near them. *English proverb*

The richer the relative is, the less he bothers you. *Kin Hubbard*

See also You can choose your FRIENDS, but you can't choose your relatives.

GOD tempers the wind to the shorn lamb. *French proverb*

For the birds that cannot soar God has provided low branches. *Turkish proverb*

Heaven takes care of children, sailors, and drunken men. *OE 289*

How many perversions of observable truth have been cherished in the sayings of past generations: "The wind is tempered to the shorn lamb," "God builds the nest of the blind bird." The wish is father of the thought; the wishful thought becomes the epigram. *J. Christopher, 1956*

I love the idea of God tempering the wind to the shorn lamb, but I'd hate to have to sell it to an American Indian. *Mignon McLaughlin*

If GOD be for us, who can be against us? *Romans 8:31*

A fanatic is a man that does what he thinks th' Lord wud do if He knew th' facts iv th' case. *Finley Peter Dunne, Mr. Dooley's Philosophy*

I care not if God is on my side. My constant hope and prayer is that I may be found upon God's side. *Abraham Lincoln*

If GOD did not exist, it would be necessary to invent Him. Voltaire (1694–1778), *Epistle to the author of Livres des Trois Imposteurs*

If God did exist, we should have to abolish Him. *Albert Camus*

If men are so wicked with religion, what would they be without it? *Benjamin Franklin*

Many people deny that there is a God, our God or the concept of God. But I have never met anybody who did not want there to be a God. *Viktor Frankel*

Some people want an affidavit from God that he really exists. *Danny Thomas, as quoted in Reader's Digest, July 1955*

The believer in God must explain one thing, the existence of suffering; the nonbeliever, however, must explain the existence of everything else. *Dennis Prager and Joseph Telushkin, The Nine Questions People Ask About Judaism*

To believe in God is to yearn for his existence and, furthermore, it is to act as if He did exist. *Miguel de Unamuno, The Tragic Sense of Life*

You need not tell a child that there is a God. *African proverb*

See also GOD is dead.

If GOD wanted us to smoke, he would have given us chimneys. *

If God had intended man to travel twelve miles an hour, He would have given him wings. *Early critics of the automobile*

If God had intended for women to wear slacks, He would have constructed them differently. *Emily Post (attributed)*

If God had intended man for racing, He would have given him four legs like a horse. *Walter "Red" Smith*

If God had intended us to fly, he would never have given us railways. *Michael Flanders*

If God had meant Wimbledon to be played in great weather, he would have put it in Acapulco. *British tennis official, as quoted in Newsweek, July 4, 1977*

If God had really intended me to fly, he'd make it easier to get to the airport. *George Winters*

If God meant for us to travel tourist class he would have made us narrower. *Air hostess Martha Zimmerman, Wall Street Journal, 1977*

If God wanted us to consume peanut butter, He would have lined our mouths with Teflon.

If nature was really interested in our welfare, it would have made health catching instead of disease. *Sydney J. Harris*

Much smoking kills live men and cures dead swine. *G. D. Prentice, Louisville Journal, ca. 1860*

*WM-65 reports the following variant, heard in Colorado and Ohio: "If boys were meant to smoke, they'd have chimneys on their heads." Perhaps this saying, and its variants, have been inspired by these words by Abraham Lincoln: "I hold that if the Almighty had ever made a set of men that should do all the eating and none of the work, He would have made them with mouths only and no hands; and if He had ever made another class that He intended should do all the work and no eating, He would have made them with hands only and no mouths" (*Address before the Wisconsin State Agricultural Society, Sept. 30, 1859*)

In GOD we trust. *

. . . All others pay cash.

. . . Everyone else is under surveillance.

In Got we trust. *L. L. Levinson*

Put your trust in God; but mind to keep your powder dry! *Oliver Cromwell*

Put your trust in God, but tie your camel. *Mohammed*

Sign in a bar: We have come to an understanding with the local banks. They don't sell beer and we don't cash checks.

Sign in a store: Cash only, please. We know that your check is good, but we don't trust the banks.

Trust everybody, but cut the cards. *Finley Peter Dunne, Mr. Dooley's Philosophy*

Trust in God, but keep a sharp lookout on your friends. *L. de V. Matthewman*

In '29 when the banks went bust,
Our coins still read "In God We Trust."
E. Y. Harburg

*An English slogan before it first appeared on American money in 1864. Only in 1956 did Congress make it the official national motto.

Man proposes, but GOD disposes. *Thomas à Kempis, Imitation of Christ, 1420; O-144*

Every drunken skipper trusts to Providence. But one of the ways of Providence with drunken skippers is to run them on the rocks. *G. B. Shaw, Heartbreak House*

Man appoints, and God disappoints. *Miguel de Cervantes*

Man proposes, woman supposes, marriage composes and divorce exposes. *Captain Billy's Whiz Bang, Jan. 1922*

The almanac writer makes the almanac, but God makes the weather. *Heard in Nebraska*

The gods thought otherwise. *Virgil, Aeneid*

See also ANYTHING can happen.

Put your trust in GOD and keep your powder dry. *1834, O-231*

See Praise the LORD and pass the ammunition.

Thank GOD it's Friday.*

*An early equivalent of this American saying is an expression once common in England: "Come day, go day, God send Sunday." Described by the Morrises (MD-144) as "the sluggard's daily prayer," it was spoken by servants whose only interest was "to serve out their time and get their wages." The expression was first documented by Draxe in 1616.

The voice of the people is the voice of GOD.* *Latin proverb*

And the Lord said unto Samuel, Hearken unto the voice of the people in all that they say unto thee. *1 Samuel 8:7*

All power to the people.

If all men say that thou art an ass, then bray. *1616, Draxe*

If everybody says so, there's some truth to it. *Yiddish proverb*

The voice of the people is the voice of humbug. *William T. Sherman, letter to his wife, 1863*

When the world goes mad, one must accept madness as sanity, since sanity is, in the last analysis, nothing but the madness on which the whole world happens to agree. *G. B. Shaw, An Open Letter to Gorki, May 1916*

*The origins of this proverb are traced by Stuart Gallacher in *Philological Quarterly* 24, Jan. 1945.

There but for the grace of GOD go I. *

Beggars get handouts before philosophers because people have some idea of what it's like to be blind and lame. *Diogenes of Sinope*

But for the grace of God. *Slogan of Alcoholics Anonymous*

Death is an arrow shot into a crowd; the only reason why it hit another is because it missed us. *Josh Billings*

Don't criticize the butter; you may be old yourself some day. *Old postcard*

Don't laugh at others' mistakes; the banana peel may be under your own feet. *Old postcard*

There are circumstantial vices and virtues. *Napoleon*

While there is a lower class, I am in it; while there is a criminal element, I am of it; while there is a soul in prison, I am not free. *Eugene V. Debs, 1917*

Whoever is spared personal pain must feel himself called to help in diminishing the pain of others. *Albert Schweitzer, Memoirs of Childhood*

There, but for the grace of God, goes God. *Winston Churchill, on Sir Stafford Cripps*

Jolly the fellow who's down today,
    Give him a smile for his sorrow.
The world sometimes has a funny way,
    And you may be down tomorrow.
Old postcard

*On seeing a criminal led to execution, John Bradford (1510?–55) is said to have uttered the words "There but for the grace of God, goes John Bradford." One of the most popular preachers of 16th-century England, Bradford was condemned as a heretic and burned on July 1, 1555. Ogden Nash (1902–71) lampoons Bradford's grave words in his verse "Oh, stop being thankful all over the place."

See also It's all a matter of LUCK.

With GOD all things are possible. *Matthew 19:26*

Faith is one of the forces by which men live, and the total absence of it means collapse. *William James*

O God, make the bad people good, and the good people nice. *Harry Emerson Fosdick, A Little Girl's Prayer*

The sovereign cure for worry is prayer. *William James*

You can't serve GOD and Mammon. *Matthew 6:24; Luke 16:13*

Dear Lord: We are in receipt of your kind favors of recent date and beg to thank you. We hope to merit your continued courtesies. *Estelle H. Ries, A Businessman's Grace*

Most people have found out, somehow, that they can't serve God and Mammon too—so they serve Mammon. *Josh Billings*

Most people sell their souls and live with a good conscience on the proceeds. *Logan Pearsall Smith*

GOD'S in his heaven; all's right with the world.[*] *1530, O-94*

The skeleton is hiding in the closet as it
should,
The needle's in the haystack and the trees are
in the wood,
The fly is in the ointment and the froth is on
the beer,
The bee is in the bonnet and the flea is in the
ear,
The meat is in the coconut, the cat is in the
bag,
The dog is in the manger and the goat is on
the crag,
The worm is in the apple and the clam is on
the shore,
The birds are in the bushes and the wolf is at
the door.
Arthur Guiterman

[*]Popularized in Robert Browning's radiantly
optimistic verse, "Pipa Passes":
The year's at the spring
And the day's at the morn;
Morning at seven;
The hillside's dew-pearled;
The lark's on the wing;
The snail's on the thorn:
God's in his heaven
All's right with the world.

See also All is for the BEST in the best of all possible worlds.

So many GODS, so many creeds,
   So many paths that wind and wind,
   While just the art of being kind
Is all the sad world needs.
Ella Wheeler Wilcox, The World's Need

Basis for a workable religion: when you have nothing better to do, do something for someone else. *Mignon McLaughlin*

God made Truth with many doors to welcome every believer who knocks on them. *Kahlil Gibran*

I do not think God cares much if we believe in Him as long as we display love of our fellow man; and I don't think He cares much for those who profess to believe in Him and use that belief to bludgeon people who do not share it. *Sydney J. Harris*

One religion is as true as another. *Robert Burton, Anatomy of Melancholy; M-827*

So many pedestrians, so little time. *Bumper sticker, 1987*

What's the matter with the world? There ain't nothing but one word wrong with every one of us, and that's selfishness. *Will Rogers*

All that glitters is not GOLD. *Latin proverb*

... nor is all that does not glitter pig-iron. *George Jean Nathan*

... How perfectly ridiculous! Everybody in the days in which we live knows—even a child knows—that all is gold that glitters. Put on clothes enough, appearance enough and you will be accepted anywhere. Just do a little glittering and everybody will think you are gold. Make a show, be a humbug, and you will succeed so fast that presently, being very wealthy and prominent, you will really think yourself a person of great merit and intellect. In other words, the glitter makes the gold. That is all there is to it. Gold is really one of the most useless of all material objects. Even now we have found no real use for it, except to fill our teeth. Any other employment of it is just glitter. So the proverb might be revised to read:

> Every thing or person may be said to stand in high esteem and to pass at a high value provided that it or he makes a sufficient show, glitter, or appearance, the estimation being in inverse ratio to the true quantitative measurement of the reality of it, them or her.

That makes a neat workable proverb, expressed with up-to-date accuracy. *Stephen Leacock, Old Proverbs*

All is not butter that comes from a cow. *Yiddish proverb*

All is not gold that glitters; all isn't garbage that smells.

All is not sex that appeals. *Hamilton Chaperon, ca. 1925*

All that is gold does not glitter; not all those that wander are lost. *J.R.R. Tolkien, The Fellowship of the Ring*

It sometimes happens with people, as with commodities, that the packaging is worth more than the contents. *Richard Needham*

Never lose sight of the fact that diplomas are hard to earn but very easy to print. *Donald G. Smith*

Sign over an after-Christmas sale of holiday decorations: All that glitters was not sold.

All that glisters is not gold
Often have you heard this told.
Shakespeare, The Merchant of Venice 2.7.65

All that glitters is sold as gold. *Ogden Nash, Look What You Did, Christopher*

All that glitters will for gold
Glitter more a thousand-fold.
Samuel Hoffenstein, For Little Boys Destined for Big Business

See also You can't tell a BOOK by its cover.

Those days are GONE forever.

. . . when children were a necessity and cars were a luxury.

. . . when minding the children didn't mean obeying them.

If you're yearning for the good old days, just turn off the air conditioning. *Griff Niblack*

It used to be a good hotel, but that proves nothing—I used to be a good boy. *Mark Twain*

Living in the past may seem foolish to some, but the price sure is right.

Nothing is ever like it used to be. *Malcolm Forbes*

Speaking of the high cost of courting, who remembers when all a feller needed was a narrow buggy and a sack of red cinnamon drops? *Kin Hubbard*

The people who are always hankering loudest for some golden yesteryear usually drive new cars. *Russell Baker, 1972*

To campaign against colonialism is like barking up a tree that has already been cut down. *Andrew Cohen, 1958*

You never get what you want for Christmas after you grow up. *Kin Hubbard*

See also Things are going to the DOGS.

GOOD things come in small packages. *French proverb; O-13*

See LESS is more; SMALL is beautiful.

If you can't be GOOD, be careful. 1303, O-97

Be good and if you can't be good be careful. *Refrain of a World War I song popular among U.S. soldiers in France*

If you can't be good, belittle. *D. V. Cubberley*

If you can't be funny, be interesting. *Harold Ross*

If you can't be virtuous, you can at least be discreet. *Bob Levinson*

If you can't laugh at yourself, make fun of other people. *Bobby Slayton*

The GOOD die young. *Herodotus* (4th century B.C.); F-70

. . . of loneliness.

. . . which is a standing invitation for the small boy to be bad. *New Orleans Picayune*

. . . particularly if their parents get drunk and neglect them. *Ambrose Bierce*

. . . [If you] believe it . . . go out and raise the dickens by way of prolonging your life. *George Jean Nathan*

. . . because they see it's no use living if you've got to be good. *John Barrymore*

. . . because the young die in innocence.

If you wish praise, die; if you wish blame, marry. *Heard in New York*

On seeing a grandmotherly face crowned by jet-black hair: Only the young dye good.

Only the young die good. *Oliver Herford*

The good die young; the bad live on,
And sin grows bold and haughty.
They even cut the good trees first
And leave behind the knotty.
Philadelphia Press

The good die young, so men have sadly sung
Who do not know the happier reason why
Is never that they die while they are young,
But that the good are young until they die.
Arthur Guiterman, Thus Spoke Theodore Roosevelt

The greatest GOOD to the greatest number.

. . . which is the measure of right and wrong. *Jeremy Bentham*

There is so much GOOD in the worst of us,
And so much bad in the best of us,
That it hardly behooves any of us
To talk about the rest of us.[*]

No man is as good as he ought to be, and few men are as bad as they seem. *Old postcard*

Sign in Springdale, Connecticut: There is so much good in the worst of us and so much bad in the best of us, that it's rather hard to tell which of us ought to reform the rest of us.

Think of me at my best, old boy. *Parting remark of spoiled, self-centered Steerforth, in Charles Dickens' David Copperfield*

It's the bad that's in the best of us
Leaves the saint so like the rest of us!
It's the good in the darkest-curst of us
Redeems and saves the worst of us!
It's the muddle of hope and madness;
It's the tangle of good and badness;

It's the lunacy linked with sanity
Makes up, and mocks, humanity!
Arthur Stringer

*From "Good and Bad," a poem first published in the *Marion (Kans.) Record,* ca. 1900; author unknown. It has been attributed to American politician Edward Wallis Hoch (1849–1925)

See also NOBODY is perfect.

What's sauce for the GOOSE is sauce for the gander. *1670, Ray*

As well for the cow as for the bull. *1546, Heywood*

If strokes be good to give, they are good to get. *1721, Kelly.* Spoken to one who is beaten for beating others.

I'm not denying that women are foolish; God Almighty made them to match the men. *George Eliot*

Law makers should not be law breakers. *14th century*

Men and women are kneaded from the same dough. *Russian proverb*

Those who deny freedom to others deserve it not for themselves. *Abraham Lincoln, 1859*

What is sauce for the goose may be sauce for the gander but it is not necessarily sauce for the chicken, the duck, the turkey, or the guinea hen. *Alice B. Toklas*

See also Fair PLAY.

A little GOSSIP goes a long way.

Gossip isn't scandal and it's not merely malicious. It's chatter about the human race by lovers of the same. *Phyllis McGinley, Woman's Home Companion, Jan. 1957*

I hate to spread rumors, but what else can one do with them? *Amanda Lear, 1978*

If you can't say anything good about someone, sit right here by me. *Alice Roosevelt Longworth*

Nobody's interested in sweetness and light. *Hedda Hopper*

There goes the good time that was had by all. *Bette Davis, said of a passing starlet*

The biggest liar in the world is They Say. *Douglas Mallock, as quoted in Reader's Digest, Feb. 1947*

They say. What do they say? Let them say! *Inscription on a ring found in the ruins of Pompeii.* These words are inscribed on the walls of Marischal College at Aberdeen and are displayed over the fireplace in the home of G. B. Shaw.

What will the neighbors say? *1942, B-1043*

What's nobody's business is everybody's curiosity.

See also PEOPLE will talk; STICKS and stones may break my bones, but names will never hurt me.

That GOVERNMENT is best which governs least.*

The legitimate object of government is to do for a community of people, whatever they need to have done, but cannot do at all, or cannot so well do for themselves, in their separate and individual capacities. *Abraham Lincoln*

*Often quoted from Thoreau's "Civil Disobedience," 1849, but traceable to a statement of Thomas Jefferson: "That government is best which governs the least, because its people discipline themselves." Keyes (K-93) questions whether Jefferson ever said it, but notes that in 1837 John L. O'Sullivan founded a publication to champion the view that "the best government is that which governs least."

Sour GRAPES.

It is easy to despise what you cannot get. *Aesop, The Fox and the Grapes*

Envy assails the noblest: the winds howl around the highest peaks. *Ovid*

If he calls it a silly and childish game, that means his wife can beat him at it. *Heard in North Dakota*

If we have lost an interest in sex, we may claim the advantage that we are less driven by strong passion and hence less likely to get into trouble. *B. F. Skinner and M. E. Vaughan, Enjoy Old Age*

Many speak the truth when they say they despise riches, but they mean the riches possessed by other men. *Charles Colton*

My best consolation is the hope that the things I failed to get weren't really worth having. © *Ashleigh Brilliant*

Never speak disrespectfully of society. . . . Only people who can't get into it do that. *Oscar Wilde, The Importance of Being Earnest*

There is a sort of hatred which is never extinguished: it is the hatred that superiority inspires in mediocrity. *Paul Bourget*

Those who condemn wealth are those who have none and see no chance of getting it. *William Penn Patrick*

Wise men care not for what they cannot have. *1640, T-439*

'Tis eminence makes envy rise,
As fairest fruits attract the flies.
Jonathan Swift, To Dr. Delany

See also OPPORTUNITY makes the thief.

GRASP all, lose all. *1205, OE-262*

All covet, all lose. *1297, OE-7*

Be not thou envious of evil men, neither desire to be with them. *Proverbs 24:1*

Most people would succeed in small things if they were not troubled with great ambitions. *Henry Wadsworth Longfellow*

Neither shalt thou desire thy neighbour's wife . . . his field, or his manservant, or his maidservant, his ox, or his ass, or any thing that is thy neighbour's. *Deuteronomy 5:21*

Real happiness don't consist so much in what a man don't have, as it does in what he don't want. *Josh Billings*

Thou shalt not covet. *Romans 7:7*

When all sins grow old, covetousness is young. *1732, Fuller*

The GRASS is always greener on the other side of the fence.* *1550, Erasmus*

. . . but our kids are much smarter than our neighbor's.

. . . but it needs mowing more often on this side. *R. J. Jensen*

. . . but their water bill is bigger.

Families with babies and families without babies are sorry for each other. *Ed Howe*

Happiness is an imaginary condition, formerly attributed by the living to the dead, now usually attributed by adults to children, and by children to adults. *Thomas Szasz, The Second Sin*

Life's like a game of marbles. No matter how pretty yours are, the other guy's are prettier. *Gilligan's Island, TV show*

Other people's goats always have the biggest udders. *Latin proverb*

The neighbor's cooking always smells better. *Maltese proverb*

There are numerous individuals in the land who look upon what they ain't got as the only things worth having. *Josh Billings*

Your neighbor's troubles are not as bad as yours, but their children are worse.

I know my neighbor's grass is greener,
The sidewalks and his windows cleaner;
His flowers taller, weeds are fewer,
The paint job on his house is newer.
But I don't envy him one bit,
Because—as follows and to wit;
His view of my place is much drearier
While mine of his yard is superior.
Harold Coffin

*This proverb originates from the habit of cows grazing through the fence that separates them from the next field.

GRASS never grows on a busy street.

Grass grows not upon the highway. *1659, Howell*

We dig our GRAVES with our teeth.

Gluttony kills more than the sword. *16th century*

See also You are what you EAT.

Some are born GREAT, some achieve greatness, and some have greatness thrust upon them. *Shakespeare, Twelfth Night 2.5.59*

Some are born great, others have greatness thrust upon them, and [Richard Nixon] pursues it like a thief with a booster bag. *Jeff Jacks, Door County (Wisc.) Advocate, July 24, 1973)*

Some are born great, some achieve greatness, and others thrust greatness upon themselves. *Boston Post, ca. 1925*

Some are born great, some achieve greatness, and others just grate.

Some are born great, some achieve greatness, and some hire public relations officers. *Daniel J. Boorstin, The Image*

Some men are born mediocre, some men achieve mediocrity, and some men have mediocrity thrust upon them. *Joseph Heller*

Some people marry happily, some acquire happiness after marriage, while others get a divorce and have happiness thrust upon them. *Old postcard*

Some thirst after fame, some thirst after power, but we all thirst after salted peanuts. *Laurence Peter*

The real hero is always a hero by mistake; he dreams of being an honest coward like everybody else. *Umberto Eco, Travels in Hyper Reality*

We may achieve climate, but weather is thrust upon us. *O. Henry*

Beware of GREEKS bearing gifts. *Virgil (70–19 B.C.), Aeneid*

After shaking hands with a Greek, count your fingers. *Albanian proverb*

Beware of Greeks bearing gifts, colored men looking for loans, and whites who understand the Negro. *Adam Clayton Powell*

Take gifts with a sigh; most men give to be paid. *Irish proverb*

There's no GRIEF that hasn't its relief.

See Every CLOUD has a silver lining.

GRIN and bear it.

. . . unless you can smile and change it.

Bear it like a man, even if you feel it like an ass. *G. B. Shaw, Man and Superman*

Blessed are they who have learned to accept the impossible, do without the indispensable, and bear the intolerable.

Cease to lament for that thou canst not help. *Shakespeare, The Two Gentlemen from Verona 3.1.241*

Don't grin, or you'll have to bear it. *Ogden Nash, 1938*

God gave burdens, also shoulders. *Yiddish proverb*

Gnaw the bone that has fallen to thy lot. *1676, Ray*

Grin and ignore it.

Grin to win.

If you can't do what you like, try and like what you can do. *Old postcard*

No man can smile in the face of adversity and mean it. *Ed Howe*

Take the bad with the good.

The man who smiles when things go wrong has thought of someone he can blame it on.

The teakettle is up to its neck in hot water, but sings a merry tune.

There is only one thing for a man to do who is married to a woman who enjoys spending money, and that is to enjoy earning it. *Ed Howe*

Thou shalt not whine. *Wall plaque inscription, 1992.*

See also BEAR and forbear; HANG in there; 'Tis easy enough to be PLEASANT . . .

All is GRIST to the mill. * *1583, WM-269*

*Grist is corn for grinding, i.e., something that keeps the mill operating profitably.

Nice GUYS finish last. *Leo Durocher**

Last guys don't finish nice. *Stanley Kelley, quoted in The Official Rules, by P. Dickson*

Nice guys are winners before the game ever starts. *Addison Walker*

*Interviewed in 1946 by sportswriter Jimmy Cannon, Durocher recalled the New York Giants of the mid-1940s and said, "Take a look at them. All nice guys. They'll finish last. Nice guys. Finish last." Cannon put Durocher's statement in print as "Nice guys finish last." Keyes (K-142–143) offers a slightly different story.

See also The END justifies the means; MIGHT makes right.

HABIT is second nature. *Michel de Montaigne (1533–92), Essays*

Habit frees us by enslaving us.

Nothing is difficult if you're used to it. *Indonesian proverb*

Habit is . . . not to be flung out of the window, but coaxed downstairs one step at a time. *Mark Twain*

The chains of habit are generally too small to be felt until they are too strong to be broken. *Samuel Johnson*

The dogmas of the quiet past are inadequate to the stormy present. . . . As our case is new, so must we think anew and act anew. We must disenthrall ourselves. *Abraham Lincoln*

The first problem for all of us, men and women, is not to learn, but to unlearn. *Gloria Steinem, New York Times, 1971*

There isn't anything you can't stand if you are only born and bred into it. *Mark Twain, A Connecticut Yankee in King Arthur's Court*

We become charlatans without realizing it, and actors without wanting to. *Henri Amiel, Journal Intime*

Habit with him was all the test of truth;
"It must be right: I've done it from my youth."
George Crabbe: The Borough

See also CUSTOM is a second nature.

Never do anything by HALVES. 1753, WM-273

Half measures are always fatal. *1930, BJW-280*

If you're looking for a helping HAND, you'll find one at the end of your arm.

176

See GOD helps those who help themselves; HELP yourself; PADDLE your own canoe.

Let not thy left HAND know what thy right hand doeth.[*]

. . . for it is probably not worth knowing.

To enjoy a good reputation, give publicly and steal privately. *Josh Billings*

[*]When thou doest alms, let not thy left hand know what thy right hand doeth. *Matthew 6:3*

One HAND washes the other. *6th century B.C., F-140*

One hand washeth the other, and both wash the face. *James Sanford, The Garden of Pleasure*

One hand will not wash the other for nothing. *James Kelley, A Complete Collection of Scottish Proverbs*

One mule scratches another. *1550, Erasmus*

You scratch my back and I'll scratch yours.

The HAND is quicker than the eye.

. . . but somewhat slower than the fly. *Richard Armour*

The HAND that rocks the cradle rules the world. *William Ross Wallace, 1865; O-105*

Baby-sitter: The hand that rocks the cradle raids the refrigerator.

HANDSOME is as handsome does. *1580, T-161*

. . . as the sow said to the boar. *H. C. Bailey, 1941; BJW-286*

A good face is a letter of recommendation. It naturally makes the beholders inquisitive into the person who is the owner of it, and generally prepossesses them in his favour. *Joseph Addison, The Spectator*

Beauty is a blessing. *1616, T-35*

Charles Lamb, recalling Edmund Spenser's observation that "Many a gentle mind/ Dwells in [a] deformed tabernacle," tells of an unforgettably ugly person who could do you a thousand kindnesses, and "her face remains the same" (*Popular Fallacies*).

Handsome is what makeup does.

He is a man who acts like a man. *Danish proverb*

Recipe for Good Looks: Take five ounces of patience, six ounces of goodwill, a pinch of hope and a bunch of faith. Then take two hands full of industry, a packet of prudence, a few sprays of sympathy, a bowl of humility and a jarful of spirit-of-humor. Season with strong commonsense and simmer gently in a pan of daily content. *British church recipe book*

HANG in there.

Heroism is endurance for one moment more. *Caucasian Mountain proverb*

Victory belongs to the most persevering. *Napoleon*

When you get into a tight place and everything goes against you, till it seems as though you could not hold on a minute longer, never give up then, for that is just the place and time that the tide will turn. *Harriet Beecher Stowe*

When you get to the end of your rope, tie a knot and hang on. *Franklin D. Roosevelt*

See also BEAR and forbear; GRIN and bear it; 'Tis easy enough to be PLEASANT . . .

HANG loose.

Let go and let God. *Slogan of Alcoholics Anonymous*

See also GO with the flow; Take it EASY.

We must all HANG together, or we shall all assuredly hang separately. *Benjamin Franklin (attributed), 1776*

Either men must learn to live like brothers or they will die like beasts. *Max Lerner, 1949*

They came for the Jews and I did not speak out—because I was not a Jew.

Then they came for the communists and I did not speak out—because I was not a communist.

Then they came for the trade unionists and I did not speak out—because I was not a trade unionist.

Then they came for me—and there was no one left to speak out for me. *Martin Niemöller*

*First to sign the Declaration of Independence on July 4, 1776, John Hancock turned to Benjamin Franklin and said, "We must all hang together." (Hancock had reason to be serious; over a year ago, the British General Gage had put a price on Hancock's head.) Franklin made the witty reply: "Ay, we must all hang together, else we shall all hang separately." Fogg, page 183.

As well be HANGED for a sheep as a lamb.* 1678, *Ray*

I don't believe in knocking a man down by inches—if you have anything against him, let him have it. *Josh Billings*

*Until 1832, in England, stealing even a lamb was punishable by death.

If you're born to be HANGED, you'll never be drowned. 1503, *T-33*

Mark Twain recalled his mother saying, "People born to be hanged are safe in water." *A. B. Paine, Mark Twain: A Biography*

HAPPINESS comes from work well done.*

. . . so find out what you don't do well, then don't do it.

A man is a worker. If he is not that, he is nothing. *Joseph Conrad*

Blessed is he who has found his work; let him ask no other blessedness. *Thomas Carlyle, Past and Present*

Choose a job you love, and you will never have to work a day in your life.

Don't undertake a project unless it is manifestly important and nearly impossible. *Edwin H. Land*

Every man loves what he is good at. *Thomas Shadwell*

Freud was once asked what he thought a normal person should be able to do well. The questioner probably expected a complicated answer. But Freud . . . is reported to have said, *"Lieben und arbeiten"* (to love and to work). *Erik Erikson, Childhood and Society*

Get your happiness out of your work or you will never know what real happiness is. *Elbert Hubbard*

Halfway through exiting work is halfway to heaven. *Mignon McLaughlin*

Have a purpose in life and having it, throw into your work such strength of mind and muscle as God has given you. *Thomas Carlyle*

Honest toil is holy service, faithful work is praise and prayer. *Henry Van Dycke*

I don't want to make money. I just want to be wonderful. *Marilyn Monroe*

I know I was writing stories when I was five. I don't know what I did before that. Just loafed, I suppose. *P. G. Wodehouse*

If a man has a talent and cannot use it, he has failed. If he has a talent and uses only half of it, he has partly failed. If he has a talent and learns somehow to use the whole of it, he has gloriously succeeded, and won a satisfaction and a triumph few men ever know. *Thomas Wolfe*

If a man love the labor of any trade, apart from any question of success or fame, the gods have called him. *Robert Louis Stevenson*

If I cannot do great things, I can do small things in a great way. *James Freeman Clarke*

If work is so good, how come they got to pay us to do it? *Mike Royko*

If you have to do it every day, for God's sake learn to do it well. *Mignon McLaughlin*

It is better to be in love with your work than in love with yourself. *B. C. Forbes*

It's not the sugar that makes the tea sweet, but the stirring. *Sam Levenson, You Can Say That Again*

Laziness may appear attractive, but work gives satisfaction. *Anne Frank, The Diary of a Young Girl*

Look at a day when you are supremely satisfied at the end. It's not a day when you lounge around doing nothing; it's when you've had everything to do, and you've done it. *Margaret Thatcher*

Love, at best, is joy; work, though, can be ecstasy. *Mignon McLaughlin*

Pleasure is a by-product of doing something that is worth doing. *A. Lawrence Lowell*

Problems are only opportunities in work clothes. *Henry J. Kaiser*

The man who is born with a talent that he is meant to use finds his greatest happiness in using it. *Johann Wolfgang von Goethe*

The more I want to get something done, the less I call it work. *Richard Bach, Illusions*

The only advice I ever give to young people who come to me for career counseling consists of ten one-syllable words: "Find out what you do best, and stick with it." *Sydney J. Harris*

The secret of joy in work is contained in one word—excellence. To know how to do something well is to enjoy it. *Pearl Buck, The Joy of Children*

The reward of a thing well done is to have it done. *Ralph Waldo Emerson*

The test of a vocation is the love of the drudgery it involves. *Logan Pearsall Smith, Afterthoughts*

There is always something useful to be done. I have no respect for those idle rich who discharge their duty to be useful by staging charity balls. *Marlene Dietrich*

They are happy men whose nature sort with their vocations. *Francis Bacon*

Three rules of work: 1. Out of clutter, find simplicity. 2. From discord, find harmony. 3. In the middle of difficulty lies opportunity. *Albert Einstein*

To love what you do and feel that it matters— how could anything be more fun. *Katharine Graham*

To work is to pray. *Latin proverb*

When love and skill work together, expect a masterpiece. *John Ruskin*

Work is love made visible. *Kahlil Gibran*

Work is much more fun than fun. *Noel Coward*

Work keeps us from three evils: boredom, vice and need. *Voltaire*

We are not here to play, to dream, to drift,
We have hard work to do, and loads to lift.
Shun not the struggle, face it, 'tis God's gift.
M. D. Babcock, 1936 office calendar

*Keyes (K-173–74) discusses the expression of this thought by Leo Tolstoy and Theodor Reik.

HAPPINESS is a warm puppy. *Charles Schulz*

. . . with an empty bladder.

HAPPINESS is just a state of mind.

. . . like insanity.

. . . Not all. Some occasionally is in the stomach and some frequently is some inches farther down. *George Jean Nathan*

A fool's paradise is better than none. *E. Bonett, 1944*

A fool's paradise is nevertheless a paradise. *Cynic, 1905*

Happiness? A good cigar, a good meal, a good cigar and a good woman—or a bad woman; it depends on how much happiness you can handle. *George Burns, 1984*

Happiness is a habit. *Elbert Hubbard, Epigrams*

Happiness is a positive cash flow.

Happiness is so fragile that one risks the loss of it by talking of it. *Jules Lemaître*

No mockery in the world ever sounds to me as hollow as that of being told to cultivate happiness. . . . Happiness is not a potato, to be planted in mould, and tilled with manure. *Charlotte Brontë*

See also There is nothing either good or bad but THINKING makes it so.

HAPPINESS is where you find it.

Life is a tragedy full of joy. *Bernard Malamud*

What seems nasty, painful, evil, can become a source of beauty, joy and strength, if faced with an open mind. Every moment is a golden one for him who has the vision to recognize it as such. *Henry Miller*

Be good and you will be HAPPY.

. . . but you will miss a lot of fun. *Old postcard*

Always do right; it will gratify some people and astonish the rest. *Mark Twain, Pudd'nhead Wilson's Calendar*

Be good and you will be lonesome. *Mark Twain, Pudd'nhead Wilson's New Calendar*

Be good or you'll be sorry. *Old postcard*

Be good, even at the cost of your self-respect. *Don Herold*

Be virtuous and you will be eccentric. *Mark Twain*

Be virtuous and you'll be happy? Nonsense! Be happy and you'll begin to be virtuous. *James Gould Cozzens, as quoted in Reader's Digest, Mar. 1922*

Being nice is overrated. *Jim Davis, Garfield: Words to Live By*

Don't be on the side of the angels, it's too lowering. *D. H. Lawrence, 1927*

He who does kind deeds becomes rich. *Hindu proverb*

Human happiness is like Joseph's coat—a thing of many colors. *Josh Billings*

I begin to find that too good a character is inconvenient. *Walter Scott*

If your morals make you dreary, depend on it they are wrong. *Robert Louis Stevenson, A Christmas Sermon; M-473*

My first wish is to do for the best. *George Washington*

Rise early, work hard and late, live on what you can't sell, give nothing away, and if you don't die rich and go to the devil, you may sue me for damages. *Josh Billings*

To enjoy yourself and make others enjoy themselves, without harming yourself or any other; that, to my mind, is the whole of ethics. *Sébastien-Roch Nicolas Chamfort, Maximes et Pensées*

To those who are good to me, let me be good. To those who are not good to me, let me also be good. Thus shall goodness be increased. *Lao-tzu*

We are here on earth to do good to others. What the others are here for, I do not know. *W. H. Auden*

We ought never to do wrong when people are looking. *Mark Twain*

We should live our lives as though Christ was coming this afternoon. *Jimmy Carter, 1976*

Be good, sweet maid, and let who can be
   clever;
Do noble things, not dream them, all day
   long;
And so make Life, and Death, for that for
   ever,
One grand sweet song.
Charles Kingsley, Farewell

See also VIRTUE is its own reward.

HARM watch, harm catch. *1481, WM-283*

No HARM in asking.

Ask much to have a little. *1640, Herbert*

There's many a good thing lost by not asking for it. *William C. Hunter*

HASTE makes waste. *Latin proverb*

A hasty man drinks his tea with a fork. *Chinese proverb*

Do nothing in great haste, except catching fleas and running from a mad dog. *Ole Farmer's Almanac, 1811*

Don't be rushed into making an important decision. People will understand if you say, "I'd like a little more time to think it over. Can I get back to you tomorrow?" *H. Jackson Brown, Jr., Life's Little Instruction Book*

Haste is from hell. *1633, Howell*

Haste makes waste and waste makes want and want makes strife between the good man and his wife. *1678, Ray*

If you go mo' slow, you'll go mo' fast. *Heard in Mississippi and New York*

If you hurry, you stumble.

Measure your cloth ten times; you can cut it but once. *Vermont proverb*

The slow and dopey waste far more than the swift and able. *Leo Rosten*

We mustn't act hastily! Let's wait until our enthusiasm evaporates. © *Ashleigh Brilliant*

Wisely and slow. They stumble that run fast. *Shakespeare, Romeo and Juliet 2.3.94*

Don't lose your head
To gain a minute.
You need your head.
Your brains are in it.
Burma-Shave road sign

Make HASTE slowly. *Latin proverb borrowed from the Greek*

. . . except when killing mosquitoes.

. . . but don't dawdle.

All haste is from the devil. *Latin proverb*

Courting is like strawberries and cream, wants to be did slow, then you git the flavor. *Josh Billings*

Go up hill as fast as you please, but go down hill slow. *Josh Billings*

God did not create hurry. *Finnish proverb*

Good and quickly seldom agree.

If you want to get there quick, go slow. *Josh Billings*

In bad things be slow; in good things be quick. *Afghan proverb*

More haste, less speed. *English proverb*

Nothing must be done hastily but killing of fleas. *1670, Ray*

Nothing valuable can be lost by taking time. *Abraham Lincoln, first inaugural speech, 1861*

One-half the troubles of this life can be traced to saying yes too quickly and not saying no soon enough. *Josh Billings*

People forget how fast you did a job—but they remember how well you did it. *Howard W. Newton*

Slowness comes from God and quickness from the devil. *African proverb*

The slower you go, the farther you get. *Russian proverb*

To a quick question, give a slow answer. *Italian proverb*

Too swift arrives as tardy as too slow. *Shakespeare, Romeo and Juliet 2.6.15*

Wait a minute. *Sam Rayburn, on "the three most important words in the English lan-*

guage," *Jack Valenti, New York Times, May 5, 1958*

See also EASY does it; HASTE makes waste.

Make HAY while the sun shines. *1509, T-295*

. . . and make rye while the moon shines.

. . . There's many a lemon dries up unsqueezed. *Old postcard*

Cy Sez: When I was a young fellow I never took the gals out buggy ridin' but nowadays, well sometimes I wish I was young again. *Old postcard*

Success comes from making hay with the grass that grows under other people's feet.

The sun shines hot, and if we use delay,
Cold biting winter mars our hop'd for hay.
Shakespeare, 3 Henry VI 4.8.60

Two HEADS are better than one. *1390, O-233*

. . . on a drum.

. . . at a barbershop.

. . . even if one is a cabbage-head. *1864, WM-288*

. . . quoth the Woman, when she had her dog with her to the Market. *1732, Fuller*

A glass of beer helps me think. Two heads are better than one.

The Pope and a peasant know more than the Pope alone. *Italian proverb*

Two heads are better than none. *Jean Green*

HEALTH is wealth.

The preservation of health is a duty. Few seem conscious that there is such a thing as physical morality. *Herbert Spencer, Education*

There is an Arab philosophy about health. They say that health is the digit one, love is zero, glory zero, success zero. Put the one of health beside the others and you are a rich man. But without the one of health, everything is zero. *Jack Denton Scott, Passport to Adventure*

See also A good WIFE and health are a man's best wealth.

It is better to be poor and HEALTHY than to be rich and sick.[*]

[*]Often facetiously misquoted as, "It is better to be rich and healthy than to be poor and sick."

Don't believe everything you HEAR.

Don't believe everything you read.

Do not all you can; spend not all you have; believe not all you hear; and tell not all you know. *1855, Bohn*

If you speak with a cunning mouth, I listen with a cunning ear. *Annang (African) proverb*

Men were born to lie, and women to believe them. *John Gay*

My sources are unreliable, but their information is fascinating. © *Ashleigh Brilliant*

The art of pleasing is the art of deceiving. *French proverb*

The man who writes the advertisements for the bank is not the guy who makes the loans. *Peter's Almanac*

See also CAVEAT emptor.

A merry HEART maketh a cheerful countenance. *Proverbs 15:13*

See SMILE.

As a man thinks in his HEART, so is he. *Proverbs 23:7*[*]

Man is a masterpiece of creation, if only because no amount of determinism can prevent him from believing that he acts as a free being. *Georg Lichtenberg*

Man is what he believes. *Anton Chekhov*

Success is a state of mind. If you want success, start thinking of yourself as a success. *Joyce Brothers*

The man who is a genius and doesn't know it probably isn't. *Stanislaw J. Lec*

They can ... because they think they can. *Virgil*

[*]"For as he thinketh in his heart, so is he": given as a warning not to be fooled by the generosity of a wicked person.

See also LIFE is what you make it; The power of positive THINKING; There is nothing either good or bad but THINKING makes it so.

Faint HEART ne'er won fair lady. *1390, O-75*

... but a faint whisper often catches her.

...True. But prepare to have your face slapped any number of times nonetheless. *George Jean Nathan*

A timid horseman does not stay mounted long. *Heard in Indiana*

A woman kissed is half enjoyed. *1607, T-744*

Chutzpah succeeds! *Yiddish proverb*

Every woman likes to be taken with a grain of assault.

Faint heart ne'er won fur, lady.

Faint praise ne'er won fair lady. *Life, ca. 1925*

He who begs timidly, courts refusal. *Heard in Ontario*

No one ever became immortal through cowardice. *Sallust, ca. 40 B.C.*

Politeness is a pleasant way for a man to get nowhere with a girl.

Some I could love if I cared to—others I would love if I dared to. *Old postcard*

Affection faints not like a pale-fac'd coward,
But then woos best when most his choice is
    froward.
Shakespeare, Venus and Adonis

See also FORTUNE favors the bold.

Out of the abundance of the HEART the mouth speaketh. *Matthew 12:34*

The HEART has its reasons, which reason does not know. *Blaise Pascal, Pensées, F-367*

A hunch is creativity trying to tell you something. *Frank Capra*

A loving heart is the truest wisdom. *Charles Dickens*

Dare to err and to dream; a higher meaning often lies in childish play. *Schiller, Thekla*

Faith is under the left nipple. *Martin Luther*

Good conduct is not dictated by reason but by a divine instinct that is beyond reason. *G. B. Shaw*

Good instincts usually tell you what to do long before your head has figured it out. *Michael Burks, Outrageous Good Fortune*

Hearts may agree, though heads differ. *1732, Fuller*

I will always stick by the people I love. Even though I don't know why I love them.

If the heart is right, the head can't be very wrong. *Josh Billings, 1865*

If you can explain it, it's not worth doing. *David Thomas, 1979*

Man lives by the mind, woman by the heart. *Eduard Herve*

May I never use my reason against truth. *Elie Wiesel, quoting a Hasidic rabbi's prayer*

One of the functions of intelligence is to take account of the dangers that come from trusting solely to intelligence. *Louis Mumford, The Transformation of Man*

Reason deceives us; conscience never. *Jean-Jacques Rosseau*

Some problems are just too complicated for rational, logical solutions. They admit of insights, not answers. *Jerome Weisner*

The feller that puts off marryin' till he kin support a wife hain't much in love. *Kin Hubbard*

The head never rules the heart, but just becomes its partner in crime. *Mignon McLaughlin*

The heart has its prisons that intelligence cannot unlock. *Marcel Jouhandeau, De la grandeur*

The man who listens to Reason is lost; Reason enslaves all whose minds are not strong enough to master her. *G. B. Shaw, Man and Superman*

The road to the head lies through the heart. *American proverb*

The world talks to the mind. Parents . . . talk to the heart. *Haim Ginott*

To live is like to love—all reason is against it, and all healthy instinct is for it. *Samuel Butler, Higgledy-Piggledy: Lifes and Love*

Trust your hunches. They're usually based on facts filed away just below the conscious level. *Joyce Brothers*

What the heart knows today the head will understand tomorrow. *James Stephens*

When you fish for love, bait with your heart, not your brain. *Mark Twain's Notebook, 1935*

You can go home when you can't go anywhere else. *Heard in Illinois and North Carolina*

I put my hand upon my heart
And swore that we should never part—
I wonder what I should have said
If I had put it on my head.
C.D.B. Ellis

The way to a man's HEART is through his stomach. *1814, O-242*

A starving man is a dangerous man, no matter how respectable his political opinions may be. A man who has had his dinner is never a revolutionist; his politics are all talk. *G. B. Shaw, The Intelligent Woman's Guide*

Men are conservative after dinner. *Ralph Waldo Emerson*

Men are like bagpipes: no sound comes from them till they're full. *Irish proverb*

The surest way to hit a woman's heart is to take aim kneeling. *Douglas Jerrold, ca. 1850*

The way to a man's heart is through his ego. *Heard in Kansas*

The way to a woman's heart is through the door of a good restaurant. *Richard Needham*

There is no love sincerer than the love of food. *G. B. Shaw, Man and Superman*

When meat is in, anger is out. *English proverb*

We may live without poetry, music, and art;
We may live without conscience, and live
   without heart;
We may live without friends, we may live
   without books;
But civilized man cannot live without cooks.
Owen Meredith, Lucile; F-141

See also KISSING don't last . . .

A HEART ATTACK is nature's way of telling us to slow down.

A yawn is nature's way of giving the person listening to a bore an opportunity to open his mouth. *Henny Youngman*

Cocaine is God's way of saying you're making too much money. *Robin Williams*

Death is nature's way of preventing you from inhaling smog. *Peter's Almanac*

Death is nature's way of telling you to slow down.

Healing is nature's way of telling you that you really do matter. © *Ashleigh Brilliant*

If you can't stand the HEAT, get out of the kitchen.*

Be not a baker if your head be of butter. *1640, Herbert*

Don't dish it out if you can't take it.

He that hath a head of wax, must not walk in the sun. *1640, Herbert*

He that's afraid of every grass must not sleep in the meadow. *1710, T-273*

My version [of Truman's proverb] is If you can't stand the heat, go back to the kitchen. *U.N. Ambassador Jeane Kirkpatrick, on her wish to retire from the pressures of political life*

Who has skirts of straw needs fear the fire. *1659, T-610*

*President Harry S. Truman, who popularized this saying, said this was a favorite expression of his military aide Major General Harry Vaughan (*Time, April 28, 1952*).

Everybody wants to go to HEAVEN but nobody wants to die.

. . . Heaven for climate; hell for society. *Mark Twain's Speeches*

Do not go gentle into that good night. *Dylan Thomas, title and first line of 1952 poem*

How much can I get away with, and still go to heaven? *Bumper sticker*

I think immortality is an over-rated commodity. *S. N. Behrman*

Millions long for immortality who do not know what to do with themselves on a rainy Sunday afternoon. *Susan Ertz*

Of course there's a heaven, but I don't think you can get there from here. © *Ashleigh Brilliant*

You could say people are living longer because of the decline of religion. Not many people believe in the hereafter, so they keep going. *Cyril Clarke, 1986*

The road to HELL is paved with good intentions. 1574, T-307

The path of civilization is paved with tin cans. *Elbert Hubbard*. Advance notice of environmental pollution.

Everyone knows the harm the bad do, but who knows the mischief done by the good? *William Makepeace Thackeray*

Hell is full of good meanings, but heaven is full of good works. *1574, WM-296*

Hell is not so bad as the road that leads to it. *Yiddish proverb*

Hell is paved with big pretensions. *Cynic, 1903*

Hell isn't merely paved with good intentions; it's walled and roofed with them. *Aldous Huxley, 1944*

I suppose the reason why the "road to ruin" is broad, is to accommodate the great amount of travel in that direction. *Josh Billings*

"Mean to" don't pick no cotton. *African American proverb*

The road to health is paved with food abstentions. *Louis Safian*

The road to hell is always in good repair because its users pay so dearly for its upkeep.

The road to hell is paved with good conventions.

The road to hell is paved with inattentions.

The road to hell is paved. It has to be; it gets a lot of traffic.

The road to success always seems to be under construction.

The road to the patent office is paved with good inventions.

Let Mr. Tomorrow go to the devil
And send us, O Lord,
The man who gets things done today:
And we will pay the freight.
Amen.
The Business Man's Prayer, on an old postcard

Hell is paved with good intentions,
Curbed with broken promises
And gutted with excuses.

HELP yourself.[*]

. . . while nobody's looking.

Be selfish. Nothing else makes the human race predictable. *John Ciardi*

God gives the nuts, but does not crack them. *German proverb*

He that has a mouth of his own, must not say to another, Blow. *1640, Herbert*

Most people are neither for you nor against you; they are thinking about themselves. *John W. Gardner*

Nobody pities the cook who goes hungry. *Yiddish proverb*

Take care to get what you like, or you will end up liking what you get. *G. B. Shaw*

The fool is thirsty in the midst of water. *Ethiopian proverb*

The older a man grows, the more convinced he becomes he will have to be his own best friend. *Ed Howe*

The world is your cow, but you have to do the milking. *Vermont proverb*

A poor cook that may not lick his own fingers. *1546, Heywood*

When a man is drowning, it may be better for him to try to swim than to thrash around waiting for divine intervention. *William Sloane Coffin*

In battle or business, whatever the game,
In law or in love, it is ever the same;
In the struggle for power, or the scramble for pelf,
Let this be your motto: rely on yourself!
John Godfrey Saxe

*Help yourself, and heaven will help you. *Jean de La Fontaine (1621–97), Fables*

See also CHARITY begins at home; The door to SUCCESS is always marked Push; Faint HEART ne'er won fair lady; Don't HIDE your light under a bushel; GOD helps those who help themselves; If you're looking for a helping HAND, you'll find one at the end of your arm; Put your best FOOT forward.

Every little bit HELPS. *1590, O-67*

. . . said the old lady as she piddled in the sea.

. . . but that's a small consolation to him who gets less than his share.

"Every little bit helps to lighten the load," said the captain as he threw his wife overboard.

Every HERO becomes a bore at last. *Ralph Waldo Emerson, Representative Men, 1850*

At fifty you begin to be tired of the world, and at sixty the world is tired of you. *Count Oxenstierna, Reflexions and Maxims*

Show me a hero and I will write you a tragedy. *F. Scott Fitzgerald, The Crack-Up*

Somebody's boring me . . . I think it's me. *Dylan Thomas*

The minute a man is convinced that he is interesting, he isn't. *Stephen Leacock*

This thing of being a hero, about the main thing to it is to know when to die. Prolonged life has ruined more men than it ever made. *Will Rogers*

Time makes heroes but dissolves celebrities. *Daniel J. Boorstin*

What is success? It is a toy balloon among children armed with pins. *Gene Fowler*

No Man is a HERO to his valet.*

. . . not because the hero is no hero, but because the valet is a valet. *Georg Hegel*

. . . Heroes never have valets. *Elbert Hubbard*

. . . To that it may be added that few men are heroes to themselves. *Agatha Christie, The Patriotic Murders*

A valet's testimony tells you more about valets than heroes. *Leo Rosten*

All celebrated people lose dignity on a close view. *Napoleon*

Even if a man was delightful, no woman would marry him if she knew what he was like. *E. F. Benson, Paul*

Many a man has been a wonder to the world, whose wife and valet have seen nothing in him that was even remarkable. Few men have been admired by their servants. *Michel de Montaigne*

No author is a man of genius to his publisher. *Heinrich Heine*

No man is a hero to a bill collector. *Louisville Times, ca. 1925*

No man is a hero to his children. He has far more chance with his valet. *V. Williams, 1937; BJW-399*

No man is a hero to his mother-in-law. *Henny Youngman*

No man is a hero to his wallet. *Wall Street Journal*

People are like birds: on the wing, all beautiful; up close, all beady little eyes. *Mignon McLaughlin*

The nearer one approaches to great persons, the more one sees that they are but men. Rarely are they great in the eyes of their valets. *Jean de La Bruyère, Les Caractères*

*The line was popularized in the 17th century by Madame de Cornuel, but the thought goes back 2000 years, according to Fogg (page 101). The King of Thessaly, Antigonus Gonatas responded to a poem addressing him as "son of the sun, and a god," by commenting, "My valet-de-chambre sings me no such song."

See also DISTANCE lends enchantment.

No man is a HERO to his wife.

A captain of industry is nothing but a buck private to his wife. *Heard in Illinois*

No man is a hero to his wife's psychiatrist. *Eric Berne*

He who HESITATES is lost. 1713, O-111

. . . Bachelors think otherwise.

He who hesitates is a damned fool. *Mae West*

He who hesitates is bossed.

He who hesitates is honked. *Kin Hubbard*

He who hesitates is last.

He who hesitates is not only lost, but several miles from the next freeway exit.

He who hesitates is sometimes saved. *James Thurber, The Thurber Carnival*

He who hesitates gets bumped from the rear. *Homer Phillips, as quoted in Reader's Digest, July 1952*

He who hesitates may know what he's doing.

In Utah . . . he who hesitates is lost—to Mormonism. *John H. Beadle, Western Wilds*

No business opportunity is ever lost. If you fumble it, your competitor will find it.

She who hesitates is won. *Oscar Wilde*

The girl who hesitates too long,
And when she gets in, gets in wrong.
Old postcard

He who dallies is a dastard, he who doubts is damned.

A bog is not the place to stop and think;
Trip fast across; he who hesitates may sink.
Arthur Guiterman

Don't HIDE your light under a bushel. *

A modest person is usually admired—if people ever hear of him. *Ed Howe*

A boy's gotta hustle his book. *Truman Capote, Esquire magazine, 1971*

God helps those who help themselves. Upon the same principle, mankind praises those who praise themselves. *Josh Billings*

Hide not your Talents, they for Use were made. What's a Sun-Dial in the Shade? *Poor Richard's Almanac, 1750*

I am here to live out loud. *Émile Zola*

Ideas are like children—if you don't send them out into the world, they die with you. *Jacob L. Moreno*

If you don't toot your own horn, no one else will toot it for you. *Heard in U.S. and Canada*

Modesty is for those who have no talent.

Noise proves nothing. Often a hen who has merely laid an egg cackles as if she laid an asteroid. *Mark Twain, Pudd'nhead Wilson's New Calendar*

Toot your horn, but deliver the goods. *Heard in U.S. and Canada*

We are all salesmen every day of our lives. We are selling our ideas, our plans, our enthusiasms to those with whom we come in contact. *Charles Schwab*

*An allusion to Matthew 5:15–16, recalling how Jesus admonished his followers not to be bashful about spreading the word: "Nei-ther do men light a candle, and put it under a bushel, but on a candlestick. . . . Let your light so shine before men, that they may see your good works."

See also It pays to ADVERTISE; SELF-LOVE is better than self-hate.

HINDSIGHT is better than foresight. *1879, WM-301*

A study of economics usually reveals that the best time to buy anything is last year. *Marty Allen*

Hindsight is always 20/20. *Billy Wilder*

If one knew that he would fall, he would lie down. *Polish proverb*

If your foresight was as good as your hindsight, you would be better off by a damn sight. *Heard in Illinois*

No matter what happens, there's always somebody who knew it would. *Lonny Starr*

HISTORY is bunk. *Henry Ford* *

A lot of guys have had a lot of fun joking about Ford because he admitted one time that he didn't know history. He don't know it, but history will know him. He has made more history than his critics have ever read. *Will Rogers*

Historians are like deaf people who go on answering questions that no one has asked them. *Leo Tolstoy*

History is fiction with the truth left out. *Heard in Illinois*

History is lies agreed upon.

History is only a confused heap of facts. *Lord Chesterfield, letter to his son, Feb. 5, 1760*

History is the propaganda of the victors. *Ernest Toller*

History: An account, mostly false, of events mostly unimportant, which are brought about by rulers mostly knaves, and soldiers mostly fools. *Ambrose Bierce*

History would be a wonderful thing—if it were only true. *Leo Tolstoy*

Myths are public dreams, dreams are private myths. *Joseph Campbell*

Perhaps nothing has changed in the course of history as much as historians. *Franklin P. Jones, as quoted in Reader's Digest, Sept. 1958*

The historian is a prophet looking backwards. *Friedrich von Schlegel, Athenaeum*

The one duty we owe to history is to rewrite it. *Oscar Wilde*

The very ink with which all history is written is merely fluid prejudice. *Mark Twain*

What is history but a fable agreed upon? *Napoleon, Sayings*

You can never plan the future by the past. *Edmund Burke*

*On the eve of America's entry into World War I, Henry Ford launched a disarmament plan. When a *Chicago Tribune* reporter pressed Ford for the historical context of his views, Ford reportedly said, "What do we care what they did 500 or 1,000 years ago? . . . History is more or less bunk. It's tradition. We don't want tradition. We want to live in the present and the only history that is worth a tinker's dam is the history we make today." (K-14)

HISTORY repeats itself. 1553, WM-302

. . . Haven't I heard that before?

. . . but in such cunning disguise that we never detect the resemblance until the damage is done. *Sydney J. Harris*

. . . that's one of the things that's wrong with history. *Clarence Darrow*

God cannot alter the past, but historians can. *Samuel Butler*

History repeats itself, says the proverb, but that is precisely what it never really does. It is the historians who repeat themselves. *Clement F. Rogers, Verify Your References*

History does not repeat itself; man repeats his mistakes. *Barbara Tuchman*

History is the science of what never happens twice.

If history repeats itself, and the unexpected always happens, how incapable must Man be of learning from experience! *G. B. Shaw*

The past's a book wherein some truths are
    found,
But not a chain by which man's feet are
    bound.
Arthur Guiterman

Don't be HOLIER-THAN-THOU.*

I have never met a single man who was morally as good as I am, who has always in every situation been drawn, as I have been, to the good. Who, like me, is always ready to sacrifice everything for this ideal? *Leo Tolstoy*

Saints should always be judged guilty until they are proved innocent. *George Orwell, Reflections on Gandhi*

*From Isaiah 65:5. The prophet criticizes those who say, ". . . come not near to me; for I am holier than thou."

A woman's place is in the HOME. 467 B.C., F-205

Be it ever so humble there's no place like HOME. *John Howard Payne, Home Sweet Home, 1823*

. . . and many a man is glad of it. *F. M. Knowles, 1906*

. . . When this motto is displayed in the guest room, what's the message?

Be it ever so mortgaged, there's no place like home. *Old postcard*

Home is home, though ne'er so homely. *1666, Torriano*

There's no place like home, thank God. *Old postcard*

Be it ever so humble, there's no place like
    home
For cutting your finger or bashing your dome,
For twisting an ankle or blacking an eye
Or breaking a leg when you don't even try.
Richard Armour

See also HOME sweet home; It takes a heap o' livin' to make a HOUSE a home.

HOME sweet home.*

. . . where you can scratch where it itches. *Old postcard*

. . . the father's kingdom, the mother's world, and the child's paradise.

A house is a home when it shelters the body and comforts the soul. *Phillip Moffitt, Esquire, April 1986*

All men are not homeless, but some are home less than others.

East, west, home is best. *1855, Bohn*

Home is where we grumble the most and are treated the best.

I would like to spend the whole of my life traveling, if I could anywhere borrow another life to spend at home. *William Hazlett*

*Principal song of the opera, *Clari, the Maid of Milan*, by John Howard Payne. Inspiration for the song came to Payne when he heard a Sicilian folk song, while traveling in Italy.

See also Be it ever so humble, there's no place like HOME.

HONESTY is the best policy. *1599, T-316*

. . . but not the cheapest. *Mark Twain*

. . . when there is money in it. *Mark Twain*

. . . most of the time.

. . . There's less competition.

. . . but don't take my word for it, try it. *Josh Billings, 1865*

. . . but there are too few policy holders. *Henny Youngman*

. . . but it can be wiser to tell a lie that sounds like the truth than to tell a truth that sounds like a lie.

. . . but it does little to develop creativity.

. . . but he who is governed by that maxim is not an honest man. *Richard Whately, Detached Thoughts*

... "but," as a politician said, "there comes a time to put principle aside and do what's right."

... [but] it is better to be partly right in practice, than perfectly right in theory. *Old postcard*

A well told lie never goes into details. *Frederick H. Seymour*

Always be sincere, even if you don't mean it. *Howard Kandel*

Always do the right thing. This will gratify some people and astonish the rest. *Mark Twain*

An honest answer can get you into a lot of trouble.

Any fool can tell the truth, but it requires a man of some sense to know how to lie well. *Samuel Butler*

Be honest. That's all. *Old postcard*

Be true and you shall never rue. *Motto of Duff family*

Craftiness must have clothes, but truth loves to go naked. *English proverb*

Don't tell a lie unless you are willing to eat it. *Ed Howe*

Every man is wholly honest to himself and to God, but not to anyone else. *Mark Twain, More Maxims of Mark*

Help fight truth decay.

Honesty has been preached more and practiced less than any other two virtues. *Josh Billings*

Honest is a fine Jewel; but much out of fashion. *1732, Fuller*

Honesty is the best fallacy. *Gene Fowler*

Honest is the best policy? *L. L. Levinson*

Honesty is unbelievable.

Honesty pays, but it doesn't seem to pay enough to suit some people. *Kin Hubbard*

How do I know you honestly want me to be honest? © *Ashleigh Brilliant*

I chose honest arrogance over hypocritical humility. *Frank Lloyd Wright*

I have discovered a new way to communicate: it's called being honest. © *Ashleigh Brilliant*

I have found that nothing so deceives your adversaries as telling them the truth. *Otto Bismarck*

I'm not smart enough to lie. *Ronald Reagan*

If you tell the truth you don't have to remember anything. *Mark Twain, Notebook*

It is always the best policy to tell the truth, unless, of course, you are an exceptionally good liar. *Jerome K. Jerome*

It takes just three times as long to tell a lie, on any subject, as it does to tell the truth. *Josh Billings*

Knavery may serve a turn but honesty never fails. *1679, Ray*

Let your life be, each day, such that you can look any man in the eye and tell him to "Go to Hell." *Old postcard*

Let your voice be the sounding-board of your soul. *Elbert Hubbard*

Make yourself an honest man and then you may be sure there is one rascal less in the world. *Thomas Carlyle*

My way of joking is to tell the truth. It's the funniest joke in the world. *G. B. Shaw, John Bull's Other Island*

Never waste a lie. You never know when you may need it. *Mark Twain*

No man has a good enough memory to make a successful liar. *Abraham Lincoln*

Personality opens doors; character keeps them open.

Plain dealing is a jewel, though they that use it commonly die beggars. *16th century*

Plain dealing is praised more than practiced. *1639, Clarke*

Righteous lips are the delight of kings, and they love him that speaketh right. *Proverbs 16:13*

Tell the truth, or someone will tell it for you. *Ed Howe*

Telling the truth is a business in which there is very little competition. *Old postcard*

The fewer lies you tell, the more chance there is of being believed when you tell one. © *Ashleigh Brilliant*

The man who is brutally honest enjoys the brutality quite as much as the honesty. *Richard Needham*

The most essential gift for a good writer is a built-in, shockproof shit detector. This is the writer's radar, and all great writers have it. *Ernest Hemingway, Paris Review, Spring 1958*

The most important thing in acting is honesty. If you can fake that, you've got it made. *George Burns*

The surest way to remain poor is to be an honest man. *Napoleon*

The world is too dangerous for anything but truth and too small for anything but love. *William Sloane Coffin, address at Trinity Institute, San Francisco, Feb. 7, 1981*

There are more people in the world honest by policy than from principle. *Josh Billings*

There are two types of people through whose lips lies never pass: those who always tell the truth and those who talk through their nose.

There is no greater injury to one's character than practicing virtue with ulterior motivation. *Chuang-tzu*

Those who feel it is okay to tell white lies soon go color-blind.

Thou shalt not have in thine house diverse measures, a great and a small. But thou shalt have a perfect and just weight. . . . all that do unrighteously, are an abomination unto the Lord thy God. *Deuteronomy 25:14–16*

Thou shalt not speak falsely of thy fellow man lest he speak the truth of you, which might be worse. *Old postcard*

Though the teeth be false, let the tongue be true.

Truth is the only thing that I know of that can't be improved upon. *Josh Billings, 1865*

Truth is the safest lie.

What is intended as a little white lie often ends up as a double feature in Technicolor. *Madena R. Wallingford, as quoted in Reader's Digest, Dec. 1944*

White lies by frequent use become black ones. *Douglas Jerrold*

Don't be veneer stuck on with glue;
Be solid timber through and through.

There is HONOR among thieves. *45 B.C., B-2296*

. . . the better kind of thieves.

All this stuff about honor among thieves went out with bustles. *Stewart Sterling, 1942*

Combinations of wickedness would overwhelm the world, did not those who have long practised perfidy grow faithless to each other. *Samuel Johnson, Lives of the Poets*

You can't live on HOPE.

He that lives on hope dances without music. *1616, Draxe*

He that lives on hope has a slender diet. *1623, Wodroephe*

He who lives by hope will die by hunger. *Italian proverb*

Hope deferred maketh the heart sick. *Proverbs 13:12*

Hope is a draft on futurity—sometimes honored but generally extended. *Josh Billings*

Hope is a good breakfast, but it is a bad supper. *Francis Bacon, Apothegems*

I never knew a man who lived on hope but what spent his old age at somebody else's expense. *Josh Billings*

Who lives by hope will die by hunger. *1616, Draxe*

Don't look a gift HORSE in the mouth.[*] *ca. 400*

[A gift-giver has no right] to palm his spavined article upon us for good ware. . . . I would no more be cheated out of my thanks than out of my money. Some people have a knack of putting upon you gifts of no real money, to engage you in substantial gratitude. We thank them for nothing. *Charles Lamb, Popular Fallacies*

[*]In his Preface to his translation of Paul's Epistle to the Ephesians, Saint Jerome asks his critics not to pick fault with his message, since it is offered as a gift. Burton Stevenson (B-1182) gives equivalent proverbs in Spanish, German, French, Italian, and other languages.

It's no use to lock the stable door after the HORSE has been stolen. *1350, WM-560*

There's no use flogging a dead HORSE.

. . . or whacking a dead dog.

Denouncing colonialism is like barking up a tree that's been cut down. *British politician*

You can lead a HORSE to water but you can't make it drink.

The hell you can't: Fill his nosebag with salt before you take him to the trough. *Leo Rosten*

You can lead a boy to college, but you can't make him think. *Elbert Hubbard*

You can lead a fellar to the polls, but you can't make him think. *Kin Hubbard*

You can lead a horse to water but you can't make it a drink.

You can lead a horse to water, and if you can train it to float on its back, you've got something. *Johnny Carson*

You can lead a horse to water, but remember how a wet horse smells.

You can lead a horticulture, but you can't make her think. *Dorothy Parker*

You can lead an ass to knowledge—but you cannot make him think. *Cynic, 1905*

You may force a man to shut his eyes, but you cannot make him sleep. *Danish proverb*

Don't swap HORSES while crossing a stream. * *Abraham Lincoln, 1864*

. . . nor ever change diapers in midstream.

*Magill (M-548) quotes Lincoln's words as "It is not best to swap horses while crossing the river."

An ounce of HORSE SENSE [or mother wit] is worth a pound of book learning. *
1596, *Delamothe*

A great deal of learning can be packed into an empty head. *Karl Kraus, Aphorisms and More Aphorisms*

Agriculture is something like farming, only farming is doing it.

A pinch of probably is worth a pound of perhaps. *James Thurber, Lanterns and Lances*

An ounce of discretion is worth a pound of learning. *1670, Ray*

An ounce of fact is worth a ton of theory. *John Galsworthy, Caravan*

An ounce of performance is worth more than a pound of preachment. *Elbert Hubbard*

Book larnin spiles a man ef he's got mother wit; and ef he ain't got that, et don't do him no good. *1846, WM-61*

Colleges are places where pebbles are polished and diamonds are dimmed. *Robert G. Ingersoll, in Abraham Lincoln*

Common sense and education are highly compatible; in fact, neither is worth much without the other. *Donald G. Smith*

Common sense is genius dressed in its working clothes. *Ralph Waldo Emerson*

Everything is not in books. *Heard in North Carolina*

He was so learned that he could name a horse in nine languages; so ignorant that he bought a cow to ride on. *Benjamin Franklin*

I never let my schooling interfere with my education. *Mark Twain*

If a man has common sense, he has all the sense there is. *Sam Rayburn*

Nature is stronger than education. *Heard in Illinois*

One pound of learning requires ten pounds of common sense to use it. *Heard in Iowa, Kansas, New Jersey, Tennessee, and Ontario*

Street-learning beats book-learning.

Wisdom is ofttimes nearer when we stoop than when we soar. *William Wordsworth*

Learning to have and wisdom to lack
Is a load of books on an ass's back.
Japanese proverb

*Comments Burton Stevenson (B-1037): "Most proverbs belittle education, since they came from the common people who had no chance at it."

See also EXPERIENCE is the best teacher.

Almost counts only in HORSESHOES.

Almost never killed a fly. *Heard in Illinois, Mississippi, and New York*

Pretty near ain't quite. *Heard in New York*

The tragedy of life is not that man loses but that he almost wins. *Heywood Broun*

When you're HOT, you're hot.

. . . and when you're not, you're not.

If at first you do succeed, try, try again—when you're hot, you're hot. *Irv Kupcinet*

A man's HOUSE is his castle.[*]

. . . so let him clean it himself. *Women's lib graffiti*

A man's home is his hassle. *Paul D. Arnold*

A man's home is his wife's castle. *Alexander Chase, Perspectives*

A man's home may seem to be his castle on the outside, inside, it is more often his nursery. *Clair Boothe Luce*

A man's house is his tax deduction.

No man is the boss of his own house, but he can make up for it, he thinks, by making a dog play dead. *W. C. Fields*

[*]For a man's house is his castle and one's home is the safest refuge to everyone. *Edward Coke (1552–1634), first great English jurist.* These words have become a basic concept of English common law.

In my father's HOUSE are many mansions. *John 14:2*

It takes a heap o' living to make a HOUSE a home.[*] *Edgar A. Guest (1881–1959), Home*

[*]The remainder of the verse:

A heap o' sun an' shadder, an' ye sometimes have t' roam

Afore ye really 'preciate the things ye lef' behind,

An' hunger fer 'em somehow, with 'em allus on yer mind.

For many years, Edgar A. Guest wrote a daily poem for readers of the *Detroit Free Press.* Two of Guest's lines have become American proverbs: this one and "SOMEBODY said that it couldn't be done" (q.v.).

See HOME sweet home.

We're only HUMAN.

Being human is a privilege, not an excuse.

It's not what we don't know that HURTS, it's what we know that ain't so.[*] ***Will Rogers (1879–1935)***

It is better to know nothing than to know what ain't so. *Josh Billings*

It is what we think we know already that often prevents us from learning. *Claude Bernard*

Nothing in the world is more dangerous than sincere ignorance and conscientious stupidity. *Martin Luther King, Jr.*

[*]Sometimes phrased as, "It ain't what a man don't know that makes him a fool, but what he does know that ain't so." Keyes (K-73–74) gives other variations of this saying, and lists various other wits the saying has been attributed to.

HYPOCRISY is a homage that vice plays to virtue. *Rochefoucauld, Les Maximes, 1665*

If you're going to be a hypocrite, at least be sincere about it.

Many a man's reputation would not know his character if they met on the street. *Elbert Hubbard*

Pretended holiness is a double iniquity. *Thomas Traxe, Bibliotheca, 1633*

There are people who laugh to show their fine teeth; and there are those who cry to show their good hearts. *Joseph Roux, ca. 1870*

There is no better compliment to virtue than this: that vice always concocts her great plans in the name of virtue. *Josh Billings, 1865*

Volumes might be written upon the impiety of the pious. *Herbert Spencer*

See also Full of COURTESY, full of craft.

There's nothing so irresistible as an **IDEA whose time has come.** *Victor Hugo, 1877 (paraphrased); B-212*

. . . and there's nothing so immovable as an idea whose time hasn't expired.

"IF" stands stiff in the corner.

If "Ifs" and "Buts" were candy and nuts, every day would be Christmas.

See also If WISHES were horses, beggars would ride.

IGNORANCE is bliss.*

. . . and we're in seventh heaven.

. . . Ignorance of sawing wood, for instance. *Josh Billings*

A man doesn't always get paid for what he knows, but he seldom escapes paying for what he doesn't know. *Wall Street Journal*

A man may be a fool and not know it, but not if he is married. *H. L. Mencken*

All our knowledge merely helps us to die a more painful death than the animals that know nothing. *Maurice Maeterlinck*

All you need in this life is ignorance and confidence, and then success is sure. *Mark Twain*

Better be happy than wise. *1546, Heywood*

Everybody is ignorant, only on different subjects. *Will Rogers*

For in much wisdom is much grief; and he that increaseth knowledge increaseth sorrow. *Ecclesiastes 1:18*

God made the world round so that we would never be able to see too far down the road. *Isak Dinesen*

Happiness is the perpetual possession of being well deceived. *Jonathan Swift*

He that knows nothing, doubts nothing. *1611, Cotgrave*

He who laughs has not yet heard the bad news. *Bertolt Brecht*

I am patient with stupidity but not with those who are proud of it. *Edith Sitwell*

I honestly believe it is better to know nothing than to know what ain't so. *Josh Billings*

If ignorance is bliss, why aren't more people happy?

If ignorance is indeed bliss, it is a very low grade of the article. *Tehi Hsieh*

Ignorance and bungling with love are better than wisdom and skill without. *Heard in New York and South Carolina*

Ignorance is not bliss—it's oblivion. *Philip Wylie*

Ignorance is not innocence but sin. *Robert Browning, M69, p. 514*

Ignorance may be free but the upkeep is tremendous.

Ignorance never settles a question. *Benjamin Disraeli, 1866*

In knowing nothing is the sweetest life. *Sophocles, Ajax*

It is unfortunate to be ignorant, inexcusable to be proud of it. *Donald G. Smith*

It Pays to Be Ignorant. *Song title*

Knowing nothing is the sweetest life. *1549, T-364*

Lambs, it is true, gambol, but in due time they all get fleeced. *L. de V. Matthewman*

Laugh and show your ignorance. *Heard in New York, Ohio, and South Carolina*

Learning leaves but one lesson: doubt. *G. B. Shaw*

No brain, no headache. *TV comedian, 1992*

Nothing is more conducive to peace of mind than not having any opinion at all. *Georg Lichtenberg*

Prejudice is being down on what we are not up on. *Rachel Davis DuBois, as quoted in Reader's Digest, Nov. 1945*

Stupidity is the deliberate cultivation of ignorance. *William Gaddis, Carpenter's Gothic*

The fool is happy that he knows no more. *Alexander Pope, An Essay on Man*

The greatest obstacle to discovery is not ignorance—it is the illusion of knowledge. *Daniel J. Boorstin, Washington Post, Jan. 29, 1984*

The less wit a man has, the less he knows that he wants it. *1732, Fuller*

The less you know about how sausages are made, the better they taste.

The luck of an ignoramus is this: He doesn't know that he doesn't know. *Yiddish proverb*

There are some things children cannot know, because once they learn them, they are no longer children. © *Ashleigh Brilliant*

There are two things for which animals are to be envied: they know nothing of future evils, or of what people say about them. *Voltaire, 1739*

There is nothing more terrible than ignorance in action. *Johann Wolfgang von Goethe, 1819*

Those who like sausage or political policy should not watch it being made.

To know nothing is the safest creed. *Johan Van Olden-Barneveldt, opponent of all religious dogmas*

Too much brains is rather a hindrance than a help to a simple business man. *Josh Billings*

Uncultivated minds are not full of wild flowers, like uncultivated fields. Villainous weeds grow in them, and they are full of toads. *Logan Pearsall Smith, Afterthoughts*

Where ignorance is bliss, a little learning is a dangerous thing. *Erle Stanley Gardner, 1943*

Where ignorance is bliss, it is foolish to borrow your neighbor's newspaper. *Kin Hubbard*

Wisdom excelleth folly, as far as light excelleth darkness. *Proverbs 2:13*

Wisdom is the principal thing; therefore get wisdom: and with all thy getting get understanding. *Proverbs 4:7*

With stupidity, the gods themselves struggle in vain. *Friedrich von Schiller, Die Jungfrau von Orleans*

See the happy moron,
    He doesn't give a damn.
I wish I were a moron—
    My God, perhaps I am!

An optimist is a guy
that has never had
much experience.
Don Marquis

*Where ignorance is bliss
'Tis folly to be wise.
Thomas Gray, Ode on a Distant Prospect of Eton College, 1742

All the things I like are either ILLEGAL, immoral, or fattening.*

A woman on a diet soon feels like Joan of Arc. *Mignon McLaughlin*

Forget about calories—everything makes thin people thinner, and fat people fatter. *Mignon McLaughlin*

Go on a diet, quit smoking, give up alcohol— but not all at once. *Mignon McLaughlin*

Rules of strict self-denial may not make your life longer—but they will make it seem longer.

The only thing people like that is good for them; a good night's sleep. *Ed Howe*

*The most interesting things in life are either immoral, illegal, or too fattening—an observation often made by Alexander Wolcott, says Keyes (K-17), but not found in any of his writings.

See also You can't WIN.

IMITATION is the sincerest form of flattery.

Imitation is the highest form of flattery. *1820, M-327*

Listening, not imitation, may be the sincerest form of flattery. *Joyce Brothers*

It's nice to be IMPORTANT, but it's more important to be nice.*

*Is this saying derived from this Will Rogers

quip? "It's great to be great, but it's greater to be human."

Don't ask for the IMPOSSIBLE.

A man cannot be in two places at once. *English proverb*

A man cannot whistle and drink at the same time. *1586, OE-704*

Even God cannot make two mountains without a valley in between. *Gaelic proverb*

You can't catch a greased pig.

You can't get a quart into a pint pot. *English proverb*

You can't mow hay where the grass doesn't grow. *Vermont proverb*

See also Nothing is IMPOSSIBLE.

Nothing is IMPOSSIBLE.

. . . to a willing heart. *1509, T-506*

. . . to those who don't have to do it themselves.

. . . except dribbling a football, or sneezing with your eyes open.

. . . except getting a plumber on Sunday.

A man cannot whistle and drink at the same time. *1586, OE-704*

Accomplishing the impossible means only that the boss will add it to your regular duties. *Doug Larson*

Can't is a liar. *Heard in New York*

Determine that the thing can and shall be done, and then we shall find the way. *Abraham Lincoln*

Medicine seems to be sharpening its tools to do battle with death as though death were just one more disease. *Leon R. Kass, New York Times, Feb. 23, 1971*

President Ronald Reagan's managerial style was lauded in the book *The Intuitive Manager,* by *Fortune* magazine writer Roy Rowan, before the President's reputation as the consummate executive was shattered by the Iran-Contra Affair, the HUD scandal, and the savings and loan disaster. The author quotes Reagan's sometime campaign manager John Sears as saying of Reagan that he is "an embodiment of a peculiar American virtue that says all things are possible if you will make them so—that reality is an illusion that you can overcome."

First IMPRESSIONS are the most lasting. *1700, O-81*

First impressions are not to be trusted.

The only good INDIAN is a dead Indian. Philip Sheridan (1831–88) (attributed)[*]

An Indian scalps his enemies, a white man skins his friends. *Heard in Kansas*

Civilization or death to all American savages. *James Norris, 1779*

I don't feel we did wrong in taking this great country away from them. There were great numbers of people who needed land, and the Indians were selfishly trying to keep it for themselves. *John Wayne*

Police brutality, incompetent bureaucrats, legal incongruities, destructive educational systems, racial discrimination, ignorant politicians who are abetted by a country largely ignorant of its native population, are conditions which Indians face daily. Yes, the only good Indian is still a dead one. Not dead physically, but dead spiritually, mentally, economically and socially. *Introduction to The Only Good Indians: Essays by Canadian Indians, edited by Waubageshig*

*A Union Army hero during the Civil War, Sheridan later became an Indian fighter and was reputed to regard the Indians as savages and to favor a harsh policy toward them. He denied having originated this saying and insisted that his goal was not extermination of the Indian, but "protection for the good, punishment for the bad" (Paul A. Hutton, *Phil Sheridan and His Army*, 1985, pp. 180–81).

Mieder (WM-329) and Keyes (K-67) trace this statement to Montana Congressman J. M. Cavanaugh, recorded in the *Congressional Globe*, May 29, 1868. Keyes adds that when these words were uttered, they expressed a widespread sentiment in the western states and territories. A very thorough study of the statement, its historical context and literary usage, is Mieder's " 'The Only Good Indian Is a Dead Indian': History and Meaning of a Proverbial Stereotype," *Journal of American Folklore* 104, no. 419, pp. 38–60.

No man is INDISPENSABLE.

A man becomes so identified with his business that people think it couldn't be run without him. He dies and the business—improves. *Opie Read*

Don't be indispensable. If you can't be replaced, you can't be promoted.

Every man is wanted, and no man is wanted much. *Ralph Waldo Emerson*

I have always noticed one thing, when a person becomes disgusted with the world and concludes to withdraw from it, the world very kindly lets the person go. *Josh Billings*

If you feel that you are indispensable, put your finger in a glass of water, withdraw it, and note the hole you have left.

Many who are only useful believe they are indispensable. *Felix Leclerc*

The graveyards are full of indispensable men. *Charles de Gaulle*

They don't know what they'd do without you, but they'll think of something if they have to.

Man's INHUMANITY to man makes countless thousands mourn. *Robert Burns, Man Was Made to Mourn, 1786*

Beasts are gentle toward each other and refrain from tearing their own kind while men glut themselves with rending one another. *Seneca, 55 A.D.*

For what is history but a . . . register of crimes and miseries that man has inflicted on his fellow men? It is a huge libel on human nature. *Washington Irving, History of New York, 1809*

God's inhumanity to man makes countless thousands mourn. *Mark Twain's Notebook, 1935*

I have seen the science I worshipped, and the aircraft I loved, destroying the civilization I expected them to serve. *Charles A. Lindbergh, Time, May 26, 1967*

If you pick up a starving dog and make him prosperous, he will not bite you; that is the principal difference between a dog and a man. *Mark Twain*

Man's capacity for justice makes democracy possible; but man's inclination to injustices makes democracy necessary. *Reinhold Niebuhr, Immoral Society and Rational Man*

Man, biologically considered . . . is the most formidable of all the beasts of prey, and, indeed, the only one that preys systematically on its own species. *William James, 1911*

One cannot be deeply responsive to the world without being saddened very often. *Erich Fromm, ABC TV, May 25, 1958*

See also PEOPLE are no damn good.

Before you invest, INVESTIGATE. *Slogan of the Better Business Bureau*

Before you invest
Always read the prospectus.
It's required by laws
Designed to protect us.
Buried somewhere therein
Under mountains of prose
Are all of the risks
To which you're exposed.
Don't know where to start?
Let me give you a hint:
The greater the hazard,
The smaller the print.
Harry E. Hill, Wall Street Journal

Don't get INVOLVED.

There's no problem so big or complicated that it can't be run away from. *London graffiti, 1979*

Never interfere with nothing that don't bother you. *Heard in New York*

No man is an ISLAND.[*] *John Donne, Devotions, 1624; M-755*

. . . but each of us privately believes . . . that he ought to be a peninsula, jutting out just ahead of the rest of mankind. *Sydney J. Harris*

Human life is human relatedness. No one lives alone. Robinson Crusoe is a feat of literary imagination. *Gregory Vlastos*

I am a part of all that I have met. *Alfred, Lord Tennyson*

I believe every man is an island, but there are no limits to the bridges or harbors he can build. *Roy C. Cook*

Injustice anywhere is a threat to justice everywhere. *Martin Luther King, Jr.*

Men can get along without the help of a man, but man cannot get along without the aid of men. *Josh Billings*

This we know, all things are connected like the blood which unites one family. . . . Whatever befalls the earth, befalls the sons of the earth. Man did not weave the web of life; he is merely a strand in it. Whatever he does to the web, he does to himself. *Chief Seattle*

[*]No man is an Island, intire of it selfe; every man is a piece of the Continent, a part of the maine; if a Clod be washed away by the Sea, Europe is the less . . . any man's death diminishes me, because I am involved in Mankinde; and therefore never send to know for whom the bell tolls: It tolls for thee.

A JACK of all trades is a master of none. *ca. 1574, B-1259*

A man of many trades begs his bread on Sunday. *1606, WM-607*

He that sips many arts drinks none. *Heard in Mississippi and New York*

If you run after two hares, you will catch neither. *Desiderius Erasmus*

If you would be Pope, you must think of nothing else. *1659, OE-512*

Jack of all trades is no trade. *1732, Fuller*

The jerk-of-all-jobs is a master of none.

Moral indignation is JEALOUSY with a halo. *H. G. Wells (1866–1946)*

Age gives good advice when it is no longer able to give a bad example.

Just about in proportion that the passions are weak, men are virtuous. *Josh Billings*

Moral indignation is in most cases two percent moral, 48 percent indignation, and 50 percent envy. *Vittorio De Sica, 1961*

Of the two, I prefer those who render vice loveable to those who degrade virtue. *Joseph Joubert, Pensées*

Old men are fond of giving good advice to console themselves for their inability to set a bad example. *François de la Rochefoucauld*

Prudes are coquettes gone to seed. *Josh Billings*

Puritanism: the haunting fear that someone, somewhere, may be happy. *H. L. Mencken, 1920*

205

The denunciation of the young is a necessary part of the hygiene of older people, and greatly assists in the circulation of the blood. *Logan Pearsall Smith*

When a feller begin to complain of the immodesty of women, he's getting pretty well along in years. *Kin Hubbard*

Many a true word is said in JEST. *Geoffrey Chaucer, Monk's Tale, 1386*

. . . and many foolish words are spoken in earnest.

Jesters do oft prove prophets. *Shakespeare, King Lear 5.3.71*

Many a true word is spoken through false teeth.

There's many a knock gits across in a jest. *Kin Hubbard*

If funny men are sometimes right
It's second guessing, not second sight;

. . . This motto, child, is my bequest:
There's many a false word spoken in jest.
Ogden Nash

See also The TRUTH is not to be spoken at all times.

There's a JOHN for every Jane.

Every Jack has a Jill. *1611, O-122*

The fact that I'm not exactly what you're looking for may be more your fault than mine. © *Ashleigh Brilliant*

There is no pot so ugly that a cover cannot be found for it. *1666, T-551*

There swims no goose so gray, but soon or late
She finds some honest gander for a mate.
Alexander Pope, The Wife of Bath: Her Prologue

A rich man's JOKE is always funny.[*]

Another advantage of being rich is that all your faults are called eccentricities.

Fred Allen coined the phrase "loyalty laughter" to describe the response of unabashed toadies to the boss's attempt at joke-making.

Rich men have no faults. *Heard in Ontario*

[*]Money is honey, my little sonny,
And a rich man's joke is always funny.
Thomas E. Brown, The Doctor

A JOURNEY of a thousand miles began with a single step. *Lao-tzu (604?–531 B.C.)*

A journey of a hundred miles starts with an argument over how to load the car. *Peninsula Times Tribune*

A journey of a thousand miles begins with but a single generous donation. *Matt Groening, The Questionable Swami*

Peace is a journey of a thousand miles and it must be taken one step at a time. *Lyndon B. Johnson, 1963*

See also One STEP at a time.

Shared JOYS are doubled; shared sorrows are halved.

A trouble shared is a trouble halved. *1931, O-230*

Fun isn't much unless shared. *Malcolm Forbes*

Grief can take care of itself, but to get the full value of a joy you must have somebody to divide it with. *Mark Twain, Pudd'nhead Wilson's New Calendar*

Labor and trouble one can always get through alone, but it takes two to be glad. *Henrik Ibsen*

Justice is the only worship.
Love is the only priest.
Ignorance is the only slavery.
Happiness is the only good.
The time to be happy is now,
The place to be happy is here,
The way to be happy is to make others so.
Wisdom is the science of happiness.
Robert G. Ingersoll

Sorrow ebbs, being blown with wind of words. *Shakespeare, The Rape of Lucrece*

Speech doth cure sorrow. Culman's *Sententiae Pueriles*, a book of Latin maxims commonly memorized by Elizabethan schoolboys

Sympathy is two hearts tugging at one load.

JUDGE not, that ye be not judged. *Matthew 7:1*

. . . at least wait until all the evidence is in.

It is impossible to run a business, a school, or a governmental organization without making constant judgments of other people. Nor can we form any relationships with our fellow humans if we don't make the judgment as to whom we want, and conversely do not want, to be our friends. *Donald G. Smith*

Thrice is he armed that hath his quarrel JUST.[*]

. . . But four times he who gets his blow in fust. *Josh Billings, Sayings*

[*]What stronger breastplate than a heart untainted!
Thrice is he armed that hath his quarrel just. *Shakespeare, 2 Henry VI 3.2.232, ca. 1590*

JUSTICE delayed is justice denied.

Slow help is no help. *1853, Trench*

JUSTICE is blind. Dryden, The Wild Gallant, 1663

. . . and deaf and dumb and has a wooden leg! *Finley Peter Dunne, 1901*

Equal justice under the law. *Inscription on the U.S. Supreme Court Building, Washington, D.C.*

Injustice is relatively easy to bear; what stings is justice. *H. L. Mencken*

Laws catch flies and let hornets go. *ca. 1412, WM-363*

Supreme Court Justice is an oxymoron. *Jennifer Berman*

Let JUSTICE be done though the heavens fall. Latin proverb

Justice is such a fine thing that we cannot pay too dearly for it. *Alain-René Lesage*

One man's JUSTICE is another man's injustice.[*]

One man's blessing is another man's bane.

[*]One man's justice is another man's injustice; one man's beauty is another man's ugliness; one man's wisdom is another man's folly. *Ralph Waldo Emerson, 1837*

See also One man's MEAT is another man's poison.

Temper JUSTICE with mercy. *John Milton, Paradise Lost, 1667; F-944*

Extreme law, extreme injustice. *Latin proverb*

Tigers have courage and the rugged bear
But man alone can, whom he conquers,
    spare.
Edmund Waller, Epistle to My Lord Protector

There ain't no JUSTICE.

. . . and at best, there is justice only between equals.

. . . If you make out your income tax correctly you go to the poorhouse. If you don't, you go to jail. *MIT Voo Doo, ca. 1925*

If all the world were just, there would be no need for valor. *Plutarch*

It is very difficult for me to tell why the lion should be so strong and the ant so weak, when one is nothing but a great loafer and the other the very pattern of industry and thrift. *Josh Billings*

Justice is the sanction of established injustice. *Anatole France, Crainquebille*

Law: A machine which you go into as a pig and come out as a sausage. *Ambrose Bierce, The Devil's Dictionary*

People who work sitting down get paid more than people who work standing up. *Ogden Nash, Will Consider Situation*

The big thieves hang the little ones. *Czech proverb*

The eagle and the rabbit can never work out any kind of an agreement because there is nothing negotiable in their relationship. *Donald G. Smith*

The rules of sportsmanship do not apply when one contestant is caught in quicksand. *Donald G. Smith*

The tongue offends and the ears get the cuffing. *Poor Richard's Almanac, 1757*

The United States is a nation of laws: badly written and randomly enforced. *Frank Zappa*

The world befriends the elephant and tramples on the ant. *Hindustani proverb*

We are creating the kind of society where the criminal is out of jail before his victim is out of hospital. *Richard Needham*

We hang little thieves and take off our hats to great ones. *German proverb*

When lightning struck the steeple
Of the Church of San Jose,
It barely missed the brothel
That was just across the way.
E. Y. Harburg

Soldiers have to fight and swear
To win the stripes they proudly wear;
While zebras, most unfit for war,
Have stripes enough to fill a corps.
Such unequal distribution
Is part of Heaven's constitution.
Samuel Hoffenstein

See also JUSTICE is blind; You can't WIN; You can't fight CITY HALL.

A used KEY is always bright. *1561, T-354*

Money is like muck, not good except it be spread. *Francis Bacon, Essays*

Use it or lose it.

Medicine left in the container can't help. *Yoruba (African) proverb*

See also Better to WEAR out than to rust out.

Don't KILL the goose that lays the golden eggs. *Aesop (6th century B.C.), The Goose and the Golden Eggs*

. . . pluck it. *Cynic, 1908*

. . . It is much better to let the goose hatch out a few of its eggs, and when the young goslings grow up and begin laying golden eggs, you can kill off the old golden goose. *William C. Hunter*

You can shear a sheep many times but you can skin him only once. *Vermont proverb*

Thou shalt not KILL. * *Exodus 20:13*

Dow shalt not kill. *College graffiti*

Thou shalt not kill joy. *Wayne G. Haisley*

*This faulty translation of the Sixth Commandment has misled generations of pacifists, vegetarians, antiabortionists, and opponents of capital punishment to wrongly claim support of the commandment. A correct translation is "You shall not murder," and these are the words used in the English translation of all Bibles of Jewish publishers. Explains the editor of the Union of American Hebrew Congregations edition of the Torah, ". . . only unauthorized homicide was meant by the text, and the older translation 'You shall not kill' was too general and did not represent the more specific meaning of *tirtzah*. Hence the claims of pacifists . . . cannot be sustained. . . . Laudable as these objectives are, they find no warranty in the text itself," writes Rabbi Plaut (*The Torah: A Modern Commentary*, 1981, p. 557).

The KING can do no wrong. *Latin proverb*

A single death is a tragedy. A million deaths is a statistic. *Joseph Stalin*

Steal money, you're a thief; steal a country, you're a king. *Japanese proverb*

That the king can do no wrong is a necessary and fundamental principle of the English constitution. *William Blackstone, Commentary on the Laws of England*

The wrongs of a husband or master are not reproached. *1640, T-764*

When the president does it, that means it is not illegal. *Richard Nixon*

The world is so full of a number of things, I'm sure we should all be as happy as KINGS.
Robert Louis Stevenson (1850–94), Happy Thought

. . . and you know how happy kings are. *James Thurber*

An Indian girl once told me that at one time Indian mothers often put their crying children out to look at the stars. We ought to have sense enough to put ourselves out when we are fretful, or uneasy, or when we think we are so important that the world would have

difficulty getting along without us. *Thomas Dreier*

The world is full of a number of things, and they all seem to be piled on my desk.

The whole secret of life is to be interested in one thing profoundly, and in a thousand things well. *Hugh Walpole*

Life, happy or unhappy, successful or unsuccessful, is extraordinarily interesting. *Flyleaf of Days with Bernard Shaw, by Stephen Winsten*

KISSING don't last; cookery do! *George Meredith, The Ordeal of Richard Feverel, 1859; M-569*

Face powder may win a man, but it takes baking powder to hold him. *Heard in Kansas*

If one cooks, one knows two joys: to watch people one loves eat, and to watch people one loves eat what one has cooked. Cooking does more than just give joy. It occupies one's hands constructively. One of the greatest occupational therapies there is. *Marlene Dietrich*

See also The way to a man's HEART is through his stomach.

A KNIFE cuts both ways.

The key that opens is also the key that closes. *African proverb*

The same knife cuts bread and fingers. *1616, Draxe*

You cannot have power for good without having power for evil too. Even mother's milk nourishes murderers as well as heroes. *G. B. Shaw, Major Barbara*

See also Never the ROSE without the thorn.

KNOCK on wood.

There is a superstition in avoiding superstition. *Francis Bacon, Of Superstition*

See also Thank your lucky STARS; The RACE is not to the swift . . .

It isn't what you KNOW, it's who you know.

. . . and what you know on whom. *Heard in Indiana, Kansas, New York, and Oklahoma*

It isn't what you know that counts, it's how you use what you know. *Heard in North Carolina*

It isn't who you know, it's who you "yes."

Skill is fine, and genius is splendid, but the right contacts are more valuable than either. *Archibald McIndoe*

See also KNOWLEDGE is power.

It takes one to KNOW one.

A thief knows a thief as a wolf knows a wolf. *1616, Draxe*

KNOW thyself.[*]

. . . but don't tell anyone. *H. F. Henrichs*

. . . Don't accept your dog's admiration as conclusive evidence that you are wonderful. *Ann Landers*

A dream not interpreted is like a letter unread. *Hebrew proverb*

An intellectual is a person whose mind watches itself. *Albert Camus*

Get acquainted with yourself—with how little you know, with how little you feel, with how little you do, with how little you love, with how little you enjoy, with how little you are. *Old postcard*

He that knows himself well despises himself. *1596, Delamothe*

He who knows others is wise. He who knows himself is enlightened. *Tao-te Ching*

I compare human life to a large mansion of many apartments, two of which I can only describe, the doors of the rest being as yet shut upon me. *John Keats*

I'm in search of myself—have you seen me anywhere? © *Ashleigh Brilliant*

If a person is to get the meaning of life he must learn to like the facts about himself—ugly as they may seem to his sentimental vanity—before he can learn the truth behind the facts. And the truth is never ugly. *Eugene O'Neill*

If I knew myself less, I might have more faith in the sincerity of mankind. *Josh Billings*

In many ways the saying "Know thyself" is lacking. Better to know other people. *Menander*

It is not only the most difficult thing to know oneself, but the most inconvenient one too. *Josh Billings*

Know thyself! A maxim as pernicious as it is ugly. Whoever observes himself arrests his own development. A caterpillar who wanted to know itself well would never become a butterfly. *André Gide, Les Nouvelles Nourritures*

"Know thyself?" If I knew myself, I'd run away. *Johann Wolfgang von Goethe*

"Know thyself," said the old philosophy. "Improve thyself," saith the new. *Edward Bulwer-Lytton, The Caxtons*

Know yourself, and know your enemy; do this and you will always be victorious. *Sun-tzu*

Life ain't long enough for any man to know himself. *Josh Billings*

No man can be a good Christian who knows his neighbor better than himself. *Josh Billings*

Observe all men; thyself most. *Poor Richard's Almanac, 1740*

Only the shallow know themselves. *Oscar Wilde, Phrases and Philosophies for the Use of the Young*

Search yourself, and you will find Allah. *Kurdish proverb*

The ascetic says: No thyself.

The man who doesn't know himself is a poor judge of other people. *Josh Billings*

The ultimate object in "knowing yourself" is to be able to forget yourself; but too many questers for self-knowledge make it an end instead of a means. *Sydney J. Harris*

Therapy is like going to grad school and majoring in yourself. *Fran Drescher*

To "know thyself" must mean to know the malignancy of one's own instincts and to know, as well, one's power to deflect them. *Karl A. Menninger, Vogue, June 1961*

To become different from what we are, we must have some awareness of what we are. *Eric Hoffer*

What little I know of other people I have found out by studying myself. *Josh Billings*

When one is a stranger to oneself, then one is estranged from others too. *Anne Morrow Lindbergh*

Whoever knows himself knows God. *Muhammad*

You don't look into the mirror to see life; you gotta look out of the window. *Drew "Budini" Brown, 1973*

Your visions will become clear only when you can look into your own heart. Who looks outside, dreams; who looks inside, awakes. *Carl Jung*

The world would be a safer place,
If someone had a plan,
Before exploring Outer space,
To find the Inner man.
E. Y. Harburg

*Motto frequently ascribed to Thales, inscribed on the temple of Apollo at Delphi, 6th century B.C. When Thales was asked what was difficult, he said, "To know one's self." And what was easy? "To give advice" (Diogenes Laertius, *Lives and Opinions of Celebrated Men*).

"Know thyself" is the theme of many lines in the works of Shakespeare.

What you don't KNOW won't hurt you. 1576, O-126

. . . or help you.

. . . so relax; you're invulnerable.

. . . but what you suspect can be awfully disturbing.

. . . but it may make you act pretty stupid.

. . . but what you suspect can drive you nuts.

. . . but you can get a fatal injury from what you know that isn't so. *Herb Daniels*

What you don't owe won't hurt you. *Henny Youngman*

He that is robb'd, not wanting what is stol'n, Let him not know't, and he's not robb'd at all. *Shakespeare, Othello 3.3.342*

See also IGNORANCE is bliss.

It's all a matter of KNOWING how.

A professional is a man who can do his job when he doesn't feel like it. An amateur is a man who can't do his job when he does feel like it. *James Agate*

Name the greatest of all inventors: Accident. *Mark Twain*

Nothing is particularly hard if you divide it into small jobs. *Henry Ford*

There is a mystery [i.e., skill, art] in the meanest trade. *1678, Ray*

You hammer in the wedge narrow end first.

While honey lies in every flower, no doubt, It takes a bee to get the honey out. *Arthur Guiterman, Poet's Proverbs*

KNOWLEDGE and timber shouldn't be much used until they are seasoned. *Oliver Wendell Holmes, Autocrat at the Breakfast Table, 1858*

KNOWLEDGE is power. *Thomas Hobbes (1588–1679), Leviathan*

. . . if you know it about the right people. *Cynic, 1905*

Some people drink at the fountain of knowledge. Others just gargle.

A wise man is strong; yea, a man of knowledge increaseth strength. *Proverbs 24:5*

Be curious always! For knowledge will not acquire you; you must acquire it. *Sudie Black*

For in much wisdom is much grief: and he that increaseth knowledge increaseth sorrow. *Ecclesiastes 1:18*

Have no fear of natural science—it brings us nearer to God. *Albert Schweitzer, 1934*

He who is ignorant of foreign languages knows not his own. *Johann Wolfgang von Goethe, 1819*

He who knows he is a fool is not a big fool. *Heard in New York*

If you think education is expensive, try ignorance. *Derek Bok*

Ignorance is the curse of God. Knowledge the wing wherewith we fly to heaven. *Shakespeare, 2 Henry VI 4.7.78*

It is better to be unborn than untaught: for ignorance is the root of misfortune. *Plato*

It is not necessary to know the origin of the universe; it is necessary to *want* to know. Civilization depends not on any particular knowledge, but on the disposition to crave knowledge. *George Will*

Knowledge is folly, except grace guide it. *1640, Herbert*

Knowledge is good. *Motto of a mythical college of the movie Animal House, Hollywood farce on campus life*

Knowledge is not power by itself. It becomes power only when it is applied. *Martin S. Dangler*

Knowledge puffeth up, but charity edifieth. *1 Corinthians 8:1*

Man may even manage to defuse the time bomb around his neck, once he has understood the mechanisms which make it tick. *Arthur Koestler, London Observer, 1969*

The brighter you are, the more you have to learn. *Don Herold*

The only good is knowledge and the only evil is ignorance. *Socrates*

The saying that knowledge is power is not quite true. Put to use, knowledge is power, but mere knowledge, left unused, has not power in it. *Edward E. Free (adapted)*

The winds and waves are always on the side of the ablest navigators. *Edward Gibbon*

The wisdom of the world is foolishness with God. *1 Corinthians 3:19*

Three passions, simple but overwhelmingly strong, have governed my life: the longing for love, the search for knowledge and an unbearable pity for the suffering of mankind. *Bertrand Russell*

We are slaves to whatever we don't understand. *Vernon Howard*

What we do not understand we do not possess. *Johann Wolfgang von Goethe*

Whoever ceases to be a student has never been a student. *George Iles*

Wisdom excelleth folly, as far as light excelleth darkness. *Ecclesiastes 2:13*

Wisdom is better than rubies. *Proverbs 8:11*

Wisdom is the principal thing; therefore get wisdom: and with all thy getting get understanding. *Proverbs 4:7*

See also It isn't what you KNOW, it's who you know; An ounce of HORSE SENSE is worth a pound of book learning.

A little KNOWLEDGE is a dangerous thing.*

. . . and a lot can be lethal.

. . . but a little want of knowledge is also a dangerous thing. *Samuel Butler*

. . . which is why so many people don't fool with it.

A little widow is a dangerous thing. *Cynic, 1904*

A little knowledge is a dangerous thing; but we must take that risk because a little is as much as our biggest heads can hold; and a citizen who knows that the earth is round and older than six thousand years is less dangerous than one of equal capacity who believes it is a flat ground floor between a first floor heaven and a basement hell. *G. B. Shaw, Geneva*

Ignorance of one's ignorance is the greatest ignorance. *Peter's Almanac*

Some know just enough to excite their pride, but not to cure their ignorance. *Old Farmer's Almanac, 1844*

The college graduate is presented with a sheepskin to cover his intellectual nakedness. *Robert Hutchins*

*If a little knowledge is dangerous, where is the man who has so much as to be out of danger? *T. H. Huxley, On Elemental Instruction in Physiology, 1877*

See also A little LEARNING is a dangerous thing.

Nobody KNOWS everything.

. . . and I'm no exception.

Everybody is ignorant, only on different subjects. *Will Rogers*

If you go to someone for advice, never accept a parable as an answer. Make him admit that he doesn't know. *Donald G. Smith*

If you think you know all the answers, you probably don't understand the questions.

It wasn't until late in life that I discovered how easy it is to say, "I don't know." *W. Somerset Maugham*

My greatest strength as a consultant is to be ignorant and ask a few questions. *Peter F. Drucker*

Ole man Know-All died las' year. *Joel Chandler Harris, Uncle Remus*

One of the functions of intelligence is to take account of the dangers that come from trusting solely to the intelligence. *Lewis Mumford*

To be conscious that you are ignorant is a great step to knowledge. *Benjamin Disraeli*

The LABORER is worthy of his hire. *Luke 10:7*

An excellent plumber is infinitely more admirable than an incompetent philosopher. *John Gardner*

LADIES first.

. . . or you may get backbitten. *Cynic, 1909*

Better LATE than never. *Greek proverb; F-20*

. . . but better never late.

Another proverb that needs changing: The Society for the Diffusion of Procrastination suggests, "Better late than on time, and better never than early."

Better never, from the point of social acceptance, than late at a funeral, wedding, dinner party, or even a businessman's lunch. There are good excuses, particularly good bogus excuses, for the "never," but there is seldom an acceptable one for the "late." *George Jean Nathan*

Better come late than uninvited.

If it weren't for the last minute, nothing would get done.

It is better to copulate than never. *Robert Heinlein*

The bones for those who come late. *F-20*

"Better late than never"
　　You've often heard it said;
Still looking for a letter
　　Are you waiting 'til I'm dead?
Old postcard

216

Never too LATE. *1590, B-1563*

. . . for some folks to keep an appointment.

It's never too late to mend. *17th century*

It's never too late until it's too late.

Though no one can go back and make a brand-new start . . . anyone can start from now and make a brand-new end. *Carl Bard*

It's LATER than you think.

See ENJOY yourself . . .

In bed we LAUGH, in bed we cry.* *Isaac de Benserade, A Son Lit, 1786; F-482*

*Samuel Johnson translated an obscure 17th-century French poem and thus popularized this line from a poem that "reduces life to the twin mysteries of birth and death and to the fact that joy and sorrow are inseparably linked" (M-483).

LAUGH and the world laughs with you; weep and you weep alone.*

A good laugh is sunshine in a house. *William Makepeace Thackeray*

Cough and the world coughs with you. Fart and you stand alone. *Trevor Griffiths*

Laugh and the world laughs with you; cry and some man will comfort you. *Mignon McLaughlin*

Laugh, and the world laughs with you; weep, and they give you the laugh. *O. Henry, The Count and the Wedding Guest*

Laughter is a form of internal jogging. It moves your internal organs around. It enhances respiration. It is an igniter of great expectations. *Norman Cousins, Anatomy of an Illness*

Laughter is the shortest distance between two people. *Victor Borge*

My tears are private property; my smiles belong to the world. *Josh Billings*

Plant and the world plants with you. Weed and you weed alone. *Dennis Breeze*

Spy and the world spies with you; get caught and you're on your own. *G. Brown*

When we sing, everybody hears us; when we sigh, nobody hears us. *Russian proverb*

Laugh and the world laughs with you;
Weep and you ruin your makeup.
The Boys from Syracuse (Broadway musical)

*In 1883 the Hearst journalist and poet Ella Wheeler Wilcox wrote a poem entitled "Solitude," which began:
Laugh, and the world laughs with you;
   Weep and you weep alone;
For the sad old earth must borrow its mirth,
   But has trouble enough of its own.

According to Burton Stevenson (B-2266), John A. Joyce fraudulently claimed authorship of the poem. An avalanche of postcards quoted (or misquoted) the first line or two, perhaps with a humorous illustration, and most didn't bother acknowledging the source. Many parodied the poem, as the following examples illustrate:

Laugh and the world looks golden;
Weep and it looks like hell!

Laugh and the world laughs with you;
Snore and you sleep alone.

Laugh and the world laughs with you;
Squawk, and you squawk alone.

Drink and the world drinks with you;
Swear off, and you drink alone.

Smile and the world smiles with you;
Cry and you get a red nose.

Smile and the world smiles with you;
Kick and you kick alone;
For a cheerful grin will let you in,
Where the kicker was never known.

Eat and the world eats with you;
Fast and you fast alone.

Spend and the world spends with you;
Go broke and you go it alone.

*Oxford (O-129) regards Wilcox's opening lines as an alteration of the sentiment expressed by Horace: "Men's faces laugh on those who laugh, and correspondingly weep on those who weep." Similarly, Romans 12:15 reads, "Rejoice with them that do rejoice, and weep with them that weep."

He who LAUGHS last laughs best. *1591, OE-353*

. . . and he who laughs loudest didn't understand the joke.

After wit is best. *1579, OE-5*

He who indulges, bulges. *Eleanor S. J. Rydberg*

He who laughs has not yet heard the bad news. *Bertolt Brecht, The Caucasian Chalk Circle*

He who laughs *first* laughs best. *Leslie Fiedler, Back to China, 1965*

He who laughs first shall be last. *Diane Crosby*

He who laughs last has no sense of humor.

He who laughs last just got the joke. *Heard in Ohio*

He who laughs, lasts. *Mary Pettibone Poole, A Glass Eye at the Keyhole*

When the boss tells a joke, he who laughs, lasts. *Peter's Almanac*

LAUGHTER is the best medicine.

A sense of humor is a major defense against minor troubles. *Mignon McLaughlin*

Every time a man laughs hearty, he takes a kink out of the chain that binds him to life, and thus lengthens it. *Josh Billings*

Good humor is the suspenders that keep our working clothes on. *Heard in Minnesota*

Hearty laughter is a good way to jog internally without having to go outdoors. *Norman Cousins*

Laugh every chance you can get but don't laugh unless you feel like it, for there ain't nothing in this world more hearty than a good honest laugh nor nothing more hollow than a heartless one. *Josh Billings*

The freedom of any society varies proportionately with the volume of its laughter. *Zero Mostel*

There ain't much fun in medicine, but there's a good deal of medicine in fun. *Josh Billings*

There is not only fun, but there is virtue in a hearty laugh; animals can't laugh, and devils won't. *Josh Billings*

Time spent laughing is time spent with the gods. *Japanese proverb*

See also A little NONSENSE now and then is relished by the best of men.

No man is above the LAW.

. . . and no man is below it. *Theodore Roosevelt, Message to Congress, 1904*

The prince is not above the law, but the laws above the prince. *Pliny, Panegyricus*

See also JUSTICE is blind; The KING can do no wrong; MIGHT makes right; MONEY talks.

The LAW rules the poor man, and the rich man rules the law.

Laws are like cobwebs, which may catch small flies, but let wasps and hornets break through. *Jonathan Swift*

Laws grind the poor, and rich men rule the law. *Oliver Goldsmith, The Traveller*

Much law, little justice.

Of course there's a different law for the rich and the poor; otherwise, who would go into business? *E. Ralph Stewart*

The gallows are for the poor. *Maltese proverb*

The great thieves hang the little ones.

The law, in its majestic equality, forbids the rich as well as the poor to sleep under bridges, to beg in the streets, and to steal bread. *Anatole France, The Red Lily*

The law is like an axle: you can turn it whichever way you please if you give it plenty of grease. *Heard in Mississippi*

Well, I don't know as I want a lawyer to tell me what I cannot do. I hire him to tell me how to do what I want to do. *J. P. Morgan*

This is what has to be remembered about the law: Beneath the cold, harsh, impersonal exterior there beats a cold, harsh, impersonal heart. *David Frost and Anthony Jay, The English*

The law doth punish man or woman
That steals the goose from off the common,
But lets the greater felon loose
That steals the common from the goose.

See also JUSTICE is blind.

A man who is his own LAWYER has a fool for a client. * *1809, O-130.*

*Perhaps inspired by the 17th-century proverb, "He that teaches himself has a fool for a master."

A little LEAK will sink a big ship. 1616, WM-365

. . . Ship construction has changed a lot since this proverb was launched. *George Jean Nathan*

A little stone may upset a large cart. *Latin proverb*

One leak will sink a ship, and one sin will destroy a sinner. *John Bunyan, The Pilgrim's Progress*

We LEARN by doing. * *1651, Herbert*

. . . We also learn by teaching others.

I hear and I forget. I see and I remember. I do and I understand. *Chinese proverb*

If skills could be acquired just by watching, every dog would be a butcher. *Turkish proverb*

What we have to learn to do, we learn by doing. *Aristotle*

*This principle of learning goes back to Aristotle, is contained in George Herbert's 17th-century proverb collection, was the cornerstone of John Dewey's philosophy of education, and is a major application of behaviorism to educational practice.

You're never too old to LEARN.

. . . and what you learn is what makes you old.

You will stay young as long as you learn, form new habits and don't mind being contradicted. *Marie von Ebner-Eschenbach*

You're never too old to grow up. *Shirley Conran, Savages*

You're never too old to yearn. *Wayne G. Haisley*

A handful of good life is better than a bushel of LEARNING. *1640, Herbert*

A little LEARNING is a dangerous thing. *

A little learning is *not* a dangerous thing to one who does not mistake it for a great deal. *William Allen White, as quoted in Reader's Digest, Aug. 1958*

A little sincerity is a dangerous thing, and a great deal of it is absolutely fatal. *Oscar Wilde, The Critic as Artist*

Despite the old adage, a little learning is probably better than none. *TW-217(1)*

I am sure that an apple grower would tell Newton he did not tell all there is to be known about the apple. *Henry Kissinger*

Little earning is a dangerous thing. *Richard Armour's parody on Pope:*

"A little learning is a dangerous thing,"

The dropout muttered, leaving school last spring.

*A little learning is a dangerous thing;
Drink deep or taste not the Pierian spring;
There shallow draughts intoxicate the brain,
And drinking largely sobers us again.
Alexander Pope, An Essay on Criticism, 1704

See also A little KNOWLEDGE is a dangerous thing.

There is no royal road to LEARNING.* *Greek proverb*

Learning is not child's play; we cannot learn without pain. *Aristotle*

*The saying goes back, write the Morrises (MD-406), to a statement by Euclid to King Ptolemy of Egypt. The monarch told Euclid he was interested in mathematics but did not have a lifetime to devote to it; could Euclid teach him some shortcuts? Replied Euclid, "There is no royal road to geometry."

LEAVE well enough alone. *Geoffrey Chaucer, Envoy to Burton, ca. 1396*

A conservative is someone who believes in reform. But not now. *Mort Sahl*

Don't jump from the frying pan into the fire. *1528, WM-243*

Never do anything for the first time.

Once a job is fouled up, anything done to improve it only makes it worse.

The more you stir a turd, the worse it stinks. *1546, Heywood*

To do nothing is sometimes a good remedy. *Hippocrates*

See also If it ain't broke, don't FIX it.

Never LEND your wife or your fountain pen.

A horse, a wife, and a sword may be shewed, but not lent. *1574, OE-305*

One should never lend either one's wife or one's razor. *Maltese proverb*

Three things in life are not to be lent: the horse, the gun, and the wife. *Rumanian proverb*

A LEOPARD cannot change its spots. *1546, WM-369*

A beast's spots are on the outside, a man's on the inside. *Chinese proverb*

Cropping a donkey's ears will not produce a stallion. *Turkish proverb*

Save a thief from the gallows and he will cut your throat. *1614, Camden*

Shit never turns to cream. *Lebanese proverb*

The challenge of the animal trainer is to change not the tiger's stripes, but its habits.

You can change your clothes, not your character. *Japanese proverb*

You can straighten a worm, but the crook is in him and only waiting. *Mark Twain*

You can't change a snake by passing it through a bamboo tube. *Japanese proverb*

*Biblical version: "Can the Ethiopian change his skin, or the leopard his spots?" (Jeremiah 13:23).

LESS is more.*

Civilization is a limitless multiplication of unnecessary necessaries. *Mark Twain, More Maxims of Mark*

Everything should be made as simple as possible, but not simpler. *Albert Einstein*

From naive simplicity we arrive at more profound simplicity. *Albert Schweitzer*

Half is better than the whole. *Latin proverb*

He smells best that smells of nothing. *Latin proverb*

I am bound to praise the simple life, because I have lived it and found it good. *John Burroughs, Leaf and Tendril*

I am for a government that is vigorously frugal and simple. *Thomas Jefferson*

I had three chairs in my house; one for solitude, two for friendship, three for society. *Henry David Thoreau, Walden*

In art, economy is always beauty. *Henry James, The Altar of the Dead*

In character, in manner, in style, in all things, the supreme excellence is simplicity. *Henry Wadsworth Longfellow*

Leaving something incomplete makes it interesting, and gives one the feeling that there is room for growth. *Yoshida Kenko, Essays in Idleness*

Less is a bore. *Robert Venturi, Time, Mar. 3, 1986*

Less is more, and Moore is a bore. *Said by British art students, of sculptor Henry Moore*

Less is only more where more is no good. *Frank Lloyd Wright*

Magnitude is no virtue. *1598, T-403*

One of the first duties of the physician is to educate the masses not to take medicine. *William Osler*

. . . Our life is frittered away by detail. . . . Simplicity, simplicity, simplicity! . . . In the midst of this chopping sea of civilized life . . . a man . . . must be a great calculator indeed who succeeds. Simplify, simplify! Instead of three meals a day, if it be necessary, eat but one; instead of a hundred dishes, five. *Henry David Thoreau, Walden*

Progress is man's ability to complicate simplicity. *Thor Heyerdahl*

Size doesn't mean much. The whale is endangered, but the ant is doing very well, thank you.

The half is more than the whole. *1550, Erasmus*

The higher the truth, the simpler it is. *Abraham Isaac Kook*

There is no greatness where there is not simplicity, goodness, and truth. *Leo Tolstoy*

Those who want the fewest things are nearest to the gods. *Socrates*

*Traced to an 1855 line by Robert Browning (K-177) and popularized by the architect Ludwig Mies van der Rohe. This "principle of parsimony" is also known as "Occam's razor" because it was first documented by the 14th-century English scientist William of Occam. Three centuries later, Isaac Newton put the same idea in the following words: "Nature does nothing in vain, and *more is vain when less will serve*; for Nature is pleased with simplicity, and affects not the pomp of superfluous causes (*Principia*; emphasis added).

See also SMALL is beautiful.

LIARS should have good memories. *Latin proverb*

Don't tell any more lies than you've got to. They're a great strain on the memory. *BJW-369*

Lying is like trying to hide in a fog; if you move about, you're in danger of bumping your head against the truth, and as soon as the fog blows off, you are gone anyhow. *Josh Billings*

No man has a good enough memory to make a successful liar. *Abraham Lincoln*

See also HONESTY is the best policy.

Give me LIBERTY, or give me death!*

Give me librium or give me meth! *Graffiti*

A little rebellion now and then is a good thing. *Thomas Jefferson*

*Is life so dear, or peace so sweet, as to be purchased at the price of chains and slavery? Forbid it, Almighty God! I know not what course others may take, but as for me, give me liberty, or give me death! *Patrick Henry, speech in Virginia Convention, 1775*

Repeat a LIE often enough and people will believe it.

A lie unanswered becomes the truth.

Hitler's propaganda minister, Paul Joseph Goebbels . . . perfected this technique to the point of social predictability. It is distressing to think that a person as reprehensible as Goebbels had such a keen insight, but he knew us all too well. *Donald G. Smith*

National Socialism does not harbor the slightest aggressive intent towards any European nation. *Adolf Hitler, 1935*

Self-hypnosis through one's own propaganda is a not infrequent phase of the self-fulfilling prophecy. *Robert Merton*

We live in a world of misinformation, false premises, questionable logic, and totally unsubstantiated beliefs; and we constantly listen to the sixteen-carat rubbish that seems to be the cornerstone of our social communication process. Fighting it is like flapping our arms when we're sinking in quicksand, and accepting it is a most uncomfortable solution—a sort of betrayal of our intelligence in a quiet and very personal sellout. *Donald G. Smith*

See also The big LIE.

The big LIE[*]

A lie is like a snowball: the farther you roll it, the bigger it gets. *Heard in New York and Wisconsin*

War is Peace
Hatred is Love
Freedom is Slavery
George Orwell, the novel 1984

[*]The great masses of people . . . tend to be corrupted rather than consciously and purposely evil, and . . . they more easily fall a victim to a big lie than to a little one. *Adolf Hitler, Mein Kampf, 1925*

There are three kinds of LIES: lies, damned lies, and statistics.[*]

He uses statistics as a drunken man uses lampposts—for support rather than for illumination. *Andrew Lang*

Never try to walk across a river just because it has an average depth of four feet. *Martin*

Friedman, quoted in the Journal of Irreproducible Results, 1985

[*]Mark Twain (*Autobiography*, vol. 1, p. 246) credited Benjamin Disraeli with this remark. According to Burton Stevenson (B-802), the phrase has also been attributed to Henry Labouchère, Abraham Hewitt, and others.

See also FIGURES don't lie; FIGURES fool when fools figure.

In the midst of LIFE, we are in death. *The Book of Common Prayer, 1549*

In the midst of life, we are in debt. *Elbert Hubbard*

Is LIFE worth living?

. . . Compared to what?

. . . It depends on the liver. *Adapted from a line in Punch, 1877*

If that's the way it's going to be, I don't want to be here. *Alvin Toffler's mother, on learning about the thesis of her son's book Future Shock: that repeated change would bring dizzying psychological shock to people forced to adapt to it*

In spite of the cost of living, it's still popular. *Kathleen Norris*

Life must be worth living. The cost has doubled and we still hang on. *Henny Youngman*

Life? and worth living?
Yes, with each part of us
Hurt of us, help of us, hope of us, heart of us,
Life is worth living.
Ah! with the whole of us,
Will of us, brain of us, senses and soul of us.

Is life worth living?
Aye, with the best of us,
Heights of us, depths of us
Life is the test of us!

It's a great LIFE if you don't weaken. 1927, WM-373

Cease to struggle and you cease to live. *Chinese proverb*

It's a hard LIFE.

Big sisters are the crabgrass on the lawn of life. *Charles Schulz, Peanuts*

Everything is not all peaches and cream. *Heard in Wisconsin*

I wept when I was born and every day shows why. *Shakespeare, King Lear 4.6.187*

If you want idiot happiness, take tranquilizers, or pray for senility. Anxiety is inevitable and periodic depression is normal. *Leo Rosten*

It strikes me as gruesome and comical that in our culture we have an expectation that man can always solve his problems. This is so untrue that it makes me want to cry—or laugh. *Kurt Vonnegut, Jr., Playboy magazine, 1973*

Life is a sexually transmitted disease. *Guy Bellamy, The Sinner's Congregation*

Life is one long struggle in the dark. *Lucretius, De Rerum Natura*

Life is a zoo in a jungle. *Peter De Vries*

Life is an onion. You peel it off one layer at a time, and sometimes you cry. *Carl Sandburg*

Life is divided into the horrible and the miserable. *Woody Allen, Annie Hall*

Life is easier than you'd think; all that is necessary is to accept the impossible, do without the indespensable, and bear the intolerable. *Kathleen Norris*

Life is irritating and then you die. *Nicole Hollander, Sylvia*

Life is no bed of roses. *1853, WM-374*

Life is not a spectacle or a feast; it is a predicament. *George Santayana, Articles and Essays*

Life Is Painful, Nasty and Short . . . In My Case It Has Only Been Painful and Nasty. *Djuna Barnes, title of autobiographical essay*

Life's jes pushin' 'side yo' troubles and lookin' for de light. *Heard in Alabama and Georgia*

Man comes into the world without his consent, goes out against his will, and the trip is exceedingly rocky. *Old postcard*

Maybe this world is another planet's hell. *Aldous Huxley*

Most things break, including hearts. The lessons of life amount not to wisdom, but to scar tissue and callus. *Walter Stegner, The Spectator Bird*

Most of the time I don't have much fun. The rest of the time I don't have any fun at all. *Woody Allen*

Most people get a fair amount of fun out of their lives, but on balance life is suffering and only the very young or the very foolish imagine otherwise. *George Orwell, Shooting an Elephant*

Shit happens.

Spring, summer, and fall fill us with hope; winter alone reminds us of the human condition. *Mignon McLaughlin*

There ain't no happiness in the world, so we must be happy without it. *Heard in Oregon*

This long disease, my life. *Alexander Pope, An Epistle to Dr. Arbuthnot*

We are all serving a life sentence in the dungeon of life. *Cyril Connolly*

We are born crying, live complaining, and die disappointed. *1732, Fuller*

We are born princes and the civilizing process makes us frogs. *Eric Berne*

We come. We go. And in between we try to understand. *Rod Steiger, 1969*

When I hear somebody sigh, "Life is hard," I am always tempted to ask, "Compared to what?" *Sydney J. Harris*

Why torture yourself when life will do it for you? *Laura Walker*

Youth is a blunder; Manhood a struggle; Old Age a regret. *Benjamin Disraeli, Coningsby*

Let Nature and let Art do what they please,
When all is done, Life's an incurable disease.
Abraham Cowley, Ode to Dr. Scarborough

Pleasure is oft a visitant; but pain
Clings cruelly to us.
John Keats, Endymion

A crust of bread and a corner to sleep in,
A minute to smile and an hour to weep in,
A pint of joy and a peck of trouble,
And never a laugh but moans come double;
    And that is life!
Paul Dunbar, Life

Cervantes, Dostoevski, Poe,
Drained the dregs and lees of woe;
Gogol, Beethoven and Keats

Got but meager share of sweets.
Milton, Homer, Dante had
Reason to be more than sad . . .
Well, if such as these could be
So fordoomed to misery,
And fate despise her own elect—
What the deuce do you expect?
Samuel Hoffenstein

LIFE begins at forty. *Title of a book by Walter B. Pitkin, 1932; O-132.*

. . . Begins to do what?

. . . unless you went like sixty when you were twenty.

. . . but you'll miss a lot of fun if you wait that long. *Henny Youngman*

. . . and so do baldness, a bay window, bifocals, bridgework, and bunions.

Life begins when the kids leave home and the dog dies.

For some people life begins at 40, but most of us spend that year resting up from being 39. *George Gobel*

If life begins at 40, what is it that ends at 39? *Jim Fiebig*

Walter B. Pitkin has written a book on "Life Begins at Forty." I rise to offer a substitute, Mr. Pitkin, "Life Begins Each Morning." Whether one is twenty, forty or sixty; whether one has succeeded, failed or just muddled along; whether yesterday was full of sun or storm, or one of those dull days with no weather at all, Life Begins Each Morning! . . . Each night of life is a wall between to-day and the past. Each morning is the open door to a new world—new vistas, new aims, new tryings. *Leigh Mitchell Hodges*

*Also the title of a song often sung by Sophie Tucker.

LIFE can be beautiful.

Every child is an artist. The problem is how to remain an artist once he grows up. *Pablo Picasso*

Life is a flower of which love is the honey. *Old postcard*

See also LIFE is sweet.

LIFE is a jest.*

Everything human is pathetic. The secret source of humor itself is not joy but sorrow. There is no humor in heaven. *Mark Twain*

If life is merely a joke, the question still remains: for whose amusement? © *Ashleigh Brilliant*

Life is like an onion; you peel off layer after layer and then you find there's nothing in it. *James Hueneker*

This world is a comedy to those that think, a tragedy to those that feel. *Horace Walpole, 1857; M-1091*

We live in jest, but we die in earnest.

Life is a party at which you arrive after it has started, and leave before it has ended. *Peter's Almanac*

*Life is a jest; and all things show it.
I thought so once; but now I know it.
John Gay, My Own Epitaph

LIFE is a rat race.

. . . and the rats are winning. *Peter's Almanac*

The trouble with being in the rat race is that even if you win, you're still a rat. *Lily Tomlin*

LIFE is but a dream. *Pedro Calderón*

. . . and please don't wake me up. *Yiddish proverb*

. . . from which we are occasionally shaken awake.

. . . and how do we know that this life isn't another world's hell?

Either this life is very dream-like, or this dream I'm in is very life-like. © *Ashleigh Brilliant*

Life is a dream: when we sleep we are awake, and when awake we sleep. *Michel de Montaigne, Essays*

Life is a movie; Cine-Kodak gets it all. *Early advertising slogan of Eastman Kodak Company*

All that we see or seem
Is but a dream within a dream.
Edgar Allan Poe, A Dream Within a Dream

LIFE is cheap.

. . . but everything else keeps getting more expensive.

LIFE is funny.

Every bigot was once a child free of prejudice. *Mary de Lourdes*

Humility is funny; when you know you've got it, you've lost it.

Fate's a fiddler, Life's a dance. *W. E. Henley*

Isn't it strange that I who have written only unpopular books should be such a popular fellow? *Albert Einstein*

It's hard to create humor because of the unfair competition from the real world. *Peter's Almanac*

Life is a mystery to be lived, not a problem to be solved.

Life is a practical joke. *Paul Bocuse*

Life is a tragedy full of joy. *Bernard Malamud, New York Times, Jan. 29, 1979*

Life is an unanswered question, but let's believe in the dignity and importance of the question. *Tennessee Williams*

Life is the greatest bargain: we get it for nothing. *Yiddish proverb*

Life is what happens to you while you're busy making other plans. *John Lennon, Beautiful Boy.* A similar line appeared in *Reader's Digest*, Jan. 1957, attributed to Allen Saunders.

Life was a funny thing that happened to me on the way to the grave. *Quentin Crisp*

My own bad luck has been curious all my literary life. I could never tell a lie that anyone would doubt, or a truth that anyone would believe. *Mark Twain*

Ours is a world where people don't know what they want and are willing to go through hell to get it. *Don Marquis*

There are only three events in a man's life; birth, life, and death: he is not conscious of being born, he dies in pain, and he forgets to live. *Jean de La Bruyère, Les Caractères*

We are born princes and the civilizing process makes us frogs. *Eric Berne*

What is life? Life is stepping down a step or sitting in a chair,
And it isn't there.
Ogden Nash, 1942

The world's as ugly, ay, as sin,
And almost as delightful.
Frederick Locker-Lampson, The Jester's Plea

See also It's a COCKEYED world.

LIFE is full of surprises.

Happiness sneaks in through a door you didn't know you left open.

Pleasure is very seldom found where it is sought; our brightest blazes of gladness are commonly kindled by unexpected sparks. *Samuel Johnson, The Idler*

LIFE is just a bowl of cherries.* *Popular song, by Lew Brown, introduced by Rudy Valee in 1931*

. . . That explains why I feel so sticky all the time. *Mike Peters, Mother Goose and Grimm*

Life is just a bowl of pits. *Rodney Dangerfield*

Life is like a bunch of raisins—raisin' heck, raisin' kids, or raisin' money. *S. S. Biddle*

Life is like a mug of beer; froth at the top, ale in the middle, and settlings at the bottom. *Josh Billings*

Life is like eating artichokes—you've got to go through so much to get to so little.

*Life is just a bowl of cherries.
  Don't take it serious.
  Life's too mysterious.
  You work, you save, and you worry so,
  But you can't take your dough when you
    go, go, go.

So keep repeating it's the berries,
The strongest oak must fall.
The sweetest things in life to you were just
  loaned,
So how can you lose what you never owned?
Life is just a bowl of cherries,
So live, love, and laugh at it all.

LIFE is just one damn thing after another.
Elbert Hubbard, 1001 Epigrams.*

. . . and love is two damn fools after each
other. *Old postcard*

. . . and happiness is merely the remission of
pain.

About the time we can make the ends meet,
somebody moves the ends. *Herbert Hoover
(attributed)*

Don't look forward to the day when you stop
suffering. Because when it comes you'll know
that you're dead. *Tennessee Williams, London
Observer, 1958*

Everybody is born a genius, but the process of
living degeniuses him. *R. Buckminster Fuller,
New York Post, May 20, 1968*

Happiness is a dream, sorrow lasts a year. *Arabic proverb*

Human life is everywhere a state in which
much is to be endured and little to be enjoyed. *Samuel Johnson, Rasselas*

I have a new philosophy. I'm only going to
dread one day at a time. *Charles Schulz,
Peanuts*

I have a simple philosophy. Fill what's empty.
Empty what's full. And scratch where it
itches. *Alice Roosevelt Longworth*

If anything can go wrong, it will. *Murphy's
Law*

If it ain't one thing, it's another.

If life is a grind, use it to sharpen your wits.

If you find something you like, buy a lifetime
supply—they're going to stop making it.

It is impossible to find anyone whose life is
immune to trouble. *Meander*

It is not labor that kills, but the small attri-
tions of daily routine that wear us down. *Roy
Bedichek, Adventures with a Texas Naturalist*

It is not true that life is one damn thing after
another—it's one damn thing over and over
again. *Edna St. Vincent Millay, Letters*

It may be that we have all lived before and
died, and this is hell. *A. L. Prusick*

Just when I was getting used to yesterday . . .
along came today. © *Ashleigh Brilliant*

Life is a big headache on a noisy street. *Yiddish proverb*

Life is a concentration camp. You're stuck
here and there's no way out and you can only
rage impotently against your persecutors.
Woody Allen, Esquire magazine, 1977

Life is a series of bad jokes, and death tops
them all. *The Saint, TV show*

Life is divided into the horrible and the miserable. *Woody Allen, Annie Hall*

Life is easier to take than you'd think; all that
is necessary is to accept the impossible, do
without the indispensable, and bear the intolerable. *Kathleen Norris*

Life is like a shower; one false move and
you're in hot water.

Life is like a taxi ride—the meter keeps on ticking whether you're getting anywhere or not. *Peter's Almanac*

Life is made up of sobs, sniffles, and smiles, with sniffles predominating. *O. Henry*

Life is not a spectacle or a feast; it is a predicament. *George Santayana*

Life is one long process of getting tired. *Samuel Butler, Notebooks*

Life is unbearable, but death is not so pleasant either. *Russian proverb*

Life—the way it really is—is a battle not between Bad and Good but between Bad and Worse. *Joseph Brodsky, New York Times, Oct. 1, 1972*

Man is born unto trouble, as the sparks fly upward. *Job 5:7*

Nobody, as long as he moves about among the chaotic currents of life, is without trouble. *Carl Jung*

Puritans will never believe it, but life is full of disagreeable things that aren't even good for you. *Mignon McLaughlin*

Shut your doors and sit in your house, yet trouble will fall from the skies. *Chinese proverb*

The art of living is more like wrestling than dancing. *Marcus Aurelius, Meditations*

The basic fact about human existence is not that it is a tragedy, but that it is a bore. *H. L. Mencken*

The chief function of an executive is to keep those who really do the work from doing it in peace. *Mignon McLaughlin*

The first half of our lives is ruined by our parents, and the second half by our children. *Clarence Darrow*

The seven deadly sins . . . food, clothing, firing, rent, taxes, respectability, and children. *G. B. Shaw, Major Barbara*

There are three ingredients in the good life: learning, earning and yearning. *Christopher Morley*

Trifles make the sum of life. *Charles Dickens*

We are born crying, live complaining, and die disappointed. *English proverb*

We spend our lives doing things we detest, to make money to buy things we don't need, to impress people we don't like. We never want to be doing what we're doing. When we eat, we read; when we watch TV, we eat; when we drive, we listen to music; when we listen to music, we work around the house. When we want to be with friends, we go to a noisy restaurant; when we want to party, we spend the evening trying to converse. *Laurence Peter*

When everything's coming your way, you're probably in the wrong lane.

When the celebrated historian Louis Gottschalk faced mandatory retirement at the University of Chicago, he offered to teach at the fledgling Chicago campus of the University of Illinois. With some embarrassment, the chairman of the history department led the famous professor to the dean of the faculties for "formal approval" of the appointment. The chairman prepared Professor Gottschalk by telling him that the dean usually asks a historian, "What is your philosophy of history?"

Replied Gottschalk, "I'll tell him that history is just one damned thing after another."

When you think you have something entirely worked out, you haven't. Something you failed to consider will arise, messing you up royally.

Why is it that we rejoice at a birth and grieve at a funeral? It is because we are not the person involved. *Mark Twain*

Why shouldn't things be largely absurd, futile, and transitory? They are so, and we are so, and they and we go very well together. *George Santayana*

Why torture yourself when life will do it for you? *Laura Walker*

Youth is a blunder, manhood a struggle, old age a regret. *Benjamin Disraeli, Coningsby*

Hell is empty,
And all the devils are here.
Shakespeare, The Tempest 1.2.214

I, a stranger and afraid
In a world I never made.
A. E. Housman, Last Poems

Nothing to do but work,
Nothing to eat but food,
Nothing to wear but clothes
To keep one from going nude.
Benjamin King, The Pessimist

O life! thou art a galling load,
Along a rough, a weary road,
    To wretches such as I!
Robert Burns, Despondency

Life is as tedious as a twice-told tale,
Vexing the dull ear of a drowsy man.
Shakespeare, King John 3.4.108, ca. 1596

*Also credited to *New York Sun* reporter Frank Ward O'Malley.

LIFE is not a popularity contest.

If you're human, you might as well face it: you are going to rub a lot of people the wrong way.

The only way to succeed is to make people hate you. *Josef von Sternberg*

See also STAND up and be counted; You can't PLEASE everybody.

LIFE is short. *

. . . and full o' blisters. *Heard in Mississippi*

. . . but misfortune make its longer. *Publilius Syrus, Sententiae*

. . . but if you notice the way most people spend their time, you would suppose that life was everlasting. *Josh Billings*

. . . but it is long enough to ruin any man who wants to be ruined. *Josh Billings, 1865*

Art is long, life is short; judgment difficult, opportunity transient. *Johann Wolfgang von Goethe*

Birth is the messenger of death. *Arabic proverb*

Death rides a fast camel. *Arabic proverb*

Don't try to live forever. You will not succeed. *G. B. Shaw, 1906*

I think immortality is an over-rated commodity. *S. N. Behrman*

It is but a few short years from diapers to dignity and from dignity to decomposition. *Don Herold*

It is not the grave which so many fear so much as the long, dreary road leading thereto. *L. de V. Matthewman*

It's no use reminding yourself daily that you are mortal: it will be brought home to you soon enough. *Albert Camus*

Kick all you want while you can. You may be paralyzed some day. *Old postcard*

Let us kiss and make up; life is too short to quarrel. *Old postcard*

Life is a loan, not a gift. *Publilius Syrus*

Life is a one-way street and there's no turning back.

Life is a punctuated paragraph—diseases are the commas, sickness the semicolons, and death the full stop. *Josh Billings*

Life is too short to do everything, but too long to do nothing. © *Ashleigh Brilliant*

Life is what happens to you while you're busy making other plans. *John Lennon*

Life, which we find too short, is made of many days which we find too long. *Octave Feuillet*

Man is a walking corpse. *Russian proverb*

Man is planned obsolescence.

Man that is born of a woman is of few days, and full of trouble. *Job 14:1*

My days are swifter than a weaver's shuttle. *Job 7:6*

My lifetime is just a moment in eternity, but for me it's quite an important moment. © *Ashleigh Brilliant*

No use getting involved in life—I'm only here for a limited time. © *Ashleigh Brilliant*

Our days on earth are as a shadow. *1 Chronicles 24:15*

So much to do. So little done. *Cecil Rhodes, last words, 1902*

The fairest rose will wither at last.

The Great Wall stands, the builder is gone. *Chinese proverb*

The life of man, solitary, poor, nasty, brutish, and short. *Thomas Hobbes, Leviathan; M-614*

The meaning of life is that it stops. *Franz Kafka*

The money that men make lives after them. *Samuel Butler*

The phrase "spending time" says something important: you have only so much time to spend; spend it well.

The trouble with ingenues: by the time a pretty young girl learns anything about acting, she's no longer a pretty young girl. *Mignon McLaughlin*

There are two things to aim at in life: first, to get what you want, and after that to enjoy it. Only the wisest of mankind achieve the second. *Logan Pearsall Smith*

Time devours all things. *Ovid*

To-day a man, tomorrow none. *1500, OE-662*

Watching a peaceful death of a human being reminds us of a falling star; one of a million lights in a vast sky that flares up for a brief moment only to disappear into the endless nights forever. *Elisabeth Kubler-Ross, On Death and Dying*

What the meaning of human life may be I don't know: I incline to suspect that it has none. All I know about it is that, to me at

least, it is very amusing while it lasts. . . .
When I die I shall be content to vanish into
nothingness. No show, however good, could
conceivably be good forever. *H. L. Mencken,
letter to Will Durant, 1931*

When one is dead, it is for a long time.
French proverb

Why does life seem so short, when it's actually the longest thing anybody ever goes
through? © *Ashleigh Brilliant*

Came in
Looked about
Didn't like it
Went out.
Alleged gravestone inscription

Once I wasn't.
Then I was.
Now I ain't again.
Alleged gravestone inscription

Life is vain; a little love, a little hate, and then
    Good-day!
Life is short; a little hoping, a little dreaming,
    and then
    Good-night!
Leon de Montenaeken

The world's a bubble; and the life of man
Less than a span.
Francis Bacon

The visions of my youth are past
Too bright, too beautiful to last.
William Cullen Bryant

I wasted time, and now doth time waste me.
Shakespeare, King Richard II 5.5.1

The time of life is short;
To spend that shortness basely were too long.
Shakespeare, 1 Henry IV 5.2.81

Had we but world enough, and time,
This coyness, lady, were no crime.
Andrew Marvell, To His Coy Mistress

A little work, a little play
To keep us going—and so good-day!
A little warmth, a little light,
Of love's bestowing—and so, good-night! . . .
A little trust that when we die
We reap our sowing! and so—good-bye!
George Du Maurier

Here he lies, extinguished in his prime,
A victim of modernity:
but yesterday he hadn't time
and now he has eternity.
Piet Hein, inscription for a monument

Your days on earth
    are just so few
that there's exactly
    time to do
the things that don't
    appeal to you.
Piet Hein

When I have fears that I may cease to be,
I think, I'll have a lot of company.
*Richard Armour, parody on Keats' When I
Have Fears*

Seven stages, first puking and mewling,
Then very pissed off with one's schooling.
    Then fucks, and then fights,
    Then judging chaps' rights;
Then sitting in slippers; then drooling.
Victor Gray

Folks, I'm telling you,
birthing is hard
and dying is mean
so get yourself
a little loving
in between.
Langston Hughes

*Life is short, but art is long. Hippocrates (ca. 460–357 B.C.) was comparing the difficulties of learning the art of medicine with the shortness of life.

See also All FLESH is grass; Here TODAY and gone tomorrow.

LIFE is so unfair.

All that the comedian has to show for his years of work and aggravation is the echo of forgotten laughter. *Fred Allen*

He is a fool that is not melancholy once a day. *1670, Ray*

If I had a nickel for every time I said "Why me?" I'd have probably said "Why me?" more often. *Ziggy (Tom Wilson)*

If life was fair, Elvis would be alive and the impersonators would be dead. *Johnny Carson*

In the great game of human life, one begins by being a dupe and ends by being a rogue. *Voltaire*

Life is a lottery: most folks draw blanks. *Heard in Illinois*

Life is an incurable disease. *Abraham Cowley, Pindaric Odes; M-611*

Sometimes it's better to compromise—like giving a gunman your wallet without approv-

ing of what he's doing. *Frank A. Clark, as quoted in Reader's Digest, May 1967*

That's the way the cookie crumbles.

The world is a queer place, where blockheads win renown, fools get rich and honest men starve. *Frederick H. Seymour*

LIFE is sweet. 1350, OE-366

Books are good enough in their own way, but they are a mighty bloodless substitute for living. *Robert Louis Stevenson*

Even when I'm sick and depressed, I love life. *Arthur Rubenstein*

How sweet it is! *Stock phrase of Jackie Gleason*

I am one of those people who can't help getting a kick out of life—even when it's a kick in the teeth. *Polly Adler, A House Is Not a Home*

I like life. It's something to do. *Ronnie Shakes*

Life is a child playing at your feet, a tool you hold firmly in your grasp, a bench you sit upon in the evening, in your garden. *Jean Anouilh, Antigone*

Live your life while you have it. Life is a splendid gift—there is nothing small about it. *Florence Nightingale*

Sloppy raggedy-assed old life. I love it. I never want to die. *Dennis Trudell*

There's night and day . . . both sweet things; sun, moon and stars . . . all sweet things; there's likewise a wind on the heath. Life is very sweet . . . who would wish to die? *George Borrow*

What seems nasty, painful, evil, can become a source of beauty, joy and strength, if faced with an open mind. Every moment is a golden one for him who has the vision to recognize it as such. *Henry Miller, 1957*

The world's ugly, ay, as sin,
And almost as delightful.
Frederick Locker-Lampson

Happy the man, and happy he alone,
He who can call today his own
He who, secure within, can say:
Tomorrow do thy worst, for I have lived today.
John Dryden

LIFE is too short to spend worrying.

Life is too short to learn German. *Richard Porson*

Life is too short to stuff a mushroom. *Shirley Conran*

LIFE is what you make it. 1941, WM-374

A fellow who thinks hard times, talks hard times and dreams hard times, is sure to have hard times most of the time. *Old postcard*

A person who finds a good reason for failing can be expected to fail. *Donald G. Smith*

For a while, life is what you make it, until your children begin to make it even worse.

In the game of life, heredity deals the hand, society makes the rules, but you can still play your own cards. *Peter's Almanac*

Life is a game—do you like the part you are playing?

Life stinks, but that doesn't mean you don't enjoy it. *Dustin Hoffman, 1975*

Most folks are about as happy as they make up their minds to be. *Abraham Lincoln*

The fear of hell is hell itself, and the longing for paradise is paradise itself. *Kahlil Gibran*

The happiest people seem to be those who have no particular reason for being happy except that they are so. *W. R. Inge*

The optimist makes his own heaven, and enjoys it as he goes through life. The pessimist makes his own hell and suffers it as he goes through life. *William C. Hunter*

To the preacher life's a sermon
   To the joker it's a jest;
To the miser life is money
   To the loafer life is rest.
To the lawyer life's a trial
   To the poet life's a song;
To the doctor life's a patient
   That needs treatment right along.
To the soldier life's a battle
   To the teacher life's a school;
Life's a good thing to the grafter,
   It's a failure to the fool.
To the man upon the engine
   Life's a long and heavy grade;
It's a gamble to the gambler,
   To the merchant life is trade.
Life is but a long vacation
   To the man who loves his work;
Life's an everlasting effort
   To shun duty, to the shirk.
To one whose heart and eyes are open
   Life's a story ever new;
Life is what we try to make it
   Brother, What is life to you?
Captain Billy's Whiz Bang, May 1922 (adapted)

LIFE isn't all beer and skittles. Charles Dickens, The Pickwick Papers, 1836

. . . I can't remember when I had my last skittle.

The road of life is strewn with the banana peels of embarrassment. *Art Linkletter*

LIFE, liberty, and the pursuit of happiness. Thomas Jefferson (1743–1826), Declaration of Independence

I do not think that we have a "right" to happiness. If happiness happens, say thanks. *Marlene Dietrich*

It is true that liberty is precious—so precious that it must be rationed. *Lenin*

The Declaration of Independence guarantees the pursuit of happiness, but not its attainment.

The U.S. Constitution doesn't guarantee happiness, only the pursuit of it. You have to catch up with it yourself. *Benjamin Franklin*

To me, it's "Life, liberty, and the pursuit of golf balls." *Henny Youngman*

The unexamined LIFE is not worth living. Plato, Apology, 400 B.C.; F-1073

An intellectual is someone whose mind watches itself. *Albert Camus, Notebooks*

In relation to any act of life, the mind acts as a killjoy. *E. M. Cioran*

In the drama of existence, we ourselves are both actors and spectators. *Niels Bohr*

The man who has no inner life is the slave of his surroundings. *Henri Amiel*

The unexamined life is not worth examining. *Jules Feiffer*

When we see men of a contrary character, we should turn inwards and examine ourselves. *Confucius*

Today is the first day of the rest of your LIFE. *Charles Dederich, 1969; slogan of Synanon*

Every day is the dawn of a new error.

Yesterday is a cancelled check, tomorrow is a promissory note, today is ready cash—use it. *Kay Lyons, as quoted in Reader's Digest, Mar. 1974*

When LIFE hands you a lemon, make lemonade.[*]

If you find yourself in hot water, take a bath. *Henny Youngman*

[*]Dale Carnegie's version was: "When fate hands us a lemon, let's try to make a lemonade." But Elbert Hubbard expressed the idea even earlier: "A genius is a man who takes the lemons that Fate hands him and starts a lemonade stand with them" (quoted in *Reader's Digest*, Oct. 1927).

See also Sweet are the uses of ADVERSITY.

Where there's LIFE there's hope. *Latin proverb*

Hope is such a bait, it covers any hook. *Ben Jonson*

LIGHTNING never strikes the same place twice.[*] 1860, WM-377

. . . It doesn't have to.

. . . but it's nevertheless good practice to steer clear of the locality where it's been in the habit of hitting. *William C. Hunter*

*As a matter of historical fact, Shenandoah, Virginia, Park Ranger Roy C. Sullivan claimed to have survived seven lightning hits between 1942 and 1977. His evidence consists of scorched park ranger hats. (F-112)

All the things I LIKE are either illegal, immoral, or fattening.*

A woman on a diet soon feels like Joan of Arc. *Mignon McLaughlin*

Forget about calories—everything makes thin people thinner, and fat people fatter. *Mignon McLaughlin*

Go on a diet, quit smoking, give up alcohol—but not all at once. *Mignon McLaughlin*

Rules of strict self-denial may not make your life longer but they will make it seem longer.

The only thing people like that is good for them: a good night's sleep. *Ed Howe*

*The most interesting things in life are either immoral, illegal, or too fattening." This observation was often made by Alexander Woollcott (1887–1943) but is not found in any of his writings, says Keyes (K-17).

I never met a man I didn't LIKE. *Will Rogers (1879–1935)*

. . . better than you.

. . . to cheat.

I never met a kid I liked. *W. C. Fields*

I do not love thee, Dr. Fell,
The reason why I cannot tell;
But this alone I know full well,
I do not love thee, Dr. Fell.
Parody of an epigram by Martial, written by Thomas Brown when he was about to be expelled from Christ Church College, Oxford, by the dean of the college, Dr. John Fell

LIKE seeks like. *Latin proverb*

. . . yet proud men hate one another. 1639, T-382

Butterflies come to pretty flowers. *Korean proverb*

The mended lid belongs on the cracked pot. *Japanese proverb*

The mightiest space in fortune nature brings
To join like likes and kiss like native things.
Shakespeare, All's Well That Ends Well 1.1.237

See also BIRDS of a feather flock together; OPPOSITES attract.

Don't gild the LILY.*

A fair bride needs no finery. *Norwegian proverb*

*To gild refined gold, to paint the lily . . . is wasteful and ridiculous excess. *Shakespeare, King John 4.2.11*

Don't go out on a LIMB.

Why not go out on a limb? Isn't that where the fruit is? *Frank Scully*

A LITTLE goes a long way. 1925, WM-379

See LESS is more.

It's the LITTLE things in life that count.

. . . What good is a bathtub without a plug?

. . . Gather the crumbs of happiness and you will have a loaf of contentment. *Old postcard*

A trifle consoles us because a trifle upsets us. *Blaise Pascal, Pensées*

Beans ain't beans without sow belly.

God is in the details. *Saint Augustine*. The line was made famous by Mies van der Rohe and was also a byword for Frank Lloyd Wright and Martha Stewart.

It isn't the mountain that wears you out—it's the grain of sand in your shoe. *Robert Service*

Enjoy the little things, for one day you may look back and realize they were the big things. *Robert Brault*

Men trip not on mountains, they trip on molehills. *Chinese proverb*

The kite flies because of its tail. *Hawaiian proverb*

If you LIVE long enough, you live to see everything.

Growing old—it's not nice, but it's interesting. *August Strindberg*

If you live long enough, you'll see that every victory turns into a defeat. *Simone de Beauvoir, Tous les Hommes Sont Mortels*

See also Grow OLD gracefully; We get too soon OLD and too late smart.

LIVE and learn. *1575, WM-380*

. . . die and forget.

A man who has made a mistake and doesn't correct it is committing another mistake. *Confucius*

No man is born wise. *17th century*

We learn not in school but in life. *Seneca, Ad Lucilium*

See also EXPERIENCE is the best teacher.

LIVE and let live. *1622, O-136*

. . . as the criminal said to the hangman. *Robert S. Surtees, Handley Cross*

. . . and anyone who can't go along with that ought to be executed. *George Carlin*

Live and let live—the two go together, and in proportion. The more fully and richly a man lives, the less he concerns himself with the lives of people around him; he lets them be. It is the people with small, dull lives who mess around with those of others. Fully alive people haven't the time for this, let alone the inclination. *Richard Needham*

Make the world a better place! Go through all of this day without hassling anybody, without criticizing anybody, without trying to put anybody down. *Richard Needham*

One for the blackbird, one for the crow, one for the worm, and one for to grow. *Heard in New York*

Smokers and non-smokers cannot be equally free in the same railway carriage. *G. B. Shaw, Everybody's Political What's What?*

Here's to all people who live while they may,
Who laugh and who love in their own chosen way
Whose creed is to live while they live and to grant
To you the same right (there's a time when you can't).
Old postcard

LIVE each day as if it were your last. [*]

. . . and someday you will be right.

[*]Redeem thy mis-spent time that's past:
Live this day, as if 'twere thy last.
Thomas Ken (1637–1711), A Morning Hymn

The more you LIVE, the more you see; the more you see, the more you know.

See EXPERIENCE is the best teacher.

You can't LIVE with them, and you can't live without them.

It [marriage] is like a cage; one sees the birds outside desperate to get in, and those inside equally desperate to get out. *Michel de Montaigne, Essays*

Marriage has many pains, but celibacy has no pleasures. *Samuel Johnson, Rasselas*

Marriage may often be a stormy lake, but celibacy is almost always a muddy horsepond. *Thomas Love Peacock, Melincourt*

One has never married, and that's his hell; another is, and that's his plague. *Robert Burton, Anatomy of Melancholy*

One of the silliest wastes of time is figuring up how much money you'd have if you'd stayed single. *Kin Hubbard*

Woman is at once apple and serpent. *Heinrich Heine*

Women are necessary evils. *1550, Erasmus*

You never know a person until you LIVE with him.

You don't know anything about a woman until you meet her in court. *Norman Mailer*

You never really know a man until you've divorced him. *Zsa Zsa Gabor*

You only LIVE once. [*] *1926, F-213*

. . . but if you work it right, once is enough. *Joe E. Lewis*

How strange to use "You only live once" as an excuse to throw it away. *Bill Copeland*

It is not true that we have only one life to live; if we can read, we can live as many kinds as we wish. *S. I. Hayakawa*

The May of life blooms once and never again. *Friedrich von Schiller, Resignation*

[*]Modern wording of an ancient sentiment. Flexner (F-213) quotes from a 1600 collection of sayings, "While we live, let us live."

See also ENJOY yourself . . .

Half a LOAF is better than none. 1546, Heywood

. . . but keep your hands off of my half.

A louse in the cabbage is better than no meat at all. *Pennsylvania Dutch proverb*

A quick sixpence is better than a slow shilling.

A relationship is what happens between two people who are waiting for something better to come along.

Better a bald head than none at all. *Austin O'Malley*

Better are small fish than an empty dish. *1678, Ray*

Better bowlegs than no legs at all.

Don't make the perfect the enemy of the good. *President Bill Clinton's appeal to Re-*

publicans to compromise on budget-balancing legislation, Jan. 1996

Good taste is better than bad taste, but bad taste is better than no taste at all. *Arnold Bennett*

Half a loafer is better than no husband at all. *Louis Safian*

He who can't do any better goes to bed with his own wife. *Spanish proverb*

If you can't get half a loaf, take a whole one— a whole loaf is better than no bread. *Josh Billings*

If you cannot catch a bird of paradise, better take a wet hen. *Nikita Khrushchev's advice to Russian peasants, Time, Jan. 6, 1958*

It's better to have bad breath than no breath at all. *Heard in Kansas*

It's better to tighten your belt than to lose your pants. *Peter's Almanac*

I'd say, my friend,
That would all depend
On what sort of an oaf
Gets the other half
Of that loaf.
Paul James. Banker and member of FDR's Brain Trust, Paul J. Warburg, thrice married, wrote under the pen name of Paul James.

Crooked LOGS make straight fires. *17th century*

From an ordinary potato comes the best potato pancake. *Yiddish proverb*

It's LONELY at the top.

. . . but you get so much more space.

If you folks think it's lonely at the top, then quit your crying and come down to the bottom where you can enjoy all the company you can handle. *Donald Davitt*

The path of social advancement is, and must be, strewn with broken friendships. *H. G. Wells, Kipps*

Don't LOOK back, someone might be gaining on you.[*]

[*]Avoid fried meats which angry up the blood. If your stomach disputes you, lie down and pacify it with cool thoughts. Keep the juices jangling around gently as you move. Go very light on vices, such as carrying on in society. The social ramble ain't restful. Avoid running at tall times. Don't look back. Someone might be gaining on you. *Satchell Paige.* Keyes (K-150) favors the variation "If you look back, someone will step on you."

It's all in how you LOOK at it.

A man who married a woman because she was a good conversationalist left her because she talked too much.

Dirt is not dirt, but only matter in the wrong place. *Lord Palmerston*

I can complain because rosebushes have thorns or rejoice because thornbushes have roses. *J. Kenfield Morley*

Is dishwater dull? Naturalists with microscopes have told me that it teems with quiet fun. *G. K. Chesterton, Spice of Life*

I've never been poor, only broke. Being poor is a frame of mind. Being broke is only a temporary situation. *Mike Todd*

Weeds are only flowers that are not fully understood. Sins are often virtues in disguise. _Thomas Dreier_

See Where you STAND depends on where you sit; There is nothing either good or bad but THINKING makes it so.

LOOK before you leap. * _ca. 1350, O-138_

. . . and look ahead, not behind.

Acting without thinking is like shooting without aiming. _B. C. Forbes_

Almost everything in life is easier to get into than out of.

Always be aware of the consequences.

Before buying, calculate the selling. _Chinese proverb_

Before you fool with a fool, be sure you have a fool to fool with. _Old postcard_

He that leapeth before he look
May hap to leap into the brook!
George Pettie, 1576

When you feel tempted to marry, think of our four sons and two daughters, and look twice before you leap. _Charlotte Brontë, Shirley_

*The full proverb was originally "Look before you leap, for snakes among sweet flowers to creep."

LOOK on the sunny side.

Happiness does not depend on outward things, but on the way we see them. _Leo Tolstoy_

In the long turn the pessimist may be proved to be right, but the optimist has a better time on the trip. _Daniel L. Reardon_

Optimism is a cheerful frame of mind that enables a tea kettle to sing though it's in hot water up to its nose.

The pessimist sees the difficulty in every opportunity; the optimist sees the opportunity in every difficulty. _L. P. Jacks_

'Twixt the optimist and pessimist
    The difference is droll;
The optimist sees the doughnut
    But the pessimist sees the hole.
McLandburgh Wilson

LOOKERS-ON see most of the game. _1529, O-138_

You can observe a lot by watching. _Yogi Berra_

Praise the LORD and pass the ammunition. * _Title of a popular song by Frank Loesser_

There is a time for preaching and praying, but there is also a time for battle, and such a time has now arrived. _Peter Muhlenberg, Lutheran minister who became a colonel of the Continental Army and led the 8th Virginia regiment in the Revolutionary War._

*Navy Chaplain Howell M. Forgy is said to have used the expression to exhort his ship's gunners during the 1941 Pearl Harbor attack.

The LORD giveth and the Lord taketh away. *

. . . Sometimes the devil giveth and the Lord taketh away. _Opie Read_

God gave me my money. _John D. Rockefeller_

Junk Mail: The postman bringeth and the trashman taketh away. _Peter's Almanac_

Mother Nature giveth—Father Time taketh away. *Peter's Almanac*

The Lord giveth and Uncle Sam taketh away.

*Naked came I out of my mother's womb, and naked shall I return thither: the Lord gave, and the Lord hath taken away; blessed be the name of the Lord. *Job 1:21*

What doth the LORD require of thee, but to do justly, and to love mercy, and to walk humbly with thy God? *Micah 6:8*

Do the right thing. *Title of a movie by Spike Lee*

Always do right. This will gratify some people, and astonish the rest. *Mark Twain*

Do right and you will be conspicuous. *Mark Twain, in Mark Twain: A Biography by A. B. Paine*

Courage, brother! do not stumble,
    Though thy path be dark as night;
There's a star to guide the humble,
    Trust in God and do the Right.
Norman MacLeod

Do all the good you can,
By all the means you can,
In all the ways you can,
In all the places you can,
At all the times you can,
To all the people you can,
As long as ever you can.
John Wesley's Rule

Whom the LORD loveth, he chasteneth. *Hebrews 12:16*

You cannot LOSE what you never had. *17th century*

The naked man never mislays his wallet. *Japanese proverb*

To lose your mind, you must have a mind to lose.

One man's LOSS is another man's gain. 43 B.C., F-141

Bad luck is good luck for someone. *Heard in Ontario and Oregon*

Everybody has got a scheme to get the world right again. I can't remember when it was ever right. There have been times when it was right for you and you and you, but never all at the same time. The whole thing is a teeter-board even when it is supposed to be going good. You are going up and somebody is coming down. You can't make a dollar without taking it from somebody. So every time you wish for something for your own personal gain, you are wishing for somebody else bad luck, so maybe that's why so few of our wishes come to anything. *Will Rogers*

One man's adversity is another man's opportunity.

One man's loss is another man's umbrella.

One man's stumbling block is another man's stepping-stone.

One man's trash is another man's treasure.

One man's wage rise is another man's price increase. *Harold Wilson*

The death of the wolves is the safety of the sheep. *16th century*

The folly of one man is the fortune of another. *17th century*

The rabbit's foot that's so lucky for you wasn't so lucky for the rabbit.

See also Every CLOUD has a silver lining; Never the ROSE without the thorn; NOTHING is simple.

All is fair in LOVE and war. *17th century**

... to him whose only standard of morality is success. *L. de V. Matthewman*

... but in love, victory goes to the man who runs away. *Napoleon*

All is fair in love and ... fighting with your brother. *Baltimore grade school child's completion of the proverb, given its first six words*

All is fair in love and whoring. *BJW-8*

All's fair when you've had the roots touched up by the hairdresser.

All's unfair in love and war. *L. L. Levinson*

He who overcomes an enemy by fraud is as much to be praised as he who does so by force. *Niccolo Machiavelli, 1531*

*Flexner (F-6) traces this thought back to the 1597 *Anatomy of Wit*, by John Lyly: "Both might and mallice, decyte and treacherye, all periurye, any impietie may lawfully be committed in loue, which is lawless." In modern English: "Both might and malice, deceit and treachery, all perjury, any impiety, may lawfully be committed in love, which is lawless."

Greater LOVE has no man than this, that a man lay down his life for his friends. **John 15:13**

Greater love hath no man than this, that he lay down his friends for his political life. *Jeremy Thorpe, on Harold Macmillan's drastic reshuffle of his Cabinet, 1962*

LOVE animals—don't eat them. *Vegetarian slogan*

A man of my spiritual intensity does not eat corpses. *G. B. Shaw, in Full Length Portrait, by Hesketh Pearson*

I did not become a vegetarian for my health. I did it for the health of the chickens. *Isaac Bashevis Singer*

It was Shelley who converted me to vegetarianism.... Vegetarianism to Shelley, like marriage and atheism, was a form of poetry. *G. B. Shaw, in Days with Bernard Shaw, by Stephen Winsten*

Many refined people will not kill a fly, but eat an ox. *Isaac Peretz*

Think of the fierce energy concentrated in an acorn! You bury it in the ground, and it explodes into a giant oak. Bury a sheep, and nothing happens but decay. *G. B. Shaw, in Playboy and Prophet, by Archibald Henderson*

Vegetarianism is harmless enough, though it is apt to fill a man with wind and self-righteousness. *Robert Hutchinson, Wit and Wisdom of Medicine*

LOVE conquers all. *Virgil, 37 B.C.*

... except poverty and toothache. *Mae West*

A father complained to Rabbi Israel ben Eleazar, founder of Hasidism: "My son has forsaken God; what shall I do?" "Love him more than ever," was the rabbi's reply.

At the center of non-violence stands the principle of love. *Martin Luther King, Jr., Stride Toward Freedom*

He who wants to do good knocks at the gate; he who loves finds the gate open. *Rabindranath Tagore, Stray Birds*

Love makes all hard hearts gentle. *1586, T-397*

Many waters cannot quench love, neither can the floods drown it. *Song of Songs 8:7*

The only way to understand any woman is to love her—and then it isn't necessary to understand her. *Sydney J. Harris*

He drew a circle that left me out
Heretic, rebel, a thing to flout.
But Love and I had the wit to win:
We drew a circle that took him in.
Edwin Markham, Outwitted

See also GOD is love.

LOVE is a many-splendored thing.

A lady of 47 who has been married 27 years and has six children knows what love really is and once described it for me like this: "Love is what you've been through with somebody." *James Thurber, as quoted in Life, Mar. 14, 1960*

Age does not protect you from love. But love, to some extent, protects you from age. *Jeanne Moreau*

I am happy now that Charles calls on my bed-chamber less frequently than of old. As it is, I now endure but two calls a week, and when I hear his steps outside my door I lie down on my bed, close my eyes, open my legs and think of England. *Alice Hillingdon.* The advice "Close your eyes and think of England"

is often attributed to Queen Victoria, says Keyes (K-187).

First love is only a little foolishness and a lot of curiosity. *G. B. Shaw*

Hot love soon cold. *1546, Heywood*

I found sex hopeless as a basis for permanent relations, and never dreamt of marriage in connection with it. . . . [But] I liked sexual intercourse because of its amazing power of producing a celestial flood of emotion and exaltation of existence which, however momentary, gave me a sample of what may one day be the normal state of being for mankind in intellectual ecstasy. *G. B. Shaw, Sixteen Self-Sketches*

If love is nothing but chemistry, could sex be nothing but physics?

Immature love says, "I love you because I need you." Mature love says, "I need you because I love you." *Erich Fromm*

In love, everything is true, everything is false; and it is the one subject on which one cannot express an absurdity. *Sébastien-Roch Nicolas Chamfort, Maximes et Pensées*

In real love, you want the other person's good. In romantic love, you want the other person. *Margaret Anderson*

It is not only highly natural to love the female sex, but 'tis highly pleasant. *Josh Billings, 1865*

Kindness consists in loving people more than they deserve. *Joseph Joubert*

Life is a flower of which love is the honey. *Victor Hugo*

Love—incomparably the greatest psychotherapeutic agent—is something that professional psychiatry cannot of itself create, focus, nor release. *Gordon W. Allport, The Individual and His Religion*

Love has its roots in sex, but its foliage and flowers are in the pure light of the spirit. *Salvador de Madriaga, as quoted in Reader's Digest, May 1929*

Love is a game that two can play and both win. *Eva Gabor*

Love is a sweet torment. *English proverb*

Love is a trembling happiness. *Kahlil Gibran*

Love is an egoism of two. *Antoine De Salle*

Love is an energy which exists of itself. It is its own value. *Thornton Wilder*

Love is liking someone better than you like yourself. *Frank Tyger*

Love is only a dirty trick played on us to achieve continuation of the species. *W. Somerset Maugham, Writer's Notebook*

Love is that funny feeling you feel when you feel that you have a feeling you have never felt before.

Love is the only sane and satisfactory answer to the problem of human existence. *Erich Fromm, The Art of Loving*

Love is the salt of life. *John Sheffield, 1721*

Love's the noblest frailty of the mind. *John Dryden, 1665*

No one worth possessing can be quite possessed. *Sara Teasdale, as quoted in Reader's Digest, May 1960*

Nobody ever told me love would be such hard work. © *Ashleigh Brilliant*

Now that we're in love, what happens next? © *Ashleigh Brilliant*

Of all the delights of *this* world, man cares *most* for sexual intercourse. He will go any length for it—risk fortune, character, reputation, life itself. And what do you think [God] has done? In a thousand years you would never guess. *He has left it out of his heaven! Prayer takes its place. Mark Twain, Notebook*

One half, the finest half, of life is hidden from the man who does not love with passion. *Stendhal*

One way to define love is that it makes us feel funny and act foolish. *Josh Billings*

People talk about beautiful friendships between two persons of the same sex. What is the best of that sort, as compared with the friendship of man and wife, where the best impulses and highest ideals of both are the same. There is no place for comparison between the two friendships; the one is earthly, the other divine. *Mark Twain, A Connecticut Yankee in King Arthur's Court*

People think love is an emotion. Love is good sense. *Ken Kesey*

Perhaps at 14 every boy should be in love with some ideal woman to put on a pedestal and worship. As he grows up, of course, he will put her on a pedestal the better to view her legs. *Barry Norman, 1978*

Sex is the poor man's opera. *Italian proverb*

The best proof of love is trust. *Joyce Brothers*

The difference between sex and love is that sex relieves tension and love causes it. *Woody Allen, A Midsummer Night's Sex Comedy*

The important thing in acting is to be able to laugh and cry. If I have to cry, I think of my sex life. If I have to laugh, I think of my sex life. *Glenda Jackson*

The pleasure is momentary, the position is ridiculous, and the expense is damnable. *Lord Chesterfield (attributed)*

There may be some things better than sex, and some things may be worse. But there is nothing exactly like it. *W. C. Fields*

This being in love is great—you get a lot of compliments and begin to think you are a great guy. *F. Scott Fitzgerald, The Crack-Up*

To me you are heaven, but you are not exactly what I thought heaven would be. © *Ashleigh Brilliant*

Trust is to love as icing to cake: not strictly necessary, but it sure sweetens the taste. *Mignon McLaughlin*

Two persons who love each other are in a place more holy than the interior of a church. *William Lyon Phelps*

We love the things we love in spite of what they are. *Louis Untermeyer, Love*

When a man is in love for the first time, he thinks he invented it. *Henny Youngman*

Where love rules, there is no will to power, and where power predominates, there love is lacking. The one is the shadow of the other. *Carl Jung*

Misshapen chaos of well-seeming forms!
Feather of lead, bright smoke, cold fire, sick
    health!
. . . This love feel I.
Shakespeare, Romeo and Juliet 1.1.186

There's nothing half so sweet in life
As love's young dream.
Thomas Moore, Love's Young Dream

Love is a sour delight, a sugared grief
A living death, an ever-dying life,
A breach of reason's law.
Thomas Watson, Hecatompathia

Do you love me,
Or do you not?
You told me once,
But I forgot.

Genitalia?
Inter alia.
F. R. Scott, The Dance Is One

LOVE is blind. *Theocritus, O-140*

. . . but sees afar. *Italian proverb*

. . . and sometimes deaf.

. . . and so is faith.

. . . but marriage restores its sight. *Georg Lichtenberg*

. . . so let's just go by our sense of touch.

. . . and self-love especially.

. . . but desire just doesn't give a good goddamn. *James Thurber*

Kissing brings two people so close together, they can't see anything wrong with each other.

Love is blonde. *Herbert Gold's mother, in Herbert Gold, Family*

Love may be blind, but jealousy sees too much.

A man in passion rides a mad horse. *New England proverb*

A man will do anything to win a certain woman; afterwards, he thinks he must have been crazy. *Mignon McLaughlin*

Even a god, falling in love, would not be wise. *1539, WM-257*

Even the wisest of men make fools of themselves about women, and even the most foolish women are wise about men. *Theodor Reik*

Falling in love with love is falling for make-believe. *Lorenz Hart, popular song of 1938*

Hatred is blind, as well as love. *1732, Fuller*

If Jack's in love, he's no judge of Jill's beauty.

If you love her, you cannot see her . . . because love is blind. *Shakespeare, The Two Gentlemen of Verona 2.1.76*

In love, to be serious is to be grotesque. *French proverb*

In the eyes of the lover, pock-marks are dimples. *Japanese proverb*

It doesn't much signify whom one marries, for one is sure to find out the next morning that it was someone else. *Samuel Rogers*

It is not love, but lack of love, which is blind. *Glenway Wescott*

Judgment is blind. Only love sees. *Gerald J. Jampolsky*

Love intoxicates you; marriage wakes you up. *Old postcard*

Love is a gross exaggeration of the difference between one person and everybody else. *G. B. Shaw, as quoted in Reader's Digest, Oct. 1938*

[Love is] a temporary insanity curable by marriage. *Ambrose Bierce*

Love is a thing that sharpens all our wits. *Italian proverb*

Love is an exploding cigar we willingly smoke. *Lynda Barry*

Love is said to be blind, but I know lots of fellows who can see twice as much in their gals as I can. *Josh Billings*

Love is the delightful interlude between meeting a beautiful girl and discovering that she looks like a haddock. *John Barrymore*

Love is the triumph of imagination over intelligence. *H. L. Mencken*

Love is the wisdom of the fool and the folly of the wise. *Samuel Johnson*

Love is what happens to a man and woman who don't know each other. *W. Somerset Maugham*

Love takes up where knowledge leaves off. *Thomas Aquinas*

Love looks not with the eyes, but with the mind. *Shakespeare, A Midsummer Night's Dream 1.1.234*

Love looks through spectacles that make copper appear gold, poverty riches, and weak eyes distill pearls. *Miguel de Cervantes, 1615*

Love makes the ugly beautiful. *Spanish proverb*

Love may not be altogether blind. Perhaps there are times when it cannot bear to look.

Love may, and therefore ought to be, under the guidance of reason. *George Washington*

Love tells us things that are not so. *Ukrainian proverb*

Love's the noblest frailty of the mind. *John Dryden, The Indian Emperor*

Love, though he be blind, can smell. *A proverb twist from 16th-century England, where "a man who ran passionately after a woman" was said to have his nose in her tail*

Lovers are lunatics. *Latin proverb*

Lunacy without love is possible but love without lunacy is impossible. *Yiddish proverb*

Man is an intelligence in servitude to his organs. *Aldous Huxley*

Many a man has fallen in love with a girl in a light so dim he would not have chosen a suit by it. *Maurice Chevalier, 1955*

Many a man in love with a dimple makes the mistake of marrying the whole girl. *Stephen Leacock*

Marriage is a book of which the first chapter is written in poetry and the remaining chapters in prose. *Beverly Nichols*

Marriage is an institution. Marriage is love. Love is blind. Therefore marriage is an institution for the blind. *Sewanee Mountain Goat, ca. 1925*

The honeymoon is over when he finds out he married a big spender and she finds out she didn't.

The love game is never called off on account of darkness. *Tom Masson*

There is no wisdom below the girdle. *17th century*

To the male rattlesnake, the female rattlesnake is the loveliest thing in nature. *Ambrose Bierce*

The glances over cocktails
That seemed to be so sweet,
Don't seem quite so amorous
Over shredded wheat.
Benny Fields, as quoted in Reader's Digest, Dec. 1947

To be wise and love
Exceeds man's might: that dwells with gods
    above.
Shakespeare, Trolius and Cressida 3.2.162

Thou blind fool, Love, what dost thou to
    mine eyes
That they behold, and see not what they see?
Shakespeare, Sonnet 135

But love is blind, and lovers cannot see
The pretty follies that themselves commit.
Shakespeare, Measure for Measure 2.6.36

Oh, innocent victims of Cupid
Remember this terse little verse;
To let a fool kiss you is stupid,
To let a kiss fool you is worse.
E. Y. Harburg

Love at first sight
Is a special delight.
It's not only sublime,
But it saves lots of time.
L.K.S., Wall Street Journal

When I took you for my own,
You stood 'mong women all alone;
When I let the magic go,
You stood with women in a row.
Samuel Hoffenstein

The smile that over cocktails looks ethereal
Is not quite so charming over breakfast cereal.

Don't make love by the garden gate.
Love is blind, but the neighbors ain't.

See also BEAUTY is in the eye of the beholder.

LOVE is never having to say you are sorry.

. . . It shows from the look on your face. *Richard Needham*

Vasectomy means never having to say you're sorry.

LOVE laughs at locksmiths. *19th century*

What's so funny about locksmiths?

Were beauty under twenty locks kept fast,
Yet love breaks through and picks them all at
    last.
Shakespeare, Venus and Adonis

Love may laugh at locksmiths, but he has a profound respect for money bags. *Sidney Paternoster, The Folly of the Wise*

LOVE lightens labor.

Labor is light were love does pay. *1539, WM-357*

There is no labor in the labor of love, and there is love in honest labor. *Heard in Illinois*

LOVE makes the world go 'round. *ca. 1700, B-1473*

. . . So does a double shot of whiskey.

. . . So does tobacco juice.

. . . with that worried expression.

A good wife is a sweet smile from Heaven. *Josh Billings*

Adam could not be happy even in Paradise without Eve. *John Lubbock Avebury, Peace and Happiness*

It is said that love makes the world go 'round—the announcement lacks verification. It's wind from the dinner horn that does it. *O. Henry, Cupid a la Carte*

Love comforteth like sunshine after rain. *Shakespeare, Venus and Adonis*

Love may not make the world go 'round, but it makes the ride worthwhile. *Franklin P. Jones*

There is only one good substitute for the endearments of a sister, that is the endearments of some other fellow's sister. *Josh Billings*

There are but two boons to make life worth living: love of art and art of love. *Edmond Haraucourt*

What the world really needs is more love and less paperwork. *Pearl Bailey*

All you need is love,
Love is all you need.
John Lennon, All You Need Is Love

LOVE me, love my dog. *Latin proverb*

We lavish on animals the love we are afraid to show to people. They might not return it; or worse, they might. *Mignon McLaughlin*

LOVE thy neighbor.*

. . . as thyself, but no more. *Vermont proverb*

. . . if she is pretty.

. . . unless you happen to live next door to a pigsty.

. . . but leave his wife alone.

. . . yet pull not down your hedge. *1651, Herbert*

. . . but don't let it get around.

. . . but first make sure her husband is away.

. . . and if he happens to be tall, debonair and devastating, it will be that much easier. *Mae West*

Ain't no such thing as I can hate anybody and hope to see God's face. *Fannie Lou Hamer*

At first glance . . . altruism may strike the biologist as contrary to the broad trend and polity of life. That makes more notable the fact that evolution nevertheless has brought it about. *Charles Sherrington, Man on His Nature*

Better good neighbors near than relatives far off. *Chinese proverb*

Do not love your neighbor as yourself. If you are on good terms with yourself it is an impertinence; if on bad, an injury. *G. B. Shaw, Maxims for Revolutionists*

Fear thy neighbor as thyself. *Eugene O'Neill*

Get acquainted with your neighbor; you might like him. *H. B. Tierney, as quoted in Reader's Digest, Feb. 1947*

He that loveth not his brother whom he hath seen, how can he love God whom he hath not seen? *1 John 4:20*

I love mankind; it's people I can't stand. *Charles Schulz, Peanuts*

I sought my soul but my soul I could not see. I sought my God but my God eluded me. I sought my brother—and I found all three. *Prayer printed in London Church News, May 1986*

I was taught when I was young that if people would only love one another, all would be well with the world. This seemed simple and very nice; but I found when I tried to put it in practice, not only that other people were seldom lovable but that I was not very lovable myself. *G. B. Shaw*

Do I advise you to love the neighbor? I suggest rather to escape from the neighbor and to love those who are the farthest away from you. Higher than the love for the neighbor is the love for the man who is distant and has still to come. *Friedrich Nietzsche, Thus Spake Zarathustra*

It is easier to love humanity as a whole than to love one's neighbor. *Eric Hoffer, New York Times Magazine, Feb. 15, 1959*

Kindness consists in loving people more than they deserve. *Joseph Joubert*

No one can love his neighbor on an empty stomach. *Woodrow Wilson, speech in New York City, May 23, 1912*

No one is rich enough to do without his neighbor. *Danish proverb*

Not only is universal love an impossible goal, but I'm not at all sure that many people are interested in achieving it anyway. I know for a fact that I am not seeking love from anyone but my immediate family; courtesy most certainly and respect if I can earn it, but I have no desire to wrap my arms around a group of strangers and I would be obliged if they would keep their hands to themselves.

I would rank respect as the most important human need. If the people . . . would advance to the state of recognizing and honoring each other's rights, we would far transcend anything envisioned by the love-sweet-love fraternity. *Donald G. Smith*

People must help one another; it is nature's law. *Jean de La Fontaine, Fables*

Suspect thy neighbor as thyself. *Abraham Heschel, on contemporary man's cynicism and self-doubt*

The Bible tells us to love our neighbors, and also to love our enemies; probably because they are generally the same people. *G. K. Chesterton*

They say if one understands himself, he understands all people. But I say to you, when one loves people, he learns something about himself. *Kahlil Gibran*

This country . . . was largely built by people getting away from their neighbors. Our folk heroes, whatever their other virtues, were never famous for being neighborly. In frontier days, when you could hear the sound of your neighbor's dog, that's when it was time to "pull up stakes and head for the tall timber." © *Ashleigh Brilliant, Be a Good Neighbor, and Leave Me Alone*

To be closer to God, be closer to people. *Kahlil Gibran*

We are here on earth to do good to others. What the others are here for, I don't know. *W. H. Auden*

Who befriends his neighbor befriends himself. *Sophocles*

You must visit your neighbors lest an unused path becomes weedy. *Heard in Ontario*

Young people from small towns are not prepared for city slickers. It's a shame, but the slogan today isn't "Love your neighbors." It's "Beware of your neighbors." *Chicago Greyhound Bus Terminal manager John L. Robinson, in a 1985 Chicago Tribune interview*

Love your neighbor—he may be
Useful; and besides it's free;
But should he more than friendship seek,
Always turn the other cheek.
Samuel Hoffenstein

"Love thy neighbor as thyself?"
Hide that motto on the shelf!
Let it lie there, keep it idle
Especially if you're suicidal.
E. Y. Harburg

*"Love thy neighbor as thyself" is commonly assumed to be a uniquely Christian teaching; actually it is given in the Hebrew Bible (Leviticus 19:18) as the conduct required of "a holy nation." In the New Testament, the commandment is repeated in Matthew 5:43 and 19:19, Galatians 5:14, and James 2:8. The popular assumption that this is a uniquely Christian idea is fostered by a passage in the Gospel. According to John, where the words of Jesus are given as "A *new* commandment I give unto you, That ye love one another" (13:34; emphasis added). Uniquely Christian, however, is the reverse commandment, "Love your enemies" (Matthew 5:44).

See also DO unto others as you would have them do unto you.

LOVE will find a way. 1597, T-398

If love is the answer, could you please rephrase the question? *Lily Tomlin*

Thus love, you see, can find a way
To make both men and maids obey.
Thomas Deloney, 1637

Love will find a way
Through paths where wolves would fear to
    prey.
Lord Byron, The Giaour

See also LOVE conquers all.

**Make LOVE, not war. *Anti–Vietnam War
slogan***

. . . Get married and do both.

After a few years of marriage, a man and his
wife are apt to be at least the sort of enemies
who respect one another. *Old postcard*

You always hurt the one you LOVE.

You only nag the ones you love. *A parent's explanation*

You can't live on LOVE. 1959, WM-390[*]

A girl can live very comfortably on love, if her
lover is rich enough.

Love is like butter; it's good with bread. *Yiddish proverb*

[*] The wording is recent, but the observation is
    ancient. In 1794, George Washington
    wrote, "Love is too dainty a food to live
    upon alone."

**'Tis better to have LOVED and lost than
never to have loved at all.**[*]

. . . but not that much better.

. . . 'Tis also cheaper.

. . . [but] a whole heart is more recommend-
able than a broken one. *George Jean Nathan*

Better be courted and jilted than never be
courted at all. *Thomas Campbell, The Jilted
Nymph; M-90*

Hate leaves ugly scars, love leaves beautiful
ones. *Mignon McLaughlin*

It is better to have loafed and lost than never
to have loafed at all. *James Thurber, Fables for
Our Time*

It is better to love someone you can't have
than to have someone you can't love. *Old
postcard*

It's better to have loved a short man than
never to have loved a tall. *Old postcard*

'Tis better to have kissed amiss than never to
have kissed a miss. *Old postcard*

'Tis better to have loved and lost than never
to have lost at all. *Samuel Butler*

'Tis better to have loved and lost than never
to have loved et al. *Joseph Browman*

'Tis better to have loved and lost than to be
married and divorced.

'Tis better to have loved and lost than to
marry and be forever bossed.

[*] I hold it true, whate'er befall;
    I feel it, when I sorrow most;
    'Tis better to have loved and lost
Than never to have loved at all.
Alfred, Lord Tennyson, 1850

Expression of the opposite sentiment goes
back to a 1509 writing of Giambattista Gua-
rini:
Far worse it is
To lose than never to have tasted bliss.

All the world loves a LOVER.[*]

. . . except his wife.

. . . as long as they behave in public.

. . . unless he's hogging a telephone booth.

*All mankind loves a lover. *Ralph Waldo Emerson, Love, 1841.* Flexner (F-7) traces the thought to the Roman poet Sextus Propertius: "There is none would hurt a lover; lovers are sacred. (*Elegies, 22 B.C.*).

Each man kills the thing he LOVES. *Oscar Wilde, The Ballad of Reading Gaol, 1898*

See A MAN is his own worst enemy; Be careful of what you WISH for . . . ; You always hurt the one you LOVE.

Bad LUCK is good for something. *1636, Camden*

See Every CLOUD has a silver lining; It all DEPENDS on whose ox is gored; Never the ROSE without the thorn; Where you STAND depends on where you sit.

Don't count on LUCK.

. . . [but] when wisdom fails, luck helps. *Heard in Illinois*

Depend on the rabbit's foot if you will, but remember it didn't work for the rabbit. *R. E. Shay*

I am a great believer in luck and I find that the harder I work, the more I have of it. *Stephen Leacock*

See also WISHING won't help.

It's all a matter of LUCK.

. . . Just ask anyone who hasn't made it.

Get married on Friday the 13th; you will always have something to blame it on. *Old postcard*

It's not enough to be exceptionally mad, licentious and fanatical in order to win a great reputation; it is still necessary to arrive on the scene at the right time. *Voltaire, 1776*

Labor helps, but you get more by luck. *Heard in Illinois*

Luck is better than long legs. *Canadian proverb*

Rise early. Work late. Strike oil. *J. Paul Getty*

Take all the good luck out of this world, and millionaires and heroes would be dreadful scarce. *Josh Billings*

The only thing sure about luck is that it will change. *Bret Harte*

The race is not to the swift, nor the battle to the strong, neither yet bread to the wise, nor yet riches to men of understanding, nor yet favor to men of skill; but time and chance happeneth to them all. *Ecclesiastes 9:11*

Throw a lucky man into the sea, and he will come up with a fish in his mouth. *Arabic proverb*

We must believe in luck. For how else can we explain the success of those we don't like. *Jean Cocteau*

We're charmed by coincidence, except when it inconveniences us. *Mignon McLaughlin*

When things go right, you become rich. *Yiddish proverb*

See also The RACE is not to the swift . . .

Some folks have all the LUCK

. . . [but] a shlemiel has accidents that start out to happen to someone else. *Yiddish proverb*

It's better to be born LUCKY than rich. *1639, Clarke*

LUCKY at cards, unlucky at love. *1738, WM-83*

There's no such thing as a free LUNCH. [*]

. . . I'll settle for a cheap one.

. . . or a cheap politician.

. . . but there is always free cheese in a mousetrap.

A business conference is a meeting in which everyone agrees that there is no such thing as a free lunch while eating one.

There is no such thing as a calorie-free lunch. *Joan Beck*

[*]Title of a book of essays by Milton Friedman, who has been erroneously credited with the authorship of the saying.

See also NOTHING's for nothing.

Don't get MAD, get even. *Attributed to Robert F. Kennedy and to Everett Dirksen*

Gentlemen: You have undertaken to ruin me. I will not sue you, for law takes too long. I will ruin you. Sincerely, Cornelius Vanderbilt. *Letter written to his business associates*

Whom the gods would destroy they first make MAD. *Euripides (484?–406 B.C.)*

. . . and God only knows what they're mad at.

Whom the gods would make bigots, they first deprive of humor. *James M. Gillis, This Is Our Day*

Whom the mad would destroy they first make gods. *Bernard Levin, on Mao Tse-tung 1967*

**Every MAIDEN's weak and willin'
When she meets the proper villain.**

Kisses are like olives out of a bottle: after the first, the rest come easy. *Heard in New York, Ohio, and South Carolina*

The only thing worse than a man you can't control is a man you can. *Margo Kaufman*

The MAJORITY rules.

. . . when we happen to belong to the majority. *L. de V. Matthewman*

. . . [but] the multitude is always wrong. *Wentworth Dillon, Essay on Translated Verse; M-722*

. . . [but] the minority is always right. *Henrik Ibsen, An Enemy of the People*

A free society is one where it is safe to be unpopular. *Adlai Stevenson*

The majority, compose them how you will, are a herd, and not a very nice one. *William Hazlitt, Butts of Different Sorts*

The most dangerous foe to truth and freedom in our midst is the compact majority. Yes, the damned, compact, liberal majority. *Henrik Ibsen, An Enemy of the People*

Where the majority rules, heads are counted; where a minority rules, heads are cracked.

See also The voice of the people is the voice of GOD.

The rule of the MAJORITY, and the rights of the minority.

A civilized society is one which tolerates eccentricity to the point of doubtful sanity. *Robert Frost*

Dissent is not sacred; the right of dissent is. *Thurman Arnold, as quoted in Reader's Digest, Sept. 1967*

My definition of a free society is a society where it is safe to be unpopular. *Adlai Stevenson*

The Jews are the living embodiment of the minority, the constant reminder of what duties societies owe their minorities, whoever they might be. *Abba Eban, Wall Street Journal, Oct. 2, 1984*

The perpetual irony of government is that rule by the majority is fairest, but minorities are almost always in the right. *Sydney J. Harris*

They'd nail anyone who ever scratched his ass during the National Anthem. *Humphrey Bogart, on the House Un-American Activities Committee*

See also The MAJORITY rules.

The tyranny of the MAJORITY.

My father is dead. And he had a terrible life. Because, at the bottom of his heart, he believed what people said about him. He believed he was a "nigger." *James Baldwin, Aug. 10, 1964*

One should respect public opinion insofar as is necessary to avoid starvation and keep out of prison, but anything that goes beyond this is voluntary submission to an unnecessary tyranny. *Betrand Russell, The Conquest of Happiness*

People are broad-minded. They'll accept the fact that a person can be an alcoholic, a dope fiend, a wife beater and even a newspaperman, but if a man doesn't drive, there's something wrong with him. *Art Buchwald, Have I Ever Lied to You?*

See also MAN is a social animal; The rule of the MAJORITY, and the rights of the minority.

Behind every successful MAN you'll find a woman.

. . . ready to catch him.

. . . telling him he's wrong.

. . . pushing him along.

. . . who has nothing to wear. *Harold Coffin*

. . . and you'll find one behind most unsuccessful men too.

A man likes his wife to be just clever enough to comprehend his cleverness, and just stupid enough to admire it. *Israel Zangwill*

A man who is wise is only as wise as his wife thinks he is. *Heard in Wisconsin*

Behind every successful man is one helluva Christmas gift list. *Irv Kupcinet*

Behind every successful man is the IRS.

Behind every successful man stands a surprised mother-in-law. *Hubert Humphrey, 1964*

Behind most successful men is a public relations man. *Henny Youngman*

Every man who is high up likes to think he has done it all himself, and the wife smiles and lets it go at that. *James M. Barrie*

There's a great woman behind every idiot. *John Lennon, tribute to his wife, Yoko Ono*

Nobody else could sleep with Dick. He wakes up during the night, switches on the lights, speaks into his tape recorder, or takes notes— it's impossible. *Pat Nixon*

The road to success is filled with women pushing their husbands along. *T. R. Dewar*

Wives of all great men remind us of it. *Wayne G. Haisley*

See also Never underestimate the power of a WOMAN.

Breathes there a MAN, with soul so dead, Who never to himself hath said, This is my own, my native land.
Walter Scott, The Lay of the Last Minstrel, 1805

Breathes there a man with a soul so dead that he doesn't stick two fingers in the coin return box after completing a pay call? *Richard Needham*

Breathes there a man with hide so tough, who says two sexes aren't enough? *Samuel Hoffenstein*

Every MAN has his price. A.D. 100, B-1877

. . . Make me an offer.

. . . and you're an unbelievable bargain.

. . . This is not true. But for every man there exists a bait which he cannot resist swallowing. *Friedrich Nietzsche*

A bribe blinds the clever; how much more so the fool. *Hebrew proverb*

A good man can't be bribed: he is good for nothing. *Heard in Illinois*

He that serves God for money, will serve the devil for better wages. *1692, OE-575*

Men are more often bribed by their loyalties and ambitions than by money. *Robert H. Jackson*

Money, we know, will fetch anything and command the service of any man. *George Washington*

Political scientist Milton Rakove was often asked how he could be a paid speechwriter and adviser to Chicago politicians and still maintain his integrity as a scholar. Explained Rakove, "I make it clear to my clients that I am for rent but not for sale."

Some people are willing to do anything for money, even work.

The awful thing is not how much it costs to buy a man's soul, but how little. *Richard Needham*

The friend that can be bought is not worth buying. *Irish proverb*

The people who believe that money can do anything may be expected to do anything for money. *Sydney J. Harris*

The reason the devil buys so many of us so cheaply is that he offers cash. *Heard in California and New York*

There is no way to buy a poor saint and no way to buy a millionaire, but there is a lot of promising territory in between. *Richard Needham*

When I want to buy up any politicians, I always find the antimonopolists the most purchaseable. They don't come so high. *William H. Vanderbilt, 1882*

You can buy the average fool for a couple of bucks, but a wise and honest man will cost you plenty. Being honest, he knows what he is worth, and being wise, he knows how to get somewhat more than he is worth. *Richard Needham*

*Sometimes attributed to Sir Robert Walpole, English prime minister, who said of "pretended patriots": "All those men have their price."

Every MAN is his own best friend.

. . . and loyal admirer.

A cuckoo thinks herself a fine bird. *1616, T-133*

He is a fool that forgets himself. *ca. 1598, T-229*

He is an ill cook that cannot lick his own fingers. *1546, Heywood*

He is not wise that is not wise for himself. *1539, p. 735*

He that is ill to himself will be good to nobody. *1721, Kelly*

I am my own best friend. *The sentiment expressed by the Baron family crest [in the Latin words* Ipse amicus], *a refreshing contrast to family mottoes that advertise altruism and extol self-sacrifice*

I am nearest to myself. *1570, T-491*

If I am not for myself, who will be for me? But if I am for myself alone, what am I? *Babylonian Talmud*

Men are not against you; they are merely for themselves. *Gene Fowler, Skyline*

If you try to please yourself, you will at least please one person. If you try to please someone else, you will likely end up displeasing two. *Richard Needham*

Looking Out for #1. *Title of an "art of selfishness" book by Mark Monsky*

Selfishness is that detestable vice which no one will forgive in others and no one is without in himself. *Henry Ward Beecher*

We have to learn to be our own best friend because we fall too easily into the trap of being our worst enemies. *Robert Thorp, New York Times, Nov. 4, 1986*

When you cannot get a compliment in any other way, pay yourself one. *Mark Twain*

How can man be merciful to others
Who is merciless to himself?
Abraham Hasdai

See also I am my own EXECUTIONER; A man is his own worst ENEMY.

A MAN convinced against his will remains of his opinion still. *Samuel Butler, Hudibras, 1678*

It is useless to attempt to reason a man out of a thing he was never reasoned into. *Jonathan Swift*

Prejudices save time. *Robert Byrne*

See also You have not CONVERTED a man because you have silenced him.

A MAN is as old as he's feeling, a woman is as old as she looks. *Mortimer Collins (1827–76)*

A horse is as old as its teeth.

A man is as old as he feels before breakfast, and a woman is as old as she looks before breakfast.

A man is as old as he looks—and if he only looks, he's old.

A man is as old as his arteries. *Frequently said by John Harvey Kellogg.* Dr. Kellogg attributed it to "an eminent French physiologist," probably Pierre Cabanis, notes Stevenson (B-31). Also a favorite saying of the German pathologist Rudolph Virchow. The saying may have been originated by Thomas Sydenham, ca. 1675, adds Stevenson.

A man is only as old as the woman he feels. *Groucho Marx*

A woman is as old as she feels like admitting.

Men are old when they lose their feelings. *Mae West*

You don't stop laughing because you grow old; you grow old because you stop laughing. *Michael Pritchard*

A MAN is as young as he feels.

. . . after trying to prove it.

. . . but seldom as important.

How old would you be if you didn't know how old you was?

There's many a good tune played on an old fiddle. *Samuel Butler, The Way of All Flesh*

Winter is on my head, but eternal spring is in my heart. *Victor Hugo*

A MAN is known by the company he keeps.* *1541, O-40*

. . . away from. *Joe Creason*

. . . and a politician is known by the promises he keeps.

. . . and a woman is known by the man who keeps her.

. . . and by the enemies he makes.

A company is known by the men it keeps.

A man is known by the companies he merges. *L. L. Levinson*

A man is known by the company he thinks nobody knows he's keeping. *Irv Kupcinet*

A man is known by the company his mind keeps. *Thomas Bailey Aldrich*

A man is known by the silence he keeps. *Oliver Herford*

A woman is known by the company she keeps waiting. *Louisville Times, ca. 1925*

Be not among winebibbers; among riotous eaters of flesh. *Proverbs 23:20*

To be a big man among big men, is what proves a man's character—to be a bullfrog among tadpoles don't amount to much. *Josh Billings*

The flannel suit,
The Dacron smile,
The drip-dry zest that sweeps him.

You can always tell
A man these days
By the Company that keeps him.
E. Y. Harburg

One night in late October,
When I was far from sober,
Returning with my load with manly pride,
My feet began to stutter,
So I lay down in the gutter,
And a pig came near and lay down by my
    side.

A lady passing by was heard to say:
"You can tell a man who boozes
By the company he chooses,"
And the pig got up and slowly walked away.

*In a 1901 issue of the *Philistine*, Elbert Hubbard denounced this proverb as "the motto of a prig. . . . Little men with foot rules six inches long, applied their measuring sticks in this way."

See also BIRDS of a feather flock together; If you lie down with DOGS, you get up with fleas.

A MAN may work from sun to sun but a woman's work is never done. *1629, T-745*

Housework is what woman does that nobody notices unless she hasn't done it. *Evan Esar*

Keeping house is like stringing beads with no knot in the end of the thread.

A MAN ought to know a goose from a gridiron.

Boys, I may not know much, but I know chicken shit from chicken salad. *Lyndon B. Johnson*

I know a hawk from a handsaw. *Shakespeare, Hamlet 2.2.397, meaning "I'm not so dumb."* Scholars have puzzled over this figure of speech, and the Morrises (MD-274) offer a fresh interpretation: A hawk is a plasterer's tool—a flat piece of wood or metal with a handle on the underside; a handsaw is a carpenter's tool, and the difference between them is as plain as can be.

MAN does not live by bread alone.*

. . . Even presliced bread. *D. W. Brogan*

. . . He needs buttering up once in a while. *Max Rogers*

. . . Let's have English muffins for a change.

. . . but he assuredly canna live without it. *John Buchan, Witch Wood*

Bread may be the staff of life, but art is the wing of the soul. *Opie Read*

If there is no bread, there is no Torah; if there is no Torah, there is no bread. *Ethics of the Fathers 3:21*

Man does not live by broad alone.

Man does not live by words alone, though he often has to eat them. *Adlai Stevenson*

Man doesn't live well by bread alone.
Man is a creature who lives not by bread
    alone, but
principally by catch-words.
Robert Louis Stevenson, Virginibus Puerisque

The man who lives by bread alone, lives alone.

God have mercy on the sinner
Who must write with no dinner.
John Crowe Ransom

*A biblical idea found in both the Hebrew Bible and the New Testament. "Man doth not live by bread alone" is found in Deuteronomy 8:3. In the New Testament, we find "Man shall not live by bread alone" both in Matthew and in Luke (coincidentally, both are located 4:4).

MAN is a social animal.* *Seneca (1st century A.D.); F-609*

. . . who dislikes his fellow men. *Eugène Delacroix, Journal*

A journeyman marcher takes his place in ranks first and then asks why he's there. *Donald G. Smith*

A party spirit forces the greatest man to act as meanly as the vulgar herd. *Jean de La Bruyère, Les Caractères*

A strict observer is one who would be an atheist under an atheistic king. *Jean de La Bruyère, Les Caractères*

Any fool can make a rule and every fool will mind it. *Henry David Thoreau, Journal*

Better be quarreling than lonesome. *Irish proverb*

Cold tea and cold rice are bearable, but not cold looks and cold words. *Japanese proverb*

Conformity, humility, acceptance—with these coins we are to pay our fares to paradise. *Robert Lindner, Must You Conform?*

Conscience is, in most men, an anticipation of the opinions of others. *Henry Taylor*

Courage is the fear of being thought a coward. *Horace Smith*

Every man has a mob self and an individual self, in varying proportions. *D. H. Lawrence, Pornography and Obscenity*

Everyone has observed how much more dogs are animated when they hunt in a pack, than when they pursue their game apart. We might, perhaps, be at a loss to explain this phenomenon, if we had not experience of a similar in ourselves. *David Hume, A Treatise of Human Nature*

For us the most entertaining plane in the world is the human face. *Georg Lichtenberg*

He that converses not, knows nothing. *English proverb*

If misery loves company, then triumph demands an audience. *Brian Moore*

If you really want to annoy your enemy, keep silent and leave him alone. *Arabic proverb*

If you want to get along, go along. *Sam Rayburn*

If you would unsettle someone, call him a name. If you would destroy him, turn your back. *Donald G. Smith*

It is unpleasant to go alone, even to be drowned. *Russian proverb*

Life is not worth living for the man who has not even one good friend. *Democritus of Abdera*

Life without a friend is death without a witness. *Spanish proverb*

Man is a gregarious animal, much more so in his mind than in his body. He may like to go alone for a walk, but he hates to stand alone in his opinions. *George Santayana*

Man was formed for society, and is neither capable of living alone, nor has the courage to do it. *William Blackstone, Commentaries on the Laws of England*

Most people suspend their judgment till somebody else has expressed his own, and then they repeat it. *Ernest Dimnet*

Nothing is illegal if one hundred businessmen decide to do it. *Andrew Young*

One can acquire anything in solitude except character. *Stendahl, Love*

One is as good as none. *1591, Florio*

One may no more live in the world without picking up the moral prejudices of the world than one will be able to go to hell without perspiring. *H. L. Mencken*

People need people. *Line from the song "People," in the 1964 musical Funny Girl (words by Bob Merrill); popularized by Barbra Streisand*

Remember no one makes it alone. Have a grateful heart and be quick to acknowledge those who help you. *H. Jackson Brown, Jr., Life's Little Instruction Book*

Solitude is a good place to visit but a poor place to stay. *Josh Billings*

Talk is by far the most accessible of pleasures. It costs nothing in money, it is all profit, it completes our education, founds and fosters friendships, and can be enjoyed at any age and in almost any state of health. *Robert Louis Stevenson*

Teamwork is not always desirable. We should try to appreciate the one ox who won't go into the quicksand. *Donald G. Smith*

The lower stone can do no good without the hyer. *William Horman, 1519*

The majority, compose them how you will, are a herd, and not a very nice one. *William Hazlitt, Butts of Different Sorts*

The most dangerous foe to truth and freedom in our midst is the compact majority. Yes, the damned, compact, liberal majority. *Henrik Ibsen, An Enemy of the People*

The surest cure for vanity is loneliness. *Thomas Wolfe, as quoted in American Mercury, Oct. 1941*

There is comfort in numbers.

To be alone is to be different, to be different is to be alone. *Suzanne Gordon, Lonely in America*

To die with others is better than living alone. *Moorish proverb*

Two starving men cannot be twice as hungry as one; but two rascals can be ten times as vicious as one. *G. B. Shaw, Maxims for Revolutionists*

We are more wicked together than separately. *Seneca*

What men call social virtues, good fellowship, is commonly but the virtue of pigs in a litter, which lie close together to keep each other warm. *Henry David Thoreau, Journal*

When one man tells you you're drunk, hesitate; when two men tell you, slow up; when three men tell you, go to bed. *Yiddish proverb*

When people are free to do as they please, they usually imitate each other. *Eric Hoffer, The Passionate State of Mind*

*A viewpoint also expressed by Aristotle (384–322 B.C.) and by Baruch Spinoza (1632–77).

See also All is VANITY; Many hands make light WORK; The MAJORITY rules; the rule of the MAJORITY . . . ; MONKEY see, monkey do; PEOPLE will talk; What will PEOPLE think?

MAN is born free, and everywhere he is in chains. *Jean-Jacques Rousseau, The Social Contract, 1762*

Don't put no constrictions on da people. Leave 'em ta hell alone. *Jimmy Durante*

Lean liberty is better than fat slavery.

Newspapers are born free, and everywhere they are in chains. *F. R. Scott*

Nothing stamped with the Divine image and likeness was sent into the world to be trodden on and degraded and imbruted by its fellows. *Abraham Lincoln*

Those who deny freedom to others deserve it not for themselves. *Abraham Lincoln, 1859*

MAN is the measure of all things. *Plato, Theatetus, 4th century B.C.; M-673*

The wonder is, not that the field of stars is so vast, but that man has measured it. *Anatole France, The Garden of Epicurus*

MAN wants but little here below.*

. . . and often settles for even less.

All I desire for my own burial is not to be buried alive. *Lord Chesterfield, Letters*

My only concern was to get home after a hard day's work. *Rosa Parks, who started the Montgomery, Alabama, bus strike in 1955 when she refused to leave a "Whites Only" seat*

Man wants but little drink below,
But wants that little strong.
Oliver Wendell Holmes, A Song of Other Days

Though statisticians in our time
Have never kept the score
Man wants a great deal here below
And Woman even more.
James Thurber, Further Tales for Our Time

*Man wants but little here below,
Nor wants that little long.
Oliver Goldsmith, The Vicar of Wakefield

The proper study of mankind is MAN.*

. . . says man. *James Thurber*

I am a man; I deem nothing human alien to me. *Terence*

The proper study of mankind is woman. *Henry Adams*

*Know then thyself, presume not God to scan;
The proper study of mankind is Man.
Alexander Pope, An Essay on Man, 1732

See also What is MAN?

What is MAN?

. . . Something between God and clay. What is God? Something of which clay and man are the shadow. *Serbian proverb*

I believe that our Heavenly Father invented man because he was disappointed in the monkey. *Mark Twain, Eruption*

I have never seen an ass who talked like a human being, but I have met many human beings who talked like asses. *Heinrich Heine*

If man is but another animal species, why has no other species produced a Darwin?

It has been said that man is the only animal who laughs, and the only one who weeps; the only one who prays; the only one who walks fully erect; the only one who makes fires; the only one who guides his own destiny; the only one who is penitent; and the only one who needs to be. *David Elton Fineblood, Philosophy of Religion*

Man is a complex being: he makes deserts bloom and lakes die. *Gil Stern, Chicago Sun-Times, Oct. 10, 1970*

Man is a singular creature. He has a set of gifts which make him unique among the animals, so that unlike them he is not a figure in the landscape, he is the shaper of the landscape. *Jacob Bronowski, 1979*

Man is an animal that makes bargains; no other animal does this—no dog exchanges bones with another. *Adam Smith*

Man is at the bottom an animal, midway a citizen, and at the top divine. But the climate of this world is such that few ripen at the top. *Henry Ward Beecher*

Man is Creation's masterpiece; but who says so? Man. *Elbert Hubbard*

Man is the only animal that plays poker. *Don Herold*

Man is the only animal who blushes. Or needs to. *Mark Twain*

The question is this: Is man an ape or an angel? I am on the side of the angels. *Benjamin Disraeli*

We are as different from the lower animals as God, if he exists, must be different from us.

Wonders are many, and nothing is more wonderful than man. *Sophocles*

The seven ages of man—spills, drills, thrills, bills, ills, pills, wills. *Richard Needham*

What a piece of work is Man! how noble in reason! how infinite in faculties! in form and moving, how express and admirable! in action how like an angel! in apprehension how like a god! the beauty of the world, the paragon of animals! *Shakespeare, Hamlet 2.2.320*

What is Man? A foolish baby,
Vainly strives, and fights, and frets;
Demanding all, deserving nothing;
One small grave is what he gets.
Thomas Carlyle, Cui Bono

Man's a kind
of Missing Link,
fondly thinking
he can think.
Piet Hein

All the windy ways of men
Are but dust that rises up,
And is lightly laid again.
Alfred, Lord Tennyson, The Vision of Sin

See also The proper study of mankind is MAN.

You can't keep a good MAN down. *Title of a song by M. F. Carey, ca. 1900*

. . . which is the moral of Jonah and the Whale.

I've never been poor, only broke. Being poor is a frame of mind. Being broke is only a temporary situation. *Mike Todd, Newsweek, Mar. 31, 1958*

You can't hold a man down without staying down with him. *Booker T. Washington*

It's a MAN'S world.

I don't mind living in a man's world as long as I can be a woman in it. *Marilyn Monroe*

It's papa who pays. *Heard in Kentucky and Tennessee*

A lady is smarter than a gentleman, maybe.
She can sew a fine seam, she can have a baby,
She can use her intuition instead of her
    brain,
But she can't fold a paper on a crowded train.
Phyllis McGinley

MANY are called but few are chosen. *Matthew 20:16*

Many are called but few are called back.

Many are called, but few deliver the goods.

Many are called but few get up. *Cynic, 1903*

Text for a January sermon: Many are cold but few are frozen.

When I go
it should be by cremation,
my ashes slipped into
an 8x10 manila envelope
with a second (stamped and self-addressed)
inside, posted to God

in His capacity as editor
of Everything.

I stand
a better than even chance
of being returned to myself,
along with a neat note
acknowledging my insight and my craft,
regretting that I do not,
at that time, fit
His divine needs,
wishing me luck in placing myself
elsewhere.
Elizabeth Flynn

MARRIAGE is a fifty-fifty proposition.

Marriage is our last, best chance to grow up. *Joseph Barth*

Marriage should be a duet—when one sings, the other claps. *Joe Murray*

MARRIAGES are made in heaven.* *1566, T-445*

. . . and consummated on earth. *French proverb*

. . . but they're broken down here on earth.

. . . So is thunder and lightning.

Divorces are made in heaven. *Oscar Wilde*

Marriage is either death or life; there is no betwixt and between. *Kahlil Gibran*

Marriages are made in heaven knows what state of mind.

More matches are arranged by Satan than are ever made in heaven. *F. C. Davis, 1941*

Those whom God hath joined together let no man put asunder. *The Book of Common Prayer*

*Also found in Midrash: Genesis Rabbah 68 (A.D. 550)

It is better to MARRY than to burn. *1 Corinthians 7:9*

MARRY in haste and repent at leisure. 1566, T-293

A manuscript is something that is submitted in haste and returned at leisure. *Oliver Herford*

A sour-face wife is the liquor dealer's friend. *Old Farmer's Almanac*

Better stay chaste than marry in haste.

Courtship to marriage, as a very witty prologue to a very dull play. *William Congreve*

I lost a good secretary and found a lousy cook. *Fiorello H. La Guardia*

It's a sad house where the hen crows louder than the cock. *1573, WM-298*

Marriage halves our griefs, doubles our joys, and quadruples our expenses. *Vincent Lean, 1902*

Marriage is a lottery in which men stake their liberty and women their happiness. *Madame de Rieux*

Marriage is a lottery, but you can't tear up your ticket if you lose. *F. M. Knowles, 1906*

Marriage is an institution which teaches a man frugality, temperance and other virtues he wouldn't need if he stayed single. *Wall Street Journal*

Marry in haste and never find the leisure to repent it.

Men marry because they are tired, women because they are curious; both are disappointed. *Oscar Wilde*

There will always be a battle between the sexes because men and women want different things. Men want women and women want men. *George Burns*

Those who marry to escape something usually find something else. *George Ade*

Though women are angels, yet wedlock's the devil. *Lord Byron, Hours of Idleness*

Now hatred is by far the longest pleasure;
Men love in haste, but they detest at leisure.
Lord Byron

A man may spend
And God will send
If his wife be good to ought,
But man may spare and still be bare
If his wife be good to nought.
English verse

Men in single state should tarry;
While women, I suggest, should marry.
Samuel Hoffenstein

A young man MARRIED is a man that's marred. *Shakespeare, All's Well That Ends Well 2.3.315, ca. 1603*

A married man with a family will do anything for money. *Charles-Maurice de Talleyrand*

I have certainly seen more men destroyed by the desire to have a wife and child and keep them in comfort than I have seen destroyed by drink or harlots. *William Butler Yeats*

In marriage, a man becomes slack and selfish, and undergoes a fatty degeneration of his moral being. *Robert Louis Stevenson, Virginibus Puerisque*

The big difference between sex for money and sex for free is that sex for money usually costs a lot less. *Brendan Behan*

The chain of wedlock is so heavy that it takes two to carry it—sometimes three. *Alexandre Dumas père*

The only really happy folk are married women and single men. *H. L. Mencken*

Wedlock is a padlock. *1678, Ray*

Well-married, a man is winged—ill-matched he is shackled. *Henry Ward Beecher*

When a man marries, dies, or turns Hindoo, his best friends hear no more of him. *Percy Bysshe Shelley*

When I can no longer bear to think of the victims of broken homes, I begin to think of the victims of intact ones. *Peter De Vries*

See also WIFE and children are hostages given to fortune; A WOMAN is only a woman, but a good cigar is a smoke.

I am the MASTER of my fate; I am the captain of my soul. W. E. Henley, Invictus

Experience is not what happens to you; it is what you do with what happens to you. *Aldous Huxley, as quoted in Reader's Digest, Mar. 1956*

Every man is the architect of his own fate. *Appius Caecus, 4th century B.C.*

Hath not the potter power over the clay, of the same lump to make one vessel unto honor, and another unto dishonor? *Romans 9:21*

He conquers twice who conquers himself. *Motto of Bysse family*

In life, as in poker, you don't need a royal flush to be a winner. Sometimes a pair of deuces—a weak hand played well—is plenty. *Elks magazine*

Life is like a game of cards. The hand that is dealt you represents determinism. The way you play it is free will. *Jawaharlal Nehru*

'Tis in ourselves that we are thus or thus. *Shakespeare, Othello 1.3.322*

When a man says he's a self-made man, is he boasting or apologizing?

Your future depends on many things, but mostly on you. *Frank Tyger*

I am the captain of my soul;
I rule it with stern joy;
And yet I think I had more fun
When I was cabin boy.
Keith Preston

Men at some times are masters of their fates;
The fault, dear Brutus, is not in our stars,
But in ourselves, that we are underlings.
Shakespeare, Julius Caesar 1.2.138

Like MASTER, like servant. *Petronius, Satyricon*

Like master, like dog.

Like master, like man.

No man can serve two MASTERS. *Matthew 6:24*

. . . or mistresses.

. . . but it's interesting to see how good a try you can make.

. . . and few of us try. We are satisfied to bless God from whom all blessings flow, while we cash the checks of Mammon. *L. de V. Matthewman*

. . . which is the basis for the law against bigamy.

He who has to serve two masters, has to lie to one. *Spanish proverb*

One man's MEAT is another man's poison. *Latin proverb*

A slice of eggplant makes a dandy sink stopper. *Kin Hubbard*

Any kind of turnip crop should be considered a failure. *Kin Hubbard*

Kitty heaven is mousie hell.

News item: Pope rules that whale meat is fish, for fast-day purposes. One man's meat is another man's *poisson*.

One century's sacrilege is another's archaeology. *Boston Herald, ca. 1925*

One man's Claire is another man's affair.

One man's cliché can be another man's conviction. *Adlai Stevenson, 1969*

One man's art is another man's hokum. *F. McGerr, 1967; BJW-400*

One man's floor is another man's ceiling. *D. Bloodworth, 1967; BJW-400*

One man's folly is another man's wife. *Helen Rowland*

One man's heresy is another man's faith. *J. Atkins, 1970; BJW-400*

One man's Jill is another man's thrill.

One man's mate is another man's passion. *Eugene Healy, Mr. Sandeman Loses His Life*

One man's meat is another man's sawdust. *1951, BJW-400*

One man's truth is another man's cold broccoli. *New Yorker, 1957*

One man's Mede is another man's Persian. *George S. Kaufman; BJW-400.* Kaufman's biographer, Howard Teichmann, regards this as one of Kaufman's greatest puns.

One man's Molly is another man's folly.

One man's nerve is another man's nervousness.

One man's poetry is another man's poison. *Oscar Wilde*

One man's red tape is another man's system. *Dwight Waldo, 1946*

One man's remorse is another's reminiscence. *Ogden Nash, A Clean Conscience Never Relaxes*

One man's strawberries are another man's hives. *Lawrence Goulde, 1940*

One man's tragedy is another man's joke. *E. Bowen, 1960; BJW-400*

One man's trash is another man's treasure.

One man's weed is another man's wild flower. *Contemporary postcard*

One man's wisdom is another man's folly.

One woman's poise is another woman's poison. *Katherine Brush, as quoted in Reader's Digest, May 1941*

The religion of one seems madness unto another. *Thomas Browne, 1658*

The shoe that fits one person pinches another; there is no recipe for living that suits all cases. *Carl Jung, Modern Man in Search of a Soul*

See also Different STROKES for different folks; One man's JUSTICE is another man's injustice.

The MEDIUM is the message. [*] *Marshall McLuhan, on the impact of television, in Understanding Media, 1964*

. . . [but] the map is not the territory. *Alfred Korzybski*

The tedium is the message. *Brian Eno*

[*]McLuhan's memorable line says much about modern life. For example, why is violence so much more prevalent on TV than it ever was on radio? Because violence can be so much more vividly portrayed on TV than on radio. On the other hand, in the future there is likely to be less police violence on the streets, because it can now be so easily recorded by camcorder.

Blessed are the MEEK, for they shall inherit the earth. *Matthew 5:5*[*]

. . . six feet of it.

. . . if nobody objects.

. . . because they will be too timid to say "No, thanks."

. . . but not its mineral rights. *J. Paul Getty*

Blessed are the flexible, for they shall not be bent out of shape.

Blessed are the meek, for they shall inherit the work.

Blessed are the pure in heart for they shall inhibit the earth. *Peter's Almanac*

Blessed are the passive for they will be screwed out of everything.

Blessed are the rich and powerful for they have inherited the earth.

Blessed are they who run around in circles for they shall be known as wheels. *Old postcard*

Blessed is the man who expects nothing, for he shall never be disappointed. *Alexander Pope, 1725*

From time to time we encounter people of a cheerful, kindly, unenvious nature. They usually run elevators. *Mignon McLaughlin*

It's going to be fun to watch and see how long the meek can keep the earth after they inherit it. *Elbert Hubbard*

Let the meek inherit the earth—they have it coming to them. *James Thurber*

Blessed are the young, for they shall inherit the national debt. *Herbert Hoover*

Some modern prophets believe that by the time the meek claim title to the globe, the polluters and pillagers may have left it a poisoned and pathetic mess. *Bruce Buursma*

The meek haven't inherited the earth, but they sure do support it.

[*]The idea that the meek shall inherit the earth is contained in both the Old and New Testaments. In one of his Sermons on the Mount, Jesus says, "Blessed are the meek: for they shall inherit the earth." In the Old Testament, Psalms 37:11 reads, "But the meek shall inherit the earth; and shall delight themselves in the abundance of peace."

All MEN are brothers.

About the only difference between the poor and the rich is this, the poor *suffer* misery, while the rich have to *enjoy* it. *Josh Billings, 1865*

All mankind are my brethren; to do good is my religion. *Thomas Paine*

Am I not a man and a brother? *Motto of the Anti-Slavery Society of London, established 1823*

Every beggar is descended from some king and every king is descended from some beggar. *1602, T-39*

Every girl in love thinks she has found the only man of his kind in the world; but the married women know that the men are all fearfully alike. *Ed Howe*

In each human heart are a tiger, a pig, an ass, and a nightingale; diversity of character is due to their unequal activity. *Ambrose Bierce*

That all men should be brothers is the dream of people who have no brothers. *Charles Chincholles, Pensées de Tout le Mond*

The Lord so constituted everybody that no matter what color you are you require the same amount of nourishment. *Will Rogers*

The partition between the sage and the fool is more slender than a spider web. *Kahlil Gibran*

To my embarrassment I was born in bed with a lady. *Wilson Mizner*

We're all brothers under the skin, but some brothers get under your skin more than others. *Peter's Almanac*

While there is a lower class I am in it, while there is a criminal element I am of it, and while there is a soul in prison I am not free. *Eugene Debs, 1918*

Whoever degrades another degrades me. *Walt Whitman, 1885*

See also No man is an ISLAND; The colonel's lady and Mrs. O'Grady are SISTERS under the skin.

All MEN are created equal. * *Thomas Jefferson (1743–1826), Declaration of Independence*

. . . but some aren't equal to much. *Peter's Almanac*

. . . but some are more equal than others.

. . . but they don't stay that way very long.

. . . then some get married.

. . . and are free to try to become otherwise. *Wall Street Journal, ca. 1925*

. . . an utterly baseless fiction. *Aldous Huxley, On the Natural Inequality of Man*

A person is a person because he recognizes others as persons. *Desmond Tutu, address at enthronement as Anglican archbishop of Cape Town, Sept. 7, 1986*

All animals are equal, but some are more equal than others. *George Orwell, Animal Farm*

All men are born truthful and die liars. *Luc de Clapiers de Vauvenargues, Reflexions*

All men are equal before fish. *Herbert Hoover, on his favorite pastime*

Before God we all are equally wise—equally foolish. *Albert Einstein, Cosmic Religion*

Black is when they say ". . . one nation indivisible with liberty and justice for all" and you wonder what nation they're talking about. *Turner Brown, Jr., Black Is*

Equality may perhaps be a right, but no power on earth can ever turn it into a fact. *Honoré de Balzac*

Every man has a right to be equal to every other man. *Abraham Lincoln*

God is no respecter of persons. . . . Whosoever believeth in him shall receive remission of sins. *Acts 10:34, 43.* Luke meant that Christianity was open to Jew and Gentile alike.

I hold that the Lord didn't make one man for another man to run over. *Opie Read*

In theory, one man is as good as another, but in practice it is a lie. *Ed Howe*

Knowing what goes on behind my placid exterior, I have a strong suspicion of what goes on behind yours. *Richard Needham*

The brotherhood of man is not a mere poet's dream; it is a most depressing and humiliating reality. *Oscar Wilde*

The law, in all its majestic equality, forbids the rich as well as the poor to sleep under bridges. *Anatole France*

The only real equality is in the cemetery. *German proverb*

Who shall say, "I am the superior and you are the inferior"? *Abraham Lincoln, speech in Springfield, Illinois, 1858*

*This phrase, of course, never claimed an equality of intellect, character, financial worth, or any other attainment, but asserted that all men were morally equal, "equal in the sight of God." The abolitionists argued with defenders of the status quo over exactly who the signers of the Declaration of Independence referred to as "all men"—did they literally mean all men, slave or free, or did they mean all citizens of their time? In his Independence Hall speech of 1861, Lincoln argued that these words "gave promise that in due time the weights would be lifted from the shoulders of all men, and that all should have an equal chance." To Lincoln, the authors of the Declaration of Independence, "did not mean to say all men were equal in color, size, intellect, moral developments, or social capacity . . . [but] in 'certain inalienable rights, among which are life, liberty, and the pursuit of happiness' " (speech on the *Dred Scott* decision).

Donald Bond suggests that Jefferson's phrase was a restatement of the English legal principle that the law is no respecter of persons, that the law is open to all, that there cannot be one law for the rich and another for the poor.

See also The colonel's lady and Mrs. O'Grady are SISTERS under the skin; Fair PLAY; What's SAUCE for the goose is sauce for the gander.

All MEN are mortal. 1537, T-433

A man's dying is more the survivors' affair than his own. *Thomas Mann, The Magic Mountain*

After your death you will be what you were before your birth. *Arthur Schopenhauer, On the Doctrine of the Indestructibility of Our True Nature*

Being born is the beginning of the end. *Japanese proverb*

Cheerio, see you soon. *Gravestone inscription, reported or invented by Nick Harris*

Do not try to live for ever. You will not succeed. *G. B. Shaw, The Doctor's Dilemma*

Dying is as natural as living. *English proverb*

Every man knows he will die but no one wants to believe it. *Yiddish proverb*

Fortune-teller peering into her crystal ball: "The crystal ball reveals sadness in your future: someday you will die!" *Cartoon by Norman Dog*

Growing old—it's not nice, but it's interesting. *August Strindberg*

I owe God a death. *1581, T-2+63*

I'm not afraid to die. I just don't want to be there when it happens. *Woody Allen, Getting Even*

If some persons died, and others did not die, death would indeed be a terrible affliction. *Jean de La Bruyère, Les Caractères*

It is as natural to die as to be born; and to a little infant, perhaps, the one is as painful as the other. *Francis Bacon, Essays*

It is hard to believe, especially when young, that we are going to die. . . . No other creature on earth has been instilled with this awareness of eventual death and this is our burden. The way to lighten it is to reflect that being here at all is an adventure that none of us would have wished to miss, even though it ends on a dying note. *Sydney J. Harris*

It is unhealthy to live. He who lives, dies. *Stanislaw J. Lec*

Man is the only animal that contemplates death, and also the only animal that shows any sign of doubt of its finality. *William Ernest Hocking, The Meaning of Immortality in Human Experience*

Old and young, we are all on our last cruise. *Robert Louis Stevenson, Virginibus Puerisque*

The fact of having been born is a bad augury for immortality. *George Santayana, The Life of Reason*

The first breath is the beginning of death. *Heard in New Jersey*

There is no medicine against death. *Latin proverb*

We are born to die. *Shakespeare, Romeo and Juliet 3.4.4*

What man is he that liveth, and shall not see death? *Psalms 89:48*

When you gotta go, you gotta go.

Golden lads and girls all must,
As chimney-sweepers, come to dust.
Shakespeare, Cymbeline 4.2.262

See also All FLESH is grass; LIFE is short; O DEATH, where is thy sting?

As many MEN, so many minds. *Terence (2nd century B.C.), Phormio*

If there were two men alike, the world would not be big enough to contain them. *Kahlil Gibran*

Men's minds are as variant as their faces. *George Washington*

Some are wise, and others are otherwise. *1601, OE-603*

Where all think alike, no one thinks very much. *Walter Lippmann*

Grown MEN don't cry.

A good cry sometimes serves as an anodyne and slightly alleviates disappointment and pain. Anyway, it can't do you any harm and it may help a little. *George Jean Nathan, opposing the proverb "There's no use crying over spilt milk."*

"It opens the lungs, washes the countenance, exercises the eyes, and softens down the temper," said Mr. Bumble. "So cry away." *Charles Dickens, Oliver Twist*

Real men don't eat quiche.

MEN are all alike.

. . . except the one you've just met, who's different. *Mae West*

. . . They just have different faces so that you can tell them apart.

An unlearned carpenter of my acquaintance once said in my hearing: "There is very little difference between one man and another; but what little there is, is very important." *William James, The Will to Believe*

MEN are but children of a larger growth. John Dryden, All for Love, 1678

All that is good in man lies in youthful feeling and mature thought. *Joseph Joubert*

As men get older, the toys get more expensive. *Denver oilman Marvin Davis, after purchasing the Oakland A's for a rumored $12 million*

Every woman keeps a corner in her heart where she is always twenty-one. *Heard in Illinois and New York*

Most of us become parents long before we have stopped being children. *Mignon McLaughlin*

Our whole life is but a greater and longer childhood. *Poor Richard's Almanac*

We write not only for children but also for their parents. They, too, are serious children. *Isaac Bashevis Singer, Stories for Children*

When childhood dies, its corpses are called adults. *Brian Aldiss, Manchester Guardian, Dec. 31, 1977*

Women are but children of a larger growth. *Lord Chesterfield, Letters to His Son, advising that women should not be consulted on serious matters*

MEN are such animals.

A gentleman is a patient wolf. *Henrietta Tiarks*

All men are liars.

Don't accept rides from strange men, and remember that all men are strange. *Robin Morgan*

Every young man carries by nature a breast of passions just such as bad men have, and should not allow wicked men to approach to seduce him. *Henry Ward Beecher*

Men are nothing but lazy lumps of drunken flesh. They crowd you in bed, get you all worked up, and before you can say "Is that all there is?" that's all there is. *Taxi, TV show*

Men are those creatures with two legs and eight hands. *Jayne Mansfield*

No wisdom below the girdle. *1670, B-960*

They say two things about a stiff pecker: (1) a stiff pecker has no conscience; and (2) a stiff pecker has no sense of humor. *J. Atkins, 1970.* Mieder (M-483) cites the proverb "A stiff prick knows no conscience."

See also MEN are all alike; PEOPLE are no damned good.

**MEN seldom make passes
At girls who wear glasses.**
Dorothy Parker (1893–1967)

Boys don't make passes at female smart-asses. *Letty Cottin Pogrebin, 1972*

In Hawaii, men make passes at girls who wear grasses. *Henny Youngman*

Men do make passes at girls who wear glasses. It all depends on their frames.

Men often make passes at girls who hold glasses. *L. L. Levinson*

Men seldom make passes at a girl who surpasses. *Franklin P. Jones*

Now, aren't young men asses
Not to make passes
At girls who wear glasses?

While elderly yokels
Leer at dolls with bifocals.

The quality of MERCY is not strained. *Shakespeare, The Merchant of Venice 4.1.163, ca. 1596*

MERIT wins.
See RIGHT makes might.

When the cat's away, the MICE will play. *1470, O-32*

Many a little makes a MICKLE. *Greek proverb*

God is in the details.

A man's accomplishments in life are the cumulative effect of his attention to detail. *John Foster Dulles, in biography by Leonard Mosley*

See also A PENNY saved is a penny earned; Mighty OAKS from little acorns grow.

MIGHT makes right. *Plato (427–347 B.C.)*[*]

. . . and a good left is an asset too.

A handful of might is better than a sackful of right. *German proverb*

Every man thinks God is on his side. The rich and powerful know that he is. *Jean Anouilh, The Lark*

For de little stealin' dey gits you in jail soon or late. For de big stealin' dey makes you emperor and put you in de Hall o' Fame when you croaks. *Eugene O'Neill, The Emperor Jones*

God is always for the big battalions. *Voltaire, 1770*

It is useless for the sheep to pass resolutions in favor of vegetarianism while the wolf remains of a different opinion. *W. R. Inge*

Never argue with people who buy ink by the gallon. *Tommy Lasorda*

Not believing in force is the same as not believing in gravity. *Leon Trotsky*

Not by might, nor by power, but by my spirit, saith the Lord of hosts. *Zechariah 4:6*

Physical violence is the weapon by which stupidity and villainy can always defeat and destroy mind and virtue. *G. B. Shaw, Sixteen Self-Sketches*

Political power grows out of the barrel of a gun. *Mao Tse-tung, 1966*

Power concedes nothing without a demand. *Frederick Douglass*

Right is overcome by might. *Plautus*

The first lesson of history is the good of evil. *Ralph Waldo Emerson*

The law is protection for the mighty and punishment for the small man. *Russian proverb*

The only sure recipe to govern mankind with, is the rod; you may festoon it with flowers and case it with velvet, if you please, but it is the rod, after all, that does the business. *Josh Billings*

The strongest man's argument is always the best. *Jean de La Fontaine, Fables*

The worm is always wrong when it argues with the chicken. *Heard in Pennsylvania*

There are no manifestos like cannon and musketry. *Duke of Wellington*

There is no argument like that of a stick. *Spanish proverb*

Where might enters right departs. *Spanish proverb*

You can get much farther with a kind word and a gun than you can with a kind word alone. *Al Capone*

You can no more win a war than you can win an earthquake. *Jeannette Rankin*

Let weakness learn meekness:
God save the House of Lords.
A.C. Swinburne, A Word for the Country

Might and right are always fighting.
In our youth it seems exciting.

Right is always nearly winning.
Might can hardly keep from grinning.
Clarence Day, 1935

*I affirm that might is right, justice the interest of the stronger. *Plato, The Republic, ca. 375 B.C.*

See also The END doesn't justify the means; the END justifies the means; RIGHT makes might.

How are the MIGHTY fallen!*

The apple grows so bright and high,
And ends its days in apple pie.
Samuel Hoffenstein

*How are the mighty fallen in the midst of the battle! *2 Samuel 1:25*

The MILL cannot grind with the water that is past. *1651, Herbert*

Oh seize the instant time; you never will
With waters once passed by impel the mill.
R. C. Trench, Poems

And a proverb haunts my mind
    As a spell is cast,
"The mill cannot grind
    With water that is passed."
Sarah Doudney, The Lesson of the Water-Mill

The MILLS of the gods grind slowly, yet they grind exceedingly fine. *Greek proverb*

God comes with leaden feet but strikes with iron hands. *1578, T-260*

A MIND is a terrible thing to waste. *Slogan of the United Negro College Fund*

The waist is a terrible thing to mind. *The dieter's lament, by Ziggy ('Tom Wilson)*

What a waste it is to lose one's mind, or not to have a mind. . . . How true that is. *Dan Quayle, addressing the United Negro College Fund, 1989*

A sound MIND in a sound body. *Juvenal, Satires, A.D. 112*

A sound mind in a sound body is a short but full description of a happy state in this world. *John Locke*

I have never taken any exercise, except for sleeping and resting, and I never intend to take any. Exercise is loathsome. *Mark Twain*

Open bowels and an open mind. *Lord Berners, ca. 1930*

It's all a matter of MIND over matter.

. . . If you don't mind, it doesn't matter.

Anytime you hear someone say: "Youth is a state of mind," you can be sure that he has a lot more state of mind than he has youth. *Peter's Almanac*

Every day, in every way, I am getting better and better. *Émile Coué, 1910*

I think I can. I think I can. *The Little Engine That Could*

It can be done. *Sign posted in President Ronald Reagan's Oval Office, according to New York Times, Jan. 21. 1989*

Old age is all in your head—particularly if you wear dentures, a hearing aid, and bifocals. *Peter's Almanac*

The city of Happiness is in the state of Mind. *Old postcard*

They can because they think they can. *Virgil*

What is mind? No matter. What is matter? Never mind. *T. H. Key, quoted by F. J. Furnivall*

This very remarkable man
Commends a most practical plan:
You can do what you want
If you don't think you can't
So don't think you can't if you can.
Charles Inge, On Monsieur Coué

Keep an open MIND. *Slogan of Alcoholics Anonymous*

. . . but not one that is open at both ends.

A great many open minds should be closed for repairs. *Toledo Blade*

If you keep your mind sufficiently open, people will throw a lot of rubbish into it. *William A. Orton, Everyman Amid the Stereotype*

Many a man thinks he has an open mind, when it's merely vacant. *Henny Youngman*

Merely having an open mind is nothing. The object of opening the mind, as of opening the mouth, is to shut it again on something solid. *G. K. Chesterton*

Minds are like parachutes. They only function when they are open. *James Dewar*

What we have to do is to be forever curiously testing new opinions and courting new impressions. *Walter Pater*

Who is wise? He who learns from all men. *Talmud*

Great MINDS run in the same channel. *1640, M-411*

. . . Them's my sentiments, tew. *Will Carleton*

. . . and weak ones in the same gutter.

Great minds run in the same ditch. *Vermont proverb*

The age of MIRACLES is past.

It must be so; for miracles are ceas'd. *Shakespeare, Henry V 1.1.67*

Miracles do happen, but not often enough to be worth waiting up for. © *Ashleigh Brilliant*

Whatever a man prays for, he prays for a miracle. Every prayer reduces itself to this: "Great God, grant that twice two be not four." *Ivan Turgenev, Prayer*

Don't count on MIRACLES.

If your prayers are not answered, the answer is No.

Miracles sometimes occur, but one has to work terribly hard for them. *Chaim Weizmann*

One must not rely on miracles. *Babylonian Talmud*

When a preacher asked Thomas Edison whether to put a lightning rod on a church steeple, Edison replied, "By all means; Providence is apt to be absent-minded."

MISERY loves company. A.D. 60, B-1592

. . . cheerful company.

. . . but company does not reciprocate. *Cynic, 1903*

. . . but affluence throws better parties.

. . . but it's better to have rheumatism in one leg than both.

. . . but can't bear competition. There ain't nobody but what he thinks their boil is the sorest boil in the market.

A handsome young fellow in New York, in great distress for want of money, married last week a rich old woman of seventy. He was no doubt miserable for want of money, and she for want of a husband; and "misery makes strange bedfellows." *G. D. Prentice, Louisville Journal, ca. 1860*

Fellowship in woe doth woe assuage. *Shakespeare, The Rape of Lucrece*

Give sorrow words; the grief that does not speak whispers the o'er-fraught heart and bids it break. *Shakespeare, Macbeth 3.4.209*

I, personally, don't long for company when I am miserable. *Marlene Dietrich*

If misery loves company, misery has company enough. *Henry David Thoreau, Journal*

If misery loves company, then triumph demands an audience. *Brian Moore, An Answer from Limbo*

Nobody cares to hear your troubles, unless they are troubles he or she has also experienced; misery may love company, but company tolerates only the kinds of misery it has already known. *Sydney J. Harris*

Two in distress makes sorrow less. *1855, OE-680*

Victims of the same disease have much to talk about. *Japanese proverb*

One man's MISFORTUNE is another man's good luck.

Calamities are of two kinds: misfortune to ourselves and good fortune to others. *Ambrose Bierce*

A MISS is as good as a mile.

Affirmative action: A Ms. is as good as a male.

A miss is as good as her smile.

The easiest way to catch a plane is to miss the one before.

I'm from MISSOURI; you've got to show me.[*]

A man must now swallow more beliefs than he can digest. *Havelock Ellis, The Dance of Life*

A Miracle: An event described by those to whom it was told by men who did not see it. *Elbert Hubbard, 1001 Epigrams*

As to the gods, I have no means of knowing either that they exist or do not exist. For many are the obstacles that impede knowledge, both the obscurity of the question and the shortness of human life. *Protagoras, in Diogenes Laertius, Lives of Eminent Philosophers*

Doubt is part of all religion. All the religious thinkers were doubters. *Isaac Bashevis Singer, New York Times, Dec. 3, 1978*

Doubt is the key to knowledge. *Persian proverb*

I am an agnostic; I do not pretend to know what many ignorant men are sure of. *Clarence Darrow*

I respect faith; but doubt is what gets you an education. *Wilson Mizner*

In all affairs it's a healthy thing now and then to hang a question mark on the things you have long taken for granted. *Bertrand Russell, as quoted in Reader's Digest, Aug. 1940*

Men become civilized, not in proportion to their willingness to believe, but in proportion to their readiness to doubt. *H. L. Mencken*

Remember to distrust. *Epicharmus*

Supposing is good, but finding out is better. *Mark Twain*

Teacher says, "Question authority . . . but raise your hand first." *T-shirt maxim of Harvard law professor Alan M. Dershowitz*

The believer is happy; the doubter is wise. *Hungarian proverb*

To believe is very dull. To doubt is intensely engrossing. *Oscar Wilde*

There lives more faith in honest doubt,
Believe me, than in half the creeds.
Alfred, Lord Tennyson, In Memoriam

People sometimes
Take for gospel
Things that simply
Are impossible.

[*]From an 1899 speech by Willard Duncan Vandiver, in which the congressman, known as the Iconoclast, said, "I come from a state that raises corn and cotton and cockleburs and Democrats, and frothy eloquence neither convinces nor satisfies me. I am from Missouri. You have got to show me."

See also ACTION speaks louder than words; SEEING is believing; The proof of the PUDDING is in the eating; Never ASSUME.

Profit from your MISTAKES.

. . . or better yet, profit from the mistakes of others.

Do not look where you fell, but where you slipped. *African proverb*

Failure teaches success. *1902, O2-185*

Good judgment comes from experience. Experience comes from bad judgment.

Good people are good because they've come to wisdom through failure. *William Saroyan*

"How did it feel to fail 1,000 times?" a reporter asked Edison, who had made 1,000 unsuccessful attempts before producing the light bulb. Edison replied: "I didn't fail 1,000 times. The light bulb was an invention with 1,001 steps."

If you can profit from your mistakes, good for you; many folks pay dearly for their experience and are worse off than they were before.

Mistakes are the portals of discovery. *James Joyce*

Why make the same mistake twice, when there are so many new ones available?

True success is that which makes
Building stones of old mistakes.
Arthur Guiterman

See also EXPERIENCE is the best teacher.

We all make MISTAKES.

See To ERR is human, to forgive is divine; NOBODY is perfect.

MODERATION in all things. *Greek proverb*

. . . including moderation?

. . . said the boy to his father who was about to give his son a spanking.

A little suffering exalts us, a little success encourages us, a little pleasure comforts us. The trouble is, it never remains a little. *Mignon McLaughlin*

A successful person is one who has the horsepower of an optimist and the emergency brakes of a pessimist.

I would remind you that extremism in the defense of liberty is no vice. And let me remind you also that moderation in the pursuit of justice is no virtue. *Barry Goldwater, on being accused of representing the Republican party's most conservative wing*

All movements go too far. *Bertrand Russell*

Be a good fellow but don't make a damn fool of yourself. *Old postcard*

Be careful but not full of care. *Heard in New Jersey*

Everything to excess, but only once in a while. *TV restaurant editor, Chicago, Oct. 15, 1993*

Extremity of right is wrong. *1539, Taverner*

Fire which warms us at a distance will burn us when near. *1374*

Going beyond is as bad as falling short. *Chinese proverb*

Happiness: a way station between too little and too much. *Channing Pollock*

He is wise who knows what is enough. *Japanese proverb*

I can't tell you who is worse off—the man who is all head and no heart, or the one who is all heart and no head. *Josh Billings*

I have not been afraid of excess; excess on occasion is exhilarating. It prevents moderation from acquiring the deadening effect of a habit. *W. Somerset Maugham*

I never wanted to be a hero, but on the other hand I am not anxious to cultivate cowardice. *Gertrude Stein*

If sweetness is excessive, it is no longer sweetness. *African proverb*

It hain't a bad plan t' keep still occasionally even when you know what you're talking about. *Kin Hubbard*

It is not wise to be wiser than is necessary. *Philippe Quinault, Armide*

It's all right letting yourself go, as long as you can get yourself back. *Mick Jagger*

Measure is treasure. *1200, OE-415*

Moderation, the noblest gift of heaven. *Euripedes, Medea*

More than ever I am convinced that there is no such thing as exaggerated art. And I even believe there is salvation only in extremes. *Paul Gauguin, 1885*

My ideal qualities . . . strength without brutality, honesty without priggishness, courage without recklessness, humor without frivolity, humanity without sentimentality, intelligence without deviousness, skepticism without cynicism. *Frederick Forsyth, 1974*

One loser confessed to another, "I never listened to anybody." Said the other, "And I took everybody's advice."

One must not be more royalist than the king. *French saying which originated under Louis XVI*

Originality in writing has always been praised, but I have read some authors who were too original to be interesting. *Josh Billings*

Self-restraint is feeling your oats without sowing them. *Shanon Fife*

The best combination of parents consists of a father who is gentle beneath his firmness, and a mother who is firm beneath her gentleness. *Sydney J. Harris*

The hardest job for a politician today is to have the courage to be a moderate. It's easy to take an extreme position. *Hubert Humphrey*

Oil, poured drop by drop into the fire, revives the flames, but poured in large gushes smothers them; fields forced to produce too much become infertile. The seed sown in excess fails to grow and is destroyed; likewise those who give themselves immoderately to pleasure remove themselves from pleasure. *The virtue of moderation as expressed by an Indian mystic, quoted by F. Gonzales-Crussi in On the Nature of Things Erotic*

The worst enemy of life, freedom and the common decencies is total anarchy; the second worst enemy is total efficiency. *Aldous Huxley, Adonis and the Alphabet*

The worst people in the world are the richest and the poorest. *William C. Hunter*

There is no such thing as too much couth. *S. J. Perelman*

There is nothing wrong with sobriety in moderation. *John Ciardi, 1966*

There may be such a thing as too much conscience, but there is no such thing as too much common sense. *Frederick H. Seymour*

To spend too much time in studies is sloth. *Francis Bacon, Essays*

Too clever is dumb. *German proverb*

Too little and too much spoils everything. *Danish proverb*

Too much of a good thing can be wonderful. *Mae West*

They are as sick that surfeit with too much as they that starve with nothing. *Shakespeare, The Merchant of Venice 1.2.6*

To you who praise the "happy medium" to me as a way of life, I reply, "Who wants to be lukewarm between cold and hot, or tremble between life and death, or be a jelly, neither fluid nor solid?" *Kahlil Gibran*

Use, do not abuse; neither abstinence nor excess ever renders man happy. *Voltaire*

Valor lies just halfway between rashness and cowardice. *Miguel de Cervantes*

We all know what happens to people who stay in the middle of the road. They get run over. *Aneurin Bevan*

What the crowd requires is mediocrity of the highest order. *Auguste Préault*

You are not a carpenter until you've run one finger through the saw; if you run too many fingers through the saw, you're also not a carpenter.

You can never get too much of a good thing. *American saying*

Your dress should be tight enough to show you're a woman and loose enough to show you're a lady. *Edith Head, quoted by Joseph Laitin in Collier's*

I love excess
of fruitfulness.
Let other fools
pay more for less.
Piet Hein

The aftereffects of a mother's neglects
    May spoil her boy's orientation to sex,
But converse is worse: if she overprotects,
    The pattern of Oedipus wrecks.
Felicia Lamport

See also ENOUGH is enough; ENOUGH is as good as a feast; DO unto others as you would have them do unto you.

If the mountain won't come to MOHAMMED, Mohammed will go to the mountain.[*] **1594, T-478**

[*]The Morrises (MD-300) explain the origin of this saying thus: "When Mohammed was bringing his message to the Arabs, they demanded some miracle to prove his power. He then ordered Mount Safa to come to him. When it failed to move, he said that God was indeed merciful, for had it obeyed, it would have fallen upon them, destroying them utterly. He then proposed to go to the mountain to offer thanks to God for his mercy."

Bad MONEY drives out good money.[*]

[*]Popularly known as Gresham's Law, but actually authored in 1857 by Scottish economist Henry Dunning Macleod, says Keyes (K-180).

Don't marry for MONEY, but never let money stand between a girl and her happiness.

A girl must marry for love, and keep on marrying until she finds it. *Zsa Zsa Gabor*

Don't marry for money, but don't marry without money. *1623, WM-415*

Don't marry for money; you can borrow it cheaper. *Scotch proverb*

He that marries for money earns it.

He that marries for wealth sells his liberty. *1651, Herbert*

It's as easy to love a rich girl as a poor one. *1941, WM-251*

Love may laugh at locksmiths, but he has a profound respect for money bags. *Sidney Paternoster, The Folly of the Wise*

Marry for money, starve for love. *Poor Richard Jr.'s Almanac*

Marrying a woman for her money is very much like setting a rat-trap and baiting it with your own finger. *Josh Billings*

Marrying for love may be a little risky, but it is so honest that God can't help but smile on it. *Josh Billings*

The man who marries for money is a fool, but rarely as big a fool as he who marries for love. *L. de V. Matthewman*

When you see what some girls marry, you realize how much they must hate to work for a living. *Helen Rowland, A Guide to Men*

It takes MONEY to make money.

Starting from scratch is easy; starting without it is tough. *Peter's Almanac*

It's easy to be generous with somebody else's MONEY.

Folks is mighty generous with money they ain't got. *Heard in Mississippi*

It's not the MONEY, it's the principle of the thing.

A man will fight harder for his interests than for his rights. *Napoleon, Maxims*

It's not the money; it's the principal and interest. *Howard Kandel*

When a man says [that], it's the money. *Kin Hubbard*

It's only MONEY.

A billion here, a billion there, and pretty soon you're talking real money. *Everett Dirksen*

Love of MONEY is the root of all evil. *1 Timothy 6:10*

It is not wealth that stands in the way of liberation but the attachment to wealth. *E. P. Schumacher, Small Is Beautiful*

Lack of money is the root of all evil. *G. B. Shaw*

Money is the root of all comfort. *J. Wechsberg, 1970; BJW-387*

The love of somebody else's money is the root of all evil.

MONEY can't buy everything.

A man who has money may be anxious, depressed, frustrated and unhappy, but one thing he's not—and that's broke. *Brendan Francis*

Among the things that money can't buy is what it used to. *Max Kauffmann*

It is true that wealth won't make a man virtuous, but I notice there ain't anybody who wants to be poor just for the purpose of being good. *Josh Billings, 1865*

It's good to have money and the things that money can buy, but it's good, too, to check up once in a while and make sure you haven't lost the things that money can't buy. *George Horace Lorimer*

Money can't buy friends, but it can get you a better class of enemy. *Spike Milligan*

Money cannot buy things that are not for sale. *Chinese proverb*

Some get wealth by wit, but none by wealth can purchase wit.

The only problems that money can solve are money problems.

There are a lot of things money can't buy— for example, what it bought last year. *Peter's Almanac*

Certainly there are lots of things in life that
   money won't buy, but it's very funny
Have you ever tried to buy them without
   money?
Ogden Nash, 1933

MONEY can't buy happiness. *1792, WM-416*

. . . but I'd like a chance to prove it.

. . . the way poverty delivers misery.

. . . Neither does poverty.

. . . but with it you can be unhappy in comfort.

. . . but with it you can choose your own way to be unhappy.

. . . but it can buy a lot of solid comfort.

. . . but it makes misery easier to handle.

. . . but it will pay the salaries of a large research staff to study the problem. *Bill Vaughan*

. . . and happiness can't buy money either.

. . . and if it could, we probably couldn't afford it.

. . . the money of others, that is.

. . . but it's nice to have enough money to find that out for yourself.

. . . but it makes searching for happiness a lot easier.

. . . [but] the happiest time in any man's life is when he is in red-hot pursuit of a dollar with a reasonable prospect of overtaking it. *Josh Billings*

. . . nor can it buy much of anything else. *Hal Heverly*

Anyone who says money doesn't buy happiness doesn't know where to shop.

Hollywood is where if you don't have happiness, you send out for it. *Rex Reed*

If you can't buy happiness, charge it.

If you can't buy happiness, lease it. *BMW advertisement*

It's a kind of spiritual snobbery that makes people think they can be happy without money. *Albert Camus*

It's not that money makes everything good, it's that no money makes everything bad. *Yiddish proverb*

It's not that the rich have fewer troubles than the poor; it's just that theirs are more interesting. *Richard Needham*

It's pretty hard to tell what does bring happiness; poverty and wealth have both failed. *Kin Hubbard*

Let us remember that money . . . buys leisure, the time to do that which is personally fulfilling . . . Money does not directly buy happiness, but it buys the opportunity for happiness, if we just have the good sense to take advantage of it. *Donald G. Smith*

Money may buy the husk of things, but not the kernel. It brings you food but not appetite, medicine but not health, acquaintances but not friends, servants but not faithfulness, days of joy but not peace and happiness. *Henrik Ibsen*

Money may not buy love, but it sure can add zest to the shopping. *Henny Youngman*

Most of the rich people I have known have been fairly miserable. *Agatha Christie*

Much happiness is overlooked because it doesn't cost anything.

There are few sorrows, however poignant, in which a good income is of no avail. *Logan Pearsall Smith*

MONEY doesn't grow on trees. *1750, WM-416*

. . . You've got to beat the bushes for it. *Changing Times*

. . . unless you happen to be a successful orchardist.

Money is like promises: easier made than kept.

MONEY has no smell. *Latin proverb*

Dirty hands make clean money. *New England proverb*

Money doesn't care who makes it.

MONEY is the root of all evil.[*]

. . . but that's one evil I'm rooting for.

. . . and a man needs roots. *Howard Kandel*

. . . but the foliage is fascinating. *Val Peters*

. . . then let us root, hog, or die. *Josh Billings, 1865*

Don't knock the rich—when did a poor person ever give you a job? *Peter's Almanac*

Filthy lucre is that which never comes our way. *L. de V. Matthewman*

Gold is the devil's fishhook. *Heard in Illinois and Kentucky*

. . . Gold, worse poison to men's souls,
Doing more murder in this loathsome world,
Than these poor compounds that thou mayst
      not sell.
Shakespeare, Romeo and Juliet 5.1.80

Industry is the root of all ugliness. *Oscar Wilde*

It is easier for a camel to go through the eye of a needle than for a rich man to enter into the kingdom of God. *Matthew 19:24*

It is the wretchedness of being rich that you have to live with rich people. *Logan Pearsall Smith, 1949*

Lack of money is the root of all evil. *G. B. Shaw*

Money is the fruit of evil as often as the root of it. *Henry Fielding*

Money lays waste cities; it sets men to roaming from home; it seduces and corrupts honest men and turns virtue to baseness; it teaches villainy and impiety. *Sophocles, Antigone*

Money roots out all evil. *Leo Rosten*

One must now apologize for any success in business as if it were a violation of the moral law so that today it is worse to prosper than to be a criminal. *Isocrates*

Riches are gotten with pain, kept with care, and lost with grief.

The only thing I like about rich people is their money. *Nancy Astor*

The rich may never get into heaven, but the pauper is already serving his term in hell. *Alexander Chase, Perspectives*

The virtue of some of the rich is that they teach us to despise wealth. *Kahlil Gibran*

To have money is a fear, not to have it a grief. *1640, Herbert*

To what cannot you compel the hearts of men, O cursed lust for gold! *Virgil, Aeneid*

We may see the small value God has for riches by the people he gives them to. *Alexander Pope, Thoughts on Various Subjects*

Wealth by which some people think to get a reputation, does but expose the more their weakness and follies. *Early 18th century*

*"For the love of money is the root of all evil," goes the actual New Testament quotation (1 Timothy 6:10). It can be argued that by these words, *greed*, not money per se, is assailed. Practical experience, however, supports the belief that money *itself* leads to evils of various kinds. It is a testimony to folk wisdom, therefore, that this biblical quotation has been altered, to assert that money itself is the root of all evil.

MONEY isn't everything. *1927, O-153*

. . . You mean Confederate money?

. . . but it's a sure cure for poverty.

. . . but it's a long way ahead of whatever comes next. *Edmund Stockdale*

. . . but it's a great consolation until you have everything.

. . . but it's handy when you've mislaid your credit card.

. . . aside from its purchasing power, it's completely useless as far as I'm concerned. *Alfred Hitchcock*

. . . In fact, the way things are going, it soon won't be anything. *Changing Times*

. . . but it keeps you in touch with the kids.

A fancy cage does not make a bird sing. *Old postcard*

A man's wealth is his enemy. *Howell, 1659*

After a certain point money is meaningless. It's the game that counts. *Aristotle Onassis*

Confidentially, I wish I had a dollar for every time I've said, "Money isn't everything."

God shows his contempt for wealth by the kind of person he selects to receive it. *Austin O'Malley*

He is rich who owes nothing.
He is poor who has nothing but money.

I don't like money actually, but it quiets my nerves. *Joe Louis*

I would rather be a beggar and spend my money like a king, than be a king and spend money like a beggar. *Robert G. Ingersoll*

If you make money your god, it will plague you like the devil. *Henry Fielding*

I'm not the least bit interested in being rich, so long as I can live comfortably and have everything I want.

It is easier to praise poverty than to bear it. *1666, Torriano*

It would be all right for these wise guys to say money isn't everything if people didn't treat you like less than nothing when you haven't any. *Cincinnati Enquirer, ca. 1925*

Material possessions are just excess baggage in the journey of life. *Taxi, TV show*

Money can cure hunger: it cannot cure unhappiness. Food can satisfy the appetite, but not the soul. *G. B. Shaw, The Intelligent Woman's Guide*

Money can't buy friends but it certainly can rent them. *Henny Youngman*

Money doesn't go as far as it used to, but at least it goes faster.

Money is a fringe benefit of success. *Peter's Almanac*

Money is a stupid measure of achievement but unfortunately it is the only universal measure we have. *Charles P. Steinmetz*

Money is not the measure of a man, but it will do quite nicely if you don't have any other yardstick handy. *Charles Merrill Smith*

Money isn't important as long as you have it.

Money, it turned out, was exactly like sex; you thought of nothing else if you didn't have it and thought of other things if you did. *James Baldwin*

Money will buy a bed but not sleep; books but not brains; food but not appetite; finery but not beauty; a house but not a home; medicine but not health; luxuries but not culture; amusements but not happiness; religion but not salvation; a passport to everywhere but heaven.

I am richer than E. H. Harriman. I have all the money I want and he hasn't. *John Muir*

Nothing is everything.

O the misery of wealth! *Horace, Satires*

It is nonsense to say that gold is dirt, as many proverbs do; gold delivers "goodly legs and shoulders of mutton, exhilarating cordials, books, pictures, the opportunities of seeing foreign countries, independence, heart's ease, a man's own time to himself. . . . [Let us not scandalize] the faithful metal that provides them for us." *Charles Lamb, Popular Fallacies*

The chief value of money lies in the fact that one lives in a world in which it is overestimated. *H. L. Mencken*

The man who says, "Money isn't everything," probably is in arrears to his landlady. *Elbert Hubbard*

The man whose only pleasure in life is making money, weighs less on the moral scale than an angleworm. *Josh Billings*

There are doubtless things money won't buy, but one can't think of them at a moment's notice. *Richard Needham*

There are more things in life than money—like credit cards and overdrafts.

There is one advantage of being poor—a doctor will cure you faster. *Kin Hubbard, Abe Martin's Sayings*

There's no money in poetry, but then there's no poetry in money either. *Robert Graves*

We can get mighty rich, but if we haven't got any friends, we will find we are poorer than anybody. *Will Rogers*

The loss of wealth is loss of dirt,
As sages in all times assert;
The happy man's without a shirt.
John Heywood, Be Merry, Friends

Money cannot buy
The fuel of love
But is excellent kindling.
W. H. Auden

Ah, money isn't everything,
　　Say even folks who hoard it
But when I'm broke I feel some cash
　　Might be a good start toward it.
Robert Dennis

MONEY makes and money mars. *Scottish proverb*

Almost everything that is said about money is a little bit true and a little bit false; the subject of money, like the subject of sex, cannot be circumscribed by absolutes. *Sydney J. Harris*

Money can pay the entrance fee to Heaven only by being used for a good cause on Earth. *Old postcard*

Money changes people just as often as it changes hands. *Al Batt*

Money is power, freedom, a cushion, the root of all evil, the sum of all blessings. *Carl Sandburg*

Riches are like muck, which stink in a heap, but spread abroad make the earth fruitful. *1564, OE-541*

Too much money is as demoralizing as too little, and there's no such thing as exactly enough. *Mignon McLaughlin*

Wealth is a blessing to the good, a curse to the wicked. *Chinese proverb*

When money is seen as a solution for every problem, money itself becomes the problem. *Richard Needham*

Gold begets in brethren hate;
Gold in families debate;
Gold does friendship separate;
Gold does civil wars create.
Abraham Cowley, 1656

MONEY makes money. *1572, O-154*

. . . as well as most everything else.

Gold that's put to use more gold begets. *Shakespeare, Venus and Adonis*

Money goes where money is. *Russian proverb*

MONEY makes the man. *Greek proverb*

. . . an eccentric; if without it he would be called a crackpot.

. . . even if he was a monkey to start with. *D. H. Lawrence, 1920*

A dog with money is addressed "Mr. Dog." *Heard in New York*

Be nice to people until you have made a million—then they'll be nice to you. *Peter's Almanac*

I have been rich and I have been poor. Rich is better. *Attributed to Sophie Tucker and to Joe E. Lewis, who, Keyes notes (K-131), often performed together*

If you have money, men think you are wise, handsome, and able to sing like a bird. *Yiddish saying*

Let the learned say what they can,
'Tis ready money that makes the man.
William Somerville, Ready Money

Make money, and the whole world will conspire to call you a gentleman. *Mark Twain*

Money is like a sixth sense—you can't make use of the other five without it. *W. Somerset Maugham, New York Times, Oct. 18, 1958*

Most rich people are pretty dull. *Marlene Dietrich*

There is a certain Buddhistic calm that comes from having . . . money in the bank. *Tom Robbins*

With money you are a dragon, without it you are a worm. *Chinese proverb*

See also A rich man's JOKE is always funny.

MONEY makes the mare go. 1500, O-154

. . . and woman makes the money go. *Old postcard*

. . . but it's credit that runs the automobile.

Knowledge makes one laugh, but wealth makes one dance. *1651, Herbert*

Long Island represents the American's idea of what God would have done with Nature if he'd had the money. *Peter Fleming, a British writer visiting America in 1929*

Love does much but money does all. *French proverb*

No man but a blockhead ever wrote, except for money. *Samuel Johnson, 1776*

The most popular labor-saving device is still money. *Phyllis George*

MONEY makes the world go 'round.

A feast is made for laughter, and wine maketh merry, but money answereth all things. *Ecclesiastes 10:19*

A heavy purse makes a light heart. *1521, T-560*

A woman's best protection is a little money of her own. *Claire Boothe Luce*

Avarice, the spur of industry. *David Hume, Of Civil Liberty*

Cash is virtue. *Lord Byron*

Donations are desperately needed to support my reckless extravagance. © *Ashleigh Brilliant*

Financial independence is a many-splendored thing. It makes it easy to stick to your codes, your principles, your beliefs, and keeps you from ever having to prostitute yourself. *Marlene Dietrich*

From birth to age eighteen a girl needs good parents, from eighteen to thirty-five she needs good looks, from thirty-five she needs a good personality. From fifty-five on, she needs good cash. *Sophie Tucker*

God loves the poor but He helps the rich. *Yiddish proverb*

Happiness is a good bank account, a good cook, and a good digestion. *Jean-Jacques Rousseau*

I'm so happy to be rich, I'm willing to take all the consequences. *Howard Abrahamson*

I'm tired of Love; I'm still more tired of
    Rhyme;
But Money gives me pleasure all the time. *Hilaire Belloc*

In investing money, the amount of interest you want should depend on whether you want to eat well or sleep well. *J. K. Morley, 1937*

It isn't necessary to be rich and famous to be happy. It's only necessary to be rich. *Alan Alda*

Money cheereth man's heart. *1659, T-468*

Money gives life to the soul, cleanses the filthy, and makes the old man a bridegroom. *Tunisian proverb*

Money is a great comfort. *1616, T-468*

Money is good for bribing yourself through the inconveniences of life. *Gottfried Reinhardt*

Money is much more exciting than anything it buys. *Mignon McLaughlin*

Money is power. Money is security. Money is freedom. It's the difference between living on the slope of a volcano and being safe in the garden of the Hesperides. *G. B. Shaw, The Millionairess*

Money . . . is so much warmth, so much bread. *Ralph Waldo Emerson*

Money is the only substance which can keep a cold world from nicknaming a citizen "Hey, you!" *Wilson Mizner*

Money makes a man laugh. *John Selden*

Money, which represents the prose of life, and which is hardly spoken of in parlors without apology, is, in its effects and laws, as beautiful as roses. *Ralph Waldo Emerson*

Most men seem to have two objects in life: one is to become rich and the other is to become richer. *William C. Hunter*

No woman can be too rich or too thin. *Attributed to the Duchess of Windsor and to Truman Capote*

Nothing but money is sweeter than honey. *Poor Richard's Almanac, 1735*

Some men worship rank, some worship heroes, some worship power, some worship God, and over these ideals they dispute, but they all worship money. *Mark Twain, Notebook*

The most popular labor-saving device today is still a husband with money. *Joey Adams, Cindy and I*

The only reason to have money is to tell any S.O.B. in the world to go to hell. *Humphrey Bogart*

The seven deadly sins . . . are food, clothing, firing, rent, taxes, respectability, and children. Nothing can lift those seven millstones from Man's neck but money; and the spirit cannot soar until the millstones are lifted. *G. B. Shaw, Major Barbara*

The two most beautiful words in the English language are "Check enclosed." *Dorothy Parker*

The value of money is that with it we can tell any man to go to the devil. It is the sixth sense which enables you to enjoy the other five. *W. Somerset Maugham*

There are few sorrows, however poignant, in which a good income is of no avail. *Logan Pearsall Smith*

There are more important things in life than a little money, and one of them is a lot of money.

There are three faithful friends: an old wife, an old dog, and ready money. *Poor Richard's Almanac*

There is no messenger like money. *Arabic proverb*

Those who have some means think that the most important thing in the world is love. The poor know that it is money. *Gerald Brenan, Thoughts in a Dry Season*

Those who think money will do everything may well be suspected of doing everything for money.

Truly wealth is a sweet and pleasant thing. *Aristophanes, Plutus*

Virtue has never been as respectable as money. *Mark Twain*

Wealth . . . means power, it means leisure, it means liberty. *J. R. Lowell, speech at Harvard University, 1886*

When a man says money can do anything, that settles it: he hasn't any. *Ed Howe*

When I think of all the sorrow and the barrenness that has been wrought in my life by want of a few more pounds per annum than I was able to earn, I stand aghast at money's significance. *George Gissing, The Private Papers of Henry Ryecroft*

Young people, nowadays, imagine that money is everything; and when they grow older, they know it. *Oscar Wilde, The Picture of Dorian Gray*

Workers earn it,
Spendthrifts burn it,
Bankers lend it,
Women spend it,
Forgers fake it,
Taxes take it,
Dying leave it,
Heirs receive it,
Thrifty save it,
Misers crave it,
Robbers seize it,
Rich increase it,
Gamblers lose it . . .
I could use it.
Richard Armour

MONEY talks. 1594, T-266

. . . and it is the only conversation worth hearing when times are bad. *Fred Allen*

. . . money prints: money broadcasts: money reigns, and kings and labor leaders alike have to register its decrees, and even, by a staggering paradox, to finance its enterprises and guarantee its profits. Democracy is no longer bought: it is bilked. *G. B. Shaw, The Apple Cart*

. . . and credit goes by sign language.

. . . or does it just snicker?

. . . and in most families it keeps up a running conversation.

. . . and sometimes it gets mistaken for the voice of conscience.

. . . and a lack of it talks even louder.

. . . Even when it whispers, people listen and hear it.

. . . but have you ever noticed how hard of hearing it is when you call it?

Bein' broke is as lonesome as bein' good. *Old postcard*

Every door is barr'd with gold, and opens but to golden keys. *Alfred, Lord Tennyson, 1842*

Fish with a golden hook. *Latin proverb*

Flea has money he buys his own dog. *Jamaican proverb*

Freedom of the press is guaranteed only to those who own one. *A. J. Liebling, quoted by Richard Kluger in The Paper: The Life and Death of the New York Herald Tribune*

Go into the street and give one man a lecture on morality and another a shilling, and see which will respect you most. *Samuel Johnson*

He that has a full purse never wanteth a friend. *Scottish proverb*

I do everything for a reason. Most of the time the reason is money. *Suzy Parker*

If a patient is poor he is committed to a public hospital as a "psychotic." If he can afford a sanatorium, the diagnosis is "neurasthenia." If he is wealthy enough to be in his own home under the constant watch of nurses and physicians, he is simply "an indisposed eccentric." *Pierre Janet*

If money talks, it ain't on speaking terms with me. *Turn-of-the-century song*

If you are rich, you speak the truth; if you are poor, your words are but lies. *Chinese proverb*

Let money talk, so long as it doesn't hog the conversation.

Man prates, but gold speaks. *Italian proverb*

Money can bribe the gods. *Chinese proverb*

Money creates taste. *Jenny Holzer*

Money doesn't talk anymore; it just goes without saying. *Herb Daniels*

Money is better than poverty, if only for financial reasons. *Woody Allen, Without Feathers*

Money is the poor people's credit card. *Marshall McLuhan*

Money still talks; you just have to increase the volume.

Money talks louder when your conscience is asleep. *Henny Youngman*

No man's credit is as good as his money. *Ed Howe*

No matter how much money talks, nobody finds it boring.

Nothing is more sincere than cash in advance. © *Ashleigh Brilliant*

Ready money is a ready medicine. *1580, OE-534*

Rich men have no faults. *1732, Fuller*

Sometimes money talks in a whisper, so low that it can hardly be heard. *Oliver Herford*

The fellow with manners will always have women around, but not quite so many as the fellow with manners and money. *Richard Needham*

The rich man in a strange land is at home; the poor man at home is a stranger. *Arabic proverb*

The world stands on three things: money, money, and money. *Yiddish proverb.* Parody on the Talmudic saying (Aboth 1:18), "The world stands on three things: truth, justice, and peace."

To a shower of gold, most things are penetrable. *Thomas Carlyle, The French Revolution*

Virtue has never been as respectable as money. *Mark Twain*

When money talks it often merely remarks "Good-by." *Saturday Evening Post, 1903*

When money talks it often says, "Not guilty."

When money talks, truth keeps silent. *Russian proverb*

When red-headed people are above a certain social grade their hair is auburn. *Mark Twain*

When you ain't got no money, well you needn't come around. *Clarence S. Brewster, 1898; title and refrain of a popular song*

Where gold speaks every tongue is silent. *1581, T-267*

Without money—without hands. *Ukrainian proverb*

You can still use a dime for a screwdriver.

Put your MONEY where your mouth is. *American proverb*

. . . Lick a postage stamp.

Throw good MONEY after bad. *19th century*

Time is MONEY. *Greek proverb*

. . . and cannot be counterfeited.

. . . and money buys time.

. . . Better to steal money—that can be replaced. *L. L. Levinson*

. . . but you're never sure of your balance.

. . . and very good money too to those who reckon interest by it. *Charles Dickens, 1839*

. . . Many people take this saying in its literal sense and undertake to pay their debts with it. *Josh Billings*

. . . and overtime is big money.

Great moments in science: Einstein discovers that time is actually money. *Gary Larson, cartoon caption*

Pity the man who is always punctual—how much time he wastes waiting for others.

Since thou are not sure of a minute, throw not away an hour. *Poor Richard's Almanac*

Time is money, says the vulgarest saw known to any age or people. Turn it around, and you get a precious truth—money is time. *George Gissing, 1903*

It would be more realistic to turn the proverb around and say that "money is time"—that the best thing money can do for you is to buy the time to demonstrate your love with your presence, your interest, your concern, and your pleasure. *Sydney J. Harris, Clearing the Ground*

You pays your MONEY, and you takes your choice.[*]

In investing money the amount of interest you want should depend on whether you want to eat well or sleep well. *J. K. Morley, 1937*

*According to Oxford (O-175), the saying originated in an 1846 *Punch* cartoon by John Leech, in which a child asks, "Which is the Prime Minister?" She is answered, "Which ever you please, my little dear. You pays your money, and you takes your choice."

MONKEY see, monkey do. *

Faith, I ran when I saw others run. *Shakespeare, Henry IV 2.4.333*

People travel for the same reason as they collect works of art: because the best people do it. *Aldous Huxley*

Of all excuses this is most forbid:
"I did the thing because the others did."
Arthur Guiterman

*The catchphrase of this children's game of the 1920s did not get into print until 1934 (WM-418).

See also MAN is a social animal; THEY say.

The MORE the merrier. *1380, WM-419*

. . . The fewer, the bigger a portion for everyone.

One God, no more, but friends good store. *1615, OE-476*

The MORE you have, the more you want. *Latin proverb*

. . . and the more you want, the less you have.

He that loveth silver shall not be satisfied with silver, nor he that loveth abundance, with increase. *Ecclesiastes 5:10*

Much would have more; but often meets with less. *Fuller, 1732*

Riches enlarge rather than satisfy appetites. *Fuller, 1732*

The more you eat, the more you want. *Cracker Jacks slogan*

Youth is not enough. And love is not enough. And success is not enough. And, if we could achieve it, enough would not be enough. *Mignon McLaughlin*

See also ENOUGH is enough; You're never SATISFIED.

All that I am or hope to be I owe to my angel MOTHER.* *Abraham Lincoln*

A kiss from my mother made me a painter. *Benjamin West*

All that I am . . . I owe.

God could not be everywhere, therefore he made mothers. *Hebrew proverb*

Mother is the name for God in the lips and hearts of little children. *William Makepeace Thackeray, Vanity Fair*

*According to Burton Stevenson (B-1627), Lincoln was referring not to his biological mother, Nancy Hanks Lincoln, who died when he was nine years old, but to his stepmother, Sara Bush Lincoln, a widow whom Thomas Lincoln married the year after his first wife's death.

Like MOTHER, like daughter. *16th century*

As is the mother, so is her daughter. *Ezekiel 16:44*

Like hen, like chicken. *1632, T-308*

Varicose veins are the result of an improper selection of grandparents. *William Osler*

MOTHER knows best. *Title of a story by Edna Ferber, 1927*

College magazine humor:
Freshman's motto—Mother knows best.
Sophomore's motto—Death before dishonor.
Junior's motto—Nothing ventured, nothing gained.
Senior's motto—Boys will be boys.

I never knew
My Mother's words
Which I thought dull, didactical,
Would prove in time,
As decades sped,
So right, so sound, so practical!
Lois Muehl

A MOUNTAIN in labor and it brings forth a mouse.[*]

[*]Mountains will be in labor, and the birth will be an absurd little mouse. *Horace (65–8 B.C.) Ars Poetica*

Don't make a MOUNTAIN out of a molehill. *1560, T-467*

A bureaucrat is someone who cuts red tape lengthwise. *Scot Morris*

A small sore wants not a great plaster. *1567, T-618*

Make not a mickle of a little. *1641, Fergusson*

One way to get high blood pressure is to go mountain climbing over molehills. *Earl Wilson*

Take care of the molehill and let the mountains take care of themselves. *Laurence Peter,*

characterizing the willing cog in the bureaucratic machine. The author's 1969 Peter Principle focused attention on ineptitude at the top: "In a hierarchy, every employee tends to rise to the level of his incompetence."

Ulcers are things you get from making mountains out of molehills.

The MOUSE that has but one hole is quickly taken. *186 B.C., B-1632*

See Don't put all your EGGS in one basket.

If a man builds a better MOUSETRAP, the world will beat a path to his door.[*] *Ralph Waldo Emerson*

. . . with cruelty-to-animal complaints, patent-infringement suits, work stoppages, union problems, collusive bidding, discount discrimination, customer complaints and taxes.

Build a better door and keep the mice out.

Build a better mousetrap and the government will build a better mousetrap tax. *Peter's Almanac*

Build a better mousetrap and the world will yawn. *Ken Nakuta, promoter of fads, 1989*

Mr. Emerson must have been smoking something funny when he wrote these words. It is not true now, and it wasn't true then. He must not have known the story of Eli Whitney's cotton gin. The market was . . . ripe for it. . . . The only beaten path the world made was to produce over 300 infringement replicants within a year. Court battles ensued over and over. Whitney said he never received more than he spent in production, legal fees, and traveling to court [for an invention that revolutionized the textile industry and boosted the American economy]. It was a good thing Emerson was a philosopher, not an inventor. *Thomas E. Mosely, Jr., Marketing Your Invention*

One way the world is sure to beat a path to your front door is if you fail to pay your bills. *Henny Youngman*

Today, if you build a better mousetrap, the government comes along with a better mouse. *Ronald Reagan, 1975*

If you build a better mousetrap
and put it in your house,
Before long, Mother Nature's
Going to build a better mouse.

He built a better mousetrap,
And then sent out the word.
His visitors came flocking
As soon as they had heard.
A multitude made journeys
To take them to his doors:
Three copyright attorneys,
Eleven realtors;
Five firms of tax accountants,
Twelve processors of cheese,
Eight labor union experts,
And forty charities.
With all their coming, going,
He's busy day and night.
It's all by way of showing
That Emerson was right.
Jeanne Hopkins

*One of the sayings most often attributed to Emerson appears nowhere in his published writings! In her book *Borrowings*, Sarah Yule quotes the remark from an Emerson speech she said she heard some years before.

A closed MOUTH catches no flies. *1599, T-481*

A closed mouth gathers no foot. *Bob Cooke*

A silent fool is a wise fool. *Heard in Ontario*

A whale is harpooned only when it spouts. *Henry Hillman, on why he avoids interviews, Fortune, May 1982*

One minute of keeping your mouth shut is worth an hour's explanation.

Some folks speak from experience; others, from experience, don't speak. *Heard in Wisconsin*

The voice of experience keeps its mouth shut. *Al Bernstein*

When you get into deep water, keep your mouth shut. *Heard in Mississippi*

See also SILENCE is golden.

MURDER will out.* *ca. 1325, O-157*

Foul deeds will rise,
Though all the earth o'erwhelm them, to men's eyes.
Shakespeare, Hamlet 1.2.257

*Stems from the superstition, says Donald Bond, that a victim's body will bleed afresh in the presence of the murderer.

MUSIC hath its charms to soothe a savage breast.*

. . . That's why I keep a piccolo tucked inside my vest.

After silence, that which comes nearest to expressing the inexpressible is music. *Aldous Huxley, Music at Night and Other Essays*

Bach almost persuades me to become a Christian. *Roger Fry*

If music be the food of love, play on. *Shakespeare, Twelfth Night 1.1.1*

Music begins where words leave off.

Music: The only cheap and unpunished rapture upon earth.

Music washes away from the soul the dust of every-day life. *Berthold Auerbach*

Musicians are magicians. *1616, T-486*

Poetry heals the wounds inflicted by reason. *Novalis, Detached Thoughts*

Wagner's music is better than it sounds. *Mark Twain*

Without music, life would be a mistake. *Friedrich Nietzsche*

We are all but fellow travelers
   Along life's weary way:
If any man can play the pipes,
   In God's name let him play!
John Bennett

* . . . To soften rocks, or bend a knotted oak. *William Congreve, The Mourning Bride, 1697.* Sometimes rendered as "Music hath its charms to soothe a savage beast."

For want of a NAIL the shoe was lost, for want of a shoe the horse was lost, for want of a horse the rider was lost. *1390, O-241*

A good NAME is better than riches.[*]

... but I have also been told that ten dollars ... will go farther toward building a church ... than all the piety of Moses. *Josh Billings*

[*]A good name is rather to be chosen than great riches. *Proverbs 22:1*

Ain't NATURE wonderful!

Dung is not holy, but wherever it falls it works a miracle. *Spanish proverb*

Nature [is] that lovely lady to whom we owe polio, leprosy, smallpox, syphilis, tuberculosis, [and] cancer. *Stanley N. Cohen*

Rejecting the proposition that life on earth is merely "a vale of tears," and but the anteroom to an eternity of heavenly bliss, Corliss Lamont expresses the Humanist view that people "rejoice profoundly in the inexhaustible beauties of their earth and universe" (*Humanism as a Philosophy*).

Though Nature slay us, yet is it ever most marvelous and beautiful! *Corliss Lamont, Humanism as a Philosophy*

We glibly talk
　　of nature's laws
but do things have
　　a natural cause?

Black earth turned into
　　yellow crocus
is undiluted
　　hocus-pocus.
Piet Hein

Let NATURE take its course.

Let us permit nature to have her way; she understands her business better than we do. *Michel de Montaigne*

Our patience will achieve more than our force. *Edmund Burke, Reflections on the Revolution in France*

Patience and the passage of time do more than strength and fury. *Jean de La Fontaine, Fables*

The great secret of doctors, known only to their wives, but still hidden from the public, is that most things get better by themselves; most things, in fact, are better in the morning. *Lewis Thomas, New York Times, July 4, 1976*

Who is there that can make muddy water clear? But if permitted to remain still, it will gradually become clear of itself. *Lao-tzu*

See also PATIENCE is a virtue.

NATURE abhors a vacuum. *Latin proverb*

. . . and fills empty heads with nonsense.

Any horizontal surface is soon piled up.

If you don't run your own life, somebody else will. *John Atkinson*

Men who do not make advances to women are apt to become victims to women who make advances to them. *Walter Bagehot*

Things accumulate to fill space; there's no such thing as an empty closet, garage, shelf, or drawer.

Traffic expands to fill expressways.

When you have a bottle of champagne, along comes something to celebrate.

Work expands so as to fill the time available for its completion. *C. Northcote Parkinson*

You can't change human NATURE.

. . . I'm sure that is what one cannibal said to the other cannibal, when some daring soul proposed that they stop eating people. *Sydney J. Harris*

You can't fool Mother NATURE.

Nature, to be commanded, must be obeyed. *Francis Bacon*

Though you drive Nature out with a pitchfork, she will still find her way back. *Horace, Epistles*

See also PAINT and powder, powder and paint . . .

NECESSITY is the mother of invention. Plato, The Republic, 4th century B.C.

. . . and brains is the father.

. . . and "Patent Right" is the father. *Josh Billings*

A guilty conscience is the mother of invention. *Carolyn Wells*

Boredom is often the mother of invention.

Contentment is the smother of invention. *Ambrose Bierce*

Getting caught is the mother of invention. *Robert Byrne*

I just invent, then wait until man comes around to needing what I've invented. *R. Buckminster Fuller, Time, July 10, 1964*

Ignorance is the mother of admiration. *George Chapman*

Invention breeds invention. *Ralph Waldo Emerson, Society and Solitude*

Invention is the mother of necessity. *Thorstein Veblen*

Name the greatest of all the inventors. Accident. *Mark Twain, Notebook*

Necessity is the mother of strange bedfellows.

Necessity is the mother of taking chances. *Mark Twain*

Necessity sharpens the mind. *Yiddish proverb*

Progress is the mother of problems. *G. K. Chesterton*

Said Father, as he tried to think up a new excuse for being out late, "Mother is the necessity for invention." *Life, ca. 1925*

There ain't no logic so powerful as necessity. *Josh Billings*

NECESSITY knows no law. *Publilius Syrus* (*1st century B.C.*)

A hungry stomach has no ears. *Jean de La Fontaine, Fables*

An incompetent attorney was called Necessity because he knew no law.

The absence of alternatives clears the mind marvelously. *Henry Kissinger*

Necessity makes an honest man a knave.

There ain't no logic as powerful as necessity. *Josh Billings*

When one must, one can. *Yiddish proverb*

Don't stick your NECK out. 1963, WM-425

Never pontificate about the weather; you may be all wet. *Leo Rosten*

See also Don't make WAVES; Don't go out on a LIMB.

NEEDLES and pins, needles and pins, When a man's married his trouble begins. 19th-century English nursery rhyme

See A young man MARRIED is a man that's marred.

If you gently touch a NETTLE it'll sting you for your pains; Grasp it like a lad of mettle, and it soft as silk remains. *Aaron Hill (1685–1750)*

See The best DEFENSE is a good offense.

Never say NEVER. 1837, WM-428

Never is a long day. *14th century*

Never say Never, never say Always, and never say Forever. *Ann Landers*

Never say never, for if you live long enough, chances are you will not be able to abide by its restrictions. . . . In 1921 I told myself . . . I would never marry again. I have had four husbands since then. . . . Never is a long, undependable time, and life is too full of rich possibilities to have restrictions placed upon it. *Gloria Swanson*

There is nothing NEW under the sun.[*]

. . . but a joke is brand-new if you've never heard it before.

. . . but a lot more of it is showing at the beach.

Every man is a borrower and a mimic, life is theatrical and literature a quotation. *Ralph Waldo Emerson, Society and Solitude*

Nobody can be so amusingly arrogant as a young man who has just discovered an old idea and thinks it is his own. *Sydney J. Harris*

Originality is nothing but judicious imitation. *Voltaire*

Originality is the fine art of remembering what you hear but forgetting where you heard it. *Laurence Peter*

There is nothing so absurd or ridiculous that has not at some time been said by some philosopher. *Oliver Goldsmith*

What a good thing Adam had—when he said a good thing he knew nobody had said it before. *Mark Twain*

What is new is not true, and what is true is not new. *1772, OE-450*

What is originality? Undetected plagiarism. *W. R. Inge*

*The thing that hath been, it is that which shall be; and that which is done, is that which shall be done; and there is no new thing under the sun. *Ecclesiastes 1:9*

See also The more things CHANGE, the more they stay the same.

Bad NEWS travels fast. *Plutarch, ca. A.D. 100*

. . . and good news travels even faster.

See also No NEWS is good news.

No NEWS is good news. *1616, O-163*

"No noose is good news," says the pardoned murderer. *Annapolis Log, ca. 1925*

No nukes is good nukes. *Campus graffiti*

The real news is bad news. *Marshall McLuhan*

When young, we are disconsolate if nothing good is happening to us . . . in later age, we feel pleased merely if nothing bad is happening. . . . "No news is good news" is a maxim that must have been devised by an older person. *Sydney J. Harris*

"You're sending your mother an empty envelope?" "To cheer her up. You know, No news is good news." *The Burns and Allen Show*

They say no news is good news but
   If one's the type to fret,
The lack of news of any kind
   Makes one more nervous yet.
Robert Dennis

Be NICE to people on your way up because you'll meet them on your way down. *Wilson Mizner (1876–1933)*

. . . Treat your friend as one who may some day be your enemy, and your enemy as one who may some day be your friend. *G. B. Shaw; also identified as an Italian proverb*

If you can't say something NICE about a person, don't say anything.

If you can't say something good about someone, sit right here by me. *Alice Roosevelt Longworth, allegedly embroidered on a cushion in her living room*

If you can't say something nice about a person, say something nasty. *Howard Kandel*

Just say NO. *Nancy Reagan's one-liner contribution to America's war on drugs*

Refrain from drink, which is the source of all evil. *George Washington*

Just Say Mo'. *Title of a 1992 movie*

Never take NO for an answer. *Title of a popular song, ca. 1886*

See If at first you don't SUCCEED, try again.

NOBLESSE oblige.[*] *Duc de Lévis, Maxims, 1808*

A rich man . . . would be a double knave to cheat mankind when he had no need of it. *Daniel Defoe, Serious Reflections*

Falsehood is worse in kings than beggars. *Shakespeare, Cymbeline 3.6.13*

Gentility is what is left over from rich ancestors after the money is gone. *John Ciardi*

[*] Ralph Waldo Emerson's translation of this two-word epigram: "Superior advantages bind you to a larger generosity" (*Progress of Culture*, 1875). The Morrises (MD-403) cast a jaundiced eye at "the generosity of the rich to charity. . . . It's tax deductible."

NOBODY is all wrong.

When you tell a plain woman she is attractive, the glow on her face makes her so. Thus, what began as a lie ends as the truth. *Richard Needham*

NOBODY is perfect. *1805, WM-431*

. . . but me. *Contemporary postcard*

. . . and pretending to be . . . can be exhausting. *Nancy Drew*

A man who does not lose his reason over certain things has none to lose. *G. E. Lessing, Emilia Galotti*

Admit your errors before someone else exaggerates them. *Andrew V. Mason*

Almost all our faults are more pardonable than the methods we resort to to hide them. *François de la Rochefoucauld*

Being right half the time beats being half-right all the time. *Malcolm Forbes*

Christ died for our sins. Dare we make his martyrdom meaningless by not committing them? *Jules Feiffer*

Don't be afraid to say, "I don't know."
Don't be afraid to say, "I made a mistake."
Don't be afraid to say, "I need help."
Don't be afraid to say, "I'm sorry."
H. Jackson Brown, Jr., Life's Little Instruction Book

Even Napoleon had his Watergate. *Yogi Berra*

Even the best writer has to erase. *Spanish proverb*

Every man has his fault. *Shakespeare, Timon of Athens 3.1.29*

Every man is a damn fool for at least five minutes every day; wisdom consists in not exceeding the limit. *Elbert Hubbard*

Everybody's got a little bit of Watergate in him. *Billy Graham*

Everyone has his own devil, and some have two. *Swedish proverb*

Growing up means never having to say you're perfect. *Peter Gzowski*

He is lifeless that is faultless. *1546, Heywood*

He that is without sin among you, let him cast a stone at her. *John 8:7*

He who makes no mistakes, makes nothing. *1911, OE-400*

How much sin can I get away with and still go to heaven? *Bumper sticker by Heather Clary McAdams*

How to reduce mistakes at work: arrive late and leave early.

I have known people who had so little character that they didn't even have any failings. *Josh Billings*

I love my failings. It is these that make me feel that I have that touch of nature in me that makes me brother to every man living. *Josh Billings*

I never entertain wicked thoughts, but they sometimes entertain me. *Laurence Peter*

I'd rather have a comfortable vice than a virtue that bores. *Heard in Kentucky and Tennessee*

If God did not forgive, Paradise would be empty. *Arabic proverb*

If you are willing to admit when you are wrong, you are right.

It has been my experience that folks who have no vices have very few virtues. *Abraham Lincoln*

It is well that there is no one without a fault, for he would not have a friend in the world: he would seem to belong to a different species. *William Hazlitt, Characteristics*

It's easy to criticize the incompetent; to criticize the competent is more difficult.

Maturity is coming to terms with that other part of yourself. *Ruth Tiffany Barnhouse*

No man of honor ever quite lives up to his code, any more than a moral man manages to avoid sin. *H. L. Mencken, Minority Report: Notebooks, 1956*

Nobody is a fool always; everybody, sometimes.

Perfection falls not to the share of mortals. *George Washington*

Pretending to be perfect when you know you're not, can be exhausting. *Nancy Drew*

Show me a man who makes no mistakes and I will show you a man who doesn't do things. *Theodore Roosevelt*

Success doesn't consist of never making blunders, but in never making the same one the second time.

The bearded lady at the circus said, "Everybody's got something wrong with them. With me, you can tell what it is." *Richard Needham*

The first essential of a typist is a good eraser. *Heard in Florida*

There's one way to find out if a man is honest—ask him. If he says "Yes," you know he is crooked. *Groucho Marx, as quoted in news summaries, July 28, 1954*

There's a little bit of the whore in all of us. *Kerry Packer*

When I make a mistake, it's a beaut. *Fiorello La Guardia*

When you make a mistake, admit it. If you don't, you only make matters worse. *Ward Cleaver*

You're everything I want, and in addition, you're several things I don't want at all. © *Ashleigh Brilliant*

He without benefit of scruples
His fun and money soon quadruples.
Ogden Nash

NOBODY knows everything.

. . . and I'm no exception.

Everybody is ignorant, only on different subjects. *Will Rogers*

If you go to someone for advice, never accept a parable as an answer. Make him admit that he doesn't know. *Donald G. Smith*

If you think you know all the answers, you probably don't understand the questions.

It wasn't until late in life that I discovered how easy it is to say, "I don't know." *W. Somerset Maugham*

Ole man Know-All died las' year. *Joel Chandler Harris, Uncle Remus*

One of the functions of intelligence is to take account of the dangers that come from trusting solely to the intelligence. *Lewis Mumford*

To be conscious that you are ignorant is a great step to knowledge. *Benjamin Disraeli*

Empty vessels make the most NOISE. 1430, O-64

It is with narrow-souled people as with narrow-necked bottles—the less they have in them, the more noise they make in pouring it out. *Old Farmer's Almanac, 1803*

Poverty often deprives a Man of all Spirit and Virtue; 'Tis hard for an empty Bag to stand upright. *Benjamin Franklin, 1758*

The bell rings because it's empty. *Yiddish proverb*

The worst wheel of the cart makes most noise. *1581, T-719*

A little NONSENSE now and then is relished by the best of men. *Old nursery rhyme*

Anybody who behaved normally all of the time would not be completely normal. © *Ashleigh Brilliant*

Comedy is medicine. *Trevor Griffiths*

Don't tell me of a man's being able to talk sense; every one can talk sense. Can he talk nonsense? *William Pitt*

Fun is a safety-valve that lets the steam-pressure off from the boiler, and keeps things from busting. *Josh Billings*

He is not a wise man who cannot play the fool on occasion. *16th century*

He who laughs, lasts.

I have often daydreamed about all manner of fantastic things for hours on end, at times when people thought I was very busy. . . . Without this fantasy-cure, which I usually took at the time of day when people take the spring-waters, I would not have reached my present age, 53 years and 1½ months. *Georg Lichtenberg*

I'd rather have a fool to make me merry than experience to make me sad. *Shakespeare, As You Like It 4.1.28*

If any cleric or monk speaks jocular words, such as provoke laughter, let him be anathema. *Ordinance, Second Council of Constance, 1498*

If you are too busy to laugh, you are too busy. *Peter's Almanac*

It is meat and drink to me to see a clown. *Shakespeare, As You Like It 5.1.11*

It's OK to be a little foolish. It makes you feel home on earth. *Sam Levenson*

Laugh and grow fat. *1596, OE-352*

Laughter is a tranquilizer with no side effects. *Arnold Glasow*

Life without jokes is like a road without inns. *Henri Pourrat*

No one is exempt from talking nonsense; the mistake is to do it solemnly. *Michel de Montaigne*

Pleasure in moderation relaxes and tempers the spirit. *Seneca, De Ira*

The finest amusements are the most pointless ones. *Jacques Chardonne, Propos comme Ça*

The gift of fantasy has meant more to me than my talent for absorbing positive knowledge. *Albert Einstein*

The man who can be nothing but serious, or nothing but merry, is but half a man. *Leigh Hunt*

There are three things which are real: God, human folly, and laughter. The first two are beyond our comprehension. So we must do what we can with the third. *John F. Kennedy*

There is a foolish corner in the brain of the wisest men. *Aristotle*

There must be a spice of mischief and wilfulness thrown into the cup of our existence to give it its sharp taste and sparkling colour. *William Hazlitt, On Depth and Superficiality*

Vice goes a long way toward making life bearable. A little vice now and then is relished by the best of men. *Finley Peter Dunne*

What's the use of growing up if you can't act childish sometimes? *Dr. Who, TV show*

When Moses came down from the mountain with the clay tablets, he said, "Folks, I was able to talk Him down to ten. Unfortunately, we had to leave Adultery in there, but you will notice that Solemnity was taken out."

Who lives without folly is not so wise as he thinks. *François de la Rochefoucauld*

You must do a crazy thing once in a while to keep from going nuts. *Harry Hirschfield*

Mingle occasional pleasures with your care
That you with courage any task may bear. *Cato, Disticha*

See also LAUGHTER is the best medicine; MEN are but children of a larger growth.

Don't cut off your NOSE to spite your face.* *ca. 1560, O-47*

*Writes Flexner (F-43): "Vengeful rage has led to many pointless and foolish acts . . . but none are so stupid as those in which we try to get back at someone else by punishing ourselves."

Keep your NOSE out of other people's business. *1841, WM-432*

See Mind your own BUSINESS.

Keep your NOSE to the grindstone. *1550, Erasmus*

. . . and your shoulder to the wheel.

See also Hard WORK never killed anybody; If you've got time to kill, WORK it to death; No GAINS without pains; No SWEET without sweat.

Blessed is he who expects NOTHING, for he shall never be disappointed. *Alexander Pope, offered as "a ninth beatitude" in a 1727 letter to John Gay*

Blessed are they that expect the worst, for they shall get it!

NOTHING comes from nothing. *Latin proverb*

There are no accidents in my philosophy. Every effect must have its cause. The past is the cause of the present, and the present will be the cause of the future. All these are links in the endless chain stretching from the Infinite to the finite. *Abraham Lincoln, 1848*

In nature there are neither rewards nor punishments—there are consequences. *Robert G. Ingersoll*

NOTHING for nothing. *1704, O-164*

. . . except conversation.

. . . and not much for six-pence.

Before you take Easy Street, make sure it's not a blind alley.

Few wishes come true by themselves. *June Smith*

God gives nothing for nothing. *Yiddish proverb*

If you don't get what you want, it is a sign either that you did not seriously want it, or that you tried to bargain over the price. *Rudyard Kipling*

Sermonettes are fine for Christianettes.

Life is something like this trumpet. If you don't put anything in it you don't get anything out. And that's the truth. *W. C. Handy,* as quoted in *New York Herald Tribune, Feb. 15, 1954*

"Take what you want," says God; "but pay for it." *Ralph Waldo Emerson, Compensation*

Taxes are what we pay for a civilized society. *Oliver Wendell Holmes*

There are no shortcuts to any place worth going. *Beverly Sills*

To receive a favor is to sell one's liberty. *Japanese proverb*

What is bought is cheaper than a gift. *1813, Ray*

When people expect to get "something for nothing" they are sure to be cheated. *P. T. Barnum, Struggles and Triumphs*

Men buy success by giving up a host
Of things they want for what they want the
    most.
Arthur Guiterman

NOTHING great was ever achieved without enthusiasm. *Ralph Waldo Emerson (1803–82), Essays (Circles)*

Halfway through exciting work is halfway to heaven. *Mignon McLaughlin*

NOTHING is all wrong.

. . . Even a broken clock is right twice a day.

A well-told lie contains a germ of truth. *Dizzy Gillespie*

There is some soul of goodness in things evil,
Would men observingly distil it out.
Shakespeare, Henry V 4.1.4

NOTHING is as easy as it looks.

A good teacher is a master of simplification and an enemy of simplism. *Louis A. Berman*

Every solution breeds new problems. *Arthur Bloch*

Everything in the universe goes by indirection. There are no straight lines. *Ralph Waldo Emerson, Society and Solitude*

Everything takes longer than you think.

If anything can go wrong, it will, and at the worst possible moment.

My suspicion is that the universe is not only queerer than we suppose, but queerer than we can suppose. *J. B. S. Haldane, Possible Worlds*

The hardest thing in the world to understand is the income tax. *Albert Einstein*

There is always an easy solution to every human problem—simple, plausible, and wrong. *H. L. Mencken*

There is no job so simple that it cannot be done wrong.

When Lem Moon was acquitted fer the murder of his wife and Judge Pusey asked him if he had anything t' say, he replied: "I never would have shot her if I'd knowed I'd have t' go thru so much red tape." *Kin Hubbard*

NOTHING is perfect.

Dictionaries are like watches, the worst is better than none, and the best cannot be expected to go quite true. *Samuel Johnson*

Miniaturization has gone too far when it makes small appliances too small to repair, too easy to misplace, and too easy to steal.

There are no straight backs, no symmetrical faces, many wry noses, and no even legs. We are a crooked and perverse generation. *William Osler*

. . . There is no clothe so fine but moathes will eate it, no yron so harde but rust will fret it, no wood so sounde but wormes will putrifie it, no metall so course but fire will purifie it, nor no Maide so free but love will bring her into thraldome and bondage. *George Pettie, 1576*

There is one thing wrong with a watch that is waterproof, shockproof, and antimagnetic—you can still lose it. *Peter's Almanac*

Would you have a mule without fault? Then keep none. *Old Farmer's Almanac, 1884*

Whoever thinks a faultless piece to see,
Thinks what ne'er was, nor is, nor e'er shall
    be.
Alexander Pope, An Essay on Criticism

And, after all, what is a lie? 'Tis but
The truth in masquerade; and I defy
Historians, heroes, lawyers, priests, to put
A fact without some leaven of a lie.
Lord Byron, Don Juan

NOTHING is simple.

A little uncertainty is good for everyone. *Henry Kissinger, 1976*

A wheel in the middle of a wheel. *Ezekiel 1:16.* This phrase is one detail of a wildly complicated vision described in Ezekiel, and is the basis for the phrase "there are wheels within wheels," popularly used to describe a complicated phenomenon. Stevenson (B-2483) cites six examples.

All blessings are mixed blessings. *John Updike*

Any philosophy that can be put "in a nutshell" belongs there. *Sydney J. Harris, 1968*

Cause and effect, means and ends, seed and fruit, cannot be severed; for the effect already blooms in the cause, and the end preexists in the means, the fruit in the seed. *Ralph Waldo Emerson, Compensation*

Courage is almost a contradiction in terms. It means a strong desire to live taking the form of readiness to die. *G. K. Chesterton*

Every excess causes a defect; every defect an excess. Every sweet hath its sorrow; every evil its good. . . . For everything you have missed, you have gained something else; and for everything you gain you lose something.

   Everything in Nature contains all the powers of Nature. Everything is made of one hidden stuff. *Ralph Waldo Emerson*

Half our mistakes in life arise from feeling where we ought to think, and thinking where we ought to feel. *John Collins*

I have yet to see any problem, however complicated, which, when looked at in the right way, did not become more complicated. *Poul Anderson*

If by the time we are 60 we haven't learned what a knot of paradox and contradiction life is, and how exquisitely the good and bad are mingled in every action we take . . . we haven't grown old to much purpose. *John Cowper Powys*

In a question period following a lecture, one of the college students in the audience asked, "What is the most important lesson you've learned in life?"

   I had no hesitancy in replying, "How to accept ambiguity and live with it."

. . . The acceptance of ambiguity implies . . . that we know that good and evil are inextricably intermixed in human affairs; that they contain, and sometimes embrace, their opposites; that success may involve failure of a different kind, and failure may be a kind of triumph. *Sydney J. Harris, Clearing the Ground*

One has two duties—to be worried and not to be worried. *E. M. Forster, 1959*

Some people are too mean for heaven and too good for hell. *Heard in North Carolina*

The nature of God is a circle of which the center is everywhere and the circumference is nowhere.

The opposite of a correct statement is a false statement. But the opposite of a profound truth may well be another profound truth. *Niels Bohr*

The pure and simple truth is rarely pure and never simple. *Oscar Wilde*

There is always an easy solution to every human problem—neat, plausible, and wrong. *H. L. Mencken*

There's no limit to how complicated things can get on account of one thing always leading to another. *E. B. White*

Whenever things sound easy, it turns out there's one part you didn't hear. *Donald E. Westlake, Drowned Hopes*

NOTHING lasts forever.

See EVERYTHING has an end.

NOTHING plus nothing is still nothing.

Nothing will come of nothing.

Nothing for nothing and not much for sixpence.

A million times zero is still zero.

You can't make something out of nothing.

NOTHING ventured, nothing gained. *Geoffrey Chaucer, Troilus and Criseyde, ca. 1374*

. . . and even when you pay a lot, you can still end up with nothing.

. . . [but] he that ventures too far loses all. *1534, T-11*

A great deal of talent is lost to the world for the want of a little courage. *Sydney Smith, Elementary Sketches of Moral Philosophy*

Forbear not sowing because of birds. *1581, T-622*

He that never climbed never fell. *1546, T-103*

He that never rode never fell. *1598, T-571*

Nothing vouchered, nothing gained.

She that will not venture her eggs shall never have chickens. *1604, T-183*

You can't be afraid of stepping on toes if you want to go dancing. *Lewis Freedman*

You can't get honey unless you take a chance on getting stung. *Old postcard*

See also Take a CHANCE.

NOTHING works.

If an experiment works, something has gone wrong.

If it's good, they'll stop making it. *Herbert Block*

Inanimate objects are classified scientifically into three major categories—those that don't work, those that break down and those that get lost. *Russell Baker, New York Times, 1968*

Life is a series of rehearsals for the gala performance which is always about to take place, but never does. *Richard Needham*

Love makes fools, marriage cuckolds, and patriotism malevolent imbeciles. *Paul Leautaud, Propos d'un Jour*

See also Things are going to the DOGS.

You can't make something out of NOTHING.

O tempora! O mores![*] *Cicero, In Catilinam, 63 B.C.; M-793*

A fashion ten years before its time is indecent. Ten years after its time it is hideous. After a century it becomes romantic. *James Laver, as quoted in Today's Health*

A supermarket is a place where you can spend an hour trying to find the instant coffee.

Actresses do things onstage today that they used to do offstage to get onstage.

Advertising is the greatest art form of the 20th century. *Marshall McLuhan, 1976*

I never expected to see the day when girls would get sunburned in the places they do now. *Will Rogers*

I wonder what language truck drivers are using, now that everyone is using theirs. *Beryl Pfizer*

If you say a modern celebrity is an adulterer, a pervert and a drug addict, all it means is that you've read his autobiography. *P. J. O'Rourke, Give War a Chance*

I'm perplexed when people adopt the modish abbreviation "Ms.," which doesn't abbreviate anything except common sense. *Dick Cavett, Eye on Cavett*

In the future everyone will be famous for 15 minutes. *Andy Warhol*

Ours is the age of substitutes: Instead of language we have jargon; instead of principles, slogans; and instead of genuine ideas, bright suggestions. *Eric Bentley, The Dramatic Event: An American Chronicle*

Remember when a juvenile delinquent was a kid with an overdue library book?

Television is the bland leading the bland. *Murray Schumach, The Face on the Cutting Room Floor*

The love that dare not speak its name has become the neurosis that does not know when to shut up. *Time magazine reviewer, on "still another fictional treatment of homosexuality," Apr. 3, 1964*

The philosophers of one age have become the absurdities of the next, and the foolishness of yesterday has become the wisdom of tomorrow. *William Osler*

The thing that impresses me most about America is the way parents obey their children. *Duke of Windsor*

The wisdom of this year is the folly of the next. *African proverb*

There was no respect for youth when I was young, and now that I am old, there is no respect for age. I missed it coming and going. *J. B. Priestly*

This isn't the age of manners, it's the age of kicking people in the crotch. *Ken Russell*

What's vice today may be virtue tomorrow. *Henry Fielding*

This is the age
Of the half-read page . . .
The plane hop
With a brief stop.
The lamp tan
In a short span . . .
And the catnaps
Till the spring snaps

And the fun's done.
Virginia Brasier, in Saturday Evening Post

*"Oh, what times! Oh, what manners!"

Mighty OAKS from little acorns grow. *Laotze (6th century B.C.)* *

. . . but not overnight.

Grain by grain, a loaf of bread; stone by stone, a castle. *Yugoslavian proverb*

Great hoax from little falsehoods grow. *Boston Transcript*

Mighty oafs from little acorns grow. *George Lichty*

Wheat is at first only grass. *Achille Paysant*

Don't worry if your grades are low
And your rewards are few.
Remember that the mighty oak
Was once a nut like you.

*The tree that needs two arms to span its girth began from the tiniest shoot. *The Way of Virtue*

Sow your wild OATS. 1600, B-1708

. . . and pray for a crop failure.

Advice to young men: If you have got some wild oats . . . get them in early, and sow them deep, so that they will rot in the ground. *Josh Billings*

Don't worry too much about avoiding temptation—as you grow older it starts avoiding you.

I'm reaping my wild oats, no longer sowing. *Gelett Burgess, Lament*

The gardener's rule applies to youth and age: When young "sow wild oats," but when old, grow sage.
H. J. Byron, *An Adage*

See also YOUTH will have its fling.

OIL and water don't mix. 1783, WM-437

. . . Neither do dogs and cats, landlords and tenants, bosses and workers, publishers and authors, teetotalers and drunks, or radicals and Republicans.

Grow OLD gracefully.

Age is an ugly thing, and it goes on getting worse. *Diana Cooper*

In spite of illness, in spite even of the archenemy sorrow, one can remain alive long past the usual date of disintegration if one is unafraid of change, insatiable in intellectual curiosity, interested in big things, and happy in a small way. *Edith Wharton*

Middle age is nature's way of showing a sense of humor.

Nowadays most women grow old gracefully; most men, disgracefully. *Helen Rowland*

Old age comes at a bad time. *San Banducci*

Old age is the most unexpected of all the things that happen to a man. *Leon Trotsky, Diary in Exile*

Old age isn't so bad when you consider the alternative. *Maurice Chevalier*

The closing years of life are like the end of a masquerade party, when the masks are dropped. *Arthur Schopenhauer*

To me, old age is always fifteen years older than I am. *Bernard Baruch*

See also There's no cure for old AGE; We get too soon OLD and too late smart.

Never too OLD to learn.[*] *Latin proverb, O-161*

. . . but many people keep putting it off.

The man who is too old to learn was probably always too old to learn. *Henry S. Haskins*

You're never too old to learn something stupid.

[*]Oxford (O-160) regards "Never too late to learn" as a variant of this proverb.

OLD WAYS are the best.

The dogmas of the quiet past are inadequate to the stormy present. As our case is new, so must we think anew and act anew. We must disenthrall ourselves, and then we shall save our country. *Abraham Lincoln*

The ancients tell us what is best, but we must learn from the moderns what is fittest. *Poor Richard's Almanac, 1738*

What is new cannot be true. *1639, O-161*

There are two kinds of fools: one says, "This is old, therefore it is good"; the other says, "This is new, therefore it is better." *W. R. Inge*

What is new is not true, what is true is not new. *B-1681*

We get too soon OLD and too late smart. *Pennsylvania Dutch proverb*

A child learns to talk in about two years, but it takes about sixty years for him to learn to keep his mouth shut. *Heard in Minnesota*

A man must have grown old and lived long in order to see how short life is. *Arthur Schopenhauer, Paregra und Paralipomena*

About the only good thing you can say about old age is, it's better than being dead. *Stephen Leacock, Reader's Digest, Mar. 1940*

As we grow older we grow both more foolish and wiser at the same time. *François de la Rochefoucauld, Maximes*

At twenty we worry about what others think of us; at forty we don't care about what others think of us; at sixty we discover they haven't been thinking about us at all.

By the time we've made it, we've had it. *Malcolm Forbes, The Capitalist Handbook*

Consider well the proportion of things. It is better to be a young June bug, than an old bird of paradise. *Mark Twain*

Experience is a comb which nature gives to men when they are bald. *Belgian proverb*

Few people know how to be old. *François de la Rochefoucauld*

Find an aim in life before you run out of ammunition. *Arnold Glasow*

God gives nuts to those with no teeth. *Arabic proverb*

Hell is truth seen too late.

I think age is a very high price to pay for maturity. *Tom Stoppard*

I was young and foolish then; now I am old and foolisher. *Mark Twain, in biography by A. B. Paine*

If I'd known how old I was going to be I'd have taken better care of myself. *Adolph Zukor, on approaching his hundredth birthday*

If youth knew; if age could. *Henri Estienne*

In youth we run into difficulties; in old age difficulties run into us. *Josh Billings*

Is it not strange that desire should so many years outlive performance. *Shakespeare, 2 Henry IV 3.4.283*

It's too late to die young. *First sentence in U.S. Public Health Service brochure Healthfacts, for those fifty and over*

Life can only be understood backwards, but it must be lived forewards. *Soren Kierkegaard*

Life is a long lesson in humility. *James M. Barrie*

Life is a maze in which we take the wrong turning before we have learnt to walk. *Cyril Connolly, The Unquiet Grave*

Life is an expressway on which the exits and interchanges are so poorly marked that by the time you see them, it is too late. *Richard Needham*

Life is half spent before we know what it is. *1651, Herbert*

Middle age . . . when a man is at the peak of his yearning power. *Wall Street Journal*

Middle age is nature's way of showing a sense of humor.

Middle age is the time in life when it takes you longer to rest than it does to get tired.

Now that I see what kind of a game life is, I'm not sure I want to play. © *Ashleigh Brilliant*

Old men wish, wise men warn, young men work. *1616, T-438*

The follies which a man regrets most in his life are those which he didn't commit when he had the opportunity. *Helen Rowland*

The gods send nuts to those who have no teeth. *1929, O-95*

The first half of life consists of the capacity to enjoy without the chance; the last half consists of the chance without the capacity. *Mark Twain*

The man who is a pessimist before 48 knows too much; if he is an optimist after it, he knows too little. *Mark Twain, Notebook*

The older I grow, the more I distrust the familiar doctrine that age brings wisdom. *H. L. Mencken*

The spiritual eyesight improves as the physical eyesight declines. *Plato*

The time to begin most things is ten years ago. *Mignon McLaughlin*

The young have aspirations that never come to pass, the old have reminiscences of what never happened. *Saki, Reginald at the Carleton*

Time is a great teacher, but unfortunately it kills all its students. *Hector Berlioz, Almanach des Lettres Français*

What good is money to burn after the fire has gone out?

When you're old enough to know your way around, you are not going anywhere.

Wisdom doesn't necessarily come with age. Sometimes age just shows up all by itself. *Tom Wilson*

You never know what life means till you die. *Robert Browning, The Ring and the Book*

Youth: A boon appreciated in old age only. *Charles Narrey*

Youth is a blunder; Manhood a struggle; Old Age a regret. *Benjamin Disraeli, Coningsby*

Youth is a period of missed opportunities. *Cyril Connolly*

Youth is a wonderful thing. What a crime to waste it on children. *G. B. Shaw (attributed).* Keyes (K-165) says it should probably be credited to Oscar Wilde.

Youth is wasted on the young, and retirement is wasted on the old.

The house that I am living in
Is not the home I planned;
I built it of the little things
That came into my hand;
Of loneliness and memories
You wouldn't understand.

The house that I am living in
A fragile haven seems;
Uncertain its foundations,
Unsure its joists and beams;
I wish I had been strong enough
To build my home of dreams.
Winifred Thorn Bailey

If you knew
what you will know
when your candle
has burnt low,
it would greatly
ease your plight
while your candle
still burns bright.
Piet Hein

See also Grow OLD gracefully; There's no cure for old AGE; There's no FOOL like an old fool.

You cannot put an OLD head on young shoulders. *1591, O-167*

Plastic surgeons, dentists, and wigmakers put young heads on aging shoulders.

Young men may die, but OLD men must. *1534, O-253*

See There's no cure for old AGE.

You can't make an OMELETTE without breaking eggs. *Robespierre, 1790; B-1230*

If your mother had not lost her virginity you would not have been born. *1550, Erasmus*

It's pretty hard to be efficient without being obnoxious. *Kin Hubbard*

Sighed the theatrical director, "You can't make a Hamlet without breaking egos."

The plow is a great disturber of the spring, and yet it is the father of the sickle. *Henry Ward Beecher*

Everybody's entitled to his own OPINION.

. . . just so long as he keeps it to himself. *L. de V. Matthewman*

. . . but no man has a right to be wrong in his facts. *Bernard M. Baruch*

As many opinions as there are men; each a law to himself. *Terence, Phormio*

Comment is free but facts are sacred. *C. P. Snow, Manchester Guardian, May 6, 1926*

Differences in political opinion are as unavoidable as, to a certain point, they may perhaps be necessary. *George Washington*

It is a difference of opinion that makes horse races. *Mark Twain, Pudd'nhead Wilson's Calendar*

The more we disagree, the more chance there is that at least one of us is right. © *Ashleigh Brilliant*

While the right to talk may be the beginning of freedom, the necessity of listening is what makes the right important. *Walter Lippmann*

OPPORTUNITY knocks but once. *1567, O-171*

. . . but don't expect it to break down the door.

. . . but temptation leans on the doorbell.

. . . but temptation can bang on the door for years.

. . . while trouble calls on the telephone.

A wise man will make more opportunity than he finds. *Francis Bacon, Essays*

Importunity knocks at the door more often than op.

Learn to listen. Opportunity sometimes knocks very softly. *H. Jackson Brown, Jr., Life's Little Instruction Book, 1991*

Opporknockety only tunes once. *Campus graffiti*

Opportunity always knocks at the least opportune moment.

Opportunity doesn't knock. *You* knock, opportunity answers.

Opportunity doesn't travel on any schedule — you just have to watch for it.

Opportunity is often a silent caller.

Opportunity seldom knocks for knockers. *Heard in Mississippi and New York*

Opportunity's favorite disguise is trouble. *Frank Tyger*

The secret of success is to always take advantage of your opportunities, and other people's too.

Trouble is only opportunity in work clothes. *Henry J. Kaiser*

When opportunity knocks, some people are in the backyard looking for four-leaf clovers.

When opportunity knocks these days . . . you have to unlock both deadbolts, remove the chain and disconnect the burglar alarm. *Irv Kupcinet*

They do me wrong who say I come no more
    When once I knock and fail to find you in;
For every day I stand outside your door,
    And bid you wake, and rise to fight and win.
Old postcard

If opportunity has shut one door,
Resolve can open thrice a hundred more.
Arthur Guiterman

OPPORTUNITY makes the thief. 1220, O-171

He that shows his purse longs to be rid of it. *1611, T-560*

Lock your door and keep your neighbors honest. *Heard in Wisconsin*

News item: In Los Angeles, transit officials are making it harder for employees to steal fares—they make bus drivers wear uniforms without pockets.

Opportunities are usually disguised as hard work, so most people don't recognize them. *Ann Landers*

Shut your door and you will make your neighbor good. *Portuguese proverb*

The hole invites the thief. *1640, Herbert*

The man who has never been tempted don't know how dishonest he is. *Josh Billings*

The open door tempts a saint. *1659, Howell*

See also CHASTE is she whom no one has asked; There but for the grace of GOD go I.

OPPOSITES attract.

. . . but similarities endure. *Leo Rosten*

. . . because they are not really opposites, but complementaries. *Sydney J. Harris*

It is a mistake for a taciturn, serious-minded woman to marry a jovial man, but not for a serious-minded man to marry a lighthearted woman. *Johann Wolfgang von Goethe*

The exotic is erotic. *Abraham N. Franzblau, in a psychiatric paper on intermarriage*

See also BIRDS of a feather flock together; LIKE seeks like.

It ain't OVER till it's over. *Yogi Berra, 1973* [*]

Nothin' don't happen till it takes place. *Heard in Mississippi*

What's going to happen will happen, and what isn't is liable to happen anyway. *Heard in Illinois*

No race is won or lost
Before the line is crossed.
Arthur Guiterman

[*]Berra insisted he actually said, "It isn't over until it's over" (K-151).

See also CHURCH ain't over till the fat lady sings.

We shall OVERCOME. *Title of a spiritual popularized by the civil rights movement*

Freedom is never voluntarily given up by the oppressor; it must be demanded by the oppressed. *Martin Luther King, Jr., Why We Can't Wait*

Don't OVERDO it.

A fellow who is always declaring he's no fool usually has his suspicions. *Wilson Mizner*

PADDLE your own canoe. *1802, WM-82*

. . . then kindly return my paddle.

Do not unto others what they will not do for themselves.

Let each man pick his own nose.

Let every sack stand upon its own bottom. *1659, Howell*

The American system of rugged individualism. *Herbert Hoover, campaign speech in New York City, Oct. 22, 1928*

If you want to get rich, you son of a bitch,
    I'll tell you what to do:
Never sit down with a tear or a frown,
    And paddle your own canoe.
ca. 1880

*Every man paddle his own canoe. *Frederick Marryat, Settlers in Canada, 1844; M-844.* A favorite expression of Abraham Lincoln, say the Morrises (MD-428).

See also The door to SUCCESS is always marked Push; HELP yourself.

PAINT and powder, powder and paint, makes a woman what she ain't.

A girl who's wearing paint has a better chance than one who ain't. *Heard in Illinois*

I think every old barn could use a little paint. *Tammy Faye Messner, who as the wife of evangelist Jim Bakker displayed an extravagant use of makeup*

What God has forgotten, you can stuff with cotton.

Women who feel naked without their lipstick are well over thirty. *Mignon McLaughlin*

"Will you walk into my PARLOUR?" said the spider to the fly. *Mary Howitt (1799–1888), The Spider and the Fly*

. . . "Well, hardly," said the insect, as he winked the other eye.
"Your parlour has an entrance, but of exits it is shy,
So I'll stay outside in safety and remain a little fly."

Fine words butter no PARSNIPS. *1670, Ray*

. . . [but] a little flattery occasionally means money in the bank or a hesitant beauty's gift of favors. There is success in diplomacy where often there is only failure in brusqueness. *George Jean Nathan*

One man's words are another man's parsnips.

There's more ways to kill a cat than by buttering it with parsnips.

See also All is VANITY; FLATTERY will get you nowhere.

PARTING is such sweet sorrow.* *Shakespeare, Romeo and Juliet 2.2.184, ca. 1594*

Every parting gives a foretaste of death; every coming together again a foretaste of the resurrection. *Arthur Schopenhauer, Studies in Pessimism*

Melancholy is the pleasure of being sad. *Victor Hugo*

Partying is such sweet sorrow. *Jean Kerr*

*Good night, good night! Parting is such sweet sorrow,

That I shall say good night till it be morrow.

I shall PASS through this world but once. Any good therefore that I can do . . . let me do it now. *Étienne de Grellet (1773–1855); also attributed to others*

Don't get up from the feast of life without paying for your share of it. *W. R. Inge*

My country is the world, and my religion is to do good. *Thomas Paine, The Rights of Man*

Service is the rent we pay for room on earth and I'd like to be a good tenant. *Eddie Cantor, Take My Life*

The urge to save humanity is almost always a false front for the urge to rule. *H. L. Mencken*

We make a living by what we get; we make a life by what we give. *Winston Churchill*

This too shall PASS away.

Success isn't permanent, and failure isn't fatal. *Mike Ditka*

See also ALL is FLUX; Nothing lasts FOREVER; LIFE is short.

PATIENCE is a virtue. *1526, T-525*

. . . of the poor. *1656, B-1757*

. . . but sometimes a sign that you just don't know what to do.

. . . but patience provoked can turn into fury.

. . . but you've got to have a lot of patience to acquire it.

Adopt the pace of nature; her secret is patience. *Ralph Waldo Emerson*

Genius is eternal patience. *Michelangelo*

He that can have patience can have what he will. *Poor Richard's Almanac*

How poor are they that have not patience. What wound did ever heal but by degrees. *Shakespeare, Othello 2.3.377*

In any contest between power and patience, bet on patience. *W. B. Prescott*

Lack of pep is often mistaken for patience. *Kin Hubbard*

Patience and the mulberry leaf become a silk robe. *Chinese proverb*

Patience conquers.

Patience is a flower that grows not in every garden. *1616, Draxe*

Patience is not only a virtue—it pays. *B. C. Forbes*

Patience, time, and money accommodate all things. *1640, Herbert*

Pray for patience but don't expect immediate results.

Take your needle, my child, and work your pattern; it will work out a rose by-and-by. Life is like that. One stitch at a time taken patiently, and the pattern will come out all right, like the embroidery. *Oliver Wendell Holmes*

The key to Paradise is patience. *Turkish proverb*

The secret of patience is doing something else in the meanwhile.

The waters wear the stones. *Job 14:19*

True patience consists in bearing what is unbearable. *Japanese proverb*

See also HASTE makes waste; Make HASTE slowly.

PATRIOTISM is the last refuge of a scoundrel. *James Boswell, The Life of Samuel Johnson, 1791*

Ambition is the last refuge of the unimaginative. *Oscar Wilde*

Consistency is the last refuge of the unimaginative. *Oscar Wilde*

Good behavior is the last refuge of mediocrity. *Henry S. Haskins*

Guard against the postures of pretended patriotism. *George Washington, 1796*

In Dr. Johnson's famous dictionary, patriotism is defined as the last resort of a scoundrel. With all due respect to an enlightened but inferior lexicographer, I beg to submit that it is the first. *Ambrose Bierce*

It seems like th' less a statesman amounts to th' more he loves th' flag. *Kin Hubbard*

Nationalism: An infantile disease. It is the measles of mankind. *Albert Einstein*

Patriotism is a pernicious, psychopathic form of idiocy. *G. B. Shaw*

Patriotism is often an arbitrary veneration of real estate above principles. *George Jean Nathan, 1931*

Patriotism is your conviction that your country is superior to all other countries because you were born in it. *G. B. Shaw*

Patriotism is the egg from which wars are hatched. *Guy de Maupassant, 1885*

Patriotism is the virtue of the vicious. *Oscar Wilde*

Patriotism is the willingness to kill and be killed for trivial reasons. *Bertrand Russell*

Talking of patriotism, what humbug it is; it is a word which always commemorates a robbery. There isn't a foot of land in the world which doesn't represent the ousting and re-ousting of a long line of successive owners. *Mark Twain, Notebooks*

The flag makes an excellent blindfold.

Violence is the last refuge of the incompetent. *Isaac Asimov*

See also It is sweet and fitting to DIE for one's country; My COUNTRY right or wrong.

You get what you PAY for.

. . . if you shop around.

. . . but "The Best things in Life Are Free."

I don't believe in restaurants that serve great food cheap. If you want great food and service, you pay for it. *Irving "Swifty" Lazar*

If you think education is expensive, try ignorance. *Derek Bok, 1978*

Never assume that any item or service is better just because it is more expensive. *Donald G. Smith*

Nothing that costs only a dollar is worth having. *Elizabeth Arden, Fortune, 1973*

What costs little, is less esteemed. *1620, OE-111*

You pay peanuts, you get monkeys. *James Goldsmith*

See also The BEST is the cheapest in the long run; NOTHING for nothing.

He who PAYS the piper may call the tune. 17th century

He who has the wheel chooses the direction.

Whose bread I eat, his song I sing. *German proverb*

A PEARL of great price is not had for the asking.*

*The kingdom of heaven is like unto a merchant man, seeking goodly pearls: Who, when he had found one pearl of great price, went and sold all that he had, and bought it. *Matthew 13:45–46*

Cast not PEARLS before swine.*

. . . lest they eat them for tapioca. *L. L. Levinson*

Advice to parents—Cast not your girls before swains. *Cynic, 1905*

Education is the process of casting false pearls before real swine. *Irwin Edman*

Neither give cherries to pigs nor advice to a fool. *Irish proverb*

One day, the acid-tongued writer-wit Dorothy Parker waved comedienne Beatrice Lillie through a hotel entrance with the words "Age before beauty." As she sashayed through the entrance, Bea retorted: "Rather, pearls before swine." *As recalled by Donald J. Quigley, in the New York Times.* Parker biographer John Keats doubts that this oft-recalled encounter ever took place (K-120).

Put not meat into a pisspot. *1539, Taverner*

*. . . Neither cast ye pearls before swine, lest they trample them under their feet. *Matthew 7:6*

The PEN is mightier than the sword. *Latin proverb*

. . . but not unless you push it.

A goose quill is more dangerous than a lion's claw. *English proverb*

A scholar's ink lasts longer than a martyr's blood. *Irish proverb*

If you're using it to write a check, you'd better have enough money in your account.

In only one respect is the pen mightier than the sword: it is easier to commit suicide with. *Sydney J. Harris*

One dagger will do more than a hundred epigrams. *Oscar Wilde*

The pen is mightier than the pencil.

The pen is pointier than the sword. *Donald Elman*

A drop of ink
Can make a million think.
Old postcard

Take care of the PENCE and the pounds will take care of themselves. *Lord Chesterfield, Letters to His Son, 1750*

Economy is a way of spending money without getting any fun out of it. *Old Farmer's Almanac, 1927*

Take care of the minutes and the hours will take care of themselves. *New England proverb*

Take care of the molehill and let the mountains take care of themselves. *Credo of the bureaucrat to whom myopia is a virtue; Laurence Peter, The Peter Principle*

Take care of the pennies and the IRS will take care of the dollars.

Take care of the peonies and the dahlias will take care of themselves. *F. P. Adams*

Take care of the sense and the sounds will take care of themselves. *Lewis Carroll, Alice in Wonderland*

Never ask of money spent
Where the spender thinks it went.
Nobody was ever meant
To remember or invent
What he did with every cent.
Robert Frost, The Hardship of Accounting

A PENNY for your thoughts.

. . . but not a cent more!

If people could read each other's minds, nobody would have any friends. *Welsh proverb*

A PENNY saved is a penny earned.* 1662, Fuller

. . . [but] sometimes a penny well spent is better than a penny ill spared. *1553, T-532*

A penny saved:

. . . gathers no moss. *Henry Youngman*

. . . is a penny.

. . . is a penny out of circulation.

. . . is a penny taxed. *Peter's Almanac*

. . . is a penny to squander. *Ambrose Bierce*

. . . is a pocket burned. *Notre Dame Juggler, ca. 1925*

. . . is ridiculous.

. . . will be eaten by bank fees. *Dilbert (Scott Adams)*

A dollar saved is a penny earned. *L. L. Levinson*

Little and often fills the purse.

No hoarder of pennies ever got rich. To make money, you must risk money. If your aim in life is only to exist, only to have the bare necessities, go ahead and save your pennies. But if you hope to live more like a human being and less like an animal, if you hope to enjoy a few of the happy little luxuries, take a gambling chance now and then. *George Jean Nathan*

Old men are always advising young men to save money. That is bad advice. Don't save every nickel. Invest in yourself. I never saved a dollar until I was 40 years old. *Henry Ford*

Save a little money each month and at the end of the year you'll be surprised at how little you have. *Ernest Haskins*

Saving money is good; making money is better.

To a real con man, a ten-spot swindled is sweeter than a C-note earned.

Who recalls when folks used to git along without somethin' if it cost too much? *Kin Hubbard*

*A favorite sentiment of George Washington, among whose writings are the following:

Keep an account book and enter therein every farthing of your receipts and expenditures.

Nothing should be bought which can be made or done without.

There is no proverb in the whole catalogue of them more true than that a penny saved is a penny got.

In for a PENNY, in for a pound. *1695, O-120*

In for a dime, in for a dollar.

No two PEOPLE are alike.

Even children of the same mother look different. *Korean proverb*

PEOPLE are no damned good. *Popularized by a caption of William Steig, in his cartoon collection The Lonely Ones*

A person is after all only human—sometimes. *Yiddish proverb*

Alienation can be fun. *Graffiti*

All men are frauds. The only difference between them is that some admit it. I myself deny it. *H. L. Mencken*

All men naturally hate one another. They employ lust as far as possible in the service of the public weal. But this is only a pretence and a false image of love; for at the bottom it is only hate. *Blaise Pascal, Pensées*

As a rule men are foolish, ungrateful, jealous, covetous of others' goods, abusing their superiority when they are strong and rascals when they are weak. *Voltaire*

Beasts are gentle toward each other and refrain from tearing their own kind, while men glut themselves with rending one another. *Seneca*

Better is he [who has never been born] than both [the living and the dead] . . . who hath not seen the evil work that is done under the sun. *Ecclesiastes 4:3*

By art and deceit men live half the year and by deceit and art the other half. *1573, Sanford*

Civilisation is the lamb's skin in which barbarism masquerades. *Thomas B. Aldrich, Ponkapog Papers*

Contemporaries: Good people who would like you if you were dead. *Charles Narrey*

Conversation is more often likely to be an attempt at deliberate evasion, deliberate confusion, rather than communication. We are all cheats and liars, really. *James Jones, Writers at Work, 3rd ser.*

Don't overestimate the decency of the human race. *H. L. Mencken*

[Friends are] people who borrow books and set wet glasses on them. *Edwin Arlington Robinson*

He that resolves to deal with none but honest men must leave off dealing. *1732, Fuller*

He who holds hopes for the human condition is a fool. *Albert Camus*

Hell is other people. *Jean-Paul Sartre, No Exit*

History . . . is indeed little more than the register of the crimes, follies, and misfortunes of mankind. *Edward Gibbon*

Humanity is a pigsty where liars, hypocrites and the obscene in spirit congregate. *George Moore*

I am convinced that we have a degree of delight, and that no small one, in the real misfortunes and pains of others. *Edmund Burke, On the Sublime and the Beautiful*

I am free of all prejudices. I hate everybody equally. *W. C. Fields*

I hate mankind, for I think myself one of the best of them, and I know how bad I am. *Samuel Johnson*

I have found little that is good about human beings. In my experience, most of them are trash. *Sigmund Freud (according to Leo Rosten)*

I love mankind, it's people I can't stand. *Charles Schulz, 1963*

If I could get my membership fee back, I'd resign from the human race. *Fred Allen*

If man is only a little lower than the angels, the angels should reform. *Mary Little*

If one looks with a cold eye at the mess man has made of history, it is difficult to avoid the conclusion that he has been afflicted by some built-in mental disorder which drives him towards self-destruction. *Arthur Koestler, 1968*

If we had an earthquake in one of our North American cities, the looters would do more damage than the quake, and the sightseers would cause more trouble than the looters. *Richard Needham*

In the misfortunes of our best friends, we find something that is not unpleasing. *François de la Rochefoucauld, Maximes*

In the whole animal kingdom I recollect no family but man, steadily and systematically employed in the destruction of itself. *Thomas Jefferson, letter to James Madison, 1797*

It is a sin to believe evil of others, but it is seldom a mistake. *H. L. Mencken*

It is a wicked world, and we make part of it. *1732, Fuller*

It's a mistake that there is no bath that will cure people's manners. But drowning would help. *Mark Twain*

Life is a God-damned, stinking, treacherous game and nine hundred and ninety-nine men out of a thousand are bastards. *Theodore Dreiser*

I've always been interested in people, but I've never liked them. *W. Somerset Maugham*

Man, biologically considered, . . . is the most formidable of all the beasts of prey, and, indeed, the only one that preys systematically on its own species. *William James, Memories and Studies*

Man is the missing link between apes and human beings. *Konrad Lorenz*

Man is the only animal that can remain on friendly terms with the victims he intends to eat until he eats them. *Samuel Butler*

Man is the only animal who causes pain to others with no other object than wanting to do so. *Arthur Schopenhauer, Paregra und Paralipomena*

Man was created a little lower than the angels, and has been getting a little lower ever since. *Josh Billings, 1865*

Man's capacity for justice makes democracy possible, and man's capacity for injustice makes democracy necessary. *Reinhold Niebuhr*

Hominis cor ex natura sua malum. ("Man's heart is wicked of its own nature.") *Culman's Sententiae Pueriles, 1540, a book of Latin maxims commonly memorized by Elizabethan schoolboys*

Many people believe that they are attracted by God, or by Nature, when they are only repelled by man. *W. R. Inge, More Lay Thoughts of a Dean*

Men have never been good, they are not good, they never will be good. *Karl Barth, 1954*

Men, my dear, are very queer animals—a mixture of horse-nervousness, ass-stubbornness and camel-malice. *T. H. Huxley, 1895*

More than any other time in history, mankind faces a crossroads. One path leads to despair and utter hopelessness. The other, to total extinction. Let us pray we have the wisdom to choose correctly. *Woody Allen, Side Effects*

Oh! How bitter a thing it is to look into happiness through another man's eyes. *Shakespeare, Coriolanus 5.2.48*

One has to look out for engineers—they begin with sewing machines and end up with the atomic bomb. *Marcel Pagnol, Critique des Critiques*

One man is another man's obstacle. *African proverb*

One man's beard is on fire, and another warms his hands at it. *Kashmiri proverb*

Our great error is that we suppose mankind to be more honest than they are. *Alexander Hamilton*

People are not essentially good, the sun doesn't shine all the time, the deserving are rarely rewarded, and most of the power is in the hands of the wrong people . . . I can't change it and neither can you. *Donald G. Smith*

People are to be taken in very small doses. *Ralph Waldo Emerson*

Real misanthropes are not found in solitude, but in the world; since it is experience of life, and not philosophy, which produces real hatred of mankind. *Giacomo Leopardi, Pensieri*

Science has improved everything except people.

Society is a hospital of incurables. *Ralph Waldo Emerson*

The average dog is a nicer person than the average person. *Andrew Rooney*

The belief in a supernatural source of evil is not necessary; men alone are quite capable of every wickedness. *Joseph Conrad, Under Western Eyes*

The chief obstacle to the progress of the human race is the human race. *Don Marquis*

The danger is not that a particular class is unfit to govern. Every class is unfit to govern. *Lord Acton*

The earth has a skin, and that skin has diseases; one of its diseases is called man. *Friedrich Nietzsche*

The human animal must be just naturally ornery or he would have reformed a long time ago. *Cal Tinney*

The longer we live the more we should be convinced that it is reasonable to love God and despise man. *Jonathan Swift*

The more I see of men the more I like dogs. *Marie de Sévigné*

The nature of men and women—their essential nature—is so vile and despicable that if you were to portray a person as he really is, no one would believe you. *W. Somerset Maugham, Conversations with Willie*

The one thing your friends will never forgive you is your happiness. *Albert Camus*

The only way to amuse some people is to slip and fall on an icy pavement. *Ed Howe*

The world is populated in the main by people who should not exist. *G. B. Shaw*

There is more amity among serpents than among men. *Juvenal*

This is an evil among all things that are done under the sun . . . the heart of the sons of men is full of evil, and madness is in their heart while they live, and after that they go to the dead. *Ecclesiastes 9:3*

There is no escape from the mournful, melancholy fact that the whole race is sinful. *Henry Ward Beecher, 1887*

There's always something about your success that displeases even your best friends. *Mark Twain*

There's nothing level in our cursed natures
But direct villany. *Shakespeare, Timon of Athens 4.3.19*

Though I love my country, I do not love my countrymen. *Lord Byron*

We hate all people, regardless of race, creed, or color. *Graffiti*

We have just enough religion to make us hate, but not enough to make us love one another. *Jonathan Swift, Thoughts on Various Subjects*

We have to distrust each other. It's our only defense against betrayal. *Tennessee Williams*

Why did nature create Man? Was it to show that she is big enough to make mistakes, or was it pure ignorance? *Holbrook Jackson*

With the exception of certain rodents, no
other vertebrate [except *Homo sapiens*] habit-
ually destroys members of his own species.
Anthony Storr, Human Destructiveness

Alas! For the rarity
Of Christian charity
Under the sun!
Thomas Hood, The Bridge of Sighs

Man's a ribald—Man's a rake,
Man is nature's sole mistake!
W. S. Gilbert, Princess Ida

A Christian is a man who feels
    Repentance on a Sunday
For what he did on Saturday
    And is going to do on Monday.
Thomas Russell Ybarra

I wish I loved the Human Race;
I wish I liked its silly face;
I wish I liked the way it walks;
I wish I liked the way it talks;
And when I'm introduced to one
I wish I thought *What Jolly Fun!*
Walter Raleigh, Wishes of an Elderly Man

Take a heavy dose of ego,
    And a good supply of sin.
Self-confidence aplenty.
    Mix some haut and grandeur in.
Some greed and hate and envy,
    Pour in a lot of gall,
Add a tiny bit of patience,
    Almost none of that at all,
A bit of business judgement,
    A drop or two's enough.
Some admiration, self- of course,
    A large amount of bluff.
A pinch of courage, not too much,
    Be as careful as you can,

For when you have it finished,
    You've got Mr. Average Man.
Orrin Alden DeMass, Modern Man

To be honest, as this world goes,
Is to be one man picked out of ten thousand.
Shakespeare, Hamlet 2.2.179

"Etiquette requires us to admire the human
race," wrote Mark Twain (quoted in *More
Maxims of Mark*, 1927). But etiquette aside,
his writings often expressed the idea that
"People are no damned good":

Is the human race a joke? Was it devised and
patched together in a dull time when there
was nothing important to do? *Mark Twain,
North American Review, Mar. 1905*

Man is the only animal that blushes. Or
needs to. *Mark Twain, Pudd'nhead Wilson's
New Calendar*

The first man was a hypocrite and a coward . . . it is the foundation upon which all
civilizations have been built. *Mark Twain,
The Mysterious Stranger*

The human race consists of the damned and
the ought-to-be-damned. *Mark Twain, Notebook*

When I get over on the other side, I shall use
my influence to have the human race
drowned again, and this time drowned good,
no omissions, no Ark. *Mark Twain, in J.
Macy, 1913*

Whenever you find that you are on the side of
the majority, it is time to reform (or pause
and reflect). *Mark Twain, Notebook*

See also GOD defend me from my
friends . . . ; MAN'S inhumanity to man . . .

PEOPLE rise to the level of their own incompetence. *Laurence Peter, The Peter Principle, 1969**

A sign of a celebrity is often that his name is worth more than his services. *Daniel J. Boorstin*

An expert is a man who has stopped thinking. Why should he think? He is an expert. *Frank Lloyd Wright, London Daily Express, 1959*

Bureaucracy is a giant mechanism operated by pygmies. *Honoré de Balzac*

In any group endeavor, the final decision will be made by that person who is the least qualified to make it. *Donald G. Smith, 1984*

It is easier to appear worthy of a position one does not hold, than of the office which one fills. *François de la Rochefoucauld, Maximes*

It isn't the incompetent who destroy an organization. The incompetent never get into a position to destroy it. It is those who have achieved something and want to rest on their achievements who are forever clogging things up. To keep an industry pure, you've got to keep it in perpetual ferment. *Henry Ford*

The art of governing consists in not letting men grow old in their jobs. *Napoleon*

The higher the monkey climbs the more he shows his arse. *16th century*

Time goes by, reputation increases, ability declines. *Dag Hammarskjöld, Markings*

*Peter, a Canadian professor of education, conducted a twenty-five-year study on teacher competence, and his findings moved him to conclude, "People rise to the level of their own incompetence." He went on to explain that "work is accomplished by those employees who have not yet reached their level of incompetence." His words were labeled "the Peter Principle," and not just one but six books followed: *The Peter Principle, The Peter Prescription, The Peter Plan, Peter's Quotations, Peter's People,* and *Peter's Almanac.*

The inverse correlation between status and competence has been noted by observers of human behavior for many years, as the above quotations indicate. Dr. Peter's words were a fresh reminder of this dismal fact of life.

PEOPLE who live in glass houses should never throw stones.* *1616, Draxe*

People who live in glass houses:

　. . . gather no moss.

　. . . shouldn't get stoned.

　. . . shouldn't throw parties. *Judge, ca. 1925*

　. . . make interesting neighbors.

　. . . have to answer the doorbell.

　. . . should take hot baths and steam up the windows.

　. . . should undress in the dark.

If the proverb is taken to mean that people who have faults of their own ought not to talk of other people's faults, it is . . . mistaken. They ought to talk of other people's faults all the time so as to keep attention away from their own. *Stephen Leacock*

People who live in hay houses shouldn't throw pitchforks. *Heard in Ontario*

People who live in wood houses shouldn't raise termites.

People who make love in glass houses should pull down the blinds.

People who live in stone houses shouldn't throw glasses.

*Archer Taylor has observed that the Spanish idiom for "a house with glass windows" would be translated word for word as "a glass house." Therefore, says Taylor, it is likely that this proverb is a translation from the Spanish. Benjamin Franklin (1736) made this meaning explicit when he rephrased the proverb, "Don't throw stones at your neighbors', if your own windows are of glass." Flexner (F-149) relates this proverb to a 17-century historical incident involving the Duke of Buckingham, whose many-windowed mansion was called the Glass House.

PEOPLE will talk.

Gettin' talked about is one o' th' penalties fer bein' purty, while bein' above suspicion is about th' only compensation fer bein' homely. *Kin Hubbard*

There isn't much to talk about at some parties until after one or two couples leave. *Heard in Mississippi*

See also THEY say.

Some PEOPLE never learn.

But a fool must follow his natural bent
Even as you and I!
Rudyard Kipling, The Vampire

What will PEOPLE think?

Other people are not thinking about you, and, if perchance you do enter their con-sciousness, they are wondering what you think of them. *Richard Needham*

Five little words which have prevented more sins and crimes than all of the priests and policemen put together—"What will the neighbors think?" *Richard Needham*

There are many who dare not kill themselves for fear of what the neighbors will say. *Cyril Connolly, 1944*

See also PEOPLE will talk; THEY say.

A PERSON is innocent until proved guilty.

All are presumed good until they are found in a fault. *1640, Herbert*

There are more things in heaven and earth than are dreamt of in your PHILOSOPHY. *Shakespeare, Hamlet 1.5.166, ca. 1600*

Woe be to him that reads but one book. *1651, T-739*

PHYSICIAN, heal thyself. *Luke 4:23*

. . . Your doctor doesn't make house calls either.

Dog trainer, heel thyself!

First keep the peace within yourself, then you can also bring peace to others. *Thomas à Kempis*

Happy are physicians! Their successes shine in the sunlight and the earth covers their failures. *Michel de Montaigne*

He copes, like everybody else, as well as he can, that's all. And it's usually deplorable enough. *Carl Jung, on how a psychiatrist deals with his own personal problems, as quoted in Portraits of Greatness, by Yousef Karsh*

Let him that would move the world first move himself. *Heard in Ontario*

Never go to a doctor whose office plants have died. *Erma Bombeck, 1978*

No man can, with propriety or a good conscience, correct others for a fault he is guilty of himself. *George Washington*

Psychiatrists are terrible ads for themselves, like dermatologists with acne. *Mignon McLaughlin*

Psychiatry is the care of the id by the odd.

The best reformers the world has ever seen are those who commence on themselves. *Josh Billings*

The fortune-teller never knows his own. *Japanese proverb*

One PICTURE is worth a thousand words.* 1921, WM-463

. . . and a documentary is both.

A good snapshot stops a moment from running away. *Eudora Welty*

Draw me a picture of the Gettysburg Address. *Leo Rosten*

One picture is worth 1,000 denials. *Ronald Reagan, to White House News Photographers Association, May 18, 1983*

One written sentence is worth 800 hours of film. *Elie Wiesel*

Pictures are the books of the unlearned. *1662, T-536*

*Slogan popularized by Fred R. Barnard, of the New York City Street Railways Advertising Company, to advocate the use of pictures in ads, first published in 1921,

according to Wolfgang Mieder. Oxford (O-177) says "there is no foundation to the ascription of Chinese origin."

Don't buy a PIG in a poke. 1546, B-1791

See CAVEAT emptor.

Little PITCHERS have big ears. 1546, Heywood

. . . and big mouths.

Oh, what a tangled web do parents weave
When they think that their children are naive.
Ogden Nash (attributed)

A PLACE for everything and everything in its place. 1640, Herbert

A neat house has an uninteresting person in it.

All things have their place, knew we how to place them. *1640, O-179*

Dirt is not dirt, but only matter in the wrong place. *Lord Palmerston*

Have a place for everything and keep the thing somewhere else. This is not advice, it is merely custom. *Mark Twain, Notebook*

One of the advantages of being disorderly is that one is constantly making exciting discoveries. *A. A. Milne*

No PLACE is perfect.

There's no nagging in heaven, but there is harping.

You cannot be in two PLACES at once. 1611, Cotgrave

. . . but with supersonic travel, you can come awfully close.

There are people who want to be everywhere at once and they seem to get nowhere. *Carl Sandburg*

You cannot drink and whistle at the same time.

PLAN ahead.

It wasn't raining when Noah built the ark. *Howard Ruff, How to Prosper in the Coming Bad Years*

Leave nothing to chance—be sure that all your crimes are premeditated. © Ashleigh Brilliant

Take care of which rut you use. You'll be in it for the next 20 miles. *Road sign at a desert crossroads at Patagonia, Arizona*

One possible reason why things aren't going according to plan is that there never was a plan. © Ashleigh Brilliant

See also Don't count your CHICKENS before they are hatched.

Make no small PLANS.*

Think big thoughts, but relish small pleasures. *H. Jackson Brown, Jr., Life's Little Instruction Book*

*Make no little plans, they have no magic to stir men's blood and probably themselves will not be realized. Make big plans; aim high in hope and work, remembering that a noble, logical diagram once recorded will never die, but long after we are gone will be a living thing, asserting itself with ever-growing insistency. Remember that our sons and grandsons are going to do things that would stagger us. *Daniel H. Burnham*

Fair PLAY.

Every man believes in fair play; fair to him, that is, and by his own definition of fairness. *Richard Needham*

Fair play is a jewel. *1824, OE-186*

Fairness is what Justice really is. *Potter Stewart, as quoted in Time, Oct. 20, 1958*

Give and take. *1519, OE-238*

If you want peace, work for justice. *Bumper sticker, 1993*

Law is the art of the good and the just. *Latin proverb*

Man's capacity for justice makes democracy possible; but man's inclination to injustice makes democracy necessary. *Reinhold Niebuhr, The Children of Light and the Children of Darkness*

Serious sport has nothing to do with fair play. It is bound up with hatred, jealousy, boastfulness, disregard of all rules and sadistic pleasure in witnessing violence. In other words, it is war minus the shooting. *George Orwell, Shooting an Elephant*

Thou shalt not pervert the justice due the sojourner, nor the fatherless, nor take a widow's raiment to pledge. *Deuteronomy 24:17*

Turn about is fair play. *1892, OE-676.*

The principle of fair play is expressed in eleven family mottoes listed by Urdang, p. 266. In the original Latin or French, these mottoes assume that special aura of obscurity and profundity: *Acquitate ac diligentia; Can-*

dide et constanter; Chacun sa part; and *Je veux bonne guerre.* Here is the English:

> With fair play and diligence. *Ashbury*
>
> Fairly and firmly. *Irwine, Warner*
>
> Each his share. *Gwilt*
>
> I wish fair play. *Thomson, Thompson*

The spirit of fair play is reflected in English legal proverbs:

> All are presumed innocent until proved guilty.
>
> Better ten guilty escape than one innocent suffer.
>
> Equality before the law.
>
> No man is obliged to accuse himself.
>
> No one shall be condemned unheard.
>
> Share and share alike.
>
> The law is open to all.

See also All MEN are created equal; GIVE and take is fair play; What's sauce for the GOOSE is sauce for the gander.

'Tis easy enough to be PLEASANT
When life flows by like a song.
But the one worth while
Is the one who will smile
When everything goes dead wrong.*
Ella Wheeler Wilcox, The Test of the Heart

In a calm sea every man is a pilot. *1670, Ray*

The man who can smile when things go wrong has thought of someone he can blame it on. *Arthur Bloch*

The ultimate measure of a man is not where he stands in moments of comfort, but where he stands at times of challenge and controversy. *Martin Luther King, Jr., Strength to Love*

*This verse is very widely seen on postcards of the pre–World War I era, usually without acknowledging the authorship of Mrs. Wilcox. The verse was also broadly paraphrased, or parodied, as the following examples (all quoted from old postcards) illustrate:

It's easy enough to be carefree
When you ride in your neighbor's machine;
But wouldn't you chew if it fell upon you
To pay for the gasoline.

It's easy enough to be pleasant
When there's nothing to make you blue,
But the one who can grin when it hurts like a
    sin
Is a hero through and through.

It's easy enough to be pleasant,
When your automobile is in trim,
But the man worth while
Is the man who will smile,
When he has to ride back on the rim.

It's easy enough to try spooning,
When nobody knows of the fact;
But the man worth while
Is the one who can smile
When caught in the mushy act.

It's easy to smile at the end of each mile
When you're traveling the road to wealth,
But you're never allowed in the Ha! Ha!
    crowd
If you have no money or health.

You can't PLEASE everybody. *1472, O-179*

...and sometimes it seems impossible to please anybody.

A man who trims himself to suit everybody will soon whittle himself away. *Charles Schwab, as quoted in Reader's Digest, May 1955*

A sensible man knows you can't please everybody. A wise man knows you can't please anybody. *Richard Needham*

Everything I did in my life that was worthwhile I caught hell for. *Earl Warren, as quoted in San Francisco Chronicle, Apr. 18, 1989*

He must rise early that would please everybody. *1670, Ray*

I cannot give you a formula for success, but I can give you a formula for failure: try to please everybody. *Herbert Swope*

I do not believe the people who tell me that they do not care a row of pins for the opinion of their fellows. It is the bravado of ignorance. *W. Somerset Maugham, The Summing Up*

If you try to make some people see the bright side, they will complain that it hurts their eyes. *Heard in New York*

If you want to please everybody, you'll die before your time. *Yiddish proverb*

Little souls wish you to be unhappy. It aggravates them to have you joyous, efficient and free. They like to feel that fate is disciplining you. It gives their egos wings if yours are clipped. You can ruin your life in an hour by listening to their puerile opinions. *David Seabury*

Not even God can please all, whether he rains or does not rain. *Theognis*

The ability to say no is more valuable to a man than the ability to read Latin. *William C. Hunter*

The strongest man in the world is he who stands most alone. *Henrik Ibsen, An Enemy of the People*

There is a certain exultation in being right. If one is alone, the joy is lessened, but it beats the alternative going away. *Donald G. Smith*

Whoso would be a man must be a nonconformist. *Ralph Waldo Emerson, Self-Reliance*

Women dress to please themselves, or their husbands, or their women friends. Any wardrobe that really satisfies one of these groups will enrage the other two. *Mignon McLaughlin*

You please your brother and you disappoint your sister-in-law. *Chinese proverb*

Who seeks to please all men each way,
    And not himself offend,
He may begin his work to-day,
    But God knows where he'll end.
Samuel Rowlands, ca. 1630

See also He TRAVELS the fastest who travels alone; Be YOURSELF; LIFE is not a popularity contest; PEOPLE will talk; To thine own self be TRUE; THEY say; You can't have your CAKE and eat it too.

Simple PLEASURES are best.

'Tis better than riches to scratch when it itches.

One bliss for which there is no match
Is when you itch to up and scratch. . . .

'Neath tile or thatch that man is rich
Who has a scratch for every itch.
Ogden Nash, 1938

**POEMS are made by fools like me,
But only God can make a tree.**
Joyce Kilmer, Trees

. . . But only fools like me, you see,
Can make a God, who makes a tree.
E. Y. Harburg

Poems are made by fools like me, but only
God can make real maple syrup.

I think I never shall admire
A line of poles festooned with wire,
And hope someday they'll all be found
(Before I get there) *underground.*
© *Ashleigh Brilliant*

I think that I shall never be
Sold on an artificial tree.
An evergreen with plastic limbs
Just doesn't go with Christmas hymns;
A tree with needles made of foil,
That grew in factories, not in soil;
And, though it will not burn or shed,
'Twill never be alive nor dead.
Perennial, yes; that it may be,
And formed in perfect symmetry.
But only God can make a tree
To suit old-fashioned folks like me.

I think that I shall never see
A billboard lovely as a tree.
Indeed, unless the billboards fall
I'll never see a tree at all.
Ogden Nash, Song of the Open Road

POETS born, not made. *Latin proverb*

Poets are born, not paid. *Addison Mizner*

POLITENESS costs nothing. *1706, O-37*

. . . and buys every thing. *Mary Wortley Montagu, 1765*

. . . Nothing, that is, to him that shows it; but it often costs the world very dear. *W. Allingham, Rambles*

Asking is just polite demanding. *Max Headroom, TV show*

POLITENESS is to do and say the kindest thing in the kindest way. *Ludwig Lewisohn (1882–1955)*

Basically, I try to be as charming and ingratiating as I can without making myself vomit. *Katie Couric, on getting a story*

Etiquette is getting sleepy in company and not showing it. *Hyman Maxwell Berston*

Etiquette is the noise you don't make while eating soup.

Gallantry consists in saying empty things in an agreeable manner. *François de la Rochefoucauld*

Good breeding consists of concealing how much we think of ourselves and how little we think of the other person. *Mark Twain, Notebook*

Good manners is simply good nature polished up. *Josh Billings*

Hospitality is the fine art of making your guests want to stay, without interfering with their departure.

Is it progress if a cannibal uses a knife and fork? *Stanislaw J. Lec*

Manners is the hypocrisy of a nation. *Honoré de Balzac*

Politeness is a fictitious benevolence. *Samuel Johnson, 1773*

Politeness is organized indifference. *Paul Válery*

Politeness is the science of getting down on your knees before folks without getting your pantaloons dirty. *Josh Billings*

Politeness: The art of saying in an exquisite manner the reverse of what one thinks. *Charles Narrey*

Politeness. The most acceptable hypocrisy. *Ambrose Bierce, The Devil's Dictionary*

Social tact is making your company feel at home, even though you wish they were.

The great advantage of good breeding is that it makes a fool endurable. *Josh Billings*

The test of good manners is being able to put up with bad ones.

The hallmark of good manners is mastering the ability to yawn without opening your mouth.

When ye run down politeness ye take the mortar from between the bricks of the foundations of society. *O. Henry, 1906*

Make me, dear Lord, polite and kind
    To every one, I pray.
And may I ask You how You find
    Yourself, dear Lord, today?
John Banister Tabb, A Child's Prayer

All POLITICIANS are crooked.

. . . because the honest ones are known as statesmen.

A good politician is quite as unthinkable as an honest burglar. *H. L. Mencken, 1955*

A man running for office puts me in mind of a dog that's lost—he smells everybody he meets, and wags himself all over. *Josh Billings, 1865*

A politician is an animal who can sit on a fence and yet keep both ears to the ground. *Heard in Kentucky and Tennessee*

A politician should have three hats. One for throwing in the ring, one for talking through, and one for pulling rabbits out of if elected. *Carl Sandburg*

A promising young man should go into politics so that he can go on promising for the rest of his life. *Robert Byrne*

A statesman is a politician who is held upright by equal pressure from all directions. *Eric A. Johnston, as quoted in Reader's Digest, Jan. 1944*

An honest politician is one who, when he is bought, will stay bought. *Simon Cameron*

Be a politician; no training necessary. *Will Rogers*

Congress consists of one-third, more or less, scoundrels; two-thirds, more or less, idiots; and three-thirds, more or less, idiots; and three-thirds, more or less, poltroons. *H. L. Mencken*

Every government is run by liars and nothing they say should be believed. *I. F. Stone*

Government is essentially immoral. *Herbert Spencer*

George Washington never told a lie, but it must be remembered that he entered politics when the country was very new. *New Orleans Picayune*

Governments tend not to solve problems, only rearrange them. *Ronald Reagan, 1973*

I don't know much about Americanism, but it's a damned good word with which to carry an election. *Warren G. Harding*

I used to say that politics was the second oldest profession, and I have come to know that it bears a gross similarity to the first. *Ronald Reagan, 1979*

If a politician found he had cannibals among his constituents, he would promise them missionaries for dinner. *H. L. Mencken*

If I had a son, I would sooner breed him a cobbler than a courtier, a hangman than a statesman! *Earl of Shrewsbury, Charles Talbot*

In politics, nothing is contemptible. *Benjamin Disraeli*

In politics some deceit or moral dishonesty is the oil without which the machinery will not work. *Woodrow Wilson*

Instead of giving a politician the keys to the city, it might be better to change the locks. *Doug Larson*

It is dangerous for a national candidate to say things people might remember. *Eugene McCarthy*

It's easier to vote a straight party ticket than it is to find a straight party.

My choice early in life was either to be a piano player in a whorehouse or a politician. And to tell the truth, there's hardly any difference. *Harry S. Truman*

Ninety percent of the politicians give the other ten percent a bad name. *Henry Kissinger*

Politicians are interested in people. Not that it is always a virtue. Fleas are interested in dogs. *P. J. O'Rourke*

Politicians are the same all over. They promise to build a bridge even where there is no river. *Nikita Khrushchev, 1960*

Politics . . . can turn an Eagle Scout into a pimp. *Mike Royko*

Politics is a promising career.

Politics is the gentle art of getting votes from the poor and campaign funds from the rich, by promising to protect each from the other. *Oscar Ameringer*

Politics is the noblest of all callings, but the meanest of all trades. *Goldwin Smith, 1893*

Politics: the conduct of public affairs for private advantage. *Ambrose Bierce, The Devil's Dictionary*

Practical politics consists in ignoring facts. *Henry Adams*

Some politicians can be bought, but most can only be rented. *Richard Needham*

The only difference between the Democrats and the Republicans is that the Democrats allow the poor to be corrupt, too. *Oscar Levant*

The politician is an acrobat. He keeps his balance by saying the opposite of what he does. *Maurice Barres*

The Democrats seem to be for people who don't work, and the Republicans for people who don't have to work. *Gerard Bentryn*

The proper memory for a politician is one that knows what to remember and what to forget. *John Morley*

Vote for the man who promises least—he'll be least disappointing. *Bernard Baruch, 1960*

A genuine statesman should be on his guard,
If he must have beliefs, not to believe them
   too hard.
James Russell Lowell, Biglow Papers

I could not dig: I dared not rob:
Therefore I lied to please the mob.
Rudyard Kipling

How dear to my heart are the grand politi-
   cians
   Who constantly strive for the popular
      votes,
Indulging in platitudes, trite repetitions,
   And time-honored bromides surrounded
with quotes.

They picture perfection in every effusion;
   We gaze at Utopia under their spell,
And though it is only an optic illusion
   We fall for the buncombe we all know so
well.
Robert E. Sherwood

See also A STATESMAN is a successful politician who is dead.

POLITICS makes strange bedfellows. *1839, O-180*

. . . They all seem to like the same bunk.

Bedfellows makes strange politics. *Boston Herald, 1959; BJW-504*

Divorce makes estranged bedfellows.

Marriage makes strange bedfellows.

Politics is perhaps the only profession for which no preparation is thought necessary. *Robert Louis Stevenson*

Politics makes strange postmasters. *Kin Hubbard*

Prohibition makes strange bar-fellows. *Judge, ca. 1925*

See also All POLITICIANS are crooked.

It's no disgrace to be POOR.

. . . but it might as well be. *Kin Hubbard*

Better to go to heaven in rags than to hell in embroidery. *1732, Fuller*

It's hell to be poor. *Heard in New York*

The POOR ye have with you always.*

. . . despite the fact that they were never invited.

I've known what it is to be hungry, but I always went right to the restaurant. *Ring Lardner*

Remember the poor—it costs nothing. *Josh Billings*

*This sentiment is expressed in both the Hebrew Bible and in the New Testament: "For the poor shall never cease out of the land; therefore I command thee saying, Thou shalt open thine hand wide unto thy brother, to thy poor, to thy needy, in thy land" (Deuteronomy 15:11); "Ye have the poor always with you (Matthew 26:11). An interesting difference in the contexts of these two observations that there will always be poor people: In Deuteronomy, this leads to the commandment that "thou shall open thine hand wide unto . . . thy needy. . . ." In Matthew, the observation is used to defend a woman who poured "very precious ointment" on the head of Jesus. When his disciples protested that "this ointment might have been sold for much, and given to the poor," Jesus defended the woman who had anointed him by saying, "Ye have the poor always with you, but me ye have not always" (Matthew 26:7–11).

Any PORT in a storm. *1749, O-4*

He came to pick her up for a tennis date, but it started to rain, so they spent the afternoon in her apartment. Any sport in a storm.

POSSESSION is nine points of the law.* *1595, O-181*

. . . and self-possession is the other one.

. . . Like stolen goods? Or two bigamous wives? Or even three? *George Jean Nathan*

Finders keepers, losers weepers. *"Law" of the playground*

It is an immutable law of kite flying that the one holding the string is in charge. *Donald G. Smith*

Possession isn't nine points . . . it's all ten points. *Dorothy L. Sayers, 1928; BJW-505*

*This proverb raises the question: What *are* the "points of the law"? About 1750, George Selwyn, an English attorney, offered the following list: "1. A good cause; 2. A good purse; 3. An honest and skillful lawyer; 4. Good evidence; 5. Able counsel; 6. An upright judge; 7. An intelligent jury; 8. Good luck" (F-151).

A little POT is soon hot. *1546, Heywood*

A man's as big as the things that make him mad. *Heard in Ontario*

A watched POT never boils. *1848, O-242*

. . . especially when you forget to light the gas.

Little things please little minds. *Ovid*

The POT calls the kettle black.* *1639, Clarke*

A group of politicians deciding to dump a President because his morals are bad is like the Mafia getting together to bump off the Godfather for not going to church on Sunday. *Russell Baker, New York Times, 1974*

Black arse, quoth the pot to the caldron. *1721, T-353*

He that is conscious of a stink in his Breeches, is jealous of every Wrinkle in another's Nose. *Benjamin Franklin, 1751*

We all find in others the faults that are found in ourselves. *François de la Rochefoucauld*

*In most 17th-century versions, the pot calls the kettle "burnt-arse" (T-353). The saying is common to all languages, says Stevenson (B-1841), and points to the universality of the habit of faultfinding.

POVERTY breeds strife. *1670, Ray*

A hungry louse bites hard. *Heard in West Virginia*

A hungry man is an angry man. *1659, Howell*

A poor man, though he speaks the truth, is not believed. *Meander*

An empty stomach is not a good political adviser. *Albert Einstein*

Better die ten years sooner than live those years in poverty. *Chinese proverb*

Better the grave than a fall to poverty. *Solomon ibn Gabirol.* Stevenson (B-1848) adds that "Hebrew literature is filled with such aphorisms."

If one man offers you democracy and another offers you a bag of grain, at what stage of starvation will you prefer the grain to the vote? *Bertrand Russell, 1950*

No man can worship God or love his neighbor on an empty stomach. *Woodrow Wilson, May 23, 1912*

Nobody ever listened to reason on an empty stomach. *Kin Hubbard*

On the day your horse dies and your gold vanishes, your relatives are like strangers met on the road. *Chinese proverb*

Poverty is a great enemy to human happiness; it certainly destroys liberty, and it makes some virtues impossible. *Samuel Johnson, 1782*

Poverty is a hateful blessing. *Vincent of Beauvais*

Poverty is another death. *Latin proverb*

Poverty is the mother of crime. *Cassiodorus*

Poverty makes Men ridiculous. *1732, Fuller*

Poverty parts good company and is an enemy to virtue. *Scottish proverb*

Poverty, the most destructive pest in all the world. *Aristophanes*

Principles have no real force except when one is well fed. *Mark Twain*

Riots are the voices of the unheard. *Martin Luther King, Jr.*

The devil dances in an empty pocket. *15th century*

There is no affliction in the world more severe than poverty. Place all punishments in one scale and poverty in the other, and poverty will be the heavier. *Midrash: Exodus Rabbah 31:12*

Want makes strife between the good man and his wife. *1732, T-552*

When more and more people are thrown out of work, unemployment results. *Calvin Coolidge*

Wrinkled purses make wrinkled faces.

POVERTY is no sin. *1651, Herbert*

. . . but an inconvenience. *1591, O-182*

. . . It's worse!

. . . but it's no honor either.

. . . but it doesn't get any applause either.

. . . but it might as well be. *Kin Hubbard*

. . . but it's mighty unhandy.

. . . but being ashamed of it is.

. . . as any rich man will tell you.

. . . It is a blunder, though, and is punished as such. A poor man is despised the whole world over. *Jerome K. Jerome, Idle Thoughts of an Idle Fellow*

A poor man can't be happy because a happy man is never poor. *Heard in Kansas*

Being broke isn't all that bad: at least it gives you something to think about while watching television. *Henny Youngman*

It is just as natural to be born poor as to be born naked, and it is no more disgrace. *Josh Billings*

No man should praise poverty but he who is poor. *Saint Bernard*

One thing you can say for poverty—it's inexpensive.

Poverty is bitter, but it has no harder pang than that it makes men ridiculous. *Juvenal, Satires*

Poverty is not a shame; but the being ashamed of it is. *1640, Herbert*

Poverty must have many satisfactions, else there would not be so many poor people. *Don Herold*

The rich man may never get into heaven, but the pauper is already serving his term in hell. *Alexander Chase, 1966*

There is one advantage of being poor—a doctor will cure you faster. *Kin Hubbard, Abe Martin's Sayings*

Tolerance is what enables the rich to declare that there is no disgrace in being poor. *Peter's Almanac*

Wealth is hard to come by, but poverty is always at hand. *Japanese proverb*

What mean ye that ye beat my people to pieces, and grind the faces of the poor? saith the Lord God of hosts. *Isaiah 3:15*

POVERTY is no vice, but it's mighty inconvenient. *1591, B-1848*

Poverty is no vice, it is worse. *Charles Dufresny*

An empty knapsack is heavier to carry than a full one. *Serbo-Croatian proverb*

One may conceal his riches but not his poverty. *Philippine proverb*

Poverty is very good in poems but very bad in the house; very good in maxims and sermons but very bad in practical life. *Henry Ward Beecher*

Too poor to paint and too proud to whitewash.

When POVERTY comes in the door, love flies out the window.* 1474, O-181

Love will cool 'twixt a pair of sheets if there be not wherewithal to keep them warm. *1573, T-398*

When loves comes in the door, truth flies out the window. And vice versa. *Richard Needham*

When mother-in-law comes in at the door, love flies out the window. *Helen Rowland*

When pa comes in at the door, ma's boyfriend flies out the window.

When newspapers enter the door, wives fly down to the bargain counters. *Old postcard*

When sex comes in by the window, logic leaves by the door. *BJW-509*

*Similar to "Love comes in at the window and goes out the door," a 17th-century proverb that contrasts the magical beginnings of a romance with its unceremonious ending.

POWER corrupts.*

. . . and corruption seeks power. *Michel Paul Richard*

. . . the few, and weakness corrupts the many. *Eric Hofer*

...but lack of power corrupts absolutely. *Adlai Stevenson, 1963*

A friend in power is a friend lost. *Henry Adams, The Education of Henry Adams*

Government is not reason, it is not eloquence—it is force! Like fire it is a dangerous servant and a fearful master; never for a moment should it be left to irresponsible action. *George Washington*

I am more and more convinced that man is a dangerous creature and that power, whether vested in many or a few, is ever grasping, and like the grave, cries "Give, give." *Abigail Adams, 1775*

If absolute power corrupts absolutely, does absolute powerlessness make you pure? *Harry Shearer*

If power corrupts, powerlessness corrupts even more. *Yeshua Eckstein*

If success is corrupting, failure is narrowing. *Stephen Spender*

It is true that wealth won't make a man virtuous, but I notice there ain't anybody who wants to be poor just for the purpose of being good. *Josh Billings, 1865*

Liberty, too, can corrupt, and absolute liberty can corrupt absolutely. *Gertrude Himmelfarb*

Lust of power burns more fiercely than all the passions combined. *Tacitus*

Men make counterfeit money; in many more cases, money makes counterfeit men. *Sydney J. Harris*

My opinion is that power should be distrusted, in whatever hands it is based. *William Jones, 1782*

Nearly all men can stand adversity, but if you want to test a man's character, give him power. *Abraham Lincoln*

Our dangerous class is not at the bottom, it is near the top, of society. Riches without law are more dangerous than is poverty without law. *Henry Ward Beecher, Proverbs from Plymouth Pulpit*

Power discovers the real disposition of a man.

Power intoxicates men. When a man is intoxicated by alcohol, he can recover, but when he is intoxicated by power, he seldom recovers. *James F. Byrnes*

Power, like virtue, is its own reward.

Power doesn't corrupt people; people corrupt power. *William Gaddis*

Power is the ultimate aphrodisiac. *Henry Kissinger*

Power will intoxicate the best hearts, as wine the strongest heads. *Charles Colton, Lacon*

Private passions grow tired and wear themselves out; political passions, never. *Alphonse de Lamartine*

So I returned, and considered all the oppressions that are done under the sun; and, behold, the tears of such as were oppressed, and they had no comforter; and on the side of their oppressors there was power, but they had no comforter! *Ecclesiastes 4:1*

Success makes you drunk without wine. *Yiddish proverb*

The effect of power and publicity on all men is the aggravation of self, a sort of tumor that ends by killing the victim's sympathies. *Henry Adams, The Education of Henry Adams*

The greater the power, the more dangerous the abuse. *Edmund Burke, Speech on the Middlesex Election*

The virtue of some of the rich is that they teach us to despise wealth. *Kahlil Gibran*

Wealth makes more people mean than it does generous. *Josh Billings, 1865*

To suppose, as we all suppose, that we could be rich and not behave the way the rich behave, is like supposing that we could drink all day and stay sober. *Logan Pearsall Smith, 1964*

When power corrupts, poetry cleanses. *John F. Kennedy, Oct. 26, 1963*

*Power tends to corrupt, and absolute power corrupts absolutely. Great men are almost always bad men, even when they exercise influence and not authority. *Lord Acton, Life and Letters of Mandel Creighton*

PRACTICE makes perfect. *Latin proverb*

. . . when you practice perfection.

Cab drivers are living proof that practice does not make perfect. *Howard Ogden*

If you think practice makes perfect, you don't have a child taking piano lessons.

Kissing is a bad practice; but practice makes perfect. *Old postcard*

PRACTICE what you preach. *ca.* 500 B.C.*

. . . said the wife of the minister, reminding him to rehearse his sermon.

A good example is the best sermon. *1732, Fuller*

Civilized men arrived in the Pacific, armed with alcohol, syphilis, trousers, and the Bible. *Havelock Ellis*

Deeds are fruits, words are but leaves. *1633, Draxe*

Doing is better than saying. *1633, Draxe*

Every word is vain that is not completed by deed. *Greek proverb, ca. A.D. 350*

Fair words and foul deeds cheat wise men as well as fools. *Samuel Palmer, 1710*

Going to church doesn't make you a Christian any more than going to the garage makes you a car. *Laurence Peter*

Good words make us laugh; good deeds make us silent. *French proverb*

Good words without deeds are but rushes and reeds. *1659, Howell*

He who learns in order to teach will be able both to learn and to teach. But he who learns in order to practice will be able to learn, to teach, and to practice. *Ishmael ben Elisha*

I won't take my religion from any man who never works except with his mouth. *Carl Sandburg*

It is easier to behave your way into a new way of thinking than to think your way into a new way of behaving.

Many talk like philosophers and live like fools. *1855, WM-412*

Men will wrangle for religion; write for it; fight for it; anything but—live for it. *Charles Colton, Lacon*

No man fully practices what he preaches, but this is no reason he shouldn't preach. The best temperance lecture we ever heard was delivered by a man under the influence of liquor. *William C. Hunter*

Practice what you pray. *Advertisement for "Religion in American Life," prepared by the Advertising Council, 1975*

Reflected a minister: "People look at me six days a week to see what I mean on the seventh."

The Holy One, blessed be He, hates a person who says one thing with his mouth and another in his heart. *Babylonian Talmud*

The man who don't practice what he preaches is no better than the rattlesnake, who warns and then strikes. *Josh Billings*

Things have come to a pretty pass when religion is allowed to invade the sphere of private life. *Lord Melbourne*

We have, in fact, two kinds of morality side by side; one which we preach but do not practise, and another which we practise but seldom preach. *Bertrand Russell, Sceptical Essays*

Words are mere bubbles of water, but deeds are drops of gold. *Chinese proverb*

Do not show me the steep and thorny way to
　　heaven,
Whiles, like a puff'd and reckless libertine,
Himself the primrose path of dalliance treads
And recks not his own rede.
Shakespeare, Hamlet 1.3.47

And help us, this and every day,
To live more nearly as we pray.
John Keble, The Christian Year

*In his *Analects*, Confucius wrote of the superior man, "He first practices what he preaches, and then preaches according to his practice."

See also ACTIONS speak louder than words; DEEDS, not creeds; DO as I say, not as I do; A man of words and not of DEEDS is like a garden full of weeds.

PRAISE is always pleasant. *Fuller, 1732*

A fool will always find a bigger fool to praise him. *Nicolas Boileau*

An occasional compliment is necessary to keep up one's self-respect. . . . When you cannot get a compliment in any other way, pay yourself one. *Mark Twain, Notebook*

Beauty's exilir vitae, praise. *Coventry Patmore, 1862*

Better praise yourself than find fault with others. *Yiddish proverb*

My advice to you concerning applause is this: Enjoy it but never quite believe it. *Robert Montgomery, to his daughter at the start of her acting career, Women's Home Companion, Dec. 1955*

My ear is always open for appreciation, but for criticism, you have to make an appointment. © *Ashleigh Brilliant*

No one is deaf to praise. *Yiddish proverb.*

Praise does wonders for our sense of hearing. *Arnold Glasow*

Praise loudly; blame softly. *Catherine II*

The deepest principle of Human Nature is the craving to be appreciated. *William James*

The praise of a fool is incense to the wisest of us. *Benjamin Disraeli*

We are all imbued with the love of praise. *Cicero*

Be PREPARED. *Motto of the Boy Scouts of America*

In the summer make a sledge, in winter a carriage. *Estonian proverb*

Who goes for a day in the forest should take bread for a week. *Czech proverb*

I'd rather be right than PRESIDENT. *Henry Clay, 1850*

Just PRETEND.

. . . That willing suspension of disbelief . . . which constitutes poetic faith. *Samuel Coleridge, Biographia Literaria*

Imagination is a good stick but a bad crutch.

It is now life and not art that requires the willing suspension of disbelief. *Lionel Trilling*

An ounce of PREVENTION is worth a pound of cure. * *ca. 1240, WM- 483*

. . . but try telling that to a government that would rather develop lung transplants than teach people not to smoke. *New York Times editorial, May 16, 1988*

An ounce of emotion is equal to a ton of facts. *John Junior, 1979*

An ounce of hundred-dollar bills is worth a pound of singles.

An ounce of hypocrisy is worth a pound of ambition. *Michael Korda*

Asking dumb questions is easier than correcting dumb mistakes.

Temptation may call but 'taint no use to set a chair for 'em. *Old postcard*

The best armor is to keep out of gunshot. *Heard in Mississippi*

The best time to repent of a blunder is just before the blunder is made. *Josh Billings*

The best way out of it is not to be in it. *Kin Hubbard*

The more you sweat in peace, the less you bleed in war. *Hyman G. Rickover, retirement speech*

Who is a skilled physician? He who can prevent sickness. *Sefer Hasidim*

*Mieder (1993, pages 155–162) offers an extended discussion of this proverb.

See also a STITCH in time saves nine.

PRIDE goeth before a fall. *

He who gets too big for his britches gets exposed in the end.

Humility is a strange thing. The minute you think you've got it, you've lost it. *E. D. Hulse*

Pride goes before, and shame comes after. *1500, T-555*

Pride is a fine imitation of self-esteem for those who can't afford the real thing. *Frederic Morton*

The best kind of pride is pride in your work. *B. C. Forbes*

The feeling that you've done a job well is rewarding; the feeling that you've done it perfectly is fatal.

The man who is proud is the man with a blemish. *Babylonian Talmud*

There is no such thing as being proud before man and humble before God. *Josh Billings*

*Pride goeth before destruction, and an haughty spirit before a fall. *Proverbs 16:18*

He who takes what isn't his'n must give it back or go to PRISON. *Variation of a line attributed to "Happy Webb," quoted by Lord Lennox (1899–1981)*

Better to beg than to steal, but better to work than to beg.

Thieves respect property; they merely wish the property to become their property that they may more perfectly respect it. *G. K. Chesterton*

It is easy to bear another person's PROBLEMS.

A tooth inside another man's mouth does not hurt. *Russian proverb*

All commend patience but none can endure to suffer. *1732, Fuller*

By trying we can easily learn to endure adversity. Another man's, I mean. *Mark Twain, Pudd'nhead Wilson's Calendar*

One does not get a headache from what other people have drunk.

The comforter's head never aches. *1590, T-112*

The tears of other people are only water. *Russian proverb*

See Great SPIRIT . . . ; It all DEPENDS on whose ox is gored.

PROCRASTINATION is the thief of time. *Edward Young, Night Thoughts, 1742; O-184*

. . . but compared with television, procrastination is just a piker. *Clyde M. Norcross*

Anybody can do any amount of work, so long as it isn't the work he is supposed to be doing. *Robert Benchley*

Far from being the thief of Time, Procrastination is the King of it. *Ogden Nash, Primrose Path*

He was always late on principle, his principle being that punctuality is the thief of time. *Oscar Wilde, The Picture of Dorian Gray*

It's amazing how long it takes to complete something you are not working on.

One of the greatest labor-saving inventions of today is tomorrow.

One of these days is none of these days. *1658, OE-477*

Procrastination is fun. Just wait and see.

Procrastination is the art of keeping up with yesterday. *Don Marquis, Certain Maxims of Archie*

Punctuality is the virtue of the bored. *Evelyn Waugh, Diaries*

Procrastination is the thief of other people's time. *V. McHugh, 1936; BJW-512*

Punctuality is the thief of time.

The right time is now.

We have left undone those things which we ought to have done; and we have done those things which we ought not to have done. *The Book of Common Prayer*

In putting off your tasks and ruing them
You waste more time than you would spend
   in doing them.
Arthur Guiterman

See also Never PUT OFF until tomorrow what you can do today; TOMORROW never comes.

No one was ever ruined by taking a PROFIT.

Capitalism will eventually pass. So will the moon, by the way. *Walter B. Pitkin*

Honestly if you can, but by any means make money. *Horace, Epistles*

Invest in inflation. It's the only thing going up. *Will Rogers*

It is a socialist idea that making profits is a vice. I consider the real vice is making losses. *Winston Churchill*

The best investment is land, because they ain't making any more of it. *Will Rogers*

The secret of business is to know something that nobody else knows. *Aristotle Onassis*

See also BUY cheap, and sell dear.

A PROMISE is a promise. 220 B.C., B-1895

A man is known by the promises he keeps.

He loses his thanks who promises and delays. *1616, Draxe*

If I owe Smith ten dollars, and God forgives me, that doesn't pay Smith. *Robert G. Ingersoll*

Let your yea be yea; and your nay, nay. *James 5:12*

Mankind lives on promises. *T. C. Haliburton, 1843*

Promise is debt. *Geoffrey Chaucer, Introduction to the Man of Law's Prologue*

Rather do what you have not promised, than promise what you will not do. *Solomon ibn Gabirol*

The best way to keep your word is not to give it. *Napoleon*

What is a gentleman but his word? *ca. 1553, T-253*

A promise made
Is a debt unpaid.

See also PROMISES and pie crust are made to be broken.

PROMISE little and do much. *Hebrew proverb*

He that promises too much means nothing. *1732, Fuller*

It is the part of wisdom to keep your word and the part of folly to count on other people keeping theirs. *Richard Needham*

Money is like promises, easier made than kept. *Josh Billings, 1865*

Oaths are but words, and words but wind. *Samuel Butler, Hudibras*

Promise much and do little. *L. L. Levinson*

Promises may get thee friends, but non-performance will turn them into enemies. *Poor Richard's Almanac*

Promises may make friends, but 'tis performances that keep them. *Latin proverb*

Some men divide their time equally—one-half making promises, one-half making excuses. If you make no promises you'll need no excuses, and can then devote *all* your time to getting business. *William C. Hunter*

The man of promise keeps his promise.

The righteous promise little and perform much; the wicked promise much and perform not even a little. *Babylonian Talmud*

There are two kinds of people on this earth — those who keep their word and those who have a dozen excellent reasons why they were unable to keep their word. *Richard Needham*

To make a vow for life is to make oneself a slave. *Voltaire, Philosophical Dictionary*

PROMISES and pie crust are made to be broken. *Jonathan Swift, Polite Conversation, 1738*

Always borrow from a pessimist — he never expects it back.

An unlawful oath is better broken than kept. *1481, T-511*

Bad promises are better broken than kept. *Abraham Lincoln, 1865*

Before marriage he promised her everything but the kitchen sink; after marriage, the kitchen sink was all she got. *Richard Needham*

More chorus girls are kept than promises. *Fred Allen*

Since men are wicked and do not keep their promises to you, you likewise do not need to keep yours to them. *Niccolo Machiavelli*

To make a *pledge* of any kind is to declare war against nature; for a pledge is a chain that is always clanking and reminding the wearer of it that he is not a free man. *Mark Twain, Following the Equator*

You can't live on PROMISES.

You can't heat a stove on promised wood. *Russian proverb*

You cannot live on other people's promises, but if you promise others enough, you can't live on your own. *Mark Caine, The S-Man: A Grammar of Success*

No man is a PROPHET in his own country.*

A prophet is a man that foresees trouble. *Finley Peter Dunne, 1901*

An expert is a mechanic away from home. *Charles E. Wilson*

Every society honors its live conformists and its dead troublemakers. *Mignon McLaughlin*

Honor is without profit — in most countries. *Cynic, 1904*

I can say anything I please in my home — nobody listens anyway.

If fame is to come only after death, I am in no hurry for it. *Martial*

It does not pay to be a prophet; if you hit it right, people will doubt it, and if you hit it wrong, they will damn it. *Josh Billings*

Sydney J. Harris noted that by a majority of three votes, the House of Delegates in George Washington's own state, Virginia, rejected a citation that commended him for showing "wisdom" in his administration.

Mozart died a pauper
Heine lived in dread,
Foster died in Bellevue,
Homer begged for bread.
Genius pays off handsomely
After you are dead.
E. Y. Harburg

*A prophet is not without honor, save in his own country, and in his own house. *Matthew 13:57.* Similar to Luke 4:24: "No prophet is accepted in his own country."

See also DISTANCE lends enchantment; FAMILIARITY breeds contempt.

Beware of false PROPHETS.

. . . which come to you in sheep's clothing, but inwardly they are ravening wolves. *Matthew 7:15*

PROSPERITY gains friends, and adversity tries them. *ca. 1500, WM- 488*

Friendship, like gold, needs the acid test of adversity to determine its value. *Old postcard*

Prosperity discovers Vice, and Adversity Virtue. *Poor Richard's Almanac, 1751*

Prosperity is the blessing of the Old Testament, and affliction is the blessing of the New. *A. C. Benton, 1908*

Prosperity's the very bond of love. *Shakespeare, A Winter's Tale 4.4.584*

Misery doth part
The flux of company.
Shakespeare, As You Like It, 2.1.51

PROVIDENCE is always on the side of the big battalions. *1673, O-185*

The winds are always on the side of the ablest navigator.

See also MIGHT makes right.

The PUBLIC be damned. *William H. Vanderbilt**

*New York Central Railroad executive Vanderbilt admitted to a reporter that his company was losing money on its Chicago–New York "flyer," but would continue to run it to compete with a similar run on the Pennsylvania Railroad. Asked the reporter, "Wouldn't you continue it anyway for the benefit of the public?" Roared Vanderbilt, "The public be damned; railroads are not run on sentiment but on business principles."

Vanderbilt's four memorable words characterize him as a capitalist monster, but in the interview from which the phrase is torn, he simply expresses the classic laissez-faire faith that what's good for business incidentally serves the needs of society.

Any PUBLICITY is good publicity. *20th century, O-185*

Every knock is a boost.

See also Don't HIDE your light under a bushel; It pays to ADVERTISE.

The proof of the PUDDING is in the eating. *1300, O-184*

. . . and in the subsequent metabolic effects. *Roger J. Williams*

See also SEEING is believing; I'm from MISSOURI . . . ; Never ASSUME.

Unto the PURE, all things are pure. *Titus 1:15*

. . . and to the jaundiced eye, all things look yellow.

To the filthy all things taste filthy. *1618, T-211*

To the pure, all things are impure.

To the pure all things are slightly indecent. *Margery Allingham, Black Plumes*

See also If it sounds DIRTY, you have a dirty mind.

To every thing there is a season, and a time to every PURPOSE under the sun. *Ecclesiastes 3:1*

See There is a time and place for EVERYTHING.

An empty PURSE cannot stand upright. 1642, O-64

. . . but if it does, 'tis a stout one. *Poor Richard's Almanac, 1750*

. . . fill it with credit cards.

A light Purse is a heavy Curse. *1732, Fuller*

A pocketbook with nothing in it is emptier than a knothole. *Josh Billings*

You can't make a silk PURSE out of a sow's ear. ca. 1514, WM-491

. . . or sweet wine from sour grapes.

. . . or a sow's ear out of a silk purse.

. . . but inflation has transformed my nest egg into chicken feed.

Expensive things *look* expensive. *Marlene Dietrich*

Of a pig's tail you can never make a good shaft. *1659, Howell*

The potter can fashion a wine jug from clay, but nothing out of sand and gravel. *Kahlil Gibran*

You can neither make a good knife out of bad steel, nor good business out of bad schemes. *William C. Hunter*

You can't fill a torn sack.

You can't make a racehorse out of a mule. *Heard in Oklahoma*

You can't make a silk purse out of polyester.

You can't make a whistle out of a pig's tail. *Vermont proverb*

You can't make cheesecakes out of snow. *Yiddish proverb*

You can't make pound cake outa cow manure.

You can't polish a tile into precious stone. *Japanese proverb*

You cannot make honey of a dog's turd. *1659, T-317*

A Chinese proverb says "Rotten wood cannot be carved." And two Chinese proverbs make just the opposite point: not to waste good materials on an ordinary task:

> Any water will do to wash a boat.

> Good iron is not used for nails, nor good men for soldiers.

Never PUT OFF until tomorrow what you can do today. 800 B.C., B-2340

. . . a maxim principally applied by children to postpone their bedtime.

. . . There may be a law against it by that time. *Judge, ca. 1925*

. . . But I say put off till tomorrow
   Your worry sweat and glum,
Keep steady and sweet all today,
   For tomorrow has never yet come.
Old postcard

. . . It is a maxim for sluggards. A better reading of it is, "Never do today what you can as well do to-morrow," because something may occur to make you regret your premature action. *Aaron Burr, ca. 1785*

Daniel Webster's Three Rules: First, never do today what could be deferred till tomorrow; secondly, never do yourself what you could make another do for you; and, thirdly, never pay any debts today. *Ralph Waldo Emerson, Letters and Social Aims (adapted)*

Do not put off till tomorrow what can be put off till the day after tomorrow just as well. *Mark Twain*

Don't put off for tomorrow what you can do today, because if you enjoy it today you can do it again tomorrow. *James Michener, as quoted in Reader's Digest, May 1973*

Most people put off until tomorrow that which they should have done yesterday. *E. B. Howe*

Never do today what you can put off till tomorrow. *Punch, 1849*

Never put off till tomorrow what can be avoided altogether.

Never put off till tomorrow what you can put off for good.

Never put off till tomorrow what you can put off today.

Never put off till tomorrow what you can put over today. *Henny Youngman*

Never put off until today what you can do yesterday. *e. e. cummings*

Never put off until tomorrow what your secretary can do today.

Never put off until tomorrow what you can manage to wriggle out of today. *Doug Larson*

One of the greatest labor-saving inventions of today is tomorrow. *Heard in Illinois*

One thing that's really good about procrastination is that you always have something planned for tomorrow.

Put not off till tomorrow what can be enjoyed today. *Josh Billings*

It takes two to make a QUARREL. 406 B.C., B-1924

. . . or to get married.

. . . only if you're an amateur.

. . . and one to take the blame.

. . . It takes two to make peace also. *S. MacLaren, Exposition Romans*

All it takes for an argument is two loud mouths and four deaf ears. *Peter's Almanac*

It takes in reality only one to make a quarrel. It is useless for the sheep to pass resolutions in favour of vegetarianism, while the wolf remains of a different opinion. *W. R. Inge, Outspoken Essays*

It takes two to tango. *Song popularized by Pearl Bailey*

Quarrels would not last so long if the fault were on only one side. *François de la Rochefoucauld, Maximes*

Women are dictators all, and I recommend to you this moral:
In real life it takes only one to make a quarrel.
Ogden Nash, I Never Even Suggested It

All the world is QUEER save thee and me, and even thou art a little queer.* Robert Owen (1771–1858)

. . . I'd admit my faults if I had any.

A man thinks everyone else is crazy but himself. *Heard in Ontario*

Half the world is nutty—the rest are squirrels. *Old postcard*

If other people would only be as reasonable as we are, what a heaven this earth would be. *L. de V. Matthewman*

I'm OK—You're OK. *Title of a 1969 self-help book by Thomas Anthony Harris*

Nature is a kind mother. She couldn't well afford to make us perfect, so she made us blind to our failings. *Josh Billings*

Neurotic means he is not as sensible as I am, and psychotic means he's even worse than my brother-in-law. *Karl Menninger*

Nothing so needs reforming as other people's habits. *Mark Twain*

One out of four people in this country is mentally imbalanced. Think of your three closest friends—if they seem okay, then you're the one. *Ann Landers*

The human race consists of the dangerously insane and such as are not. *Mark Twain, Notebook*

When we remember we are all mad, the mysteries of life disappear and life stands explained. *Mark Twain, Notebook*

Would it not be more economical for the governments to build asylums for the sane instead of the demented? *Kahlil Gibran*

You can see another's arse but not your own. *Japanese proverb*

Other people's lives look strange to me.
  I often wonder what they're all about.
The only view of any life that's clear,
  I think, is from the inside looking out.
Rebecca McCann

*Written when Owen was ending his partnership with William Allen.

There are two sides to every QUESTION.
Greek proverb

. . . that we're not interested in.

. . . Otherwise it would not be a question.

. . . Then how come there's only one answer?

. . . your own side, and the wrong side.

. . . and generally a third side that neither disputant is willing to concede. *Sydney J. Harris*

. . . Not always, warns Donald G. Smith, who admonishes parents that it's simply wrong to always order their kids to "stop that fighting!" "There are times when one child is simply defending his rights and damned well should be fighting."

All religions issue Bibles against Satan, and say the most injurious things against him, but we never hear his side. *Mark Twain*

He who hears one side only, hears nothing. *Thomas Smollett, 1750*

He who knows only his own side of the case knows little of that. *John Stuart Mill, On Liberty*

Hear the other side. *Latin proverb*

Quarrels would not last long if the fault were on one side only. *François de la Rochefoucauld*

The only people who listen to both sides of a family quarrel are the next-door neighbors. *Ligourian*

The opposite side has its opposite side. *Japanese proverb*

The really difficult moral issues arise, not from a confrontation of good and evil, but from a collision between two goods. *Irving Kristol*

There are also two sides to a sheet of flypaper and it makes a big difference to the fly which side he chooses.

There are three sides to every story—his, yours, and the truth. *Harry Hirschfield*

There's two sides to every flapjack. *Ozark variation*

If your devoted mother suggests that you will
    some day be rich and famous, why perish
    the suggestion
If you are afflicted with the suspicion that
    there are two sides to every question.
Ogden Nash

See also Fair PLAY.

Ask me no QUESTIONS, I'll tell you no lies. *Oliver Goldsmith, She Stoops to Conquer, 1773*

Don't ask silly questions, if you don't want foolish answers. *C. Ryland, 1934; BJW-519*

Never cross-question your husband about what kept him so late; he might discover how easy it is to lie. *Mignon McLaughlin*

Questioning is not a mode of conversation among gentlemen. *Samuel Johnson*

Asking questions
    Of the youthful
Teaches them
    To be untruthful
Angela Cypher

When inquisitive people
    Ask questions of you,
No law says your answers
    Must strictly be true.
Robert Dennis

Don't ask too many QUESTIONS.

Search not too curiously lest you find trouble. *1659, Howell*

QUIT while you're ahead.

Quit when you're behind.

The RACE is not to the swift, nor the battle to the strong . . . but time and chance happen to them all. *Ecclesiastes 9:11*

A man may *plan* as much as he wants to, but nothing of consequence is likely to come of it until the magician *circumstance* steps in and takes the matter off his hands. *Mark Twain, The Turning Point of My Life, What Is Man? and Other Essays*

After thirty-nine years of teaching the art of acting, and seeing a handful of her students rise to Hollywood stardom, or fame on Broadway, Stella Adler reflected that "fame is a matter of luck." She told a reporter, "I can't say who my favorites are, because they won the prize by accident. There are as many talented people who are not known, because the accident didn't happen, as there are ac-

tors who are known, who are God's favorites." (*New York Times*, Sept. 4, 1988)

Circumstances make man, not man circumstances. *Mark Twain, Notebook*

Good luck beats early rising. *Irish proverb*

It may be that the race is not always to the swift, or the battle to the strong, but that's the way to bet. *Damon Runyon*

Objective consideration of contemporary phenomena compels the conclusion that success or failure in competitive activities exhibits no tendency to be commensurate with innate capacity, but that a considerable element of the unpredictable must invariably be taken into account. George Orwell, satirical rephrasing of the biblical passage into "mod English," in *Politics and the English Language*

Some rise by sin, and some by virtue fall. *Shakespeare, Measure for Measure 3.1.38*

The battle is not to the strong alone; it is to the vigilant, the active, the brave. *Patrick Henry*

The battle is not to the strong, but to the tricky.

The lopsided man runs the fastest along the little side-hills of success. *Frank Moore Colby*

Full many a gem of purest ray serene
The dark unfathomed caves of ocean bear;
Full many a flower is born to blush unseen,
And waste its sweetness on the desert air.
Thomas Gray, An Elegy Written in a Country Church Yard

A few can touch the magic string,
    And noisy Fame is proud to win them;
Alas for those that never sing,
    And die with all their music in them.
Oliver Wendell Holmes, The Voiceless

See also There but for the grace of GOD go I.

Into each life some RAIN must fall. **Henry Wadsworth Longfellow, The Rainy Day, 1842**

. . . unless you never leave Las Vegas at all. *L. L. Levinson*

. . . usually on week-ends. *Sylvia Strum Bremer*

No man shall pass his whole life free from misfortune. *Aeschylus, The Libation-Bearers*

The RAIN falls on the just and on the unjust alike.*

. . . but if I had the management of such affairs I would rain softly and sweetly on the just, but if I caught a sample of the unjust outdoors I would drown him. *Mark Twain, My Father, Mark Twain, by Clara Clemens*

Robbers are like rain, they fall on the just and the unjust. *Josh Billings, 1865*

The sun shines upon all alike. *16th century*

The rain it raineth on the just
    And also on the unjust fella;
But chiefly on the just because
    The unjust steals the just's umbrella.
Lord Bowen, The Rain It Raineth

*He maketh his sun to rise on the evil and on the good, and sendeth rain on the just and on the unjust. *Matthew 5:45*

When it RAINS, it pours. A.D.390, B-1596, and Morton salt slogan since 1914.

It never rains but it pours. *1771, B-1931*

Misfortune and twins hardly ever come singly. *Josh Billings, 1865*

Trouble comes double.

Trouble comes in bunches, like bananas.

When sorrows come, they come not single spies,
But in battalions!
Shakespeare, Hamlet 4.5.78

Tomato ketchup.
If you do not shake the bottle,
None'll come and then a lot'll.

RANK has its privileges.

Don't say yes until I finish talking. *Hollywood producer Darryl Zanuck, to his fawning subordinates*

Private Berman, you stand on your rights as a private, and I'll stand on my rights as a captain. *Memorable advice of his commanding officer, from the editor's experience in World War II*

I'd like to live like a poor man with lots of money. *Pablo Picasso*

It is not every man that can afford to wear a shabby coat. *Charles Colton*

The priest never waits his turn at the mill. *Russian proverb*

A RAT can sink a ship.

Don't burn the barn to destroy the RATS.

Don't throw out the baby with the bathwater. *1853, M-33*

Don't use a cannon to shoot a sparrow. *Chinese proverb*

Do not remove a fly from your friend's forehead with a hatchet. *Chinese proverb*

Often a limb must be amputated to save a life; but a life is never wisely given to save a limb. *Abraham Lincoln, letter to Albert G. Hodges, 1864*

One does not moisten a stamp with the Niagara Falls. *Submitted by P.W.R. to the Meaningless Proverbs contest in the New Statesman, 1969*

Never spit in a man's face unless his mustache is on fire. *Ted Nowicki*

The dog had fleas so the dog was chloroformed.

RATS desert a sinking ship. *1579, WM-499*

. . . and so do people, if they have any sense.

A man's REACH should exceed his grasp, Or what's a heaven for?
Robert Browning, Andrea del Sarto, 1855

A man's reach should exceed his grasp, or what's a metaphor? *Marshall McLuhan*

See also Hitch your wagon to a STAR; Reach for the STARS.

READING maketh a full man.*

A house without books is like a room without windows. *Heard in New York and North Carolina*

Books may well be the only true magic. *Alice Hoffman, New York Times*

Some read to think,—these are rare; some to write,—these are common; some to talk,—and these form the great majority. *Charles Colton, 1820*

The library is the temple of learning, and learning has liberated more people than all the wars in history. *Carl Rowan*

Thinking maketh a full man;
Drinking maketh a man full.
Old postcard

You say that you have gone all through
The book; but has it gone through you?
Arthur Guiterman

*Reading makes a full man, conference a ready man, and writing an exact man. *Francis Bacon (1561–1626)*

There's always a good REASON, and then there's the real reason.*

Criticism is prejudice made plausible. *H. L. Mencken*

Fishing, with me, has always been an excuse to drink in the daytime. *Jimmy Cannon*

Human beings are the only creatures who are able to behave irrationally in the name of reason. *Ashley Montagu, New York Times, Sept. 30, 1975*

Idealism is the noble toga that political gentlemen drape over their will to power. *Aldous Huxley*

Most of our so-called reasoning consists in finding arguments for going on believing as we already do. *James Harvey Robinson, The Mind in the Making*

Poke any saint deeply enough, and you touch self-interest. *Irving Wallace*

The urge to save humanity is almost only a false-front for the urge to rule. *H. L. Mencken, Minority Report*

To act from pure benevolence is not possible for finite beings. Human benevolence is mingled with vanity, interest, or some other motive. *James Boswell, The Life of Samuel Johnson*

To rationalize is to make rational lies.

*Does J. P. Morgan deserve credit for phrasing this idea? *Reader's Digest,* June 1940, quotes Morgan as saying, "A man always has two reasons for doing anything—a good reason and the real reason."

See also It all DEPENDS on whose ox is gored; The HEART has its reasons.

Yours is not to REASON why; yours is but to do or die.*

Don't ask why; just memorize it.

It is much easier to do and die than it is to reason why. *G. A. Studdert-Kennedy, as quoted in Reader's Digest, Sept. 1937*

You'll understand when you're older.

Yours is not to reason why; yours is but to take it and run.

*Someone had blundered:
Theirs not to make reply,
Theirs not to reason why,
Theirs but to do and die.
Alfred, Lord Tennyson (1809–92), The Charge of the Light Brigade

Better RED than dead.

It is better to be a live jackal than a dead lion—for jackals, not men. *Sidney Hook*

It is better to die on your feet than to live on your knees. *Delores Ibarruri, stirring orator of the Spanish Civil War*

RELIGION is the opiate of the people.*
Karl Marx, 1884

A man who has never had religion before no more grows religious when he is sick, than a man who has never learnt figures can count when he has need of calculation. *Samuel Johnson, 1783*

Communism is the opiate of the intellectuals. *Clare Boothe Luce*

Formal religion was organized for slaves: it offered them consolation which earth did not provide. *Elbert Hubbard, 1908*

If men are so wicked with religion, what would they be without it? *Benjamin Franklin*

If religion is the opiate of the masses, jargon is the opiate of the intellectuals. *Leo Rosten*

In Russia religion is the opium of the people; in China opium is the religion of the people. *Edgar Snow*

Labor is the capital of our workingmen. *Grover Cleveland*

Men never do evil so completely and cheerfully as when they do it from religious conviction. *Blaise Pascal, 1660*

Most religious teachers spend their time trying to prove the unproven by the unprovable. *Oscar Wilde*

Politics is the chloroform of the Irish people. *P. W. Joyce*

Reality is just there for people who can't face drugs.

Religion is a disease, but it is a noble disease. *Heracleitus*

Religion is a morality touched by emotion. *Matthew Arnold, Literature and Dogma*

Religion is a pill best swallowed without chewing.

Religion is regarded by the common people as true, by the wise as false, and by the rulers as useful. *Seneca*

Religion is the masterpiece of the art of animal training, for it trains people as to how they shall think. *Arthur Schopenhauer*

Religion is what keeps the poor from murdering the rich. *Napoleon*

Religions are such stuff as dreams are made of. *H. G. Wells, The Happy Turning*

Theatre is the aspirin of the middle classes. *Wolcott Gibbs, More in Sorrow*

There is something feeble and a little contemptible about a man who cannot face the perils of life without the help of comfortable myths. *Bertrand Russell, 1954*

To attempt to be religious without practicing a specific religion is as possible as attempting to speak without a specific language. *George Santayana, quoted in Nine Questions People Ask About Judaism, by Prager and Telushkin*

Today, sports are the opium of the people, television is the opiate of the poor, travel is the opiate of the rich, and opium is the religion of the young. *Sydney J. Harris*

Where it is a duty to worship the sun it is pretty sure to be a crime to examine the laws of heat. *John Morley*

*Religion is the sign of the oppressed creature, the sentiment of a heartless world, and the soul of soulless conditions. It is the opium of the people." This characterization of religion was popularized by Marx, but did not originate with him, Keyes notes (K-181).

The REMEDY is often worse than the disease.

See Don't cut off your NOSE to spite your face.

Those who cannot REMEMBER the past are condemned to repeat it. *George Santayana*

He who does not remember the past forgets where he parked his car.

History, in illuminating the past, illuminates the present, and in illuminating the present, illuminates the future. *Benjamin N. Cardozo, Nature of the Judicial Process*

If we do not learn from history, we shall be compelled to relive it. True. But if we do not change the future, we shall be compelled to endure it. And that could be worse. *Alvin Toffler*

Those who don't study the past will repeat its errors; those who do study it will find other ways to err. *Charles Wolf, Jr., Wall Street Journal, 1976*

See also HISTORY is bunk; HISTORY repeats itself.

When I am right, no one REMEMBERS; when I am wrong, no one forgets.

A good executive takes the blame upon himself when things go wrong and gives the credit to his staff when things go right. *Richard Needham*

When I did well, I heard it never;
When I did ill, I heard it ever.
1721, Kelly

Living well is the best REVENGE.* 1578, T-389

The best revenge is to live long enough to be a problem to your children.

The greatest mischief you can do the envious is to do well. *1732, T-389*

*Title of a 1971 book by Calvin Tomkins, about Gerald and Sara Murphy, American expatriates in Paris after World War I. Sara Murphy popularized (and is wrongly believed to have originated) this saying.

See also CARPE diem; EAT, drink and be merry for tomorrow we die; ENJOY yourself . . . ; You only LIVE once.

REVENGE is sweet. *Greek proverb*

. . . but not when you're on the receiving end.

. . . to think about, but stupid to do.

To forget a wrong is best revenge. *1639, Clarke*

No revenge is more honorable than one not taken. *Spanish proverb*

Revenge is a dish best served cold.

Revenge is often like biting a dog because the dog bit you. *Austin O'Malley*

There is no passion in the human heart that promises so much and pays so little as revenge. *Josh Billings*

There's nothing like the sight of an old enemy down on his luck. *Euripedes*

Treacle is sweet, but revenge is sweeter. *J. V. Turner, 1930; BJW-530*

When a man steals your wife, there is no better revenge than to let him keep her. *Sacha Guitry, Elle et Toi*

REVERENCE for life.*

*Reverence for life affords me my fundamental principle of morality, namely that good consists in maintaining, assisting and enhancing life, and that to destroy, to harm or to hinder life is evil. *Albert Schweitzer, 1929*

See Be kind to ANIMALS.

The RICH get richer, and the poor get children.

He that hath plenty of goods shall have more. *1546, Heywood*

One half of the world must sweat and groan that the other half may dream. *Henry Wadsworth Longfellow*

The rich celebrate the feasts and the poor observe the fasts. *Voltaire*

The Rich Get Richer, and the Poor Write Grant Proposals. *Title of a publication of the Citizen Involvement Training Project, Amherst, Massachusetts*

The rich man has his ice in the summer and the poor man gets his in the winter. *Scottish proverb*

The rich own the land and the poor own the
    water.
The rich get richer and the poor get children.
The rich have baby napkins, and the poor
    have diapers.
The big houses have small families and the
    small houses have big families.
Why did Death take the poor man's cow and
    the rich man's child?
Carl Sandburg

It's the same the whole world over,
It's the poor what gets the blame,
It's the rich what gets the pleasure,
Isn't it a blooming shame?

If two RIDE on a horse, one must ride behind. *Shakespeare, Much Ado About Nothing 3.5.34, ca. 1598*

Be sure you're RIGHT, then go ahead. *David Crockett, motto during War of 1812*

. . . In case of doubt, go ahead anyway. *Josh Billings*

. . . but don't arbitrate. *Will Rogers*

Be sure you're right and then keep still about it.

I argue this way: if a man is right he can't be too radical, if he is wrong he can't be too conservative. *Josh Billings, 1865*

If the thing a man wants to do is right, he goes ahead and does it. If it is wrong, he consults an attorney. *Old postcard*

In war you don't have to be nice, you only have to be right. *Winston Churchill*

It's fine to believe in ourselves, but we mustn't be too easily convinced. *Burton Hillis, as quoted in Reader's Digest, Aug. 1960*

Measure twice, cut once.

RIGHT makes might.

. . . if you are the biggest. *Old postcard*

Brute force without wisdom falls by its own weight. *Horace, Odes*

Right may be might; but Wrong is often mightier. *L. De V. Matthewman*

The arm of the moral universe is long, but it bends toward justice. *Martin Luther King, Jr.*

The best way I know to win an argument is to start by being in the right. *Lord Hailsham*

Might and Right are always fighting.
In our youth it seems exciting.
Right is always nearly winning.
Might can hardly keep from grinning.
Clarence Day, Right and Might

See also MIGHT makes right.

Be not RIGHTEOUS overmuch. *Ecclesiastes 7:16*

Soon RIPE, soon rotten. *Latin proverb*

Early ripe, early rotten.

Young saint, old devil. *1493, T-580*

A prodigy at five
A gen-i-us at seven,
A meteor at eight
And senile at eleven.
E. Y. Harburg

It's a long ROAD that has no turning. *1659, Howell*

It's a long stovepipe that has no elbow. *New England proverb*

It's a long worm that has no turning. *P. C. Wren, 1941*

It's a short road that somebody hasn't written a song about.

It's a strong stomach that has no turning. *Oliver Herford*

It's a wrong road that has no turning.

All ROADS lead to Rome. *1175, B-2003*

. . . and the same roads lead away from Rome.

All detours lead to swearing.

All roads lead to rum. *W. C. Fields*

Don't ROB Peter to pay Paul. *1514, B-1783*

Spare the ROD and spoil the child.* *1639, Clarke*

A pat on the back will build character if applied low enough, hard enough, and often enough. *Heard in Colorado*

A wise parent knows which side his brood should be battered on.

Beat your child once a day. If you don't know why, the child does. *Chinese proverb*

Better a snotty child than his nose wiped off. *1640, Herbert*

Children are never too tender to be whipped. Like tough beefsteaks, the more you beat them, the more tender they become. *Edgar Allan Poe*

Do not threaten a child; either punish or forgive him. *Gemara*

Love your children with your heart, but train them with your hands. *Ukrainian proverb*

Many a man spanks his children for things his own father should have spanked out of him. *Don Marquis*

My father never raised a hand to any one of his children except in self-defense. *Fred Allen*

Permissiveness is the principle of treating children as if they were adults; and the tactic of making sure they never reach that stage. *Thomas Szasz, The Second Sin*

Spare the rod and save the child. *Elbert Hubbard*

The rod and reproof give wisdom, but a child left to himself bringeth his mother to shame. *Proverbs 29:15*

The only persons permitted to punish children should be persons who love them. *Marlene Dietrich*

Speak roughly to your little boy,
    And beat him when he sneezes:

He only does it to annoy,
  Because he knows it teases.
Lewis Carroll, Alice in Wonderland

*He that spareth the rod hateth his son.
  Proverbs 14:10

ROME was not built in a day. *Latin proverb*

Rome Was Not Burnt in a Day. *Title of a collection of sayings by Leo Rosten*

When in ROME, do as the Romans do. *Latin proverb*

. . . and think as the Romans think.

Every land has its own law. *Scottish proverb*

Fools invent fashion, and wise men . . . follow them. *Samuel Butler, Prose Observations*

Speak the language of the company that you are in; speak it purely, and unlarded with any other. *Lord Chesterfield, Letters, Feb. 22, 1748*

To be utterly reasonable in an unreasonable world is itself a form of insanity. *Sydney J. Harris*

When in Rome—one must be romantic. *E. D. Biggers, 1925; BJW-536*

See also Other DAYS, other ways.

There's always ROOM at the top.*

. . . and at the bottom.

. . . but there's no room to sit down.

. . . as the man said who looked for the gas leak with a candle. *B. Flynn, 1937; BJW-536*

America is where a young man can start at the bottom and work his way into a hole. *Wall Street Journal*

There's room at the top for the fellow with brains,
With talent and tact, if he's got 'em;
But I must confess, my experience proves,
There's also some room at the bottom.
S.S., Wall Street Journal

*So answered Daniel Webster (1782–1852) when advised not to become a lawyer because the field was overcrowded. See also O-193.

See also It's LONELY at the top.

ROOT, hog, or die. *Davy Crockett, 1834*

Don't speak of a ROPE in a house where there has been a hanging. *1599, WM- 516*

Don't talk of halters in a hanged man's house.

Give a man enough ROPE and he'll hang himself. *1639, Clarke*

Give a child enough rope and he'll trip you up. *Peter's Almanac*

Give a housewife enough rope and she'll make macramé hangers for all her houseplants.

Give a thief enough rope and he'll tie up the night watchman.

Give a man enough rope and he'll lead a horse to water. *R. Penny, 1937; BJW-537*

Give an enterprising fellow enough rope and he'll go into the rope business.

Give some men a free hand and they'll stick it right in your pocket. *Henny Youngman*

If you give a man enough rope, he'll hang you. *Leo Rosten*

Let the wicked fall into their own nets. *Psalms 141:10*

A ROSE by any other name would smell as sweet.*

. . . What name did you have in mind?

A chrysanthemum by any other name would be easier to spell. *William J. Johnston*

A hamburger by any other name costs twice as much.

A rose by any other name would smell.

Rose is a rose is a rose is a rose. *Gertrude Stein, Sacred Emily.* Popularly misquoted as "A rose is a rose . . ."

I used to think I was poor. Then they told me I wasn't poor, I was needy. They told me it was self-defeating to think of myself as needy, I was deprived. Then they told me underprivileged was overused. I was disadvantaged. I still don't have a dime. But I have a great vocabulary. *Jules Feiffer, cartoon, 1965*

*What's in a name? That which we call a rose By any other name would smell as sweet. *Shakespeare, Romeo and Juliet 1.2.44, ca. 1594*

Never the ROSE without the thorn. 300 B.C., B-2009

. . . not to mention black spot, red spiders, rose leaf hoppers, sawflies, rose chafers, Japanese beetles, leaf-cutter bees, rose midges, aphids, thrips, chlorosis and mildew. Wouldn't you rather grow marigolds?

All brew hath its dregs.

Evermore in the world is this balance of beauty and disgust, magnificence and rats. *Ralph Waldo Emerson, 1860*

Every gain has its loss.

Every good has its evil.

Every joy has its sorrow.

Every path hath a puddle. *George Herbert, 1640*

Every pleasure has its pain. *1591, O2-179*

Every sweet has its sour; every evil its good. *Ralph Waldo Emerson, Compensation*

Good for the Liver may be bad for the Spleen. *Thomas Fuller, 1732*

Honey is sweet but the bee stings.

If we're going to see a rainbow, we've got to stand some rain. *Motto under his glass desktop, according to President George Bush, Oct. 1991*

No action without its side effects. *Barry Commoner*

No garden without weeds *1732, Fuller*

No gold without some dross. *1611, Cotgrave*

No land without stones, no meat without bones.

Pleasure has a sting in its tail. *17th century*

Religion has two children, love and hatred. *Russian proverb*

Roses have thorns, and silver fountains mud. *Shakespeare, Sonnet 35*

The penalty of success is to be bored by people who used to snub you. *Nancy Astor*

The rose has thorns only for those who would pluck it. *Chinese proverb*

The unintended consequences of human actions. The black underclass is twice the victim of unintended consequences. (1) A federal welfare system made AFDC (Aid for Dependent Children) benefits in combination with food stamps of greater value than the minimum wage; discouraging education, marriage, and job-holding; and encouraging single parenthood and welfare as a way of life. (2) Civil rights legislation gave job and housing opportunities to better educated and more stable African American families, taking them to the suburbs and emptying the urban ghettos of most of its leadership, moral and economic strength. *Charles A. Murray, Losing Ground, paraphrased*

The way I see it, if you want the rainbow, you gotta put up with the rain. *Dolly Parton*

There will be ruts in the smoothest road. *Walter Scott, 1821*

You cannot pluck roses without fear of
 thorns,
Nor enjoy a fair wife without danger of horns.
Poor Richard's Almanac, 1734

You never see anything great which is not, at the same time, horrible in some respect. The genius of Einstein leads to Hiroshima. *Pablo Picasso, 1964*

Every day has its night, and every weal its woe. *Danish proverb*

He who wishes a fire must put up with the smoke. *Italian proverb*

In every pomegranate a decayed pip. *Latin proverb*

No garden without its weeds. *1732, Fuller*

There never was a good town but had a mire at one end of it. *Scottish proverb*

Wherever there is . . . wine, there is intoxication. *Sadi, 1258*

This world we are a-livin' in
 Is mighty hard to beat;
You get a thorn with every rose
 But ain't the roses sweet!
Frank L. Stanton, This World

Mother, Mother,
Tell me please,
Did God who gave us flowers and trees,
Also provide the allergies?
E. Y. Harburg

Technology replaces obvious problems with more insidious ones. That is the theme of the 1996 book by Edward Tenner, *Why Things Bite Back: Technology and the Revenge of Unintended Consequences*. For example: air-conditioned subway trains raise the temperature of platforms by as much as 10 degrees F; some computer users get painful carpal tunnel syndrome; every seventeenth hospital patient catches an infection at the hospital.

Gather ye ROSEBUDS while ye may.*

Gathering rosebuds while I may,
To hoard against a barren day.
Ogden Nash, Remembrance of Things to Come

*Gather ye Rose-buds while ye may,
 Old Time is still a flying:
 And this same flower that smiles to day
 To morrow will be dying.
 Robert Herrick, Heperides, 1648

See also CARPE diem.

Buds will be ROSES and kittens cats.

The trouble with a kitten is that
Eventually it becomes a cat.
Ogden Nash

It's a bad RULE that won't work both ways.
1837, WM-518

RULES were made to be broken.

. . . then why were they made?

Any fool can make a rule and every fool will
mind it. *Henry David Thoreau*

See also PROMISES and pie crust are made
to be broken.

**Scratch a RUSSIAN and you'll find a Tar-
tar.** *Attributed to Joseph de Maistre, to
Napoleon, and to Prince de Ligne*

Scratch a Christian and you'll find the
pagan—spoiled. *Israel Zangwill, Children of
the Ghetto*

Scratch a lover, and find a foe. *Dorothy
Parker, Enough Rope*

Remember the SABBATH to keep it holy. *Exodus 20:8*

Keep the weekdays honest and it will be easy to keep the Sabbath holy. *Heard in Minnesota*

Remember the weekday to keep it holy. *Elbert Hubbard*

The sabbath was made for man, and not man for the sabbath. *Mark 2:27*

Better be SAFE than sorry. *1837, O-15*

There's nothing like being on the safe side.

Safety first. *

Industrial Council for Industrial Safety, 1915
  *Motto of the railway industry, whose employees were indoctrinated that "the safety of the public is to be the first consideration of the staff" (1925, B-2023).

There is SAFETY in numbers. * *1914, O-196*

. . . mused the student as he changed his major from philosophy to accounting.

. . . but the bigger the flock, the more inviting a target it makes.

. . . seems to be the motto of bachelors who always have several lady friends.

One of Thurber's "Fables for Our Times" tells of a fly who landed on flypaper, thinking it was safe because so many other flies were there. Thurber moralizes: "There is no safety in numbers, or in anything else."

*An ancient idea, expressed in Proverbs 24:6, "In the multitude of counsellors there is safety," and in Juvenal's *Satires* (ca. 120), "Number is their defense."

See also MAN is a social animal.

Least SAID, soonest mended. *1460, O-131*

See SILENCE is golden.

Get thee behind me, SATAN. *Matthew 16:23*

As I grow older I find that I don't have to avoid temptation any longer—now temptation avoids me. *Henny Youngman*

I can resist everything except temptation. *Oscar Wilde*

It is good to be without vice, but it is not good to be without temptations. *Walter Bagehot*

Keep my hands from picking and stealing. *The Book of Common Prayer*

Lead us not into temptation; tell us where it is, and we'll find it. *Captain Billy's Whiz Bang, Aug. 1922*

Most people want to be delivered from temptation but would like it to keep in touch. *Robert Orben*

Strength is the capacity to break a chocolate bar into four pieces with your bare hands—and then eat just one of the pieces. *J. Vorst*

The Devil Is a Liar. *Motto displayed in housing project apartment, Chicago, 1993*

The devil tempts but doesn't force. *Guyanese proverb*

The only way to get rid of a temptation is to yield to it. *Oscar Wilde, The Picture of Dorian Gray*

There are several good protections against temptation, but the surest is cowardice. *Mark Twain*

Those who flee temptation usually leave a forwarding address. *Lane Olinghouse*

Wherever God erects a house of prayer,
The Devil always builds a chapel there;
And 'twill be found upon examination,
The latter has the largest congregation.
Daniel Defoe, The True-Born Englishman

Satan trembles when he sees
The weakest saint upon his knees.

You're never SATISFIED.

A celebrity is a person who works hard all his life to become well known, then wears dark glasses to avoid being recognized. *Fred Allen, Treadmill to Oblivion*

He that loveth silver shall not be satisfied with silver, nor he that loveth abundance, with increase. *Ecclesiastes 5:10*

Hell and destruction are never full; so the eyes of man are never satisfied. *Proverbs 27:20*

It's when you're safe at home that you wish you were having an adventure. When you're having an adventure you wish you were safe at home. *Thornton Wilder, The Matchmaker*

Marriage is like a cage; one sees the birds outside desperate to get in, and those inside equally desperate to get out. *Michel de Montaigne*

Much would have more. *1597, T-483*

Nothing is enough to the man for whom enough is too little. *Epicurus*

Of all the people in the world, those who want the most are those who have the most. *David Grayson*

Only madmen and fools are pleased with themselves; no wise man is good enough for his own satisfaction. *Benjamin Whichcote*

The dead are content. *Tunisian proverb*

The miser is always in want. *Horace*

The more you eat, the more you want. *Advertising slogan* popularized during the 1930s by Eatmore chocolates

The sea complains of want of water. *English proverb*

The trouble ain't that there is too many fools, but that the lightning ain't distributed right. *Mark Twain*

There's something in every atheist, itching to believe, and something in every believer, itching to doubt. *Mignon McLaughlin*

To be discontented with the divine discontent, and to be ashamed with the noble shame, is the very germ and first upgrowth of virtue. *Charles Kingsley, Health and Education*

Unrest of spirit is a mark of life. *Karl Menninger, This Week, Oct. 16, 1958*

What a miserable thing life is: you're living in clover, only the clover isn't good enough. *Bertolt Brecht*

When I first started working, I used to dream of the day when I might be earning the salary I'm starving on now.

Who is rich? He that is content. Who is that? Nobody.

Youth is not enough. And love is not enough. And success is not enough. And, if we could achieve it, enough would not be enough. *Mignon McLaughlin*

When I was planned,
And spawned and hatched,
My heart and mind
Were badly matched.

My heart wants roots,
My mind wants wings
I cannot bear
Their bickerings.

Oh, Lord, who wrought
This schizoid mess,
Did you forget
Togetherness?

Must I now pay
An analyst
To teach them how
To co-exist?
E. Y. Harburg

To men of greed, however great their store,
"Enough" is always "Just a little more."
Arthur Guiterman

The cat at the screen door knows
    What all new lovers doubt;
Those who are out want in,
    And those who are in want out.
Paul Breslin, Marriage

As a rule, man is a fool.
When it's hot, he wants it cool;
When it's cool, he wants it hot,
Always wanting what is not.

See also ENOUGH is enough.

SAY it right.

A word fitly spoken is like apples of gold in pictures [rather, ornaments? vessels? bowls?] of silver. *Proverbs 25:11.* A favorite saying of Abraham Lincoln.

Define your terms.

Speak the speech, I pray you . . . trippingly on the tongue. *Shakespeare, Hamlet 3.2.1*

The difference between the right word and the almost right word is the difference between lightning and the lightning bug. *Mark Twain*

He jests at SCARS that never felt a wound. *Shakespeare, Romeo and Juliet 2.2.1, ca. 1594*

See Great SPIRIT . . .

The best-laid SCHEMES o' mice and men gang aft agley. *Robert Burns, To a Mouse, 1785*

When I was a young man I vowed never to marry until I found the ideal woman. Well, I found her but, alas, she was waiting for the ideal man. *Robert Schuman*

See also There's many a SLIP 'twixt cup and lip.

Don't tell tales out of SCHOOL. *1530, WM-580*

They came to SCOFF and stayed to pray.*

They came to cough and remained to spray. *Oliver Herford, of patients in the waiting room of a throat specialist*

They came to jeer but remained to whitewash. *Mark Twain, Tom Sawyer*

*Fools, who came to scoff, remained to pray. *Oliver Goldsmith, Deserted Village, 1770*

You SCRATCH my back and I'll scratch yours. *500 B.C., B-2045*

You roll my log, and I'll roll yours. *Seneca, Apocolocyntosis, ca. A.D. 50; M-1319*

"Do unto others as you would have them do unto you." Praise in others what you would like to have praised in you—is the very sublimity of blowing your own trumpet. *Josh Billings*

See also One HAND washes the other.

Two can keep a SECRET if one of them is dead. *1558, WM-530*

. . . [and] three may keep a secret if two of them are dead. *1546, O- 224*

A secret shared is no secret. *1929, WM-528*

Gossip that is traveling around loose is a lie, or it will be, by the time it has changed hands once more. *Josh Billings*

If you want to keep a secret, keep it to yourself. *Geoffrey Chaucer, 1386*

The only secret a woman can keep is that of her age. *1732, Fuller*

The only way to keep a secret is to forget it. *Old postcard*

The more you live, the more you SEE; the more you see, the more you know.

See EXPERIENCE is the best teacher.

What you SEE is what you get.*

It is just as is and ain't no is-er. *Heard in Kentucky, Michigan, and Tennessee*

Ah caint be no hypocrite;
What you see is what you git.
Country song

*In computer technology, programs differ in how faithfully the monitor image matches the printed (hard copy) image. Programs in which the match is good are known by the acronym "wysiwyg" (What you see is what you get), pronounced *wizzy-wig*.

SEEING is believing. *1609, WM-530*

. . . but don't bet on another man's game. *Old postcard*

. . . but feeling's the truth. *1732, Fuller*

. . . but feeling is knowing.

. . . the most fallacious of all proverbs. It should be reversed. Believing is seeing. The eye does not control the mind. The mind controls the eye. *R. A. J. Walling*

"I heard" is not as good as "I saw." *Chinese proverb*

I wouldn't have seen it if I hadn't believed it. © *Ashleigh Brilliant*

It is only with the heart that one can see rightly; what is essential is invisible to the eye. *Antoine de Saint-Exupéry, The Little Prince*

One eyewitness is better than ten earwitnesses. *1519, T-197*

Seeing is deceiving. It's eating that's believing. *James Thurber, Further Fables for Our Times*

The eyes believe themselves; the ears believe other people. *German proverb*

The wise man speaks of what he sees, the idiot of what he hears. *Arabic proverb*

Why believe, when you've got eyes? *Yiddish proverb*

Words are only painted fire; a look is the fire itself. *Mark Twain, A Connecticut Yankee in King Arthur's Court*

I might not this believe
Without the sensible and true avouch
Of mine own eyes.
Shakespeare, Hamlet 1.1.56

Some things have to be believed
To be seen.
Ralph Hodgson, The Skylark and Other Poems

No, seeing's not believing
As some old stories say.
There are some folks that I don't believe,
Though I see them every day.

See also I'm from MISSOURI . . . ; One PICTURE is worth a thousand words.

SEEK and ye shall find. *Matthew 7:7*

. . . out otherwise.

Look for the ridiculous in everything and you will find it. *Jules Renard, Journal*

Seek and ye shall find that a lot of other people are looking for the same thing.

Sneak and ye shall find.

See also I'm from MISSOURI . . .

SELF-LOVE is better than self-hate.*

Don't belittle yourself—your friends will do it for you.

Every man has a right to be conceited until he is successful. *Benjamin Disraeli, Young Duke*

He who is his own friend is a friend to all men. *Seneca*

I have never seen a more lucid, better balanced, mad mind than mine. *Vladimir Nabokov*

If you are all wrapped up in yourself, you are overdressed.

It may be called the Master Passion, the hunger for self-approval. *Mark Twain*

To myself, without whose inspired and tireless efforts this book would not have been possible. *Dedication of book by Al Jaffee*

Many a man is proud of his father and mother because they are the parents of such a wonderful person.

Of all my wife's relations I like myself the best. *Joe Cook*

Place a high value on yourself and then prove that you are worth it. *Thomas Dreier*

Self-love is a cup without any bottom; you might pour all the great lakes into it, and never fill it up. *Oliver Wendell Holmes*

Self-love is the greatest of all flatterers. *François de la Rochefoucauld*

The advantage of doing one's praising for oneself is that one can lay it on so thick and exactly in the right places. *Samuel Butler, The Way of All Flesh*

*Self-love, my liege, is not so vile a sin
  As self-neglecting.
Shakespeare, Henry V, 2.4.74, ca. 1598

SELF-PRAISE is no recommendation. *French proverb*

. . . but at least you know it's sincere.

A man who isn't his own worst critic is his own worst enemy. *Frank Tyger*

Conceit is God's gift to little men. *Bruce Barton*

Nature knows best; she hasn't arranged your anatomy so as to make it easy for you to pat yourself on the back.

Self-love is a mote in every man's eye. *1758, Ray*

Self Prays is no recommendation. *F. Scully, 1943; BJW-552*

Don't praise yourself, lest others doubt and
    grieve you;
Yet don't dispraise yourself—they might be-
    lieve you.
Arthur Guiterman

SELF-PRESERVATION is the first law of nature. * *1631, O-200*

. . . and exploitation is the second.

He who is no good for himself is no good for others.

Nature is man's enemy. If you don't believe this, try spending a night in the mountains without fire, shelter, or blankets, wrapped only in the arms of Mother Nature. If you survive the night you can consider yourself fortunate indeed. Nature's plan is to kill you. *Donald G. Smith*

Self-deception is the first law of human nature.

No man was ever yet so void of sense
As to debate the right of self-defence.
Daniel Defoe, 1701

*If a man by the terror of present death, be compelled to do a fact against the Law, he is totally Excused; because no Law can oblige a man to abandon his own preservation. *Thomas Hobbes, Leviathan, 1651*

See also HELP yourself; CHARITY begins at home; PADDLE your own canoe.

Don't take yourself too SERIOUSLY.

A man without mirth is like a wagon without springs. He is jolted disagreeably by every pebble in the road. *Henry Ward Beecher*

A sense of humor . . . is the ability to understand a joke and that the joke is oneself. *Clifton Fadiman*

A sense of humor reduces people and problems to their proper proportion. *Arnold Glasow*

Good humor is the suspenders that keep our working clothes on. *Heard in Minnesota*

Imagination was given to man to compensate him for what he is not; a sense of humor to console him for what he is. *Francis Bacon*

It is our responsibilities, not ourselves, that we should take seriously. *Peter Ustinov*

Life is far too important a thing ever to talk seriously about. *Oscar Wilde*

Nothing matters very much, and in the end nothing matters at all.

The more I live, the more I think that humor is the saving sense. *Jacob Riis*

Three things are needed for success: a backbone, a wishbone, and a funnybone.

See also A little NONSENSE now and then is relished by the best of men.

SHARE and share alike. *1611, Cotgrave*

. . . pleads the latecomer. "First come, first served," says he who got there first.

Bread is to be shared. Ptahhotep

All who joy would win must share it.

Happiness was born a twin. *Lord Byron*

See also Shared JOYS are doubled . . .

If you make yourself a SHEEP, you will be eaten by the wolf. *1651, Herbert*

All lay a load on the willing horse. *1546, Heywood*

Better to be pissed off than pissed on. *College graffiti*

He that makes himself an ass must not complain if men ride him. *1732, Fuller*

If you're naturally kind, you attract a lot of people you don't like. *William Feather*

Make yourself all honey and the flies will devour you. *Italian proverb*

Nobody can walk all over me unless I lie down first.

The man who does not demand his rights is buried alive. *Greek proverb*

Those who are willing to be walked upon will eventually become footpaths. *Donald G. Smith*

There are black SHEEP in every flock.

There are black sheep in the best of families.

If the SHOE fits, wear it.*

If the shoe fits:

   . . . try a size smaller.

   . . . it's lost its shape.

   . . . ask for it in another color. *Beryl Pfizer*

   . . . get another one just like it.

   . . . I buy it in every available color. *Emelda Marcos*

A West Texas small-town editor, with some space to fill, set up the Ten Commandments and ran them without comment. Seven people left town the next morning and another wrote, "Cancel my subscription; you're getting too personal."

*Perhaps a variant of the 17th-century English proverb "If the [fool's] cap fits, wear it."

Keep your SHOP, and your shop will keep you. 1605, O-124

Sell your goods at market price; keep it not for rats and mice. *Heard in Ontario*

The SHOW must go on.*

A professional is someone who can do his best work when he doesn't feel like it. *Allistair Cooke*

*According to *Variety* editor Abel Green, this saying was inherited by show business from the circus. When a mishap or injury occurred during a circus performance, the ringmaster ordered the band to keep playing; "The show must go on" to prevent panic and loss of lives and property.

SHROUDS have no pockets. *Italian proverb, O-203; also a Yiddish proverb*

The clergy takes theirs now; you get yours after you are dead. *Kin Hubbard*

Put up or SHUT UP. 1924, WM-492

See DO it now; FISH or cut bait; If you can't stand the HEAT get out of the kitchen.

Once bitten, twice SHY. 1484, F-139

See A burnt CHILD dreads fire; FOOL me once, shame on you . . .

SIC transit gloria mundi.* *Thomas à Kempis (1380–1417),* **Imitation of Christ**

Glory is fleeting, but obscurity is forever. *Napoleon*

*"So passes away the glory of the world."

Out of SIGHT, out of mind.* *Homer,* **Odyssey, 9th century B.C.**

Absence is the enemy of love. *Italian proverb*

Far from eye, far from heart. *13th century*

Long absent, soon forgotten. *1616, Draxe*

The heart may think it knows better: the senses know that absence blots people out. *Elizabeth Bowen, The Death of the Heart*

What the eye doesn't see, the heart doesn't grieve over. *1545, O-73*

*A proverb theme common to many languages, says Burton Stevenson (B-6).

See also ABSENCE makes the heart grow fonder.

Merely to SILENCE a man is not to persuade him. 1874, WM-402

You can kill a man but you can't kill an idea. *Medgar Evers*

SILENCE gives consent. *Latin proverb and axiom of Roman law; B- 2112*

Silence gives contempt.

Silence will not cure a disease. On the contrary, it will make it worse. *Leo Tolstoy*

When you are climbing a mountain, don't talk; silence gives ascent. *Robert J. Burdett*

SILENCE if golden. *

. . . but sometimes invisibility is golder. *Ogden Nash*

. . . Maybe that's why it's so rare.

. . . so shut up and listen.

. . . Sometimes it's just yellow.

. . . but I must say that some of the most discreet and dignified fools that I have ever met have been those who never ventured an opinion on any subject. *Josh Billings*

. . . [but] The best remedy for a dispute is to discuss it. *African proverb*

Take a tip from nature: ears aren't made to shut, but a mouth is.

Silence Is Deadly. *1977 ad urging people to speak up and not let their friends drive drunk*

A fool uttereth all his mind, but a wise man keepeth it in until afterwards. *Proverbs 29:11*

A man of no conversation should smoke. *Ralph Waldo Emerson*

A politician is a man who approaches every question with an open mouth. *Adlai Stevenson*

A silent mouth is sweet to hear. *Irish proverb*

A still tongue keeps a wise head. *1562, Heywood*

A wise head makes a closed mouth. *1678, Ray*

An inability to stay quiet is one of the most conspicuous failings of mankind. *Walter Bagehot*

An open ear and a closed mouth is the best known substitution for wisdom. *Heard in Utah*

As long as a word remains unspoken, you are its master; once you utter it, you are its slave. *Solomon ibn Gabirol, The Choice of Pearls*

As we must account for every idle word, so we must for every idle silence. *Benjamin Franklin, 1738*

As you go through life, you are going to have many opportunities to keep your mouth shut. Take advantage of all of them.

Better to remain silent and be thought a fool, than to speak out and remove all doubt. *Abraham Lincoln, ca. 1862*

Big mouth, small brain.

Blessed is the man who, having nothing to say, abstains from giving us wordly evidence of the fact. *George Eliot*

Breathe through your nose; it keeps the mouth shut.

Dignity is the quality that enables a man who says nothing, does nothing and knows nothing to command a great deal of respect. *John W. Raper, 1954*

Diplomacy: thinking twice before saying nothing.

Don't let your mouth say nothing your head don't understand. *Louis "Satchmo" Armstrong*

Don't talk about your neighbors: if your jaw needs exercise, chew gum. *Old postcard*

Even a fool, when he holdeth his peace, is counted wise. *Proverbs 17:28*

Fools live to regret their words, wise men to regret their silence. *Will Henry, as quoted in Reader's Digest, Feb. 1974*

Had the pheasant not screamed, it would not have been shot. *Japanese proverb*

He cannot speak well that cannot hold his tongue. *1732, Fuller*

He that hath knowledge spareth his words. *Proverbs 17:27*

He who says nothing never lies. *Italian proverb*

If A equals success, then the formula is A equals X plus Y plus Z. X is work. Y is play. Z is keep your mouth shut. *Albert Einstein*

If a man keeps his trap shut, the world will beat a path to his door. *Franklin P. Adams*

If people find your silences interesting, don't disillusion them. *Mignon McLaughlin*

If the bird hadn't sung, it wouldn't have been shot. *Japanese proverb*

If you can't say it out loud, keep your mouth shut. *Old postcard*

If you don't say it, you won't have to unsay it.

If you have to whisper it, better not to say it. *New England proverb*

If you keep your mouth shut you will never put your foot in it. *Austin O'Malley*

If you want to save face, keep the lower half shut. *Ann Landers*

If you wouldn't write it and sign it, don't say it.

In Maine we have a saying that there's no point in speaking unless you can improve on silence. *Edmund Muskie*

Instead of opening your mouth, open your eyes. *Turkish proverb*

It is better to keep your mouth shut and appear stupid than to open it and remove all doubt. *Mark Twain*

It is better to play with the ears than the tongue. *1611, OE-506*

It is even more damaging for a minister to say foolish things than to do them. *Cardinal de Retz, Memoirs*

Keep frowning: Some people may give you credit for thinking. *Wall Street Journal*

Keep your mouth shut and your eyes open. *1710, OE-332*

Look wise, say nothing, and grunt. Speech was given to conceal thought. *William Osler*

Nature has given us two ears but one mouth. *Benjamin Disraeli*

No answer is often the best answer. *Malcolm Forbes*

No wisdom like silence. *1620, WM-659*

Nothing is more useful than silence. *Menander*

Once a word has left one's lips, even a team of four horses cannot overtake it. *Chinese proverb*

Open mouth invites foot.

People who wouldn't think of talking with their mouths full often speak with their heads empty. *Heard in Ontario*

Quietness is best. *1832, Henderson*

Save thy wind to keel thy porridge. *English dialect; EMW-172*

Saying nothing indicates a fine command of the English language. *Peter's Almanac*

Silence can't be misquoted.

Silence is a cheap virtue.

Silence is like darkness, a good place to hide. *Josh Billings*

Silence is also speech. *African proverb*

Silence is not always tact, and it is tact that is golden, not silence. *Samuel Butler*

Silence is one of the hardest arguments to refute. *Josh Billings*

Silence is sometimes an answer. *Estonian proverb*

Silence is stupid.

Silence is the most perfect expression of scorn. *G. B. Shaw, Back to Methuselah*

Silence is the safest course for any man to adopt who distrusts himself. *François de la Rochefoucauld*

Silence is the virtue of fools. *Francis Bacon*

Silence may be golden, but many a cow would be killed if it wasn't for the whistle on the engine. *Old postcard*

Silence seldom doth harm. *1670, Ray*

Speak, if you have something to say which is better than silence. *Gregory Nazianzen*

Talk less and listen more. *Old postcard*

Talk low, talk slow, and don't say too much. *John Wayne*

The cruelest lies are often told in silence. *Robert Louis Stevenson, Truth of Intercourse*

The easiest way to win an argument is to keep quiet. *Old postcard*

The heart of the fool is in his mouth, but the mouth of the wise man is in his heart. *Benjamin Franklin, 1733*

The mind is like a TV set: when it goes blank, it's a good idea to turn off the sound.

The silent man is often worth listening to.

The tongue: we spend three years learning how to use it, and the rest of our lives learning how to control it.

There is something fascinating about silence. One gets such wholesale returns of conjecture out of such a trifling investment of fact. *Mark Twain*

They say that silence resides in contentment; but I say to you that denial, rebellion, and contempt dwell in silence. *Kahlil Gibran*

Think today and speak tomorrow. *1855, Bohn*

Think twice before you speak and then talk to yourself. *Old postcard*

Those who know do not speak; those who speak do not know. *Lao-tzu*

To say the right thing at the right time, keep still most of the time.

Very often the quiet feller has said all he knows. *Kin Hubbard*

What's said cannot be unsaid.

When a fool keeps quiet, you can't tell whether he is foolish or wise. *Yiddish proverb*

When a man ain't got anything to say, then is a good time to keep still. *Josh Billings*

When I say nothing, I don't necessarily mean nothing. © *Ashleigh Brilliant*

When something defies description, let it. *Arnold Glasgow, as quoted in Reader's Digest. May 1962*

When you have nothing to say, say nothing. *Charles Colton, Lacon*

You can't know too much, but it's easy to say too much. *Ed Howe*

Here lies Sir Tact, a diplomatic fellow
Whose silence was not golden, but just yellow.
Timothy Steele

If your lips you would keep from slips,
    Five things observe with care:
Of whom you speak, to whom you speak,
    And how and when and where.

*If speech is silver, then silence is golden. *ca. 600, Midrash: Leviticus Rabbah, 16*

Speech is silver, but SILENCE is golden.*

*According to Flexner (F-163), it is an ancient idea to say, in one way or another, that silence is better than speech. This thought was first recorded in the exact words of this proverb by James Russell Lowell in *The Biglow Papers*, 1848.

Better to remain SILENT and be thought a fool than to speak out and remove all doubt. *Attributed to Abraham Lincoln in a 1931 source; B-2111*

Even a fool, when he holdeth his peace, is counted wise; and he that shutteth his lips is esteemed a man of understanding. *Proverbs 18:28*

God hath given to man a cloak whereby he can conceal his ignorance; that cloak is silence. *Bhartrhari; B-2111*

See also SILENCE is golden.

Hate the SIN, but love the sinner. *Thomas Buchanan Read, What One Word May Do, 1865*

SIN in haste and repent at leisure.

For the sin ye do by two and two ye must pay for one by one! *Rudyard Kipling, Tomlinson*

It's hard to work for money you've already spent on things you didn't really need.

Let him who sins when drunk be punished when sober. *Legal maxim*

Manuscript: something submitted in haste and returned at leisure. *Oliver Herford*

Old sins have long shadows.

One night with Venus, three years with Mercury. *BJW-448*

Reckless youth makes rueful age. *1520, OE-534*

The majority of men employ the first portion of their life in making the other portion miserable. *Jean de La Bruyère*

Turn or burn. (Turn from sin or burn in hell.) *1616, Draxe*

The wages of SIN is death. *Romans 6:23*

The wages of gin is debt. *Captain Billy's Whiz Bang, Oct. 1922*

The wages of sin are unreported.

The wages of sin is an income for life. *William Irish, 1943*

The SINS of the fathers shall be visited upon the sons.*

The virtues of the mothers shall [also] be visited upon the children. *Charles Dickens*

*I the Lord thy God am a jealous God, visiting the iniquity of the fathers upon the children unto the third and fourth generation of those that hate me. *Exodus 20:5*

Let him who has not SINNED among us cast the first stone.*

Who am I to stone the first cast? *Walter Winchell, explaining why he always praised the first show of a new theatrical season*

Let him that is without gin cast the first moan. *Northwestern Purple Parrot, ca. 1925*

*He that is without sin among you, let him first cast a stone at her. *John 8:7*

See also NOBODY is perfect; We are all SINNERS.

We are all SINNERS.

A hypocrite is a person who . . . but who isn't? *Don Marquis*

Adam ate the apple, and our teeth still ache. *Heard in Wisconsin*

As part of a general amnesty, I have decided to forgive myself. © *Ashleigh Brilliant*

Faith heightens guilt, it does not prevent sin. *Cardinal Newman*

Have mercy upon us, miserable sinners. *The Book of Common Prayer*

If after I depart this vale, you ever remember me and have thought to please my ghost, forgive some sinner and wink your eye at some homely girl. *H. L. Mencken, as quoted in Reader's Digest, Nov. 1955*

Lead me not into temptation; let me find the way myself.

No man is made a Christian once and forever. *Henry Ward Beecher*

Sign in a church vestibule: If you were on trial for being a Christian, would there be enough evidence to convict you?

The wages of war is debt. *Wall Street Journal, ca. 1925*

To adjust for inflation, the wages of sin have been increased by 10 percent.

"We are all sinners" is what we confess on Sunday and prove on Monday.

Who can say, I have made my heart clean, I am pure from my sin? *Proverbs 20:9*

You can't have the joy of repenting unless you sin first. © *Ashleigh Brilliant*

Forbear to judge for we are sinners all.
Close up his eyes and draw the curtain close;
And let us all to meditation.
Shakespeare, 2 Henry VI 3.3.31

The colonel's lady and Mrs. O'Grady are SISTERS under the skin. *Rudyard Kipling, The Ladies, 1902*

Every king springs from a race of slaves, and every slave has had kings among his ancestors. *Plato, Theaetetus*

He did not know that a keeper is only a poacher turned outside in, and a poacher a keeper turned inside out. *Charles Kingsley, The Water Babies*

I am as bad as the worst, but thank God I am as good as the best. *Walt Whitman*

In each of us there is a little of all of us. *Georg Lichtenberg*

The difference between a lady and a flower girl is not how she behaves, but how she's treated. *G. B. Shaw, Pygmalion*

The Tsarina's breasts yield milk, not wine. *Russian proverb*

No matter how high or great the throne
What sits on it is the same as your own.
E. Y. Harburg

See also All MEN are brothers.

There's many a SLIP 'twixt cup and lip. *Greek proverb*

. . . Play it safe and drink right out of the bottle.

There's many a sip 'twixt cup and lip.

See also The best-laid SCHEMES o' mice and men gang aft agley.

SLOW but sure. *1562, O-205*

In real life, of course, it is the hare who wins. Every time. Look around you. And in any case it is my contention that Aesop was writing for the tortoise market. Hares have no time to read. They are too busy winning the game. *Anita Brookner, Hotel du Lac*

Wisely and slow; they stumble that run fast. *Shakespeare, Romeo and Juliet, 2.3.94*

SMALL is beautiful. *Title of a book by Eduard Schumacher, 1973*

. . . but big pays more.

. . . like small change? . . . small comfort? . . . small minds?

The little things of life are as interesting as the big ones. *Henry David Thoreau*

See also LESS is more; Make no small PLANS.

SMILE

. . . Cheerfulness keeps up a kind of daylight in the mind, and fills it with a steady and perpetual serenity. *Joseph Addison*

A merry heart maketh a cheerful countenance: but by sorrow of heart the spirit is broken. *Proverbs 15:13*

A two-cent smile gets more for you than a ten-dollar frown. *Old postcard*

Act as if you were already happy and that will tend to make you happy. *Dale Carnegie*

All the world's a camera; look pleasant, please.

Always keep smiling, and the whole world will know you're an idiot.

Be pleasant every morning until ten o'clock; the rest of the day will take care of itself. *William C. Hunter*

Don't open a shop unless you know how to smile. *Yiddish proverb*

Grin and win. *Office sign seen in Sylvia, comic strip by Nicole Hollander*

Is it bliss or is it Prozac? Only her pharmacist knows.

It takes thirteen muscles to frown and only two to smile. Why strain yourself?

Keep smiling. It makes people wonder what you've been up to.

People who are resolutely cheerful can be just as taxing as people who are chronically grumpy. *Sydney J. Harris*

Start off each day with a smile and get it over with. *W. C. Fields*

The bitterest misfortune can be masked by a smile. *Yiddish proverb*

Wear a smile on your face,
Keep a laugh in your heart,
Let your lips bubble over with song;
'Twill lighten your load
As you travel life's road
And help some other sinner along.
Old postcard

The thing that goes the farthest towards making life worthwhile,
That costs the least and does the most, is just a pleasant smile.

Where there's SMOKE, there's fire. *ca. 1375, WM-549*

Oft fire is without smoke, and peril without show. *Heard in California and Pennsylvania*

Where bees are, there is honey. *1670, Ray*

Where there's a dog, there's fleas. *Heard in Arkansas and Kansas*

Where there's smoke, there's burnt toast.

Where there's smoke, there's pollution.

Where there's smoking, there's cancer, heart disease, and emphysema.

Whoever said, "Where there's smoke, there's fire," never had a fireplace. *Laurence Peter*

Thank you for not SMOKING. *Saying popularized by the American Heart Association*

A cigarette has a fire at one end and a fool at the other.

A custom loathsome to the eye, hateful to the nose, harmful to the brain, dangerous to the lungs, and in the black, stinking fume thereof nearest resembling the horrible Stygian smoke of the pit that is bottomless. *James I of England, 1604*

A pack of cigarettes: It costs a penny to make. Sell it for a dollar. It's addictive. And there's fantastic brand loyalty. *Warren Buffett*

A person's right to smoke ends where the next person's nose begins. *Public service announcement, WNET-TV, 1986*

Smoking is one of the leading causes of statistics. *Fletcher Knebel*

Smoking is, as far as I'm concerned, the entire point of being an adult. *Fran Lebowitz, Social Studies*

To cease smoking is the easiest thing I ever did. I ought to know because I've done it a thousand times. *Attributed to Mark Twain (in an issue of Coronet magazine) but never found in his works (K-110)*

What smells so? Has somebody been burning a rag, or is there a dead mule in the backyard? No, the man is smoking a five-cent cigar. *Eugene Field, Tribune Printer, 1882*

When you smoke cigarettes, you're likely to burn yourself to death; with chewing tobacco the worst thing you can do is drown a midget. *Fred Allen*

Tobacco is an evil weed,
It was the Devil sowed the seed;
It stains your fingers, burns your clothes
And makes a chimney of your nose.

See also If GOD wanted us to smoke, he would have given us chimneys.

Old SOLDIERS never die; they just fade away. *1920 Army song by J. Foley**

Old soldiers never die; but alas for the young ones!

Old accountants never die; they just lose their balance.

Old bankers never die; they just lose their interest.

Old basketball players never die; they just dribble away.

Old bureaucrats never die; they just waste away.

Old burglars never die; they just steal away. *Glen Gilbreath, seventy-two-year-old burglar, as quoted in Chicago Sun-Times, April 26, 1985*

Old college presidents never die; they just lose their faculties.

Old chemists never die; they just stop reacting.

Old female lawyers never die; they just lose their appeals.

Old fishermen never die; they just smell that way.

Old gardeners never die; they just spade away.

Old jokes never die; they just sound that way.

Old ladies never die; they just play bingo.

Old landlords sometimes die, but are quickly replaced with real estate management companies.

Old mailmen never die; they just lose their zip.

Old physicians never die; they just lose their patients.

Old refrigerators never die; they just lose their cool.

Old rock hounds never die; they just petrify.

Old salesmen never die; they just go out of commission.

Old textbooks never die; they just get paraphrased. *Diana B. Paul*

*Keyes (K-69) notes that this song parodied the hymn "Kind Words Can Never Die."

If you're not part of the SOLUTION, you're part of the problem.* 1975, O-207

. . . but the perpetual human predicament is that the answer soon poses its own problems. *Sydney J. Harris*

Either lead, follow or get out of the way. *Sign on the desk of Ted Turner, 1987*

Government does not solve problems—it subsidizes them. *Ronald Reagan, 1972*

If one views his problem closely enough, he will recognize himself as part of the problem. *Logan Pearsall Smith, Afterthoughts*

If you don't know who's to blame, you are!

It's all right if you're not part of the solution because there really isn't one.

*According to Jonathan Green, a 1968 slogan of Black Power leader Eldridge Cleaver, expressed as "You're either part of the solution or part of the problem." Keyes (K- 40) notes that on June 18, 1964, the president of New York's City College, Buell Gallagher, had told his graduating class, "Be part of the answer, not part of the problem, as the American revolution proceeds."

SOMEBODY said that it couldn't be done.*

. . . so forget it.

Genius is the faculty of doing a thing that nobody supposed could be done at all. *Josh Billings*

If it's impossible, let's do it.

Nothing is so embarrassing as watching someone do something that you said couldn't be done. *Sam Ewing, Mature Living*

Only he who attempts the ridiculous can achieve the impossible. *Will Henry*

The greatest pleasure in life is doing what people say you cannot do. *Walter Bagehot*

The person who says it cannot be done should never interrupt the one who is doing it.

The world is moving so fast these days that the man who says it can't be done is generally interrupted by someone doing it. *Elbert Hubbard*

The Wright Brothers flew right through the smokescreen of impossibility. *Charles F. Kettering*

Somebody said that it couldn't be done,
And the fellow was right, the son of a gun.
Richard Armour

The world would sleep if things were run
By men who say, "It can't be done!"
Philander Johnson, It Can't Be Done

*Somebody said it couldn't be done,
 But he with a chuckle replied
 That maybe it couldn't, but he would be one
 Who wouldn't say so till he tried.
 Edgar A. Guest, It Couldn't Be Done

SOMETHING is better than nothing. 1546, O-207

Better are small fish than an empty dish. 1687, T-217

August Wilson recalls that his mother, "a fiercely independent and stubborn woman," once entered a contest in which the prize was a new washing machine, and she won. The sponsor regarded her as "a simple Negro woman," and offered her a used washing machine. Her friends urged her to accept it but she refused, saying "Something is not always better than nothing." Comments her son, "She would rather have had her dignity than to have traded it for such a small thing." *New York Times, May 12, 1996*

See also A BIRD in the hand is worth two in the bush; Half a LOAF is better than none.

A wise SON makes a glad father.

. . . but a foolish son is the heaviness of his mother. 1732, WM-552

My SON is my son till he gets him a wife,
My daughter's my daughter all her life.
1670, *Ray*

When a young man marries, he divorces his mother. *Talmud*

Your son isn't your son for life—if he's normal. *Marlene Dietrich*

I felt SORRY for myself because I had no shoes, until I met a man who had no feet.

Every man is sorry for himself. *Terence*

What is a man profited, if he shall gain the whole world, and lose his own SOUL? Matthew 16:26*

. . . I suppose this depends somewhat upon the size of the soul. I think there are cases where the trade would do. *Josh Billings*

How the Hollywood star system becomes an actor's undoing: First the actor gets an image; then the image gets the actor. *John Payne*

The danger of the past was that men became slaves. The danger of the future is that men may become robots. *Erich Fromm*

*The same thought is expressed in Mark 8:36.

Consider the SOURCE.

He that would know the Nature of the Water . . . must find out its Source. *William Temple, 1673; B-2174*

As you SOW, so shall you reap.*

. . . unless you're a week-end gardener.

As ye smoke, so shall ye reek.

Every man reaps what he sows—except the amateur gardener. *Cholly Knickerbocker, as quoted in Reader's Digest, Sept. 1960*

Now You Can Reap What We Have Sewn. *Advertisement by Brooks Brothers, Chicago Tribune, Oct. 7, 1993*

Whatever a bad seamstress seweth, that shall she also rip.

You commit the crime, you do the time.

You may sow thorns, but you won't reap jasmine. *Iranian proverb*

*Whatsoever a man soweth, that shall he also reap. *Galatians 6:7*. In Hosea 8:7 appear the words "They have sown the wind, and they shall reap the whirlwind."

Call a SPADE a spade. *Latin proverb*

The beginning of wisdom is calling things by their right names. *Chinese proverb*

You must not call a spade a spade;
    It isn't nice any more.
It now is termed a workman's aid,
    For spade's a word kicked out the door.
And other words are on the run,
    For instance, janitors no more.
For now is a custodian
    Who vacuums or mops up the floor.
Assistant used to be the word,
    But now if you'd be up-to-date,
And not thought of as quite absurd,
    You use the word associate.
It used to be in the olden days
    We simply said we had a cold,
But now a virus is the craze;
It sounds more dignified, we're told.
It used to be when we got old
    We were referred to as old men,
But times have changed—lo and behold,
    I'm now a senior citizen!
I guess I've ranted on enough,
    And maybe I my point have made
To be considered up to snuff
    You just don't call a spade a spade.
Tenney Call, Spades Ain't Spades

See also TELL it like it is.

SPEAK or forever hold your peace.*

Dumb folks heirs no land. *English proverb*

The lame tongue gets nothing. *1636, Camden*

*Let him now speak, or else hereafter for ever hold his peace. *Solemnization of Matrimony, The Book of Common Prayer*

SPEAK softly and carry a big stick.* *Theodore Roosevelt (1858–1919)*

*There is a homely adage that runs, "Speak softly and carry a big stick; you will go far." If the American nation will speak softly and yet build and keep at a pitch of the highest training a thoroughly efficient navy, the Monroe Doctrine will go far. *Speech at Minnesota State Fair, Sept. 2, 1901.* Flexner (F-162) believes that Roosevelt's "homely adage" is a West African proverb. A kindred thought was expressed in an item in Herbert's 1640 collection of proverbs: "One sword keeps another in the sheath."

SPEAK when you are spoken to, come when you are called. *1670, Ray*

Showing up is 80 percent of life. *Woody Allen*

Big SPENDERS are bad lenders. *1639, Clarke*

Great SPIRIT, teach me never to judge another until I have walked at least two weeks in his moccasins. *American Indian prayer*

He whose belly is full believes not him that is fasting. *English proverb*

How gravely the glutton counsels the famished to bear the pangs of hunger. *Kahlil Gibran*

I have walked in your moccasins for ten days and I still don't like you. *Donald G. Smith*

Never take the advice of someone who has not had your kind of trouble. *Sydney J. Harris*

No one who has not sat in prison knows what the State is like. *Leo Tolstoy*

None knows the weight of another's burden. *1651, Herbert*

Of all the preposterous assumptions of humanity over humanity, nothing exceeds most of the criticisms made on the habits of the poor by the well-housed, well-warmed, and well-fed. *Herman Melville, Poor Man's Pudding and Rich Man's Crumbs*

Pretend not thou to scorn the pomp of the world before thou knowest it. *1732, Fuller*

Until you walk a mile in another man's moccasins, you can't imagine the smell. *Robert Byrne*

Before you walk in another guy's boot
Make sure he doesn't have athlete's foot.

See also CHASTE is she whom no one has asked; OPPORTUNITY makes the thief; Where you STAND depends on where you sit; You measure everyone's CORN by your own bushel.

The letter killeth but the SPIRIT giveth life.*

*Not of the letter, but of the spirit: for the letter killeth, but the spirit giveth life. *2 Corinthians 3:6*

The SPIRIT is willing but the flesh is weak. *Matthew 26:41*

For I do not do what I want, but I do the very thing I hate. *Romans 17:15*

I can resist everything except temptation. *Oscar Wilde, Lady Windermere's Fan*

The trouble with drinking today is that the flesh is willing but the spirits are too strong. *Judge, ca. 1925*

The ant, he lays aside some dough
Against the time of cold and snow;
He doesn't trust a bit to luck,
But gathers his assorted truck:
If I could live just like the ant
I'd be as thrifty—but I can't.
Samuel Hoffenstein

In the SPRING a young man's fancy lightly turns to thoughts of love. Alfred, Lord Tennyson, Locksley Hall, 1842

In the spring a young man's fancy.

In the spring a young man's fancy turns—and turns—and turns. *Helen Rowland*

In the spring a young man's fancy
Lightly turns to love, they say.
And some, who otherwise are smart,
Get hooked—and how!—for life that way.

All the world's a STAGE. *1549, T-759*

. . . and it's putting on a mighty poor show. *Edward H. Dreschnach*

. . . but the play is badly cast. *Oscar Wilde*

. . . and most of the actors are desperately underrehearsed.

All the world's an analog stage, and digital circuits play only bit parts.

The world's a stage—as Shakespeare said one day;
The stage a world—was what he meant to say.
Oliver Wendell Holmes, Prologue

STAND up and be counted.

Each man must for himself alone decide what is right and what is wrong, which course is patriotic and which isn't. You cannot shirk this and be a man. *Mark Twain*

Shut up and be appreciated.

The dissenter is every human being at those moments of his life when he resigns momentarily from the herd and thinks for himself. *Archibald MacLeish, as quoted in New York Times, Dec. 16, 1956*

The ultimate measure of a man is not where he stands in moments of comfort and convenience, but where he stands at times of challenge and controversy. *Martin Luther King, Jr., Strength to Love*

Where you STAND depends on where you sit.

A "just peace" is when our side gets what it wants. *Bill Maudlin*

A citizen is influenced by principle in direct proportion to his distance from the political situation. *Milton Rakove, Virginia Quarterly Review, 1965*

A liberal is a radical with a wife and child; a conservative is a liberal with property.

A rotten log is truth to a bed of violets; while sand is truth to a cactus. *Elbert Hubbard*

Acquaintance: a person whom we know well enough to borrow from, but not well enough to lend to. *Ambrose Bierce*

Every way of a man is right in his own eyes, but the Lord weigheth the hearts. *Proverbs 21:2*

In a strong position, even a coward is a lion. *Hindu proverb*

In Haiti, when they make statues of Christ and Satan, they make Christ black and Satan white. *Bertrand Russell*

It is your interest to sell high: it is mine to buy low. *George Washington*

It's easy to spot the winners—they're the ones not complaining about the rules. *Peter's Almanac*

It's strange, but wherever I take my eyes, they always see things from my point of view. © *Ashleigh Brilliant*

Knaves imagine nothing can be done without knavery. *1732, Fuller*

Who to whom? As Lenin said.
> Who rules whom?
> Who hands out the soup to whom?
> Who is a better person than whom?
> Who is more democratic than whom?
> Who says "Who whom" to whom?

Michael Frayn, Constructions. Lenin was once asked, "In Communism, how do you define morality?" Lenin reportedly answered, "It all depends on who does what to whom." (The Russian idiom *kto kvo* could be literally translated as "who to whom.")

Many people consider the things government does for them to be social progress, but they regard the things government does for others as socialism. *Earl Warren, as quoted in Reader's Digest, Nov. 1952*

Mother says no because she loves you. Grandma says yes for the same reason.

Nobody wants to be married to a doctor who works weekends and makes house calls at 2 A.M. But every patient would like to find one. *Ellen Goodman, Keeping in Touch*

Nothing like leather. *1692, T-506.* A fable of L'Estrange tells of a town council which was deciding how to build a town wall. The town mason said, "Surely, there's nothing better than a wall of stone." The town carpenter countered by proposing a wall of heavy timbers. In the midst of the discussion that followed, the town tanner shouted, "Nothing like leather."

Nothing makes you more tolerant of a neighbor's noisy party than being there. *Franklin P. Jones, as quoted in Reader's Digest, Jan. 1953*

Poor and liberal, rich and covetous. *1631, OE-510*

Show me a man who claims to be objective and I'll show you a man with illusions. *Henry R. Luce, New York Times, Mar. 1967*

The fascination of shooting as a sport depends almost wholly on whether you are at the right or wrong end of the gun. *P. G. Wodehouse*

The only war is the war you fought in. Every veteran knows that. *Allan Keller, 1965*

The symbol of the race ought to be a human being carrying an ax, for every human being has one concealed about him somewhere, and is always seeking the opportunity to grind it. *Mark Twain, Biography, by A. B. Paine*

The white man's Heaven is the black man's Hell. *James Baldwin, quoting a Black Muslim minister, in The Fire Next Time*

The winners decide what were war crimes. *Gary Wills, New York Times, 1975*

The wrongdoer forgets, but not the wronged. *African proverb*

Truth is a jewel of many facets.

War hath no fury like a non-combatant. *C. E. Montague*

What a woman admires in a man depends on whether she is married or single. *L. de V. Matthewman*

Where your treasure is there will your heart be also. *Matthew 6:21*

Whether the road goes uphill or downhill depends on where you stand.

Why is it that we rejoice at a birth and grieve at a funeral? It is because we are not the person involved. *Mark Twain, Pudd'nhead Wilson's Calendar*

A salesman's motto:
To sell John Brown what John Brown buys,
You've got to see things through John Brown's
    eyes.

See also BEAUTY is in the eye of the beholder; DISTANCE lends enchantment; It all DEPENDS on whose ox is gored.

Hitch your wagon to a STAR. * *Ralph Waldo Emerson, Civilization, 1870*

A map of the world that does not include Utopia is not worth glancing at. *Oscar Wilde*

A press agent is a man who hitches his braggin' to a star. *Heard in Indiana*

Aim at heaven and you will get earth thrown in. Aim at earth and you will get neither. *C. S. Lewis, Mere Christianity*

All my life I wanted to be somebody. I see now that I should have been more specific. *Jane Wagner, writer for Lily Tomlin*

Better aim at the moon than shoot into the well. *Heard in Indiana*

Don't aim for success if you want it; just do what you love and believe in, and it will come naturally. *David Frost*

Don't part with your illusions. When they are gone, you may still exist, but you have ceased to live. *Mark Twain, Pudd'nhead Wilson's New Calendar*

Far away there in the sunshine are my highest aspirations. I may not reach them, but I can look up and see their beauty, believe in them and try to follow where they lead. *Louisa May Alcott*

Follow your bliss. *Joseph Campbell*

Go confidently in the direction of your dreams. Live the life you have imagined. *Henry David Thoreau*

He that strives to touch the stars, oft stumbles at a straw. *Edmund Spenser, The Shepheardes Calendar; M-413*

I teach you the Superman. Man is something that is to be surpassed. *Friedrich Nietzsche*

I hitched my wagon to a star, and then the harness broke.

I was very ambitious when I was young; but all I try to do now is get through the day. *Ed Howe*

Idealism is fine; but as it approaches reality, the cost becomes prohibitive. *William F. Buckley, Jr.*

If a man happens to find himself, he has a mansion which he can inhabit with dignity all the days of his life. *James Michener*

If you have built castles in the air, your work need not be lost; that is where they should be. Now put the foundation under them. *Henry David Thoreau*

Keep your eyes on the stars, and your feet on the ground. *Theodore Roosevelt*

Live beyond your means; then you're forced to work hard—you have to succeed. *Edward G. Robinson*

Never hitch your wagon to another man's star. You never know where the fool will take you. *The Wild, Wild West, TV show*

No bird soars too high if he soars with his own wings. *William Blake*

Reach for the high apples first; you can get the low ones anytime. *Heard in Mississippi*

Some men see things as they are and say "Why?" I dream things that never were and say "Why not?" *G. B. Shaw*

Spit on the ceiling—anyone can spit on the floor. *Peter's Almanac*

The measure of success is not whether you have a tough problem to deal with, but whether it's the same problem you had last year. *John Foster Dulles*

The biggest human temptation is . . . to settle for too little. *Thomas Merton*

The toughest thing about success is that you've got to keep on winning. *Irving Berlin*

What you want to do, and what you can do, is limited only by what you can dream. *Mike Melville*

You aim at the impossible to get the unusual. *Floyd Patterson, 1972*

Climb high
Climb far
Your goal the sky
Your aim the star.
Inscription on Hopkins Memorial Steps, Williams College, Williamstown, Massachusetts

Hew not too high,
Lest the chips fall in thine eye.
14th century proverb

*Hitch your wagon to a star. Let us not fag in paltry works which serve our pot and bag alone. *Ralph Waldo Emerson (1803–82), Society and Solitude (Civilization)*

See also Follow your BLISS; A man's REACH should exceed his grasp, or what's a heaven for?; Reach for the STARS.

Only the STARS are neutral.

I cannot remain impartial as between the fire brigade and the fire. *Winston Churchill*

Reach for the STARS.

. . . settle for the bucks. *Jim Davis, Garfield: Words to Live By*

See also Hitch your wagon to a STAR; Follow your BLISS; A man's REACH should exceed his grasp, or what's a heaven for?

Don't START up.

Kindle not a fire that you cannot extinguish. *1584, O2-336*

Never argue with a fool—people might not know the difference.

A STATESMAN is a successful politician who is dead. *Thomas B. Reed* (1839–1902)

A politician is a person with whose politics you don't agree; if you agree with him, he is a statesman. *David Lloyd George, 1935*

A statesman is a politician who places himself at the service of the nation. A politician is a statesman who places the nation at his service. *Georges Pompidou, London Observer, 1973*

See also All POLITICIANS are crooked.

Thou shalt not STEAL. *Exodus 20:15*

God help those who help themselves! *L. L. Levinson*

It is rascally to steal a purse, daring to steal a million, and a proof of greatness to steal a crown. *Friedrich von Schiller, Fiesco*

There is no sixth commandment in art. The poet is entitled to lay his hands on whatever material he finds necessary for his work. *Heinrich Heine, Letters on the French Stage*

He who STEALS an egg today will steal a hen tomorrow. *1659, Howell*

. . . Absurd. It might as soundly be argued that because you steal a cookie from the kitchen you are on the criminal way to steal-

ing your mother's jewelry. *George Jean Nathan*

Don't steal; you'll never thus compete successfully in business. Cheat. *Ambrose Bierce*

He that will cheat at play, will cheat you anyway. *1721, OE-89*

If he steals a needle, he will steal a cow. *Korean proverb*

If once a man indulges himself in murder, very soon he comes to think little of robbing; and from robbing he next comes to drinking and Sabbath-breaking, and from that to incivility and procrastination. *Thomas De Quincey, On Murder*

Minor vices lead to major ones, but minor virtues stay put. *Mignon McLaughlin*

Who STEALS my purse steals trash.*

Who steals my purse steals cash.

*Who steals my purse steals trash; 'tis something, nothing;
'Twas mine, 'tis his, and has been slave to thousands;
But he that filches from me my good name
Robs me of that which not enriches him,
And makes me poor indeed.
Shakespeare, Othello 3.3.155, ca. 1604

Why did Shakespeare put his smoothest lines of wisdom into the mouths of villains and fools? The above lines are spoken by the villain Iago. Shakespeare's famous lines "To thine own self be true" were spoken in *Hamlet* by Polonius, a senile meddler. What is Shakespeare telling us—to beware of the facile dispensers of fine words?

One STEP at a time. *1901, O-212*

A successful individual typically sets his next goal somewhat but not too much above his last achievement. In this way, he steadily raises his level of aspiration. *Kurt Lewin*

Feather by feather the goose is plucked.

Grasp a little and you may secure it; grasp too much and you will lose everything. *ca. 1205, WM-264*

It is necessary for me to establish a winner image. Therefore, I have to beat somebody. *Richard Nixon, 1968*

One thing at a time
And that done well
Is a very good thing
As many can tell.

Life is hard,
By the yard;
But by the inch,
Life's a cinch!
Jean L. Gordon, as quoted in Reader's Digest, June 1974

See also A JOURNEY of a thousand miles began with a single step; Mighty OAKS from little acorns grow; The BEGINNING is the hardest.

The first STEP is the hardest. *1596, O-82*

The worst is at first. *1672, T-41*

See also The BEGINNING is the hardest.

STICKS and stones may break my bones, but names will never harm me. *1562, Heywood, and 19th-century children's rhyme*

A sadomasochist's secret: Sticks and stones will break my bones, but whips and chains excite me.

A thick skin is a gift from God. *Konrad Adenauer*

Spit in a whore's face and she'll say it's raining. *Heard in Illinois*

Words may be mere wind, but then so is a tornado. *L. de V. Matthewman*

Sticks and stones are hard on bones,
Aimed with angry art.
Words can sting like anything.
But silence breaks the heart.
Phyllis McGinley, 1954

See also An ill WOUND is cured, but not an ill name.

A STITCH in time saves nine. *1732, Fuller*

A lie in time saves nine. *Addison Mizner*

A stitch in time saves embarrassment.

A stitch in time saves exposure. *Old postcard*

A stitch too late is my fate. *Ogden Nash, 1938*

A word before is worth two after; let's talk it over! *Old postcard*

Men say that a stitch in time saves nine, and so they take a thousand stitches to save nine tomorrow. *Henry David Thoreau*

Unless you stop the crack, you will rebuild a wall. *African proverb*

Who repairs not his gutter, repairs his whole house. *1849, OE-538*

See also An ounce of PREVENTION is worth a pound of cure.

A rolling STONE gathers no moss.* *Greek proverb*

. . . but it gains a certain polish. *Oliver Herford*

. . . but neither does it pay rent.

. . . but a rolling stone doesn't care; momentum is what it wants to gather. *Brink Stillwater*

This was supposed to show that a young man who wandered from home never got on in the world. In very ancient days it was true. The young man who stayed at home and worked hard and tilled the ground and goaded oxen with a long stick like a lance found himself as he grew old a man of property, owning four goats and a sow. The son who wandered forth in the world was either killed by the cannibals or crawled home years afterwards doubled up with rheumatism. So the old men made the proverb. But nowadays it is exactly wrong. It is the rolling stone that trudges off to the city leaving his elder brother in the barnyard and who later makes a fortune and founds a university. While his elder brother still has only the old farm with three cows and a couple of pigs, he has a whole department of agriculture. . . .

In short, in modern life it is the rolling stone that gathers the moss. And the geologists . . . say that the moss on the actual stone was first started in exactly the same way. It was the rolling of the stone that smashed up the earth and made the moss grow. *Stephen Leacock*

A revolving fan gathers no flies.

A rolling pin gathers no sass.

A rolling stone can give you a helluva bruise.

A rolling stone gathers no boss.

The Rolling Stones gather screaming teenagers.

We keep repeating the silly proverb that rolling stones gather no moss, as if moss were a desirable parasite. *G. B. Shaw, Misalliance*

You had better be a round peg in a square hole than a square peg in a square hole. The latter is in for life, while the first is only an indeterminate sentence. *Elbert Hubbard*

The stone that is rolling can gather no moss;
For master and servant oft changing is loss.
Thomas Tusser, Preface to the Book of Housewifery

They say a rolling stone's a loss
And yet I see no use in moss;
I'd rather gypsy through Cockaigne
Than vegetate a dubious gain.
Samuel Hoffenstein

*Mieder has noted that the Scots and the English differ in their interpretation of this proverb. To the Scots, the proverb extols the virtues of action. The English see the beautiful growth of moss on a stone in a stream as a sign of tradition and stability.

After the STORM comes the calm. *410 B.C., B-2222*

. . . and after a calm may come a storm.

After the storm comes the calamity.

Gladness follows sadness.

Nothing so rousingly raises your spirits as emerging from a gloomy movie into a sunny afternoon. *Mignon McLaughlin*

STRIKE while the iron is hot. *Geoffrey Chaucer, 1386*

Bake while the oven is hot. *Yiddish proverb*

Know thy opportunity. *Pittacus*

Seize opportunity by the beard, for it has a bald behind. *Bulgarian proverb*

Strike while the irony is hot. *Don Quinn*

Strike while your employer has a big contract. *Ambrose Bierce*

Take what the gods give while their hands are open, for none know what they will withhold when they are shut. *African proverb*

The best time to frame an answer to the letters of a friend, is the moment you receive them. Then the warmth of friendship, and the intelligence received, most forcibly cooperate. *William Shenstone, Essays on Men and Manners*

When fortune smiles, embrace her. *1611, Cotgrave*

Women's lib slogan: Don't iron while the strike is hot!

See also Make HAY while the sun shines.

There is no right to STRIKE against the public safety. *Calvin Coolidge**

*There is no right to strike against the public safety by anybody, anywhere, any time. *Telegram to Samuel Gompers, president of AFL, on threatened Boston Police strike of 1919. This stand made Coolidge, who at the time was governor of Massachusetts, a national political figure.*

Different STROKES for different folks. *African American proverb, and title of a TV show*

Different hopes for different folks. *Advertisement promoting U.S. Savings Bonds*

Different Volks for different folks. *Volkswagen advertisement*

Every shoe fits not every foot. *1616, T-600*

See also One man's MEAT is another man's poison; TASTES are tastes.

Little STROKES fell great oaks. *ca. 1370, WM-569*

Dripping moisture hollows out a stone. *Latin proverb*

Feather by feather, the goose is plucked. *Italian proverb*

Be STRONG and of good courage. *Deuteronomy 31:6*

Courage comes and goes. Hold on for the next supply. *Thomas Merton*

Courage is fear that has said its prayers.

Courage is not the absence of fear but the ability to carry on with dignity in spite of it. *Scott Turow, The Burden of Proof*

Courage is the ladder on which all other virtues mount. *Claire Boothe Luce, Reader's Digest, May 1979*

Fear less, hope more; eat less, chew more; whine less, breathe more; talk less, say more; hate less, love more; and all good things will be yours.

For they conquer who believe they can. *John Dryden*

Grace under pressure. *Ernest Hemingway, definition of guts, 1929*

Just pray for a tough hide and a tender heart. *Ruth Graham*

Never bend your head. Always hold it high. Look the world straight in the eye. *Helen Keller, advice to a five-year-old*

The first and greatest commandment is, Don't let them scare you. *Elmer Davis*

Life is mostly froth and bubble,
Two things stand like stone,
Kindness in another's trouble,
Courage in your own.
Adam Lindsay Gordon, Ye Wearie Wayfarer

See also FORTUNE favors the bold; Faint HEART ne'er won fair lady.

Against STUPIDITY the very gods themselves contend in vain. *Friedrich von Schiller, The Maid of Orleans, 1801*

No medicine cures stupidity. *Japanese proverb*

Rascality has limits; stupidity has none. *Heard in Ontario*

The trouble with the world is that the stupid are cocksure and the intelligent full of doubts. *Bertrand Russell*

From the SUBLIME to the ridiculous is only a step.* *Napoleon, reflection on his retreat from Moscow, 1812*

. . . but there's no road that leads back from the ridiculous to the sublime. *Lion Feuchtwanger, Paris Gazette, 1940*

Here the sublime and the ridiculous are blended without the step between. *A critic's barb*

There's only a hairsbreadth between a hero and a fool. *Heard in Oregon*

*Keyes (K-45) notes that seventeen years earlier, Thomas Paine had written, "One step above the sublime makes the ridiculous, and one step above the ridiculous makes the sublime again" (*The Age of Reason*, 1795).

If at first you don't SUCCEED, try again.*

. . . when nobody's looking.

. . . but make sure the prize you chase is worth the effort.

. . . just to show how stubborn and stupid you can be.

. . . Then quit. There's no use being a damn fool about it. *W. C. Fields*

. . . It is often the last key in the bunch that opens the lock. *Old postcard*

If at first you don't succeed:

  . . . the heck with it.

  . . . cheat.

  . . . blame somebody.

  . . . you're fired. *Jean Graman*

  . . . find someone who knows what he's doing.

  . . . clutch for whatever you can get.

  . . . read the instructions.

  . . . you're running about average.

  . . . try something else.

  . . . destroy all evidence that you tried.

  . . . failure may be your thing. *Peter's Almanac*

  . . . blame your wife.

. . . blame the teacher. *Grade school cop-out*

. . . so much for skydiving.

. . . transform your data set.

. . . date the boss's daughter.

If at first you do succeed:

. . . try to hide your astonishment.

. . . try not to be a bore.

. . . quit. Don't spoil a perfect record.

Character consists of what you do on the third and fourth tries. *James Michener, Chesapeake*

Energy and persistence conquer all things. *Poor Richard's Almanac*

She married a man for companionship and didn't get it, so she had children for companionship and didn't get it, so she had an affair for companionship and didn't get it, and now she has goldfish. *Richard Needham*

You never really lose until you quit trying. *Mike Ditka*

Experiment with many things, until
Through learning what won't work, you find
  what will.
Arthur Guiterman

Talent made a poor appearance.
Until he married Perseverance.
Arthur Guiterman

Ladies, to this advice give heed
In controlling men:
If at first you don't succeed,
Cry, cry again.

*'Tis a lesson you should heed:
  Try, try, again.

If at first you don't succeed,
  Try, try, again.
T. H. Palmer, Teacher's Manual

The door to SUCCESS is always marked Push.

. . . and the door on City Hall is marked Pull.

Boldness has genius, power and magic in it. *Johann Wolfgang von Goethe*

Guts gets there. *B. C. Forbes*

If you itch for something, scratch for it. *Heard in Kentucky*

No one ever excused his way to success. *David del Dotto, How to Make Nothing but Money*

Prudence is no doubt a valuable quality, but prudence which degenerates into timidity is very seldom the path to safety. *Robert Cecil*

The dictionary is the only place where success comes before work. *Heard in Kentucky and New Jersey*

The successful man puts his trust in God, and works like the devil. *Old postcard*

There is no luck in laziness. *Heard in North Carolina and Ontario*

See also Faint HEART ne'er won fair lady; Don't count on LUCK; Don't HIDE your light under a bushel; Every MAN for himself . . . , HELP yourself; Put your best FOOT forward; SELF-PRESERVATION is the first law of nature.

Nothing succeeds like SUCCESS.

. . . and the law of averages occasionally lets a fool be right by chance.

. . . because without it, a man is a failure.

A celebrity is someone who is known for being known. *Studs Terkel, 1978*

A definition of fame: When people don't cash your check because your signature is worth more than the amount of the check. © *Ashleigh Brilliant*

A genius is a crackpot whose crazy idea actually works.

A man with a new idea is a crank—until the idea succeeds. *Mark Twain*

After all is said and done, the grand secret of winning is to win. *Josh Billings, 1865*

Failure has no friends. *John F. Kennedy*

He who once hits will be ever shooting. This is literally true, for I have known many a foolish fellow spend much time and money in shooting to no purpose, because he happened one day to hit a turkey by chance. *Old Farmer's Almanac, 1811.* What this editor observed in the woodlands of 1811 was apparent in the gambling parlors of Las Vegas a century and a half later, where one stroke of luck would generate a lifetime of enthusiasm for the gaming table. Psychologist B. F. Skinner recognized this paradox, that scarce and unpredictable rewards can be a powerful learning tool. He used this principle of "aperiodic partial reinforcement" to teach "simian-level" skills to mice and pigeons.

I believe that the power to make money is a gift from God. *John D. Rockefeller*

It signifies nothing to play well if you lose. *1732, Fuller*

Jascha Heifetz, in the days of his fame, played his violin in the streets, receiving no more attention than any blind fiddler. *Syd-ney J. Harris, Clearing the Ground.* Harris recalls other incognito—and unappreciated—performances of Caruso and Chaplin to underscore the fact that nothing succeeds like success: "The name makes the game.... Fame creates its own generative power of response."

It is not enough to succeed; others must fail. *Gore Vidal*

It's not for stealing that you are punished, but for getting caught. *Russian proverb*

Losers are always in the wrong. *1855, Bohn*

Luck begets luck, and failure suckles failure. *Opie Read*

Moderation is a fatal thing. Nothing succeeds like excess. *Oscar Wilde, A Woman of No Importance*

Nothing fails like success. *G. K. Chesterton*

Nothing recedes like success. *Helen Gurley Brown*

Nothing succeeds like the appearance of success. *Christopher Lasch, The Culture of Narcissism*

Sometimes nothing succeeds like excess.

Stupidities that succeed are still stupidities. *Yiddish proverb*

Success begets success.

Success covers a multitude of blunders. *G. B. Shaw*

Success has many parents, but failure is an orphan.

Success is a good deodorant. It takes away all your past smells. *Elizabeth Taylor, 1984*

Success is never blamed. *1732, T-607*

Success is the fine art of making mistakes when nobody is looking.

Success, in men's eyes, is God and more than God. *Aeschylus*

Success makes a fool seem wise. *1707, OE-628*

Successful and fortunate crime is called virtue. *Seneca, Hercules Furens*

Successful sin passes for virtue. *Francis Bacon*

The desire for success lubricates secret prostitutions in the soul. *Norman Mailer*

The man who takes a dollar is a thief, but if he steals a million, he is a genius. *Josh Billings*

The one who wins plays best. *German proverb*

The only infallible criterion of wisdom to vulgar minds—success. *Edmund Burke*

The poor man's wisdom is despised, and his words are not heard. *Ecclesiastes 9:16*

The world rewards the appearance of merit oftener than merit itself. *François de la Rochefoucauld*

There are only two ways of getting on in the world: by one's own industry, or by the stupidity of others. *Jean de La Bruyère*

When the play works, you keep running it. *Old football adage*

Watergate was worse than a crime—it was a blunder. *Richard Nixon, 1978*

We don't want any losers around. In this family we want winners. *Joseph P. Kennedy*

We don't know who we are until we see what we can do. *Martha Grimes*

When you win, nothing hurts. *Joe Namath*

When you win, you're an old pro. When you lose, you're an old man. *Charles Conerly*

Why they call a feller who keeps losing all the time a good sport gits me. *Kin Hubbard*

Winning has a joy and discrete purity to it that cannot be replaced by anything else. *A. Bartlett Giamatti*

You can't beat winning.

The law doth punish man or woman
That steals the goose from off the common,
But lets the greater felon loose,
That steals the common from the goose.
18th century

Treason doth never prosper: what's the reason?
For if it prosper, none dare call it treason.
John Harington, Epigrams

See also If it ain't broke, don't FIX it.

You can't argue with SUCCESS.

I never question a success, any more than I do the right of a bulldog to lie in his own gateway. *Josh Billings*

Now when I bore people at a party, they think it's their fault. *Henry Kissinger*

Success is the sole earthly judge of right and wrong. *Adolf Hitler, Mein Kampf*

The only man who is really free is the one who can turn down an invitation to dinner without giving an excuse. *Jules Renard*

The successful revolutionary is a statesman, the unsuccessful one is a criminal. *Erich Fromm, Escape from Freedom*

See also Nothing succeeds like SUCCESS.

Never give a SUCKER an even break.*

It is morally wrong to allow suckers to keep their money. *"Canada Bill" Jones*

*Keyes (K-114) conjectures that Wilson Mizner picked up this phrase during his gambling days in Alaska and San Francisco and brought it to New York in 1905. He was a good friend of W. C. Fields, who popularized the line by "ad-libbing" it in the 1923 musical comedy *Poppy*. "Never Give a Sucker an Even Break" was the title of Fields' last movie.

There's a SUCKER born every minute.*

. . . and two to take him. *Wilson Mizner*

Anyone who can be hustled will be hustled. *Donald G. Smith*

Every crowd has a silver lining. *P. T. Barnum*

If something sounds too good to be true, it probably is.

If the world will be gulled, let it be gulled. *Robert Burton*

People will buy anything that's one to a customer. *Sinclair Lewis*

Remember this: the house doesn't beat a player. It merely gives him a chance to beat himself. *Nick "The Greek" Dandalos*

The world likes to be cheated. *Dutch proverb*

There's a thumb-sucker born every minute.

There is no crime in the cynical American calendar more humiliating than to be a sucker. *Max Lerner*

*Attributed to P. T. Barnum, although there is no evidence that he ever said it, says the Barnum Museum curator, Robert S. Pelton. The word *sucker*, meaning a gullible person, was not idiomatic in Barnum's time. Barnum did say, "The American people like to be humbugged." Burton Stevenson (B-2237) compares the saying with the proverb "A fool is born every minute."

The same SUN softens wax and hardens clay. 1550, Erasmus

From the same flower the bee extracts honey and the wasp gall. *Heard in Illinois*

Hammering hardens steel and breaks rocks.

The same sun bleaches linen and darkens Gypsies. *Yiddish proverb*

The same fire melts the butter and hardens the egg.

The wind that blows out candles, kindles the fire. *1732, T-729*

The SUN don't shine on the same dog's tail all the time.*

*Every dog has his day; things are bound to change. Listed as a Southern saying by Smith.

SURVIVAL of the fittest. *Herbert Spencer, Principles of Biology, 1864*

At least in the law of the jungle, you've survival of the fittest. In Congress, you've just got survival. *Robert W. Packwood*

If there is anything in the theory of the survival of the fittest, a lot of people we know must have been overlooked. *William C. Hunter*

Survival of the luckiest.

Then why do "the good die young"?

The best swimmers are drowned. *T-645*

The best climbers do fall. *T-645*

The bravest fencers are the soonest run through. *T-645*

"The unfit die—the fit both live and thrive." Alas, who say so? They who do survive. *Sarah N. Cleghorn, The Survival of the Fittest*

One SWALLOW doesn't make a summer. Aesop (6th century B.C.)

. . . but it may break a New Year's resolution.

. . . but too many swallows make a fall. *George Prentice*

. . . nor one woodcock a winter. *1636, Camden*

. . . Perhaps not. But there are ever so many occasions when one swallow—just one single swallow—is better than nothing to drink at all. And if you get enough of them they *do* make a summer. *Stephen Leacock*

One fly makes a summer. *Mark Twain*

No SWEET without sweat. 1639, Clarke

Elbow grease gives the best polish. *1672, OE-170*

Expecting something for nothing is the most popular form of hope. *Arnold Glasow*

I am a great believer in luck, and find the harder I work, the more I have of it. *Stephen Leacock*

If only I could get that wonderful feeling of accomplishment without having to accomplish anything. © *Ashleigh Brilliant*

No joy without annoy. *1598, T-350*

No money, no honey.

No rule for success will work if you won't. *Elmer C. Leterman*

Sweat: the cologne of accomplishment. *Heywood Broun*

See also Don't count on LUCK; No GAINS without pains.

SWEETS to the sweet. *Shakespeare, Hamlet 5.1.266, ca. 1600*

. . . bring business to dentists.

Who lives by the SWORD dies by the sword.*

A man may build himself a throne of bayonets, but he cannot sit on it. *W. R. Inge*

Four decades of nuclear weapon production have polluted the air, soil and water at 16 plants and research laboratories in the United States. The contaminants include uranium, plutonium, cesium, strontium, PCB's, chromium, arsenic, mercury and solvents used in making nuclear weapons. *New York Times, 1989*

Injure others, you injure yourself. *1578, Florio*

Malice drinks its own poison. *1572, WM-395*

The god of war is alike to all, and slayeth him that would slay. *Homer, Iliad*

Who is created by television can be destroyed by television. *Theodore H. White, 1984*

Whoso diggeth a pit shall fall therein, and he that rolleth a stone, it will return upon him. *Proverbs 26: 27*

*All they that take the sword shall perish with the sword. *Matthew 26:52*. He that killeth with the sword must be killed with the sword. *Revelation 3:10*

It's all in how you TAKE it.

A letter depends on how you read it, a melody on how you sing it. *Yiddish proverb*

A man's life is dyed the color of his imagination.

Illusion is the first of all pleasures. *Voltaire*

Life is ten percent what you make it and 90 percent how you take it. *Irving Berlin, as quoted in Reader's Digest, May 1949*

Men are disturbed not by the things that happen, but by their opinion of the things that happen. *Epictetus*

The difference between stumbling blocks and stepping-stones is the way you use them.

There is nothing either good or bad, but thinking makes it so. *Shakespeare, Hamlet 2.2.11*

Two men look out through the same bars:
One sees the mud, and one the stars.
Frederick Langebridge, A Cluster of Quiet Thoughts

The optimist sees the doughnut,
The pessimist, the hole.
McLandburgh Wilson, Optimist and Pessimist

TALK is cheap. *1800, B-2279*

. . . except when you hire a lawyer. *Joey Adams*

. . . but you can seldom buy it back.

. . . because the supply always exceeds the demand.

. . . but it takes money to buy whiskey. *New England proverb*

. . . but it don't pay off mortgages. *Boston Herald, 1957; BJW-612*

Anybody who thinks talk is cheap has never argued with a traffic cop. *Henny Youngman*

Deeds are fruit, words are but leaves. *1616, Draxe*

Good words cost nought. *1599, T-755*

I thought talk was cheap until I saw our telephone bill. *Henny Youngman*

It's not the same to talk of bulls as to be in the bullring. *Spanish proverb*

Kind words will never die—neither will they buy groceries. *Bill Nye*

Life is far too important a thing ever to talk about. *Oscar Wilde*

Talk is easy, but work is hard. *Heard in Ontario*

Words are but sands, it's money buys lands. *1659, Howell*

Words are but wind. *1486, T-756*

See also ACTIONS speak louder than words; EASIER said than done; STICKS and stones may break my bones, but names will never harm me.

It takes two to TANGO.* *Title of a 1952 song by Hoffman and Manning, popularized by Pearl Bailey*

Success in marriage does not come merely through finding the right mate, but through being the right mate. *Barnett Brickner*

You cannot shake hands with a clenched fist. *Indira Gandhi, 1982*

*You can sail in a ship by yourself,
  Take a nap or a nip by yourself.

You can get into debt on your own.
There are lots of things that you can do
  alone.

But it takes two to tango, two to tango,
Two to really get the feeling of romance.
Let's do the tango, do the tango,
Do the dance of love.

A TASK well begun is half done.

See The BEGINNING is the hardest.

TASTES are tastes.

Each to his taste, and a taste to each. *Ogden Nash, Seaside Serenade*

Everyone as they like, as the good woman said when she kissed her cow. *Jonathan Swift, Polite Conversation; M-261*

Everyone carries his own inch-rule of taste, and amuses himself by applying it triumphantly wherever he travels. *Henry Adams, The Education of Henry Adams*

"Everything's a matter of taste," said the devil, as he helped himself to another forkful of roast infant. *Sydney J. Harris*

If a man does not keep pace with his companions, perhaps it is because he hears a different drummer. Let him step to the music which he hears, however measured or far away. *Henry David Thoreau.* "A different drummer" is perhaps the most memorable phrase from the writings of Thoreau.

In the cuisine of love, there are flavors for all tastes. *James Huenecker, Painted Veils*

Nearly all men are married. Some are married to cars, some to booze, some to money, some to power, some to fame, some to golf, some to gambling. A small minority are married to a woman. *Richard Needham*

People say that life is the thing, but I prefer reading. *Logan Pearsall Smith*

There is no disputing about tastes. *Latin proverb*

Well, for those who like that sort of thing, I should think that is just about the sort of thing they would like. *Abraham Lincoln, 1863, when he was asked to endorse a book on communicating with spirits of the deceased.*

See also One man's MEAT is another man's poison; EVERYBODY'S entitled to his own opinion; I don't know what ART is, but I know what I like; There's no accounting for TASTES.

There's no accounting for TASTES. *Latin proverb*

. . . as the woman said when somebody told her her son was wanted by the police. *F. P. Adams*

See also One man's MEAT is another man's poison; TASTES are tastes.

TAXATION without representation is tyranny.* *James Otis, 1761*

If Patrick Henry thought that taxation without representation was bad, he would see how bad it is *with* representation. *Old Farmer's Almanac*

Rebellion to tyrants is obedience to God. *Thomas Jefferson*

*Watchword of the American Revolution, popularized by James Otis (1725–83) (K-58–59).

Don't TEACH fish to swim. *1611, T-219*

Don't teach your grandmother to suck eggs. *1701, O-221*

Must you teach your grandfather how to cough? *Hindu proverb*

Tell me it snows. *1585, T-653*

You teach your father to get children. *1641, Fergusson*

Those who can, do; those who can't, TEACH.*

. . . Those who can't teach, teach the teachers. Those who can't teach the teachers, get government grants. *Peter's Almanac*

A critic is a gong at a railroad crossing clanging loudly and vainly as the train goes by. *Christopher Morley*

A critic is a legless man who teaches running. *Channing Pollock*

A critic is a man who knows the way but can't drive the car. *Kenneth Tynan, New York Times Magazine, Jan. 9, 1966*

A good writer is not, per se, a good critic. No more than a good drunk is automatically a good bartender. *Jim Bishop*

Asking a working writer what he thinks about critics is like asking a lamppost what it thinks about dogs. *John Osborne*

Critics are like eunuchs in a harem: they know how it's done, they've seen it done every day, but they're unable to do it themselves. *Brendan Behan*

Eighty-seven percent of all people in all professions are incompetent. *John Gardner*

It is only the learned who care to learn, the ignorant prefer to teach. *Edouard le Berquier*

Only those become priests who cannot earn a living. *Heard in Indiana*

There is one thing more exasperating than a wife who can cook and won't, and that's a wife who can't cook and will. *Robert Frost*

Those who can't teach, administrate. Those who can't administrate, run for office.

Those who can't, criticize. *Heard in New York and South Carolina*

Those who can, do. Those who can't, attend conferences.

Those who think they can't are generally right. *Heard in New Jersey*

He who can, does. He who cannot, teaches. G. B. Shaw, Maxims for Revolutionists

TELL it like it is.

If you can't be direct, why be? *Lily Tomlin, 1974*

We have enough people who tell it like it is—now we could use a few who tell it like it can be. *Robert Orben*

See also Call a SPADE a spade; Speak the TRUTH and shame the devil; A WORD fitly spoken is like apples of gold in pictures of silver.

You never can TELL.

Always put on clean underwear in the morning, in case you're in an accident. *A parent's advice*

Marriage is a covered dish. *Swiss proverb*

We know what we are, but know not what we may be. *Shakespeare, Hamlet 4.5.42*

See also ANYTHING can happen.

TEMPUS fugit. *Latin proverb*

See TIME flies.

THANK your lucky stars.

An agnostic thanks whomever this may concern.

As Thanksgiving approaches, turkeys are thankful for vegetarians.

Hollywood producers thank their lucky stars.

See also KNOCK on wood; The RACE is not to the swift . . . ; There but for the grace of GOD go I.

You can't live on THANKS.

Kind words will never die—neither will they buy groceries. *Edgar Nye*

Praise without profit puts nothing in the pocket.

Praises fill not the belly. *1666, Torriano*

Thanks is poor pay on which to keep a family. *Heard in Mississippi*

You can't put THANKS in your pocket. *Russian proverb*

Honor will buy no beef. *17th century*

See also You can't live on THANKS.

THEM that has, gets.*

A girl with a pretty knee can grin and bare it. *Captain Billy's Whiz Bang, Oct. 1922*

*Them ez wants, must choose.
  Them ez hez, must lose.
  Them ez knows, won't blab.
  Them ez guesses, will gab.
  Them ez borrows, sorrows.

Them ez lends, spends.
Them ez gives, lives.
Them ez keeps dark, is deep.
Them ez kin earn, kin keep.
Them ez aims, hits.
Them ez hez, gits.
Them ez waits, win.
Them ez will, kin.
Edward R. Sill, A Baker's Duzzen uv Wize Saws, 1880

See also The RICH get richer, and the poor get children; MONEY makes money.

THEM that has it shows it. *Diamond Jim Brady (1856–1917)*

See When you've got it—FLAUNT it.

It takes a THIEF to catch a thief. *ca. 250 B.C., B-2300*

. . . and a jury to let him go.

An old poacher makes the best keeper. *Geoffrey Chaucer, Physician's Tale*

Put an old cat to catch an old rat. *1668, B-296*

Rats know the way of rats. *Chinese proverb*

Set a thief to catch a thief. *1670, Ray*

Once a THIEF, always a thief.* *1706, O-168–69*

*Among variants listed by Oxford (O-168–69) are "Once a bishop and ever a bishop," "Once a whore, always a whore" (1613), "Once a priest, always a priest," "Once a patsy, always a patsy" (1953). Other variants of this proverb are "Once a drunkard, always a drunkard," "Once a fool, always a fool," and "Once a liar, always a liar."

One THING leads to another.

One calamity leads to another.

Women are the flowers of life as children are its fruits. *Bernardin de Saint Pierre*

THINGS are not always what they seem. *Latin proverb*

. . . Skim milk masquerades as cream. *W. S. Gilbert, H. M. S. Pinafore*

See also APPEARANCES are deceiving; You can't tell a BOOK by its cover.

THINGS could be worse.

. . . Suppose your errors were counted and published every day, like those of a baseball player?

. . . and when they are . . . find hope in the thought that things are so bad they have to get better. *Malcolm Forbes, The Sayings of Chairman Malcolm*

THINK*

. . . or thwim.

. . . and if you can't think, frown and look like you're thinking.

A great many people think they are thinking when they are merely rearranging their prejudices. *William James*

Act as men of thought; think as men of action. *Henri Bergson*

Few people think more than two or three times a year. I have made an international reputation for myself by thinking once or twice a week. *G. B. Shaw*

If you don't do your own thinking, someone else will do it for you. *Edward de Bono*

If you make people think they're thinking, they'll love you; but if you really make them think, they'll hate you. *Don Marquis*

If you think twice before you speak, you'll find that about ninety percent of the time you will have no occasion to say a word. *William C. Hunter*

It is impossible to live without brains, either one's own or borrowed. *Baltasar Gracian*

It occurred to me lately that nothing has occurred to me lately. © *Ashleigh Brilliant*

It's always best to stop and taste your words before you let them pass through your teeth.

Machines should work. People should think.

Most men, when they think they are thinking, are merely rearranging their prejudices. *Knute Rockne, as quoted in Reader's Digest, Oct. 1927*

Nobody is hanged for thinking. *Hungarian proverb*

Say as men say, but think for yourself. *1639, Clarke*

See into life. Don't just look at it. *Anne Baxter*

Sometimes I sits and thinks, and sometimes I just sits.

Taking thought is strength. *African proverb*

The best use one can make of his mind is to distrust it. *François Fénelon*

The chief function of the body is to carry the brain around. *Thomas Edison*

The only food for thought is more thought. *Peter's Almanac*

The real problem is not whether machines think but whether men do. *B. F. Skinner*

There is a greater difference between really thinking and only thinking that we think than most of us think. *L. de V. Matthewman*

There is no expedient to which a man will not go to avoid the real labor of thinking. *Thomas Edison*. Posted on signs about the Edison laboratory, ca. 1895.

Think before you speak is criticism's motto; speak before you think creation's. *E. M. Forster, Two Cheers for Democracy*

Think before you think! *Stanislaw J. Lec, Unkempt Thoughts*

Think twice before you speak and then say it to yourself. *Elbert Hubbard, 1895*

think twice before you think. *e. e. cummings*

Thinking is like loving and dying. Each of us must do it for himself. *Josiah Royce*

Thinking is the hardest work there is, which is the probable reason why so few engage in it. *Henry Ford, 1929*

Thinking is the one thing no one has ever been able to tax. *Charles F. Kettering*

What is the hardest task in the world? To think. *Ralph Waldo Emerson, 1841*

Wishful thinking is a contradiction in terms. *Malcolm Forbes*

Said first and thought after
Brings many to disaster.
H. W. Thompson, 1940

Think wisely, weighing word and fact,
But never think too much to act.
Arthur Guiterman

*Motto popularized by IBM's Thomas Watson.

THINK big.

Better to fail in attempting exquisite things than to succeed in the department of the utterly contemptible. *Arthur Machen, The Hill of Dreams*

Think globally, but act locally. *Abbie Hoffman, theme of his last public address, Jericho (New York) High School, Mar. 27, 1989*

Bite off more than you can chew,
    Then chew it.
Plan more than you can do,
    Then do it.

See also LESS is more; Make no small PLANS; SMALL is beautiful.

I THINK, therefore I am. René Descartes, Discourse on Method, 1637

I am, therefore I think. *G. B. Shaw*

I tape, therefore I am. *Studs Terkel*

Cartoonist: I ink, therefore I am.
Coward: I think, therefore I scram.
Critic: I think, therefore I damn.
Drunkard: I drink, therefore I ham.
Flirt: I wink, therefore I am.
Hypocrite: I think, therefore I sham.
Obsessive: I think that I think, therefore I think that I am.
Panhandler: I think, therefore I bum.
Pessimist: I think, therefore I'm worried.
Rake: Coito, ergo sum.

Man is no more than a reed, the weakest in nature. But he is a thinking reed. *Blaise Pascal, Pensées*

The power of positive THINKING. *Title of a book by Norman Vincent Peale, 1952*

A positive attitude may not solve all your problems, but will annoy enough people to make it worth the effort. *Herm Albright*

Attitudes are more important than facts. *Karl Menninger.* Quoted by Norman Vincent Peale, with the comment: "That is worth repeating until its truth grips you."

Believe in yourself! Have faith in your abilities! Without a humble but reasonable confidence in your own powers you cannot be successful or happy. *Norman Vincent Peale*

But the power of positive thinking will not turn paraplegics into quarterbacks or blind men into sportscasters.

Enthusiasm is the greatest asset—more than power or influence or money. *Motto on a needlepoint pillow in the Kennebunkport, Maine, bedroom of George and Barbara Bush, New York Times, Nov. 26, 1988*

I think there is one smashing rule: Never face the facts. *Ruth Gordon, New York Post, 1971*

I was going to buy a copy of *The Power of Positive Thinking,* and then I thought: What the hell good would that do? *Ronnie Shakes*

One of the most powerful concepts, one that is a sure cure for lack of confidence, is the thought that God is actually with you and helping you. . . . To practice it simply affirm "God is with me; God is helping me; God is guiding me." Spend several minutes each day visualizing His presence. . . . Go about your business on the assumption that what you have affirmed and visualized is true. Affirm it, visualize it, believe it, and it will actualize itself. The release of power which this procedure stimulates will astonish you. *Norman Vincent Peale*

They are able who think they are able. *Virgil*

"Think positively and good things will happen" . . . [promises that] good thoughts are going to trigger all kinds of provident vibrations and sweet blessings to that person who has done nothing but sit on his can and let the good thoughts flow. . . . This is a very easy message to sell because it comes down to the idea of getting something for nothing. *Donald G. Smith*

When I hear Norman Vincent Pealing,
I get that awful run-down feeling.

See also It's all a matter of MIND over matter.

There is nothing either good or bad but THINKING makes it so. *Shakespeare, Hamlet 2.2.259, ca. 1600*

A man's no better than he thinks he is. *Heard in Michigan and Minnesota*

Do not be afraid of life. Believe that life is worth living and your belief will help create that fact. *William James*

Everything is but what we think it. *Marcus Aurelius, Meditations*

See also It's all a matter of MIND over matter; It's all in how you LOOK at it; Nothing is IMPOSSIBLE; The power of positive THINKING.

THOUGHT is free. *1390, O-223*

There is no hanging a man for his thoughts. *New England proverb*

See also THINK; You have not CONVERTED a man because you have silenced him.

Second THOUGHTS are best. *Greek proverb*

See HASTE makes waste.

He that would THRIVE must rise at five; he that has thriven may lie till seven. *16th century*

There is a TIDE in the affairs of men.*

. . . but the trick is in learning how to tell a tide from an undertow. *Sydney J. Harris*

Nothing is as inevitable as a mistake whose time has come.

The wave of the future is coming and there is no stopping it. *Anne Morrow Lindbergh*

There is a tide in the affairs of women,
Which, taken at the flood, leads—God knows
   where.
Lord Byron, Don Juan

*There is a tide in the affairs of men,
  Which, taken at the flood, leads on to fortune.
  Shakespeare, Julius Caesar, 4.3.217, ca. 1600
See also STRIKE while the iron is hot.

Blest be the TIE that binds. *Title of a hymn by Johann G. Nägeli (1773–1836)*

No TIME like the present. *1562, O-226*

I gave my wife a watch for her birthday. I figure there's no present like the time. *Henny Youngman*

No time like the pleasant.

The graveyard is too lonesome. Give me my flowers now. *Old postcard*

See also CARPE diem; The MILL cannot grind with the water that is past.

TIME and tide wait for no man. *Geoffrey Chaucer, Prologue to Clerk's Tale, 1386*

. . . and for very few women.

. . . but time always stands still for a woman of thirty. *Robert Frost*

Time and tide and newspapers wait for no man.

TIME flies. (Tempus fugit.) *Latin proverb*

. . . and eternity waits. *Polish proverb*

. . . death urges, knells call, heaven invites, Hell threatens.
Edward Young, Night Thoughts

Don't worry about middle age; you'll outgrow it. *Peter's Almanac*

Hourglasses remind one not only of the quick passage of time, but also of the dust to which we shall come one day. *Georg Lichtenberg*

Lost: Somewhere between sunrise and sunset, two golden hours, each set with sixty diamond minutes. No reward is offered, for they are gone forever. *Horace Mann*

Sweetest hours fly fastest.

Time has wings. *1600, T-670*

Time is an illusion—to orators. *Kin Hubbard*

Time is but a freckle on the face of eternity. *Evan Esar*

Here hath been dawning another blue day;
Think, wilt thou let it slip useless away?
Thomas Carlyle

The noiseless foot of time steals swiftly by,
And, ere we dream of manhood, age is nigh!
Juvenal, trans. by William Gifford

TIME heals all wounds. *Geoffrey Chaucer, Troilus and Criseyde, ca. 1374*

. . . and wounds all heels.

What wound did ever heal but by degrees?
Shakespeare, Othello 2.3.337

TIME is of the essence. 1629, M-599

All of us complain about the shortness of life, yet we waste more time than we use. *Josh Billings, 1865*

I wasted time; now doth time waste me. *Shakespeare, Richard II 5.5.49*

If you have a half hour to spare, don't spend it with someone who hasn't.

Time is the coin of your life. It is the only coin you have, and only you can determine how it will be spent. Be careful lest you let other people spend it for you. *Carl Sandburg*

TIME marches on. *Heard in California, Michigan, and New York*

A man who dares to waste one hour of life has not discovered the value of life. *Charles Darwin*

Dime is money, as the Dutchman says. *Heard in California and New York*

Nothing is ours except time. *Seneca*

The Future is something which everyone reaches at the rate of sixty minutes an hour, whatever he does, whoever he is. *C. S. Lewis, The Screwtape Letters*

Time is nature's way of keeping everything from happening at once.

Time is slippery. *Kim Linder*

Time makes a wise person wiser and a fool more foolish—but so does everything else. *Peter's Almanac*

We mustn't waste time, for that's the stuff life's made of. *David Belasco, 1911*

What greater crime than loss of time? *Thomas Tusser, 1573*

Who kills time murders opportunity. *Frederick H. Seymour*

TIME waits for no one.

Time devours all things. *1732, Fuller*

TIME will tell. *Latin proverb*

There are many events in the womb of time, which will be delivered. *Shakespeare, Othello 1.3.377*

Time and chance reveal all secrets. *18th century*

TIME works wonders. *1588, M-599*

Old droppings do not stink. *Swahili proverb*

Nature, time, and patience are the three great physicians. *Bulgarian proverb*

Snow and adolescence are the only problems that disappear if you ignore them long enough. *Earl Wilson, as quoted in Reader's Digest, Jan. 1963*

These are the TIMES that try men's souls. *Thomas Paine, The American Crisis, 1776*

More than any other time in history, mankind faces a crossroads. One path leads to despair and utter hopelessness. The other, to total extinction. Let us pray we have the wisdom to choose correctly. *Woody Allen, Side Effects*

TIMES change and we with them. *Latin proverb*

Don't limit a child to your own learning, for he was born in another time. *Rabbinical saying*

Since the beginning, each generation has fought nature. Now, in the life-span of a single generation, we must turn around 180 degrees and become the protector of nature. *Jacques Cousteau*

The automobile changed our dress, manners, social customs, vacation habits, the shape of our cities, consumer purchasing patterns, common tastes, and positions in intercourse. *John Keats, The Insolent Chariot*

The heresy of one age becomes the orthodoxy of the next. *Helen Keller*

Times change and men deteriorate. *Gesta Romanorum, 1440*

Times sure change; today cars are a necessity and children are a luxury.

Times, they are a-changin'.

We ain't what we want to be, and we ain't what we are gonna be, but we ain't what we was. *Heard in Mississippi*

Yes, the old-fashioned family doctor is disappearing—but, then, again, so is the old-fashioned family. *Wall Street Journal*

A truth
Looks freshest in the fashion of the day.
Alfred, Lord Tennyson, Morte D'Arthur

See also O tempora! O mores!; Things are going to the DOGS.

TIT for tat.* 1546, Heywood

. . . quoth the wife when she farted at the thunder. *1721, T-672*

He that speaks me fair and loves me not, I'll speak him fair and trust him not. *1616, Draxe*

*A senseless proverb spoken when we give as good as we get (T-672). OE-661 says the proverb is apparently a variation of "tip for tap."

TO BE, or not to be; that is the question. Shakespeare, Hamlet 3.1.55

Poisons pain you;
Rivers are damp;
Acids stain you;
And drugs cause cramp.
Guns aren't lawful;
Nooses give;
Gas smells awful;
You might as well live.
Dorothy Parker

Here TODAY and gone tomorrow. 1549, F-86

Fret today, regret tomorrow. *Heard in Ontario*

Hair today, gone tomorrow.

Hero today, gone tomorrow. *Herb Daniels*

To-day gold, to-morrow dust. *1869, Hazlitt*

Today above ground, tomorrow under. *1611, Cotgrave*

Today at good cheer, tomorrow on the bier. *C. H. Spurgeon, 1880*

Today's newspaper is tomorrow's fish-wrapper. *Ben Hecht*

Today's peacock is tomorrow's feather-duster.

What we think we have but have not: money. *Japanese proverb*

See also All FLESH is grass; LIFE is short.

TODAY is the tomorrow you worried about yesterday.

. . . Now you know why.

. . . and in two days, tomorrow will be yesterday.

The future has a way of arriving unannounced. *George Will*

There's always TOMORROW.

An American living in Mexico was berating a worker for stalling on a job for several weeks. "Señor," the worker patiently explained, "I think I know what is wrong with you gringos. You Americans think *mañana* means *tomorrow*. It does not mean tomorrow. It means not today."

Men think foolishly they may abuse and misspend life as they please and when they get to heaven turn over a new leaf. *Henry David Thoreau, Journal*

Tomorrow is often the busiest day of the year. *Spanish proverb*

Tomorrow is a new day. *1527, T-674*

TOMORROW is another day.* *1527, O-227*

. . . to waste.

Because you have occasional low spells of despondency, don't despair. The sun has a sinking spell every night but it rises again all right the next morning. *Henry Van Dycke*

Successful people do what failures put off until tomorrow. *Heard in Minnesota*

Yesterday is experience, tomorrow is hope, and today is getting from one to another as best we can. *Peter's Almanac*

*The Spanish expression (not the word per se) *Mañana* may be an elliptical form of the proverb *Mañana sera otro día.*

TOMORROW never comes. *1539, Taverner*

Mañana is often the busiest day of the week. *Spanish proverb*

Tomorrow never gets here; when it gets here, it's today. *Heard in U.S. and Canada*

TOMORROW will be better. *Theocritus, ca. 270 B.C.*

A windy March and a rainy April make a beautiful May. *1657, T-443*

Tomorrow will be worse.

TOO MUCH of anything is not good. *ca. 1500, T-658*

. . . but so can not enough. © *Ashleigh Brilliant*

It is not good to eat much honey. *Proverbs 25:27*

Too much of a good thing is simply wonderful. *Liberace*

Too much of anything is worse than none at all. *Geoffrey Chaucer, 1390*

See MODERATION in all things.

One TOUCH of nature makes the whole world kin. *Shakespeare, Trolius and Cressida 3.3.1, ca. 1601*

Human nature's human nature.

Human nature is the same all the world over.

When the going gets tough, the TOUGH get going.*

The tougher the fight, the sweeter the triumph. *Heard in Oregon*

When the going gets tough, the smart get lost. *Robert Byrne*

When the going gets tough, the tough go shopping.

When the going gets tough, the tough take a vacation. *Harry Browne*

When you get to the end of your rope, tie a knot and hang on. *Franklin D. Roosevelt*

*A decades-old (perhaps centuries-old) maxim, says Keyes (K-86), who recalls hearing it from his high school coach in 1959, and it was a favorite saying of Joseph P. Kennedy, (1888–1969). Biographer J. H. Cutler wrote, "Joe made his children stay on their toes. . . . He would bear down on them and tell them, 'When the going gets tough, the tough get going' " (*Honey Fitz*).

Of all sad words of TONGUE or pen, the saddest are these: It might have been. *John Greenleaf Whittier, Maude Muller, 1854*

The follies which a man REGRETS most are those which he didn't commit when he had the opportunity. *Helen Rowland, Reflections of a Bachelor Girl*

It is not impossibilities which fill us with the deepest despair, but possibilities which we have failed to realize. *Robert Mallet, Apostilles*

Life consists of wishing you had if you didn't and wishing you hadn't if you did. *Heard in Mississippi*

The saddest words of tongue or pen,
We sold the crib and baby buggy, then . . .
The saddest words of tongue or pen
If I had only bought it then.
Ruth J. Perot, Wall Street Journal

Saddest words of tongue or pen,
Are these two words, Stung again.
Old postcard

The trouble with opportunities is that they always look much better going than coming.

The oldest words of pen or tongue:
We didn't do that when I was young.
Suzanne Douglass

More sad are these we daily see:
"It is, but hadn't ought to be."
Bret Harte, Mrs. Judge Jenkins

Of all cold words of tongue or pen,
The worst are these, I knew him when.
Heard in Mississippi

The way of TRANSGRESSORS is hard.
Proverbs 13:15

. . . but it isn't lonely.

. . . because the traffic is so heavy.

TRAVEL broadens the mind. *1933, O-229*

. . . and reduces the bank balance.

. . . and lengthens the conversation.

. . . and loosens the bowels.

An ox goes to town and when it comes back it's still an ox. *Yiddish proverb*

Be a tourist! Hard work, no pay, uncertain conditions, and long periods away from home. © *Ashleigh Brilliant*

Generally the net cerebral broadening that the average man derives from travel is merely a greater knowledge of hotels, restaurants, barrooms, tipping customs, acquiescent hussies, and bargains in the way of walking sticks, neckties and bandana handkerchiefs, with here and there possibly an art gallery, which he generally dislikes intensely, thrown in. *George Jean Nathan*

He that travels far knows much. *1670, Ray*

If an ass goes a-travelling, he'll not come home a horse. *1732, Fuller*

If you reject the food, ignore the customs, fear the religion and avoid the people, you might better stay home. You are like a pebble thrown into water; you become wet on the surface, but never part of the water. James *Michener, in Good Advice, by William and Leonard Safire*

It isn't the travel that's broadening; it's all that rich foreign food.

Nothing thickens one like travel. *Will Rogers*

Send a donkey to Paris, he'll return no wiser than he went. *Flemish proverb*. There are many variants, says Stevenson (B-2363).

Send a fool to the market and a fool he will return again. *ca. 1598, T-230*

This summer one-third of the nation will be ill-housed, ill-nourished and ill-clad. Only they call it vacation. *Joseph Salak*

Travel is educational; it teaches you how to get rid of money in a hurry. *S. Barry Lipkin*

Travel makes a wise man better but a fool worse. *1623, T-679*

Traveling is the ruin of all happiness. *Fanny Burney, Cecilia; M-1147*

Traveling is a brutality. It forces you to trust strangers and to lose sight of all that familiar comfort of home and friends. You are constantly off-balance. *Caesar Pavase, New York Times Book Review, 1981*

Travelling is almost like talking with men of other centuries. *René Descartes, Discourse on Method*

You can never really get away—you can only take yourself somewhere else. *Peter's Almanac*

Some of our sparks to London town do go,
Fashions to see, and learn the world to know;
Who at return have nought but these to show,
New wig above, and new disease below.
Benjamin Franklin, 1734

Travel: some good advice
　From one who knows;
Take twice the cash
　And half the clothes.

He TRAVELS the fastest who travels alone. *Rudyard Kipling (1865–1936), The Winners*

He that hath wife and children hath given hostages to fortune, for they are impediments to great enterprises, either of virtue, or mischief. *Francis Bacon, Of Marriage and Single Life*

The man who goes alone can start today; but he who travels with another must wait till that other is ready. *Henry David Thoreau, Walden*

See also A young man MARRIED is a man that's marred; You can't LIVE with them, and you can't live without them.

Don't TREAD on me.*

I am a person. Do not bend, fold, spindle, or mutilate. *Picket sign at the Berkeley riots, 1964.* In the early days of data processing, this warning, "Do not bend . . ." routinely appeared on bills, which were also to be used as data cards.

*In the early days of the American Revolution, naval forces and militiamen adopted rattlesnake flags. Coiled or crawling, the reptile became a symbol of the American cause and frequently appeared with the motto "Don't Tread on Me."

Both Presidents Reagan and Clinton have used this phrase to characterize American foreign policy. In a speech of June 26, 1993, announcing an American naval strike against the Iraqi intelligence establishment, President Clinton introduced the variant "Don't tread on *us.*"

If this be TREASON, make the most of it. *Patrick Henry, 1765*

Rebellion to tyrants is obedience to God. *Motto on Thomas Jefferson's seal, ca. 1776*

The TREE is known by its fruit. *Matthew 12:33*

See DEEDS, not creeds.

There are TRICKS to every trade. *1632, O-230*

. . . and it's all a matter of knowin' how.

Knavery in All Trades. *Title of a 1632 book by M. Parker*

If you haven't TRIED it, don't knock it.

Prove all things; hold fast to that which is good. *1 Thessalonians 5:21*

Try everything once except incest and folk-dancing. *Thomas Beecham*

Don't ask for TROUBLE.

Don't go near the water unless you know how to swim. *Old postcard*

Don't marry an automobile wife on a wheel-barrow salary. *Old postcard*

Don't piss against the wind.

Finding extreme pleasure will make you a better person if you are careful about what thrills you. *Jenny Holzer*

He that seeks trouble never misses it. *1612, T-683*

He who a wolf-cub kept, the beast to tame,
Was torn to pieces when a wolf it became. *Sadi, 1250*

If a man puts a rope around his neck, God will provide someone to pull it. *African proverb*

If you don't want to be crucified, don't hang around crosses.

If you invite trouble, it's sure to accept.

Never invest your money in anything that eats or needs repairing. *Billy Rose*

Never play cards with a man named Doc. Never eat at a place called Mom's. Never sleep with a woman whose troubles are worse than your own. *Nelson Algren*

Never stand between a dog and the hydrant.

The nail that sticks up gets hammered down. *Japanese proverb*

Spit against the wind and you spit in your own face. *Armenian proverb*

See also Don't monkey with the BUZZSAW.

Don't borrow TROUBLE. *1719, WM-612*

. . . It is cheerfully given.

. . . Be patient and you'll have some of your own.

. . . Get married and have troubles of your own.

. . . Borrow money; it gives a lot more satisfaction.

Borrow trouble for yourself, if that's your nature, but don't lend it to your neighbors. *Rudyard Kipling, Rewards and Fairies*

Some people are so fond of ill luck that they run halfway to meet it. *Douglas Jerrold*

Worry [is] the interest paid by those who borrow trouble. *George W. Lyon, in Judge, 1924*

Don't go looking for TROUBLE.

He that seeks trouble never misses. *1640, Herbert*

If you're going looking for trouble, you don't need to get ready for a long trip.

See also Don't borrow TROUBLE; Never trouble TROUBLE till trouble troubles you.

Man is born unto TROUBLE, as the sparks fly upward. *Job 5:7*

The art of living lies not in eliminating but in growing with troubles. *Bernard M. Baruch*

See also It's a hard LIFE; LIFE is just one damn thing after another.

Never trouble TROUBLE till trouble troubles you. *1884, O-230*

Anxiety is the interest paid on trouble before it is due. *W. R. Inge*

Are you come to meet your trouble? The fashion of the world is to avoid cost, and you encounter it. *Shakespeare, Much Ado About Nothing 1.1.98*

It's bad form to go half-way to meet troubles which are not coming to your house. *Ethel White, The Wheel Spins*

Never go out to meet trouble. If you will just sit still, nine times out of ten, someone will intercept it before it reaches you. *Calvin Coolidge*

Stay away from trouble. Presence of mind is good, but absence of body is better.

The fellow who courts trouble often marries her. *Old postcard*

Troubles, like babies, grow larger by nursing. *Old postcard*

Better never trouble Trouble
  Until trouble troubles you;
For you only make your trouble
  Double-trouble when you do.
David Keppel, Trouble

There's a saying old and rusty,
  But as good as any new;
'Tis Never trouble trouble
  Till trouble troubles you.

See also Don't go looking for TROUBLE.

Keep your TROUBLES to yourself.

The best remedy for a dispute is to discuss it. *African proverb*

Most TROUBLES never occur. *1817, B-2378*

Of all our troubles great and small, the greatest are those that don't happen at all. *Heard in Ontario*

Real difficulties can be overcome; it is only the imaginary ones that are unconquerable. *Theodore N. Vail*

The misfortunes hardest to bear are those which never come. *James Russell Lowell, Democracy*

Worry often gives a small thing a big shadow. *Swedish proverb*

See also Why WORRY?

Keep on TRUCKIN'. *Hippie maxim of the 1960s meaning Don't give up**

Even if you're on the right track, you'll get run over if you just sit there. *Will Rogers*

I'm doing what I can to prolong my life, hoping that someday I'll learn what it's for. © *Ashleigh Brilliant*

Life is like riding a bicycle: you don't fall off unless you stop pedaling. *Claude Pepper*

*Popularized by cartoonist R. Crumb. Keyes (K-39) notes that the expression "trucking it" emerged in the 1890s to describe riding a train by holding onto the trucking hardware between the wheels. In the Depression-era blues song "Trucking," the singer vows to "Keep on truckin' . . . truckin' my blues away."

To thine own self be TRUE. *Shakespeare, Hamlet 1.3.75*

A man ought to do what he thinks is right. *Line spoken by John Wayne in the 1953 film Hondo*

Be careless in your dress if you must, but keep a tidy soul. *Mark Twain, Pudd'nhead Wilson's New Calendar*

Be so true to thyself, as thou be not false to others. *Francis Bacon, Of Wisdom for a Man's Self*

Be true to your own self, aim high, never give up, and you will surely win. *Old postcard*

Brush and floss every day. Be true to your teeth or your teeth will be false to you.

If I am like others, who will be like me? *Yiddish proverb*

It is better to be defeated on principle than to win on lies. *Arthur Calwell, 1968*

Keep true to the dreams of thy youth. *Friedrich von Schiller*

The greatest of all freedoms is that of non-participation. When you stop applauding on cue, you are reborn. You are free. Until then, you are merely picking cotton for the master. *Donald G. Smith*

Try not to become a man of success but rather to become a man of value. *Albert Einstein*

When someone else writes your script, you're not living. You're just playing a part. *Donald G. Smith*

When you betray someone else, you also betray yourself. *Isaac Bashevis Singer, New York Times, Nov. 26, 1978*

Never TRUST anyone over thirty. *

. . . What ever happened to that asinine, divisive, and useless dictum so popular in the sixties? Answer: It has been unabashedly abandoned because its perpetrators are now themselves over thirty. *Garson Kanin*

Every man over forty is a scoundrel. *G. B. Shaw, Stray Sayings*

Never trust anyone over-dirty. *Robert Byrne*

One of the privileges of old age seems to be to give advice that nobody will follow and relating experiences that everybody mistrusts. *Josh Billings*

Young people don't know what age is, and old people forget what youth was. *Vermont proverb*

*Popularized by Jerry Rubin, 1966, but first said in 1964 by Jack Weinberg, says Keyes (K-10).

Half the TRUTH is often a great lie. *Poor Richard's Almanac, 1758*

Speak the TRUTH and shame the Devil. *François Rabelais (1494?–?1553), Gargantua and Pantagruel; F-898*

. . . You will also surprise him very often. *L. de V. Matthewman*

He that hath truth on his side is a fool as well as a coward if he is afraid to own it because of other men's opinions. *Daniel Defoe*

He who speaks the truth should have one foot in the stirrup. *Hindu proverb*

I never give them hell. I just tell the truth and they think it is hell. *Harry S. Truman, as quoted in Look, Apr. 3, 1956*

In every generation there has to be some fool who will speak the truth as he sees it. *Boris Pasternak*

It's almost got so you can't speak the truth without committing an indescretion. *Kin Hubbard*

It's better to tell the truth and run, than to lie and get caught in the act. *William C. Hunter*

Man is a born liar. Otherwise he would not have invented the proverb "Tell the truth and shame the devil."

My way of joking is to tell the truth. It is the funniest thing in the world. *G. B. Shaw*

Publicity is justly commended as a remedy for social and industrial diseases. Sunlight is said to be the best of disinfectants; electric light the most efficient policeman. *Louis D. Brandeis, Other People's Money*

Say as you think and speak it from your souls. *Shakespeare, 2 Henry VI 3.1.247*

Tell the truth and run. *Yugoslav proverb*

Ten people who speak make more noise than ten thousand who are silent. *Napoleon*

The tongue of a man is his weapon, and speech is mightier than fighting. *Khati I*

There can be no higher law in journalism than to tell the truth and to shame the devil. . . . Remain detached from the great. *Walter Lippmann, 1974*

To knock a thing down, especially if it is cocked at an arrogant angle, is a deep delight of the blood. *George Santayana*

Truth makes the devil blush. *1732, I-687*

We seek the truth and will endure the consequences. *Charles Seymour*

See also SILENCE is golden; The PEN is mightier than the sword.

The TRUTH hurts.

. . . Not the searching after, the running from. *John Eyberg*

. . . Sometimes it ought to.

A remark generally hurts in proportion to its truth. *Will Rogers*

Better a dish of illusion and a hearty appetite for life, than a feast of reality and indigestion therewith. *H. A. Overstreet, The Enduring Quest*

Cynicism is an unpleasant way of saying the truth. *Lillian Hellman*

Honest criticism is hard to take, particularly from a relative, a friend, an acquaintance, or a stranger. *Franklin P. Jones*

Humor is really laughing off a hurt, grinning at misery. *Bill Mauldin, Time, July 21, 1961*

If the Republicans will stop telling lies about us, we will stop telling the truth about them. *Adlai Stevenson, waggishly proposing a compromise to the Republican charge that he was misrepresenting them.*

If we were all given by magic the power to read each other's thoughts, I suppose the first effect would be to dissolve all friendships. *Bertrand Russell*

Men occasionally stumble over the truth, but most of them pick themselves up and hurry off as if nothing had happened. *Winston Churchill*

The reason for the sadness of this modern age and the men who live in it is that it looks for the truth in everything, and finds it. *Edmond and Jules Goncourt*

The truth makes one angry. *Italian proverb*

The truth, naked and unashamed, is always unpleasant. *James Huneker, 1905*

Truth is disagreeable only to a fool. *Arabic proverb*

Truth is truth. *1576, T-686*

We can easily forgive a child who is afraid of the dark; the real tragedy of life is when men are afraid of the light. *Plato*

See also Ye shall know the TRUTH, and the truth shall make you free.

The TRUTH is not to be spoken at all times. *Pindar, 485 B.C.*

. . . because honesty can be a catastrophic policy.

A fool's soul is always dancing on the tip of his tongue. *Arabic proverb*

A good lie finds more believers than a bad truth. *German proverb*

A lie is an abomination unto the Lord and a very present help in trouble. *Adlai Stevenson*

A little inaccuracy sometimes saves tons of explanation. *Saki, The Square Egg*

A man may, in some circumstances, disguise the truth, . . . for were it always to be spoken, and upon all occasions, this were no world to live in. *Walter Scott, 1821*

A man who won't lie to a woman has very little consideration for her feelings. *Heard in New York*

A person that always says just what he thinks at last gets just what he deserves. *Austin O'Malley*

A necessary lie is harmless.

A wise woman puts a grain of sugar into everything she says to a man, and takes a grain of salt with everything he says to her. *Helen Rowland*

Always tell the truth, even if you have to lie to do so.

An ounce of hypocrisy is worth a pound of ambition. *Michael Korda*

An untruth is not always a lie. Romancing, as we use the term, means the telling of untruths that are not falsehoods. *Edward A. Strecker and Vincent T. Lathbury, Their Mothers' Daughters*

Any fool can tell the truth, but it requires a man of some sense to know how to lie well. *Samuel Butler*

As a politician never believes what he says, he is always astonished when others do. *Charles de Gaulle, 1962*

Better a lie that soothes than a truth that hurts. *Czech proverb*

Beware of telling an improbable truth. *1732, Fuller*

Blunt truths cause more mischief than nice falsehoods do. *Alexander Pope, An Essay on Criticism*

Bureaucrats are the only people in the world who can say absolutely nothing and mean it. *James Harlan Boren*

George Washington, as a boy, was ignorant of the commonest accomplishments of youth. He could not even lie. *Mark Twain*

God is not adverse to untruth in a holy cause. *Aeschylus*

He that cannot dissemble knows not how to live. *Latin proverb*

He that will live in this world must be endowed with the three rare qualities of dissimulation, equivocation, and mental reservation. *Aphra Behn*

He who speaks the truth will lose his head. *Arabic proverb*

Homely truth is unpalatable. *Mark Twain, The Adventures of Tom Sawyer*

Honesty has ruined more marriages than infidelity. *Charles McCabe*

Honesty is often in the wrong. *Lucan*

Hypocrisy is the all-purpose lubricant of social intercourse.

If every man were straightforward in his opinions, there could be no conversation. *Benjamin Disraeli*

If you always tell the truth, nobody will trust you. © *Ashleigh Brilliant*

Insincerity is merely a method by which we can multiply our personalities. *Oscar Wilde*

It is better to be quotable than honest. *Tom Stoppard*

It is dangerous to be sincere unless you are also stupid. *G. B. Shaw*

Lie, but don't overdo it. *Russian proverb*

Lying increases the creative faculties, expands the ego, and lessens the frictions of social contacts. *Clare Boothe Luce*

Lying is an indispensable part of making life tolerable. *Bergen Evans*

Many people today don't want honest answers insofar as honest means unpleasant or disturbing. They want a soft answer that turneth away anxiety. *Louis Kronenberger, as quoted in Reader's Digest, Feb. 1972*

Most writers regard truth as their most valuable possession, and therefore are most economical in its use. *Mark Twain*

Never tell a lie till the truth doesn't fit. *Heard in Ontario*

Never waste a lie; you never know when you may need it. *Mark Twain*

No real gentleman will tell the naked truth in the presence of ladies. *Mark Twain*

Optimistic lies have such immense therapeutic value that a doctor who cannot tell them convincingly has mistaken his profession. *G. B. Shaw, Misalliance*

People have lost their jobs, gone bankrupt, destroyed their marriages, gone to jail, and even faced the executioner for telling the truth. I am not advocating a life of prevarication, but I think it should be pointed out that honesty . . . can . . . be very painful. *Donald G. Smith*

Please don't lie to me, unless you're absolutely sure I'll never find out the truth. © *Ashleigh Brilliant*

Society can only exist on the basis that there is some amount of polished lying and that no one says exactly what he thinks. *Lin Yu-tang*

Speak fair and think what you will. *1598, OE-610*

The history of our race, and each individual's experience, are sown thick with evidence that truth is not hard to kill and that a lie well told is immortal. *Mark Twain*

The lie is a condition of life. *Friedrich Nietzsche*

The secret of staying young is to live honestly, eat slowly, and lie about your age. *Lucille Ball*

The true use of speech is not so much to express our wants as to conceal them. *Oliver Goldsmith*

There are only two ways of telling the complete truth—anonymously and posthumously. *Thomas Sowell*

Truth is a rare virtue; be sparing of it. *Mark Twain, 1893*

Truth is a science but lying is an art, since you're stuck with the truth but you can be wonderfully creative with a lie.

You don't tell deliberate lies, but sometimes you have to be evasive. *Margaret Thatcher, 1976*

When my love swears that she is made of truth,
I do believe her though I know she lies.
Shakespeare, Sonnet 138

A truth that's told with bad intent
Beats all the lies you can invent.
William Blake, Auguries of Innocence

The truth is so top secret,
It only stands to reason,
That any one exposing it
Is culpable of treason.
E. Y. Harburg

Too much truth
Is uncouth.
Franklin P. Adams

See also HONESTY is the best policy.

The TRUTH will out. *1439, O-231*

A lie stands on one leg, truth on two. *New England proverb*

Carlyle said, A lie cannot live; it shows he did not know how to tell them. *Mark Twain*

Rumor travels faster, but it don't stay put as long as truth. *Will Rogers*

Thaw shows up what the snow has hidden. *Heard in Ontario*

The truth never dies—but it lives a wretched life. *Yiddish proverb*

The truth will ouch. *Arnold Glasow*

Time hatcheth truth. *Robert Greene, 1592*

Truth alone can stand strict and stern investigation, and rejoices to come to the light. *Moses Harvey, on old postcard*

Truth is the daughter of Time. *Aulus Gellius*

Truth surfaces like oil on water. *Yiddish proverb*

Truth wins out. *Latin proverb*

TRUTH, crushed to the earth, shall rise again. *William Cullen Bryant, The Battlefield, 1837*

. . . A lie will do the same thing. *Albany (Ore.) Herald, ca. 1925*

Truth, crushed to earth, burrows out of sight. *J. Mistletoe*

The truth is the most robust and indestructible and formidable thing in the world. *Woodrow Wilson, 1919*

Truth is tough. It will not break, like a bubble, at a touch; nay, you may kick it about all day, like a football, and it will be round and full at evening. *Oliver Wendell Holmes, 1860*

Truth never dies, but leads a tortured life. *Sign in a lawyer's office*

See also FACTS are facts.

TRUTH is beauty.*

If truth is beauty, how come no one has their hair done in the library? *Lily Tomlin*

The good is nothing but the beautiful in action. *Jean-Jacques Rousseau*

True words are not always pretty; pretty words are not always true. *Japanese proverb*

Truth is beautiful. Without doubt; and so are lies. *Ralph Waldo Emerson*

What is art? A semblance of truth more beautiful than truth. *Opie Read*

*"Beauty is truth, truth beauty,"—that is all ye know on earth, and all ye need to know. *John Keats (1795–1821), Ode on a Grecian Urn*

TRUTH is often spoken in jest. *14th century*

A jest is something that is sharp enough to be noticed, and not rude enough to be resented. *Josh Billings*

A true jest is no jest. *14th century*

Comedy is simply a funny way of being serious. *Peter Ustinov*

Fortunately there is one outlet for the truth. We are permitted to discuss in jest what we may not discuss in earnest. A serious comedy about sex is taboo: a farcical comedy is privileged. *G. B. Shaw, Overruled*

Good nonsense is good sense in disguise. *Josh Billings*

Humor is also a way of saying something serious. *T. S. Eliot*

It always hurts a bit when you strike your funny bone. That's the essence of humor. *Jim Fiebig*

My way of joking is telling the truth. That is the funniest joke in the world. *G. B. Shaw, as quoted in Reader's Digest, Jan. 1939*

There are people who can talk sensibly about a controversial issue; they're called humorists. *Cullen Hightower*

There is more logic in humor than in anything else. Because, you see, humor is truth. *Victor Borge, London Times, Jan. 3, 1984*

When a thing is funny, search it for a hidden truth. *G. B. Shaw, Back to Methuselah*

Wit has truth in it, wisecracking is merely calisthenics with words. *Dorothy Parker*

You cannot jest an enemy into a friend, but you can jest a friend into an enemy. *Heard in Illinois, Texas, and Wisconsin*

TRUTH is stranger than fiction.*

. . . and more embarrassing.

. . . That's why it's not so popular.

. . . and publicity is stranger than both.

. . . and often it is also more artistic.

. . . It is to most folks! *Josh Billings*

. . . but I am measurably familiar with it. *Mark Twain, Pudd'nhead Wilson's New Calendar*

. . . but it is because fiction is obliged to stick to possibilities; truth isn't. *Mark Twain, Pudd'nhead Wilson's New Calendar.* Sydney J. Harris expressed the same thought: "The reason that truth is stranger than fiction is that fiction has to have a rational thread running through it in order to be believable, whereas reality may be totally irrational."

Fact is richer than diction. *J. L. Austin, Philosophical Papers*

Fiction reveals truths that reality obscures. *Jessamyn West*

I don't know if truth is stranger than fiction; it can certainly be more disconcerting.

I don't make jokes—I just watch the government and report the facts. *Will Rogers*

I have seen the truth, and it doesn't make sense.

It is easier to believe a lie that one has heard a thousand times than to believe a fact that no one has heard before. *Grit*

Nowadays, truth is not only stranger than fiction, it's a lot cleaner.

Telling the truth is a business in which there is very little competition. *Old postcard*

The difference between truth and fiction is that fiction has to make sense. *Mark Twain*

The main difference between living people and fictitious characters is that the writer takes great pains to give the characters coherence and inner unity, whereas the living people may go to extremes of incoherence because their physical existence holds them together. *Hugo von Hofmannsthal, The Book of Friends*

Truce is stronger than friction. *L. L. Levinson*

Truth is always duller than fiction. *Piers Paul Read, 1981*

Truth is not only stranger than fiction but far more interesting. *Margaret Echard, 1943*

Truth may be stranger than fiction, but fiction is truer. *Frederic Raphael, 1976*

Truth must necessarily be stranger than fiction; for fiction is the creation of the human mind and therefore congenial to it. *G. K. Chesterton, The Club of Queer Trades*

We learn from experience that not everything which is incredible is untrue. *Cardinal de Retz, Memoirs*

Youth is stranger than fiction. *J. D. Fenna*

*'Tis strange but true; for truth is always strange;
　Stranger than fiction.
　Lord Byron (1788–1824), Don Juan

What is TRUTH?

A philosopher looking for absolute truth is like a blind man in a dark room looking for a black cat that isn't there. *Laurence Peter*

Dear Lord: Help me seek the truth, but spare me the company of those who have found it.

What kind of truth is it that is true on one side of the mountain and false on the other? *Michel de Montaigne*

Ye shall know the TRUTH, and the truth shall make you free. *John 8:32*

. . . but first it shall make you miserable.

All truths are half-truths. *Alfred North Whitehead*

Chase after truth like hell and you'll free yourself, even though you never touch its coat-tails. *Clarence Darrow*

I have seen the truth and it doesn't make sense.

Let the people know the truth and the country is safe. *Abraham Lincoln*

Tell your boss what you think of him, and the truth shall set you free.

The search for truth is really a lot of good fun. *Vernon Howard*

The terrible thing about the quest for truth is that you find it. *Rémy de Gourmont*

Universities should be safe havens where ruthless examination of realities will not be distorted by the aim to please or inhibited by the risk of displeasure. *Kingman Brewster*

Veritas vos liberabit. ("The truth shall make you free.") *Motto of the Johns Hopkins University*

What for centuries raised man above the beast is not the cudgel but the irresistible power of unarmed truth. *Boris Pasternak, Doctor Zhivago*

Ye shall know the truth and the truth shall make you mad. *Aldous Huxley*

Ye shall know the truth and the truth shall make you flee. *Helen Wieselberg*

See also RIGHT makes might.

Let every TUB stand on its own bottom. 1564, WM-618

See PADDLE your own canoe.

One good TURN deserves another. 412 B.C., B-2400

. . . thought the dog, as he prepared to lie down.

. . . and one dirty trick ought to get paid back with interest.

If you don't go to other people's funerals, how can you expect them to come to yours?

One good turn and you have most of the bedcovers. *Elaine C. Moore*

TURNABOUT is fair play. 1755, O-232

To deceive a deceiver is no deceit. *Ulpian Fulwell, 1580*

As the TWIG is bent, the tree's inclined.* 1530, *Palsgrave*

Birth is much, but breeding is more. 1639, *Clarke*

Conscience is what your mother told you before you were six years old. *Brock Chisholm, Ladies' Home Journal, 1949*

Parenting is a negative thing. Keep your children from killing themselves, or anyone else, and hope for the best. *Donald G. Smith*

To reform a man, you must begin with his grandmother. *Old postcard*

As the twig is bent—so the saying goes,
And I do my darndest, goodness knows.
But nevertheless, when day is done
And at last in bed is my little son,

It isn't the twig that is bent, I sigh,
It is I.
Richard Armour

*The popularity of this 16th-century proverb probably comes from its use two centuries later by Alexander Pope in his 1732 poem, "Epistles to Several Persons":

'Tis Education forms the common mind,
Just as the Twig is bent, the Tree's inclined.

TWO can live as cheaply as one.

. . . if both are working.

. . . for half as long.

. . . if they don't eat. *Harold Jones*

. . . but it's worth the difference to stay single.

. . . but it takes both of them to earn enough to do it. *Frances Rodman*

. . . but it costs them twice as much. *Frank Sullivan*

The only two who can live as cheaply as one are a dog and a flea. *Evan Esar*

The UNEXPECTED always happens.
Latin proverb

Nothing is certain but the unforeseen. *1886, O-164*

Unexpected things happen more often than those you hope for. *Latin proverb*

See also ANYTHING can happen.

In UNION there is strength.*

A cloth is stronger than the threads from which it is made. *Richard Nixon*

In onion there is strength.

Man is like a banana: when he leaves the bunch, he gets skinned. *Heard in Ohio*

One leg cannot dance alone. *East African proverb*

One voice, no voice. *Italian proverb*

Snowflakes are one of nature's most fragile things, but just look what they can do when they stick together. *Vesta M. Kelly*

Sticks in a bundle are unbreakable. *African proverb*

*Aesop (6th century B.C.), "The Bundle of Sticks." Attributed to Homer by Oxford (O-236).

See also MAN is a social animal; Many hands make light WORK.

UNITED we stand, divided we fall. *Aesop (6th century B.C.), The Four Oxen and the Lion*

Then join hand in hand, brave Americans all,
By uniting we stand, by dividing we fall!

John Dickinson's Liberty Song, published in the Boston Gazette, 1768. This proverb became a watchword of the American Revolution.

See also We must all HANG together, or we shall all assuredly hang separately.

Whatever goes UP must come down. *1939, O-237*

. . . except the cost of living.

. . . only if it goes up with a velocity of less than 4.8 miles per second.

Gardening is based on the faith that what goes down must come up.

Whatever goes up will go up some more after the first of the year.

What's the USE?

He is a fool that is not melancholy once a day. *1678, Ray*

I could tell you some real funny jokes but you'd only laugh at them.

I should have stood in bed. *Joe Jacobs.* John Lardner attended the frigid opening of the 1935 World Series and overheard a companion ask Jacobs what he thought of the game. Lardner claims to have heard Jacobs' memorable reply: "The only time I ever heard a famous quotation in the making." (K-149)

Life is a dead-end job.

Motto of a drug rehabilitation institute: Abandon all dope ye that enter here.

There is no use in your walking five miles to fish when you can depend on being just as unsuccessful near home. *Mark Twain*

There is nothing to express, nothing from which to express, no power to express, no desire to express, together with the obligation to express. *Samuel Beckett*

You leap out of bed; you start to get ready;
You dress and you dress till you feel unsteady;
Hours go by, and you're still busy
Putting on clothes, till your brain is dizzy.
Do you flinch, do you quit, do you go out naked?
The least little button, you don't forsake it.
What thanks do you get? Well, for all this mess yet
When night comes around, you've got to undress yet.
Samuel Hoffenstein

"What's the use?" was a popular theme on old postcards, which offered a variety of contraries like those listed below:

If you save your money, you're a grouch; if you spend it, you're a loafer.

If you get it, you're a grafter; if you don't get it, you're a bum.

When a man is little, the big girls kiss him; when he's big, the little girls kiss him.

If he is poor, he is a bad manager; if he is rich, he's dishonest.

If he needs credit, he can't get it; if he is prosperous, everybody wants to do him a favor.

If he is in politics, it is for graft; if he stays out of politics, he is no good to the country.

If he does not give to charity, he is a stingy cuss; if he does, it is for show.

If he is actively religious, he is a hypocrite; if he takes no interest in religion, he is a hardened sinner.

If he gives affection, he is a soft specimen; if he care for no one, he is cold blooded.

If he lives to an old age, he missed his calling; if he dies young, there was a great future for him.

One old postcard lists a few contraries in verse:

If you dance the jazz and shimmy, you're a bounder.

If you do not jazz and shimmy, you're a rube.

If you stay out in the evening, you're a rounder.

If you stick around the house, you're a boob.

If you dress well, they will call you a cake-eater.

If you don't regard your clothes, you are a mark.

If you lose your wad on Wall Street, you're a bleater.

If you win out down on Wall Street, you're a shark.

No matter what we do, they're going to slam you.

We all come in for our share of abuse.

So live to suit yourself, and let them lam you.

But, to please everyone, aw, what's the use?

See also You can't WIN.

You can get USED to anything.

Servitude debases men to the point where they end up liking it. *Luc de Clapiers de Vauvenargues, Reflections and Maxims*

You could get used to hangin' if it didn't kill you.

See also HABIT is second nature.

All is VANITY.*

. . . except words of wisdom like these.

. . . But if all were only vanity, who would mind? Alas, it is too often worse than vanity: agony, darkness, death also. *Thomas Hardy, in The Later Years of T. H., by F. E. Hardy*

A gossip is one who talks to you about others; a bore is one who talks to you about himself; a brilliant conversationalist is one who talks to you about yourself. *Lisa Kirk, New York Journal-American, Mar. 9, 1954*

Conceit is God's gift to little men. *Bruce Barton*

Fashion makes fools of some, sinners of others, and slaves of all. *Josh Billings*

Flattery is soft soap, and soft soap is ninety percent lye. *1840, WM-215*

He who is in love with himself has at least this advantage: he won't encounter many rivals. *Georg Lichtenberg*

How I like to be liked, and what I do to be liked! *Charles Lamb, letter to Dorothy Wadsworth, 1821*

Humility is not renunciation of pride but the substitution of one pride for another. *Eric Hoffer*

If a man is vain, flatter. If timid, flatter. If boastful, flatter. In all history, too much flattery never lost a gentleman. *Kathryn Cravens, Pursuit of Gentlemen*

If egoism were a disease, the world would be one big hospital.

If there is a single quality that is shared by all great men, it is vanity. *Yousuf Karsh, Cosmopolitan, Dec. 1955*

It is not to be imagined by how many different ways vanity defeats its own purpose. *Lord Chesterfield*

Nothing makes you a better listener than hearing your name mentioned.

One is vain by nature, modest by necessity. *Pierre Reverdy*

Take all the vanity and selfishness out of a man, and there ain't much of anything left. *Josh Billings*

The sweetest sound to anyone's ear is the sound of his own name. *Dale Carnegie*

To love oneself is the beginning of a life-long romance. *Oscar Wilde, Phrases and Philosophies*

Vanity dies hard; in some obstinate cases it outlives the man. *Robert Louis Stevenson, Prince Otto*

We are more anxious to speak than to be heard. *Henry David Thoreau, Journal*

We are offended and resent it when people do not respect us; and yet no man, deep down in the privacy of his heart, has any considerable respect for himself. *Mark Twain*

What makes the vanity of other people intolerable is that it wounds our own. *François de la Rochefoucauld*

Whenever cannibals are on the brink of starvation, Heaven in its infinite mercy sends them a nice plump missionary. *Oscar Wilde, (adapted)*

Women and maidens must be praised, whether truly or falsely. *German proverb*

From the sayings of Malcolm Forbes:

> To seduce most anyone, ask for and listen to his opinion.

> The ideal conversationalist is one who listens—and agrees.

> Attention is to people what fertilizer is to flowers.

'Tis an old maxim in the schools,
That flattery's the food of fools;
Yet now and then your men of wit
Will condescend to take a bit.
Jonathan Swift, Cadenus and Vanessa

Vanity, vanity, all is vanity
That's any fun at all for humanity. . . .
The prophets chant and the prophets chatter,
But somehow it never seems to matter,
For the world hangs on to its ancient sanity
And orders another round of vanity.
Ogden Nash

*Vanity of vanities . . . all is vanity. *Ecclesiastes 1:2; 12:8.* An inspection of the Hebrew text shows that the subject is not self-love but *futility*, the emptiness of things.

See also FLATTERY will get you nowhere; PRAISE is always pleasant; SELF-LOVE is better than self-hate.

VANITY, thy name is woman.

If a woman were on her way to an execution, she would demand a little time to put on makeup. *Sébastien-Roch Nicolas Chamfort*

Vanity is what makes a woman look for shoes that are larger inside than outside.

Women are wacky,
Women are vain:
They'd rather be pretty
Than have a good brain.
Dorothy Fishback, Lip Service

VARIETY is the spice of life.*

. . . when it is not for its own sake. *Marlene Dietrich*

A change of work is as good as a rest. *Irish proverb*

It destroys one's nerves to be amiable every day to the same human being. *Benjamin Disraeli, The Young Duke*

Let a hundred flowers blossom and a hundred schools of thought contend. *Mao Tsetung, Feb. 27, 1957, as he was about to launch a major political campaign to flush out dissenters*

Let it be worse, so long as it's different. *Yiddish proverb*

Love is like linen: often changed, the sweeter. *Phineas Fletcher*

Sour, sweet, bitter, pungent, all must be tasted. *Chinese proverb*

Such is the state of life, that none are happy but by the anticipation of change: the change itself is nothing; when we have made it the next wish is to change again. *Samuel Johnson, Rasselas*

Suicide is despise of life. *Cynic, 1905*

The love of change is as natural to man as it is to nature. *Josh Billings*

Variety is the one simply and absolutely foolproof aphrodisiac. *Norman Douglas*

We all become great explorers during our first few days in a new city, or a new love affair. *Mignon McLaughlin*

*The sweetness of variety was extolled by the ancient Greeks, but it was first called the spice of life by William Cowper:
Variety's the very spice of life,
That gives it all its flavour.
The Task, ca. 1783

VENGEANCE is mine . . . sayeth the Lord.* *Romans 12:19*

When the Italians hear how God hath reserved vengeance to himself, they say blasphemously, He knew it was too sweet a bit for man, therefore kept it for His own tooth. *Samuel Pepys*

*The Hebrew Bible similarly reserves vengeance to God: "O Lord God, to whom vengeance belongeth" (Psalms 94:1).

To the VICTOR belong the spoils. *Aristotle (384–322 B.C.), B-2200*

The man who pulls the plow gets the plunder. *Huey Long, 1934*

VICTORY is sweet.

I hope the other side plays well. I hope they play to their limit, because if they don't, there's no fun beating them. *Joe Paterno*

The harder the battle, the sweeter the victory. *Heard in Rhode Island*

See also It matters not whether you WON or lost, but how you played the game.

Eternal VIGILANCE is the price of liberty.* *Wendell Phillips, Public Opinion, 1852*

Eternal boredom is the price of vigilance.

Eternal vigilance is the price of celibacy. *Poor Richard Jr.'s Almanac, 1906*

Eternal vigilance is the price, not only of liberty, but of a great many other things. It is the price of everything good. It is the price of one's own soul. *Woodrow Wilson, speech in Washington, D.C., Oct. 1914*

*Popularly regarded as the words of Thomas Jefferson. Wendell Phillips wrote that he believed he had originated the phrase, but Keyes (K-59) traces the line to a speech by an Irish statesman half a century earlier.

VIOLENCE begets violence.

Blood will have blood. *1559, O-22*

Whoso sheddeth man's blood, by man shall his blood be shed; for in the image of God made he man. *Genesis 9:6*

See also Who lives by the SWORD dies by the sword.

VIRTUE is its own reward. *Latin proverb*

. . . alas! *L. L. Levinson*

. . . but has no sale at the box office. *Mae West*

. . . and that is what deters so many from carrying out their own good intentions.

Chastity is no more a virtue than malnutrition. *Alex Comfort*

Don't be misled into the paths of virtue. *Oscar Wilde*

Good girls go to heaven; bad girls go everywhere. *Embroidered on a pillow displayed in office of Cosmopolitan editor Helen Gurley Brown*

If virtue were its own reward, it would no longer be a human quality, but supernatural. *Vauvenargues*

Of all the sexual aberrations, the most peculiar is chastity. *Rémy de Gourmond*

Once you have done a man a service, what more would you have? Is it not enough to have obeyed the laws of your own nature, without expecting to be paid for it? That is like the eye demanding a reward for seeing, or the feet for walking. *Marcus Aurelius, Meditations*

Our virtues are most frequently but vices in disguise. *François de la Rochefoucauld*

Righteous people terrify me . . . virtue is its own punishment. *Aneurin Bevan*

Service is the rent we pay for room on earth and I'd like to be a good tenant. *Eddie Cantor, Take My Life*

Sin is its own reward. *L. L. Levinson*

The greatest pleasure I have known is to do a good action by stealth, and to have it found out by accident. *Charles Lamb, Table Talk*

The liar's punishment is not in the least that he is not believed but that he cannot believe anyone else. *G. B. Shaw*

The one sure way to escape ingratitude is to do good without expecting gratitude as your reward. If you do not get your joy out of the act of self-expression you cannot find it elsewhere. *Thomas Dreier*

The reward is *in* keeping the Commandments, not *for* keeping them.

Those who genuinely believe that virtue is its own reward should also believe, as a corollary, that vice is its own retribution—and should not desire to add society's revenge to nature's punishment. *Sydney J. Harris*

Virtue has never been as respectable as money. *Mark Twain*

Virtue is her own reward, is but a cold principle. *Thomas Browne, Religio Medici*

Virtue is its own—and only—reward. *L. de V. Matthewman*

Virtue is its own disappointment. *Philip Moeller, 1917*

Virtue is its own punishment. *Aneurin Bevan (attributed)*

Virtue is its own revenge. *E. Y. Harburg*

Virtue is learned at Mother's knee—and vice at other joints.

Virtue is more to be feared than vice, because it excesses are not subject to the restraints of conscience. *Albert Jay Nock*

Virtue is praised but hated. People run away from it, for it is ice-cold and in this world you must keep your feet warm. *Denis Diderot, Rambeau's Nephew*

Virtue is simply vice at rest. *Harry Hirschfield*

When a man does a good turn just for the fun of the thing, he has got a good deal more virtue in him than he is aware of. *Josh Billings*

When I do good, I feel good; when I do bad, I feel bad, and that is my religion. *Abraham Lincoln*

If virtue is its own reward,
   Then why—I'd like to know
Does doing only what I should,
   So often bore me so!

Robert Dennis

My only aversion to vice,
Is the price.
Victor Buono

Vice
Is Nice
But a little virtue
Won't hurt you.
Felicia Lamport, 1961

Make a VIRTUE of necessity. *Saint Jerome, ca. 400, B-1668*

Of necessity, one makes a virtue out of virtue.

Where there is no VISION, the people perish. *Proverbs 29:18*

VIVE la difference.

An unlearned carpenter of my acquaintance once said in my hearing: "There is very little difference between one man and another, but what there is is very important." *William James*

Early in World War II, a speaker to a group of factory workers in France was rallying the workers to redouble their efforts: "Today, men and women of France are working together to help win the war. Today, there is a very small difference between men and women." A voice from the crowd of workers shouted, *"Vive la petite difference!"*

The VOICE of the people in the voice of God. *

All power to the people.

And the Lord said unto Samuel, Hearken to the voice of the people in all they say unto thee. . . . *I Samuel 8:7*

If all men say that thou art an ass, then bray. *1616, Draxe*

If everybody says so, there's some truth to it. *Yiddish proverb*

The voice of the people is the voice of humbug. *William Tecumseh Sherman, 1863, letter to his wife*

When the world goes mad, one must accept madness as sanity, since sanity is, in the last analysis, nothing but the madness on which the whole world happens to agree. *G. B. Shaw, an open letter to Gorki, May 1916*

*The supreme law of all is the weal of the people *(Salus populi supreme lex). Lex XII Jabularum, the earliest code of Roman law, adopted 451 B.C.*

They also serve who only stand and WAIT. *John Milton, On His Blindness, M-985*

A good spectator also creates. *Swiss proverb*

They also swear who only stand and wait. *Addison Mizner*

We can't all be heroes because somebody has to sit on the curb and clap as they go by. *Will Rogers*

The weakest go to the WALL.* 1450, B-2469

*A proverb so old, its meaning is now obscure. Burton Stevenson (B-2470) relates it to three customs: (1) putting the youngest and feeblest to bed close to the wall; (2) letting ladies walk next to the walls along the street, where it was cleaner and safer than at the curb; and (3) allowing the old and weak to sit on benches along the church wall while the congregation stood.

Stone WALLS do not a prison make.*

*. . . Nor iron bars a cage;
Minds innocent and quiet take
    That for a hermitage.
    Richard Lovelace (1618–58), To Althea, from Prison

The WALLS have ears. A.D. 450, B-654

. . . and bottles have mouths. *Japanese proverb*

See also Little PITCHERS have big ears; Two can keep a SECRET if one of them is dead.

If you WANT something badly enough, you can get it.

An oak tree is just a nut that held its ground. *Fred Shero, 1975*

Let me tell you the secret that has led me to my goal. My strength lies solely in my tenacity. *Louis Pasteur*

Oversleeping will never make your dreams come true.

Work seven days a week and nothing can stop you. *John Moores*

You always WANT what you can't get.

Adam was but human—this explains it all. He did not want the apple for the apple's sake, he wanted it only because it was forbidden. *Mark Twain*

As soon as you stop wanting something, you get it. I've found that to be absolutely axiomatic. *Andy Warhol*

Money, it turned out, was exactly like sex; you thought of nothing else if you didn't have it and thought of other things if you did. *James Baldwin*

The average man is an irrational creature who's always looking for home atmosphere in a hotel, and hotel service at home.

See also You're never SATISFIED.

Save energy—help win the WAR. *World War II slogan*

Keep America beautiful—throw away something lovely.

Save energy—shower with a friend.

Save energy—on a cold night, go to bed with the person of your choice.

Save a tree—eat a beaver.

Support wildlife—throw a party.

Sometime they'll give a WAR and nobody will come. *Carl Sandburg, The People, Yes.*
Thirty years after it was written, this line became popular as an expression of protest against the Vietnam War.

Either war is obsolete, or men are. *R. Buckminster Fuller, New Yorker magazine, 1966*

Maybe they can't make you fight, said the draft officer, but they can take you where the fighting is, and you can use your own judgment.

We must not depend on any sort of Divine Providence to put a stop to war. Providence says, Kill one another, my children. Kill one another to your hearts' content. There are plenty more where you came from. Consequently, if we want war to stop we must all become conscientious objectors. *G. B. Shaw, This Danger of War*

There never was a good WAR or a bad peace. *Benjamin Franklin, 1775*

I learned that war was a profit-making business, and that there are men in the world who stir up war for profit. It is a terrible thing to think of. War is a man-made affair—it is not natural. It never settles anything. *Henry Ford*

If peace is equated simply with the absence of war, it can become abject pacifism that turns the world over to the most ruthless. *Henry Kissinger, Years of Upheaval*

See also WAR is hell; Sometime they'll give a WAR and nobody will come; WAR is not healthy for children and other living things.

WAR is hell.*

A just war is better than an unjust peace. *Tacitus*

A revolution is not a dinner party. *Mao Tsetung, 1973*

As long as war is regarded as wicked it will always have its fascination. When it is looked upon as vulgar, it will cease to be popular. *Oscar Wilde, Intentions*

Civil War: a conflict which cost more than ten billion dollars. For less than half, the freedom of all the four million slaves could have been purchased. *Charles and Mary Beard*

Don't be a fool and die for your country. Let the other sonofabitch die for his. *George S. Patton*

Fondly do we hope, fervently do we pray, that this mighty scourge of war may speedily pass away. *Abraham Lincoln*

I hate war only as a solider who has lived it can, only as one who has seen its brutality, its futility, its stupidity. *Dwight D. Eisenhower*

I'm tired of feeling rejected by the American people. I'm tired of waking up in the middle of the night worrying about the war. *Lyndon B. Johnson, to a friend following his renomination-withdrawal speech, Newsweek, Apr. 15, 1968*

In peace, sons bury their fathers; in war, fathers bury their sons. *Herodotus*

Is not life miserable enough, comes not death soon enough, without resort to the hideous enginery of war? *Horace Greeley*

Isn't it surprising what terrible things people will do just to change the line on a map? © *Ashleigh Brilliant*

It is well that war is so terrible—we would grow too fond of it. *Robert E. Lee, 1862*

It takes 15,000 casualties to train a major-general. *Ferdinand Foch*

Military justice is to justice what military music is to music. *Groucho Marx*

One should never put on one's best trousers to go out to battle for freedom and truth. *Henrik Ibsen*

Revolutions are not made with rosewater. *Edward Lytton, The Partisans*

There mustn't be any more war. It disturbs too many people. *Said by an old French peasant woman to Aristide Briand, 1917*

Unloose the dogs of war; but muzzle the darn critters; if you don't, somebody will get hurt. *Josh Billings, probably written during the Civil War*

War doesn't decide who's right—only who's left. *Antiwar bumper sticker, 1970s*

War is death's feast. *1611, Cotgrave*

War is fear cloaked in courage. *William C. Westmoreland, 1966*

War is not a solution—it is an aggravation. *Benjamin Disraeli*

War is the greatest plague that can afflict mankind. . . . Any scourge is preferable to it. *Martin Luther, 1569*

War is the unfolding of miscalculations. *Barbara Tuchman, The Guns of August*

War, after all, is simply a letting loose of organized murder, theft, and piracy on a foe. *G. B. Shaw, What I Really Wrote About the War*

War, at its best, is terrible; and this war of ours, in its magnitude and duration, is one of the most terrible. *Abraham Lincoln, speech at Great Central Sanitary Fair, 1864*

War is a series of catastrophes that result in a victory. *Georges Clemenceau*

War leaves the country with three armies: an army of cripples, an army of mourners, and an army of thieves. *German proverb*

War, which used to be cruel and magnificent, is now cruel and squalid. *Winston Churchill*

Wars are never won. Wars are only and always lost both by the victor and vanquished alike. *Bernard M. Baruch*

We are the unwilling, led by the unqualified, doing the unnecessary for the ungrateful. *Scribbled on their helmets by U.S. soldiers serving in Vietnam*

When war begins, hell opens. *1651, Herbert*

When war comes, the devil enlarges hell. *German proverb*

You can no more win a war than you can win an earthquake. *Jeannette Rankin*

You can't say civilization don't advance . . . for in every war, they kill you in a new way. *Will Rogers, Autobiography*

This is the soldier brave enough to tell
The glory-dazzled world that 'war is hell.'
from a poem by Henry Van Dyke eulogizing General Sherman

*I am tired and sick of war. Its glory is all moonshine. Only those who have never fired a shot or heard the shrieks and groans of the wounded cry aloud for blood, more

vengeance, more desolation. War is Hell. *William T. Sherman (1820–91), letter, in a biography by Lloyd Lewis*

WAR is not healthy for children and other living things.

The time not to become a father is 18 years before a world war. *E. B. White*

See also Sometime they'll give a WAR and nobody will come.

WAR is much too important a matter to be left to the generals. *Georges Clemenceau*

Government is too . . . important to be left to the politicians. *Chester Bowles*

Law reform is far too serious a matter to be left to the legal profession. *Leslie Scarman, 1955*

Military intelligence is a contradiction in terms. *Groucho Marx*

The army is a dangerous instrument to play with. *George Washington*

Don't WASH your dirty linen in public. *1809, O-241*

The amount of women in London who flirt with their husbands is perfectly scandalous. It looks bad. It is simply washing one's clean linen in public. *Oscar Wilde, The Importance of Being Earnest*

It will all come out in the WASH. *Miguel de Cervantes, 1620*

. . . and don't get caught in the wringer.

What goes on in the dark will come out in the light. *ca. 1390, WM-134*

What won't come out in the wash will come out in the rinse. *Heard in Wisconsin*

WASTE not, want not. 1732, *Fuller*

Never cut what can be untied. *H. Jackson Brown, Jr., Life's Little Instruction Book*

Never throw away food that will make a pig open his mouth. *Vermont proverb*

Recycle; we all live downstream. *Motto of Bass Pro Shops*

Reincarnation: a philosophy of spiritual recycling.

Using a Kleenex twice does not make you a conservationist.

Use it up, wear it out;
Make it do, or do without.
New England maxim

See also Save energy—help win the WAR.

Who will WATCH the watchman?*

When the fox turns preacher, beware of the geese. *1546, Heywood*

*Who is to guard the guards themselves? *Juvenal*

See also Never send a DOG to deliver a steak.

Don't go near the WATER.*

Games are a compromise between intimacy and keeping intimacy away. *Eric Berne, Games People Play*

The desire engendered in the male glands is a hundred times more difficult to control than the desire bred in the female glands. All girls [who] . . . limit their actions to arousing

desire and then defend their virtue, should be horsewhipped. *Marlene Dietrich*

*Mother, may I go out to swim?
Yes, my darling daughter:
Hang your clothes on a hickory limb
And don't go near the water.

See also CATCH-22.

Still WATER runs deep. *Latin proverb*

. . . and dirty.

. . . and the devil lays wait at the bottom.

. . . Nonsense; still water doesn't run at all.

. . . This simply is not so. The turbulent oceans run a bit deeper than any placid lake. . . . Most silent men are silent because they haven't a thought in their heads and do not wish to be found out. *George Jean Nathan*

Beware of the fury of a patient man.

Don't think there are no crocodiles because the water is calm. *Malayan proverb*

Every martyr comes with a built-in bully. *Mignon McLaughlin*

Some folks are too polite to be up to any good. *Kin Hubbard*

The rage is the most dangerous which is the most silent. *Frederick H. Seymour*

There's no one so ruthless as a timid woman striking back. *Mignon McLaughlin*

See also SILENCE is golden.

WATER never rises above its level.

Water seeks its own level. *1778, WM-642*

You never miss the WATER till the well runs dry. 1721, *Kelly*

. . . but it's also true that we often don't know what we have been missing until it arrives. *Elaine McCreight, Thoughts for All Seasons*

A man never appreciates ashes until he slips on the ice. *Heard in Mississippi*

Blessings are not valued till they are gone. *1732, Fuller*

I have always thought it would be a blessing if each person could be blind and deaf for a few days during his early adult life. Darkness would make him appreciate sight; silence would teach him the joys of sound. *Helen Keller*

The easiest way to find a use for something is to throw it away.

We never miss the waiter till our throats go dry. *Old postcard*

When you are accustomed to anything, you are estranged from it. *George Cabot Lodge*

You can't appreciate home till you've left it, money till it's spent, your wife till she joins a woman's club. *O. Henry, 1909*

You never know how dirty your hands are until you peel a hardboiled egg or go into politics. *L. L. Levinson*

You never miss the water while the champagne runs dry. *Cynic, 1905*

You are only young once.

The WATERS wear the stones.

It's a steady stream that wears a stone. *1250, M-567*

Don't make WAVES.

A protruding nail gets hit. *Japanese proverb*

Don't Make No Waves, Don't Back No Losers. *Title of a book on Chicago politics by Milton Rakove*

Don't shout for help at night. You may wake the neighbors. *Stanislaw J. Lec, Unkempt Thoughts*

Go with the flow.

It is a great folly to struggle against such things as thou canst not overcome. *Desiderius Erasmus, 1523*

One must make himself liked, for men are just only with those that they like. *Joseph Joubert*

What we want is brand-new ideas that don't upset our old ideas. *Peter's Almanac*

Who pisseth against the wind wets his shirt. *1666, Torriano*

Who spits against heaven, it falls in his face. *1583, T-304*

See also Don't rock the BOAT; If you're going to GET ALONG, you've got to go along.

There's always a WAY.

There ain't no rules around here! We're trying to accomplish something! *Thomas Edison, in Historians' Fallacies, by D. Fischer*

There is no problem so big and complicated that it can't be run away from.

They feed the baby garlic so they can find it in the dark.

See also Where there's a WILL, there's a way.

WEALTH maketh many friends.*

In wealth many friends; in poverty, not even relatives. *Japanese proverb*

Lots of people want to ride with you in the limo, but what you want is someone who will take the bus with you when the limo breaks down. *Oprah Winfrey*

Men ain't apt to get kicked out of good society for being rich. *Josh Billings*

The rich have more relatives, but the poor have more children.

The rich knows not who is his friend. *1640, Herbert*

When you ain't got no money, well, you needn't come around. *Title of a popular song, 1898*

When you are down and out, something always turns up—and it is usually the noses of your friends. *Orson Welles, New York Times, 1962*

Every man will be thy friend
Whilst thou hast wherewith to spend.
Shakespeare, The Passionate Pilgrim

*Wealth maketh many friends; but the poor is separated from his neighbour. *Proverbs 19:4*

See also MONEY makes the world go 'round; PROSPERITY gains friends, and adversity tries them.

Better to WEAR out than to rust out. *1557, WM-646*

Isn't life difficult enough without exercise? © *Ashleigh Brilliant*

Money is like an arm or leg—use it or lose it. *Henry Ford, New York Times, Nov. 8, 1931*

Rest makes rust.

The rhubarb that no one picks goes to seed.

We can now prove that large numbers of Americans are dying from sitting on their behinds. *Bruce B. Dan, New York Times, 1984*

Active minds that think and study,
Like swift brooks are seldom muddy.
Arthur Guiterman

See also A used KEY is always bright.

Everybody talks about the WEATHER but nobody does anything about it. *Mark Twain (1835–1925), K-195*

Whether it's cold or whether it's hot
We're going to have weather, whether or not.

You can always grumble about the weather: spring is too rainy, summer is too hot, fall is too soon over, and winter is not.

You never know when you're WELL OFF.

Health is not valued till sickness comes. *1732, Fuller*

If a man could have half of his wishes, he would double his troubles. *Poor Richard's Almanac*

The reason some married men never know when they are well off is because they never are. *Everybody's Weekly, ca. 1925*

See also Be careful of what you WISH for . . .

Go WEST, young man. *Horace Greeley (1811–72)**

*Greeley was quoting an 1851 editorial in the *Terre Haute Express*. When the slogan became popular, Greeley tried to credit the originator, John B. L. Soule, but to no avail.

WHATEVER will be will be.

See CHE sera sera.

The WHEEL that squeaks the loudest is the one that gets the grease.*

. . . but the quacking duck gets shot.

. . . and the wheel that makes too much of a nuisance of itself gets replaced.

A creaking door hangs longest. *1776, O-44*

A grouch escapes so many little annoyances that it almost pays to be one. *Kin Hubbard*

A noisy man is always in the right. *William Cowper, Conversation; M-765*

It pays to pester. *Heard in Nebraska*

It's the crying baby that gets the milk. *Heard in California*

The horseshoe that clatters wants a nail.

The tongue is ever turning to the aching tooth. *New England proverb*

*The thought goes back to the 15th century, but Josh Billings popularized the most familiar wording of this proverb:
I hate to be a kicker,
I always long for peace,
But the wheel that squeaks the loudest
Is the one that gets the grease.
Josh Billings (1818–85), The Kicker

They have sown the wind, and they shall reap the WHIRLWIND. *Hosea 8:7*

The WHOLE is greater than the sum of its parts.

Every WHY hath a wherefore. *Shakespeare, the Comedy of Errors 2.2.45., ca. 1593*

In nature there are neither rewards nor punishments—there are consequences. *Robert G. Ingersoll*

There's no rest for the WICKED.*

. . . and none for the virtuous either.

No arrest for the wicked who are politically connected.

No arrest for the wary. *Heard in Wisconsin*

Peace of mind is elusive when the past haunts us, the future taunts us, and the present flaunts us.

*There is no peace, saith the Lord, unto the wicked. *Isaiah 48:22; 57:21*

A good WIFE and health are a man's best wealth. *1732, Fuller*

A man's best fortune or his worst is a wife. *1655, T-431*

A happy marriage is the world's best bargain. *O. A. Battista*

A man in love is incomplete until he has married. Then he's finished. *Zsa Zsa Gabor, Newsweek, Mar. 28, 1960*

People don't judge a man by his wife as much as by the way he treats his wife. *Sydney J. Harris*

Two things doth prolong thy life: a quiet heart and a loving wife. *1607, OE-519*

When a marriage works, nothing on earth can take its place. *Helen Gahagan Douglas, A Full Life*

Who of us is mature enough for offspring before the offspring themselves arrive? The value of marriage is not that adults produce children but that children produce adults. *Peter De Vries*

O! what's a table richly spread,
Without a woman at its head?
Thomas Wharton, The Progress of Discontent

A plump WIFE and a big barn never did any harm. *Pennsylvania Dutch proverb*

Better two hundred pounds of curves than one hundred pounds of nerves.

See also A good WIFE and health are a man's best wealth.

He took defeat like a man; he blamed it on his WIFE.

When you're bored with yourself, marry and be bored with someone else. *David Pryce-Jones*

He wrecked his car, he lost his job
   And yet throughout his life,
He took his troubles like a man:
   He blamed them on his wife.

The shoemaker's WIFE never has shoes.

See A COBBLER'S children always go barefoot.

WIFE and children are hostages given to fortune.*

A married man with a family will do anything for money. *Charles-Maurice de Talleyrand*

Wedlock is a padlock. *1678, Ray*

Women, as some witty Frenchman once put it, inspire us with the desire to do masterpieces, and always prevent us from carrying

them out. *Oscar Wilde, The Picture of Dorian Gray*

Who drags the fiery artist down?
Who keeps the pioneer in town?
Who hates to let the seaman roam?
It is the wife, it is the home.
Clarence Day, Wife and Home

If ye've got one [child] you can run,
If ye've got two you may goo,
But if ye've got three
You must bide where you be.
English dialect proverb

*He that hath wife and children, hath given hostages to fortune, for they are impediments to great enterprises, either of virtue, or mischief. *Francis Bacon, Of Marriage and Single Life, 1612*

See also A young man MARRIED is a man that's marred.

He that complies against his WILL is of his own opinion still. *1678, O-41*

See You have not CONVERTED a man because you have silenced him.

Where there's a WILL, there's a way. *1651, Herbert*

. . . out of it.

Where there's a will:

   . . . there are relatives.

   . . . there are thousands of ruses; when there is none, then a thousand excuses. *Malayan proverb*

   . . . there's a fee.

   . . . there's a lawyer who can break it.

. . . there's an inheritance tax.

. . . there's apt to be a contest.

Determine that the thing can and shall be done, and then we shall find the way. *Abraham Lincoln*

Man has his will, but woman has her way. *Oliver Wendell Holmes*

Them ez will, kin. *Edward R. Sill, a Baker's Duzen uv Wize Saws.* (For entire verse, see THEM that has, gets.)

Where there's a bill, we're away.

Have ye vices that ask a destroyer?
    Or passions that need your control?
Let Reason become your employer,
    And your body be ruled by your soul.

Fight on, though ye bleed in the trial,
    Resist with all strength that ye may;
Ye may conquer sin's host by denial;
    For Where there's a will there's a way.
Eliza Cook

See also If at first you don't SUCCEED, try again; It's up to YOU.

Heads I WIN, tails you lose. 1687, OE-285

You can't WIN.

Aren't women prudes if they don't and prostitutes if they do? *Kate Millett*

As necessity is the lash that falls upon common people, so ennui is the lash of the upper classes. *Arthur Schopenhauer*

Adultery is in your heart not only when you look with excessive sexual desire at a woman who is not your wife, but also if you look in the same manner at your wife. *John Paul II, 1980*

Before you love, learn to run through snow leaving no footprints. *Turkish proverb*

Beggars should be abolished entirely! It is annoying to give to them and it is annoying not to give to them. *Friedrich Nietzsche, Thus Spake Zarathustra*

Best let a woman have her own way; she'll take it anyhow; and it is well to have the appearance of being generous. *L. de V. Matthewman*

Call a lady "a chicken," and ten to one, she is angry. Tell her she is "no chicken," and twenty to one, she is still angrier. *G. D. Prentice, Louisville Journal, ca. 1860*

Child's complaint: If I don't wash my hands, they're dirty; if I do, I'm wasting water.

Drink wine, and have the gout; drink none, and have the gout. *16th century*

Every decision you make is a mistake. *Edward Dahlberg*

Every time you learn all the answers, they change all the questions.

Every wise man makes provisions for possible disasters. Unfortunately, the disasters coming his way are not the ones he made provision for. *Richard Needham*

His wife complains that he makes too much noise while fixing breakfast.

I feel much better, now that I've given up hope. © *Ashleigh Brilliant*

I Feel So Miserable Without You, It's Almost Like Having You Here. *Title of a song by Stephen Bishop*

I have abandoned my search for truth, and am now looking for a good fantasy. © *Ashleigh Brilliant*

I phoned my dad to tell him I had stopped smoking. He called me a quitter. *Steven Pearl*

I spend all my time trying to improve myself, and then people complain that I'm self-centered. © *Ashleigh Brilliant*

If you drink, you die. If you don't drink, you die. So it is better to drink. *Russian proverb*

I'm not happy when I'm writing, but I'm more unhappy when I'm not. *Frannie Hurst*

If a husband dislikes his work, he will never be happy; if he likes it, he will never be home.

If you husband your funds to provide against poverty in your old age, people say you have no soul and money is your God. If you are a spendthrift, people say you are shiftless and some day you'll be sorry. *William C. Hunter*

If you keep anything long enough, you can throw it away. If you throw it away, you will need it the next day.

If you travel to an underdeveloped country, you can't drink the water. If you travel to a developed country, you can't breathe the air. *Robert J. Beran*

It doesn't pay to fight a skunk, because if you win, you lose. *Vermont proverb*

It's disgusting when we're together, and it's lonesome when we're apart. *Russian proverb*

Just as you manage to make ends meet, something breaks in the middle.

Life consists of wishing you had if you didn't and wishing you hadn't if you did. *Heard in Mississippi*

Life is a constant oscillation between the sharp horns of a dilemma. *H. L. Mencken*

Life is a gamble, at terrible odds—if it was a bet, you wouldn't take it. *Tom Stoppard, Rosencrantz and Guildenstern Are Dead*

Life is an incurable disease. *Abraham Cowley, Pindaric Odes;* M-611

Life is rather like a tin of sardines: we're all of us looking for the key. *Alan Bennett, Beyond the Fringe*

Man is incapable of living alone. And he is also incapable of living in society. *Georges Duhamel, Le Désert de Bievres*

Man's unique agony as a species consists in his perpetual conflict between the desire to stand out and the need to blend in. *Sydney J. Harris*

Not every problem has a good solution, and good solutions have unwanted side effects.

One must choose in life between boredom and torment. *Madame de Staël*

People who avoid the mistakes their parents made often make the mistakes their parents avoided.

Pessimism, when you get used to it, is just as agreeable as optimism. *Arnold Bennett*

Rule A: Don't. Rule A-1: Rule A does not exist. Rule A-2: Do not discuss the existence or non-existence of Rules A, A-1 or A-2. *R. D. Laing, 1968*

Since I gave up hope, I feel much better. *Office sign*

Solitude is impracticable, and society fatal. *Ralph Waldo Emerson*

Success and failure are both difficult to endure. Along with success come drugs, divorce, fornication, bullying, travel, meditation, medication, depression, neurosis and suicide. With failure, comes failure. *Joseph Heller, Playboy magazine, 1973*

Talk about others, you're a gossip; talk about yourself, you're a bore. *Henny Youngman*

The evils of the world flow from the envy of the have-nots, and the selfishness of the haves.

The greatest and most important problems of life are all in a certain sense insoluble. They can never be solved but only outgrown. *Carl Jung*

The inherent vice of capitalism is the unequal sharing of blessings; the inherent vice of communism is the equal sharing of miseries. *Winston Churchill*

The two hardest things to handle in life are failure and success.

The universe is like a safe to which there is a combination. But the combination is locked up in the safe. *Peter De Vries, Let Me Count the Ways*

There are two tragedies in life. One is not to get your heart's desire. The other is to get it. *G. B. Shaw, Man and Superman*

To have money is a fear, not to have it a grief. *1640, T-470*

Tragedy is the conflict not of right and wrong, but of right and right. *Georg Hegel*

Walk fast and you catch misfortune; walk slowly and it catches you. *Russian proverb*

We all live in a house on fire, no fire department to call; no way out, just the upstairs window to look out of while the fire burns the house down with us trapped, locked in it. *Tennessee Williams*

Whichever you do, you will repent it. *Socrates, when asked whether a man should marry*

When you argue with a fool, that makes two. *Vermont proverb*

Whenever you take a mouthful of too-hot soup, the next thing you do will be wrong.

Whether the pitcher strikes the stone, or the stone the pitcher, it is bad for the pitcher. *17th century*

Everything's either
concave or convex,
so whatever you dream
will be something with sex.
Piet Hein

Born 1914
Gave up smoking 1959
Gave up booze 1973
Gave up red meat 1983
Died anyway..............1989

See also CATCH-22; What's the USE?

You can't WIN them all. *1953, O-246*

. . . but you can sure lose them all.

Losing is part of winning. *Dick Munro*

I think and think for months and years. Ninety-nine times, the conclusion is false.

The hundredth time I am right. *Albert Einstein*

Sometimes you eat the bear, and sometimes the bear eats you.

There is no good in arguing with the inevitable. The only argument available with an east wind is to put on your overcoat. *James Russell Lowell*

You WIN some and you lose some.

Great gains cover many losses.

You win a few and you lose a few. *Rudyard Kipling, Captains Courageous*

Success covers a multitude of blunders. *G. B. Shaw*

Win some, lose some. *1897, O-246*

See also You can't WIN them all.

It's an ill WIND that blows nobody any good. *1546, Heywood*

An oboe is an ill wind that nobody blows good. *P. Dennis, 1961; BJW-658*

Coffin-makers love the plague. *Japanese proverb*

It's an ill wind that blows when you leave the hairdresser. *Phyllis Diller*

No man loses but another wins. *1550, Erasmus*

Sun is good for cucumbers, rain for rice. *Vietnamese proverb*

Whichever way the wind doth blow
Some heart is glad to have it so;
Then blow it east or blow it west
The wind that blows, *that* wind is best.
Caroline H. Mason, on old postcard

See also Every CLOUD has a silver lining.

Don't tilt at WINDMILLS.*

*From an episode in Cervantes' *Don Quixote*, in which the hero mistakes a row of windmills for giants and attacks them.

Good WINE needs no bush.* 1430, O-99

The sharp point comes out of the bag. *Chinese proverb*

The best ad is a good product. *Alan H. Meyer*

*When illiteracy was widespread, signs bore pictures rather than words. The sign of a wine merchant pictured a bush (or grapevine?).

WINE is a mocker.*

A drunkard is like a whiskey bottle, all neck and belly and no head. *Austin O'Malley*

Alcohol removes inhibitions—like that scared little mouse who got drunk and shook his whiskers and shouted: Now bring on that damn cat! *Eleanor Early*

Alcoholic rheumatism: getting stiff in the joints.

Bacchus has drowned more men than Neptune. *1732, Fuller*

Because some men are ruined by intemperance, it does not follow that all should become abstainers, any more than because some men are ruined by marriage all men should remain single. *L. de V. Matthewman*

Booze: milk of amnesia. *Wall Street Journal*

Conscience is that part of the personality that dissolves in alcohol. *Harold D. Lasswell*

Drink in, wit out. *English proverb*

Drinking makes such fools of people, and people are such fools to begin with, that it's compounding a felony. *Robert Benchley*

Drunkenness does not create vice; it merely brings it into view.

First the man takes a drink, then the drink takes a drink, then the drink takes the man. *Japanese proverb*

For when the wine is in, the wit is out. *Thomas Becon, Catechism*

A wife's defense of her husband's difficulty in managing his alcoholic intake: He doesn't have a drinking problem; he has a stopping problem.

I'm not so think as you drunk I am.

It provokes the desire, but it takes away the performance. *Shakespeare, Macbeth 2.3.30*

Liquor talks mighty loud when it gets loose from the jug. *Joel Chandler Harris, Uncle Remus*

Man ages whiskey, and whiskey ages man. *Henny Youngman*

One drink: I'm rich. Two drinks: I'm good-looking. Three drinks: I'm bulletproof. Four drinks: I'm invisible. *T-shirt saying*

One of the disadvantages of wine is that it makes a man mistake words for thoughts. *Samuel Johnson*

Rum is, in my opinion, the bane of morals and the parent of idleness. *George Washington*

The vine brings three kinds of grapes: the first of pleasure, the next of intoxication, and the third of disgust. *Anacharsis*

They who drink beer will think beer. *Washington Irving*

Watch your drinking—patronize a bar with mirrors.

What soberness conceals drunkenness reveals. *1616, T-616*

When some people drink, they see double and feel single.

When ale is in, the wit is out. *1546, Heywood*

Wine and women make fools of everybody. *German proverb*

Wine brings out the truth. *Chinese proverb*

Wine has drowned more men than the sea. *New England proverb*

Wine makes old wives wenches. *1639, T-732*

Wine neither keeps secrets nor fulfills promises. *1620, T-732*

Wine, women and song will get a man wrong. *1580, WM-658*

Wonderful, varied words. Blitzed, blasted, blotto, bombed, cockeyed, crocked, ripped, looed, loaded, leveled, wasted, wiped, soused, sozzled, smashed and schnockered. Stewed, stinko, stupid, tanked, totalled, tight and tipsy. Not to mention feeling no pain, three sheets to the wind, in one's cups, intoxicated, addle-pated and pixilated. *Bruce Weber, in Esquire, Sept. 1984*

*Wine is a mocker, strong drink is raging, and whosoever is deceived thereby is not wise. *Proverbs 20:1*

WINE maketh glad the heart of man.*

A woman drove me to drink, and I never even had the courtesy to thank her. *W. C. Fields*

Drink no longer water, but use a little wine for thy stomach's sake and thy frequent infirmities. *1 Timothy 5:23*

I am not a problem drinker; I never drank a problem in my life.

I have taken more out of alcohol than alcohol has taken out of me. *Winston Churchill*

Poetry in a bottle. *Clifton Fadiman, Manhattan Inc., July 1958*

Two pints make one cavort. *Wall Street Journal*

Water taken in moderation cannot hurt anybody. *Mark Twain*

Whiskey make rabbit hug lion. *1928, WM-651*

Why be small and weak, when with two drinks you can be big and strong? *Peter's Almanac*

Wine makes a man better pleased with himself. I don't say that it makes him more pleasing to others. *Samuel Johnson*

*Bless the Lord . . . [who causeth] wine that maketh glad the heart of man, and oil to make his face to shine, and bread which strengtheneth man's heart. *Psalms 104:1, 15*

See also Who loves not WOMEN, wine and song remains a fool his whole life long.

You don't put new WINES in old bottles.*

The new wines of industrialism and democracy have been poured into old bottles and they have burst the old bottles beyond repair. *A. J. Toynbee, Civilization on Trial*

*Neither do men put new wine in old bottles, else the bottles break, and the wine runneth out, and the bottles perish; but they put new wines into new bottles, and both are preserved. *Matthew 9:17*. With these words, Jesus is saying that one cannot insert new details into old ways of thinking, but must cast off one's old assumptions, and think anew: put new wine into new bottles. Actually, Jesus spoke not of old bottles, but of old wineskins, which are subject to deterioration, which glass bottles are not.

A WINNER never quits, and a quitter never wins.

A knocker never wins, and a winner never knocks. *Heard in Ontario*

Success is the good fortune that comes from aspiration, desperation, perspiration, and inspiration. *Evan Esar*

See When the going gets tough, the TOUGH get going.

WINNING isn't everything, it's the only thing.*

Winning isn't everything, but defeat has absolutely nothing to recommend it.

Winning isn't everything, but it beats anything that comes in second. *Paul W. "Bear" Bryant*

Every time you win, you're reborn; when you lose, you die a little. *George Allen*

Pick battles big enough to matter, small enough to win. *Jonathan Kozol, On Being a Teacher*

The person who said "Winning isn't everything" never won anything.

Winning has a joy and discrete purity to it that cannot be replaced by anything else. *A. Bartlett Giamatti*

*Slogan popularly attributed to Vince Lombardi, but was more likely said first by WCLA football coach Red Sanders, says Keyes (K-2). In a book on football published after his 1970 death, Lombardi wrote, "I have been quoted as saying, Winning is the only thing. That's a little out of context. What I said is that Winning is not everything—but making an effort to win is" (K-155).

See also It matters not whether you WON or lost, but how you played the game; Nothing succeeds like SUCCESS; VICTORY is sweet.

If WINTER comes, can spring be far behind? *Percy Bysshe Shelley, Ode to the West Wind, 1820*

One man's WISDOM is another man's folly.

WISDOM is better than rubies. *1590, WM-660*

It is easy to be WISE after the event. *ca. 1590, O-247*

See HINDSIGHT is better than foresight.

A WISE MAN changes his mind; a fool never does. *Geoffrey Chaucer, Tale of Melibee, ca. 1386*

If in the last few years, you haven't discarded a major opinion or acquired a new one, investigate and see if you're not growing senile. *Gelett Burgess, as quoted in Reader's Digest, Oct. 1947*

There is no stigma attached to recognizing a bad decision in time to install a better one. *Laurence Peter*

See also A foolish CONSISTENCY is the hobgoblin of little minds.

A WISE MAN learns from the mistakes of others; a fool by his own. *Latin proverb*

It's a wise man who profits from his experience, but it's a good deal wiser one who lets the rattlesnake bite the other fellow. *Josh Billings*

Learn from the mistakes of others, because you can't live long enough to make them all by yourself.

See also EXPERIENCE is the best teacher.

Be careful of what you WISH for; you might get it.

A man's worst enemies can't wish on him what he can think up himself. *Yiddish proverb*

Almost everything in life is easier to get into than out of.

Every man is wise when pursued by a mad dog; fewer when pursued by a mad woman; only the wisest survive when attacked by a mad notion. *Robertson Davies*

Granting our wish is one of Fate's saddest jokes. *James Russell Lowell*

How many of our daydreams would darken into nightmares were there any danger of their coming true. *Logan Pearsall Smith, Afterthoughts*

If a man could have half his wishes, he would double his troubles. *Poor Richard's Almanac*

More tears are shed over answered prayers than unanswered ones. *Theresa of Avila.* A favorite quotation of Truman Capote, and source of the title of his unfinished book.

Protect me from what I want. *Jenny Holzer*

There are two things to aim for in life; first to get what you want; and, after that, to enjoy it. *Logan Pearsall Smith*

There are two tragedies in life. One is to lose your heart's desire. The other is to gain it. *G. B. Shaw, Man and Superman*

. . . When the Gods wish to punish us, they answer our prayers. *Oscar Wilde, An Ideal Husband*

*Keyes (K-164) notes similar mots attributed to Thomas Huxley, Elbert Hubbard, and Irving Kristol.

See also A MAN is his own worst enemy; I am my own EXECUTIONER; You never know when you're WELL OFF.

The WISH is father to the thought. **Latin proverb**

To deceive oneself is very easy. *1640, T-147*

We soon believe what we desire. *Latin proverb*

Wishing Can Make It So. *Title of a popular song*

See also There is nothing either good or bad but THINKING makes it so.

If WISHES were horses, beggars would ride. *1670, Ray*

. . . If turnips were watches, I would wear one by my side. *Nursery Rhymes of England, 1844*

If frogs had wings, they wouldn't bump their asses on rocks. *Heard in North Carolina and Virginia*

If hope worked half the time, there wouldn't be one-third as much trouble in the world. *Opie Read*

If my aunt had been a man, she'd have been my uncle. *John Ray, 1813*

Stealing would be a pleasant occupation if only they hanged you round the middle. *Spanish proverb*

Wish in one hand and shit in the other and see which will be full first. *1659, Howell*

If ifs and an's
Were pot's an' pans
There'd be naya trade for tinkers.
English dialect

See also IF stands stiff in the corner.

WISHING won't help.

If you wish for a thing and don't get it, try working for it. *Old postcard*

Is that an itch for achievement or an inflammation of the wishbone?

Wishing isn't doing. *Vermont proverb*

Wishes won't do dishes. *Vermont proverb*

See also Don't count on LUCK.

WIVES are young men's mistresses; companions for middle age; and old men's nurses. *Francis Bacon, Of Marriage and Single Life, 1612; F-1185*

The first wife is from God, the second from people, and the third from the devil. *Yiddish proverb*

The first wife is matrimony, the second company, the third heresy. *1659, T-722*

Don't cry "WOLF!" *Aesop (6th century B.C.), The Shepherd's Boy*

A liar is not believed when he speaks the truth. *Latin proverb*

He that swears till no man trust him,
He that lies till no man believe him,
He that borrows till no man will lend him,
Let him go where no man knows him.
1530, T-414

A WOMAN is as old as she looks.

. . . before breakfast. *Ed Howe*

. . . to the man who likes to look at her. *Finley Peter Dunne*

. . . but a man isn't old till he quits looking. *Heard in Ontario and Texas*

The same old charitable lie
Repeated as the years scoot by
Perpetually makes a hit—
"You really haven't changed a bit"
Margaret Fishback

See also A MAN is as old as he's feeling, a woman is as old as she looks.

A WOMAN is only a woman, but a good cigar is a smoke.*

. . . Though a woman's not made of tobacco, she's often the butt of a joke. *Richard Armour*

A good cigar is as great a comfort to a man as a good cry is to a woman. *Edward Bulwer-Lytton*

If you would be happy for a week, take a wife; if you would be happy for a month, kill a pig; but if you would be happy all your life, plant a garden. *1661, O-106*

Ravi Shankar, in New York for a concert, returned to his hotel to find it in flames. As he ran toward it, a beautiful woman flung herself into his arms. Rushing on, he cast her aside, exclaiming: A woman is only a woman, but a good sitar is asmoke. *Paula A. Franklin, New York magazine*

*The line is taken from Rudyard Kipling's poem "The Betrothed." A young man proposes marriage, and the maiden answers, only if he will give up smoking cigars. The man muses that when a cigar is used up, he can toss away the butt and light up a fresh one; something he cannot do with a wife. He rejects her conditions, and the reader is left to wonder whether the young man was too strongly hooked on tobacco, or only lukewarm about the maiden.

See also There are plenty more FISH in the sea; Why buy a COW when you can get milk free?

Frailty, thy name is WOMAN! *Shakespeare, Hamlet 1.2.146, ca. 1600*

As is the body, so is the soul of tender women frail. *Ovid*

And when weak women go astray,
Their stars are more in fault than they.
Robert Bland, Proverbs

It's the WOMAN who pays.

. . . but look at whose money she uses.

Never underestimate the power of a WOMAN. *An advertising slogan of the Ladies' Home Journal, used since about 1946*

A good woman inspires a man; a brilliant woman interests him; a beautiful woman fascinates him; and a sympathetic woman gets him. *Helen Rowland*

A man chases a woman until she catches him (Leo Rosten recalls this as the first wisecrack he ever heard.)

A man thinks he knows, but a woman knows better. *Chinese proverb*

A mother takes twenty years to make a man of her boy, and another woman makes a fool of him in twenty minutes. *Robert Frost; also attributed to Helen Rowland*

A pious man married a wicked woman, and she made him wicked. A pious woman married a wicked man, and she made him righteous. This indicates that all depends on the woman. *Talmud*

A woman with true charm is one who can make a youth feel mature, an old man youthful, and a middle-aged man completely sure of himself. *Bob Talbert, as quoted in Reader's Digest, Jan. 1968*

A woman without a man is like a fish without a bicycle. *Women's lib slogan, 1970s*

A woman's guess is much more accurate than a man's certainty. *Rudyard Kipling, Plain Tales from the Hills*

A woman's heart sees more than ten men's eyes. *Swedish proverb*

A woman's tears are a man's terrors. *Arnold Haultain, Hint for Lovers*

All I was doing was trying to get home from work. *Rosa Parks, on her refusal, in 1955, to give up her bus seat to a white man, an action leading to the Birmingham bus boycott and to the civil rights movement*

Any man who thinks he's smarter than his wife is married to a smart woman.

Better than being the head of the family is being the heart of it.

Brains are an asset, if you hide them. *Mae West*

Even the wisest men make fools of themselves about women, and even the most foolish women are wise about men. *Theodor Reik*

Feminine intuition is a fiction and a fraud. It is nonsensical, illogical, emotional, ridiculous and practically foolproof. *Henry Haenigsen, as quoted in Reader's Digest, Jan. 1967*

Feminine passion is to masculine as an epic to an epigram. *Karl Kraus*

For the female of the species is more deadly than the male. *Rudyard Kipling, The Female of the Species*

Girls have an unfair advantage over men: if they can't get what they want by being smart, they can get it by being dumb. *Yul Brynner*

God has given more understanding to a woman than to a man. *Babylonian Talmud*

Happy is the man with a wife to tell him what to do and a secretary to do it. *Lord Mancroft, London Observer, 1966*

He married his secretary and thought he could go on dictating to her.

I expect that Woman will be the last thing civilized by Man. *George Meredith, The Ordeal of Richard Feverel*

I have learned that only two things are necessary to keep one's wife happy. First, let her think she's having her way. And second, let her have it. *Lyndon B. Johnson, to Lord Snowden at a White House reception, Nov. 1965*

If Mama ain't happy, ain't nobody happy. *T-shirt saying, 1993*

If there hadn't been women, we'd still be squatting in a cave eating raw meat, because we made civilization in order to impress our girlfriends. *Orson Welles.* President Ronald Reagan made a similar tribute to women, and was roundly denounced for expressing a sexist attitude.

If people think I'm a dumb blonde because of the way I look, then they're dumber than they think I am. *Dolly Parton*

If women didn't exist, all the money in the world would have no meaning. *Aristotle Onassis*

If you educate a man, you have an educated man; but if you educate a woman, you educate a family.

In politics, if you want anything said, ask a man; if you want anything done, ask a woman. *Margaret Thatcher, 1975*

It takes a smart woman to be a fool. *Heard in Maryland*

Man has his will—but woman has her way. *Oliver Wendell Holmes, The Autocrat at the Breakfast Table*

Man proposes, woman disposes. *Herb Daniels*

Men play the game; women know the score. *Roger Woddis*

Nature has given women so much power that the law has very wisely given them very little. *Samuel Johnson, letter to Dr. Taylor, Aug. 18, 1763*

Never argue with a woman when she's tired—or rested. *H. C. Diefenbach, as quoted in Reader's Digest, Nov. 1960*

Never underestimate a woman, unless you're estimating her age or weight.

Some leaders are born women. *Saying on a T-shirt worn on International Women's Day, 1983*

The cock crows, but the hen lays the eggs.

The Lord makes a man, but the wife makes a husband. *Heard in New York and South Carolina*

The way to fight a woman is with your hat. Grab it and run. *John Barrymore*

The weaker sex is really the stronger sex because of the weakness of the stronger sex for the weaker sex.

What passes for woman's intuition is often nothing more than man's transparency. *George Jean Nathan*

Whatever women do, they must do twice as well as men to be thought half as good. Luckily this is not difficult. *Charlotte Whitton*

When the fine eyes of a woman are veiled with tears, it is the man who no longer sees clearly. *Achille Tournier*

When [women] are intelligent, I prefer their conversation to that of men: One finds in it a certain gentleness that is lacking in us; and besides that, they express themselves with more clarity and give a more pleasant turn to their speech. *François de la Rochefoucauld*

Woman begins by resisting a man's advances and ends by blocking his retreat. *Oscar Wilde*

Woman—she needs no eulogy; she speaks for herself.

Woman would be more charming if one could fall into her arms without falling into her hands. *Ambrose Bierce*

Women are afraid of mice and murder, and of very little in between. *Mignon McLaughlin*

Women have served all these centuries as looking-glasses possessing the magic and delicious power of reflecting the figure of man at twice its natural size. *Virginia Woolfe, A Room of One's Own*

Women in mischief are wiser than men. *ca. 1526, T-748*

Women run to extremes; they are either better or worse than men. *Jean de La Bruyère, Les Caractères*

Women's Rights are men's duties. *Karl Kraus, Aphorisms and More Aphorisms*

Women's styles may change, but their designs remain the same. *Oscar Wilde*

Four things greater than all things are Women and Horses and Power and War. *Rudyard Kipling, The Ballad of the King's Jest*

It is a WOMAN'S privilege to change her mind. *1616, Draxe*

A woman's mind is cleaner than a man's— she changes it oftener. *Oliver Herford*

All WOMEN are vain.

. . . and men are no different.

With men, as with women, the main struggle is between vanity and comfort; but with men, comfort often wins. *Mignon McLaughlin*

Women are wacky,
　　Women are vain:
They'd rather be pretty
　　Than have a good brain.
Margaret Fishback, Lip Service

Who loves not WOMEN, wine and song remains a fool his whole life long. *Martin Luther (1483–1546)*

A good drink makes old men young. *German proverb*

A wonderful drink, wine. . . . Did you ever hear of an Italian grape crusher with athlete's foot? *W. C. Fields*

An aversion to women is like an aversion to life. *Heard in New York*

Beware of the man who does not drink.

Drink no longer water, but use a little wine for thy stomach's sake and thine often infirmities. *1 Timothy 5:23*

Drink wine in winter for cold, and in summer for heat.

I only drink to make other people seem more interesting. *George Jean Nathan*

It used to be wine, women and song. Now it's beer, the old lady, and TV.

The best audience is intelligent, well-educated and a little drunk. *Alben W. Barkley*

There is nothing wrong with sobriety in moderation. *John Ciardi*

Water taken in moderation cannot hurt anybody. *Mark Twain, Notebook*

We drink one another's healths and spoil our own. *Jerome K. Jerome*

Wine is the best broom for troubles. *Japanese proverb*

Wine is the drink of the gods, milk the drink of babes, tea the drink of women, and water the drink of beasts. *John Stuart Blackie*

Wine is the king of medicines. *Japanese proverb*

Wine is the old man's milk. *1584, T-732*

Wine, women, and song will get a man wrong. *1580, WM-658*

God made Man
   Frail as a bubble;
God made Love,
   Love made Trouble.
God made the Vine,
   Was it a sin
That Man made Wine
   To drown Trouble in?
Oliver Herford, A Plea

I often wonder what the Vintners buy
One half so precious as the Goods they sell.
Omar Khayyam, The Rubaiyat

Here's to champagne, the drink divine
   That makes us forget our troubles.
It is made of a dollar's worth of wine
   And three dollars' worth of bubbles.

See also EAT, drink, and be merry for tomorrow we die; WINE maketh glad the heart of man.

WOMEN are all alike.

. . . a notion not shared by men who divorce and remarry.

It matters not whether you WON or lost, but how you played the game. *

. . . until you lose.

. . . In that case, why keep score? *Donald Dell*

A cynic is one who believes it matters not whether you win, *nor* how you play the game. *Mignon McLaughlin*

A good sport has to lose to prove it.

A poor winner is better than a good loser.

As in a game of cards, so in the game of life we must play what is dealt to us; and the glory consists, not so much in winning as in playing a poor hand well. *Josh Billings*

Everyone likes a good loser, especially if he's on the other side.

Fear of losing is what makes competitors so great. Show me a gracious loser and I'll show you a perennial loser. *O. J. Simpson*

It isn't whether you win or lose, it's how you place the blame.

It matters not whether you win or lose; what matters is whether *I* win or lose. *Darin Weinberg*

It may be no disgrace to be defeated. It is a disgrace to stay defeated. *B. C. Forbes*

It requires no particular skill to win the game when Fortune has dealt you all the trumps. *L. de V. Matthewman*

Learn how to fail intelligently, for failing is one of the greatest arts in the world. *Charles Kettering*

Losers are always in the wrong. *1855, Bohn*

Losing is the only American sin. *John R. Tunis*

Show me a good and gracious loser, and I'll show you a failure. *Knute Rockne*

Show me a good loser and I'll show you a loser.

Show me a good loser and I'll show you a salesman playing golf with his best customer.

The cheerful loser is a sort of winner. *William Howard Taft*

The only thing that's bad about being a good sport is that you have to lose to prove it.

There are two kinds of losers: (1) the good loser and (2) those who can't act. *Laurence Peter*

Let others cheer the winning man,
There's one I hold worth while;
'Tis he who does the best he can,
Then loses with a smile.
Beaten he is, but not to stay
Down with the rank and file;
That man will win some other day,
Who loses with a smile.

"It isn't if you win or lose,
But how you play the game."
It's an admirable philosophy
And true; but just the same
I note it's mostly uttered with
A condescending grin
By people whom I play against,
That is, by those who win.
F.W., Wall Street Journal

*For when the One Great Scorer comes
  To write against your name,
  He marks—not that you won or lost—

But how you played the game.
Grantland Rice, Alumnus Football

Sometimes you WONDER if it's all worth it.

See What's the USE?; You can't WIN.

WONDERS will never cease! *1776, WM-670*

See Ain't NATURE wonderful!

Chop your own WOOD and it warms you twice. *1819, WM-670*

Burn gas or oil and when the bill comes in, you will get hot under the collar all over again. *Cal Craig*

An honest man's WORD is as good as his bond. *1616, Draxe*

. . . but many an honest man has a poor memory. It's better to get it on paper. *George Jean Nathan*

An honest politician is one who when he is bought will stay bought. *Simon Cameron*

See also A PROMISE is a promise.

A WORD fitly spoken is like apples of gold in pictures of silver.* *Proverbs 25:11*

A gentle word opens an iron gate. *Bulgarian proverb*

How forcible are right words! *Job 6:25*

Kind words are the music of the world. *Frederick W. Faber*

The best remedy for a dispute is to discuss it. *African proverb*

*The Hebrew meaning of what the King James Version translates as "pictures" is uncertain; perhaps "bowls" or "vessels" would be a better guess.

See also A soft ANSWER turneth away wrath; SPEAK or forever hold your peace; Speak the TRUTH and shame the Devil.

A WORD to the wise is sufficient.* *Latin proverb*

. . . only when the word is wise.

. . . but an entire library could not convince the fool otherwise.

A nod for a wise man, a rod for a fool. *The Alphabet of Ben Sira*

A word to the wise is resented.

A word to the wise is superfluous.

Advice to a fool goes in one ear and out the other. *Heard in Mississippi and New York*

Nuf sed.

One word to the wife is sufficient: say "Yes."

When you say one thing, the clever person understands three. *Chinese proverb*

*The Morrises (MD-587) give the Latin phrase as *verbum sapienti satis*, which is known in its short form, they say: *verb sap.*

A woman's WORK is never done. 1570, O-249

. . . by a man.

A woman's word is never done. *J. Adams*

If she really hates housework, a woman's work is never done; and sometimes it never even gets started.

Man's work lasts till set of sun,
Woman's work is never done.
Roxburghe Ballads

See also A MAN may work from sun to sun but a woman's work is never done.

All at once makes light WORK.

See Many hands make light WORK.

All WORK and no play makes Jack a dull boy. 1659, Howell*

. . . and Jill a well-to-do widow. *Raymond Duncan*

. . . but all play and no work makes him something greatly worse. *S. Smiles, Self-Help*

A life spent in constant labor is a life wasted, save a man be such a fool as to regard a fulsome obituary notice as ample reward. *George Jean Nathan*

All play and no work makes Jack a dull jerk. *BJW-701*

All work and no pay—that's housework.

All work and no plagiarism makes a dull speech. *Jacob M. Braude*

All work and no play. *Advertising slogan of Timken Roller Bearing Company*

All work and no play makes jack.

All work and no play makes jack for the psychiatrist.

All work and no play makes jack the dull way. *Henny Youngman*

All work and no play makes Jack the new manager.

All work and no spree makes Jill a dull she. *Heard in U.S. and Canada*

Don't overwork a willing horse.

For the happiest life, days should be rigorously planned, nights left open to chance. *Mignon McLaughlin, Atlantic, July 1965*

From beavers, bees should learn to mend their ways. A bee works; a beaver works and plays. *Heard in New York*

Jack considered himself an actor by profession but he spent his whole life shifting from job to job, waiting for the acting role he was never offered.

He that never eases himself faints. *1616, Draxe*

Lots of jack makes all work play. *Judge, ca. 1925*

*Flexner (F-8) traces this thought back to ca. 2400 B.C., when the Egyptian sage Ptahhotep wrote: "One that reckoneth accounts all the day, passeth not a happy moment. One that gladdeneth his heart all the day provideth not for his house. The bowman hitteth the mark, as the steersman reacheth land, by diversity of aim."

Hard WORK never killed anybody.

. . . but why take a chance?

. . . but it sure has scared a lot of folks.

. . . but who wants to be its first victim?

. . . but you never heard of anyone relaxing to death either. *Wall Street Journal*

Blessed be the horned hands of toil. *Heard in New York and Ontario*

Hard work is the yeast that raises the dough.

The problem with success is that its formula is the same as the one for ulcers. *Peter's Almanac*

See also If you've got time to kill, WORK it to death.

If you've got time to kill, WORK it to death.

A loafer is an abomination, but a man who is busy doing foolish things is worse than a loafer. *William C. Hunter*

As a cure for worry, work is better than whiskey. *Heard in Utah*

I am only an average man but, by George, I work harder at it than the average man. *Theodore Roosevelt*

Killing time can be suicide.

One should labor so hard in youth that everything one does subsequently is easy by comparison. *Ashley Montagu, The American Way of Life*

To be *busy* is man's only happiness. *Mark Twain's Letters, 1917*

When your work speaks for itself, don't interrupt. *Henry J. Kaiser*

Work is the best method devised for killing time. *William Feather*

Work only half a day. It makes no difference which half—the first 12 hours or the last 12 hours. *Kemmons Wilson*

You ask . . . why go on working. I go on working for the same reason a hen goes on laying eggs. *H. L. Mencken, letter to Will Durant, 1933*

See also HAPPINESS comes from work well done.

Many hands make light WORK. *Latin proverb*

. . . and a heavy payroll.

Don't bite the many hands that make light work. *M. G. Eberhart, 1961; BJW-283*

Many hands make a good jackpot.

Many hands make light of work. *Judge, ca. 1925*

Many light hands make light work.

One is none. *1591, Florio*

There's always plenty of help when it's not needed.

See also MAN is a social animal; Too many COOKS spoil the broth.

One does all the WORK and the other takes all the credit.

A successful executive is one who can delegate all the responsibility, shift all the blame, and take all the credit.

One beats the bush, and another catches the birds. *14th century*

One sows, another reaps. *John 4:37*

Take care of those who work for you and you'll float to greatness on their achievements. *H. S. M. Burns, 1959*

The coat and pants do the work but the vest gets the gravy. *Carl Sandburg*

The horse does the work and the coachman is tipped.

The soldier's blood, the general's name. *Jamaican proverb*

The successful people are the ones who can think up things for the rest of the world to keep busy at. *Don Marquis*

There is no finer revenge than that which others inflict on your enemy. *Cesare Pavese, This Business of Living: Diaries 1935–1950*

Two dogs strive for a bone and the third runs away with it. *1560, T-170*

War hath no fury like a non-combatant. *C. E. Montague, Disenchantment*

The seed ye sow, another reaps;
The wealth ye find, another keeps.
Percy Bysshe Shelley

Who invented WORK?

A lazy man goes to work like a thief to the gallows. *Heard in Wisconsin*

Better sit idle than work for nothing. *17th century*

For every feller what lookin' for work, there's nine hidin' from it. *Kin Hubbard*

Hard work is damn near as overrated as monogamy. *Huey P. Long*

I am a friend of the working man, and I would rather be his friend than be one. *Clarence Darrow*

I do not like work even when somebody else does it. *Mark Twain, The Lost Napoleon, Europe and Elsewhere*

I have never liked working. To me a job is an invasion of privacy. *Danny McGoorty, 1968*

I like work: it fascinates me. I can sit and look at it for hours. *Jerome K. Jerome, Three Men in a Boat*

I never forget that work is a curse—which is why I've never made it a habit. *Blaise Cendrars, 1967*

If hard work were such a wonderful thing, surely the rich would have kept it all to themselves. *Lane Kirkland*

If you are good, you'll be assigned all the work. If you are really good, you'll get out of doing it.

I'm lazy. But it's lazy people who invented the wheel and the bicycle because they didn't like walking or carrying things. *Lech Walesa*

Like every man of sense and good feeling, I abominate work. *Aldous Huxley, 1936*

My father taught me to work; he did not teach me to love it. *Abraham Lincoln*

Next to debt, the hardest thing to get out of is a warm bed on a cold morning.

Samuel Gompers has spent his life trying to keep labor from working too hard and he has succeeded beyond his own dreams. *Will Rogers*

Slump, and the world slumps with you. Push, and you push alone. *Laurence Peter*

The only one who got everything done by Friday was Robinson Crusoe.

The paths of glory at least lead to the grave, but the paths of duty may not get you anywhere. *James Thurber*

The world is full of willing people; some willing to work, the rest willing to let them. *Robert Frost*

Wanting to work is so rare a merit that it should be encouraged. *Abraham Lincoln, in a letter of recommendation he consented to write for a woman who said her son was looking for work*

When one has no money, it is amusing to work. *Alfred de Musset*

When someone else decides when you are through, it's work. *Donald G. Smith*

Work is a form of nervousness. *Don Herold*

Work is the crabgrass of life, but money is the water that keeps it green.

Work is the greatest thing in the world, so we should always save some of it for tomorrow. *Don Herold*

Work is the refuge of people who have nothing better to do. *Oscar Wilde, 1897*

It's nice to get up in the mornin',
But it's nicer to stay in bed.
Harry Lauder, Song

Who first invented work and bound the free
And holiday-rejoicing spirit down?
Charles Lamb, Work

Labor raises honest sweat;
Leisure puts you into debt.

Labor gives you rye and wheat;
Leisure gives you naught to eat.

Labor makes your riches last;
Leisure gets you nowhere fast.

Labor makes you bed at eight;
Leisure lets you stay up late.

Labor makes you swell with pride;
Leisure makes you shrink inside.

Labor keeps you fit and prime,
But give me leisure every time.
Robert Bersohn, The Dignity of Labor

See also HAPPINESS comes from work well done; If you've got time to kill, WORK it to death; Take it EASY; Thank GOD it's Friday.

WORK expands so as to fill the time available.*

News expands to fill the time and space allotted to its coverage. *William Safire, 1973*

*Parkinson's Law was first enunciated by C. Northcote Parkinson in a Nov. 1955 issue of the *Economist* and was the subject of his 1958 book, *Parkinson's Law*.

WORKERS of the world, unite. *Karl Marx (1818–83), The Communist Manifesto*

Bad spellers of the world, untie! *Graffiti*

I'm a Marxist, Groucho variety. *Graffiti*

Under capitalism, man exploits man; under socialism, the reverse is true. *Polish proverb, according to Leo Rosten*

Workers of the World, Relax. *Sign in an anarchist bookstore in San Francisco's Haight-Ashbury District*

A bad WORKMAN quarrels with his tools. *1640, Herbert*

It takes all sorts to make a WORLD.* *Miguel de Cervantes, 1620*

. . . a comforting thought for one of those people.

. . . and we've *got* all sorts.

Don't expect much of a country in which half of the people are below average. *Peter's Almanac*

Society is like a pot of soup: It needs different, and contrasting, ingredients to give it body and flavor and lasting nourishment. It is compound, not simple; not like wine that drugs us, or caffeine that agitates us, but a blend to satisfy the most divergent palates. *Sydney J. Harris*

The two most successful insects are the ant and the hornet: one trusts to industry and patience, and the other to nerve and dispatch. Take your choice, Gentlemen! *Josh Billings*

There is no pack of cards without a knave. *16th century*

We should expect the best and the worst from mankind, as from the weather. *Luc de Clapiers de Vauvenargues*

What a dull world it would be for us honest men if it weren't for its sinners. *H. L. Mencken*

*Variant: "It takes all kinds to make up a world."

It's a small WORLD. *1886, WM-677*

One half of the WORLD does not know how the other half lives. *1640, Fuller*

. . . but it is trying to find out. *Ed Howe*

. . . and it's none of their business.

Society is composed of two great classes: those who have more dinners than appetite, and those who have more appetite than dinners. *Sébastien-Roch Nicolas Chamfort*

The WORLD doesn't stand still.

Civilization requires slaves. Human slavery is wrong, insecure and demoralizing. On mechanical slavery, on the slavery of the machine, the future of the world depends. *Oscar Wilde*

See also All is FLUX; TIME marches on; TIMES change and we with them.

The WORM turns.*

. . . my stomach. *Twila Van Leer, chapter title of Life Is Just a Bowl of Kumquats*

. . . and it often does so without giving the proper signal.

. . . but it's still a worm, just going in another direction, isn't it? *Sydney J. Harris*

Good to eat, and wholesome to digest, as a worm to a toad, a toad to a snake, a snake to a pig, a pig to a man, and a man to a worm. *Ambrose Bierce, The Devil's Dictionary*

*Most older variants follow Heywood's 1546 entry, which reads, "Tread on a worm and it will turn." The proverb warned that a patient and long-suffering person if pushed too far will eventually strike back.

Why WORRY?

. . . It won't last; nothing does.

. . . Many a man loses his hair through worrying about losing his hair.

Blessed is the person who is too busy to worry in the daytime and too sleepy to worry at night. *Leo Aikman*

Do not take life too seriously; you will never get out of it alive. *Elbert Hubbard*

Don't Worry, Be Happy. *Title of a song popularized by Bobby McFerrin*

I've had many troubles in my day—most of which didn't happen. *Old postcard*

More men die of worry than of work, because more men worry than work. *Robert Frost*

Of all your troubles great and small,
The greatest are those that don't happen at all.
Heard in Ontario

Put your troubles in a pocket with a hole in it. *Old postcard*

The traveler with empty pockets will sing in the thief's face. *Juvenal, Satires*

Troubles are like babies. They only grow bigger by nursing. *Old postcard*

What, me worry? *Motto of Mad magazine's fictional Alfred E. Neuman*

Worry affects the circulation, the heart, the glands, the whole nervous system. I have never known a man who died from overwork, but many who died from doubt. *Charles H. Mayo*

WORRYING won't help.

. . . We know better; the things we worry about don't happen.

Assumptions keep us awake nights. *Earl Shorris*

If worry were an effective weight-loss program, women would be invisible. *Nancy Drew*

Worry is like a rocking chair: both give you something to do, but neither gets you anywhere. *Heard in Washington and Wisconsin*

Worrying helps you some. It seems as if you are doing something when you're worrying. *Lucy M. Montgomery*

See also Most TROUBLES never occur; Why WORRY?

It could be WORSE.

Fat sorrow is better than lean sorrow. *1820, OE-318*

He who sees a dead man is thankful to be alive. *Tunisian proverb*

If your dreams don't come true, be thankful that neither do your nightmares. *Peter's Almanac*

I'm a congenital optimist. . . . You might call that denial of reality, but as they say, what's the alternative? *Barry Commoner, Chicago Tribune, Dec. 14, 1993*

I'm very pleased with each advancing year. It stems back to when I was forty. I was a bit upset about reaching that milestone, but an older friend consoled me. "Don't complain about growing old—many people don't have that privilege." *Earl Warren*

The best medicine that I know for rheumatism is to thank the Lord it ain't gout. *Josh Billings*

The only thing worse than a flooded basement is a flooded attic.

The first rule of holes: when you're in one, stop digging. *Molly Ivins*

Things are never so bad that they can't get worse. But they're sometimes so bad they can't get better. *Mignon McLaughlin*

When things get rough, visit the graveyard. *Tunisian proverb*

Which would you rather have, a bursting planet or an earthquake here and there? *John Joseph Lynch, New York Times, Dec. 5, 1963*

An ill WOUND is cured, but not an ill name. *1640, Herbert*

A wicked tongue is worse than an evil hand. *Yiddish proverb*

If criticism had any real power to harm, the skunk would be extinct by now. *Fred Allen*

If you want to give a man credit, put it in writing. If you want to give him hell, do it on the phone. *Lee Iacocca*

It takes your enemy and your friend, working together, to hurt; the one to slander you, and the other to bring the news to you. *Mark Twain*

Pain is forgotten; insult lingers on.

The stroke of the whip maketh marks in the flesh; but the stroke of the tongue breaketh bones. *Ecclesiasticus 28:17*

The words of a talebearer are as wounds, and they go down into the innermost parts. *Proverbs 18:8*

We make more enemies by what we say than friends by what we do. *Churton Collins, Aphorisms, English Review, 1914*

See also STICKS and stones may break my bones, but names will never harm me.

Time heals all WOUNDS. *Greek proverb*

. . . and daily routine keeps them bandaged.

. . . but doesn't reset broken bones.

. . . lacerations today, scars tomorrow.

Dirt will rub off when it is dry. *New England proverb*

In the end, things will mend. *1659, Howell*

People who think time heals everything haven't tried sitting it out in a doctor's office. *San Francisco Chronicle*

Time doesn't heal all wounds. Now, as before, I'm astonished at the permanence of sadness and its power over humans. Perhaps time does heal superficial wounds, but it has no power over deep wounds. Over the years, the scars hurt as much as the wounds. *Marlene Dietrich, Marlene*

Time heals and time kills. *Mexican proverb*

Time is a great healer but a poor beautician.

Time is the great healer but is also the great sickener.

Time solves every problem and, in the process, adds a couple of new ones. *Richard Needham*

Time wounds all heels. *Attributed to Groucho Marx, Bennett Cerf, Jane Ace, W. C. Fields, and Irving Brecher.* Keyes (K-124) favors crediting Frank Case, manager of the Algonquin Hotel in its literary heyday, who included this pun in his 1938 memoir.

This, too, will pass. O heart, say it over and
   over,
Out of your deepest sorrow, out of your deep-
   est grief,
No hurt can last forever—perhaps tomorrow
Will bring relief.
Grace Noll Crowell

Put it in WRITING.

A mother's advice: I can forget and you can forget, but a piece of paper never forgets.

An oral contract isn't worth the paper it's written on. *Louis B. Mayer (attributed)*

He who lives without keeping records dies without leaving an inheritance. *Yiddish proverb*

Spoken words fly away; written words remain. *Latin proverb*

If something can go WRONG, it will. Murphy's Law*

. . . and at the worst possible moment.

If anything can go wrong, sometime it will. *Original version*

*Murphy's Law expresses our anguish over the fact that we live in an imperfect world and that modern technology often escalates imperfections into disasters. Where did Murphy's Law come from? Who's Murphy?

According to an article in *People* (Jan. 31, 1983), in 1949, when the U.S. Air Force was conducting critical experiments on space travel, Major John Paul Stapp was blasted off across the Mojave Desert in a rocket sled, to set a new record in defiance of the force of gravity, but no record was set because the recording mechanism failed. Assigned to investigate the goof, Captain Edward A. Murphy discovered that an absentminded technician had installed six sensors backward. Murphy sighed, "If there's more than one way to do a job and one of those ways will end in disaster, then somebody will do it that way."

A few weeks after the incident, the major, who had risked his life in the experiment, attended an Air Force press conference and attributed the blunder to Murphy's Law. A reporter asked him to define it. Said Stapp: "If something can go wrong, it will."

Major Stapp's sharpened paraphrase of Captain Murphy's comment caught on, spreading from aviation journals to the popular press. Murphy didn't really like Stapp's paraphrase. "My original statement was to warn people to be sure that they cover all the bases, because if you haven't, you're in trouble," he explained. "It was never meant to be fatalistic."

Murphy's misquotation inspired posters, calendars, and books. Beginning in 1977, a California writer, Arthur Bloch, published three Murphy's Law books, and several Murphy's Law calendars. Millions of copies were sold and not a penny ever went to Edward Murphy. Said the publisher: "It never occurred to me that I had infringed on Ed Murphy. I felt that his law was in the public domain." Murphy may have been disappointed with these turns of events, but he probably was not altogether surprised.

See also The BREAD always falls buttered side down.

Two WRONGS don't make a right. *1783, O-234*

. . . and three rights will get you back on the freeway.

. . . but two Wrights made an airplane.

Bigamy: when two rites make a wrong.

It's up to YOU.

Be master of mind rather than be mastered by mind. *Zen saying*

Each man is the architect of his own fate. *Appius Caecus; B-870*

Genes may make us susceptible to diabetes, but we can reduce the risk by avoiding obesity. Nature may play a role in lung cancer, but we can quit smoking. Inheritance may include a bad heart, but the right physical exercise may make a difference. *The Elks (adapted)*

Hath not the potter power over the clay, of the same lump to make one vessel unto honor, and another unto dishonor? *Romans 9:21*

It's not the gale but the set of the sail that determines the way you go.

Most folks are about as happy as they make up their minds to be. *Abraham Lincoln*

No one can make you feel inferior without your consent. *Eleanor Roosevelt, 1960*

Teachers open the door, but you must enter by yourself. *Chinese proverb*

The kingdom of God is within you. *Luke 17:21*

The Zen master said, Who binds you? The seeker of liberty said, No one binds me. The Zen master said, Then why seek liberation? *Zen Mondo*

We have to believe in free-will. We've got no choice. *Isaac Bashevis Singer, quoted in Times Diary, June 21, 1982*

When the student is ready, the master appears. *Buddhist proverb*

See also CHE sera sera; I am the MASTER of my fate; The power of positive THINKING.

YOU can't take it with you. 472 B.C., B-1984

. . . That's okay; you can't use it there anyway.

. . . Then Father won't go. *Moss Hart and George Kaufman, You Can't Take It with You*

. . . You're lucky if it doesn't go before you do.

. . . but these days where can you go without it? *Pearl Bailey*

As he came forth of his mother's womb, naked shall he return to go as he came, and shall take nothing of his labour, which he may carry away in his hand. *Ecclesiastes 5:15*

I'm not sure I even have enough to get there.

I've never seen a Brink's truck follow a hearse to the cemetery. *Barbara Hutton, quoted in Poor Little Rich Girl*

Philosophy teaches a man that he can't take it with him; taxes teach him he can't leave it behind either. *Mignon McLaughlin*

Save your money and die rich. *Heard in Ohio*

You can't take it with you when you go,
There is no doubt about it;
But that's about the only place
That you can go without it.
Kathryn Gelander, Wall Street Journal

See also SHROUDS have no pockets.

You're only YOUNG once.

. . . After that, you have to think up some other excuse. *Billy Arthur*

. . . but you can stay immature indefinitely.

It is better to be a young June-bug than an old bird of paradise. *Mark Twain, Pudd'nhead Wilson's Calendar*

Rejoice, O young man, in thy youth; and let thy heart cheer thee in the days of thy youth. *Ecclesiastes 11:9*

The best substitute for experience is being 16. *Raymond Duncan*

The rising, not the setting, sun is worshipped by most men. *1550, Erasmus*

You're Only Old Once! A Book for Obsolete Children. *Title of a 1986 book by Dr. Seuss (Theodor Seuss Geisel)*

Youth is a quality and if you have it, you never lose it. *Frank Lloyd Wright*

Youth is a wonderful thing. What a crime to waste it on children. *G. B. Shaw*

Youth is the best time to be rich, and the best time to be poor. *Euripides*

Youth is wasted on the young, and retirement is wasted on old fogies.

See also YOUTH will have its fling.

What's YOURS is mine, and what's mine is my own. A.D. 450, B-1834

Whatever is not nailed down is mine. Whatever I can pry loose is not nailed down. *Collis P. Huntington, on fair competition*

What kind of society isn't structured on greed? The problem of social organization is how to set up an arrangement under which greed will do the least harm; capitalism is that kind of a system. *Milton Friedman, Playboy magazine, 1973*

Be YOURSELF.

. . . but do everything you can to make a good impression.

. . . is about the worst advice you can give to some people. *Tom Masson*

. . . Who else is better qualified? *Frank J. Giblin, II*

. . . An original is always better than a copy. *Thomas F. Coonan*

Be what you seem, and seem what you are. *Scottish proverb*

Don't be yourself—be someone a little nicer. *Mignon McLaughlin*

Eagles fly alone, but sheep flock together.

Every man has three temperaments: the one he has, the one he shows, and the one he thinks he has. *Alphonse Karr*

Follow your own bent no matter what people say. *Karl Marx*

If a man does not keep pace with his companions, perhaps it is because he hears a different drummer. Let him step to the music which he hears, however measured or far away. *Henry David Thoreau, Walden*

If I do not appear to keep pace with my neighbor, perhaps it is because I am paying a different piper. *T. Dubois, 1964; BJW-495*

If I'm going to sing like someone else, then I don't need to sing at all. *Billie Holiday (attributed)*

If you ain't what you is, you is what you ain't.

If you want to be original, be yourself. God never made two people exactly alike.

If you're honest about yourself, somebody might even be impressed. *Donald G. Smith*

I would like to be myself. I tried to be other things, but I always failed. *A third grader, answering the question, "What do you want to be?"*

Rabbi Noah of Lekivitz was asked, "Why do you not conduct yourself like your father, the late rabbi?" Replied Rabbi Noah, "I do conduct myself like him. He did not imitate anybody, and I do likewise."

The first duty in life is to be as artificial as possible; what the second duty is, no one has yet discovered. *Oscar Wilde*

The most exhausting thing in life, I have discovered, is being insincere. That is why so much social life is exhausting: one is wearing a mask. *Anne Morrow Lindbergh, Gift from the Sea*

Three sure ways to confuse and annoy people—by keeping your word, by telling the truth, by being yourself. *Richard Needham*

To be nobody-but-myself—in a world which is doing its best, night and day, to make you everybody else—means to fight the hardest battle which any human being can fight, and never stop fighting. *e. e. cummings*

We forfeit three-fourths of ourselves to be like other people. *Arthur Schopenhauer*

When all men are what they pretend to be, jails will be torn down, churches turned into storehouses, and policemen will be cab drivers. *William C. Hunter*

Whoso would be a man must be a noncon-formist. . . . Nothing is at last sacred but the integrity of your own mind. *Ralph Waldo Emerson*

You can pretend to be serious, but you can't pretend to be witty. *Sacha Guitry*

To follow you, I'm not content,
Unless I know which way you went.

Let YOURSELF go.

It's all right letting yourself go, as long as you can get yourself back. *Mick Jagger*

Sex is a natural function. You can't make it happen, but you can teach people to let it happen. *William H. Masters, New York Times, Oct. 29, 1984*

Under certain circumstances, profanity pro-vides a relief denied even to prayer. *Mark Twain*

YOUTH will be served. *1579, F-213*

. . . but old age and treachery will always de-feat youth and skill.

. . . pollution, inflation, and a burdensome national debt.

. . . Young turkeys are served stuffed with chestnuts. *James Thurber*

Note on the police station bulletin board: Youth will be observed.

YOUTH will have its fling. *1562, WM-688*

. . . but can't they be careful about what they throw?

. . . and the flingier the better. *George Jean Nathan*

Adolescence is a time of rapid changes. Be-tween the ages of 12 and 17, for example, a parent ages as much as 20 years. *Changing Times*

As adolescents are too old to do the things kids do and not old enough to do things adults do, they do things nobody else does.

Ask the young; they know everything. *French proverb*

Death is just a distant rumor to the young. *Andy Rooney*

He was a Boy Scout until he was 16—then he became a girl scout.

I don't say we all ought to misbehave, but we out to look as if we could. *Orson Welles*

If you want a symbolic gesture, don't burn the flag, wash it. *Norman Thomas*

It is better to waste one's youth than to do nothing with it at all. *Georges Courteline, La Philosophie de Georges Courteline*

It is the obligation of every new generation to outrage its elders. *Offered as Page's First Law of Youth Attitudes by Chicago Tribune colum-nist Clarence Page*

No member of our generation who wasn't a Communist or a dropout in the thirties is worth a damn. *Lyndon B. Johnson, 1960*

No young man believes he shall ever die. *William Hazlitt, On the Feeling of Immortal-ity in Youth*

Rejoice, O young man, in thy youth; and let thy heart cheer thee in the days of thy youth, and walk in the ways of thine heart, and in the sight of thine eyes: but know thou, that for all these things God will bring thee into judgment. *Ecclesiastes 11:9*

The young always have the same problem—how to rebel and conform at the same time. They have now solved this by defying their parents and copying one another. *Quentin Crisp*

We can endure vices in the young that we would despise in the old. *Josh Billings*

When a nation's young men are conservative, its funeral-bell is already rung. *Henry Ward Beecher*

Young men are apt to think themselves wise enough, as drunken men are apt to think themselves sober enough. *Lord Chesterfield, Letters, Jan. 15, 1753*

Young men are fitter to invent than to judge; fitter for execution than for counsel; fitter for new projects than for settled business. *Francis Bacon, Essays*

Youth is a disease from which we all recover. *Dorothy Fuldheim, A Thousand Friends*

A boy's will is the wind's will,
And the thoughts of youth are long, long thoughts.
Henry Wadsworth Longfellow, My Lost Youth

See also BOYS will be boys.

Proverbs and Sayings of Contrast

Almost every wise saying has an opposite one, no less wise, to balance it. George Santayana, *The Life of Reason*

Absence makes the heart grow fonder
BUT: Out of sight, out of mind

Actions speak louder than words
BUT: A word to the wise is sufficient

Advice is cheap
BUT: A fool's counsel is sometimes worth the weighing

Advice that ain't paid for ain't no good
BUT: A word to the wise is sufficient

Ah, but a man's reach should exceed his grasp
BUT: Take it easy

All at once makes light work
BUT: Too many cooks spoil the broth

All for one and one for all
BUT: Every man for himself
& What's yours is mine, and what's mine is my own
& Help yourself
& Heads I win, tails you lose
& Paddle your own canoe

All is flux
BUT: The more things change, the more they stay the same

All is for the best in the best of all possible worlds
BUT: Things are going to the dogs
& It's a cockeyed world
& Nothing works
& The bread always falls buttered side down
& If anything can go wrong, sometime it will

All is vanity
BUT: Flattery will get you nowhere

All men are brothers
BUT: People are no damned good
& East is East and West is West and never the twain shall meet

All men are created equal
BUT: The only good Indian is a dead Indian
& The apple doesn't fall far from the tree

All roads lead to Rome
BUT: East is East and West is West, and never the twain shall meet

All things come to him who waits
BUT: He who hesitates is lost
& Justice delayed is justice denied

All work and no play makes Jack a dull boy
BUT: Hard work never killed anybody
& Happiness comes from work well done

Always speak well of the dead
BUT: Tell the truth and shame the devil

Any port in a storm
BUT: There's no place like home

Anything can happen
BUT: The die is cast
& History repeats itself

Apparel oft proclaims the man
BUT: Clothes do not make the man

Appearances are deceiving
BUT: What you see is what you get

The apple doesn't fall far from the tree
BUT: Many a good cow has a bad calf
& Straight logs have crooked roots

As many men, so many minds
BUT: Great minds think alike
& Men are all alike

As the twig is bent, the tree's inclined
BUT: Anything can happen

As you sow, so shall you reap
BUT: Anything can happen
& The race is not to the swift, nor the battle to the strong, but time and chance ruleth over them all
& You can't win
& You never can tell

Bad news travels fast
BUT: No news is good news

A bad wound heals, a bad name kills
BUT: Sticks and stones may break my bones, but names will never harm me

Be all that you can
BUT: Take it easy

Be careful of what you wish for; you might get it
BUT: Hitch your wagon to a star

Be good and you will be happy
BUT: The good die young
& Sow your wild oats
& Youth will have its fling

Be it ever so humble, there's no place like home
BUT: Variety is the spice of life
& No place is perfect

Be sure you're right, then go ahead
BUT: Make haste slowly

Be yourself
BUT: Put your best foot forward
& When in Rome, do as the Romans do

Beauty is in the eye of the beholder
BUT: What you see is what you get

The bee that gets the honey doesn't hang around the hive
BUT: A rolling stone gathers no moss
& Stay in your own backyard
& The higher they climb, the harder they fall

Behind every successful man is a woman
BUT: No man is a hero to his wife

The best defense is a good offense
BUT: He who fights and runs away lives to fight another day

The best is yet to be
BUT: Things are going to the dogs
& Life is one damned thing after another

The best things in life are free
BUT: Money makes the world go 'round
& You get what you pay for
& No gains without pains
& No sweet without sweat

The best way to kill time is to work it to death
BUT: Take it easy

& Thank God it's Friday
& Who invented work?

Better late than never
BUT: Justice delayed is justice denied

Better Red than dead
BUT: It is sweet and fitting to die for one's country

Better the devil you know than the devil you don't know
BUT: Variety is the spice of life

Better to be born lucky than rich
BUT: Money makes the man

Better to wear out than to rust out
BUT: Take it easy

The big lie
BUT: Honesty is the best policy

A bird in the hand is worth two in the bush
BUT: A man's reach should exceed his grasp, or what's heaven for?

Birds of a feather flock together
BUT: Opposites attract

Blood is thicker than water
BUT: A near friend is better than a distant relative

Bragging saves advertising
BUT: Self-praise is no recommendation

The bread always falls buttered side down
BUT: Anything can happen

Business before pleasure
BUT: Enjoy yourself, it's later than you think
& Take it easy
& Who invented work?

Call a spade a spade
BUT: The truth is not to be spoken at all times

Carpe diem
BUT: Make haste slowly
& Patience is a virtue
& There's a time and a place for everything
& There's always tomorrow
& Look before you leap

Charity begins at home
BUT: Love thy neighbor as thyself

Che sera sera
BUT: I am the captain of my fate
& It's up to you

Cheaters never win
BUT: Nothing succeeds like success

Circumstances alter cases
BUT: Let justice be done!

A closed mouth catches no flies
BUT: Bragging saves advertising
& Don't hide your light under a bushel
& Speak or forever hold your peace

Clothes don't make the man
BUT: Clothes make the man
& Fine feathers make fine birds

Clothes make the man
BUT: You can't make a silk purse out of a sow's ear

Comparisons are odious
BUT: Wisdom is better than rubies

Confession is good for the soul
BUT: Keep your troubles to yourself
& Never apologize

Conscience is that still, small voice within you
BUT: What, me worry?

Covet nothing overmuch
BUT: A man's reach should exceed his grasp, or what's heaven for?

A coward dies a thousand deaths, the brave just one
BUT: He who fights and runs away lives to fight another day

Crime does not pay
BUT: Nothing succeeds like success
& There ain't no justice

Crooked logs make straight fires
BUT: What you see is what you get
& You can't make a silk purse out of a sow's ear

Curiosity killed the cat
BUT: Knowledge is power

The curse of bigness
BUT: Make no small plans

A deal is a deal
BUT: Promises and pie crusts are made to be broken

Death before dishonor
BUT: He who fights and runs away lives to fight another day

Delays are dangerous
BUT: Make haste slowly

Desperate diseases must have desperate remedies
BUT: The end does not justify the means

The devil finds work for idle hands
BUT: Take it easy

The devil is an ass
BUT: The devil is not as black as he is painted

Diplomacy is to do and say the nastiest thing in the nicest way
BUT: Honesty is the best policy

Discretion is the better part of valor
BUT: Nothing ventured, nothing gained

Distance lends enchantment
BUT: Out of sight, out of mind

Do as you would be done by
BUT: Every man for himself

Do it now
BUT: Make haste slowly
& Patience is a virtue
& There's a time and a place for everything
& There's always tomorrow
& Look before you leap

Do or die
BUT: He that fights and runs away lives to fight another day

Do unto others as you would have them do unto you
BUT: Dog eat dog

Do your own thing
BUT: When in Rome do as the Romans do

The dog that trots about will find a bone
BUT: A rolling stone gathers no moss

Don't be too fussy
BUT: Hitch your wagon to a star

Don't borrow trouble
BUT: Fools rush in where angels fear to tread

Don't count on miracles
BUT: Faith is the substance of things hoped for
& If you have faith as a grain of mustard seed, nothing is impossible for you

Don't count your chickens before they're hatched
BUT: Hope deferred maketh the heart sick

Don't cross your bridges before you come to them
BUT: Plan ahead

Don't get involved
BUT: A friend in need is a friend indeed
& Man is a social animal

Don't go by appearances
BUT: What you see is what you get

Don't hide your light under a bushel
BUT: Good wine needs no bush
& Self-praise is no recommendation

Don't let the cat out of the bag
BUT: Tell the truth and shame the devil

Don't lock the stable door after the horse has bolted
BUT: It's never too late

Don't look a gift horse in the mouth
BUT: Nothing's for nothing

Don't make waves
BUT: Tell the truth and shame the devil

Don't start up
BUT: If this be treason, let us make the most of it

Don't stick your neck out
BUT: Take a chance

Don't take yourself too seriously
BUT: I am the captain of my soul

Don't tell tales out of school
BUT: Honesty is the best policy

The door to success is always marked Push
BUT: Easy does it

Drink is the curse of the working class
BUT: Eat, drink, and be merry

Each man kills the thing he loves
BUT: Love is a many-splendored thing

The end does not justify the means
BUT: The end justifies the means
& Fight fire with fire

Enjoy yourself; it's later than you think
BUT: Work never killed anybody

Enough is enough
BUT: You're never satisfied

Every little bit helps
BUT: Too many cooks spoil the broth

Every man has his price
BUT: You can't buy friendship

Every man is his own best friend
BUT: I am my own executioner
& A man is his own worst enemy

Everyone has his cross to bear
BUT: Some folks have all the luck

Everything comes to him that waits
BUT: He who hesitates is lost
& Strike while the iron is hot

Experience is the best teacher
BUT: Experience is the name that everyone gives to their mistakes
& Wise men learn from the mistakes of others
& Some people never learn

Facts are facts
BUT: It's all in how you look at it
& There's nothing either good or bad but thinking makes it so
& To the pure all things are pure

Faint heart never won fair maid
BUT: The meek shall inherit the earth

Faith is the substance of things hoped for
BUT: I'm from Missouri; you've got to show me
& Never assume

Familiarity breeds contempt
BUT: Be it ever so humble, there's no place like home
& Home sweet home
& Out of sight, out of mind

Fight fire with fire
BUT: The end does not justify the means

Flattery will get you nowhere
BUT: Praise is always pleasant

Foresight is better than hindsight
BUT: Hindsight is better than foresight

Frailty, thy name is woman
BUT: Never underestimate the power of a woman

A friend in need is a friend indeed
BUT: Rats desert a sinking ship
& Fools run in where angels fear to tread
& God defend me from my friends

Full of courtesy, full of craft
BUT: Politeness costs nothing

Genius is born, not made
BUT: Genius is one percent inspiration and ninety-nine percent perspiration

God is dead
BUT: God's in heaven, all's right with the world
& If God did not exist, it would be necessary to invent him
& Keep the faith
& There are no atheists in foxholes

God tempers the wind to the shorn lamb
BUT: God helps those who help themselves

God's in heaven, all's right with the world
BUT: Things are going to the dogs

Good guys finish last
BUT: The race is not to the swift, nor the battle to the strong, but time and chance happen to them all

A good wife and health are a man's best wealth
BUT: A young man married is a man that's marred

Good wine needs no bush
BUT: It pays to advertise

Grasp all, lose all
BUT: Help yourself

The grass is always greener on the other side of the fence
BUT: Be it ever so humble, there's no place like home

Grown men don't cry
BUT: Let yourself go

Half a loaf is better than none
BUT: Never do anything by halves
& Hitch your wagon to a star
& A man's reach should exceed his grasp

A half-truth is often a whole lie
BUT: The truth is not to be spoken at all times

The hand is quicker than the eye
BUT: What you see is what you get

A handful of good life is better than a bushel of learning
BUT: Knowledge is power

Hang loose
BUT: Happiness comes from work well done
& If you have time to kill, work it to death

Happiness comes from work well done
BUT: Who the hell invented work?
& Hang loose
& Take it easy

Hard work never killed anybody
BUT: Take it easy

Haste makes waste
BUT: He who hesitates is lost

He that fights and runs away lives to fight another day
BUT: It is sweet and fitting to die for one's country

He that would thrive must rise at five; he that has thriven may lie till seven
BUT: Who the hell invented work?

He took defeat like a man; he blamed it on his wife
BUT: Never underestimate the power of a woman

He who hesitates is lost
BUT: Marry in haste, repent at leisure
& Look before you leap

Help yourself
BUT: Share and share alike

The higher they climb, the harder they fall
BUT: There's plenty of room at the top

History is bunk
BUT: History repeats itself
& Those who cannot remember the past are condemned to repeat it

Hitch your wagon to a star
BUT: Keep both feet on the ground
& Stay in your own backyard

Honesty is the best policy
BUT: The truth is not to be spoken at all times
& The truth hurts

I am my own executioner
BUT: Your best friend is yourself

I am the master of my fate: I am the captain of my soul
BUT: Anything can happen
& Better to be born lucky than rich
& If I own a cow, the cow owns me
& It's all a matter of luck
& There but for the grace of God go I

If at first you don't succeed, try, try again
BUT: The race is not to the swift
& Let well enough alone
& You can't win

If God be for us, who can be against us?
BUT: Providence is always on the side of the big battalions

If thine enemy offends thee, turn the other cheek
BUT: Tit for tat
& What's sauce for the goose is sauce for the gander

If you can't say something nice about a person, don't say anything
BUT: Tell the truth and shame the devil

If you have time to kill, work it to death
BUT: Take it easy
& Who invented work?

If you haven't tried it, don't knock it
BUT: You don't have to be able to lay an egg to tell a bad one

If you want a thing done well, do it yourself
BUT: Many hands make light work
& Let George do it

Ignorance is bliss
BUT: Knowledge is power
& Think

& Keep an open mind
& Keep your ears open
& I'm from Missouri; you've got to show me
& The unexamined life is not worth living

In God we trust
BUT: God is dead

In time of peace, prepare for war
BUT: War is not healthy for children and other living things
& War is hell
& Who lives by the sword dies by the sword

Is life worth living?
BUT: It's great to be alive

It's not the money, it's the principle of the thing
BUT: Money talks

It's not what you know, it's who you know
BUT: Knowledge is power
& Merit wins

It is not good for man to be alone
BUT: A young man married is a man that's marred

It is sweet and fitting to die for one's country
BUT: He that fights and runs away lives to fight another day
& Patriotism is the last refuge of the scoundrel

It's a hard life
BUT: Life is sweet

It's a man's world
BUT: Never underestimate the power of a woman

It's all a matter of luck
BUT: No sweat, no sweet

It's better to be born lucky than rich
BUT: Money makes the world go 'round

It's never too late
BUT: A miss is as good as a mile

It's the woman who pays
BUT: Never underestimate the power of a woman

It matters not whether you won or lost, but how you played the game
BUT: Nothing succeeds like success

Join the army and see the world
BUT: War is hell

Keep your troubles to yourself
BUT: Confession is good for the soul
& Let it all hang out
& Let yourself go

Knowledge is power
BUT: There's no fool like an educated fool
& What you don't know won't hurt you

Less is more
BUT: Make no small plans
& Think big

Let well enough alone
BUT: Whatever is worth doing is worth doing well

Life can be beautiful
BUT: Things are going to the dogs

Life is hard
BUT: Life is sweet

Life is so unfair
BUT: The mills of the gods grind slowly, yet they grind exceedingly fine

Life is sweet
BUT: Most men lead lives of quiet desperation

Life is what you make it
BUT: The race is not to the swift

Like father, like son
BUT: Many a good cow has a bad calf

Like seeks like
BUT: Opposites attract

Live and learn
BUT: Some people never learn

Love conquers all
BUT: A young man married is a man that's marred
& Spare the rod and spoil the child
& You can't live on love

Love is blind
BUT: Love makes the world go 'round

Love is never having to say you're sorry
BUT: You always hurt the one you love

Love thy neighbor
BUT: Mind your own business

Love will find a way
BUT: When poverty enters the door, love flies out the window

Make haste slowly
BUT: Strike while the iron is hot

Make hay while the sun shines
BUT: Take it easy

Make no small plans
BUT: Less is more
& The curse of bigness
& Small is beautiful

Man is a social animal
BUT: To thine own self be true

A man is his own worst enemy
BUT: Your best friend is yourself

Man is the measure of all things
BUT: People are no damned good
& What fools these mortals be

A man who is his own doctor has a fool for a patient
BUT: Physician, heal thyself

Many a good cow has a bad calf
BUT: Train up a child in the way he should go; and when he is old, he will never depart from it

Many hands make light work
BUT: Too many cooks spoil the broth

The meek shall inherit the earth
BUT: There ain't no justice

Merit wins
BUT: It's all a matter of luck
& It's not what you know, it's who you know
& The race is not to the swift, nor the battle to the strong, but time and chance happen to them all

Might is not right
BUT: Might makes right
& The end justifies the means

Might makes right
BUT: The pen is mightier than the sword
& The end doesn't justify the means

The mills of the gods grind slowly, yet they grind exceedingly fine
BUT: There ain't no justice

Money doesn't buy happiness
BUT: Wealth makes many friends

Money is the root of all evil
BUT: Money makes the world go 'round

Money isn't everything
BUT: Money makes the world go 'round
& Money talks

Money makes the world go 'round
BUT: Wisdom is better than rubies

Money talks
BUT: Power corrupts

The more, the merrier
BUT: Two's company, three is a crowd
& Too much of anything is not good

The more things change, the more they stay the same
BUT: Other days, other ways
& There's nothing permanent except change

Never put off until tomorrow what you can do today
BUT: Take it easy
& There's always tomorrow
& Tomorrow is another day

Never too old to learn
BUT: You can't teach an old dog new tricks

Never underestimate the power of a woman
BUT: A woman's place is in the home

No time like the present
BUT: There's always tomorrow

Nothing is impossible
BUT: You can't make an omelette without breaking eggs

Nothing succeeds like success
BUT: Who lives by the sword dies by the sword

Nothing ventured, nothing gained
BUT: Play it safe
& A rolling stone gathers no moss

O tempora! o mores!
BUT: There's nothing new under the sun

Oh what a tangled web we weave, when first we practice to deceive
BUT: The truth is not to be told at all times

Oil and water don't mix
BUT: Opposites attract

Old friends and old wine are the best
BUT: Variety is the spice of life

Old ways are best
BUT: Other days, other ways
& Times change and we with them

One error leads to another
BUT: Profit from your mistakes
& To err is human, to forgive is divine

Opportunity knocks but once
BUT: There's always tomorrow

Other days, other ways
BUT: The more things change, the more they stay the same

Out of the abundance of the heart the mouth speaketh
BUT: Silence is golden

Paddle your own canoe
BUT: It is not good for man to be alone

People are no damned good
BUT: This is the best of all possible worlds
& There is honor among thieves

Plan ahead
BUT: Take one day at a time

Poverty breeds strife
BUT: Poverty is no sin
& Sweet are the uses of adversity

A promise is a promise
BUT: Promises and pie crust are made to be broken

Put your nose to the grindstone and your shoulder to the wheel
BUT: Who invented work?

Quit while you're ahead
BUT: Throw good money after bad
& A quitter never wins and a winner never quits

Rank has its privileges
BUT: What's sauce for the goose is sauce for the gander

Right is might
BUT: There ain't no justice
& Providence is always on the side of the big battalions

Root, hog, or die
BUT: Take it easy

See no evil, hear no evil, speak no evil
BUT: Ye shall know the truth, and the truth shall make you free

Seeing is believing
BUT: You can't tell a book by its cover

Self-love is better than self-hate
BUT: Self-praise is no recommendation

The shoemaker should stick to his last
BUT: Variety is the spice of life

Silence gives consent
BUT: Silence is golden
& You have not converted a man because you have silenced him

Silence is golden
BUT: Tell the truth and shame the devil
& Speak or forever hold your peace
& The wheel that squeaks the loudest is the one that gets the grease

Slow but sure
BUT: Strike while the iron is hot

Small is beautiful
BUT: Think big

Sow your wild oats
BUT: You can't be too careful

Stay in your own backyard
BUT: There's plenty of room at the top

Take a chance
BUT: You can't be too careful
& There's nothing like being on the safe side

Take it easy
BUT: Tend to business

Tell the truth and shame the devil
BUT: The truth is not to be spoken at all times

There is a time and a place for everything
BUT: There's no time like the present

There's always tomorrow
BUT: There's no time like the present

Things are going to the dogs
BUT: This is the best of all possible worlds

Tomorrow never comes
BUT: Tomorrow will be better

Too many cooks spoil the broth
BUT: Many hands make light work
& Two heads are better than one

Victory is sweet
BUT: You can't win

We get too soon old and too late smart
BUT: You're never too old to learn

Wine is a mocker
BUT: Wine maketh glad the heart of man

Wishing will make it so
BUT: Wishing won't help

You can't win
BUT: You get what you pay for

Bibliography

Proverb Wit and Wisdom draws upon three distinct groups of sources: (1) classic proverb collections. Dates indicate the years of the first edition. If date is followed by + (e.g., 1614+), editions were also published at a later date, often containing new items; (2) modern proverb studies; and (3) a browser's paradise of books that yield a rich harvest of proverb twists, witticisms, verses, and reflections on proverb lore.

I. Classic Collections

Bohn, H. *A Handbook of Proverbs.* 1855.

Breton, N. *Crossing of Proverbs.* 1616.

Camden, W. *Remains Concerning Britain.* 1614+.

Clarke, J. *Paroemiologia Anglo-Latina.* 1639.

Cotgrave, Randis. *A Dictionary of the French and English Tongue.* 1611.

Delalmothe, G. *The French Alphabet.* 1592+.

Draxe, T. *Bibliotheca Scholastica.* 1616+.

Erasmus, D. *Adagiorum Opus.* 1550.*

Fergusson, D. *Scottish Proverbs.* 1641.*

Florio, J. *First Fruites.* 1578.

_____. *Second Frutes.* 1591+.

Fuller, T. *Gnomologia.* 1732+.

Hazlitt, W. *English Proverbs.* 1869+.

Herbert, G. *Outlandish Proverbs.* 1640.*

_____. *Jacula Prudentum, an Expanded Version of Outlandish Proverbs.* 1651.

Heywood, J. *A Dialogue Containing the Number in Effect of All the Proverbs in the English Tongue.* 1546.

_____. *Two Hundred Epigrams upon Two Hundred Proverbs with a Third Hundred Newly Added.* 1555.

Kelly, J. *A Complete Collection of Scottish Proverbs.* 1721.

Lean, V. S. *Collectanea.* 1902–4.

Palsgrave, J. *L'Éclaircissement de la Langue Française.* 1530.

Ramsay, A. *A Collection of Scots Proverbs.* 1737.

Ray, J. *A Collection of English Proverbs.* 1670 and 1678.

Taverner, R. *Proverbs or Adages with New Additions, Gathered out of the Chiliades of Erasmus.* 1539.

Torriano, G. *Select Italian Proverbs.* 1642.

_____. *Piazza Universale di Proverbi Italiani.* 1666.

Trench, R. C. *On the Lessons in Proverbs.* 1853.

*These, and perhaps others on this list, were published posthumously.

II. Modern Studies and Informational Sources

Barnes-Harden, Alene L. *African American Verbal Arts: Their Nature and Communicative Interpretation.* Dissertation of The State University of New York at Buffalo, 1980.

Boller, Paul F. Jr., and John George. *They Never Said It; a Book of Fake Quotes, Misquotes and Misleading Attributes.* New York: Oxford University Press, 1989.

Bond, Donald. "English Legal Proverbs," *PMLA,* vol. 51, pp. 921–35, 1936.

Flexner, Stuart, and Doris Flexner. *Wise Words and Wives' Tales.* New York: Avon Books, 1993. (*Abbreviated in this book as F.*)

Fogg, Walter. *1000 Sayings of History.* Boston: Beacon Press, 1929.

Keyes, Ralph. *Nice Guys Finish Seventh: False Phrases, Spurious Sayings, and Familiar Misquotations.* New York: Harper-Collins, 1992.

Magill, Frank N., and Tench F. Tilghman. *Magill's Quotations in Context.* 2 vols. New York: Salem Press, 1965. (*Abbreviated in this book as M.*)

_____. *Magill's Quotations in Context.* 1969 ed. New York: Harper & Row, 1969. (*Abbreviated in this book as M69.*)

McNamara, M. Frances. *2000 Famous Legal Quotations.* Rochester: Aqueduct Books, 1967.

Mieder, Wolfgang. *Talk Less and Say More: Vermont Proverbs.* Shelburne, Vt.: New England Press, 1986.

_____. *American Proverbs: A Study of Texts and Contexts.* Berne: Peter Lang, 1989.

_____. ed. *A Dictionary of American Proverbs.* New York: Oxford University Press, 1992. (*Abbreviated in this book as WM.*)

_____. *Proverbs are Never Out of Season: Popular Wisdom in the Modern Age.* New York: Oxford University Press, 1993.

Morris, William, and Mary Morris. *Morris Dictionary of Word and Phrase Origins.* New York: Harper & Row, 1977. (*Abbreviated in this book as MD.*)

Simpson, John A. *Concise Oxford Dictionary of Proverbs.* New York, Oxford University Press, 1982. (*Abbreviated in this book as O.*)

Smith, Charles G. *Shakespeare's Proverb Lore.* Cambridge: Harvard University Press, 1963.

Smith, Diann Sutherlin. *Down Home Talk: An Outrageous Dictionary of Colorful Country Expressions.* New York: Collier, 1988.

Smith, William G., ed. *Oxford Dictionary of English Proverbs.* New York: Oxford University Press, 1935. (*Abbreviated in this book as OE.*)

_____. *Oxford Dictionary of English Proverbs,* 2nd ed. Oxford University Press: New York, 1952. (*Abbreviated in this book as O2.*)

Stevenson, Burton. *The Home Book of Proverbs, Maxims, and Familiar Phrases.* New York: Macmillan, 1948. (*Abbreviated in this book as B.*)

Taylor, Archer. *The Proverb.* Cambridge: Harvard University Press, 1931.

_____, and Bartlett Jere Whiting. *A Dictionary of American Proverbs and Proverbial Phrases, 1820–1880*. Cambridge: Belknap Press of Harvard University Press, 1967. *(Abbreviated in this book as TW.)*

Tilley, George Palmer. *A Dictionary of the Proverbs in England in the Sixteenth and Seventeenth Centuries*. Ann Arbor: University of Michigan Press, 1950. *(Abbreviated in this book as T.)*

Urdang, Lawrence, ed. *Mottoes: A Compilation of More Than 9000 Mottoes from Around the World and Throughout History*. Detroit: Gale Research, 1986.

Whiting, Bartlett Jere. *Early American Proverbs and Proverbial Phrases*. Cambridge: Belknap Press of Harvard University Press, 1977. *(Abbreviated in this book as EAP.)*

_____. *Modern Proverbs and Proverbial Sayings*. Cambridge: Harvard University Press, 1989. *(Abbreviated in this book as BJW.)*

III. A BROWSER'S PARADISE

Adams, A. K. *The Home Book of Humorous Quotations*. New York: Dodd, Mead, 1969.

Bierce, Ambrose. *The Devil's Dictionary*. New York: Boni, 1911.

Brilliant, Ashleigh. *I May Not Be Totally Perfect, but Parts of Me Are Excellent*. Santa Barbara: Woodbridge Press, 1979. Some of the author's epigrams are taken from his "Pot-shot" postcards.

Brookes, Stella Brewer. *Joel Chandler Harris, Folklorist*. Athens: University of Georgia Press, 1950. See chapter 8, "Proverbs and Folk-say."

Dennis, Robert. *Alec the Great*. New York: Crown, 1946.

Esar, Evan. *The Comic Encyclopedia*. Garden City, N.Y.: Doubleday, 1978.

Forbes, B. C. *Forbes Epigrams: 1000 Thoughts on Life and Business*. New York: B. C. Forbes Publishing, 1922.

_____. ed. *Thoughts on the Business of Life*. New York: B. C. Forbes Publishing, 1937.

Guiterman, Arthur. *A Poet's Proverbs*. New York: Dutton, 1924.

Harburg, E. Y. *Rhymes for the Irreverent*. New York: Grossman Publishers, 1965.

Harnsberger, Caroline Thomas, ed. *Mark Twain at Your Fingertips*. New York: Beechurst Press, 1948.

_____. ed. *Bernard Shaw, Selections of His Wit and Wisdom*. Chicago: Follett, 1965.

Harris, Sydney J. *Clearing the Ground*. Boston: Houghton Mifflin, 1986. Quotations from the author are also drawn from his syndicated newspaper column, "Strictly Personal," and from other collections of his works.

Hein, Piet. *Grooks*. Garden City, N.Y.: Doubleday, 1969.

_____. *Grooks 2*. Garden City, N.Y.: Doubleday, 1969.

_____. *Grooks 3*. Toronto: General Publishing, 1970.

Hoffenstein, Samuel. *Poems in Praise of Practically Nothing*. Garden City, N.Y.: Garden City Publishing, 1941.

Howe, Ed. *Country Town Sayings*. Amarillo: Russell Stationery, 1911.

Hubbard, Elbert. A *Thousand and One Epigrams*. 1914.

Hunter, William C. *Brass Tacks*. Chicago: Reilly & Britton, 1910.

Lamb, Charles, and Mary Lamb. *The Works of Charles and Mary Lamb*. London: Methuen, 1903. "Popular Fallacies," pp. 252–75.

Leacock, Stephen C. *Winnowed Wisdom*. Toronto: Macmillan, 1926.

Lec, Stanislaw J. *Unkempt Thoughts*. Funk & Wagnalls, 1967.

Levinson, Leonard. *Left-Handed Dictionary*. Macmillan, 1963.

_____. *Webster's Unafraid Dictionary*. New York: Collier Books, 1967.

_____. *Bartlett's Unfamiliar Quotations*. Cowles, 1971.

Leonard Levinson merits a special annotation as a prolific inventor of proverb twists. He was an actor, journalist, and Broadway, television, and radio comedy writer (cowriter of the *Fibber McGee and Molly* show), and also the author of many cookbooks.

McLaughlin, Mignon. *The Neurotic's Notebook*. Indianapolis: Bobbs-Merrill, 1963.

_____. *The Second Neurotic's Notebook*. Indianapolis: Bobbs-Merrill, 1966.

Nathan, George Jean. *Beware of Parents*. New York: Farrar & Rinehart, 1943.

Needham, Richard J. *The Wit and Wisdom of Richard Needham*. Edmonton, Alberta: Hurtig Publishers, 1977.

Peter, Laurence J., and Raymond Hull. *The Peter Principle: Why Things Always Go Wrong*. New York: Morrow, 1969.

_____. *Peter's Almanac*. New York: Morrow, 1982.

Preston, Charles, ed. *The Light Touch: Verses, Epigrams, Aphorisms and Jokes Selected from the Pepper . . . and Salt Column of the Wall Street Journal*. Chicago: Rand McNally, 1965.

Rosten, Leo. *The Power of Positive Nonsense*. New York: McGraw-Hill, 1977.

Safian, Louis A. *The Book of Updated Proverbs*. New York: Abelard Schuman, 1967.

Shaw, Henry W. *The Complete Works of Josh Billings*. Chicago, 1919.

Smith, Donald G. *. . . And They Also Kick You When You're Down*. New York: Dodd, Mead, 1984.

Index of Main Entries

Supplementary Index by Subject

In many proverbs, the subject is stated in the KEY-WORD. For example, consider the proverbs "It pays to ADVERTISE" or "ABSENCE makes the heart grow fonder" or "ACTIONS speak louder than words." These proverbs can be easily found by the KEYWORD in the main part of the book, or in the Index of Main Entries. They are not listed in this Supplementary Index.

Other proverbs are completely figurative or metaphorical; the subject is implied rather than stated. For example, "You never miss the WATER till the well runs dry" is a good proverb about Absence. The purpose of this index is to help you locate figurative or metaphorical proverbs by their unstated subject.

Also included in this Supplementary Index are proverbs that have two subjects; for example: "HAPPINESS comes from work well done." This is a statement about happiness, but it is also about work. Since the keyword is HAPPINESS, this proverb is listed in the Supplementary Index under Work.

Absence. You never miss the WATER till the well runs dry.

Achievement. The DIFFICULT we do promptly . . . EASIER said than done. There's always ROOM at the top. *See also* Success, Work.

Action. HANDSOME is as handsome does. PROMISE little and do much. Be sure you're RIGHT, then go ahead. TALK is cheap. No TIME like the present. WISHING won't help.

Adversity. EVERYBODY has his cross to bear. FORTUNE makes friends and adversity tries them. It's a HARD life. It's easy enough to be PLEASANT . . . PROSPERITY gains friends, and adversity tries them. These are the TIMES that try men's souls. When the going gets tough, the TOUGH get going. Man is born unto TROUBLE as the sparks fly upward. You can get USED to anything. See Hardship, Perseverence.

Advice. A fool's COUNSEL . . .

Aesthetics. FORM follows function.

Agape. Love your ENEMIES. GOD is love. Hate the SIN but love the sinner.

Age. You can't teach an old DOG new tricks. Respect your ELDERS. There's no FOOL like an old fool. You're never too old to LEARN. LIFE begins at forty. A MAN is as young as he feels. Grow OLD gracefully. Never too OLD to learn. We get too soon OLD and too late smart. Young men may die, OLD men must. Never TRUST anyone over thirty.

Aggressiveness. Desperate DISEASES must have desperate remedies. DOG eat dog. Fight FIRE with fire. Big FISH eat little fish. No HARM in asking. Faint HEART . . . He who HESITATES is lost. If you gently touch a NETTLE . . . The door to SUCCESS is always marked Push.

Alertness. Keep your EARS open.

Ambition. Be ALL that you can be. The BEE that gets the honey. . . . FAME is the spur. Make no small PLANS. A man's REACH should exceed his grasp, or what's a heaven for? Hitch your wagon to a STAR. Reach for the STARS. THINK big.

Appearance. You can't tell a BOOK . . . All BRIDES are beautiful. When the CANDLES are out . . . At night all CATS are gray. CLOTHES don't make the man. CLOTHES make the man.

Barking DOGS seldom bite. Fine FEATHERS do not make a peacock. Fine FEATHERS make fine birds. Beware of the FURY of a patient man. GENTLEMEN prefer blondes. All that glitters is not GOLD. GOOD things come in small packages.

The HAND is quicker than the eye. First IMPRESSIONS are the most lasting. Crooked LOGS make straight fires. NOTHING is as easy as it looks. NOTHING is simple. What you SEE is what you get. SEEING is believing. Out of SIGHT, out of mind. THINGS are not always what they seem.

Argument. The PEN is mightier than the sword. There are two sides to every QUESTION.

Bargaining. Fair EXCHANGE is no robbery.

Bed. In bed we LAUGH, in bed we cry.

Boasting. SELF-PRAISE is no recommendation.

Bravery. The COWARD dies a thousand deaths . . . DISCRETION is the better part of valor. FORTUNE favors the bold. Grown MEN don't cry.

Brevity. BREVITY is the soul of wit. A WORD to the wise is sufficient.

Brotherhood. Ask not for whom the BELL tolls. Let them eat CAKE. No man is an ISLAND. All MEN are brothers.

Business. CAVEAT emptor. COMPETITION is the life of trade. The CURSE of bigness. The CUSTOMER is always right. No one was ever ruined by taking a PROFIT. Keep your SHOP and your shop will keep you.

Calm Yourself!* Don't rock the BOAT. Don't upset the apple CART. Take one DAY at a time. EASY does it. Take it EASY. Take time to stop and smell the FLOWERS. Don't be too FUSSY. If you're going to GET ALONG . . . GO with the flow. GOD grant me the serenity . . . HANG loose. LEAVE well enough alone. LIFE is too short to spend worrying. MUSIC hath its charms to soothe a savage breast. SMILE. Let NATURE take its course. After the STORM comes the calm. Why WORRY? WORRYING won't help. *See also* Patience.

*The above category merits a special comment. Psychologically, "Calm Yourself!" proverbs may be regarded as the internalized voice of Mother, calming the child who has been hurt or frightened or agitated. Philosophically, it suggests the basic principle of Tao-te Ching, *wu-wei:* "noninterference, letting things take their natural course: 'Do nothing and everything is done'" (*Encyclopedia Britannica*). An example of *wu-wei* is the Lao-tsu quotation that appears on page 297: "Who is there that can make muddy water clear? But if permitted to remain still, it will gradually become clear of itself."

Caution. Don't monkey with the BUZZSAW. You can't be too CAREFUL. Don't get INVOLVED. Don't go out on a LIMB. LOOK before you leap. Don't stick your NECK out. Just say NO. Better be SAFE than sorry. SAFETY first. SLOW but sure. Don't START up. Don't ask for TROUBLE. Don't borrow TROUBLE. Don't go looking for TROUBLE. Never trouble TROUBLE till trouble troubles you. Don't go near the WATER. Don't make WAVES.

Chance. ANYTHING can happen. There but for the grace of GOD go I. LIGHTNING never strikes the same place twice. The RACE is not to the swift . . .

Change. All good things must come to an END. Everything has an end. All is FLUX. Nothing lasts FOREVER. Those days are GONE forever. The MILL cannot grind with the water that is past. There is nothing NEW under the sun. O tempora! O mores! This too shall PASS away. It's a long ROAD that has no turning. Buds will be ROSES and kittens cats. SIC transit gloria mundi. TEMPUS fugit. TIMES change and we with them. The WORLD doesn't stand still. The WORM turns.

Character. The CHILD is father of the man. As a man thinketh in his HEART . . . A LEOPARD cannot change its spots. Great MINDS run in the same channel.

Charity. It is more blessed to GIVE . . . There is no grace in GIVING . . . GOD loveth a cheerful giver. Let not thy left HAND . . .

Children. Little PITCHERS have big ears. *See* Upbringing.

Choice. BEGGARS can't be choosers. You can't have your CAKE . . . There are more ways than one to kill a CAT.

Closedmindedness. None so DEAF as those who will not hear.

Commitment. In for a PENNY, in for a pound. Put up or SHUT UP. If you're not part of the SOLUTION, you're part of the problem. STAND and be counted. Put it in WRITING.

Communication. The MEDIUM is the message. SAY it right. SPEAK or forever hold your peace. SPEAK softly and carry a big stick. A WORD fitly spoken is like apples of gold in pictures of silver.

Compensation. Every CLOUD has a silver lining. When one DOOR shuts, another opens. There's no

GRIEF that hasn't its relief. One man's LOSS is another man's gain. Bad LUCK is good for something. One man's misfortune . . . Never the ROSE without the thorn. You can't live on THANKS. You can't put THANKS in your pocket. It's an ill WIND that blows nobody any good.

Competence. There's a SUCKER born every minute. Those who can, do; those who can't, TEACH. The weakest go to the WALL. WATER never rises above its level.

Competition. If you can't BEAT 'em, join 'em. Don't LOOK back . . . All is fair in LOVE and war. SURVIVAL of the fittest.

Complaint. The WHEEL that squeaks the loudest is the one that gets the grease.

Compromise. A BIRD in the hand is worth two in the bush. Better an EGG today than a hen tomorrow. Half a LOAF is better than none. SOMETHING is better than nothing.

Consequences. As you make your BED, so must you lie in it. That's the way the COOKIE crumbles. The DEER that goes too often to the lick meets the hunter at last.

Conservation. Save energy—help win the WAR.

Conservatism. OLD ways are best. WIFE and children are hostages given to fortune.

Consolation. THINGS could be worse.

Context. CIRCUMSTANCES alter cases. It all DEPENDS on how you look at it. It all DEPENDS on how you take it. It won't make any DIFFERENCE a hundred years from now. If it sounds DIRTY, you have a dirty mind. DISTANCE lends enchantment. All's well that ENDS well. EVERYTHING is relative. There is a time and a place for EVERYTHING. You can't see the FOREST for the trees. The GRASS is always greener . . . It's all in how you LOOK at it. MAN is the measure of all things. Where you STAND depends on where you sit. One man's WISDOM is another man's folly.

Cooperation. ALL for one . . . A CHAIN is as strong as its weakest link. One HAND washes the other. We must all HANG together . . . Two HEADS are better than one. You SCRATCH my back and I'll scratch yours. It takes two to TANGO. All at once makes light WORK.

Courage. None but the BRAVE . . . Faint HEART . . . NOTHING ventured . . . Once bitten, twice SHY.

STAND and be counted. Be STRONG and of good courage.

Courtesy. The age of CHIVALRY is not dead. DIPLOMACY is to do and say . . . NOBLESS oblige. *See also* Good manners and Politeness.

Criticism. It's easier to pull down than to BUILD up. If you don't DIG it don't knock it. You don't have to be able to lay an EGG to tell a bad one. FAULTS are thick where love is thin. Don't make a MOUNTAIN out of a molehill. *See also* Faultfinding.

Curiosity. A PENNY for your thoughts. Little PITCHERS have big ears. Don't ask too many QUESTIONS.

Custom. Other DAYS, other ways. EAST is east . . . EVERYBODY'S doing it. When in ROME, do as the Romans do. Thank you for not SMOKING. TIMES change and we with them.

Danger. A little spark kindles a great FIRE. If you play with FIRE, you'll get burnt.

Death. Everybody wants to go to HEAVEN . . . In the midst of life, we are in DEATH.

Debt. You can't get BLOOD from a stone.

Deception. CAVEAT emptor. FOOL me once, shame on you . . . Ill gotten GAINS never prosper. Never give a SUCKER an even break. There's a SUCKER born every minute. Heads I WIN, tails you lose.

Decision. Don't cross the BRIDGE before you get there. FISH or cut bait. You cannot be in two PLACES at once.

Defeat. How the MIGHTY have fallen.

Deliberation. THINK. Second THOUGHTS are best.

Desperation. A DROWNING man will grasp at a straw. Any PORT in a storm.

Destiny. CHE sera sera. The DIE is cast. There's a DIVINITY that shapes our ends . . . If you're born to be HANGED . . . All ROADS lead to Rome. WHATEVER will be will be. Why WORRY?

Diligence. Go to the ANT, thou sluggard. ANYTHING worth having is worth working for. Well BEGUN is half done. The early BIRD catches the worm. DO it now. DO your best . . . The DOG that trots about finds the bone. The shortest answer is DOING. If you want a thing DONE well . . . Nothing worthwhile is ever EASY. FIRST come, first served. Never do anything by HALVES. *See also* Work.

Discretion. Don't let the CAT out of the bag. A living DOG is better than a dead lion. Let sleeping DOGS lie. When in DOUBT, abstain. Don't put all your EGGS in one basket. He that FIGHTS and runs away . . . Better RED than dead. Least SAID, soonest mended. The TRUTH is not to be spoken at all times.

Diversity. In my father's HOUSE are many mansions. The MOUSE that has but one hole is quickly taken.

Dog. HAPPINESS is a warm puppy. LOVE me, love my dog.

Drinking. CANDY is dandy, but liquor is quicker.

Duplicity. Full of COURTESY, full of craft. Beware of false PROPHETS. *See also* Integrity.

Economy. What this country really needs is a good five-cent cigar. WASTE not, want not.

Education. There's no FOOL like an educated fool. An ounce of HORSE SENSE . . . A MAN ought to know a goose from a gridiron. A MIND is a terrible thing to waste. READING maketh a full man. TRAVEL broadens the mind.

Effort. FIGHT the good fight. The FIRST hundred years are the hardest. Put your best FOOT forward. No GAINS without pains. GENIUS is one percent inspiration and ninety-nine percent perspiration. LOOKERS-ON see most of the game. A MOUNTAIN in labor and it brings forth a mouse. NOTHING is as easy as it looks. NOTHING ventured, nothing gained. PADDLE your own canoe. Better to WEAR out than to rust out. Chop your own WOOD and it warms you twice. *See also* Work.

Egocentricity. You measure everyone's CORN . . . Every CROW thinks . . . What DUST do I raise! Every man thinks his own GEESE swans. O wad some pow'r the GIFTIE gie us . . . It is easy to bear another person's PROBLEMS. All the world is QUEER save thee and me, and even thou art a little queer.

Egotism. When you've got it—FLAUNT it. PRIDE goeth before a fall. SELF-LOVE is better than self-hate. Don't take yourself too SERIOUSLY. THEM that has it, shows it. VANITY, thy name is woman.

Endurance. What can't be CURED must be endured. GRIN and bear it. If you can't stand the HEAT . . . When LIFE hands you a lemon, make lemonade. *See also* Forbearance.

Enthusiasm. NOTHING great was ever achieved without enthusiasm.

Equality. All ANIMALS are equal . . . All MEN are created equal.

Example. DO as I say, not as I do. What you DO speaks so loudly . . . One PICTURE is worth a thousand words.

Experience. If you LIVE long enough, you live to see everything. LIVE and learn. The more you LIVE, the more you see; the more you see, the more you know. You cannot put an OLD head on young shoulders. The proof of the PUDDING is in the eating. Those who cannot REMEMBER the past are condemned to repeat it. He jests at SCARS that never felt a wound. The more you live, the more you SEE; the more you see, the more you know. If you haven't TRIED it, don't knock it. It is easy to be WISE after the event. A WISE man learns from the mistakes of others; a fool by his own. WONDERS will never cease!

Facing Reality. The shortest DISTANCE . . . What's DONE is done. You can't unscramble EGGS. EPPUR si muove. EVERYTHING that goes up must come down. No FIGS from thistles. FIGURES don't lie. GARBAGE in, garbage out. Almost counts only in HORSESHOES. "IF" stands stiff in the corner. No man is INDISPENSABLE. A KNIFE cuts both ways. A little LEAK . . . There's no such thing as a free LUNCH. The age of MIRACLES is past. Don't count on MIRACLES. If the mountain won't come to MOHAMMED . . . NOBODY is all wrong. NOTHING comes from nothing. NOTHING is all wrong. NOTHING is perfect. NOTHING plus nothing is still nothing. You can't make something out of NOTHING. You can't make an OMELETTE without breaking eggs. It ain't OVER till it's over. No PLACE is perfect. You cannot be in two PLACES at once. To every thing there is a season, and a time to every PURPOSE under the sun. You cannot make a silk PURSE out of a sow's ear. When it RAINS it pours. A ROSE by any other name would smell as sweet. Buds will be ROSES and kittens cats. Where there's SMOKE, there's fire. All the world's a STAGE. One SWALLOW doesn't make a summer.

You never can TELL. One THING leads to another. Whatever goes UP must come down. The WHOLE is greater than the sum of its parts. Every WHY has a wherefore. If WINTER comes, can spring be far behind? It takes all sorts to make a WORLD. It's a small WORLD. It could be WORSE.

Failure. A MISS is as good as a mile.

Fairness. Don't DISH it out if you can't take it. DO as you would be done by. DO unto others . . . GIVE and take is fair play. What's sauce for the GOOSE . . . You get what you PAY for. A PERSON is innocent until proven guilty. Fair PLAY. Don't ROB Peter to pay Paul. One good TURN deserves another. TURNABOUT is fair play. *See also* Justice.

Faith. GOD never sends mouths . . . GOD tempers the wind . . . If GOD be for us, who can be against us? In GOD we trust. Put your trust in GOD and keep your powder dry. With GOD all things are possible. GOD'S in heaven; all's right with the world. They came to SCOFF and stayed to pray.

Familiarity. Better the DEVIL you know . . .

Family. You can choose your FRIENDS, but you can't choose your relatives.

Fate. *See* Destiny.

Faultfinding. JUDGE not, that ye be not judged. The POT calls the kettle black. Great SPIRIT, teach me never to judge another until I have walked at least two weeks in his moccasins. *See also* Criticism.

Fear. A burnt CHILD dreads fire.

Flattery. You can catch more FLIES with honey than with vinegar. IMITATION is the sincerest form of flattery. Fine words butter no PARSNIPS. SWEETS to the sweet.

Flexibility. Better BEND than break. Keep an open MIND. A REED bends, an oak tree breaks. A WISE man changes his mind; a fool never does.

Fool. *See* Stupidity.

Forbearance. BEAR and forbear. Take the BITTER with the sweet. *See also* Endurance.

Foresight. It's no use to lock the stable door after the HORSE has been stolen. PLAN ahead. Be PREPARED. Where there is no VISION, the people perish.

Forgiveness. Let BYGONES be bygones. JUDGE not, that ye be not judged.

Freedom. Follow your BLISS. CARPE DIEM. If I own a COW, the cow owns me. It's a FREE country. Give me LIBERTY or give me death. LIFE, liberty, and the pursuit of happiness. MAN is born free . . . Everyone's entitled to his own OPINION. We shall OVERCOME. THOUGHT is free.

Friendship. Should auld ACQUAINTANCE . . . ? BIRDS of a feather flock together. If you lie down with DOGS . . . Greater LOVE has no man than this . . . A MAN is known by the company he keeps. Better an open ENEMY than a false friend. A friend to EVERYBODY . . . GOD defend me from my friends . . . GOD sends our relatives, but we can choose our friends. Shared JOYS are doubled, shared sorrows are halved. PROSPERITY gains friends, and adversity tries them.

Frustration. CATCH-22. You always WANT what you can't get.

Futility. You're DAMNED if you do and damned if you don't.

Don't tilt at WINDMILLS.

Generosity. Cast your BREAD upon the waters. It's easy to be generous with somebody else's MONEY. SHARE and share alike.

God. POEMS are made by fools like me, but only God can make a tree.

Good manners. Keep your NOSE out of other people's business.

Don't WASH your dirty linen in public.

Gossip. There's so much GOOD in the worst of us . . . Don't believe everything you HEAR. If you can't say something NICE about a person . . . PEOPLE will talk. Don't tell tales out of SCHOOL. THEY say. *See also* Secrets.

Government. TAXATION without representation is tyranny.

Gradualism. Mighty OAKS from little acorns grow. ROME was not built in a day. One STEP at a time. Little STROKES fell great oaks. The WATERS wear the stones. *See also* Patience.

Gratitude. Don't BITE the hand that feeds you. Count your BLESSINGS. Know which side your BREAD is buttered on. Out of the abundance of the HEART . . . Don't look a gift HORSE in the mouth. Don't KILL the goose that lays the golden eggs. I felt SORRY for myself because I had no shoes, until I met a man who had no feet. You can't live on THANKS.

Greed. The MORE you have, the more you want. You're never SATISFIED. What's YOURS is mine, and what's mine is my own.

Greeting. Have a nice DAY.

Gregariousness. It is not good for man to be ALONE. The voice of the people is the voice of GOD. The MAJORITY rules. The rule of the MAJORITY . . . MAN is a social animal. There is SAFETY in numbers.

Guests. FISH and visitors stink after three days.

Gullibility. Repeat a LIE often enough . . .

Habit. You can take the BOY out of the country . . . FINGERS were made before forks. It takes three generations to make a GENTLEMAN. If GOD wanted us to smoke . . .

Happiness. A merry HEART . . .

Hardship. It's a hard LIFE. LIFE is a rat race. LIFE is just one damn thing after another. All the things I LIKE are either illegal, immoral, or fattening. LOVE lightens labor. Into each life some RAIN must fall. The RAIN falls on the just and unjust alike. Sometimes you WONDER if it's all worth it. *See also* Adversity, Endurance, Work.

Health. An APPLE a day keeps the doctor away. We dig our GRAVES with our teeth. A sound MIND in a sound body.

Helpfulness. Better to light a CANDLE . . .

Heredity. The APPLE doesn't fall far from its tree. BLOOD will tell. What's bred in the BONE . . . Many a good COW has a bad calf. Like FATHER, like son. Like MOTHER, like daughter.

Hindsight. EVERYBODY is wise after the event.

Home. GOD bless our home. A man's HOUSE is his castle. It takes a heap o' living to make a HOUSE a home.

Honesty. You can't CHEAT an honest man. O what a tangled web we weave, when first we practice to DECEIVE. An honest man is the noblest work of GOD. I'd rather be right than be PRESIDENT. Ask me no QUESTIONS, I'll tell you no lies. TELL it like it is. An honest man's WORD is as good as his bond. *See also* Integrity.

Honor. DEATH before dishonor.

Hope. It's always DARKEST just before the dawn. Where there's LIFE there's hope.

Hopelessness. CATCH-22. LIFE is just one damn thing after another. All the things I LIKE are either illegal, immoral, or fattening. NOTHING works. What's the USE? You can't WIN. Why WORRY? WORRYING won't help.

Human Limitations. To ERR is human . . . HINDSIGHT is better than foresight. We're only HUMAN. Profit from your MISTAKES. We all make MISTAKES. NOBODY is perfect. NOBODY knows everything. We get too soon OLD and too late smart. PEOPLE rise to the level of their own incompetence. PEOPLE who live in glass houses should never throw stones. There are more things in heaven and earth than are dreamt of in your PHILOSOPHY. You can't PLEASE everybody. There's many a SLIP 'twixt cup and lip. The SPIRIT is willing but the flesh is weak. You never know when you're WELL OFF. You can't WIN them all. You WIN some and you lose some. Be careful of what you WISH for, you might get it.

Human Nature. There are no ATHEISTS in a foxhole. LIKE seeks like. MAN is a social animal. MONKEY see, monkey do. You can't change human NATURE. OPPOSITES attract. The colonel's lady and Mrs. O'Grady are sisters under the skin. One TOUCH of nature makes the whole world kin.

Hypocrisy. Full of COURTESY, full of craft. DIPLOMACY is . . . PATRIOTISM is . . . All POLITICIANS are crooked.

Idleness. The DEVIL finds work for idle hands.

Ignorance. It's not what we don't know that HURTS, it's what we know that ain't so. What you don't KNOW won't hurt you.

Illegitimacy. There are no illegitimate CHILDREN . . .

Imagination. Just PRETEND.

Importance of Small Things. A CHAIN is as strong as its weakest link. A little spark kindles a great FIRE. For want of a NAIL the shoe was lost . . . A RAT can sink a ship. SMALL is beautiful.

Individuality. One man's MEAT is another man's poison. MEN are all alike. No two PEOPLE are alike. There are black SHEEP in every flock. Different STROKES for different folks. The same SUN softens wax and hardens clay. TASTES are tastes. There's no accounting for TASTES. VIVE la difference.

Individualism. EVERYONE should row his own boat. EVERYONE to his own taste. Every FELLOW ought to cut his own fodder. As many MEN, so many minds. PADDLE your own canoe. He TRAVELS the fastest who travels alone. Let every TUB stand on its own bottom.

Ingratitude. Give a FINGER and they'll want a hand.

Injustice. A COBBLER'S children always go barefoot. It's a COCKEYED world. EVERYTHING happens to me. It isn't what you KNOW, it's who you know. LIFE is so unfair. The RAIN falls on the just and unjust alike. When I am right, no one REMEMBERS; when I am wrong, no one forgets. The shoemaker's WIFE never has shoes. One does all the WORK and the other takes all the credit.

Initiative. What you don't ASK for, you don't get. Don't just stand there; DO something.

Insight. It takes one to KNOW one. It takes a THIEF to catch a thief.

Interference. Too many COOKS spoil the broth.

Integrity. PRACTICE what you preach. What is a man profited if he shall gain the whole world, and lose his own SOUL? To thine own self be TRUE. Be YOURSELF.

Interest. It all DEPENDS on whose ox is gored.

Introspection. KNOW thyself. The unexamined LIFE is not worth living. I THINK therefore I am. THINK. TO BE or not to be; that is the question.

Interruption. The SHOW must go on.

Intuition. The HEART has its reasons . . .

Investigate. Don't buy a PIG in a poke. SEEK, and ye shall find.

Invention. NECESSITY is the mother of invention.

Justice. From each according to his ABILITIES . . . What goes AROUND comes around. CURSES, like chickens, come home to roost. No good DEED goes unpunished. Whoso DIGGETH a pit shall fall therein. Every DOG has his day. The END doesn't justify the means. The END justifies the means. EVERYTHING will come out in the wash. An EYE for an eye. Nobody has the right to shout "FIRE" in a crowded theater. Thrice is he armed that hath his quarrel JUST. No man is above the LAW. The LAW rules the poor man . . . The MILLS of the gods grind slowly . . . MURDER will out. You get what you PAY for. A PERSON is innocent until proven guilty. He that diggeth a PIT shall fall into it. Fair PLAY. RIGHT makes might. Who lives by the SWORD dies by the sword. TIT for tat. Two WRONGS don't make a right.

Kindness. Be kind to ANIMALS. So many GODS . . . Now abideth . . . but the greatest of these is CHARITY. Be NICE to people on your way up . . . I shall PASS through this world but once . . . REVERENCE for life.

Knowledge. NOBODY knows everything. There are more things in heaven and earth than are dreamt of in your PHILOSOPHY. There are TRICKS to every trade. *See also* Education.

Leadership. A FISH stinks from the head. One bad GENERAL is better than two good ones.

Learning. PRACTICE makes perfect.

Life. It's great to be ALIVE.

Loss. 'Tis better to have LOVED and lost . . . For the want of a NAIL . . .

Love. If a BODY kiss a body . . . The way to a man's HEART is through his stomach. When POVERTY comes in the door, love flies out the window. In the SPRING a young man's fancy lightly turns to thoughts of love.

Loyalty. BLOOD is thicker than water. Theirs not to reason why, theirs is but to DO or die. If you're not FOR us, you're against us. No man can serve two MASTERS. RATS desert a sinking ship. Only the STARS are neutral.

Luck. BEGINNER'S luck. The BREAD always falls buttered side down. A FOOL for luck, a poor man for children. FORTUNE favors fools. Some are born GREAT . . . One man's MISFORTUNE is another man's luck. The SUN don't shine on the same dog's tail all the time. THANK your lucky stars.

Marriage. It is not good for man to be ALONE. Why buy a COW when you can get milk free? Better to be an old man's DARLING . . . There are plenty more FISH in the sea. No man is a HERO to his wife.

There is a JOHN for every Jane. KISSING don't last . . . Never LEND your wife or your fountain pen. You never know a person until you LIVE with him. Don't marry for MONEY . . . NEEDLES and pins . . . Blessed be the TIE that binds. TWO can live as cheaply as one. A good WIFE and health . . . A plump WIFE and a big barn . . . He took defeat like a man; he blamed it on his WIFE. WIFE and children are hostages given to fortune. WIVES are young men's mistresses . . . *See also* Women.

Mastery. DIVIDE and conquer.

Maturity. When I was a CHILD . . .

Measure. Don't throw out the BABY with the bathwater. Don't GALLOP when you're going downhill. Strain at a GNAT and swallow a camel. Don't ask the IMPOSSIBLE. LESS is more. Don't gild the LILY. A LITTLE goes a long way. It's the LITTLE things in life that count. MAN wants but little here below. Don't make a MOUNTAIN out of a molehill. Quit while you're ahead. Don't burn the barn to destroy the RATS. The REMEDY is often worse than the disease. Don't TEACH fish to swim. TOO MUCH of anything is not good. You don't put new WINES in old bottles.

Memory. Everyone COMPLAINS of his memory . . .

Moderation. Don't BITE off more than you can chew. You can't burn the CANDLE . . . EAT to live, and do not live to eat. ENOUGH is as good as a feast. ENOUGH is enough. GRASP all, lose all. Don't OVERDO it.

Modesty. Be not RIGHTEOUS overmuch.

Money. SHROUDS have no pockets.

Morality. Everything's got a moral, if only you can find it. Thou shalt not KILL. What doth the LORD require of thee . . .

Mortality. ASHES to ashes, dust to dust. EAT, drink and be merry . . . All FLESH is grass. LIFE is short. LIVE each day as if it were your last. You only LIVE once. The LORD giveth and the Lord taketh away. What doth the LORD require of thee . . . All MEN are mortal. NOTHING lasts forever. Young men may die, OLD men must. SHROUDS have no pockets. Old SOLDIERS never die . . . Here TODAY and gone tomorrow. YOU can't take it with you.

Moving. Three moves is as bad as a FIRE.

Naivete. CHILDREN and fools speak the truth.

Unto the PURE, all things are pure. If you haven't TRIED it, don't knock it.

Nature. GOD made the country, and man made the town. Buds will be ROSES and kittens cats. SURVIVAL of the fittest.

Necessity. Make a VIRTUE of necessity.

Neighborliness. Good FENCES make good neighbors. LOVE thy neighbor.

Nonsense. No matter how you slice it, it's still BALONEY.

Obedience. Yours is not to REASON why; yours is but to do or die. SPEAK when you are spoken to, come when you are called.

Obesity. EVERYBODY loves a fat man. Inside every FAT person is a thin person trying to get out.

Opinion. Who shall decide when DOCTORS disagree? A MAN convinced against his will . . . Merely to SILENCE a man is not to persuade him. He that complies against his WILL is of his own opinion still.

Opportunity. CHASTE is she . . . When the fox turns preacher, beware of the GEESE. Make HAY while the sun shines. STRIKE while the iron is hot. There is a TIDE in the affairs of men. TIME and tide wait for no man.

Optimism. All is for the BEST . . . The BEST is yet to be. All is GRIST to the mill. Nothing is IMPOSSIBLE. The world is so full of a number of things, I'm sure we should all be as happy as KINGS. LOOK on the sunny side. The power of positive THINKING. There's always TOMORROW. TOMORROW will be better.

Order. A PLACE for everything and everything in its place.

Parenthood. Train up a CHILD . . . The HAND that rocks the cradle . . . A wise SON makes a glad father. My SON is my son till he gets him a wife, My daughter's my daughter all her life.

Patience. Don't count your CHICKENS . . . CHURCH ain't over till the fat lady sings. Don't jump to CONCLUSIONS. We have to CREEP before we can walk. Take one DAY at a time. EVERYTHING comes to him that waits. EVERYTHING takes longer than you think it will. GENIUS is an infinite capacity for taking pains. HANG in there. HASTE makes waste. Make HASTE slowly. A JOURNEY of a thousand miles . . . Many a little makes a MICKLE. Mighty OAKS from little acorns grow. A watched POT never boils. TIME works wonders. They also serve who only stand and WAIT.

Patriotism. Don't sell AMERICA short. Ask not what your COUNTRY can do for you . . . My COUNTRY right or wrong. It is sweet and fitting to DIE for one's country. GOD bless America. Breathes there a MAN, with soul so dead . . .

People. GOD must love the common people . . . I never met a man I didn't LIKE. The proper study of mankind is MAN. What is MAN? OIL and water don't mix.

Perfectionism. ANYTHING worth doing is worth doing well.

Perseverence. Never say DIE. Constant DRIPPING wears away a stone. Don't GIVE UP. You can't keep a good MAN down. Never say NEVER. Never take NO for an answer. SOMEBODY said that it couldn't be done. If at first you don't SUCCEED, try again. The door to SUCCESS is always marked Push. Keep on TRUCKIN'. A WINNER never quits, and a quitter never wins.

Personality. The CHILD is father of the man.

Perspective. Don't let the tail wag the DOG.

Pessimism. Things are going to the DOGS. PEOPLE are no damn good. If something can go WRONG, it will.

Piety. The DEVIL was sick . . .

Planning. Man proposes, but GOD disposes. The best-laid SCHEMES o' mice and men gang aft agley.

Play. Who loves not WOMEN, wine and song remains a fool his whole life long. All WORK and no play makes Jack a dull boy. *See also* Nonsense.

Pleasure. ENJOY yourself; it's later than you think. Living well is the best REVENGE. A WOMAN is only a woman, but a good cigar is a smoke.

Point of View. BEAUTY is in the eye of the beholder. It all DEPENDS on how you look at it. It all DEPENDS on how you take it. If it sounds DIRTY, you have a dirty mind. EVERYTHING is relative. It's all in how you LOOK at it. Where you STAND depends on where you sit. It's all in how you TAKE it. There is nothing either good or bad but THINKING makes

it so. Stone WALLS do not a prison make. One man's WISDOM is another man's folly.

Politics. You can't fight CITY HALL. A STATESMAN is a successful politician who is dead.

Possessions. DIAMONDS are a girl's best friend. The EARTH is the Lord's . . . EASY come, easy go. You can't have EVERYTHING. The best things in life are FREE. You cannot LOSE what you never had.

Poverty. A FOOL for luck, a poor man for children. GOD help the poor . . . GOD help the rich, the poor can beg. It's better to be poor and HEALTHY than rich and sick. An empty PURSE cannot stand upright. The RICH get richer, and the poor get children.

Power. PROVIDENCE is always on the side of the big battalions. SPEAK softly and carry a big stick.

Prayer. The FAMILY that prays together stays together.

Precocity. Soon RIPE, soon rotten.

Prevention. A STITCH in time saves nine.

Priority. FIRST things first.

Privacy. Two is COMPANY . . . Don't WASH your dirty linen in public.

Procrastination. There's always TOMORROW. TOMORROW is another day.

Promise. A DEAL is a deal.

Promptness. The EARLY bird . . . Better LATE than never. Never PUT OFF until tomorrow what you can do today. TOMORROW never comes.

Publicity. Don't HIDE your light under a bushel.

Punishment. As well be HANGED for a sheep as a lamb. Whom the LORD loveth he chasteneth. *See* Retribution.

Quarreling. A little POT is soon hot. It takes two to make a QUARREL. STICKS and stones may break my bones, but names will never harm me. After the STORM comes the calm.

Racial Prejudice. The only good INDIAN is a dead Indian. Scratch a RUSSIAN and you'll find a Tartar.

Rationalization. Sour GRAPES. There's always a good REASON, and then there's the real reason. He took defeat like a man; he blamed it on his WIFE. A bad WORKMAN quarrels with his tools.

Rebellion. If this be TREASON, make the most of it. WORKERS of the world, unite.

Reciprocity. You SCRATCH my back and I'll scratch yours. One good TURN deserves another. TURN-ABOUT is fair play. *See also* Fairness.

Regret. It is no use CRYING over spilt milk. Of all sad words of TONGUE or pen, The saddest are these: It might have been.

Religion. Ye must be BORN again. Give unto CAE-SAR . . . GOD is dead. GOD is our refuge . . . GOD moves in a mysterious way . . . If GOD did not exist . . . Praise the LORD and pass the ammunition. The LORD giveth and the Lord taketh away. What doth the LORD require of thee . . . Whom the LORD loveth he chasteneth. MAN does not live by bread alone. The letter killeth but the SPIRIT giveth life. *See* Agape, Faith.

Remembering. An ELEPHANT never forgets.

Reputation. Good WINE needs no bush. CAE-SAR'S wife . . . A man is known by the COMPANY he keeps. Give a DOG a bad name and hang him. Every HERO becomes a bore at last. No man is a HERO to his valet. A good NAME is better than riches. What will PEOPLE think? No man is a PROPHET in his own country. Consider the SOURCE. A STATESMAN is a successful politician who is dead. The TREE is known by its fruit. Don't WASH your dirty linen in public. Good WINE needs no bush. Don't cry "WOLF!" An ill WOUND is cured, but not an ill name.

Responsibility. Everybody's BUSINESS . . . You've buttered your BREAD . . . Am I my BROTHER'S keeper? The BUCK stops here. Who will bell the CAT? Uneasy lies the head that wears a CROWN. He who DANCES must pay the piper. Let you and him FIGHT. Let GEORGE do it. NOBLESSE oblige. PADDLE your own canoe. The PUBLIC be damned. It's up to YOU.

Retribution. What goes AROUND comes around. CURSES, like chickens, come home to roost. No good DEED goes unpunished. Whoso DIGGETH a pit shall fall therein. EVERYTHING will come out in the wash. An EYE for an eye. Be NICE to people on your way up . . . Who lives by the SWORD dies by the sword. TIT for tat. They have sown the wind, and

they shall reap the WHIRLWIND. There is no rest for the WICKED.

Revenge. Don't get MAD, get even. VENGEANCE is mine . . .

Reverence. Always speak well of the DEAD.

Reward. If a man builds a better MOUSETRAP, the world will beat a path to his door. NOTHING for nothing. NOTHING ventured, nothing gained. You get what you PAY for. As you SOW, so shall you reap. No SWEET without swear.

Risk. Take a CHANCE.

Sacrifice. No CROSS, no crown. Greater LOVE has no man than this . . .

Scripture. The DEVIL can cite Scripture for his purpose.

Secrecy. The WALLS have ears.

Self-consciousness. Don't speak of a ROPE in a house where there has been a hanging.

Self-control. It's all a matter of MIND over matter.

Self-defense. Don't TREAD on me.

Self-deception. A man who is his own DOCTOR . . . A man who is his own LAWYER . . . PHYSICIAN, heal thyself.

Self-destruction. A man is his own worst ENEMY. We have met the ENEMY . . . I am my own EXE-CUTIONER. The road to HELL is paved with good intentions. Don't cut off your NOSE to spite your face. Give a man enough ROPE and he'll hang himself.

Self-effacement. Blessed be he who expects NOTH-ING, for he shall never be disappointed. If you make yourself a SHEEP . . .

Self-interest. It's an ill BIRD that fouls its own nest. Every man for himself, and the DEVIL take the hindmost. DO your own thing. To EACH his own. EVERYBODY knows where his shoe pinches. Your best FRIEND is yourself. Every man for himself, and GOD for all of us. GOD helps those who help themselves. Nice GUYS finish last. HELP yourself. Every MAN is his own best friend. SELF-LOVE is better than self-hate. SELF-PRESERVATION is the first law of nature. Where you STAND depends on where you sit.

Self-reliance. If you're looking for a helping HAND . . . I am the MASTER of my fate . . . *See also* Will.

Selfishness. Don't be a DOG in the manger.

Separation. PARTING is such sweet sorrow.

Skepticism. I'm from MISSOURI; you've got to show me.

Sickness. A HEART ATTACK . . .

Side-effects. You always hurt the one you LOVE. Each man kills the thing he LOVES. Never the ROSE without the thorn.

Silence. CHILDREN should be seen but not heard. You have not CONVERTED a man . . . Even a FOOL, when he holds his peace . . . A closed MOUTH catches no flies. Keep your TROUBLES to yourself. Still WATER runs deep.

Simplicity. Simple PLEASURES are the best.

Sin. The way of TRANSGRESSORS is hard.

Skill. It's all a matter of KNOWING how. There's always a WAY.

Slander. Throw enough DIRT . . .

Small. *See* Importance of Small Things.

Sociability. The MORE the merrier.

Social Welfare. The greatest GOOD to the greatest number. That GOVERNMENT is best which governs least. There is no right to STRIKE against the public safety.

Sportsmanship. It matters not whether you WON or lost, but how you played the game.

Stability. A rolling STONE gathers no moss.

Station in Life. Stay in your own BACKYARD. The higher they CLIMB . . . Let the COBBLER stick to his last. The KING can do no wrong. It's LONELY at the top. NOBLESSE oblige. OIL and water don't mix. Rank has its privileges. If two RIDE on a horse, one must ride behind. One half of the WORLD does not know how the other half lives. *See also* Leadership.

Statistics. Figures FOOL when fools figure.

Stealing. He who takes what isn't his'n must give it back or go to PRISON. Once a THIEF, always a thief.

Strategy. The best DEFENSE is a good offense.

Strength. DIAMOND cuts diamond.

Stupidity. Empty vessels make the most NOISE. Some PEOPLE never learn. A WISE man changes his mind; a fool never does. A WISE man learns from the mistakes of others; a fool by his own.

Style. It ain't what you DO . . .

Success. The higher they CLIMB . . . MANY are called but few are chosen. The RACE is not to the swift . . . From the SUBLIME to the ridiculous is only a step. He that would THRIVE must rise at five; he that has thriven may lie till seven. VICTORY is sweet. You can't WIN them all. You WIN some and you lose some. WINNING isn't everything; it's the only thing.

Superfluity. Don't carry COALS to Newcastle.

Superstition. KNOCK on wood.

Supervision. The EYE of the master does more work than both his hands. Like MASTER, like servant. When the cat's away the MICE will play. Who will WATCH the watchman?

Talkativeness. Babbling BROOKS are noisy.

Teaching. Give me a FISH and I will eat today; teach me to fish and I will eat all my life.

Temptation. Never send a DOG to deliver a steak. Don't put the FOX to guard the henhouse. Forbidden FRUIT is sweetest. Stolen FRUIT is sweetest. All the things I like are either ILLEGAL, immoral, or fattening. Every MAN has his price. OPPORTUNITY makes the thief. "Will you walk into my PARLOUR?" said the spider to the fly. Give a man enough ROPE and he'll hang himself. Get thee behind me, SATAN.

Temperment. A little POT is soon hot.

Theater. There's no BUSINESS like show business.

Thrift. Take care of the PENCE and the pounds will take care of themselves. A PENNY saved is a penny earned. Big SPENDERS are bad lenders.

Time. It's LATER than you think. Today is the first day of the rest of your LIFE. Time is MONEY. Here TODAY and gone tomorrow. TODAY is the tomorrow you worried about yesterday. Time heals all WOUNDS.

Timing. DELAYS are dangerous. Don't swap HORSES . . . When you're HOT, you're hot. There's nothing so irresistible as an IDEA whose time has come.

Tolerance. LIVE and let live.

Trust. Who will WATCH the watchman?

Trouble. Little CHILDREN, little troubles . . .

Truth. The EMPEROR has no clothes. Many a true word is said in JEST. LIARS should have good memories. NOTHING is all wrong. If the SHOE fits, wear it. Call a SPADE a spade. It will all come out in the WASH.

Uncertainty. ANYTHING can happen. Nothing is certain but DEATH and taxes. The UNEXPECTED always happens.

Unfairness. *See* Injustice.

Unpleasantness. Every man must eat a peck of DIRT . . .

Unity. A CHAIN is as strong as its weakest link. We must all HANG together . . .

Upbringing. Spare the ROD and spoil the child. Train up a CHILD in the way he should go . . . As the TWIG is bent, the tree's inclined.

Value. A PEARL of great price is not had for the asking.

Vegetarianism. LOVE animals—don't eat them.

Victory. It matters not whether you WON or lost, but how you played the game. *See also* Success.

Vigilance. Beware of GREEKS bearing gifts.

Virtue. CHASTE is she whom no one has asked. GIRLS who are chaste . . . If you can't be GOOD, be careful. The GOOD die young. Be good and you will be HAPPY. Don't be HOLIER-THAN-THOU. It's nice to be IMPORTANT, but it's more important to be nice. Blessed are the MEEK . . .

War. Make LOVE, not war. Yours is not to REASON why; yours is but to do or die. Who lives by the SWORD dies by the sword. To the VICTOR belong the spoils.

Waste. Cast not PEARLS before swine. *See also* Conservation and Thrift.

Wealth. It is easier for a CAMEL . . . A rich man's JOKE is always funny. It's better to be born LUCKY than rich. He who PAYS the piper may call the tune. PROSPERITY gains friends, and adversity tries them. The RICH get richer, and the poor get children. What is a man profited if he shall gain the whole world, and lose his own SOUL? THEM that has, gets.

Will. DO or die. You can lead a HORSE to water . . . A MAN convinced against his will . . . If you WANT something badly enough, you can get it.

Women. CHERCHEZ la femme. A woman's place is in the HOME. LADIES first. You can't LIVE with them, and you can't live without them. Every MAIDEN'S weak and willin' . . . Behind every successful MAN you'll find a woman. A MAN is as old as he's feeling, a woman is as old as she looks. A MAN may work from sun to sun but a woman's work is never done. It's a MAN'S world. MEN seldom make passes at girls who wear glasses. PAINT and powder, powder and paint, makes a woman what she ain't. VANITY, thy name is woman. A woman's WORK is never done. *See also* Marriage.

Work. Don't send a BOY . . . He that would have the fruit must CLIMB the tree. Thank GOD it's Friday. GRASS never grows on a busy street. Never do anything by HALVES. HAPPINESS comes from work well done. Every little bit HELPS. A JACK OF ALL TRADES is a master of none. A used KEY is always bright. The LABORER is worthy of his hire. A MAN may work from sun to sun . . . Keep your NOSE to the grindstone. PADDLE your own canoe. ROOT, hog, or die. The first STEP is the hardest. *See also* Achievement, Diligence, Perseverance, Reward, Success.

Worry. Care killed the CAT. TODAY is the tomorrow you worried about yesterday. Most TROUBLES never occur.

Youth. Sow your wild OATS. You cannot put an OLD head on young shoulders. Gather ye ROSEBUDS while ye may. Never TRUST anyone over thirty. Go WEST, young man. You're only YOUNG once.